Exploring Writing
Paragraphs and Essays
FOURTH EDITION

Zoé L. Albright
Metropolitan Community College–Longview

John Langan
Atlantic Cape Community College

McGraw
Hill
Education

EXPLORING WRITING: PARAGRAPHS AND ESSAYS, FOURTH EDITION

Published by McGraw-Hill Education, 2 Penn Plaza, New York, NY 10121. Copyright © 2020 by McGraw-Hill Education. All rights reserved. Printed in the United States of America. Previous editions © 2013, 2010, and 2008. No part of this publication may be reproduced or distributed in any form or by any means, or stored in a database or retrieval system, without the prior written consent of McGraw-Hill Education, including, but not limited to, in any network or other electronic storage or transmission, or broadcast for distance learning.

Some ancillaries, including electronic and print components, may not be available to customers outside the United States.

This book is printed on acid-free paper.

1 2 3 4 5 6 7 8 9 LWI 21 20 19

ISBN 978-0-07-353479-4 (bound edition)
MHID 0-07-353479-X (bound edition)
ISBN 978-1-260-16455-8 (loose-leaf edition)
MHID 1-260-16455-1 (loose-leaf edition)

Portfolio Manager: *Penina Braffman*
Product Developer: *Beth Tripmacher*
Marketing Manager: *Byron Kanoti*
Content Project Manager: *Lisa Bruflodt*
Buyer: *Laura Fuller*
Designer: *Jessica Cuevas*
Content Licensing Specialist: *Brianna Kirschbaum*
Cover Image: *(Hands): ©mYanis/Shutterstock; (computer): ©CostinT/iStock.com; (woman using computer): ©Dragon Images/Shutterstock*
Compositor: *Lumina Datamatics, Inc.*

All credits appearing on page or at the end of the book are considered to be an extension of the copyright page.

Library of Congress Cataloging-in-Publication Data

Names: Albright, Zoe L., author. | Langan, John, author.
Title: Exploring writing : paragraphs and essays / John Langan, Atlantic Cape
    Community College ; Zoâe L. Albright, Metropolitan Community
    College—Longview.
Description: Fourth edition. | New York, NY : McGraw-Hill Education, [2020] |
    Includes bibliographical references and index.
Identifiers: LCCN 2018032683 (print) | LCCN 2018046001 (ebook) | ISBN
    9781260164541 | ISBN 9780073534794 (bound edition : acid-free paper) |
    ISBN 007353479X (bound edition : acid-free paper) | ISBN 9781260164558
    (loose-leaf edition) | ISBN 1260164551 (loose-leaf edition)
Subjects: LCSH: English language—Paragraphs—Problems, exercises, etc. |
    English language—Rhetoric—Problems, exercises, etc. | Report
    writing—Problems, exercises, etc.
Classification: LCC PE1439 (ebook) | LCC PE1439 .L36 2020 (print) | DDC
    808/.042076—dc23
LC record available at https://lccn.loc.gov/2018032683

The Internet addresses listed in the text were accurate at the time of publication. The inclusion of a website does not indicate an endorsement by the authors or McGraw-Hill Education, and McGraw-Hill Education does not guarantee the accuracy of the information presented at these sites.

mheducation.com/highered

ABOUT THE AUTHORS

Zoé L. Albright has been involved in diverse aspects of education for twenty-two years. For the last eighteen years, she has been a faculty member at Metropolitan Community College—Longview, teaching developmental writing, composition, and literature. She has created and implemented traditional and online curricula for high school and college English and composition courses and for a variety of literature courses. She continues to research new educational theory and practices. In addition to this extensive teaching experience, Zoé is the co-author of *College Writing Skills with Readings 10/e* and *English Skills with Readings 9/e*. She has also contributed to other Langan texts, including the *Exploring Writing 3/e books* and *College Writing Skills with Readings 9/e*. She received her M.A. from Goldsmiths, University of London; B.S. and B.A. from the University of Idaho; and A.A. from Cottey College. She is currently pursuing a Ph.D. in Curriculum and Instruction at the University of Kansas. Travel is one of Zoé's main passions. Whenever she travels, she incorporates what she has experienced and learned into her writing and teaching. Zoé currently resides outside Kansas City, Missouri, with her husband and teenage son.

Zoé L. Albright
Courtesy of Zoé L. Albright

John Langan has taught reading and writing at Atlantic Cape Community College near Atlantic City, New Jersey, for more than twenty-five years. The author of a popular series of college textbooks on both writing and reading, John enjoys the challenge of developing materials that teach skills in an especially clear and lively way. Before teaching, he earned advanced degrees in writing at Rutgers University and in reading at Rowan University. He also spent a year writing fiction that, he says, "is now at the back of a drawer waiting to be discovered and acclaimed posthumously." While in school, he supported himself by working as a truck driver, a machinist, a battery assembler, a hospital attendant, and an apple packer. John now lives with his wife, Judith Nadell, near Philadelphia. In addition to his wife and Philly sports teams, his passions include reading and turning on non-readers to the pleasure and power of books. Through Townsend Press, his educational publishing company, he has developed the nonprofit "Townsend Library"—a collection of more than one hundred new and classic stories that appeal to readers of any age.

John Langan
Courtesy of Judith Nadell

BRIEF CONTENTS

CONTENTS

READINGS LISTED BY RHETORICAL MODE

Note: Some selections are cross-listed because they illustrate more than one rhetorical method of development.

EXEMPLIFICATION

DESCRIPTION

NARRATION

PROCESS

CAUSE AND/OR EFFECT

COMPARISON AND/OR CONTRAST

DEFINITION

DIVISION-CLASSIFICATION

ARGUMENT

Preface

Exploring Personal, Academic, and Workplace Writing

Exploring Writing: Paragraphs and Essays 4/e is flexible. Throughout the book, students are exposed to examples of writing that reflect the three key realms of their lives—personal, academic, and workplace. Seeing these different types of writing can help them understand the critical way in which writing will have an impact on the many facets of their lives.

To help students learn the different characteristics of each type of writing, icons identifying specific writing pieces, examples, and assignments are integrated throughout the chapters. Writings that employ first-person point of view, narrative, and/or an informal tone are marked "Personal." Writings that employ a third-person point of view, a formal tone, and focus on academic topics are identified as "Academic." Writings that employ a third-person point of view, a formal tone, and focus on employment-related topics are marked "Work."

Students will see models and examples for many writing situations. Parts Three and Four, for example, include new sample paragraphs reflecting academic and workplace writing while continuing to offer familiar as well as updated personal writing examples. Writing assignments and grammar assignments have also been updated to provide practice with multiple writing situations. This variety provides great flexibility in the kinds of assignments you prefer to give.

New Focus on Information Literacy and Research Writing

Exploring Writing: Paragraphs and Essays 4/e has a new, updated focus on information literacy, working with sources, and writing research papers. Students are introduced to using and locating online sources effectively and efficiently and employing critical thinking skills to determine the reliability and validity of sources found. Resources available at most college libraries—including the expertise of resource librarians and how to make best use of that expertise—are discussed in detail. In addition to learning how to choose sources, students are exposed to a new, more in-depth look at the skill of incorporating their sources into a source-based essay. Paraphrasing, summarizing, and direct quoting are explained in more depth, and multiple activities are provided to give students the practice they need. Finally, writing a research paper is explained in detail, including how to create a plan to meet deadlines set by instructors, how to take good notes, how to incorporate sources to avoid plagiarism, and how to use proper MLA format. In addition to the sample research paper, students are also given the opportunity to read and work with additional source-based essays, including a literary analysis.

Exploring and Mastering the Four Bases: Unity, Support, Coherence, Sentence Skills

Exploring Writing emphasizes writing skills and process. By referring to a set of four skills for effective writing, *Exploring Writing* encourages new writers to see writing as a skill that can be learned and a process that must be explored. The four skills, or bases, for effective writing are as follows:

- **Unity:** Discover a clearly stated point or topic sentence, and make sure that all other information in the paragraph or essay supports that point.

- **Support:** Support the points with specific evidence, and plenty of it.

- **Coherence:** Organize and connect supporting evidence so that paragraphs and essays transition smoothly from one bit of supporting information to the next.

- **Sentence skills:** Revise and edit so that sentences are error-free for clearer and more effective communication.

The four bases are essential to effective writing, whether it be a narrative paragraph, a cover letter for a job application, or an essay assignment.

UNITY

Discover a clearly stated point, or topic sentence, and make sure all the other information in the paragraph or essay is in support of that point.

SUPPORT

Support points with specific evidence, and plenty of it.

COHERENCE

Organize and connect supporting evidence so that paragraphs and essays transition smoothly from one bit of supporting information to the next.

SENTENCE SKILLS

Revise and edit so that sentences are error-free for clearer and more effective communication.

CHAPTER-BY-CHAPTER CHANGES

In addition to maintaining its hallmark, the four bases framework for writing and revising, *Exploring Writing: Paragraphs and Essays 4/e* includes the following chapter-by-chapter emphases and changes:

Part 1: Writing Skills and Process

* New sample paragraphs that reflect personal, academic, and workplace writing
* New section on using technology to write and study efficiently
* Inclusion of Diagram of a Paragraph, with color-coded annotations that explain the parts of a paragraph and how they flow
* Revised and updated coverage of MLA formatting in research writing
* Revised and enhanced coverage of audience and purpose
* Enhanced discussion of peer and personal review
* Targeted instruction and illustration of proper e-mail and discussion forum post writing

Part 2: Basic Principles of Effective Writing

* New sample paragraphs that reflect personal, academic, and workplace writing
* Inclusion of brand-new section, "The Writing Process in Action," demonstrating a student's working through all stages of the writing process from prewriting through peer review, self-evaluation, and revising

Part 3: Paragraph Development

* Several new student paragraphs and Writing Assignments that reflect personal, academic, and workplace writing and that address high-interest topics
* Inclusion in each chapter of one complete Checklist that is more focused on the specific needs of the targeted mode
* Inclusion of multiple across-chapter cross-references to related topics

Part 4: Essay Development

* Inclusion of Diagram of an Essay with brand-new accompanying walk-through of an annotated essay, illustrating the parts of the essay and how they work together
* Introductory text for each pattern with explanation of how multiple modes function together in one essay
* All sample essays emphasize one pattern or mode, but include other modes as well to more fully reflect real writing
* Inclusion of multiple across-chapter cross-references to related topics
* Updated Essay Checklist

Part 5: Research-Based Writing

Brand-new Part updating and coalescing previous coverage and weaving in new relevant topics

Chapter 19: Information Literacy

- New chapter with updated coverage of students' use of the Internet, technology, and the library in the digital age

Chapter 20: Working with Sources

- Revised, newly focused, and enhanced treatment of summarizing and paraphrasing
- Updated and increased coverage of identifying and avoiding plagiarism
- New, visually called out and identified examples of source-based essay writing and literary analysis
- Revised and updated coverage of MLA formatting in research writing

Chapter 21: Writing a Research Paper

- Updated discussion of key research skills including how to create a workable timeline for writing a research paper
- Revised and updated coverage of MLA formatting in research writing

Part 6: Handbook of Sentence Skills

- Revised and strengthened coverage of key sentence skills such as pronoun usage and verbs
- Revised and newly focused treatment of irregular and regular verbs
- New grammar activities, exercises, and Review Tests that continue to incorporate personal, academic, and workplace-related themes
- New and existing test and activity material is typically focused on one issue so that it reads as a unified passage

Part 7: Readings for Writers

- Newly organized and titled sub-sections:
    - Goals and Values
    - Education and Learning
    - Challenging Society
- Readings updated to include eleven new selections by diverse and well-respected authors:
    - "What Students Need to Know about Today's Job Crisis" by Don Bertram
    - "The Great Spirit" by Zitkala-Ša
    - "A Few Good Monuments Men" by Noah Charney
    - "On Homecomings" by Ta-Nehisi Coates
    - "L.A. Targets Full-Time Community College Students for Free Tuition" by Anna M. Phillips
    - "Carol Dweck Revisits the 'Growth Mindset'" by Carol Dweck
    - "Mayor of Rust" by Sue Halpern
    - "Why You May Need Social Media for Your Career" by John Warner
    - "Lincoln's Second Inaugural Address" (1865) by Abraham Lincoln
    - "Serena Williams Is the Greatest" by Vann R. Newkirk II
    - "Raise the Minimum Wage, Reduce Crime?" by Juleyka Lantigua-Williams
- Each new reading accompanied by new full set of questions and assignments
- All assignments reflect personal, academic, or workplace-related themes

Connect Writing and the *Exploring Writing* Master Course

Connect is a highly reliable, easy-to-use homework and learning management solution that embeds learning science and award-winning adaptive tools to improve student results. Connect Writing offers comprehensive, reliable writing and research content that is designed to actively engage students and help prepare them to be successful writers. LearnSmart Achieve's adaptive technology creates an optimal learning path for each individual student, so that students spend less time in areas they already know and more time in areas they don't. Connect Writing provides a systematic and easily deployed option for instructors and administrators to assess their program's learning outcomes.

In this master course, which you can copy to your own Connect account and adapt as you wish, you will find various Connect Writing assignment types aligned to every chapter of the *Exploring Writing: Paragraphs and Essays* text to accelerate learning. Zoé L. Albright sets up

- *LearnSmart Achieve* topics
- *Power of Process* assignments
- writing prompts
- concept *PowerPoint* presentations

Contact your local McGraw-Hill representative to copy the course to your Connect account.

LearnSmart Achieve

LearnSmart Achieve offers students an adaptive, individualized learning experience designed to ensure the efficient mastery of reading and writing skills in tandem. By targeting students' strengths and weaknesses, LearnSmart Achieve customizes its lessons and facilitates high-impact learning at an accelerated pace.

Evaluate and Revise a Thesis Statement for Effectiveness   3/3

Student Essay Excerpt: Final Draft

The introductory paragraph below is adapted from the final draft of the essay "Fraud Alert." The <u>thesis</u> includes the following elements: a **clearly stated topic** and a **clearly stated and supportable controlling idea.**

A new brand of retail store has developed over the past several years. The superstore overwhelms smaller, independent competitors with its larger inventory, lower prices, and multiple locations. The chain bookstore is a unique kind of superstore: part store, part library, part café, it's a place where the emphasis has shifted from selling books to getting people to visit, apparently. It is the policy of these stores not to pressure customers, and they usually provide ample tables and sofas. This laid-back atmosphere has created a new breed of bookstore patron. In fact, <u>there are specific types of customers at these bookstores,</u> and they can be easily distinguished by their

< BACK   GIVE FEEDBACK   BACK TO LIBRARY

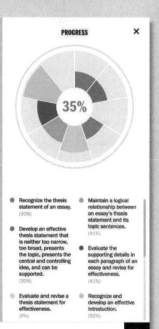

Power of Process

One overarching goal is at the heart of Power of Process: for students to become self-regulating, strategic readers and writers. Power of Process facilitates engaged reading and writing processes using research-based best practices suggested by major professional reading and writing organizations.

Text-Specific Resources for Instructors

The **Annotated Instructor's Edition** consists of the student text, complete with answers to all activities and tests. We also offer a number of instructional materials including:

- an instructor's manual
- sample syllabi
- PowerPoint presentations

Customize *Exploring Writing* in Create™ with Bonus Content

With McGraw-Hill Create™, you can easily arrange your book to align with your syllabus. You can eliminate chapters you do not assign, include material from other content sources (including chapters from other McGraw-Hill textbooks), and quickly upload content you have written, such as your course syllabus or teaching notes. You may also customize the readings in Part Seven by eliminating or adding readings from other Langan titles or from other McGraw-Hill collections.

We are offering two additional chapters and three appendices, specific to *Exploring Writing: Paragraphs and Essays*, through Create™:

- ESL Pointers
- Spelling Improvement
- Appendix: Writing a Résumé and Cover Letter
- Appendix: Writing a Formal E-mail
- Appendix: Transition Words and Phrases

You control the net price of the book as you build it, and can choose its format: color, black and white, and eBook. When you build a CREATE book, you'll receive a complimentary print review copy in three to five business days or a complimentary electronic review copy (eComp) via e-mail in about one hour.

Go to www.mcgrawhillcreate.com and register today!

Connect Learning Management System Integration

Connect Writing integrates with your local Learning Management System (Blackboard, Canvas, and others).

McGraw-Hill Campus™ is a new one-stop teaching and learning experience available to users of any learning management system. This complimentary integration allows faculty and students to enjoy single sign-on (SSO) access to all McGraw-Hill Higher Education materials and synchronized grade-books with our award-winning McGraw-Hill *Connect* platform. For more information on McGraw-Hill Campus please visit our website at **www.mhcampus.com** or contact your local McGraw-Hill representative to find out more about installations on your campus.

ACKNOWLEDGMENTS

Market Development Acknowledgments

The quality of *Exploring Writing: Paragraphs and Essays 4/e* is a testament to the suggestions and insights from instructors around the country. Many thanks to all of those who helped improve this project.

- Barbara Brown, *City Colleges of Chicago–Olive-Harvey College*
- Emily Cosper, *Delgado Community College*
- Marcia Dawson, *Prince George's Community College*
- Margie Dernaika, *Southwest Tennessee Community College*
- Dane Galloway, *Ozarks Technical Community College–Springfield Campus*
- Cynthia Galvan, *Milwaukee Area Community College*
- Melody Hargraves, *St. Johns River State College–Orange Park*
- Andrew Howard, *UDC Community College*
- Brian Kehler, *Alcorn State University*
- Katherine Kellen, *Seminole State College of Florida*
- Rosalind Manning, *Atlanta Technical College*
- Amarilis Martinez, *Milwaukee Area Community College*
- Kimberly Murphy, *Montgomery College–Rockville*
- Lonetta Oliver, *St. Louis Community College–Florissant Valley*
- James R. Sodon, *St. Louis Community College–Florissant Valley*

Personal Acknowledgments

We are incredibly grateful for the talent and support of our developmental team without which this edition would not have happened. Thank you to Mark Schaefer, DeAnna Dausener, and Brianna Kirschbaum for their hard work in obtaining text and photo permissions despite the many challenges. To Val Brandenburg and her composition team, thank you for all the dedication you showed. Thank you to Lisa Bruflodt who handled the production process masterfully. To the marketing team, Suzie Flores and Byron Kanoti, thank you for all your research and planning to market this new edition. Jessica Cuevas, thank you for the great design. To Kelly Villella, we are ever thankful for the professional and personal support you have given over this and past projects. To Penina Braffman and Beth Tripmacher—you kept us on schedule, vetted our ideas, laughed and cried with us, and genuinely became more than just our editors. Finally, to Merryl Maleska Wilbur, a colleague and friend, thank you for pushing and developing our abilities as writers and thinkers; we have grown beyond our imagination and remain immensely grateful.

Zoé L. Albright

John Langan

Exploring Writing

Writing:
Skills and Process

PART ONE WILL

- introduce you to the basic principles of effective writing

- present writing as a skill and as a process of discovery

- present writing as a way to communicate with others

- discuss the efficient and effective use of technology in writing

- explain and illustrate the sequence of steps in writing an effective paragraph, including:

  - prewriting

  - revising

  - editing

- ask you to write a paragraph

EXPLORING WRITING PROMPT:

This part of the text explains writing as an invaluable tool in college and beyond. Focus on one of your favorite activities—playing basketball, cooking, watching movies, listening to music alone in your room, or just taking a walk, for example. Then, pretend that you have been asked to explain the reasons you enjoy this activity to the other students in your writing class. Now, on a piece of paper or on a computer, write the answers to the following questions:

©McGraw-Hill Education/Jill Braaten

1. Would you rather stand up in front of the class and explain these reasons in person, or would you rather explain them in a written note or letter?

2. What advantages might speaking have over writing in this example? What advantages might there be in writing your reasons in a note or letter?

3. Which method would you find harder? Why?

4. What are the differences between speaking about this topic and writing about it?

An Introduction to Writing

TEACHING TIP
Ask students to complete this writing prompt in class. Encourage them to take an inventory of their strengths and weaknesses.

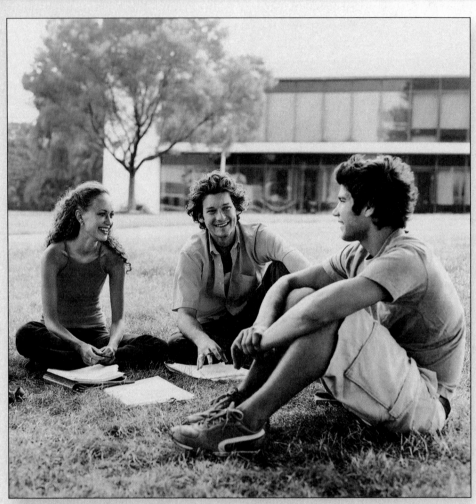

©Digital Vision/Getty Images

RESPONDING TO IMAGES

College offers many different challenges for students. In order to be a successful student, you should know your individual strengths and weaknesses. Take some time to think about your strengths and weaknesses as a student. Later in this chapter you will be asked to write a paragraph on this topic.

The experience I had writing my first college essay helped shape this book. I received a C– for the essay. Scrawled beside the grade was the comment "Not badly written, but ill-conceived." I remember going to the instructor after class, asking about his comment as well as the word *Log* that he had added in the margin at various spots. "What are all these logs you put in my paper?" I asked, trying to make a joke of it. He looked at me a little wonderingly. "Logic, Mr. Langan," he answered, "logic." He went on to explain that I had not thought out my paper clearly. There were actually two ideas rather than one in my thesis, one supporting paragraph had nothing to do with either idea, another paragraph lacked a topic sentence, and so on. I've never forgotten his last words: "If you don't think clearly," he said, "you won't write clearly."

I was speechless, and I felt confused and angry. I didn't like being told that I didn't know how to think. I went back to my room and read over my paper several times. Eventually, I decided that my instructor was right. "No more logs," I said to myself. "I'm going to get these logs out of my papers."

My instructor's advice was invaluable. I learned that clear, disciplined thinking is the key to effective writing. *Exploring Writing: Paragraphs and Essays* develops this idea by breaking down the writing process into a series of four logical, easily followed steps. These steps, combined with practical advice about prewriting and revision, will help you write strong papers.

Here are the four steps in a nutshell:

1. Discover a clearly stated point.

2. Provide logical, detailed support for your point.

3. Organize and connect your supporting material.

4. Revise and edit so that your sentences are effective and errorfree.

Part 2 of this book explains each of these steps in detail and provides many practice materials to help you master them.

TEACHING TIP
Students might enjoy hearing about your writing experiences. Recount a vivid memory.

Point and Support

An Important Difference between Writing and Talking

In everyday conversation, you make all kinds of points or assertions. You say, for example, "My boss is a hard person to work for"; "It's not safe to walk in our neighborhood after dark"; or "Poor study habits keep getting me into trouble." Your points concern personal matters as well as, at times, outside issues: "That trade will be a disaster for the team"; "*CSI* is the most entertaining drama on TV"; "Students are better off working for a year before attending college."

The people you are talking with do not always challenge you to give reasons for your statements. They may know why you feel as you do, or they may already agree with you, or they simply may not want to put you on the spot; and so they do not always ask "Why?" But the people who read what you write may not know you, agree with you, or feel in any way obliged to you. If you want to communicate effectively with readers, you must provide solid evidence for any point you make. An important difference, then, between writing and talking is this: *In writing, any idea that you advance must be supported with specific reasons or details.*

TEACHING TIP
Have students come up with their own examples of bold statements made in school, at work, or among friends. Ask them if these assertions were challenged. You may want to offer examples of your own.

ESL NOTE
Some nonnative speakers have learned English from their peers. Therefore, they may not readily distinguish between writing and talking.

Think of your readers as reasonable people. They will not take your views on faith, but they are willing to consider what you say as long as you support it. Therefore, remember to support with specific evidence any point that you make.

Point and Support in a Paragraph

In conversation, you might say to a friend who has suggested a movie, "No, thanks. Going to the movies is just too much of a hassle. Parking, people, everything." From shared past experiences, your friend may know what you are talking about so that you will not have to explain your statement. But in writing, your point would have to be backed up with specific reasons and details.

Below is a paragraph, written by a student named Diane Woods, on why moviegoing is a nuisance. A *paragraph* is a short paper of 150 to 200 words. It usually consists of an opening point called a *topic sentence* followed by a series of sentences that support that point.

The Hazards of Moviegoing

Although I love movies, I have found that there are drawbacks to moviegoing. One problem is just the inconvenience of it all. To get to the theater, I have to drive for at least fifteen minutes, or more if traffic is bad. It can take forever to find a parking spot, and then I have to walk across a huge parking lot to the theater. There I encounter long lines, sold-out shows, and ever-increasing prices. And I hate sitting with my feet sticking to the floor because of other people's spilled snacks. Another problem is my lack of self-control at the theater. I often stuff myself with unhealthy calorie-laden snacks. My choices might include a bucket of popcorn dripping with butter, a box of Milk Duds, a large Coke, or all three. Finally, the worst problem is some of the other moviegoers. As kids run up and down the aisle, teenagers laugh and shout at the screen. People of all ages drop soda cups and popcorn tubs, cough and burp, and squirm endlessly in their seats. All in all, I would rather stay home and watch movies on cable TV or Netflix in the comfort of my own living room.

Notice what the supporting evidence does here. It provides you, the reader, with a basis for understanding *why* the writer makes the point that is made. Through this specific evidence, the writer has explained and successfully communicated the idea that moviegoing can be a nuisance.

The evidence that supports the point in a paragraph often consists of a series of reasons followed by examples and details that support the reasons. That is true of the paragraph above: three reasons are provided, with examples and details that back up those reasons. Supporting evidence in a paper can also consist of anecdotes, personal experiences, facts, studies, statistics, and the opinions of experts.

The paragraph on moviegoing, like almost any piece of effective writing, has two essential parts: (1) a point is advanced, and (2) that point is then supported. Taking a minute to outline the paragraph will help you understand these basic parts clearly. Add the words needed to complete the outline of the paragraph.

Point: There are drawbacks to moviegoing.

Support:

1. Inconvenience

    a. Fifteen-minute drive to theater

    b. Long time to find parking spot, and long walk to theater

    c. Long lines, sold-out shows, and increasing prices

    d. Sticky floor

2. Lack of self-control

    a. Often stuff myself with unhealthy snacks

    b. Might have popcorn, candy, soda, or all three

3. Other moviegoers

    a. Running kids

    b. Laughing, shouting teenagers

    c. People of all ages make noise

TEACHING TIP
You may want to do this activity with the entire class. Copy this partial outline onto the board, and then ask students to fill in the blanks.

An excellent way to get a feel for the paragraph is to write one. Your instructor may ask you to do that now. The only guidelines you need to follow are the ones described here. There is an advantage to writing a paragraph right away, at a point where you have had almost no instruction. This first paragraph will give a quick sense of your needs as a writer and will provide a baseline—a standard of comparison that you and your instructor can use to measure your writing progress during the semester.

Here, then, is your topic: The opening photo of this chapter asked you to think about your strengths and weaknesses as a student. Select one of your strengths or weaknesses and write a paragraph on why you believe it to be a strength or weakness. Provide three reasons why you consider it a strength or weakness, and give plenty of details to develop each of your three reasons.

Notice that the sample paragraph, "The Hazards of Moviegoing," has the same format your paragraph should have. You should do what this writer has done:

- State a point in the first sentence.

- Give three reasons to support the point.

- Introduce each reason clearly with signal words (such as *First of all,* *Second,* and *Finally*).

- Provide details that develop each of the three reasons.

TEACHING TIP
Have students complete paragraph and submit for instructor feedback.

Benefits of Paragraph Writing

Paragraph writing offers at least three benefits. First of all, mastering the structure of the paragraph will help make you a better writer. For other courses, you'll often do writing that will be variations on the paragraph form—for example, exam answers, summaries, response papers, and brief reports. In addition, paragraphs serve as the basic building blocks of essays, the most common form of writing in college. The basic structure of the traditional paragraph, with its emphasis on a clear point and well-organized, logical support, will help you write effective essays and almost every kind of paper that you will have to do.

Second, the discipline of writing a paragraph will strengthen your skills as a reader and listener. You'll become more critically aware of other writers' and speakers' ideas and the evidence they provide—or fail to provide—to support those ideas.

Most important, paragraph writing will make you a stronger thinker. Writing a solidly reasoned paragraph requires mental discipline and close attention to a set of logical rules. Creating a paragraph in which there is an overall topic sentence supported by well-reasoned, convincing evidence is more challenging than writing a free-form or expressive paper. Such a paragraph obliges you to carefully sort out, think through, and organize your ideas. You'll learn to discover and express just what your ideas are and to develop those ideas in a sound and logical way. Traditional paragraph writing, in short, will train your mind to think clearly, and that ability will prove to be of value in every phase of your life.

Diagram of a Paragraph

The following diagram shows you at a glance the different parts of a standard college paragraph. The diagram will serve as a helpful guide when you are writing or evaluating paragraphs.

Topic sentence	The *topic sentence* states the main idea advanced in the paragraph.
Support point 1 Specific evidence	The *support point* advances the first point for the main idea and provides *specific evidence* that develops that point.
Support point 2 Specific evidence	The *support point* advances the second point for the main idea and provides *specific evidence* that develops that point.
Support point 3 Specific evidence	The *support point* advances the third point for the main idea and provides *specific evidence* that develops that point.
Concluding sentence	The *concluding sentence* is the final thought that stems from and reinforces the topic of the paragraph.

Sample Annotated Paragraph

Dr. Seuss, born Theodor Seuss Geisel, wrote and illustrated more than forty books for children, but his three most important books are *Horton Hears a Who!*, *The Lorax*, and *The Sneetches*. In *Horton Hears a Who!*, Horton finds and protects a speck of dust that turns out to be a tiny planet. Because the other animals cannot see nor hear the people on the planet, they tease Horton for his beliefs. Despite danger and bullying, Horton stands up for the community and saves it from being destroyed by the other animals. In *The Lorax*, the Lorax stands up for the environment and the Truffula trees. The trees are being cut down to be turned into Thneeds, garments that are knitted out of the trees' silk-like leaves. As more and more people want Thneeds, the factories grow, the forests are cut down, and the air is filled with smog. Through it all, the Lorax keeps pleading with the factory owners to stop killing the forests and pay attention to the environment. In *The Sneetches*, the Sneetches learn about discrimination. The Sneetches with stars on their bellies don't treat the Sneetches without stars nicely. A shady businessman creates a machine that stamps stars onto Sneetches bellies. This causes the original Sneetches to get upset because they lose their specialness and leads to a series of events in which Sneetches get stars stamped on their bellies and removed from their bellies until no one has any more money. The Sneetches eventually learn that discrimination is hurtful. While Dr. Seuss wrote many other books, these three have very powerful messages.

Writing as a Way to Communicate with Others: Audience and Purpose

When you talk, chances are you do not treat everyone the same. For example, you are unlikely to speak to your boss in the same way that you chat with a young child. Instead, you adjust what you say to suit the people who are listening to you—your *audience*. Similarly, you probably change your speech each day to suit whatever *purpose* you have in mind when you are speaking. For instance, if you wanted to tell someone how to get to your new apartment, you would speak differently than if you were describing your favorite movie.

To communicate effectively, people must constantly adjust their speech to suit their purpose and audience. This same idea is true for writing. When you write for others, it is crucial to know both your purpose for writing and the audience who will be reading your work. The ability to adjust your writing to suit your purpose and audience will serve you well, not only in the classroom but also in the workplace and beyond.

TEACHING TIP
Ask students to suggest a topic, and then reinforce the three purposes by creating a topic sentence to inform, to persuade, and to entertain.

ESL NOTE
Students from other cultures may not be used to arguing a point or stating an opinion.

Purpose

The three most common purposes of writing are to inform, to persuade, and to entertain. Each is described briefly below.

- To **inform**—to give information about a subject. Authors who are writing to inform want to provide facts that will explain or teach something to readers. For example, an informative paragraph about Veterans Day might begin, "Veterans Day became a national holiday in 1938."

- To **persuade**—to convince the reader to agree with the author's point of view on a subject. Authors who are writing to persuade may give facts, but their main goal is to argue or prove a point to readers. A persuasive paragraph about Veterans Day might begin, "Everyone in America should have the day off on Veterans Day in order to attend celebrations to honor all those who have served America so honorably."

- To **entertain**—to amuse and delight; to appeal to the reader's senses and imagination. Authors write to entertain in various ways, through fiction and nonfiction. An entertaining paragraph about Veterans Day might begin, "My grandfather's most embarrassing moment occurred on Veterans Day when he was just a private."

Considering Purpose within Different Contexts

Typically, the *purpose* of completing any college writing assignment is to fulfill a course requirement and get a grade. But all writing—whether done for a class, a job, or any other reason—is aimed at accomplishing something far more specific. In most cases, you will be given an assignment that explains or at least hints at that purpose. You will be able to spot clues about purpose by looking for key words in the assignment such as *define, contrast, argue, illustrate*, or *explain causes and/or effects*.

For example, an assignment for a history paper might ask you to *explain* the causes of the Iraq War. An essay question on a chemistry midterm might call for the *definition* of an ionic bond. A criminal justice assignment might ask you to *contrast* the American criminal justice system with the Australian criminal justice system. If you are enrolled in a technical writing course, you may be asked to *describe* a machine or *analyze* a natural or mechanical *process*. Each of these tasks asks you to accomplish a specific aim.

Having a clear idea of your purpose is just as important for writing you do outside of college (what many call "real-world writing"). For example, say your employer asks you to write a report that recommends the purchase of a standing desk from a choice of three. You might have to *contrast* each on the basis of cost, ease of use, features, and reliability. Then you might have to *argue* that even though standing desk A is more expensive than standing desks B and C, it is preferable because it is more durable and will hold multiple monitors. Note that unlike a college writing assignment, the job you have been given by your employer does not specify the approaches (in this case *contrasting* and *arguing*) that you will have to take to complete the project. You will have to figure that out for yourself by considering the writing's purpose before you begin.

As you gather information for your paragraph or essay, keep your purpose in mind. You might want to read your assignment several times, looking for key words such as those mentioned above, and then summarize your purpose in a short sentence of your own on a piece of scrap paper. Keep this sentence in front of you throughout the prewriting stage.

As noted previously, much of the writing in this book will involve some form of argumentation or persuasion. You will advance a point or thesis and then support it in a variety of ways. To some extent, also, you will write papers to inform—to provide readers with information about a particular subject. And because, in practice, writing often combines purposes, you might also find yourself including vivid or humorous details in order to entertain your readers.

Audience

The audience for a piece of writing is its reader or readers. Like purpose, audience should be considered early in the writing process. In college, your primary audience will be your instructor. Your instructor, though, is really representative of the larger audience you should see yourself writing for—an audience of educated adults who expect you to present your ideas in a clear, direct, organized way.

Some instructors will also require you to share your work with other students, either in small groups or with the class as a whole. In some cases, your writing will be judged on how well it informs or persuades your classmates. Therefore, you must keep them in mind as you write. Other academic situations in which you will want to keep your audience in mind include writing a letter to a college newspaper to express an opinion, applying for a transfer to another college, or applying for a scholarship.

After you graduate, you will have ample opportunity to write to a wide range of audiences. This is when you will have to pay even more attention to evaluating your audience. For example, careers in science and technology require employees to write to other experts, who may know a great deal about the subject. On the other hand, scientists and technologists are often required to write to laypersons, whose knowledge of a subject might vary from adequate to nonexistent. The same is true of those who pursue careers in business, law enforcement, the legal and medical professions, the military, education, or government work.

Let's say you get a job as a city engineer, and the town decides to change an intersection from a four-way stop to a roundabout. You may be asked to write a letter to residents who live along that road explaining why the job is necessary, what will be done, how long it will take, and why they may experience delays in getting home during construction. Explaining such a project to another civil engineer might not be difficult, since he or she will know about the technicalities of traffic flow studies, intersection studies, and paving. Your explanation will be fairly straightforward and will use technical terminology that this reader is sure to understand. In addition, you won't have to convince your engineering colleague that the inconvenience to residents will be worthwhile; it will be obvious that the improvements will make the road much safer and more efficient. However, if you were writing to the residents—people who may not have any knowledge about road and intersection design—you would avoid using technical terminology, which they might not understand. In addition, you might have to make a real effort to convince these readers that the inconvenience they will experience during construction is worth the outcome—a much safer and more efficient intersection.

Evaluating the Nature of Your Audience

Here are a few questions you should ask yourself when evaluating any audience. The answers to these questions will help determine your approach to any writing project.

1. *How much does the audience already know about the subject?* If you assume that your readers know very little, you might bore them with too much basic information. On the other hand, if you incorrectly assume that they know more than they do, you might confuse them by using unfamiliar technical terminology or neglecting to provide enough informative detail.

2. *Why might the reader need or want to read this material?* In college, your English professor will use your papers to evaluate your writing skills and determine how you can strengthen them. He or she will probably also use them to establish your course grade. If, however, you are writing to a group of residents whose road is going to be intermittently closed for improvements, you will have to meet different expectations. They will want to know why the improvements are being made, how long the work will take, and what benefits they will reap from it. As taxpayers, they may also want to know how much the new intersection will cost.

3. *Is your purpose simply to inform the audience? Or is it to convince readers of something as well?* If your purpose is to convince or persuade, you may want to use some of the techniques for writing arguments in Chapter 14. For example, if you are writing a letter to the editor of your local newspaper in support of the new school budget, you may have to persuade voters to approve the budget even though it is sure to raise their property taxes.

4. *What type of language should be used?* Are you writing to peers—other college students—or are you communicating with professors, business and community leaders, or government officials? With peers, you might want to use language that is relaxed, friendly, and informal, language that will win their confidence. If you're writing to a professor, a government official, or an employer, you will have to be more formal.

Writing as a Skill

A sure way to ruin your chances of learning how to write competently is to believe that writing is a "natural gift" rather than a learned skill. People with such an attitude think that they are the only ones for whom writing is unbearably difficult. They feel that everyone else finds writing easy or at least tolerable. Such people typically say, "I'm not any good at writing" or "English was not one of my good subjects." They imply that they simply do not have a talent for writing, while others do. The result of this attitude is that people try to avoid writing, and when they do write, they don't try their best. Their attitude becomes a self-fulfilling prophecy: Their writing fails chiefly because they have brainwashed themselves into thinking that they don't have the "natural talent" needed to write. Unless their attitude changes, they probably will not learn how to write effectively.

A realistic attitude about writing must build on the idea that *writing is a skill.* It is a skill like driving, typing, or cooking, and like any skill, it can be learned. If you have the determination to learn, this book will give you the extensive practice needed to develop your writing skills.

Many people find it difficult to do the intense, active thinking that clear writing demands. (Perhaps television has made us all so passive that the active thinking necessary in both writing and reading now seems harder than ever.) It is frightening to sit down before a blank sheet of paper or a computer screen and know that, an hour later, nothing on it may be worth keeping. It is frustrating to discover how much of a challenge it is to transfer thoughts and feelings from one's head into words. It is upsetting to find that an apparently simple writing subject often turns out to be complicated. But writing is not an automatic process: we will not get something for nothing—and we should not expect to. For almost everyone, competent writing comes from plain hard work—from determination, sweat, and head-on battle. The good news is that the skill of writing can be mastered, and if you are ready to work, you will learn what you need to know.

TEACHING TIP
Get students to talk about other skills they have mastered. Draw parallels to writing.

To get a sense of just how you regard writing, read the following statements. Put a check (✓) beside those statements with which you agree. This activity is not a test, so try to be as honest as possible.

ACTIVITY 3

TEACHING TIP
Consider doing this activity with the entire class. Ask students if they agree with each statement and keep a tally of their answers on the board.

_____ 1. A good writer should be able to sit down and write a paper straight through without stopping.

_____ 2. Writing is a skill that anyone can learn with practice.

_____ 3. I'll never be good at writing because I make too many mistakes in spelling, grammar, and punctuation.

_____ 4. Because I dislike writing, I always start a paper at the last possible minute.

_____ 5. I've always done poorly in English, and I don't expect that to change.

Now read the following comments about the five statements. The comments will help you see if your attitude is hurting or helping your efforts to become a better writer.

TEACHING TIP
You may want to provide additional statements, such as "Good writers don't need any help" and "The teacher is the only one who can help me."

Comments

- **A good writer should be able to sit down and write a paper straight through without stopping.**

  Statement 1 is not true. Writing is, in fact, a process. It is done not in one easy step but in a series of steps, and seldom at one sitting. If you cannot do a paper all at once, that simply means you are like most of the other people on the planet. It is harmful to carry around the false idea that writing should be easy.

• **Writing is a skill that anyone can learn with practice.**

Statement 2 is absolutely true. Writing is a skill, like driving or cooking, that you can master with hard work. If you want to learn to write, you can. It is as simple as that. If you believe this, you are ready to learn how to become a competent writer.

Some people hold the false belief that writing is a natural gift, which some have and others do not. Because of this belief, they never make a truly honest effort to learn to write—and so they never learn.

• **I'll never be good at writing because I make too many mistakes in spelling, grammar, and punctuation.**

The first concern in good writing should be content—what you have to say. Your ideas and feelings are what matter most. You should not worry about spelling, grammar, or punctuation while working on content.

Unfortunately, some people are so self-conscious about making mistakes that they do not focus on what they want to say. They need to realize that a paper is best done in stages, and that applying the rules can and should wait until a later stage in the writing process. Through review and practice, you will eventually learn how to follow the rules with confidence.

• **Because I dislike writing, I always start a paper at the last possible minute.**

This habit is all too common. You feel you are going to do poorly, and then behave in a way that ensures you *will* do poorly! Your attitude is so negative that you defeat yourself—not even allowing enough time to really try.

TEACHING TIP
Comment on the other statements made in class.

Again, what you need to realize is that writing is a process. Because it is done in steps, you don't have to get it right all at once. If you allow yourself enough time, you'll find a way to make a paper come together.

• **I've always done poorly in English, and I don't expect that to change.**

How you may have performed in the *past* does not control how you can perform in the *present*. Even if you did poorly in English in high school, it is in your power to make English one of your best subjects in college. If you believe writing can be learned and then work hard at it, you *will* become a better writer.

In conclusion, your attitude is crucial. If you believe you are a poor writer and always will be, chances are you will not improve. If you realize you can become a better writer, chances are you *will* improve. Depending on how you allow yourself to think, you can be your own best friend or your own worst enemy.

TEACHING TIP
Ask students to recall a time in their lives when they embarked on a journey without having a clear destination (for example, an unplanned road trip). Inquire if they made any discoveries.

Writing as a Process of Discovery

In addition to believing that writing is a natural gift, many people believe, mistakenly, that writing should flow in a simple, straight line from the writer's head onto the written page. But writing is seldom an easy, one-step journey in which a finished paper comes out in a first draft. The truth is that *writing is a process of discovery* involving a series of steps, and those steps are very often a zigzag journey. Look at the following illustrations of the writing process:

Seldom the Case

Starting point ⟶ Finished paper

Usually the Case

Starting point ⟿ Finished paper

Very often, writers do not discover just what they want to write about until they explore their thoughts in writing. For example, Diane Woods, the author of the paragraph on moviegoing, had been assigned to write about some annoyance in everyday life. She did not know what annoyance she would choose; instead, she just began writing about annoyances in general, in order to discover a topic. One of those annoyances was traffic, which seemed promising, so she began putting down ideas and details that came to her about traffic. One detail was the traffic she had to deal with in going to the movies. That made her think of the traffic in the parking lot at the theater complex. At that point, she realized that moviegoing itself was an annoyance. She switched direction in midstream and began writing down ideas and details about moviegoing.

As Diane wrote, she realized how much other moviegoers annoyed her, and she began thinking that other movie patrons might be her main idea in a paper. But when she was writing about patrons who loudly drop popcorn tubs onto the floor, she realized how much all the snacks at the concession stand tempted her. She changed direction again, thinking now that maybe she could talk about patrons and tempting snacks. She kept writing, just putting down more and more details about her movie experiences, still not having figured out exactly how she would fit both patrons and snacks into the paragraph. Even though her paragraph had not quite jelled, she was not worried, because she knew that if she kept writing, it would eventually come together.

The point is that writing is often a process of continuing discovery; as you write, you may suddenly switch direction or double back. You may be working on a topic sentence and realize suddenly that it could be your concluding thought. Or you may be developing a supporting idea and then decide that it should be the main point of your paper. Chapter 2 will treat the writing process more directly. What is important to remember here is that writers frequently do not know their exact destination as they begin to write. Very often they discover the direction and shape of a paper during the process of writing.

Keeping a Journal

Because writing is a skill, it makes sense that the more you practice writing, the better you will write. One excellent way to get practice in writing, even before you begin composing formal paragraphs, is to keep a daily or almost daily journal. Writing a journal will help you develop the habit of thinking on paper and will show you how ideas can be discovered in the process of writing. A journal can make writing a familiar part of your life and can serve as a continuing source of ideas for papers.

TEACHING TIP
Provide visual pictures of the writing process, such as a spiral or zigzag line. Emphasize to your students that writers often repeat steps. For example, a writer may brainstorm ideas after writing a first draft.

in a writer's words
" *I fill notebooks with ideas, and I may take six to eight months writing about a situation that interests me. My ideas get better as time goes on.*"
—Ross Macdonald

TEACHING TIP
Bring a variety of "journals" to class to show students. For example, bring a spiral-bound notebook, loose-leaf paper, a composition notebook, an artist's sketchpad, and even a laptop computer. Encourage students to find a "journal" that suits their personality and style.

At some point during the day—perhaps during a study period after your last class of the day, or right before dinner, or right before going to bed—spend fifteen minutes or so writing in your journal. Keep in mind that you do not have to plan what to write about, or be in the mood to write, or worry about making mistakes as you write; just write down whatever words come out. You should write at least one page in each session.

You may want to use a notebook that you can easily carry with you for on-the-spot writing. Or you may decide to write on loose-leaf paper that can be transferred later to a journal folder on your desk. Many students elect to keep their journals on their home computer or laptop. No matter how you proceed, be sure to date all entries.

Your instructor may ask you to make journal entries a specific number of times a week, for a specific number of weeks. He or she may have you turn in your journal every so often for review and feedback. If you are keeping the journal on your own, try to make entries three to five times a week every week of the semester. Your journal can serve as a sourcebook of ideas for possible papers. More important, keeping a journal will help you develop the habit of thinking on paper or at the computer, and it can help you make writing a familiar part of your life.

TEACHING TIP
You may want to devote the first ten minutes of class to journal writing. Model this practice by making journal entries, too.

TEACHING TIP
Get students to discuss how blogs are public online journals. In a computer lab, you could ask students to share their blogs with the class.

| ACTIVITY 4 | Following is an excerpt from one student's journal. As you read, look for a general point and supporting material that could be the basis for an interesting paper. |

September 6

My first sociology class was tonight. The parking lot was jammed when I got there. I thought I was going to be late for class. A guard had us park on a field next to the regular lot. When I got to the room, it had the usual painted construction. Every school I have ever been in since first grade seems to be made of cinder block. The students all sat there without saying anything, waiting for the instructor to arrive. I think they were all a bit nervous like me. I hoped there wasn't going to be a ton of work in the course. I think I was also afraid of looking foolish somehow. This goes back to grade school, when I wasn't a very good student and teachers sometimes embarrassed me in class. I didn't like grade school, and I hated high school. Now here I am six years later-in college, of all places. Who would have thought I would end up here? The instructor appeared-a woman who I think was a bit nervous herself. I think I like her. Her name is Barbara Hanlin. She says we should call her Barbara. We got right into it, but it was interesting stuff. I like the fact that

continued

> she asks questions but then she lets you volunteer. I always hated it when teachers would call on you whether you wanted to answer or not. I also like the fact that she answers the questions and doesn't just leave you hanging. She takes the time to write important ideas on the board. I also like the way she laughs. This class may be OK.

1. If the writer of the journal entry above was looking for ideas for a paragraph, he could probably find several in this single entry. For example, he might write a story about the roundabout way he apparently wound up in college. See if you can find in the entry an idea that might be the basis for an interesting paragraph, and write your point in the space below.

   <u>Answers will vary</u>

2. Take fifteen minutes now to write a journal entry on this day in your life. Just start writing about anything that you have seen, said, heard, thought, or felt today, and let your thoughts take you wherever they may.

ESL NOTE
Journals are not evaluated or marked for errors, so remind nonnative speakers they can feel free to express experiences and perceptions they would readily write about in their native language.

Using Technology to Work Efficiently

- If you use computers at school to work on your essays, allow enough time. You may have to wait for a computer or printer to be free. In addition, you may need several sessions at a computer and printer to complete your paper.

- There are numerous programs you can use to type and save your work. Google Docs, Pages, Open Office, and Microsoft Office are all programs that offer helpful features for typing and saving students' papers.

- Every program allows you to save your writing by clicking one or more icons. Save your work frequently as you write your draft. A saved file is stored safely on the computer or network. A file that is not saved will be lost if the computer crashes or if there is a loss of power.

- Keep your work in two places—the hard drive or network you are working on and a backup USB drive. At the end of each session, copy your work onto the USB drive or e-mail a copy to yourself. Then, if the hard drive or network fails, you'll have the backup copy.

- Print out your work at least at the end of every session. Then you will have not only your most recent draft to work on away from the computer but also a backup hard copy in case something should happen to your electronic file.

- Work in single spacing so that you can see as much of your writing on the screen at one time as possible. Just before you print out your work, change to double spacing.

- Before making major changes in a paper, create a copy of your file. For example, if your file is titled "Worst Job," create a file called "Worst Job 2." Then make all your changes in that new file. If the changes don't work out, you can always go back to the original file.

Using Technology to Communicate Effectively

Much communication that takes place between instructors and students occurs electronically, either through e-mail or a discussion forum on a learning management system like Blackboard or Schoology.

A Proper Formal E-mail

Students should keep the following points in mind when corresponding via e-mail with an instructor:

- E-mail should be treated like a formal writing assignment.

- You should include a subject line, a formal greeting, an explanation of who you are and what class you are enrolled in, a detailed message, and a formal closing.

- You should revise for clarity and edit for mistakes prior to sending your message.

- You should not expect immediate responses from instructors. You may have to wait up to forty-eight hours before hearing back from an instructor.

in a writer's words

" *The computer is the most liberating because it is the fastest: I can sneak up on myself and write things that I would never dare to say or write it out longhand or if I had to say it publicly.*"

—Russell Banks

Send now   **Send Later**   **Draft**   **Trash**   **Attachment**   **Signature**

To: Professor Williams

Cc:

Subject: English 101 Literary Analysis Assignment

Dear Professor Williams:

My name is Finn Boller, and I am a student in your English 101 class that meets on Monday/Wednesday/Friday at 9:00 a.m. I have a question about the literary analysis assignment.

I wrote down that the assignment is due next Wednesday, but in class you stated it was due on Friday instead. I wanted to make sure that I understood you correctly, and that you are giving us an extension.

Thank you so much.

Sincerely,
Finn Boller

A Proper Discussion Forum Post

Students should keep the following points in mind when posting on a discussion forum:

- Discussion forums should be treated like formal writing assignments.

- You should include a title line that explains what the post will be about.

- You don't need to explain who you are and what class you are in, as forums are set up in individual classes and are automatically attached to students' accounts.

- You should revise for clarity and edit for mistakes prior to sending your message.

- You should not expect immediate responses from instructors. You may have to wait up to forty-eight hours before hearing back from an instructor.

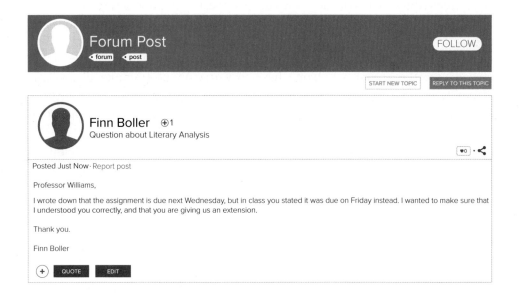

Either write a formal e-mail to your instructor or post the following information to your class discussion forum.

ACTIVITY 5

Your formal e-mail should include:

- full name
- class you are enrolled in
- class schedule
- work schedule
- concerns about the class

Your discussion forum post should include:

- class schedule
- work schedule
- concerns about the class

TEACHING TIP
Have students complete this activity in the first week of class to ensure they understand proper communication techniques. The results of students' concerns can also be compiled and shared with the class.

Using a Computer at Each Stage of the Writing Process

Following are some ways to make computer use a part of your writing. Note that this section may be more meaningful *after* you have worked through Chapter 2 of this book.

Prewriting

If you're a fast typist, many kinds of prewriting will work well on a computer. With freewriting in particular, you can get ideas onto the screen almost as quickly as they occur to you. A passing thought that could be productive is not likely to get lost. You may even find it helpful, when freewriting, to dim the monitor screen so that you can't see what you're typing. If you temporarily can't see the screen, you won't have to worry about grammar or spelling or typing errors (none of which matter in prewriting); instead, you can concentrate on getting down as many ideas and details as possible about your subject.

After any initial freewriting, questioning, and list making on a computer, it's often very helpful to print out a hard copy of what you've done. With a clean printout in front of you, you'll be able to see everything at once and revise and expand your work with handwritten comments in the margins of the paper. Don't underestimate the power of working on a printed copy. By allowing yourself the freedom to mark up the printed copy, you will free up more ideas.

If you prepared a list of items, you may be able to turn that list into a scratch outline right on the screen. Create a copy of your list below the original. Next, using the copy, delete the ideas you feel should not be in your paper and add any new ideas that occur to you. Then use the cut and paste functions to shuffle the supporting ideas around until you find the best order for your paper. If you find that you accidentally deleted an idea that would now work, you can use the copy and paste feature to take that idea from your original list and place it in your scratch outline.

Using the computer also makes it easy for you to experiment with the wording of your paper's point. You can try a number of versions in a short time. After you have decided on the version that works best, you can easily delete the other versions—or simply move them to a temporary "leftover" section at the end of the paper.

Writing Your First Draft

Like many writers, you may want to write out your first draft by hand and then type it into the computer for the next steps in writing. Even as you type your handwritten draft, you may find yourself making some changes and improvements. And once you have a draft on the screen, or printed out, you will find it much easier to revise than a handwritten one.

If you feel comfortable composing directly on a computer and you typed your prewriting, you can benefit from its special features. For example, if you wrote an anecdote in your freewriting that you plan to use in your paper, simply copy the story from your freewriting file and insert it where it fits in your paper. You can refine it then or later. Or if you discover while typing that a sentence is out of place, cut it out from where it is and paste it wherever you wish. And if while writing you realize that an earlier sentence can be expanded, just move your cursor back to that point and type in the additional material.

Revising

It is during revision that the virtues of using a computer really shine. All substituting, adding, deleting, and rearranging can be done easily within an existing file. All changes instantly take their proper places within the paper, not scribbled above the line or squeezed into the margin. You can concentrate on each change you want to make, because you never have to type from scratch or work on a messy draft. You can carefully go through your paper to check that all your supporting evidence is relevant and to add new support as needed here and there. Anything you decide to eliminate can be deleted in a keystroke. Anything you add can be inserted precisely where you choose. If you change your mind, all you have to do is delete or cut and paste. Then you can sweep through the paper, focusing on other changes, such as improving word choice, increasing sentence variety, and eliminating wordiness.

Editing and Proofreading

Editing and proofreading also benefit richly from computers. Most programs have spell-checker and grammar-checker features. If your own program doesn't have these options, your college computers will likely provide them, or you can use an online program like Grammarly or SpellCheckPlus.

The spell-checker function tells you when a word is not in the program's dictionary. Keep in mind, however, that the spell-checker cannot tell you how to spell a name correctly or when you have mistakenly used, for example, *their* instead of *there*. To a spell-checker, *Thank ewe four the complement* is as correct as *Thank you for the compliment*. The grammar-checker is a good feature, but use it with caution. It will look for mistakes like fragments and run-ons, but it isn't always correct. Any errors it doesn't uncover are still your responsibility.

Once you have checked your essay, you should print it out for a final read-through. Reading aloud, slowly, will help you catch any typos or awkward sentences the programs didn't identify.

A typed paper, with its clean appearance and handsome formatting, often looks so good that you may feel it is in better shape than it really is. Do not be fooled. Take sufficient time to review your grammar, punctuation, and spelling carefully.

Even after you hand in your paper, save the computer file. Your teacher may ask you to do some revising, and then the file will save you from having to type the paper from scratch.

MLA Format

Assignments in English classes must be submitted in MLA format. While many students might think this only applies to source-based essays, MLA format also dictates the formal characteristics of the paper, including paper size, margins, spacing, and font. All writing assignments should be formatted like this:

Model First Page of a Paper in MLA Style

Double-space lines. Leave a one-inch margin on all sides.

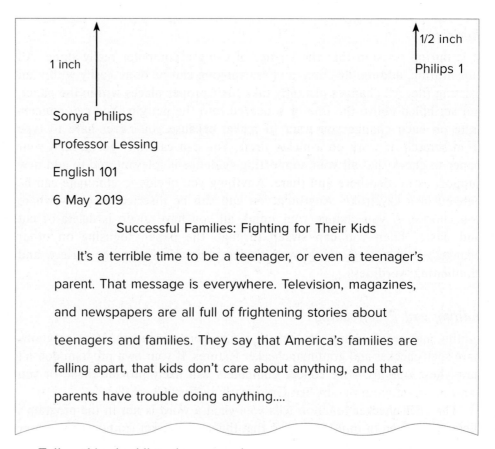

1 inch

1/2 inch

Philips 1

Sonya Philips

Professor Lessing

English 101

6 May 2019

Successful Families: Fighting for Their Kids

It's a terrible time to be a teenager, or even a teenager's parent. That message is everywhere. Television, magazines, and newspapers are all full of frightening stories about teenagers and families. They say that America's families are falling apart, that kids don't care about anything, and that parents have trouble doing anything....

Follow this checklist when preparing a paper:

- Is there a heading that includes your name, your professor's name, your class, and the date?

- Is there a header with your last name and the page number?

- Are your margins one inch all around the paper?

- Is the title of your paper about two inches from the top of the page, centered, and separate from the body of the text? Have you been careful *not* to put quotation marks around the title and *not* to underline it? Have you capitalized all the words in the title except short connecting words like *of, for, the, and, it,* and *to*?

- Have you indented the first line of each paragraph five spaces (half an inch or tab) from the left-hand margin?

- Is your paper double-spaced?

- Does your paper use Times New Roman 12-point font throughout, including your title? (This is the standard MLA font unless your professor directs you otherwise.)

Also ask yourself these important questions about the title and the first sentence of your paper:

- Is your title made up of several words that tell what the paper is about? (The title should hint at the topic, not focus on what assignment it fulfills.)

- Does the first sentence of your paper stand independent of the title? (The reader should *not* have to use the words in the title to make sense of the opening sentence.)

| Answering the following questions will help you evaluate your attitude about writing. | **ACTIVITY 6** |

Answers will vary.

TEACHING TIP
After students complete this activity, ask them to share their answers with a partner. Students are often surprised to learn that others share their attitudes about writing.

1. How much practice were you given writing compositions in high school?

    _____ Much   _____ Some   _____ Little

2. How much feedback (positive or negative comments) from teachers were you given on your compositions?

    _____ Much   _____ Some   _____ Little

3. How did your teachers seem to regard your writing?

    _____ Good   _____ Fair   _____ Poor

4. Do you feel that some people simply have a gift for writing and others do not?

    _____ Yes   _____ Sometimes   _____ No

5. When do you start writing a paper?

    _____ Several days before it is due

    _____ About a day before it is due

    _____ At the last possible minute

Many people who answer *Little* to questions 1 and 2 often answer *Poor, Yes,* and *At the last possible minute* to questions 3, 4, and 5. On the other hand, people who answer *Much* or *Some* to questions 1 and 2 also tend to have more favorable responses to the other questions. The point is that people with little practice in the skill of writing often have understandably negative feelings about their writing ability. They need not have such feelings, however, because writing is a skill that they can learn with practice.

6. Did you learn to write traditional paragraphs in high school?

    _____ Yes   _____ No

7. If so, did your teacher explain to you the benefits of writing such essays?

    _____ Yes, very clearly

    _____ Maybe, but not that I remember

    _____ No

If you answered *Maybe* or *No* to question 7, you may not be looking forward to taking the course in which you are using this book. It will be worth your while to read and consider again the enormous benefits that can come from practice in writing traditional paragraphs (discussed in an earlier section, "Benefits of Paragraph Writing").

8. In your own words, explain what it means to say that writing is often a zigzag journey rather than a straight-line journey.

    _____

    _____

    _____

    _____

    _____

REFLECTIVE ACTIVITY

©mavo/Shutterstock

1. Read the journal entry on a day in your life (Activity 4). What does it tell you about your ability to generate ideas that might later be used as topics for more complete and more formal writing?

2. You read that writing is a process of discovery, a series of steps. You also learned that going through the process will be like a zigzag journey. How is this different from the way you thought about writing before?

The Writing Process

©Noel Hendrickson/Getty Images

RESPONDING TO IMAGES

Everyone approaches writing differently. Some people dive right in. Others wait until the last minute. How would you describe your approach? Think about the steps you follow when asked to write for school. Keep in mind that there is no one right way to get started.

TEACHING TIP
Ask students to complete this writing prompt in class.

Chapter 1 introduced you to the paragraph form and some basics of writing. This chapter will explain and illustrate the sequence of steps in writing an effective paragraph. In particular, the chapter will focus on prewriting and revising—strategies that can help with every paper that you write.

For many people, writing is a process that involves the following steps:

1. Discovering a point—often through prewriting

2. Developing solid support for the point—often through more prewriting

3. Organizing the supporting material, making an outline, and writing it out in a first draft

4. Revising and then editing carefully to ensure an effective, error-free paper

Learning this sequence will help give you confidence when the time comes to write. You'll know that you can use prewriting as a way to think on paper (or on the screen) and to discover gradually just what ideas you want to develop. You'll understand that there are four clear-cut goals to aim for in your writing—unity, support, organization, and error-free sentences. You'll realize that you can revise a paper until it is strong and effective. As well, you'll be able to edit a paper so that your sentences are clear and free of errors.

Prewriting

Like many people, you may have trouble getting started writing. A mental block may develop when you sit down before a blank sheet of paper. You may not be able to think of an interesting topic sentence. Or you may have trouble coming up with relevant details to support a possible topic sentence. And even after starting a paper, you may hit snags—moments when you wonder, "What else can I say?" or "Where do I go next?"

The following pages describe five prewriting techniques that will help you think about and develop a topic and get words on paper: (1) freewriting, (2) questioning, (3) making a list, (4) diagramming, and (5) preparing a scratch outline. These techniques help you think about and create material, and they are a central part of the writing process.

Technique 1: Freewriting

Freewriting means jotting down in rough sentences or phrases everything that comes to mind about a possible topic. See if you can write nonstop for ten minutes or more. Do not worry about spelling or punctuating correctly, about erasing mistakes, about organizing material, or about finding exact words. Instead, explore an idea by putting down whatever pops into your head. If you get stuck for words, repeat yourself until more words come. There is no need to feel inhibited, since mistakes *do not count* and you do not have to hand in your freewriting.

Freewriting will limber up your writing muscles and make you familiar with the act of writing. It is a way to break through mental blocks about writing. Since you do not have to worry about mistakes, you can focus on discovering what you want to say about a subject. Your initial ideas and impressions will often become clearer after you have gotten them down on paper, and they may lead to other impressions and ideas. Through continued practice in freewriting, you will develop the habit of thinking as you write. And you will learn a technique that is a helpful way to get started on almost any paper.

Freewriting: A Student Model

Diane Woods's paragraph "The Hazards of Moviegoing" in Chapter 1 was developed in response to an assignment to write about some annoyance in everyday life. Diane began by doing some general freewriting and thinking about things that annoy her. At first, she was stuck for words; she had writer's block, a common experience for writers. However, Diane pushed through and just kept putting words on the page. Even writing "stuck, stuck, stuck!" helped her stay focused, and eventually, good ideas began to emerge. Here is her freewriting:

continued

There are lots of things I get annoyed by. One of them that comes to mind is politishans, in fact I am so annoyed by them that I don't want to say anything about them the last thing I want is to write about them. Stuck, stuck, stuck! . . what else annoys me?? (besides this assignment)–now I'm whining again. That's annoying. OK–Another thing that bothers me are people who keep complaining about everything. If you're having trouble, do something about it just don't keep complaining and just talking. I am really annoyed by traffic. There are too many cars in our block and its not surprising. Everyone has a car, the parents have cars and the parents are just too induljent and the kids have cars, and they're all coming and going all the time and often driving too fast. Speeding up and down the street. We need a speed limit sign but here I am back with politiks again. I am really bothered when I have to drive to the movie theater all the congestion along the way plus there are just so many cars there at the mall. No space even though the parking lot is huge it just

TEACHING TIP
Point out that writers often want to correct their mistakes or pause during freewriting. Stress the importance of nonstop writing.

TEACHING TIP
To help students limber up their writing muscles have them limber up their physical muscles. You might ask them to stretch their fingers.

TEACHING TIP
Ask a volunteer to read Diane Woods's general freewriting. Next, ask a volunteer to read her focused freewriting. As a class, discuss the changes that the author made to her paragraph.

> fills up with cars. Movies are a bother anyway because the people can be annoying who are sitting there in the theater with you, talking on their cell phones, squirming in their seats, and dropping popcorn tubs and acting like they're at home when they're not.

TEACHING TIP
Suggest to students that they can use a computer to freewrite.

At this point, Diane read over her notes and, as she later commented, "I realized that I had several potential topics. I said to myself, 'What point can I make that I can cover in a paragraph? What do I have the most information about?' I decided that maybe I could narrow my topic down to the annoyances involved in going to the movies. I figured I would have more details for that topic." Diane then did more focused freewriting to accumulate details for a paragraph on problems with moviegoing:

> I really find it annoying to go see movies anymore. Even though I love films, Traffic to Cinema Six is awful. I hate looking for a parking place, the lot isn't big enough for the theaters and other stores. You just keep driving to find a parking space and hoping someone will pull out and no one else will pull in ahead of you. Then you don't want there to be a long line and to wind up in one of the first rows with this huge screen right in front of you. Then I'm in the theater with the smell of popcorn all around. Sitting there smelling it trying to ignore it and just wanting to pour a whole bucket of popcorn with melted butter down my throat. I can't stop thinking about the choclate bars either. I love the stuff but I don't need it. The people who are there sometimes drive me nuts. Talking and laughing, kids running around, packs of teens hollaring, who can listen to the movie? And I might run into my old boyfriend—the last thing I need. Also sitting thru all the previews and commercals. If I arrive late enough to miss that junk the movie may be selled out.

Notice that there are errors in spelling, grammar, and punctuation in Diane's freewriting. Diane is not worried about such matters, nor should she be. At this stage, she just wants to do some thinking on paper and get some material down on the page. She knows that this is a good first step, a good way of getting started, and that she will then be able to go on and shape the material.

You should take the same approach when freewriting: explore your topic without worrying at all about being "correct." Figuring out what you want to say and getting raw material down on the page should be your primary focus at this early stage of the writing process.

TEACHING TIP
Get students to talk about why writers worry so much about being "correct." Offer a few reasons (for example, being a perfectionist, feeling insecure).

a. To get a sense of the freewriting process, take a sheet of paper and freewrite about some of the everyday annoyances in your life. See how much material you can accumulate in ten minutes. And remember not to worry about "mistakes"; you're just thinking on paper.

b. Read over the material that you generated and decide which annoyance you have the most information about. Then do more focused freewriting on that specific annoyance.

ACTIVITY 1

Answers will vary.

Technique 2: Questioning

In *questioning,* you generate ideas and details by asking questions about your subject. Such questions include *Who? What? Where? When? Why?* and *How?* Ask as many questions as you can think of.

Here are some questions that Diane Woods might have asked while developing her paragraph.

TEACHING TIP
Teach your students the acronym 5WH (*Who, What, Where, When, Why, How*).

Questioning: A Student Model

Questions	Answers
Why don't I like to go to a movie?	Just too many problems involved.
What annoys me about going to the movies?	Everything! Getting to the theater, waiting for the movie to start, eating snacks that I shouldn't be eating, and putting up with others during the movie.

continued

<u>When</u> is going to the movies a problem?	Could be any time—when a movie is popular, the theater is too crowded; when traffic is bad, the trip is a drag.
<u>Where</u> are problems with moviegoing?	On the highway, in the parking lot, at the concession stand, in the theater itself.
<u>Who</u> creates the problems?	I do by wanting to eat too much. The patrons do by creating disturbances. The theater owners do by not having enough parking space and showing too many commercials.
<u>How</u> can I deal with the problem?	I can stay home and watch movies on cable TV or Netflix.

TIP   Asking questions can be an effective way of getting yourself to think about a topic from different angles. The questions can help you generate details about a topic.

ACTIVITY 2

Answers will vary.

To get a sense of the questioning process, use a sheet of paper to ask yourself and answer a series of questions about a specific recent experience you've had involving your everyday annoyance. What happened? Why did the situation annoy you? How did you respond? See how many details you can accumulate in ten minutes. And remember again not to be concerned about "mistakes," because you are just thinking on paper.

Technique 3: Making a List

In *making a list,* also known as *brainstorming,* you collect ideas and details that relate to your subject. Pile these items up, one after another, without trying to sort out major details from minor ones, or trying to put the details in any special order. Your goal is just to make a list of everything about your subject that occurs to you.

After Diane did her freewriting about moviegoing, she made up the following list of details.

TEACHING TIP
Explain to your students that writers often use several prewriting techniques. Each technique may provide different results.

Making a List: A Student Model

Traffic is bad between my house and theater

Noisy patrons

Don't want to run into Jeremy

Hard to be on a diet

Kids running in aisles

I'm crowded into seats between strangers who push me off armrests

Not enough parking

Parking lot needs to be expanded

Too many previews

Can't pause or fast-forward as you can with Netflix

Long lines

High ticket prices

Too many temptatons at snack stand

Commercials for food on the screen

Can prepare healthy snacks for myself at home

Tubs of popcorn with butter

Huge choclate bars

Candy has always been my downfall

Movie may be sold out

People talking on their cell phones

People squirming in their seats

People coughing and sneezing

Icky stuff on floor

Teenagers yelling and showing off

One detail led to another as Diane expanded her list. Slowly but surely more details emerged, some of which she could use in developing her paragraph. By the time she was done with her list, she was ready to plan an outline of her paragraph and then to write her first draft.

TEACHING TIP
You may want to do Activity 3 with the entire class. Write the topic "Things that drive me crazy" on the board, and then ask your students to freely shout out their ideas. Be prepared to write quickly.

To get a sense of list-making, list on a sheet of paper all the details that you can think of about your particular everyday annoyance.

Technique 4: Clustering

Clustering, also known as *diagramming* or *mapping,* is another strategy that can be used to generate material for a paper. This method is helpful for people who like to do their thinking in a visual way. In clustering, you use lines, boxes, arrows, and circles to show relationships among the ideas and details that occur to you.

Begin by stating your subject in a few words in the center of a blank sheet of paper. Then, as ideas and details come to you, put them in boxes or circles around the subject and draw lines to connect them to each other and to the subject. Put minor ideas or details in smaller boxes or circles, and use connecting lines to show how they relate as well.

Keep in mind that there is no right or wrong way of clustering or diagramming. Remember, too, that as with other prewriting strategies, spelling mistakes are acceptable at this stage. Most importantly, this is a way to think on paper about how various ideas and details relate to one another. Below is an example of what Diane might have done to develop her ideas.

TEACHING TIP
Mention to your students that clustering helps them "see" their ideas.

TEACHING TIP
Students who find clustering helpful may want to use other graphic organizers (for example, Venn diagram or fishbone map). Provide images of these organizers.

Clustering: A Student Model

TEACHING TIP
Remind students that their ideas can overlap in clustering.

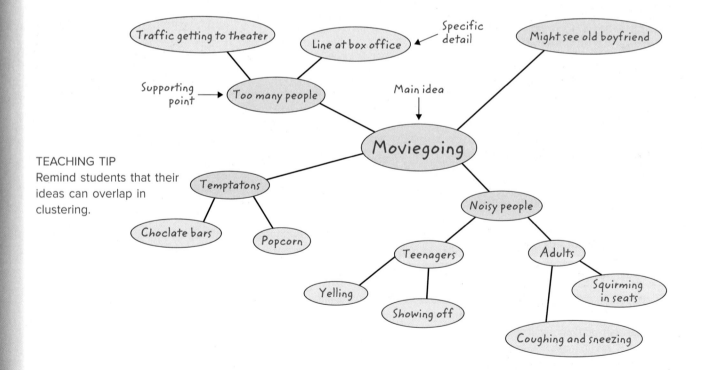

TIP In addition to helping generate material, clustering often suggests ways to organize ideas and details.

Use clustering (diagramming) to organize the list of details that you created for the previous activity (Activity 3).

ACTIVITY 4

Answers will vary.

TEACHING TIP
You may want to do this activity with the entire class. Use clustering to organize the details that students created for the previous activity.

Technique 5: Preparing a Scratch Outline

A *scratch outline*, or informal outline, is an excellent sequel to the first four prewriting techniques. A scratch outline often follows freewriting, questioning, list-making, or diagramming; or it may gradually emerge in the midst of these strategies. In fact, trying to make a scratch outline is a good way to see if you need to do more prewriting. If you cannot come up with a solid outline, then you know you need to do more prewriting to clarify and support your main point.

In a scratch outline, you think carefully about the point you are making, the supporting items for that point, and the order in which you will arrange those items. The scratch outline is a plan or blueprint to help you achieve a unified, supported, well-organized composition.

Scratch Outline: A Student Model

As Diane was working on her list of details, she suddenly realized what the plan of her paragraph could be. She could organize many of her details into one of three supporting groups: (1) annoyances in going out; (2) too many tempting snacks; and (3) other people. She then went back to the list, crossed out items that she now saw did not fit, and numbered the items according to the group where they fit. Here is what Diane did with her list:

TEACHING TIP
Ask students what the word "scratch" means in "scratch outline." Point out that a scratch outline can be prepared quickly.

1   Traffic is bad between my house and the theater

3   Noisy patrons

~~Don't want to run into Jeremy~~

2   Hard to be on a diet

3   Kids running in aisles

3   I'm crowded into seats between strangers who push me off armrests

1   Not enough parking

1   Parking lot needs to be expanded

1   Too many previews

~~Can't pause or fast forward as you can with Netflix~~

1   Long lines

1   High ticket prices

2   Too many temptations at snack stand

~~Commercials for food on the screen~~

2   Can prepare healthy snacks for myself at home

2   Tubs of popcorn with butter

continued

2   Huge choclate bars

~~Candy has always been my downfall~~

1   Movie may be sold out

3   People talking on their cell phones

3   People squirming in their seats

3   People coughing and sneezing

1   Icky stuff on floor

2   Teenagers yelling and showing off

Under the list, Diane was now able to prepare her scratch outline:

Moviegoing a problem

• inconvenience of going out

• tempting snacks

• other moviegoers

After all her prewriting, Diane was pleased. She knew that she had a promising paragraph—one with a clear point and solid support. She saw that she could organize the material into a well-developed paragraph with a topic sentence, supporting points, and vivid details. She was now ready to write the first draft of her paragraph, using her outline as a guide.

TEACHING TIP
Call attention to this point.

 TIP Chances are that if you do enough prewriting and thinking on paper, you will eventually discover the point and support of your paragraph.

ACTIVITY 5   Create a scratch outline that could serve as a guide if you were to write a paragraph about your particular annoyance.

Answers will vary.

TEACHING TIP
Remind students to look over all their prewriting notes when creating a scratch outline.

ESL NOTE
Remind nonnative speakers to write multiple drafts, and emphasize that it's not an indication of poor or weak writing skills.

Writing a First Draft

When you write a first draft, be prepared to put in additional thoughts and details that did not emerge during prewriting. And don't worry if you hit a snag. Just leave a blank space or add a comment such as "Do later" and press on to finish the paragraph. Also, don't worry yet about grammar, punctuation, or spelling. You don't want to take time correcting words or sentences that you may decide to remove later. Instead, make it your goal to state your main idea clearly and develop the content of your paragraph with plenty of specific details.

Writing a First Draft: A Student Model

Here is Diane's first draft:

> ~~Although I love movies, there are just too many problems involved in going to the movies.~~ Although I love movies, I've found that there are drawbacks to moviegoing. One problem is just the inconveneince of it all. To get to the theater you have to drive for at least 15 minutes, or more if traffic is bad. Because of a nearby supermarket and restaurants, it can take forever to find a parking spot and then I have to walk across a huge parking lot to the theater. There I deal with lines that are long, sold-out shows, and ever-increasing prices. I hate sitting with my feet sticking to the floor because of other people's spilled snacks. Another problem is my lack of self-control, I often stuff myself with ~~snacks~~ unhealthy, calorie-laden snacks. My choices might include a bucket of popcorn, a box of milk duds, a giant soda, or all three. My friends are as bad as I am. The worst problem is some of the other moviegoers. Little kids run up and down the aisle. Teenagers laugh and shout at the screen. Other people drop food and soda cups on the floor. They are also talking a lot and doing other stuff—bms! I would rather stay home and watch movies on cable TV or Netflix in the comfort of my own living room.

TIP After Diane finished the first draft, she was able to put it aside until the next day. You will benefit as well if you can allow some time between finishing a draft and starting to revise.

See if you can fill in the missing words in the following explanation of Diane's first draft.

ACTIVITY 6

1. Diane presents her topic sentence/main idea in the first sentence and then crosses it out and revises it right away to make it read smoothly and clearly.

2. There are some misspellings—for example, inconveneince (answers vary). Diane doesn't worry about spelling at this point. She just wants to get down as much of the substance of her paragraph as possible.

TEACHING TIP
Writers may feel pressured to write a perfect first draft. Emphasize the importance of revision and editing.

TEACHING TIP
Ask students to think about why writers should put their draft aside for a while. Mention that a cake needs to cool before it is frosted and a turkey needs to stand before it is carved.

TEACHING TIP
Suggest to your students that they work in pairs to complete this activity.

3. There are various punctuation errors, especially the run-on near the (beginning, (middle,) end) of the paragraph. Again, Diane is focusing on content; she knows she can attend to punctuation and grammar later.

4. Notice that she continues to accumulate specific supporting details as she writes the draft. For example, she crosses out and replaces "snacks" with the more specific unhealthy, calorie-laden snacks.

5. Near the end of her draft, Diane can't think of added details to insert so she simply puts the letters "_____bms_____" at that point to remind herself to "be more specific" in the next draft. She then goes on to finish her first draft.

ACTIVITY 7	Use the prewriting that you generated in this chapter to write a paragraph about a particular annoyance in everyday life. Provide three reasons why you consider your topic an annoyance, and give plenty of details to support each of your three reasons.

TEACHING TIP
Get students to talk about how they revise. Often students simply fix superficial features, such as spelling and punctuation.

Revising

Revising is as much a stage in the writing process as prewriting, outlining, and doing the first draft. *Revising* means rewriting a paper, building on what has already been done, in order to make it stronger. One writer has said about revision, "It's like cleaning house—getting rid of all the junk and putting things in the right order." But it is not just "straightening up"; instead, you must be ready to roll up your sleeves and do whatever is needed to create an effective paper. Too many students think that the first draft *is* the paper. They start to become writers when they realize that revising a rough draft three or four times is often at the heart of the writing process.

Here are some quick hints that can help make revision easier. First, set your first draft aside for a while. A few hours will do, but a day or two would be better. You can then come back to the draft with a fresh, more objective point of view. Second, work from typed or printed text. You'll be able to see the paper more impartially in this way than if you were just looking at your own familiar handwriting. Next, read your draft aloud. Hearing how your writing sounds will help you pick up problems with meaning as well as with style. Finally, as you do all these things, add your thoughts and changes above the lines or in the margins of your paper. Your written comments can serve as a guide when you work on the next draft.

There are two stages to the revision process:

- Revising content
- Revising sentences

in a writer's words

" *It would be crazy to begin revising immediately after finishing the first draft, and counter to the way the mind likes to create. You're exhausted. You deserve a vacation.* "

—Kenneth Atchity

TEACHING TIP
Use these tips to help your students revise a paragraph they created for a previous activity.

Revising Content

To evaluate and revise the content of your paragraph, ask these questions:

1. Is my paragraph **unified**?

   - Do I have a clear, single point in the first sentence of the paragraph?

   - Does all my evidence truly support and back up my main idea?

2. Is my paragraph **supported**?

   - Are there separate supporting points for the main idea?

   - Do I have *specific* evidence for each supporting point?

   - Is there *plenty of* specific evidence for the supporting point?

3. Is my paragraph **organized**?

   - Do I have a clear method of organizing my paragraph?

   - Do I use transitions and other connecting words?

Chapters 3 and 4 will give you practice in achieving **unity, support,** and **organization** in your writing.

Revising Sentences

To evaluate and revise sentences in your paragraph, ask yourself:

1. Do I use parallelism to balance my words and ideas?

2. Do I have a consistent point of view?

3. Do I use specific words?

4. Do I use active verbs?

5. Do I use words effectively by avoiding slang, clichés, pretentious language, and wordiness?

6. Do I vary my sentences?

Chapter 4 will give you practice in revising sentences.

Editing

After you have revised your paragraph for content and style, you are ready to *edit*—check for and correct—errors in grammar, punctuation, and spelling. Students often find it hard to edit their writing carefully. They have put so much, or so little, work into their writing that it's almost painful for them to look at it one more time. You may simply have to *will* yourself to perform this important closing step in the writing process. Remember that eliminating sentence-skills mistakes will improve an average paragraph and help ensure a strong grade on a good paper. Further, as you get into the habit of checking your work, you will also get into the habit of using the sentence skills consistently. They are an integral part of clear and effective writing.

Once you have completed your editing, you should always double-check everything by proofreading what you have written. During proofreading, you look for small errors like typos and spacing issues. Proofreading focuses on careless mistakes rather than grammar and content.

TEACHING TIP
Photocopy these lists for your students to use as checklists for revising content and sentences.

TEACHING TIP
Draw attention to the word "revision." During this stage of the writing process, writers are able to "see" their draft in a new light.

ESL NOTE
Get students to read their paragraph beginning with the last sentence. Nonnative speakers will find they can concentrate on the errors with missing articles, wrong prepositions, verb tenses, and so on, without being concerned about content.

TEACHING TIP
Get students to talk about how they edit. Often students submit papers without carefully editing their work. They may expect teachers to correct their errors.

Chapter 4 and Part 6 of this book will serve as a guide while you are editing your paragraphs for mistakes in **sentence skills.**

An Illustration of the Revising and Editing Processes

Revising with a Second Draft: A Student Model

Since Diane Woods was working on a computer, she was able to print out a double-spaced version of her paragraph about movies, leaving her plenty of room for revisions. Here is her revised paragraph:

Although I love movies, I've found that there are drawbacks to moviegoing. One problem is just the inconveneince of it all. To get to the theater ~~you~~ have to drive for at least 15 minutes, or more if traffic is bad. ~~Because of a nearby supermarket and restaurants,~~ it can take forever to find a parking spot and then I have to walk across a huge parking lot to the theater. There I deal with ~~lines that are long~~ long lines, sold-out shows, and ever-incresing prices. I hate sitting with my feet sticking to the floor because of other people's spilled snacks. Another problem is my lack of self-control, I often stuff myself with unhealthy, calorie-laden snacks. My choices might include a bucket of popcorn *dripping with butter*, a box of milk duds, a ~~giant soda~~ large Coke, or all three. ~~My friends are as bad as I am.~~ Finally The worst problem is some of the other moviegoers. As Little kids run up and down the aisle, Teenagers laugh and shout at the screen. ~~Other people~~ People of all ages drop ~~food~~ popcorn tubs and soda cups and squirm endlessly in their seats. I would rather stay home and watch movies on cable TV or Netflix in the comfort of my own living room.

Diane made her changes in longhand as she worked on the second draft. As you will see when you complete the activity below, her revision serves to make the paragraph more unified, better supported, and better organized.

TEACHING TIP
You may want to ask students to provide additional changes and additions to Diane's second draft. Remind them that there is no right or wrong way to revise.

ACTIVITY 8	Fill in the missing words.

1. To achieve better organization, Diane sets off the third supporting point with the word "_____Finally_____."

2. In the interest of (unity, support, coherence) _____unity_____, Diane crosses out the sentence "My friends are as bad as I am." She realizes this sentence is not a relevant detail, but really another topic.

TEACHING TIP
Suggest to your students that they work in pairs to complete this activity. Then go over the answers in class.

3. To add more (unity, support, coherence) _____support_____, Diane changes "giant soda" to "_____large Coke_____"; she changes "food" to "_____popcorn tubs_____"; and she adds "_____dripping with butter_____" after "bucket of popcorn."

4. To eliminate wordiness, she removes the words "_Because of a nearby_ _supermarket and restaurants_" from the fourth sentence.

5. In the interest of parallelism, Diane changes "lines that are long" to "_____long lines_____."

6. For greater sentence variety, Diane combines two short sentences, beginning the first sentences with the subordinating word "____As____."

7. To create a consistent point of view, Diane changes "you have to drive" to "_____I have to drive_____."

8. Finally, Diane replaces the somewhat vague "other people" with the more precise "_____People of all ages_____."

Editing: A Student Model

After typing in the changes to her document and saving it as a second draft, Diane printed out another clean draft of the paragraph. The paragraph required almost no more revision, so Diane turned her attention mostly to editing changes, illustrated below.

> Although I love movies, I've found that there are drawbacks to moviegoing. One problem is just the ~~inconveneince~~ *inconvenience* of it all. To get to the theater, I have to drive for at least ~~15~~ *fifteen* minutes, or more if traffic is bad. It can take forever to find a parking spot, and then I have to walk across a huge parking lot to the theater. There I deal with long lines, sold-out shows, and ~~ever-incresing~~ *ever-increasing* prices. I hate sitting with my feet sticking to the floor because of other people's spilled snacks. Another problem is my lack of self-control, I often stuff myself with unhealthy, calorie-laden snacks. My choices might include a bucket of popcorn dripping with butter, a box of Milk Duds, a large Coke, or all three. Finally, the worst problem is some of the other moviegoers. As little kids run up and down the aisle,

continued

TEACHING TIP
Ask students to provide additional changes and additions to Diane's third draft. Remind them that there is no right or wrong way to edit.

teenagers laugh and shout at the screen. People of all ages drop
, cough and burp,
popcorn tubs and soda cups, and squirm endlessly in their seats. I

would rather stay home and watch movies on cable TV or Netflix in

the comfort of my own living room.

Once again, Diane makes her changes in longhand right on the printout of her paragraph. To note these changes, complete the activity below.

| ACTIVITY 9 | Fill in the missing words. |

1. As part of her editing, Diane checked and corrected the ____spelling____ of two words, *inconvenience* and *ever-increasing*.

2. She added ____commas____ to set off an introductory phrase ("To get to the theater") and an introductory word ("Finally") and also to connect the two complete thoughts in the fourth sentence.

3. She realized that "milk duds" is a brand name and added ____capital letters____ to make it "Milk Duds."

TEACHING TIP
Explain why a comma is needed to set off an introductory phrase.

4. She realized that a number like "15" should be ____written out____ as "fifteen."

5. And since revision can occur at any stage in the writing process, including editing, she makes one of her details more vivid by adding the descriptive words "__cough and burp__."

| ACTIVITY 10 | Write a paragraph about the everyday annoyance you've been prewriting about throughout this chapter. Draft your work, and then revise and edit it, using the guidelines on the previous pages. You might want to work with a partner to revise and edit even more effectively. |

Using Peer Review

TEACHING TIP
Ask students to list the benefits of peer review. Often students think that peer review is a waste of time.

It is a good idea to have another student or peer respond to your writing before you hand it in to the instructor. On the day a rough draft is due, or on a day when you are writing paragraphs or essays in class, your instructor may ask you to pair up with another student or group of students. Each student's essay will be read and responded to by those in the group.

Ideally, read the other person's paragraph or essay aloud while your partner listens. If that is not practical, read it in a whisper while he or she looks on. As you read, both you and your partner should look and listen for spots where the composition does not read smoothly and clearly. Check or circle the trouble spots where your reading snags.

Your partner should then reread your work, marking possible trouble spots while doing so. Then each of you should do the following three things.

1. Identification

At the top of a separate sheet of paper, write the title and author of the paper you have read. Under it, write your name as the reader of the paper.

2. Scratch Outline

"X-ray" the paper for its inner logic by making up a scratch outline. The scratch outline need be no more than twenty words or so, but it should show clearly the logical foundation on which the paragraph or essay is built. It should identify and summarize the overall point of the paper and the three areas of support for the point.

Your outline can look like this:

> Point: _____
>
> Support:
>
> (1) _____
>
> (2) _____
>
> (3) _____

For example, here is a scratch outline of the paragraph on moviegoing in Chapter 1.

> Point: Moviegoing a problem _____
>
> Support:
>
> (1) inconvenience of going out _____
>
> (2) tempting snacks _____
>
> (3) other moviegoers _____

3. Comments

Under the outline, write the heading "Comments." Many people are sensitive to criticism, so it is very important to be specific and constructive with your comments. Try to avoid vague comments like "it's good"; instead offer helpful suggestions like "your topic sentence is very broad and should be narrowed down." Here are some of the general areas you should comment on while peer reviewing:

- Is there a topic sentence or a statement that makes a main point? If not, try to suggest ways the author could improve it.

- Are there spots in the paragraph where you see problems with *unity*, *support*, or *organization*? (You'll find it helpful to refer to the checklist on the inside back cover of this book.) If so, offer comments.

For example, you might say, "More details are needed to support your first point," or "Some of the details don't really back up your point."

- Make a note of at least two things the author did really well, such as good use of transitions or an especially realistic or vivid specific detail.

- Make a note of at least two things the author could do to improve the paragraph, such as adding details in specific areas or using more vibrant and active language.

- Finally, go back to the spots where your reading of the composition snagged: Are words or ideas missing? Is there a lack of parallel structure? Is the meaning of a sentence confusing? Try to figure out what the problems are and suggest ways of fixing them.

- Although *sentence skills* are important, try not to simply edit a student's paper as you are reviewing; extra attention to grammar and punctuation should be given during the editing stage and not the revising stage.

After you have completed your evaluation of the composition, give it to your partner and talk about the comments. As the author, it is important you understand the reviewer's comments, so you should ask for clarification about anything that you don't understand. Remember not to get defensive, but see this as one part of the process of writing and a chance to improve your skills as a writer.

Doing a Personal Review

Follow these steps as you do a personal review of your paper:

1. While you're writing and revising a paper, you should be constantly evaluating it in terms of *unity*, *support*, and *organization*. Use as a guide the detailed checklist on the inside back cover of this book.

2. After you've finished the next-to-final draft of a composition, check it for the *sentence skills* listed on the inside back cover. It may also help to read your work out loud. If a given sentence does not sound right—that is, if it does not read clearly and smoothly—chances are something is wrong. In that case, revise or edit as necessary until your composition is complete.

Review Activities

To reinforce much of the information about the writing process that you have learned in this chapter, you can now work through the following activities:

- Taking a writing inventory
- Prewriting
- Outlining
- Revising

Taking a Writing Inventory

Answer the questions below to evaluate your approach to the writing process. Think about the writing you have done for other classes. This activity is not a test, so try to be as honest as possible. Becoming aware of your writing habits will help you realize changes that may be helpful.

Answers will vary.

TEACHING TIP
Consider having your students discuss their answers with a partner.

1. When you start to work on a paragraph, do you typically do any prewriting?

   _____ Yes   _____ Sometimes   _____ No

2. If so, which prewriting techniques do you use?

   _____ Freewriting   _____ Diagramming

   _____ Questioning   _____ Scratch outline

   _____ List-making   _____ Other (please describe on the lines below)

   _____

   _____

3. Which prewriting technique or techniques work best for you, or which do you think will work best for you?

   _____

   _____

   _____

4. Many students say they find it helpful to handwrite a first draft and then type that draft on a computer. They then print out the draft and revise it by hand. Describe the way you proceed in drafting and revising a paragraph.

   _____

   _____

   _____

5. After you write the first draft of a paragraph, do you have time to set it aside for a while so that you can come back to it with a fresh eye?

   _____ Yes   _____ No

6. How many drafts of a paragraph do you typically write? _____

7. When you revise, are you aware that you should be working toward a paragraph that is unified, solidly supported, and clearly organized? Has this chapter given you a better sense that unity, support, and organization are goals to aim for?

   _____

   _____

   _____

8. Do you revise a paragraph for the clarity and quality of its sentences as well as for its content?

   _____ Yes   _____ No

9. Do you typically do any editing of the almost-final draft of a paragraph, or do you tend to "hope for the best" and hand it in without carefully checking it?

_____ Edit   _____ Hope for the best

10. What (if any) information has this chapter given you about *prewriting* that you will try to apply in your writing?

_____

_____

_____

TEACHING TIP
Follow up to see what
information students
applied to their writing.

11. What (if any) information has this chapter given you about *revising* that you will try to apply in your writing?

_____

_____

_____

12. What (if any) information has this chapter given you about *editing* that you will try to apply in your writing?

_____

_____

_____

Prewriting

REVIEW ACTIVITY 2

TEACHING TIP
Students can do this
activity alone or in pairs.

On the following pages are examples of how the five prewriting techniques could be used to develop the topic "Problems of Combining Work and College." Identify each technique by writing F (for freewriting), Q (for questioning), L (for list-making), C (for clustering), or SO (for the scratch outline) in the answer space.

_____L_____   Never enough time
Miss campus parties
Had to study (only two free hours a night)
Give up activities with friends
No time to rewrite papers
Can't stay at school to hang out with or talk to friends
Friends don't call me to go out anymore
Sunday no longer relaxed day—have to study
Missing sleep I should be getting
Grades aren't as good as they could be
Can't watch favorite TV shows
Really need the extra money
Tired when I sit down to study at 9 o'clock

Q	*What* are some of the problems of combining work and school?	Schoolwork suffers because I don't have time to study or rewrite papers. I've had to give up things I enjoy, like sleep and touch football. I can't get into the social life at college, because I have to work right after class.
	How have these problems changed my life?	My grades aren't as good as they were when I didn't work. Some of my friends have stopped calling me. My relationship with a girl I liked fell apart because I couldn't spend much time with her. I miss TV.
	What do I do in a typical day?	I get up at 7 to make an 8 a.m. class. I have classes till 1:30, and then I drive to the supermarket where I work. I work till 7 p.m., and then I drive home and eat dinner. After I take a shower and relax for a half hour, it's about 9. This gives me only a couple of hours to study—read textbooks, do math exercises, write essays. My eyes start to close well before I go to bed at 11.
	Why do I keep up this schedule?	I can't afford to go to school without working, and I need a degree to get the accounting job I want. If I invest my time now, I'll have a better future.

SO

major difficulties juggling job and college

- little time for studying
  - textbooks not read
  - papers not revised
  - no study time for tests

- no time for socializing
  - during school
  - after school

- no time for personal pleasures
  - TV shows
  - Sunday touch football
  - sleeping late

C

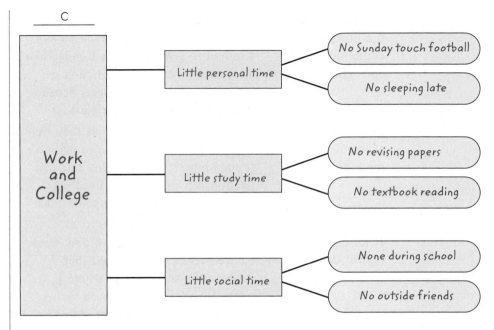

F   It's hard working and going to school at the same time. I never realized how much I'd have to give up. I won't be quitting my job because I need the money. And the people are friendly at the place where I work. I've had to give up a lot more than I thought. We used to play touch football games every Sunday. They were fun and we'd go out for drinks afterwards. Sundays now are for catch-up work with my courses. I have to catch up because I don't get home every day until 7, I have to eat dinner first before studying. Sometimes I'm so hungry I just eat cookies or chips. Anyway, by the time I take a shower it's 9 p.m. or later and I'm already feeling tired. I've been up since 7 a.m. Sometimes I write an English paper in twenty minutes and don't even read it over. I feel that I'm missing out on a lot in college. The other day some people I like were sitting in the cafeteria listening to music and talking. I would have given anything to stay and not have to go to work. I almost called in sick. I used to get invited to parties, I don't much anymore. My friends know I'm not going to be able to make it, so they don't bother. I can't sleep late on weekends or watch TV during the week.

Outlining

There are two types of outlines that will help you create strong compositions. The first is a scratch, or informal, outline. As we have seen earlier in this chapter, it can be a very helpful tool in the prewriting stage. The second, a formal outline, is useful during the drafting and revision stages. You should have a working thesis before you begin a formal outline. Unlike a scratch outline, a formal outline employs specific formatting and uses complete sentences.

Another way to use a formal outline is as a check. Once you have written your draft, you can go through and outline your paper. This will help you decide whether any information is out of place and will help you find a better location for it.

One key to effective outlining is the ability to distinguish between general ideas (or main points) and specific details that fit under those ideas. Read each group of specific details below. Then circle the letter of the general idea that tells what the specific details have in common. Note that the general idea should not be too broad or too narrow. Begin by trying the example item, and then read the explanation that follows.

EXAMPLE

Specific details: runny nose, coughing, sneezing, sore throat

The general idea is:

a. cold symptoms.

b. symptoms.

c. throat problems.

EXPLANATION

It is true that the specific ideas are all symptoms, but they have in common something even more specific—they are all symptoms of the common cold. Therefore, answer *b* is too broad; the correct answer is *a*. Answer *c* is too narrow because it doesn't cover all the specific ideas; it covers only the final item in the list ("sore throat").

 TIP   Remember that the general idea is the main point.

1. *Specific details:* leaking toilet, no hot water, broken window, roaches
   The general idea is:
   a. problems.
   b. kitchen problems.
   c. apartment problems.

2. *Specific details:* count to ten, take a deep breath, go for a walk
   The general idea is:
   a. actions.
   b. ways to calm down.
   c. ways to calm down just before a test.

3. *Specific details:* Mark Twain, Kate Chopin, Nathaniel Hawthorne, Toni Morrison
   The general idea is:
   a. famous people.
   b. authors.
   c. American authors.

4. *Specific details:* going to bed earlier, eating healthier foods, reading for half an hour each day, trying to be nicer to my mother

The general idea is:

ⓐ resolutions.

b. problems.

c. solutions.

5. *Specific details:* money problems, family problems, relationship problems, health problems

The general idea is:

a. poor grades.

ⓑ causes of poor grades.

c. effects of poor grades.

| **REVIEW ACTIVITY 4** | In each of the following items, specific ideas (details) are given but a general idea is unstated. Fill in each blank with a general heading that accurately describes the list provided. |

EXAMPLE

General idea: Household Chores

Specific ideas:
washing dishes
preparing meals
taking out trash
dusting furniture

1. *General idea:*   Features of a Good Job

Specific ideas:
convenient work hours
short travel time to job
good pay
considerate boss

2. *General idea:*   Negative Qualities/Vices

Specific ideas:
greed
cowardice
selfishness
dishonesty

3. *General idea:*   How to Prepare for a Wedding

Specific ideas:
order the invitations
get the bride's gown
rent the tuxedos
hire a photographer

4. *General idea:*   Insults

Specific ideas:
"Your cologne stinks."
"You look terrible."
"You've got no common sense."
"Your writing sucks."

5. *General idea:* Compliments

   Specific ideas:
   "I love your hair."
   "You look great in red."
   "You're so smart."
   "Your writing is outstanding."

Major and minor ideas are mixed together in the two scratch outlines below. Put the ideas into logical order.

TEACHING TIP
Students may find this activity challenging, so encourage them to work in pairs.

1. *main idea:* people classified by treatment of cars

   seldom wax or vacuum car

   keep every mechanical item in top shape

   protective owners

   ignore needed maintenance

   indifferent owners

   wash and polish car every week

   never wash, wax, or vacuum car

   abusive owners

   inspect and service car only when required by state law

   - protective owners
     - keep every mechanical item in top shape
     - wash and polish car every week

   - indifferent owners
     - inspect and service car only when required by state law
     - seldom wax or vacuum car

   - abusive owners
     - ignore needed maintenance
     - never wash, wax, or vacuum car

2. *main idea:* benefits of living with elderly parents

   advantages for elderly person

   live-in caretaker

   learn about the past

   advantages for adult children

   serve useful role in family

   help with household tasks

   advantages for grandchildren

   stay active and interested in young people

   more attention from adults

- advantages for elderly person _____
  - live-in caretaker _____
  - stay active and interested in young people _____
- advantages for adult children _____
  - serve useful role in family _____
  - help with household tasks _____
- advantages for grandchildren _____
  - learn about the past _____
  - more attention from adults _____

| **REVIEW ACTIVITY 6** | Major and minor ideas are mixed together in the two formal outlines below. In addition, in each outline, one of the three major ideas is missing and must be added. Put the ideas in logical order and add a third major idea. |

Wording of missing idea may vary.

TEACHING TIP
Students may find this activity challenging, so encourage them to work in pairs.

1. *Topic sentence:* Extending the school day would have several advantages.

   Help children academically

   Parents know children are safe at the school

   More time to spend on basics

   Less pressure to cover subjects quickly

   More time for extras like art, music, and sports

   Help working parents

   More convenient to pick up children at 4 or 5 p.m.

   Teachers' salaries would be raised

   (1) Help children academically _____
      a. More time to spend on basics _____
      b. More time for extras like art, music, and sports _____
   (2) Help working parents _____
      a. Parents know children are safe at the school _____
      b. More convenient to pick up children at 4 or 5 P.M. _____
   (3) Help teachers _____
      a. Less pressure to cover subjects quickly _____
      b. Teachers' salaries would be raised _____

2. *Topic sentence:* By following certain hints about food, exercise, and smoking, people can increase their chances of dying young.

   Don't ever walk if there is a ride available

   Choose foods such as bacon and lunch meats that are laced with nitrites and other preservatives

   Be very selective about what foods are eaten

   Keep smoking, even if it causes coughing or shortness of breath

   Don't play an outdoor sport; open a beer instead and head for a La-Z-Boy recliner

Resist the urge to exercise

Choose foods from one of four essential groups: fat, starch, sugar, and grease

Smoke at least a pack a day

(1) Be very selective about what foods are eaten

    a. Choose foods from one of four essential groups: fat, starch, sugar, and grease

    b. Choose foods such as bacon and lunch meats . . . preservatives

(2) Resist the urge to exercise

    a. Don't ever walk if there is a ride available

    b. Don't play an outdoor sport . . . head for a La-Z-Boy recliner

(3) Develop the habit of smoking

    a. Smoke at least a pack a day

    b. Keep smoking, even if it causes coughing or shortness of breath

---

REVIEW ACTIVITY 7

Read the following two paragraphs. Then outline each one in the space provided. Write out the topic sentence in each case and summarize in a few words the supporting points and details that fit under the topic sentence.

1.

TEACHING TIP
Suggest to your students that they first annotate this paragraph, underlining the topic sentence and major ideas.

Why I'm a Stay-at-Home Baseball Fan

I'd much rather stay at home and watch ball games on television than go to the ballpark. First, it's cheaper to watch a game at home. I don't have to spend twenty-five dollars for a ticket and another ten dollars for a parking space. If I want some refreshments, I can have what's already in the refrigerator instead of shelling out another six dollars for a limp, lukewarm hot dog and a watery Coke. Also, it's more comfortable at home. I avoid a bumper-to bumper drive to the ballpark and pushy crowds who want to go through the same gate I do. I can lie quietly on my living-room sofa instead of sitting on a hard stadium seat with noisy people all around me. Most of all, watching a game on television is more informative. Not only do I see all the plays that I might miss from my twenty-five-dollar seat, but I see some of them two and three times in instant replay. In addition, I get each play explained to me in glorious detail. If I were at the ballpark, I wouldn't know that the pitch our third baseman hit was a high and inside slider or that his grand-slam home run was a record-setting seventh in his career. The other fans can spend their money; put up with traffic, crowds, and hard seats; and guess at the plays. I'll take my baseball lying down—at home.

Topic sentence: I'd much rather stay at home and watch ball games on television than go to the ballpark.

  (1) Cheaper at home

      a. No charge for ticket or parking

      b. No charges for refreshments

  (2) More comfortable at home

      a. No drive or crowds

      b. Comfortable sofa

  (3) Televised game more informative

      a. See every play

      b. Explanations of plays

2.

TEACHING TIP
Suggest to your students that they first annotate this paragraph, underlining the topic sentence and major ideas.

Good Employees

Employers are always looking for great employees who are conscientious, focused, and analytical. First, conscientious employees are people who take pride in their work and want to do their best. These employees make sure they contribute the best work possible and meet set deadlines. If they run into a problem, they first try to solve the problem on their own, but if they cannot solve the problem, they seek the help necessary to complete the task. Second, focused employees are people who don't waste time. They arrive on time and use the time at work to do work. They don't unnecessarily talk to their friends or family on the phone, they don't surf the Internet for amusing YouTube videos, and they don't stand around chatting with other employees for long periods of time. Finally, analytical employees are people who see a problem and work to solve the problem. They strive to make things better. If they see a better way that something could be done, they try to implement it. Employees who have these three qualities will always be in demand.

Topic Sentence: Employers are always looking for great employees who are conscientious, focused, and analytical.

  (1) Conscientious employees take pride and want to do their best

      a. Contribute the best work within the time period

      b. Try to solve the problem; then ask for help

  (2) Focused employees don't waste time

      a. Arrive on time and work

      b. Don't spend unnecessary time chatting or surfing the Internet

(3) Analytical employees work to solve problems
    a. Strive to make things better
    b. If they see a way to change something, they will try to implement it

Revising

Listed in the box below are five stages in the process of composing a paragraph titled "Dangerous Places."

REVIEW ACTIVITY 8

TEACHING TIP
You may want to do this activity with the entire class.

1. Prewriting (list)

2. Prewriting (freewriting, questioning, and scratch outline)

3. First draft

4. Revising (second draft)

5. Revising (final draft)

The five stages appear in scrambled order below and on the next page. Write the number 1 in the blank space in front of the first stage of development and number the remaining stages in sequence.

    3   There are some places where I never feel safe. For example, public rest rooms. The dirt and graffiti dirt on the floors and the graffiti scrawled on the walls make the room seem dangerous create a sense of danger. I'm also afraid in parking lots. Late at night, I don't like walking in the lot After class, I don't like the parking lot. When I leave my night class or the shopping mall late the walk to the car is scary. Most parking lots have large lights which make me feel at least a little better. I feel least safe in our laundry room. . . . It is a depressing place . . . Bars on the windows, . . . pipes making noises, . . . cement steps the only way out. . . .

    1   Dangerous Places
        Highways
        Cars—especially parking lots
        Feel frightened in our laundry room
        Big crowds—concerts, movies
        Closed-in places
        Bus and train stations
        Airplanes
        Elevators and escalators

TEACHING TIP
Have students underline or
highlight the editing
changes on the final draft.

_____5_____

Dangerous Places

There are some places where I never feel completely safe. For example, I seldom feel safe in public rest rooms. I worry that I'll suddenly be alone there and that someone will come in to attack me. The ugly graffiti often scrawled on the walls, along with the grime and dirt in the room and crumpled tissues and paper towels on the floor, add to my sense of unease and danger. I also feel unsafe in large, dark parking lots. When I leave my night class a little late, or I am one of the few leaving the mall at 10 p.m., I dread the walk to my car. I am afraid that someone may be lurking behind another car, ready to attack me. And I fear that my car will not start, leaving me stuck in the dark parking lot. The place where I feel least safe is the basement laundry room in our apartment building. No matter what time I do my laundry, I seem to be the only person there. The windows are barred, and the only exit is a steep flight of cement steps. While I'm folding the clothes, I feel trapped. If anyone unfriendly came down those steps, I would have nowhere to go. The pipes in the room make sudden gurgles, clanks, and hisses, adding to my unsettledness. Places like public rest rooms, dark parking lots, and the basement laundry room give me the shivers.

_____4_____

There are some places where I never feel completely safe. For example, I never feel safe in public rest rooms. If I'm alone there, I worry that someone will come in to rob and attack me. The dirt on the floors and the graffiti scrawled on the walls create a sense of danger. I feel unsafe in large, dark parking lots. When I leave my night class a little late or I leave the mall at 10 P.M., the walk to the car is scary. I'm afraid that someone may be behind a car. Also that my car won't start. Another place I don't feel safe is the basement laundry room in our apartment building. No matter when I do the laundry, I'm the only person there. The windows are barred and there are steep steps. I feel trapped when I fold the clothes. The pipes in the room make frightening noises such as hisses and clanks. Our laundry room and other places give me the shivers.

_____2_____

Some places seem dangerous and unsafe to me. For example, last night I stayed till 10:15 after night class and walked out to parking lot alone. Very scary. Also, other places I go to every day, such as places in my apartment building. Also frightened by big crowds and public rest rooms.

<u>Why was the parking lot scary?</u>
Dark
Only a few cars
No one else in lot
Could be someone behind a car
Cold

What places in my building scare me?
Laundry room (especially)
Elevators
Lobby at night sometimes
Outside walkway at night
2 Parking lots
3 Laundry room
1 Public rest rooms

The author of "Dangerous Places" in Review Activity 8 made a number of editing changes between the second draft and the final draft. Compare the two drafts and, in the spaces provided below, identify five of the changes.

1. _____

2. _____

3. _____

4. _____

5. _____

See note below for possible answers.

EXPLORING WRITING ONLINE

In this chapter, you learned how to cluster or diagram your ideas. Use your favorite search engine, such as Google, to discover other ways to visually organize your ideas. Do a search for the phrase "graphic organizers" to find the many different types of printable organizers available. Find at least three that you would like to use during prewriting.

©Tetra Images/Shutterstock

Note: Each of the following changes in details could count as one of the five answers that students may provide.

A title ("Dangerous Places") has been added.

A sentence-skills mistake (the fragment "Also that my car won't start") has been corrected.

A number of specific details have been added:

"The dirt on the floors" has become "the grime and dirt in the room and crumpled tissues and paper towels on the floor."

"The graffiti scrawled on the walls" has become "ugly graffiti often scrawled on the walls."

"When I leave my night class a little late or I leave the mall at 10 p.m., the walk to the car is scary" has become "When I leave my night class a little late, or I am one of the few leaving the mall at 10 p.m., I dread the walk to my car."

"Also that my car won't start" has become "And I fear that my car will not start, leaving me stuck in the dark parking lot."

"The windows are barred and there are steep steps" has become "The windows are barred, and the only exit is a steep flight of cement steps."

"The pipes in the room make frightening noises such as hisses and clanks" has become "The pipes in the room make sudden gurgles, clanks, and hisses, adding to my uneasiness."

As a college student, you will be asked to write in many of your classes. The writing that you do in these classes will often involve making a point and supporting that point with reasons and details. Keep this in mind when you read the first draft of the paragraph below written by Lashawna for an introductory history class, and then answer the questions that follow.

Three Great Women in History

Three important women who have had a significant impact on others are Elizabeth Cady Stanton, Sandra Day O'Connor, and Malala Yousafzai. Elizabeth Cady Stanton was a leader of the women's rights movement in the nineteenth century. Sandra Day O'Connor was the first woman on the US Supreme Court. Malala Yousafzai became known when she was shot by the Taliban for standing up for the rights of girls to be educated.

©Jacob Lund/
Shutterstock

TEACHING TIP
Ask students to think about what makes a specific detail memorable.

Collaborative Activity

Lashawna, the writer of the above paragraph, provided three reasons to support her opening point, but not much else. With a classmate, together complete the outline below by providing two specific supporting details for each of Lashawna's three reasons.

Title: Three Great Women in History

Topic sentence: Three important women who have had a significant impact on others are Elizabeth Cady Stanton, Sandra Day O'Connor, and Malala Yousafzai.

1. Elizabeth Cady Stanton was a leader of the women's rights movement in the nineteenth century.

    a. She was the main author of the *Declaration of Sentiments and Resolutions*.

    b. In her *Declaration*, she proclaimed that men and women were equal and that women be given the right to vote.

2. Sandra Day O'Connor was the first woman on the US Supreme Court.

    a. She was nominated by President Ronald Reagan in 1981 and was confirmed unanimously.

    b. She has been a deciding vote in many cases involving sexual harassment, the death penalty, and affirmative action.

3. Malala Yousafzai became known when she was shot by the Taliban for standing up for the rights of girls to be educated.

   a. She founded the nonprofit organization Malala Fund, which advocates for girls around the world.

   b. She has shared her story in the book *I Am Malala* and through many speaking engagements.

Explore Writing Further
Using your outline, revise Lashawna's paragraph.

PART 2

Basic Principles of Effective Writing

PART TWO SHOWS YOU HOW TO

- begin a paper with a point of some kind

- provide specific evidence to support that point

- write a paragraph

- organize specific evidence by using a clear method of organization

- connect the specific evidence by using transitions and other connecting words

- revise so that your sentences flow smoothly and clearly

- edit so that your sentences are error-free

- evaluate a paragraph for unity, support, coherence, and sentence skills

EXPLORING WRITING PROMPT:

So much of what we do involves communication. In addition to talking, we spend a lot of time writing. We may not write essays, but we send off e-mails and text messages, jot down notes, and write up lists. Take a few minutes to think about how you use writing in everyday life. You may be asked to write down your ideas or share them with others.

©damircudic/Getty Images

The First and Second Steps in Writing

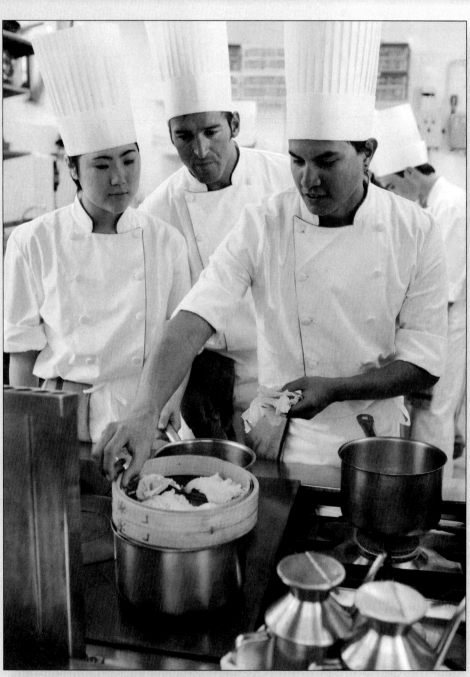

©Pixtal/AGE Fotostock

TEACHING TIP
You may want to do this activity with the entire class. Write the topic "Reasons for Attending College" on the board, and then ask students to freely shout out their ideas. Be prepared to write quickly.

RESPONDING TO IMAGES

There are many different reasons for going to college. Maybe you are fulfilling a dream of yours or maybe you are studying for a specific career. What are your reasons? Take a few minutes to write nonstop, make a list, or draw a diagram of your ideas. In this chapter you will read two separate paragraphs detailing each writer's reasons for being in college, and later you will be asked to write a paragraph of your own on this topic.

Chapter 2 emphasized how prewriting and revising can help you become an effective writer. This chapter will focus on the first two steps in writing an effective paragraph:

1. Begin with a point.

2. Support the point with specific evidence.

Chapter 4 will then look at the third and fourth steps in writing:

3. Organize and connect the specific evidence.

4. Write clear, error-free sentences.

Four Steps ➡ **Four Bases**

1. **If you make one point and** ➡ your writing will have *unity*.
   stick to that point,

2. **If you back up the point** ➡ your writing will have *support*.
   with specific evidence,

3. If you organize and connect ➡ your writing will have *coherence*.
   the specific evidence,

4. If you write clear, error-free ➡ your writing will demonstrate
   sentences, effective *sentence skills*.

Step 1: Begin with a Point

Your first step in writing is to decide what point you want to make and to write that point in a single sentence. The point is commonly known as a *topic sentence*. As a guide to yourself and to the reader, put that point in the first sentence of your paragraph. Everything else in the paragraph should then develop and support in specific ways the single point given in the first sentence.

TEACHING TIP
You may want to remind students that a topic sentence usually appears as the first sentence but may appear later in the paragraph.

Read the two student paragraphs below about families today. Which paragraph clearly supports a single point? Which paragraph rambles on in many directions, introducing a number of ideas but developing none of them?

ACTIVITY 1

PARAGRAPH A

ESL NOTE
Nonnative students may not be accustomed to writing a topic sentence that presents a strong or direct point. In some cultures, this is considered rude and impolite.

Changes in the Family

The demands of modern society in recent years have changed family life. First of all, today's parents spend much less time with their children. Several generations ago, most parents were able to pick their children up from school. Now parents work longer hours, and their children attend an after-school program, stay with a neighbor or older sibling, or go home to an empty house. Another

continued

TEACHING TIP
Ask volunteers to read these paragraphs aloud so that students can "hear" how a rambling paragraph sounds.

change is that families no longer eat together. In the past, Mom would be home and fix a full dinner—salad, pot roast, potatoes and vegetables, with homemade cake or pie to top it off. Dinner today is more likely to be takeout food or frozen dinners eaten at home, or fast food eaten out, with different members of the family eating at different times. Finally, television and the Internet have taken the place of family conversation and togetherness. Back when there were traditional meals, family members would have a chance to eat together at the dining room table, talk with each other, and share events of the day in a leisurely manner. Now, families are more likely to be looking at the TV or browsing the Internet than talking to each other. Clearly, modern life is a challenge to family life.

PARAGRAPH B

The Family

Family togetherness is very important. However, today's mothers spend much less time at home than their mothers did, for several reasons. Most fathers are also home much less than they used to be. In previous times, families had to work together running a farm. Now children are left at other places or are home alone much of the time. Some families do find ways to spend more time together despite the demands of work. Another problem is that with parents gone so much of the day, nobody is at home to prepare wholesome meals for the family to eat together. The meals Grandma used to make would include pot roast and fried chicken, mashed potatoes, salad, vegetables, and delicious homemade desserts. Today's takeout foods and frozen meals can provide good nutrition. Some menu choices offer nothing but high-fat and high-sodium choices. People can supplement prepared foods by eating sufficient vegetables and fruit. Finally, television and the Internet are also big obstacles to togetherness. It sometimes seems that people are constantly watching TV or browsing the Internet and never talking to each other. Even when parents have friends over, it is often to watch something on TV. TV and the Internet must be used wisely to achieve family togetherness.

Complete the following statement: Paragraph __A__ is effective because it makes a clear, single point in the first sentence and goes on in the remaining sentences to support that single point.

Paragraph A starts with a point—that demands of modern society in recent years have changed family life—and then supports that idea with examples about parents' work hours, families' eating habits, TV, and the Internet.

Paragraph B, on the other hand, does not make and support a single point. At first we think the point of the paragraph may be that "family togetherness is very important." But there is no supporting evidence showing how important family togetherness is. In the second sentence, we read that "today's mothers spend much less time at home than their mothers did, for several reasons." Now we think for a moment that this may be the main point and that the author will go on to list and explain some of those reasons. But the paragraph then goes on to comment on fathers, families in previous times, and families who find ways to spend time together. Any one of those ideas could be the focus of the paragraph, but none is. The paragraph ends with yet another idea that does not support any previous point and that itself could be the point of a paragraph: "TV and the Internet must be used wisely to achieve family togetherness." No single idea in this paragraph is developed, and the result for the reader is confusion.

In summary, while paragraph A is unified, paragraph B shows a complete lack of unity.

TEACHING TIP
For added practice, ask students to revise Paragraph B.

Identifying Common Errors in Topic Sentences

When writing a point, or topic sentence, people sometimes make mistakes that undermine their chances of producing an effective paragraph. One mistake is to substitute an announcement of the topic for a true topic sentence. Other mistakes include writing statements that are too broad or too narrow. Following are examples of all three errors, along with contrasting examples of effective topic sentences.

TEACHING TIP
Use the analogy of Goldilocks and the Three Bears to teach students about topic sentences. Tell them that a topic sentence cannot be "too broad" or "too narrow" but must be "just right."

Announcement

My car is the concern of this paragraph.

The statement above is a simple announcement of a subject, rather than a topic sentence expressing an idea about the subject.

Statement That Is Too Broad

Many people have problems with their cars.

The statement is too broad to be supported adequately with specific details in a single paragraph.

Statement That Is Too Narrow

My car is a Ford Focus.

The statement above is too narrow to be expanded into a paragraph. Such a narrow statement is sometimes called a *dead-end statement* because there is no place to go with it. It is a simple fact that does not need or call for any support.

ESL NOTE
Nonnative students may not be accustomed to writing a topic sentence that presents a strong or direct point. Instead, they may use a pattern of circular reasoning that simply restates a point. You may want to include some examples of such ineffective topic sentences.

Effective Topic Sentence

I hate my car.

The statement above expresses an opinion that could be supported in a paragraph. The writer could offer a series of specific supporting reasons, examples, and details to make it clear why he or she hates the car.

Here are additional examples:

Announcements

The subject of this paper will be my apartment.
I want to talk about increases in the divorce rate.

Statements That Are Too Broad

The places where people live have definite effects on their lives.
Many people have trouble getting along with others.

Statements That Are Too Narrow

I have no hot water in my apartment at night.
Almost one of every two marriages ends in divorce.

Effective Topic Sentences

My apartment is a terrible place to live.
The divorce rate is increasing for several reasons.

ACTIVITY 2	For each pair of sentences below, write A beside the sentence that only *announces* a topic. Write OK beside the sentence that *advances an idea* about the topic.

TEACHING TIP
For added practice, ask students to revise the sentences that announce a topic.

1. __A__ a. This paper will deal with flunking math.

   __OK__ b. I flunked math last semester for several reasons.

2. __A__ a. I am going to write about my job as a gas station attendant.

   __OK__ b. Working as a gas station attendant was the worst job I ever had.

3. __A__ a. Obscene phone calls are the subject of this paragraph.

   __OK__ b. People should know what to do when they receive an obscene phone call.

4. __OK__ a. In several ways, my college library is inconvenient to use.

   __A__ b. This paragraph will deal with the college library.

5. __A__ a. My paper will discuss the topic of procrastinating.

   __OK__ b. The following steps will help you stop procrastinating.

ACTIVITY 3	For each pair of sentences below, write TN beside the statement that is *too narrow* to be developed into a paragraph. Write OK beside the statement in each pair that could be developed into a paragraph.

TEACHING TIP
For added practice, ask students to revise the statements that are too narrow.

1. __TN__ a. Employers notice how applicants dress for a job interview.

   __OK__ b. First impressions are important in a job interview.

2. __TN__ a. Sophia plans to audition for *American Idol*.

   __OK__ b. Sophia is destined for stardom.

3. __TN__ a. Jerome left college to serve in the US Army, but now he is back to earn a degree in computer programming.

    __OK__ b. Some people "stop out" of college, and then they return more determined.

4. __OK__ a. There are many different attractions at Walt Disney World.

    __TN__ b. Water park enthusiasts can enjoy Typhoon Lagoon and Blizzard Beach.

5. __OK__ a. My daughter Celia has the potential to become a college athlete.

    __TN__ b. Celia holds the state track record for the 400-meter dash.

For each pair of sentences below, write TB beside the statement that is *too broad* to be supported adequately in a short paper. Write OK beside the statement that makes a limited point.

ACTIVITY 4

TEACHING TIP
For added practice, ask students to revise the statements that are too broad.

1. __OK__ a. Professional football is a dangerous sport.

    __TB__ b. Professional sports are violent.

2. __TB__ a. Married life is the best way of living.

    __OK__ b. Teenage marriages often end in divorce for several reasons.

3. __OK__ a. Aspirin can have several harmful side effects.

    __TB__ b. Drugs are dangerous.

4. __TB__ a. School has always been challenging.

    __OK__ b. I have struggled in school for several reasons.

5. __TB__ a. Computers are changing our society.

    __OK__ b. Using computers to teach schoolchildren is a mistake.

Understanding the Two Parts of a Topic Sentence

As stated earlier, the point that opens a paragraph is often called a *topic sentence*. When you look closely at a point, or topic sentence, you can see that it is made up of two parts:

1. The *limited topic*

2. The writer's idea about or attitude toward the limited topic

The writer's idea or attitude is usually expressed in one or more *key words*. All the details in a paragraph should support the idea expressed in the key words. In each of the topic sentences below, a single line appears under the

TEACHING TIP
To reinforce this lesson, ask students to draw a line under the topic and a double line under the idea for the "OK" sentences in the previous activities.

topic and a double line under the idea about the topic (expressed in a key word or key words):

My girlfriend is very assertive.

Highway accidents are often caused by absentmindedness.

The kitchen is the most widely used room in my house.

Voting should be required by law in the United States.

My pickup truck is the most reliable vehicle I have ever owned.

In the first sentence, the topic is *girlfriend,* and the key word that expresses the writer's idea about his topic is that his girlfriend is *assertive.* In the second sentence, the topic is *highway accidents,* and the key word that determines the focus of the paragraph is that such accidents are often caused by *absentmindedness.* Notice each topic and key word or key words in the other three sentences as well.

ACTIVITY 5

TEACHING TIP
Ask students to identify statements that can be further narrowed. For example, "insects" in the statement "Insects serve many useful purposes" may be too broad, so the topic can be narrowed to "ants."

For each point below, draw a single line under the topic and a double line under the idea about the topic.

1. Billboards should be abolished.

2. My boss is an ambitious person.

3. Politicians are often self-serving.

4. The apartment needed repairs.

5. Television commercials lack originality.

6. My parents have rigid racial attitudes.

7. The middle child is often a neglected member of the family.

8. The language in many movies today is inappropriate for children.

9. Doctors are often insensitive.

10. People today are more energy-conscious than ever before.

11. My car is a temperamental machine.

12. My friend Debbie, who is only nineteen, is extremely mature.

13. Looking for a job can be a degrading experience.

14. The daily life of students is filled with conflicts.

15. Regulations in the school cafeteria should be strictly enforced.

16. The national speed limit should be raised.

17. Our vacation turned out to be a disaster.

18. The city's traffic-light system has both benefits and drawbacks.

19. Insects serve many useful purposes.

20. Serious depression often has several warning signs.

Selecting a Topic Sentence

Remember that a paragraph is made up of a topic sentence and a group of related sentences developing the topic sentence. It is also helpful to remember that the topic sentence is a *general* statement. The other sentences provide specific support for the general statement.

Each group of sentences below could be written as a short paragraph. Circle the letter of the topic sentence in each case. To find the topic sentence, ask yourself, "Which is a general statement supported by the specific details in the other three statements?"

ACTIVITY 6

Begin by trying the example item below. First circle the letter of the sentence you think expresses the main idea. Then read the explanation.

EXAMPLE

    a. By no longer carrying matches or a lighter, people can cut down on impulse smoking.

    b. People who sit in no-smoking areas will smoke less.

    (c.) There are ways to behave that will help people smoke less.

    d. By keeping personal records of where and when smoking occurs, people can identify the most tempting situations and avoid them.

TEACHING TIP
After students complete this activity, review the answers with the class. Encourage students to explain how they identified topic sentences.

EXPLANATION

Sentence *a* explains one way to smoke less. Sentences *b* and *d* also provide specific ways to smoke less. In sentence *c,* however, no one specific way is explained. The words *ways to behave that will make people smoke less* refer only generally to such methods. Therefore, sentence *c* is the topic sentence; it expresses the author's main idea. The other sentences support that idea by providing examples.

1. a. "I couldn't study because I forgot to bring my textbook home."

    b. "I couldn't do my homework because my printer ran out of toner."

    (c.) Students give instructors some common excuses.

    d. "I couldn't come to class because I had a migraine headache."

2. a. Its brakes are badly worn.

    (b.) My old car is ready for the salvage yard.

    c. Its floor has rusted through, and water splashes on my feet when the highway is wet.

    d. My mechanic says its engine is too old to be repaired, and the car isn't worth the cost of a new engine.

3. a. The last time I ate at the restaurant, I got food poisoning and was sick for two days.

    b. The city inspector found roaches and mice in the restaurant's kitchen.

(c.) The restaurant on 23rd street is a health hazard and ought to be closed down.

d. The toilets in the restaurant often back up, and the sinks have only a trickle of water.

4. a. Part-time employees can be easily laid off.

b. Most part-time employees do not receive fringe benefits.

c. A part-time employee earns 25 to 40 percent less than a full-time employee.

(d.) Part-time employment has several disadvantages.

5. a. In early colleges, students were mostly white males.

(b.) Colleges of two centuries ago were quite different from today's schools.

c. All students in early colleges had to take the same courses.

d. The entire student body at early schools consisted of only a few dozen people.

Writing a Topic Sentence I

ACTIVITY 7

The following activity will give you practice in writing an accurate point. Often you will start with a general topic or a general idea of what you want to write about. You may, for example, want to write a paragraph about some aspect of school life. To come up with a point about school life, begin by limiting your topic. One way to do this is to make a list of all the limited topics you can think of that fit under the general topic. Each of the general topics below is followed by a series of limited topics. Make a point out of *one* of the limited topics in each group.

To create a topic sentence, ask yourself, "What point do I want to make about _____ (*my limited topic*)?"

EXAMPLE

Recreation

* Movies
* Dancing
* TV shows
* Reading
* Sports parks

Your point: Sports parks today have some truly exciting games.

Answers will vary; examples are given.

1. Your school

* Instructor
* Cafeteria
* Specific course
* Particular room or building

- Particular policy (attendance, grading, etc.)
- Classmate

   Your point: Business Writing 101 has proved to be the most useful college

   course I've taken.

2. Job

   - Pay
   - Boss
   - Working conditions
   - Duties
   - Coworkers
   - Customers or clients

   Your point: After having worked at several jobs, I've concluded that there

   are three kinds of coworkers.

3. Money

   - Budgets
   - Credit cards
   - Dealing with a bank
   - School expenses
   - Ways to get it
   - Ways to save it

   Your point: There are some foolproof ways for students to save money.

   _____

4. Cars

   - First car
   - Driver's test
   - Road conditions
   - Accident
   - Mandatory speed limit
   - Safety problems

   Your point: Passing the driver's test can be easy if a person is well prepared.

   _____

5. Sports

   - A team's chances
   - At your school

- Women's team
- Recreational versus spectator
- Favorite team
- Outstanding athlete

    Your point: <u>My school's sports teams have come a long way this season.</u>

Writing a Topic Sentence II

ACTIVITY 8   The following activity will give you practice in writing an accurate point, or topic sentence—one that is neither too broad nor too narrow for the supporting material in a paragraph. Sometimes you will construct your topic sentence after you have decided which details you want to discuss. An added value of this activity is that it shows you how to write a topic sentence that will exactly match the details provided in the outline.

Wording of answers may vary.

1. Topic sentence: <u>There are steps that students can take to do well in college.</u>

    a. They should study the hardest subjects first when their minds are most alert.
    b. They should form study groups and meet regularly at the library.
    c. They should ask teachers for help when they don't understand something.
    d. They should reward themselves when they do well.

TEACHING TIP
Emphasize to students that topic sentences often need to be revised.

2. Topic sentence: <u>My mom lived and died by the Golden Rule.</u>

    a. My mom always said, "Do unto others as you would have them do unto you."
    b. She believed that everyone should be treated with respect and kindness.
    c. When my brother got caught up in the wrong crowd, she had him promise her that he would never hurt anyone.
    d. At my mom's funeral, so many people talked about how she had helped them.

3. Topic sentence: <u>The new Thai restaurant is worth a visit.</u>

    a. My friends recommended that I try the new Thai restaurant.
    b. The waiter was friendly and explained the daily lunch specials.
    c. The Evil Jungle Prince was the best red curry I had ever eaten.
    d. I plan to take my family to that restaurant for dinner.

4. Topic sentence: <u>Sports have always played a major role in my school life.</u>

    a. In elementary school, my favorite subject was morning recess.

    b. All I remember about junior high was playing volleyball in P.E. class.

    c. In high school, I kept my grades up so that I could stay on the basketball team.

    d. Before my knee injury, I had hoped to go to college on an athletic scholarship.

5. Topic sentence: <u>Breakfast is the most important meal of the day.</u>

    a. People who skip breakfast usually snack a lot.

    b. People who eat breakfast feel less grouchy.

    c. People who eat breakfast are more alert mentally.

    d. Breakfast can help people lose—not gain—weight.

Step 2: Support the Point with Specific Evidence

The first essential step in writing effectively is to start with a clearly stated point. The second basic step is to support that point with specific evidence. Consider the supported point that you read at the beginning of this chapter.

Point

The demands of modern society in recent years have changed family life.

Support

(1) Parents
    (a) Today's parents spend much less time with their children
    (b) Most work longer hours now, leaving children at an after-school program, or with a neighbor, or in an empty house

(2) Eating habits
    (a) Formerly full homemade meals, eaten together
    (b) Now prepared foods at home or fast food out, eaten separately

(3) Television and the Internet
    (a) Watching TV or browsing the Internet instead of conversing

The supporting evidence is needed so that we can *see and understand for ourselves* that the writer's point is sound. The author of "Changes in the Family" has supplied specific supporting examples of how changes in our society have weakened family life. The paragraph has provided the evidence that is needed for us to understand and agree with the writer's point.

ESL NOTE
Remind nonnative students to avoid using circular reasoning, which simply restates the main idea and does not provide supporting details. Although this pattern may be used in some cultures, it is not acceptable in academic writing. In English, it is important to begin with a strong point and provide relevant support.

TEACHING TIP
Cluster these details on the board for your visual learners.

Now consider the following paragraph:

> ### Good-Bye, Tony
>
> I have decided not to go out with Tony anymore. First of all, he was late for our first date. He said that he would be at my house by 7:30, but he did not arrive until 8:30. Second, he was bossy. He told me that it would be too late to go to the new *Star Wars* film that I wanted to see, and that we would go instead to the new action film starring Liam Neeson. I told him that I didn't want to see that movie, but he said that he was paying, so he got to choose. Only because it was a first date did I let him have his way. Finally, he was abrupt. After the movie, rather than suggest a bite to eat or a drink, he drove right out to a back road near Oakcrest High School to meet his friends. What he did a half hour later angered me most of all. His friends all decided they wanted to go to a club. He didn't want to take me, so he told me he was going to immediately take me home. When he dropped me off, I said, "Good-bye, Tony," in a friendly enough way, but I thought, "Good-bye *forever*, Tony."

The author's point is that she has decided not to go out with Tony anymore. See if you can summarize in the spaces below the three reasons she gives to support her decision:

Reason 1: He was late.

Reason 2: He was bossy.

Reason 3: He was abrupt.

Notice what the supporting details in this paragraph do. They provide you, the reader, with a basis for understanding why the writer made the decision she did. Through specific evidence, the writer has explained and communicated her point successfully. The evidence that supports the point in a paragraph often consists of a series of reasons introduced by signal words (the author here uses *First of all, Second,* and *Finally*) and followed by examples and details that support the reasons. That is true of the sample paragraph above: three reasons are provided, followed by examples and details that back up those reasons.

The Point as an "Umbrella" Idea

You may find it helpful to think of the point as an "umbrella" idea. Under the writer's point fits all of the other material of the paragraph. That other material is made up of specific supporting details—evidence such as examples, reasons, or facts. The diagram to the left shows the relationship for the paragraph "Good-Bye, Tony."

Both of the paragraphs that follow resulted from an assignment to "Write a paper that details your reasons for being in college." Both writers make the point that they have various reasons for attending college. Which paragraph then goes on to provide plenty of specific evidence to back up its point? Which paragraph is vague and repetitive and lacks the concrete details needed to show us exactly why the author decided to attend college?

ACTIVITY 9

TIP Imagine that you've been asked to make a short film based on each paragraph. Which one suggests specific pictures, locations, words, and scenes you could shoot?

TEACHING TIP
Bring a movie script to class. Show students how the screenwriter includes specific details. If possible, show a clip from the film so that your students can "see" these details.

PARAGRAPH A

Personal

Reasons for Going to College

I decided to attend college for various reasons. One reason is self-respect. For a long time now, I have had little self-respect. I spent a lot of time doing nothing, just hanging around or getting into trouble, and eventually I began to feel bad about it. Going to college is a way to start feeling better about myself. By accomplishing things, I will improve my self-image. Another reason for going to college is that things happened in my life that made me think about a change. When I lost my job, I realized I would have to do something in life, so I thought about school. I was in a rut and needed to get out of it but did not know how. But when something happens that is out of your control, then you have to make some kind of decision. The most important reason for college, though, is to fulfill my dream. I know I need an education, and I want to take the courses I need to reach the position that I think I can handle. Only by challenging myself can I get what I want. Going to college will help me fulfill this goal. These are the main reasons why I am attending college.

PARAGRAPH B

Personal

Why I'm in School

There are several reasons I'm in school. First of all, my father's attitude made me want to succeed in school. One night last year, after I had come in at 3 A.M., my father said, "Jake, you're a loser. When I look at my son, all I see is a good-for-nothing loser." I was angry, but I knew my father was right in a way. I had spent the last two years working at odd jobs at a convenience store and gas station, while experimenting with all kinds of drugs with my friends.

continued

That night, though, I decided I would prove my father wrong. I would go to college and be a success. Another reason I'm in college is my girlfriend's encouragement. Marie has already been in school for a year, and she is doing well in her computer courses. Marie helped me fill out my application and register for courses. She even lent me two hundred dollars for textbooks. On her day off, she lets me use her car so I don't have to take the bus. The main reason I am in college is to fulfill a personal goal: for the first time in my life, I want to finish something. For example, I quit high school in the eleventh grade. Then I enrolled in a government job-training program, but I dropped out after six months. I tried to get a G.E.D., but I started missing classes and eventually gave up. Now I am in a special program where I will earn my G.E.D. by completing a series of five courses. I am determined to accomplish this goal and to then go on and work for a degree in hotel management.

Complete the following statement: Paragraph ___B___ provides clear, vividly detailed reasons why the writer decided to attend college.

Paragraph B is the one that solidly backs up its point. The writer gives us specific reasons he is in school. On the basis of such evidence, we can clearly understand his opening point. The writer of paragraph A offers only vague, general reasons for being in school. We do not get specific examples of how the writer was "getting into trouble," what events occurred that forced the decision, or even what kind of job he or she wants to qualify for. We sense that the feeling expressed is sincere; but without particular examples we cannot really see why the writer decided to attend college.

Reinforcing Point and Support

You have now learned the two most important steps in writing effectively: making a point and supporting that point. Take a few minutes now to do the following activity. It will strengthen your ability to recognize a *point* and the *support* for that point.

ACTIVITY 10	In the following groups, one statement is the general point and the other statements are specific support for the point. Identify each point with a P and each statement of support with an S.

ESL NOTE
This is an important activity for nonnative students. Since the organization and details in a paragraph may be different in other cultures, students need to learn to distinguish between the main point and supporting details.

EXAMPLE

____S____   A city bus pass costs less than a tank of gas.

____S____   Brewing coffee at home is cheaper than buying coffee at Starbucks.

____S____   Coupons help reduce the grocery bill.

____P____   There are several ways to cut down on daily expenses.

EXPLANATION

The point—that daily spending can be reduced—is strongly supported by the three specific ways stated.

1. __S__ A person with depression might have sleep problems.

__S__ A person with depression might withdraw from friends.

__P__ Depression can affect a person's life in negative ways.

__S__ A person with depression might feel hopeless all the time.

2. __S__ Kim takes online classes, which fit into her busy schedule.

__P__ Kim is able to juggle the demands of school, family, and work.

__S__ Kim taught her kids how to help around the home.

__S__ Kim's supervisor gives her a flexible work schedule.

3. __P__ There are serious consequences to plagiarism.

__S__ A student can fail a class for turning in someone else's work.

__S__ Some schools award a grade of FD for academic dishonesty.

__S__ Some schools expel students who plagiarize.

4. __S__ Artificial sweeteners provide an alternative to refined sugar.

__S__ Regular exercise helps regulate a person's blood sugar level.

__S__ Blood sugar meters are sold over the counter at pharmacies.

__P__ Diabetes can be managed successfully.

5. __S__ Keisha was promoted to shift manager at work.

__S__ Mel received a two-year scholarship from the Rotary Club.

__P__ Keisha and Mel considered themselves fortunate.

__S__ Keisha and Mel were able to find an affordable apartment.

6. __S__ Be cautious about what is shared on social media and on online sites.

__S__ Shred all bank statements and credit card statements with a cross cut shredder.

__S__ Make sure all passwords use random letters, numbers, and symbols.

__P__ Everyone should take precautions to avoid identity theft.

7. __S__ White Castle sells microwavable hamburgers and cheeseburgers.

__S__ Hooters sells frozen Buffalo-style chicken strips.

__P__ Restaurant chains are selling their products in frozen food sections of supermarkets.

__S__ T.G.I. Friday's sells its popular appetizers, such as potato skins and onion rings.

8. __S__ People take personal phone calls during meetings.

__P__ Workplace etiquette is sorely lacking.

TEACHING TIP
Consider making a game out of this activity. See how quickly your students can complete the activity correctly. You may want to ask them to create a set of game rules first.

    S   People "borrow" coworkers' supplies without asking first.

    S   People leave their dirty dishes in the workplace kitchen.

9.   P   Ms. Lee is an outstanding teacher.

    S   She always asks if students have questions.

    S   She promptly answers e-mail and phone messages.

    S   She adds humor to her class lectures.

10.   S   I am able to do my homework while on my way to school.

    S   I am able to take a nap between school and work.

    S   I am able to stream videos on the way home.

    P   I prefer to use the city's public transportation.

11.   P   The musical group The Who performed all the theme songs for the *CSI* shows.

    S   The theme song for *CSI: Vegas* is "Who Are You."

    S   The theme song for *CSI: Miami* is "Won't Get Fooled Again."

    S   The theme song for *CSI: New York* is "Baba O'Riley."

12.   S   Mars has a rocky surface.

    S   Mercury has a rocky surface.

    S   Venus has a rocky surface.

    P   In addition to Earth, three planets in our solar system have rocky surfaces.

13.   S   Some courses have a prerequisite grade of C or better.

    S   Some employers look at a student's grade point average (GPA).

    P   Students should understand the importance of grades.

    S   Students who transfer need to meet that school's minimum GPA.

14.   S   He rearranged his work schedule so he could drop off and pick up his daughter from day care.

    S   He takes online classes to reduce his commuting time to and from school.

    P   Kyong Li takes his parenting responsibilities seriously.

    S   He is working toward an associate degree so he can better support his family.

15.   P   College students depend on technology to assist them in their learning.

    S   Professors may make class lectures available as podcasts.

    S   Campus classes may have an online component.

    S   Students often communicate with professors and classmates through e-mail.

The Importance of *Specific* Details

The point that opens a paper is a general statement. The evidence that supports a point is made up of specific details, reasons, examples, and facts.

Specific details have two key functions. First of all, details *excite the reader's interest.* They make writing a pleasure to read, for we all enjoy learning particulars about other people—what they do and think and feel. Second, details *support and explain a writer's point;* they give the evidence needed for us to see and understand a general idea. For example, the writer of "Good-Bye, Tony" provides details that make vividly clear her decision not to see Tony anymore. She specifies the exact time Tony was supposed to arrive (7:30) and when he actually arrived (8:30). She mentions the kind of film she wanted to see (a new *Star Wars* movie) and the one that Tony took her to instead (an action film). She tells us what she may have wanted to do after the movie (have a bite to eat or a drink) and what Tony did instead (met up with his friends); she even specifies the exact location of the place Tony took her (a back road near Oakcrest High School).

The writer of "Why I'm in School" provides equally vivid details. He gives clear reasons for being in school (his father's attitude, his girlfriend's encouragement, and his wish to fulfill a personal goal) and backs up each reason with specific details. His details give us many sharp pictures. For instance, we hear the exact words his father spoke: "Jake, you're a loser." He tells us exactly how he was spending his time ("working at odd jobs at a convenience store and gas station while experimenting with all kinds of drugs with my friends"). He describes how his girlfriend helped him (filling out the college application, lending money and her car). Finally, instead of stating generally that "a person has to make some kind of decision," as the writer of "Reasons for Going to College" does, he specifies that he has a strong desire to finish college because he dropped out of many schools and programs in the past: high school, a job-training program, and a G.E.D. course.

In both "Good-Bye, Tony" and "Why I'm in School," then, the vivid, exact details capture our interest and enable us to share in the writer's experience. We see people's actions and hear their words; the details provide pictures that make each of us feel "I am there." The particulars also allow us to understand each writer's point clearly. We are shown exactly why the first writer has decided not to see Tony anymore and exactly why the second writer is attending college.

Recognizing Specific Details

Each of the five points below is followed by two attempts at support (*a* and *b*). Write S (for *specific*) in the space next to the one that succeeds in providing specific support for the point. Write X in the space next to the one that lacks supporting details.

1. My three-year-old son was in a stubborn mood today.

   ___X___ a. When I asked him to do something, he gave me nothing but trouble. He seemed determined to make things difficult for me, for he had his mind made up.

TEACHING TIP
Have students look at a previously written paragraph to see if they used specific details.

ACTIVITY 11

TEACHING TIP
Consider making a game out of the next three activities. See how quickly your students correctly complete an activity. You may want to ask them to create a set of game rules first.

_____ S _____   b. When I asked him to stop playing in the yard and come indoors, he looked me squarely in the eye and shouted "No!" and then spelled it out, "N ... O!"

2. The prices in the amusement park were outrageously high.

_____ X _____   a. The food seemed to cost twice as much as it would in a supermarket and was sometimes of poor quality. The rides also cost a lot, and so I had to tell the children that they were limited to a certain number of them.

_____ S _____   b. The cost of the log flume, a ride that lasts roughly three minutes, was ten dollars a person. Then I had to pay four dollars for an eight-ounce cup of Coke and six dollars for a hot dog.

3. My brother-in-law is accident prone.

_____ S _____   a. Once he tried to open a tube of Krazy Glue with his teeth. When the cap came loose, glue squirted out and sealed his lips shut. They had to be pried open in a hospital emergency room.

_____ X _____   b. Even when he does seemingly simple jobs, he seems to get into trouble. This can lead to hilarious, but sometimes dangerous, results. Things never seem to go right for him, and he often needs the help of others to get out of one predicament or another.

4. The so-called bargains at the yard sale were junk.

_____ X _____   a. The tables were filled with useless stuff no one could possibly want. They were the kinds of things that should be thrown away, not sold.

_____ S _____   b. The "bargains" included two headless dolls, blankets filled with holes, scorched potholders, and a plastic Christmas tree with several branches missing.

5. The key to success in college is organization.

_____ X _____   a. It is a big help for students to know what they are doing, when they have to do it, and so on. A system is crucial in achieving an ordered approach to study. Otherwise, things become very disorganized, and it is not long before grades will begin to drop.

_____ S _____   b. Organized students never forget paper or exam dates, which are marked on a calendar above their desks. And instead of having to cram for exams, they study their clear, neat classroom and textbook notes on a daily basis.

EXPLANATION

The specific support for point 1 is answer *b*. The writer does not just tell us that the little boy was stubborn but provides an example that shows us. In particular, the detail of the son's spelling out "N . . . O!" makes his stubbornness vividly

continued

real for the reader. For point 2, answer *b* gives specific prices (ten dollars for a ride, four dollars for a Coke, and six dollars for a hot dog) to support the idea that the amusement park was expensive. For point 3, answer *a* vividly backs up the idea that the brother-in-law is accident-prone by detailing an accident with Krazy Glue. Point 4 is supported by answer *b,* which lists specific examples of useless items that were offered for sale—from headless dolls to a broken plastic Christmas tree. We cannot help agreeing with the writer's point that the items were not bargains but junk. Point 5 is backed up by answer *b,* which identifies two specific strategies of organized students: they mark important dates on calendars above their desks, and they take careful notes and study them on a daily basis.

In each of the five cases, the specific evidence enables us to *see for ourselves* that the writer's point is valid.

| Follow the directions for Activity 11. | **ACTIVITY 12** |

1. The house has been neglected by its owners.

    ___X___ a. As soon as I looked at the house from the outside, I could tell that repairs need to be made. The roof is badly in need of attention. But it is very obvious that other outside parts of the house also are badly in need of care.

    ___S___ b. The roof is missing a number of shingles. The house's paint is peeling and spotted with mold. Two windows have been covered with plywood.

2. Students have practical uses for computers.

    ___S___ a. Students stay in touch with friends by e-mail. They often shop over the Internet. They do all their research online.

    ___X___ b. Students have an easier way now to communicate with their friends. They can also save time now: they have no need to go out and buy things but can do it at home. Also, getting information they need for papers no longer requires spending time in the library.

3. Rico knew very little about cooking when he got his first apartment.

    ___X___ a. He had to live on whatever he had in the freezer for a while. He was not any good in the kitchen and had to learn very slowly. More often than not, he would learn how to cook something only by making mistakes first.

    ___S___ b. He lived on frozen macaroni and cheese dinners for three weeks. His idea of cooking an egg was to put a whole egg in the microwave, where it exploded. Then he tried to make a grilled cheese sandwich by putting slices of cheese and bread in a toaster.

4. Speaking before a group is a problem for many people.

_____X_____ a. They become uncomfortable even at the thought of speaking in public. They will go to almost any length to avoid speaking to a group. If they are forced to do it, they can feel so anxious that they actually develop physical symptoms.

_____S_____ b. Stage fright, stammering, and blushing are frequent reactions. Some people will pretend to be ill to avoid speaking publicly. When asked to rank their worst fears, people often list public speaking as even worse than death.

5. Small children can have as much fun with ordinary household items as with costly toys.

_____S_____ a. A large sheet thrown over a card table makes a great hideout or playhouse. Banging pot covers together makes a tremendous crash that kids love. Also, kids like to make long, winding fences out of wooden clothespins.

_____X_____ b. Kids can make musical instruments out of practically anything. The result is a lot of noise and fun. They can easily create their own play areas as well by using a little imagination. There is simply no need to have to spend a lot of money on playthings.

Providing Supporting Evidence

ACTIVITY 13

©Jacob Lund/
Shutterstock

Answers will vary;
examples are given.

Working in groups of two or three, provide three details that logically support each of the following points, or topic sentences. Your details can be drawn from your own experience, or they can be invented. In each case, the details should show in a specific way what the point expresses in only a general way. You may state your details briefly in phrases, or as complete sentences.

EXAMPLE

Each holiday season, several "hot" items are on kids' wish lists.

1. One year, every preschooler wanted a Tickle Me Elmo doll.

2. Kids always want the most up-to-date video game console.

3. Electronic toys are popular among both girls and boys.

1. Everyone has a cure for the common cold.

a. Some people believe that chicken soup cures a cold.

b. Some people believe that one should "starve" a cold.

c. Many people take vitamin C when they have a cold.

2.   Nothing can take the place of home cooking.

   a.   My grandma makes the best frijoles refritos. _____

   b.   Everyone loves my dad's marinade for carne asada. _____

   c.   When I feel homesick, I make myself tortilla soup. _____

3.   We can help save our environment in small but powerful ways.

   a.   Recycle our old newspapers and magazines. _____

   b.   Bring our cans and bottles to a recycling center. _____

   c.   Use compact fluorescent lightbulbs. _____

4.   I could never understand the wisdom of my father until I became one.

   a.   My dad wanted me home by eleven, but now I worry when my kids are out past ten. _____

   b.   My dad scolded me when I fell asleep with the TV on, and now I nag my kids when they forget to turn off anything that requires electricity. _____

   c.   My dad grilled me about who my friends were, and now I want to know who my kids are chatting with online. _____

5.   People should look for certain qualities when selecting a doctor.

   a.   They should feel comfortable asking their doctor questions. _____

   b.   They should know what their doctor's credentials are. _____

   c.   They should trust that their doctor will be honest with them. _____

The Importance of *Adequate* Details

One of the most common and most serious problems in students' writing is inadequate development. You must provide *enough* specific details to support fully the point you are making. You could not, for example, submit a paragraph about your brother-in-law being clumsy and provide only a single short example. You would have to add several other examples or provide an extended example of your brother-in-law's clumsiness. Without such additional support, your paragraph would be underdeveloped.

At times, students try to disguise an undersupported point by using repetition and wordy generalities. You saw this, for example, in paragraph A ("Reasons for Going to College") earlier in this chapter. Be prepared to do the plain hard work needed to ensure that each of your paragraphs has full, solid support.

TEACHING TIP
Students often use repetition and wordy generalizations when faced with a word-count or minimum-page requirement. Remind them that brainstorming can be done after a draft is written to generate more support.

ACTIVITY 14

The following paragraphs were written on the same topic, and each has a clear opening point. Which one is adequately developed? Which one has few particulars and uses mostly vague, general, wordy sentences to conceal the fact that it is starved for specific details?

ESL NOTE
"Wordy generalities" and "repetition" may be examples of using circular reasoning, a typical paragraph development in some cultures and languages. Nonnative students may need some closer guidance and examination to understand that this is not acceptable or expected in academic writing.

PARAGRAPH A

Abuse of Public Parks

Some people abuse public parks. Instead of using the park for recreation, they go there, for instance, to clean their cars. Park caretakers regularly have to pick up the contents of dumped ashtrays and car litter bags. Certain juveniles visit parks with cans of spray paint to deface buildings, fences, fountains, and statues. Other offenders are those who dig up and cart away park flowers, shrubs, and trees. One couple were even arrested for stealing park sod, which they were using to fill in their lawn. Perhaps the most widespread offenders are the people who use park tables and benches and fireplaces but do not clean up afterward. Picnic tables are littered with trash, including crumpled bags, paper plates smeared with ketchup, and paper cups half-filled with stale soda. On the ground are empty beer bottles, dented soda cans, and sharp metal bottle caps. Parks are made for people, and yet—ironically—their worst enemy is "people pollution."

PARAGRAPH B

Mistreatment of Public Parks

Some people mistreat public parks. Their behavior is evident in many ways, and the catalog of abuses could go on almost without stopping. Different kinds of debris are left by people who have used the park as a place for attending to their cars. They are not the only individuals who mistreat public parks, which should be used with respect for the common good of all. Many young people come to the park and abuse it, and their offenses can occur in any season of the year. The reason for their inconsiderate behavior is known only to themselves. Other visitors lack personal cleanliness in their personal habits when they come to the park, and the park suffers because of it. Such people seem to have the attitude that someone else should clean up after them. It is an undeniable fact that people are the most dangerous thing that parks must contend with.

Complete the following statement: Paragraph ___A___ provides an adequate number of specific details to support its point.

Paragraph A offers a series of detailed examples of how people abuse parks. Paragraph B, on the other hand, is underdeveloped. Paragraph B speaks only of "different kinds of debris," while paragraph A refers specifically to "dumped ashtrays and car litter bags"; paragraph B talks in a general way of young people abusing the park, while paragraph A supplies such particulars as "cans of spray paint" and defacing "buildings, fences, fountains, and statues." And there is no equivalent in paragraph B for the specifics in paragraph A about people who steal park property and litter park grounds. In summary, paragraph B lacks the full, detailed support needed to develop its opening point convincingly.

©mavo/Shutterstock

REFLECTIVE ACTIVITY

To check your understanding of the chapter so far, see if you can answer the following questions.

1. It has been observed: "To write well, the first thing you must do is decide what nail you want to drive home." What is meant by *nail?*

    The "nail" is the point you want to make, or "drive home."

2. How do you "drive home the nail" in the paragraph?

    You drive home the nail—or point—in the paragraph with specific supporting

    details.

3. What are the two reasons for using specific details in your writing?

    a.   Details excite the reader's interest.

    b.   Details support and explain your point.

4. Look back at the paragraph you wrote in Chapter 2 (Activity 10) about an everyday annoyance. How could you further "drive home the nail"? In other words, what could you do to improve that paragraph?

TEACHING TIP
You may want to use this activity to assess student learning.

Identifying Adequate Supporting Evidence

Two of the following paragraphs provide sufficient details to support their topic sentences convincingly. Write AD, for *adequate development,* beside those paragraphs. There are also three paragraphs that, for the most part, use vague, general, or wordy sentences as a substitute for concrete details. Write U, for *underdeveloped,* beside those paragraphs.

ACTIVITY 15

TEACHING TIP
For added practice, ask students to revise the underdeveloped paragraphs by providing adequate, specific details.

_____U_____ 1.

Social Saving

The power of the group is often stronger than the power of the individual. This is demonstrated by the blossoming of online group coupon sites like LivingSocial, Yipit, and Groupon. By exercising group buying power, users are able to save money of food, clothing, and entertainment. Most sites offer discounts of at least 50 percent for consumers. These are good sites not just for people to use in their local areas, but also for savvy travelers. In preparation for a visit to another city, travelers can select that particular city and start finding deals at restaurants, spas, and hotels to use during their vacation.

_____AD_____ 2.

The Dangers of Being Charitable

People need to be aware of the hazards of charity and helping those in need because giving often starts small, but soon takes over and becomes a lifestyle. Charity usually begins with a minor donation of change to the local firefighters' boot drive. The philanthropist feels good for a while, but then that feeling fades. The next time the patron drops change in the boot, it isn't enough—that helpful feeling just isn't there, so she begins to purchase large quantities of bottled water and ready-to-eat foods, and drives around delivering food and water to the homeless. The feeling of doing good returns, but then, a disaster happens—earthquake in Haiti, hurricanes in Puerto Rico, tornadoes in the Midwest—and the donor fumbles to reclaim that gratifying feeling. Just sending monetary donations doesn't seem to be enough. Just sending food, clothing, and products doesn't seem to be enough. The philanthropist starts charity drives to raise awareness and support, and the humanitarian feeling settles back in. Unfortunately, the feeling still doesn't last and the withdrawal begins to set in. The giver frantically begins to research more and more ways to get involved, chasing that altruistic feeling that has become so elusive. Soon, the donor is spending time at local soup kitchens, adopting needy families, and opening doors to those who have no place to live. Like an addict, the philanthropist is no longer a free agent, but a servant to humanitarian causes.

_____U_____ 3.

School Lunch Woes

Most school lunches are not pleasing to the eye or taste buds. Too often, the food lacks a variety of color and pretty texture. Green beans should be green, macaroni and cheese should be bright yellow or orange, and hamburger should be brown. The food tends to be either mushy or burned. More than half of the food has once been frozen or in a can. Frozen vegetables are usually over-steamed and become tasteless and flavorless. Mashed potatoes look lumpy and colorless. Meats that have been frozen too long have rubbery textures and never taste right. If the cafeteria worker hadn't told me that the meat on my tray was chicken, I would never have figured it out.

_____U_____   4.

Qualities in a Friend

There are several qualities I look for in a friend. A friend should give support and security. A friend should also be fun to be around. Friends can have faults, like anyone else, and sometimes it is hard to overlook them. But a friend can't be dropped because he or she has faults. A friend should stick around, even in bad times. There is a saying that "a friend in need is a friend indeed." I believe this means that there are good friends and fair-weather friends. The second type is not a true friend. He or she is the kind of person who runs when there's trouble. Friends don't always last a lifetime. Someone who is believed to be a best friend may lose contact if they move to a different area or go around with a different group of people. A friend should be generous and understanding. Friends do not have to be exactly like each other. Sometimes friends are opposites, but they still like each other and get along. Since I am a very quiet person, I can't say that I have many friends. But these are the qualities I believe a friend should have.

_____AD_____   5.

Learning Outside the Classroom

Colleges should require that all students take a service learning course. Service learning not only combines classroom study and community service, but it introduces students to hands-on training and helps create a sense of well-being in students. Students in biology classes often take part in waterway clean-up projects. These students not only gain a sense of contributing to their community and helping improve the environment, but they also get to study the local plants and wildlife and learn just how humans positively and negatively impact the ecosystems. Students in theater classes can expand their knowledge about costumes, set design, and lighting while they participate in community theater programs. Additionally, students can learn how the theater programs can enhance individuals through better social, communication, and problem-solving skills. This, in turn, improves local communities through cross-generational participation. Students in education classes can volunteer at local schools, offering services like free tutoring, aiding teachers, and campus clean-up programs. Not only will this volunteer work have a positive impact on the schools' communities, but it will introduce future teachers to ways of improving the environments they will be

continued

working in. Students who are in English composition classes can participate in local adult literacy programs, helping tutor adults in reading and writing. Not only will these students gain a sense of purpose, but they will be increasing their knowledge of reading and writing skills. Service learning improves both classroom learning and lifelong learning and should be a requirement for every college graduate.

Adding Details to Complete a Paragraph

ACTIVITY 16

Each of the following paragraphs needs specific details to back up its supporting points. In the spaces provided, add a sentence or two of realistic details for each supporting point. The more specific you are, the more convincing your details are likely to be.

Answers will vary; examples are given.

1.

A Pushover Instructor

We knew after the first few classes that the instructor was a pushover. First of all, he didn't seem able to control the class. Most students conversed loudly with each other during the entire class period. A group of students soon got into the habit of leaving class after five minutes to eat a very early lunch.

In addition, he made some course requirements easier when a few students complained. Students persuaded him to give ten-question open-book tests. Melodramatic students convinced him that they couldn't possibly write a final paper, so he dropped it.

Finally, he gave the easiest quiz we had ever taken. He asked simple fourth-grade-level questions. Some students got him to allow open books even for this quiz.

2.

Helping a Parent in College

There are several ways a family can help a parent who is attending college. First, family members can take over some of the household chores that the parent usually does. The other parent and the children can insist on cooking and cleaning on the day before and the day of the parent's classes. They can also help by doing the parent's laundry, freeing the parent to study.

Also, family members can make sure that the student has some quiet study time. They can establish a study space and time for the parent and avoid disturbing him or her. They can try not to yell and not to turn on the TV or play gaming consoles loudly when the parent is studying.

Last, families can take an interest in the student's problems and accomplishments. They should be sure to ask how classes went when the parent comes home and to listen with interest when he or she answers.

Writing a Paragraph

You know now that an effective paragraph does two essential things: (1) it makes a point, and (2) it provides specific details to support that point. You have considered a number of paragraphs that are effective because they follow these two basic steps or ineffective because they fail to follow them.

The following writing assignments will give you practice in writing a paragraph of your own. Choose one of the three assignments below, and follow carefully the guidelines provided.

DEVELOPING AND SUPPORTING A POINT

Turn back to Activity 13 and select the point for which you have the best supporting details. Develop that point into a paragraph by following these steps:

a. If necessary, rewrite the point so that the first sentence is more specific or suits your purpose more exactly. For example, you might want to rewrite the second point so that it includes a specific time and place: "Dinner at the Union Building Cafeteria was terrible yesterday."

b. Provide several sentences of information to develop each of your three supporting details fully. Make sure that all the information in your paragraph truly supports your point.

c. Use the words *first of all, second,* and *finally* to introduce your three supporting details.

WRITING ASSIGNMENT 1

Academic

TEACHING TIP
Remind students that writing is a recursive process, so they may need to revise their topic sentence or do additional prewriting.

d. Conclude your paragraph with a sentence that refers to your opening point. This last sentence "rounds off" the paragraph and lets the reader know that your discussion is complete. For example, the paragraph "Changes in the Family" in Activity 1 begins with, "The demands of modern society in recent years have changed family life." It closes with a statement that refers to, and echoes, the opening point: "Clearly, modern life is a challenge to family life."

e. Supply a title based on your point. For instance, point 3 in Activity 13 might have the title "Ways to Save the Environment."

Use the following list to check your paragraph for each of the above items:

Yes No

☐ ☐ Do you begin with a point?

☐ ☐ Do you provide relevant, specific details that support the point?

☐ ☐ Do you use the words *first of all, second,* and *finally* to introduce your three supporting details?

☐ ☐ Do you have a closing sentence?

☐ ☐ Do you have a title based on your point?

☐ ☐ Are your sentences clear and free of obvious errors?

Answers will vary.

TEACHING TIP
Photocopy this section for your students to use as a checklist.

WRITING ASSIGNMENT 2

Personal

ESL NOTE
A variation on this topic could be: Reasons nonnative students, especially international students, attend American colleges.

Answers will vary.

EXPLAINING YOUR DECISION

In this chapter you have read two paragraphs (Activity 9) on reasons for being in college. The writing prompt at the opening of this chapter asked you to consider your own reasons for being in college and to write nonstop, make a list, or draw a diagram of your ideas. For this assignment, look back at the ideas you wrote down in response to the chapter opening writing prompt and write a paragraph describing your reasons for being in college. You might also want to look at the following list of common reasons students give for going to school. Write a check mark next to each reason that applies to you. Using this list and the ideas you have written down, select your three most important reasons for being in school and generate specific supporting details for each reason.

Before starting, reread paragraph B in Activity 9. *You must provide comparable specific details of your own.* Make your paragraph truly personal; do not fall back on vague generalities like those in paragraph A. As you work on your paragraph, use the checklist for Assignment 1 as a guide.

*Applies in
My Case*   **Reasons Students Go to College**

_____   To have some fun before getting a job

_____   To prepare for a specific career

_____ To please their families

_____ To educate and enrich themselves

_____ To be with friends who are going to college

_____ To take advantage of an opportunity they didn't have before

_____ To find a husband or wife

_____ To see if college has anything to offer them

_____ To do more with their lives than they've done so far

_____ To take advantage of Veterans Administration benefits or other special funding

_____ To earn the status that they feel comes with a college degree

_____ To get a new start in life

_____ Other:

in a writer's words

" *Write what you want to read. The person you know best in the world is you. Listen to yourself. If you are excited by what you are writing, you have a much better chance of putting that excitement over to a reader.*"

—Robin McKinley

IDENTIFYING GOALS

Write a paragraph about your goals for the coming year. First, list a series of realistic goals, major and minor, that you would like to accomplish between today and one year from today. Your goals can be personal, academic, and/or career related. Next, organize your list by using clustering or a scratch outline. Use the checklist for Writing Assignment 1 as a guide while you are working on the paragraph.

WRITING ASSIGNMENT 3

Personal

ESL NOTE
Nonnative students might want to write about goals for learning/studying English.

EXPLORING WRITING ONLINE

Go to your school's Web site. What can you learn about your school from its Web site? Which details might appeal to a student who is considering attending your school? Using specific details from the Web site, write a paragraph explaining why this student should attend your school.

©Tetra Images/ Shutterstock

The Third and Fourth Steps in Writing

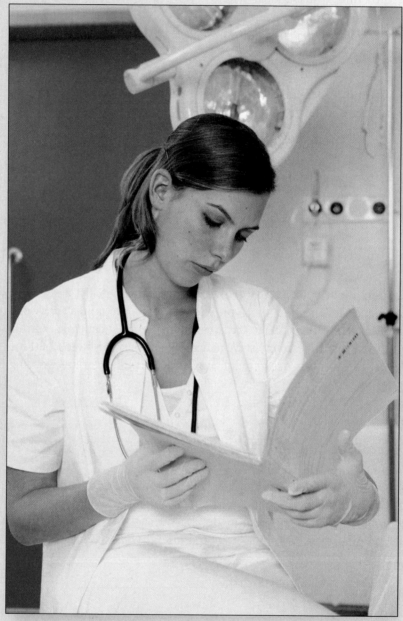

©Cultura Motion/Shutterstock

RESPONDING TO IMAGES

Many jobs require clear, accurate writing. What would happen if an insurance agent wrote a confusing claim report—or if a nurse recorded an incomplete description of a patient's medical history? Think about how you write. Do you usually check your work for mistakes? Take a few minutes to jot down your thoughts on this topic. In this chapter you will learn strategies to help you write clear, error-free sentences.

You know from Chapter 3 that the first two steps in writing an effective para-graph are making a point and supporting the point with specific evidence. This chapter will deal with the third and fourth steps. You'll learn the chief ways to organize and connect the supporting information in a paragraph, and how to write clear, error-free sentences.

Four Steps		Four Bases
1. If you make one point and stick to that point,	➡	your writing will have *unity*.
2. If you back up the point with specific evidence,	➡	your writing will have *support*.
3. **If you organize and connect the specific evidence,**	➡	**your writing will have *coherence*.**
4. **If you write clear, error-free sentences,**	➡	**your writing will demonstrate effective *sentence skills*.**

Step 3: Organize and Connect the Specific Evidence

At the same time that you are generating the specific details needed to support a point, you should be thinking about ways to organize and connect those details. All the details in your paper must cohere, or stick together; when they do, your reader is able to move smoothly from one bit of supporting informa-tion to the next. This chapter will discuss the following ways to organize and connect supporting details:

1. Common methods of organization

2. Transition words, or signals

3. Other connecting words

Common Methods of Organization: Time Order and Emphatic Order

Time order and emphatic order are common methods used to organize the supporting material in a paper. (You will learn more specialized methods of development in Part 3 of the book.)

Organizing through Time Order

Time order, or *chronological order*, means that details are listed as they occur in time. *First* this is done; *next* this; *then* this; *after* that, this; and so on. Here is a paragraph that organizes its details through time order.

TEACHING TIP
To illustrate coherence, bring a spiral- or comb-bound book to class. Tell your students that the pages of the book are supporting details and the spine serves as the method of organization. You might also use the analogy of a human skeleton. The bones are supporting details, the spine is the method of organization, and the joints are transitions and connecting words.

TEACHING TIP
Explain to students that spatial organization can also be used, but generally only for describing something or someone.

Crazy Fad Diets

People often resolve to lose weight and get healthy, but many choose a popular diet without thinking about the adverse side effects. In the early twentieth century, the "Chew Yourself Thin" diet became popular. People could eat whatever they wanted, but each bite of food needed to be chewed until no taste remained. For some foods, this could be as few as thirty bites, but for others, a jaw-dropping one hundred bites might be needed. Losing weight came about because people never finished their plates—their jaws were too tired. By the middle of the century, "The Sleeping Beauty" diet gained popularity. Dieters would be drug-induced to sleep for extra-long periods of time—days even—in order to lose weight. Of course, avoiding eating caused dieters to lose weight, but in addition to malnutrition, there was a terrible epidemic of bed-head. Decades later, dieters became more varied in their quest for thinness. The "Cotton Ball" diet had dieters ingesting cotton balls filled with fiber, but it was the wrong type of fiber. Despite the softness of the cotton, dieters became very prickly and cranky. The "Baby Food" diet, in which participants ate baby food instead of regular food, contained more nutrients than many of the previous diets, but there was a high incidence of incessant crying as dieters felt hungry and needed their mommies. The "Cookie Diet" was the answer to the hungry baby food dieters and was very popular, especially with the sweets-loving, snacking crowd. All dieters had to do was eat cookies to get thin, but the problem was dieters were supposed to purchase specially formulated cookies, not the chocolate chip and iced-sugar cookies from the local grocery store. In the future, maybe someone will come up with a Chewy Cotton Cookie diet that involves exercising by sleeping and has no side effects; until then, dieters may have to try eating healthily and exercising regularly.

Fill in the missing words: "Crazy Fad Diets" uses five phrases to help show time order: In the early twentieth century; By the middle of the century; Decades later; In the future; until then.

ACTIVITY 1

Use time order to organize the scrambled list of sentences below. Write the number 1 beside the point that all the other sentences support. Then number each supporting sentence as it occurs in time.

10   The table is right near the garbage pail.

6   So you reluctantly select a gluelike tuna-fish sandwich, a crushed apple pie, and watery, lukewarm coffee.

12   You sit at the edge of the table, away from the garbage pail, and gulp down your meal.

1	Trying to eat in the cafeteria is an unpleasant experience.
9	Suddenly you spot a free table in the center.
13	With a last swallow of the lukewarm coffee, you get up and leave the cafeteria as rapidly as possible.
11	Flies are flitting into and out of the pail.
4	By the time it is your turn, the few things that are almost good are gone.
8	There does not seem to be a free table anywhere.
3	Unfortunately, there is a line in the cafeteria.
5	The hoagies, coconut-custard pie, and iced tea have all disappeared.
7	You hold your tray and look for a place to sit down.
2	You have a class in a few minutes, and so you run in to grab something to eat quickly.

Organizing through Emphatic Order

Emphatic order is sometimes described as "save-the-best-for-last" order. It means that the most interesting or important detail is placed in the last part of a paper. (In cases where all the details seem equal in importance, the writer should impose a personal order that seems logical or appropriate to the details.) The last position in a paper is the most emphatic position because the reader is most likely to remember the last thing read. *Finally, last of all,* and *most important* are typical words showing emphasis. The following paragraph organizes its details through emphatic order.

US Weekly

There are several reasons why *US Weekly* is so popular. First of all, editors from the magazine are often interviewed by popular entertainment news television shows, such as *Entertainment Tonight,* for their insights into the world of celebrity gossip. This exposure helps convince people that the editors at *US Weekly* are the experts on the inside scoop in Hollywood, and that the stories they print are truthful. In addition, the magazine is easily available. In supermarkets, convenience stores, and drugstores, *US Weekly* is always displayed in racks close to the cash register. As customers wait in line, they can't help being attracted to the magazine's glaring headlines. Then, on impulse, customers will add the magazine to their other purchases. Most of all, people read *US Weekly* because they love gossip. We find other people's lives fascinating, especially if those people are rich and famous. We want to see and read

continued

about their homes, their clothes, and their friends, lovers, and families. We also take a kind of mean delight in their unflattering photos and problems and mistakes, perhaps because we envy them. Even though we may be ashamed of our interest, it's hard to resist buying a paper that promises "Brad and Angelina's Deep Secret," or "Film Stars Without Makeup," or even "Hollywood Star Wars: Who Hates Whom and Why." *US Weekly* knows how to get us interested and make us buy.

Fill in the missing words: The paragraph lists a total of <u>three</u> different reasons people read *US Weekly*. The writer of the paragraph feels that the most import-ant reason is <u>our love of gossip</u>. He or she signals this reason by using the emphasis words <u>Most of all</u>.

ACTIVITY 2	Use emphatic order (order of importance) to arrange the following scrambled list of sentences. Write the number 1 beside the point that all the other sentences sup-port. Then number each supporting sentence, starting with what seems to be the least important detail and ending with the most important detail.

    __3__   The people here are all around my age and seem to be genuinely friendly and interested in me.

    __1__   The place where I live has several important advantages.

    __10__   The schools in this neighborhood have a good reputa-tion, so I feel that my daughter is getting a good education.

    __9__   The best thing of all about this area, though, is the school system.

    __7__   Therefore, I don't have to put up with public trans-portation or worry about how much it's going to cost to park each day.

    __11__   The school also has an extended day-care program, so I know my daughter is in good hands until I come home from work.

    __2__   First of all, I like the people who live in the other apartments near mine.

    __5__   Another positive aspect of this area is that it's close to where I work.

    __4__   That's more than I can say for the last place I lived, where people stayed behind locked doors.

    __6__   The office where I'm a receptionist is only a six-block walk from my house.

    __8__   In addition, I save a lot of wear and tear on my car.

Organizing through a Combination of Time Order and Emphatic Order

Some paragraphs use a *combination of time order and emphatic order*. For example, "Good-Bye, Tony" in Chapter 3 includes time order: it moves from the time Tony arrived to the end of the evening. In addition, the writer uses emphatic order, ending with her most important reason (signaled by the words *most of all*) for not wanting to see Tony anymore.

Use a combination of time and emphatic order to arrange the scrambled list of sentences below. Write the number 1 beside the point that all the other sentences support. Then number each supporting sentence. Paying close attention to transitional words and phrases will help you organize and connect the supporting sentences.	**ACTIVITY 3**

TEACHING TIP
Ask your students to identify words that signal time order and emphatic order.

___3___ For months, I dreamt of gigantic spiders crawling into my bed and devouring me.

___7___ I saw the bandage on his hand and the puffy swelling when the bandage was removed.

___9___ My most traumatic experience with spiders happened when another friend and I were hiking in the mountains.

___14___ For an hour afterward, I constantly rubbed the fingers of my hand to reassure myself that the spider was no longer there.

___2___ The first experience was the time I stayed up late to watch the horror movie *Tarantula.*

___10___ As we approached several bushes, I felt a presence on my left hand.

___1___ I had three experiences that are the cause of my arachnophobia, a terrible and uncontrollable fear of spiders.

___8___ For several weeks afterward, I saw the ugly red scab on my friend's hand and the yellow pus that continued oozing from under the scab.

___11___ Almost completely covering my finger was a monstrous brown spider, with white stripes running down each of a seemingly endless number of long, furry legs.

___4___ I even imagined seeing these hairy, vicious creatures every time I turned a corner.

___15___ After my three experiences, I suspect that my fear of spiders will be with me until I die.

___6___ I did not see the spider but visited my friend in the hospital, where he suffered through a few days of nausea and dizziness because of the poison.

___12___ I cried out "Arghh!" and flicked my hand violently back and forth to shake off the spider.

___5___ The second experience was the time when my best friend received a bite from a black widow spider.

___13___ For a long, horrible second it clung stickily, as if permanently intertwined among the fingers of my hand, but then it flew off my hand.

Transitions

Look at the following items. Then check (✓) the one that is easier to read and understand.

_____   Our landlord repainted our apartment. He replaced the dishwasher.

____✓____   Our landlord repainted our apartment. Also, he replaced the dishwasher.

You probably found the second item easier to understand. The word *also* makes it clear that the writer is adding a second way the landlord has been of help. *Transitions* are signal words that help readers follow the direction of the writer's thought. They show the relationship between ideas, connecting one thought to the next. They are "bridge" words, carrying the reader across from one idea to the next.

Two major types of transitions are of particular help when you write: words that show *time* and words that show *addition*.

Words That Show Time

Check (✓) the item that is easier to read and understand.

1. _____   a. I had blood work done. I went to the doctor.

   ____✓____   b. I had blood work done. Then I went to the doctor.

The word *Then* in the second item makes clear the relationship between the sentences. After having blood work done, the writer goes to the doctor. *Then* and words like it are time words, carrying the reader from one idea to the next.

I had blood work done. ————— I went to the doctor.

Here are some more pairs of sentences. Check (✓) the item in each pair that contains a time signal and is easier to read and understand.

2. _____   a. Every week my uncle studies the food ads to see which stores have the best specials. He clips all the coupons.

   ____✓____   b. Every week my uncle studies the food ads to see which stores have the best specials. Next, he clips all the coupons.

3. _____   a. Carmen took a very long shower. There was no hot water left for anyone else in the house.

   ____✓____   b. Carmen took a very long shower. After that, there was no hot water left for anyone else in the house.

In the pair of sentences about the uncle, the word *Next* helps make the relationship between the two sentences clear. The uncle studies ads, and then he clips coupons. In the second pair of sentences, the word *after* makes the relationship clear: after Carmen's long shower, there was no hot water left for anyone else.

Time signals tell us *when* something happened in relation to when something else happened. They help writers organize and make clear the order of events, stages, and steps in a process. Below are some common words that show time.

Time Signals

first	soon	by then	by that time
then	now	since	previously
next	during	suddenly	at last
after	finally	then	later
as before	after a while	thereafter	all this time
while	as soon as	by then	shortly
meanwhile	at that time	in a few hours	formerly

Fill in each blank with the appropriate time signal from the box. Use each transition once.

then	first	after	as	later

ACTIVITY 4

TEACHING TIP
For the next three activities, read each paragraph aloud as your students fill in the blanks.

A Victory for Big Brother

In one of the most terrifying scenes in all of literature, George Orwell in his classic novel *1984* describes how a government known as Big Brother destroys a couple's love. The couple, Winston and Julia, fall in love and meet secretly, knowing the government would not approve. _____After_____ informers turn them in, a government agent named O'Brien takes steps to end their love. _____First_____ he straps Winston down and explains that he has discovered Winston's worst fear. _____Then_____ he sets a cage with two giant, starving sewer rats on the table next to Winston. He says that when he presses a lever, the door of the cage will slide up, and the rats will shoot out like bullets and bore straight into Winston's face.

_____As_____ Winston's eyes dart back and forth, revealing his terror, O'Brien places his hand on the lever. Winston knows that the only way out is for Julia to take his place. Suddenly, he hears his own voice screaming, "Do it to Julia! Not me! Julia!" Orwell does not describe Julia's interrogation, but when Julia and Winston see each other _____later_____, they realize that each has betrayed the other. Their love is gone. Big Brother has won.

Words That Show Addition

Check (✓) the item that is easier to read and understand.

1. _____   a. A drinking problem can destroy a person's life. It can tear a family apart.

  ___✓___   b. A drinking problem can destroy a person's life. In addition, it can tear a family apart.

2. _____   a. One way to lose friends is always to talk and never to listen. A way to end friendships is to borrow money and never pay it back.

  ___✓___   b. One way to lose friends is always to talk and never to listen. Another way to end friendships is to borrow money and never pay it back.

In the pair of sentences about a drinking problem, the words *In addition* help make the relationship between the two sentences clear. The author is describing two effects of a drinking problem: it can destroy a life and a family. *In addition* and words like it are known as addition signals. In the pair of sentences about losing friends, you probably found the second item easier to understand. The word *Another* is an addition signal that makes it clear that the writer is describing a second way to lose friends.

Addition signals indicate added ideas. They help writers organize information and present it clearly to readers.

Some common words that show addition follow.

Paperback books cost less than hardbacks. _ALSO_____, they are easier to carry.

Addition Signals		
one	also	further
first	in addition	furthermore
first of all	next	similarly
for one thing	last (of all)	likewise
to begin with	finally	as well
another	and	too
second	moreover	besides

ACTIVITY 5

Fill in each blank with the appropriate addition signal from the box. Use each transition once.

in	finally	second	first

Social Not-Working

The workplace environment is being affected by social

networking sites such as Twitter, Reddit, and Facebook. ___First___,

continued

most people don't consider it a negative habit to check Twitter during the work day, but it is actually stealing. People who constantly check Twitter when they should be working are stealing time from the company. If, for example, "Sam" gets paid ten dollars an hour and he spends one hour a week looking at Twitter, he is being paid for one hour that he is not working. In other words, he is stealing ten dollars a week from the company. Over the course of a year, that could add up to over $500. __Second__, people who check Reddit during the work day and are using company computers are misusing company equipment. Although it might seem harmless, this use of company equipment is no different from driving a company car or using company furniture; maintenance, service, and upgrades cost money and must be budgeted. Taking a company car on a personal trip or borrowing company furniture to decorate a house are not allowed; most companies don't allow personal use of company computers either. __In addition__, many company computers contain private and sensitive material that could be compromised if an employee is on a social networking site. __Finally__, people who check Facebook during work hours can lose focus on their work, causing delays and poor performance. If something exciting or terrible is posted, it could affect the attitude of the employee, which in turn could affect how that employee functions the rest of the day. Although people like to stay connected with each other during the day, company employees need to limit their use of social networking sites to private equipment during lunch hours, breaks, or nonworking hours.

Other Kinds of Transitions

In the following box are other common transitional words, grouped according to the kind of signal they give readers. In the paragraphs you write, you will most often use addition signals (words like *first, also, another,* and *finally*), but all of the following signals are helpful to know as well.

ESL NOTE
Nonnative speakers may require a more in depth explanation of these transitional words. Again, some transitions that are part of a phrase may be written incorrectly (i.e., on the other hand → *in* the other hand; as a result → as *the* result).

> **Other Common Transitional Signals**
>
> *Space signals:* next to, across, on the opposite side, to the left, to the right, in front, in back, above, below, behind, nearby, near, beside, on top of, under, over, underneath, far from
>
> *Change-of-direction signals:* but, however, yet, in contrast, otherwise, still, on the contrary, on the other hand, although, nevertheless, instead, nonetheless, even though, unfortunately, alternatively
>
> *Illustration signals:* for example, for instance, specifically, as an illustration, once, such as
>
> *Conclusion signals:* therefore, consequently, thus, then, as a result, in summary, to conclude, last of all, finally, in review

ACTIVITY 6

1.   Underline the three *space* signals in the following paragraph:

Standing in the burned-out shell of my living room was a shocking experience. Above my head were charred beams, all that remained of our ceiling. In front of me, where our television and sound system had once stood, were twisted pieces of metal and chunks of blackened glass. Strangely, some items seemed little damaged by the fire. For example, I could see the TV remote and a dusty DVD under the rubble. I walked through the gritty ashes until I came to what was left of our sofa. Behind the sofa had been a wall of family photographs. Now, the wall and the pictures were gone. I found only a waterlogged scrap of my wedding picture.

2.   Underline the four *change-of-direction* signals in the following paragraph:

In some ways, train travel is superior to air travel. People always marvel at the speed with which airplanes can zip from one end of the country to another. Trains, on the other hand, definitely take longer. But sometimes longer can be better. Traveling across the country by train allows people to experience the trip more completely. They get to see the cities and towns, mountains and prairies that too often pass by unnoticed when they fly. Another advantage of train travel is comfort. Traveling by plane means wedging adult-sized bodies into narrow seats, bumping knees on the back of the seat, and having to pay five dollars for a tiny bag of pretzels. In contrast, the seats on most trains are spacious and comfortable, permitting even the longest-legged traveler to stretch out and watch the scenery just outside the window. And when train travelers grow hungry, they can get up and stroll to the dining car, where they can order anything from a simple snack to a gourmet meal. There's no question that train travel is definitely slow and old-fashioned compared with air travel. However, in many ways it is much more civilized.

3. Underline the three *illustration* signals in the following selection:

Americans are obsessed with status symbols. The cars we drive, <u>for instance</u>, say something about who we are and how successful we have been. Automakers depend on this perception of automobiles, which is clear in their commercials. Hip young people are shown driving sports cars and SUVs, and well-dressed, gorgeous middle-aged people are shown driving luxury vehicles. Clothing, too, has always been a status symbol. <u>Specifically</u>, teens and young adults spend hours trying to recreate outfits they see on celebrities in order to be "as cool" as that person. Another <u>example</u> of a status symbol is the cell phone. People regularly spend hundreds of dollars to own the latest version of the iPhone, Samsung Galaxy, or Pixel. Status symbols are Americans' way of trying to show that they are someone important.

4. Underline the *conclusion* signal in the following paragraph:

A hundred years ago, miners used to bring caged canaries down into the mines with them to act as warning signals. If the bird died, the miners knew that the oxygen was running out. The smaller animal would be affected much more quickly than the miners. In the same way, animals are acting as warning signals to us today. Baby birds die before they can hatch because pesticides in the environment cause the adults to lay eggs with paper-thin shells. Fish die when lakes are contaminated with acid rain or poisonous mercury. The dangers in our environment will eventually affect all life on earth, including humans. <u>Therefore</u>, we must pay attention to these early warning signals. If we don't, we will be as foolish as a miner who ignored a dead canary—and we will die.

Fill in each blank with the appropriate transition signal from the box. Use each transition once.

ACTIVITY 7

> *Addition transitions:* first of all, second, finally
> *Time transition:* when
> *Illustration transition:* once
> *Change-of-direction transition:* however
> *Conclusion transition:* as a result

Joining an International Club

One of the best things I've done in college is to join the International Students Club. <u>First of all</u>, the club has helped me become friendly with a diverse group of people, including other students who share my Dominican heritage. At any time in my

continued

apartment, I can hear someone from Pakistan chatting about music to someone from Sweden, or someone from Russia talking about politics to someone from Uganda. ____Once____, I made fried sweet plantains for three students from China. They had never tasted such a dish before, but they liked it. A ____second____ benefit of the club is that it's helped me realize how similar people are. ____When____ the whole club first assembled, we wound up having a conversation about dating and sex that included the perspectives of fifteen countries and six continents! It was clear we all shared the feeling that sex was fascinating. The talk lasted for hours, with many different people describing the wildest or funniest experience they had had with the opposite sex. Only a few students, particularly those from the United States and Japan, seemed bashful.

____Finally____, the club has reminded me about the dangers of stereotyping. Before I joined the club, my only direct experience with people from China was ordering meals in the local Chinese restaurant. ____As a result____, I believed that most Chinese people ate lots of rice and worked in restaurants. In the club, ____however____, I met Chinese people who were soccer players, English majors, and math teachers. I've also seen Jewish and Muslim students—people who I thought would never get along—drop their preconceived notions and become friends. Even more than my classes, the club has been an eye-opener for me.

Other Connecting Words

In addition to transitions, three other kinds of connecting words help tie together the specific evidence in a paragraph: *repeated words, pronouns,* and *synonyms.* Each will be discussed in turn.

Repeated Words

Many of us have been taught by English instructors—correctly so—not to repeat ourselves in our writing. On the other hand, repeating key words can help tie ideas together. In the paragraph that follows, the word *retirement* is repeated to remind readers of the key idea on which the discussion is centered. Underline the word the five times it appears.

Oddly enough, <u>retirement</u> can pose more problems for the spouse than for the retired person. For a person who has been accustomed to a demanding job, <u>retirement</u> can mean frustration and a feeling of uselessness. This feeling will put pressure on the spouse to provide challenges at home equal to those of the workplace. Often, these tasks will disrupt the spouse's well-established routine. Another problem arising from <u>retirement</u> is filling up all those empty hours. The spouse may find himself or herself in the role of social director or tour guide, expected to come up with a new form of amusement every day. Without sufficient challenges or leisure activities, a person can become irritable and take out the resulting boredom and frustration of <u>retirement</u> on the marriage partner. It is no wonder that many of these partners wish their spouses would come out of <u>retirement</u> and do something—anything—just to get out of the house.

Pronouns

Pronouns (*he, she, it, you, they, this, that,* and others) are another way to connect ideas as you develop a paper. Using pronouns to take the place of other words or ideas can help you avoid needless repetition. (Be sure, though, to use pronouns with care in order to avoid the unclear or inconsistent pronoun references described in Chapters 29 and 30 of this book.) Underline the eight pronouns in the passage below, noting at the same time the words that the pronouns refer to.

A professor of nutrition at a major university recently advised <u>his</u> students that <u>they</u> could do better on <u>their</u> examinations by eating lots of sweets. <u>He</u> told <u>them</u> that the sugar in cakes and candy would stimulate <u>their</u> brains to work more efficiently, and that if the sugar was eaten for only a month or two, <u>it</u> would not do <u>them</u> any harm.

Synonyms

Using synonyms—words that are alike in meaning—can also help move the reader from one thought to the next. In addition, the use of synonyms increases variety and interest by avoiding needless repetition of the same words. Underline the three words or phrases used as synonyms for *false ideas* in the following passage.

There are many false ideas about suicide. One <u>wrong idea</u> is that a person who talks about suicide never follows through. The truth is that about three out of every four people who commit suicide speak about it ahead of time. Another <u>misconception</u> is that a person who commits suicide is poor or downtrodden. Actually, poverty appears to be a deterrent to suicide rather than a predisposing factor. A third <u>myth</u> about suicide is that people bent on suicide will eventually take their lives one way or another, whether or not the most obvious means of suicide is removed from their reach. In fact, since an attempt at suicide is often a kind of cry

TEACHING TIP
Explain pronoun–antecedent agreement and pronoun reference to your students.

ESL NOTE
Nonnative speakers have difficulty using correct pronouns/forms. Possessive adjectives can present a particular problem for Spanish speakers, who use definite articles to refer to parts of the body (*see sentence 2 in the passage*).

TEACHING TIP
Suggest that your students consult a thesaurus to locate synonyms but caution against using unfamiliar words.

ESL NOTE
Nonnative speakers may use a thesaurus to check for synonyms.

for help, removing a convenient means of taking one's life, such as a gun, can show people thinking about suicide that others are aware of them and want to prevent it.

| ACTIVITY 8 | This activity will give you practice in identifying connecting words that are used to help tie ideas together. |

REPEATED WORDS:

In the space provided, write the repeated words.

1. We absorb radiation from many sources in our environment. Our television sets and microwave ovens, among other things, give off low-level radiation.

   radiation

2. Many researchers believe that people have weight set-points their bodies try to maintain. This may explain why many dieters return to their original weight.

   weight

3. At the end of the concert, thousands of fans held up cell phones in the darkened arena. The sea of cell phones signaled that the fans wanted an encore.

   cell phones

4. Establishing credit is important for everyone. A good credit history is often necessary when applying for a loan or charge account.

   credit

SYNONYMS:

In the space provided, write in the synonym for the underlined word.

5. I checked my <u>car</u>'s tires, oil, water, and belts before the trip. But the ungrateful machine sputtered and died about fifty miles from home.

   machine

6. Women's <u>clothes</u>, in general, use less material than do men's clothes. Yet women's garments usually cost more than men's.

   garments

7. The temperance movement in this country sought to ban <u>alcohol</u>. Drinking liquor, movement leaders said, led to violence, poverty, prostitution, and insanity.

   liquor

8. For me, <u>apathy</u> quickly sets in when the weather becomes hot and sticky. This listlessness disappears when the humidity decreases.

   listlessness

TEACHING TIP
Remind students to use a dictionary to look up unfamiliar words (for example, "apathy").

PRONOUNS:

In the space provided, write in the word referred to by the underlined pronoun.

9. At the turn of the twentieth century, bananas were still an oddity in the United States. Some people even attempted to eat <u>them</u> with the peel on.

<u>bananas</u>

10. Canning vegetables is easy and economical. <u>It</u> can also be very dangerous.

<u>Canning vegetables</u>

11. There are a number of signs that appear when students are under stress. For example, <u>they</u> start to have trouble studying, eating, and even sleeping.

<u>students</u>

REFLECTIVE ACTIVITY

1. Look over the paragraph you wrote in response to Writing Assignment 1, 2, or 3 in Chapter 3. Is the paragraph organized well? If not, rewrite it using time or emphatic order as explained in the first section of this chapter.

2. Is your paragraph easy to follow? If not, see if adding transitions and connective words as explained in the "Transitions" section of this chapter will help.

©mavo/Shutterstock

Step 4: Write Clear, Error-Free Sentences

Up to now this book has emphasized the first three steps in writing an effective paragraph: making a point, supporting the point, and organizing and connecting the evidence. This section will focus on the fourth step: writing clear, error-free sentences. You'll learn how to revise a paragraph so that your sentences flow smoothly and clearly. Then you'll review how to edit a paragraph for mistakes in grammar, punctuation, and spelling.

Revising Sentences

The following strategies will help you to revise your sentences effectively.

- Use parallelism.
- Use a consistent point of view.
- Use specific words.
- Use concise wording.
- Vary your sentences.

in a writer's words

" *When I was seven, I said to my mother, may I close my door? And she said yes, but why do you want to close your door? And I said because I want to think. And when I was eleven, I said to my mother, may I lock my door? And she said yes, but why do you want to lock your door? And I said because I want to write.* "

—Dorothy West

Use Parallelism

Words in a pair or a series should have a parallel structure. By balancing the items in a pair or a series so that they have the same kind of structure, you will make a sentence clearer and easier to read. Notice how the parallel sentences that follow read more smoothly than the nonparallel ones.

Nonparallel (Not Balanced)	Parallel (Balanced)
I resolved to lose weight, to study more, and *watching* less TV.	I resolved to lose weight, to study more, and to watch less TV. (A balanced series of *to* verbs: *to lose, to study, to watch*)
A consumer group rates my car as noisy, expensive, and *not having much safety.*	A consumer group rates my car as noisy, expensive, and unsafe. (A balanced series of descriptive words: *noisy, expensive, unsafe*)
Lola likes wearing soft sweaters, eating exotic foods, and *to bathe* in scented bath oil.	Lola likes wearing soft sweaters, eating exotic foods, and bathing in scented bath oil. (A balanced series of -ing words: *wearing, eating, bathing*)
Single life offers more freedom of choice; *more security is offered by marriage.*	Single life offers more freedom of choice; marriage offers more security. (Balanced verbs and word order: *single life offers . . .; marriage offers . . .*)

You need not worry about balanced sentences when writing first drafts. But when you rewrite, you should try to put matching words and ideas into matching structures. Such parallelism will improve your writing style.

ACTIVITY 9

Cross out the unbalanced part of each sentence. In the space provided, revise the unbalanced part so that it matches the other item or items in the sentence. The first one is done for you as an example.

1. Our professor warned us that he would give surprise tests, ~~the assignment of term papers~~, and allow no makeup exams.
   assign term papers

2. Making a big dinner is a lot more fun than ~~to clean up after it~~.
   cleaning up after it

3. The street-corner preacher stopped people walking by, ~~asking them questions~~, and handed them a pamphlet.
   asked them questions

4. My teenage daughter enjoys shopping for new clothes, ~~to try different cosmetics~~, and reading beauty magazines.
   trying on different cosmetics

5. Many of today's action movies have attractive actors, fantastic special effects, and ~~dialogue that is silly~~.

   silly dialogue
   _____

6. While I am downtown, I need to pick up the dry cleaning, return the library books, and ~~the car needs washing too~~.

   wash the car, too
   _____

7. I want a job that pays high wages, provides a complete benefits package, and ~~offering opportunities for promotion~~.

   offers opportunities for promotion
   _____

8. As the elderly woman climbed the long staircase, she breathed hard and ~~was grabbing the railing tightly~~.

   grabbed the railing tightly
   _____

9. I fell into bed at the end of the hard day, grateful for the ~~sheets that were clean~~, soft pillow, and cozy blanket.

   clean sheets
   _____

10. Ray's wide smile, clear blue eyes, and ~~expressing himself earnestly~~ all make him seem honest, even though he is not.

    earnest self-expression
    _____

Cross out the unbalanced part of each sentence. In the space provided, revise the unbalanced part so that it matches the other item or items in the sentence.

ACTIVITY 10

1. The preschool teacher asked the children to put away their art supplies and ~~that their hands needed to be washed~~ for lunch.

   wash their hands
   _____

2. Boring lectures, ~~labs that are long~~, and mindless homework make college uninteresting.

   long labs
   _____

3. The vending machines on campus offer ~~oily chips that shouldn't be eaten~~, sugary beverages I shouldn't drink, and stale cookies I don't like.

   oily chips I shouldn't eat
   _____

4. My new apartment has new appliances, ~~storage that are plentiful~~, and a spacious bedroom.

   plentiful storage
   _____

5. The badly maintained sales showroom needs the displays replaced, the outlets rewired, and ~~cleaning the carpet~~.

   the carpet cleaned
   _____

6. I edited my paper for comma splices, sentence fragments, and ~~there were comma mistakes~~.

   comma mistakes
   _____

7. Rob does not want to spend two hours a day commuting to work, but ~~employment nearby is something he cannot find~~.

   he cannot find employment nearby

8. Watching DVD movies, ~~buttered popcorn that I eat~~, and drinking Diet Coke make up my Friday night routine.

   eating buttered popcorn

9. Raising a two-year-old, a ~~child that is four years old~~, and a twelve-year-old makes life extremely hectic.

   four-year-old

10. The Elton John AIDS Foundation is a global organization that not only educates people about HIV/AIDS prevention but also ~~providing~~ health services to people living with this disease.

    provides

Use a Consistent Point of View

Consistency with Verbs Do not shift verb tenses unnecessarily. If you begin writing a paper in the present tense, don't shift suddenly to the past. If you begin in the past, don't shift without reason to the present. Notice the inconsistent verb tenses in the following example:

> The shoplifter *walked* quickly toward the front of the store. When a clerk *shouts* at him, he *started* to run.

The verbs must be consistently in the present tense:

> The shoplifter *walks* quickly toward the front of the store. When a clerk *shouts* at him, he *starts* to run.

Or the verbs must be consistently in the past tense:

> The shoplifter *walked* quickly toward the front of the store. When a clerk *shouted* at him, he *started* to run.

TEACHING TIP
Writers sometimes may not realize that they are shifting tenses. Stress to your students that verb consistency can be achieved during editing.

ESL NOTE
Nonnative speakers need to know that time is an important message expressed by a verb in English. If you shift tenses, readers will have difficulty following the sequence of events in your writing.

| **ACTIVITY 11** | Change verbs as needed in the following passage so that they are consistently in the past tense. Cross out each incorrect verb and write the correct form above it, as shown in the example. You will need to make nine corrections. |

TEACHING TIP
Read this paragraph aloud. Students should be able to "hear" many of the verb shifts.

Late one rainy night, Mei Ling woke to the sound of steady dripping. When she got out of bed to investigate, a drop of cold water ~~splashes~~ [splashed] onto her arm. She ~~looks~~ [looked] up just in time to see another drop form on the ceiling, hang suspended for a moment, and fall to the carpet. Stumbling to the kitchen, Mei Ling ~~reaches~~ [reached] deep into one of the cabinets and ~~lifts~~ [lifted] out a large roasting pan. As she did so, pot lids and baking tins clattered out and ~~crash~~ ^{crashed} onto the counter. Mei Ling ignored them, stumbled back to the bedroom, and ~~places~~ ^{placed} the pan on the floor under the drip. But a minute after sliding her icy feet under the covers, Mei Ling realized she ~~is~~ ^{was} in trouble. The sound of each drop hitting the metal pan echoed like a gunshot in the quiet room. Mei Ling ~~feels~~ ^{felt} like crying, but she finally thought of a solution. She got out of bed and ~~returns~~ ^{returned} a minute later with a thick bath towel. She lined the pan with the towel and ~~crawls~~ ^{crawled} back into bed.

Consistency with Pronouns Pronouns should not shift point of view unnecessarily. When writing a paper, be consistent in your use of first-, second-, or third-person pronouns.

Type of Pronoun	Singular	Plural
First-person pronouns	I (my, mine, me)	we (our, ours, us)
Second-person pronouns	you (your, yours)	you (your, yours)
Third-person pronouns	he (his, him) she (her) it (its)	they (their, them)

 TIP Any person, place, or thing, as well as any indefinite pronoun like *one, anyone, someone,* and so on (Chapter 29), is a third-person word.

For instance, if you start writing in the third person *she,* don't jump suddenly to the second person *you.* Or if you are writing in the first person *I,* don't shift unexpectedly to *one.* Look at the following examples.

Inconsistent

I enjoy movies like *The Return of the Vampire* that frighten *you.* (A very common mistake people make is to let *you* slip into their writing after they start with another pronoun.)

As soon as a person walks into Addison's apartment, *you* can tell that Addison owns a cat. (Again, *you* is a shift in point of view.)

Consistent

I enjoy movies like *The Return of the Vampire* that frighten me.

As soon as a person walks into Addison's apartment, *he or she* can tell that Addison owns a cat. (See also the note on *his or her* references in Chapter 29.)

ACTIVITY 12

TEACHING TIP
Read each sentence aloud to help students "hear" the shifts in point of view.

Cross out the inconsistent pronouns in the following sentences and revise by writing the correct form of the pronoun above each crossed-out word.

EXAMPLE

I like solving math problems, for ~~you~~ [I] can always find the correct answer.

1. My grades are so low that ~~one~~ [I] may be placed on academic probation.

2. Wanting a more attractive smile, Jenna asked her dentist if teeth whitening could really do ~~you~~ [her] any good.

3. I drink green tea every day because ~~you~~ [I] want to experience its many health benefits.

4. As we entered the café, ~~you~~ [we] could smell the delicious aroma of freshly roasted coffee beans.

5. I hate going to the doctor because ~~you~~ [I] always am told to eat less and exercise more.

6. In my workplace, every employee is encouraged to express ~~your~~ [his or her] opinion.

7. The Furtado twins are fraternal, but most people cannot tell ~~her~~ [them] apart.

8. As we listened to Mika give her speech, ~~you~~ [we] could hear the nervousness in her voice.

9. Gavin refuses to quit smoking, even though he knows that smoking is not good for ~~you~~ [him].

10. I love playing *Guitar Hero* on my PlayStation, for ~~you~~ [I] have always wanted to be a rock star.

ESL NOTE
Nonnative speakers should consult a thesaurus for synonyms and more specific words. Extensive reading can also help ESL students develop a richer vocabulary.

Use Specific Words

To be an effective writer, you must use specific words rather than general words. Specific words create pictures in the reader's mind. They help capture interest and make your meaning clear. Compare the following sentences:

General	Specific
The boy came down the street.	Theo ran down 125th Street.
A bird appeared on the grass.	A blue jay swooped down onto the frost-covered lawn.
She stopped the car.	Jackie slammed on the brakes of her Camry.

The specific sentences create clear pictures in our minds. The details *show* us exactly what has happened.

Here are four ways to make your sentences specific.

TEACHING TIP
Ask students to create a sentence using vague, general words, and then replace those words with specific ones.

1. Use exact names.

   She loves her *car.*

   Renée loves her *Honda.*

2. Use lively verbs.

The garbage truck *went* down Front Street.

The garbage truck *rumbled* down Front Street.

3. Use descriptive words (modifiers) before nouns.

A girl peeked out the window.

A *chubby six-year-old* girl peeked out the *dirty kitchen* window.

4. Use words that relate to the five senses: sight, hearing, taste, smell, and touch.

That woman is a karate expert.
That *tiny, silver-haired* woman is a karate expert. (*Sight*)

When the dryer stopped, a signal sounded.
When the *whooshing* dryer stopped, a *loud buzzer* sounded. (*Hearing*)

Terence offered me an orange slice.
Terence offered me a *sweet, juicy* orange slice. (*Taste*)

The real estate agent opened the door of the closet.
The real estate agent opened the door of the *cedar-scented* closet. (*Smell*)

I pulled the blanket around me to fight off the wind.
I pulled the *fluffy* blanket around me to fight off the *chilling* wind. (*Touch*)

TEACHING TIP
For a memorable lesson, do something outrageous or unexpected as you enter the classroom. When students complete this activity, ask them to recall what you did.

ACTIVITY 13

This activity will give you practice in replacing vague, indefinite words with sharp, specific words. Add three or more specific words to replace the general word or words underlined in each sentence. Make changes in the wording of a sentence as necessary.

EXAMPLE

My bathroom cabinet contains <u>many drugs</u>.

My bathroom cabinet contains aspirin, antibiotics, tranquilizers, and codeine cough medicine.

Wording will vary; examples are given.

1. At the shopping center, we visited <u>several stores</u>.

At the shopping center, we visited Target, Macy's, Staples, and Petco.

2. Sunday is my day to take care of <u>chores</u>.

Sunday is my day to take care of vacuuming the carpets, dusting the furniture, and doing the laundry.

3. Lauren enjoys <u>various activities</u> in her spare time.

Lauren enjoys exploring the Internet, devising new recipes, and writing in her journal in her spare time.

4. I spent most of my afternoon <u>doing homework</u>.

I spent most of my afternoon solving calculus equations, writing a lab report, and reading a Russian novel.

5. We returned home from vacation to discover that <u>several pests</u> had invaded the house.

We returned home from vacation to discover that several mice, two squirrels, and a garden snake had invaded the house.

ACTIVITY 14

TEACHING TIP
You may want to ask students to work in pairs. Encourage them to create funny, imaginative sentences.

With the help of the methods described in the previous section and summarized below, add specific details to the sentences that follow. Note the examples.

- Use exact names.
- Use lively verbs.
- Use descriptive words (modifiers) before nouns.
- Use words that relate to the senses—sight, hearing, taste, smell, touch.

EXAMPLES

The person got out of the car.

The elderly man painfully lifted himself out of the white Buick station wagon.

The fans enjoyed the victory.

Many of the fifty-thousand fans stood, waved banners, and cheered wildly when Barnes scored the winning touchdown.

Answers will vary; examples are given

1. The crowd grew restless.

The monied, upscale audience began to squirm and chatter after waiting thirty minutes for the moody tenor to appear on the stage.

2. I relaxed.

I flopped onto my sofa, kicked up my heels, and stretched out my body with relief.

3. The room was cluttered.

Mario's bedroom was hidden beneath strewn dirty laundry, wads of crumpled paper, and scattered textbooks.

4. The child threw the object.

The eight-year-old flung her brother's baseball glove into the neighbor's yard.

5. The driver was angry.

The school bus driver slammed on the brakes and shouted at the raucous ninth-graders to sit down.

Use Concise Wording

Wordiness—using more words than necessary to express a meaning—is often a sign of lazy or careless writing. Your readers may resent the extra time and energy they must spend when you have not done the work needed to make your writing direct and concise.

Here are examples of wordy sentences:

Anne is of the opinion that the death penalty should be allowed.

I would like to say that my subject in this paper will be the generous person that my father was.

Omitting needless words improves the sentences:

Anne supports the death penalty.

I will write about my father, who was a generous person.

The following box lists some wordy expressions that could be reduced to single words.

Wordy Form	Short Form
a large number of	many
a period of a week	a week
arrive at an agreement	agree
at an earlier point in time	before
at the present time	now
big in size	big
owing to the fact that	because
during the time that	while
five in number	five
for the reason that	because
good benefit	benefit
in every instance	always
in my own opinion	I think
in the event that	if
in the near future	soon
in this day and age	today
is able to	can
large in size	large
plan ahead for the future	plan
postponed until later	postponed
red in color	red
return back	return

TEACHING TIP
Take an opinion poll in class to see if students think that wordiness is a sign of lazy and careless writing. Writers may not realize that their readers resent having to wade through unnecessary words.

ESL NOTE
What might appear as "wordiness" might actually be an attempt to translate an expression from a native language. Encourage nonnative speakers to think in English. Extensive reading might help them learn equivalent expressions in English and learn idiomatic and figurative language.

TEACHING TIP
Ask your students to cover the right column with a sheet of paper. Then ask them to replace the wordy expressions with single words.

| **ACTIVITY 15** | Rewrite the following sentences, omitting needless words. |

Wording may vary slightly.

1. After a lot of careful thinking, I have arrived at the conclusion that drunken drivers should receive jail terms.

   I believe drunken drivers should be jailed.

2. The movie that I went to last night, which was fairly interesting, I must say, was enjoyed by me and my girlfriend.

   My girlfriend and I enjoyed the movie we saw last night.

3. Ben finally made up his mind after a lot of indecisions and decided to look for a new job.

   Ben finally decided to look for a new job.

4. Due to inclement weather conditions of wind and rain, we have decided not to proceed with the athletic competition about to take place on the baseball diamond.

   Owing to the weather, the baseball game is canceled.

5. Beyond a doubt, the only two things you can rely or depend on would be the fact that death comes to everyone and also that the government will tax your yearly income.

   The only sure things are death and taxes.

| **ACTIVITY 16** | Rewrite the following sentences, omitting needless words. |

Wording may vary slightly.

TEACHING TIP
Ask your students to create their own wordy sentences. Then have them exchange papers with a partner and rewrite each sentence for conciseness.

1. There is this one worker at the warehouse who rarely if ever arrives on time.

   One worker at the warehouse rarely arrives on time.

2. Judging by the looks of things, it seems to me that no one studied for the quiz.

   It looks as if no one studied for the quiz.

3. Seeing as how gas prices are increasing in every instance, in the very near future I will ride my bike everywhere.

   Since gas prices are constantly increasing, soon I will ride my bike everywhere.

4. In this day and age it is almost a certainty that someone you know will experience the crime of identity theft.

Someone you know will probably experience identity theft.

5. In my personal opinion it is correct to say that organic chemistry is the most difficult course in the science curriculum.

Organic chemistry is the most difficult science course.

ESL NOTE
Nonnative speakers may still be struggling to write grammatically correct simple sentences. Once they have learned to combine sentences effectively with coordinating conjunctions and subordinating conjunctions, remind them that varying sentences will add interest in their writing style.

TEACHING TIP
Provide an example for each method. Students may need to see these sentences, which you could write on the board. Caution your students against relying too much on *be* verbs, which may become monotonous.

Vary Your Sentences

One aspect of effective writing is to vary your sentences. If every sentence follows the same pattern, writing may become monotonous. This chapter explains four ways you can create variety and interest in your writing style. The first two ways involve coordination and subordination–important techniques for achieving different kinds of emphasis.

The following are four methods you can use to make your sentences more varied and more sophisticated:

1. Add a second complete thought (coordination).

2. Add a dependent thought (subordination).

3. Begin with a special opening word or phrase.

4. Place adjectives or verbs in a series.

Revise by Adding a Second Complete Thought When you add a second complete thought to a simple sentence, the result is a *compound* (or double) sentence. The two complete statements in a compound sentence are usually connected by a comma plus a joining, or *coordinating*, word (*and, but, for, or, nor, so, yet*).

Use a compound sentence when you want to give equal weight to two closely related ideas. The technique of showing that ideas have equal importance is called *coordination*. Following are some compound sentences. Each contains two ideas that the writer regards as equal in importance.

Bill has stopped smoking cigarettes, but he is now addicted to chewing gum.

I repeatedly failed the math quizzes, so I decided to drop the course.

Darrell turned all the lights off, and then he locked the office door.

TEACHING TIP
Teach your students the acronym FANBOYS (*For, And, Nor, But, Or, Yet,* and *So*).

Combine the following pairs of simple sentences into compound sentences. Use a comma and a logical joining word (*and, but, for, so*) to connect each pair. If you are not sure what *and, but, for,* and *so* mean, turn to Chapter 25.

ACTIVITY 17

TEACHING TIP
Caution students against using the word "and" too often. Encourage them to use a variety of coordinating conjunctions.

EXAMPLE

• The cars crept along slowly.

• Visibility was poor in the heavy fog.

The cars crept along slowly, for visibility was poor in the heavy fog.

Wording may vary slightly.

ESL NOTE
Writing complex sentences is a tremendous challenge for nonnative speakers. They may confuse or not understand some dependent words (*even if* vs. *even though*; *who* vs. *that*). They may also write fragments because they don't understand subordination, as this structure may not be used in their first language. Dependent words that indicate a time relationship will also present a problem for nonnative speakers. They might select the wrong verb tense.

1. • Lee thought she would never master her new computer.

   • In two weeks she was using it comfortably.

   Lee thought she would never master her new computer, but in two weeks she was using it comfortably.

2. • Vandals smashed the car's headlights.

   • They slashed the tires as well.

   Vandals smashed the car's headlights, and they slashed the tires as well.

3. • I married at age seventeen.

   • I never got a chance to live on my own.

   I married at age seventeen, so I never got a chance to live on my own.

4. • A volcano erupts.

   • It sends tons of ash into the air.

   • This creates flaming orange sunsets.

   When a volcano erupts, it sends tons of ash into the air, creating flaming orange sunsets.

5. • The phone rings late at night.

   • We answer it fearfully.

   • It could bring tragic news.

   Whenever the phone rings late at night, we answer it fearfully because it could bring tragic news.

Revise by Adding a Dependent Thought When you add a dependent thought to a simple sentence, the result is a complex sentence.* A dependent thought begins with a word or phrase like one of the following:

Dependent Words		
after	if, even if	when, whenever
although, though	in order that	where, wherever
as	since	whether
because	that, so that	which, whichever
before	unless	while
even though	until	who, whoever
how	what, whatever	whose

*The two parts of a complex sentence are sometimes called an *independent clause* and a *dependent clause. A clause* is simply a word group that contains a subject and a verb. An independent clause expresses a complete thought and can stand alone. A dependent clause does not express a complete thought in itself and "depends on" the independent clause to complete its meaning. Dependent clauses always begin with a dependent, or subordinating, word.

A *complex* sentence is used to emphasize one idea over another. Look at the following complex sentence:

Although I lowered the thermostat, my heating bill remained high.

The idea that the writer wants to emphasize here—*my heating bill remained high*—is expressed as a complete thought. The less important idea—*Although I lowered my thermostat*—is subordinated to this complete thought. The technique of giving one idea less emphasis than another is called *subordination*.

Following are other examples of complex sentences. In each case, the part starting with the dependent word is the less emphasized part of the sentence.

Even though I was tired, I stayed up to watch the horror movie.

Before I take a bath, I check for spiders in the tub.

When Vera feels nervous, she pulls on her earlobe.

TEACHING TIP
Ask students to underline the dependent words in these sentences.

Use logical subordinating words to combine the following pairs of simple sentences into sentences that contain a dependent thought. Place a comma after a dependent statement when it starts the sentence.

ACTIVITY 18

Wording may vary slightly.

EXAMPLE

- Our team lost.
- We were not invited to the tournament.

  Because our team lost, we were not invited to the tournament.

  _____

1. • I receive my degree in June.
   • I will begin to apply for jobs.

   When I receive my degree in June, I will begin to apply for jobs.

   _____

2. • Robyn doesn't enjoy cooking.
   • She often eats at fast-food restaurants.

   Because Robyn doesn't enjoy cooking, she often eats at fast-food restaurants.

   _____

3. • I sent several letters of complaint.
   • The electric company never corrected my bill.

   Although I sent several letters of complaint, the electric company

   never corrected my bill.

4. • Neil felt his car begin to skid.
   • He took his foot off the gas pedal.

   When Neil felt his car begin to skid, he took his foot off the gas pedal.

   _____

5. • The final exam covered sixteen chapters.

    • The students complained.

      Because the final exam covered sixteen chapters, the students complained.

ACTIVITY 19

©Jacob Lund/
Shutterstock

Wording may vary slightly.

Using coordination, subordination, or both, combine each of the following groups of simple sentences into two longer sentences. Omit repeated words. Various combinations are possible, so for each group, try to find the combination that flows most smoothly and clearly. Work in pairs to complete this activity.

1. • Lynn pretended not to overhear her coworkers.

    • She couldn't stop listening.

    • She felt deeply embarrassed.

    • They were criticizing her work.

      Lynn pretended not to overhear her coworkers, but she couldn't
stop listening. She felt deeply embarrassed because they were
criticizing her work.

2. • Nigel got home from the shopping mall.

    • He discovered that his rented tuxedo did not fit.

    • The jacket sleeves covered his hands.

    • The pants cuffs hung over his shoes.

      When Nigel got home from the shopping mall, he discovered that his
rented tuxedo did not fit. The jacket sleeves covered his hands and the
pants cuffs hung over his shoes.

3. • The boys waited for the bus.

    • The wind shook the flimsy shelter.

    • They shivered with cold.

    • They were wearing thin jackets.

      While the boys waited for the bus, the wind shook the flimsy shelter.
They shivered with cold, for they were wearing thin jackets.

4. • The engine almost started.

    • Then it died.

    • I realized no help would come.

    • I was on a lonely road.

    • It was very late.

      The engine almost started, but then it died. I realized no help would
come, for I was on a lonely road and it was very late.

5. • Justin was leaving the store.

   • The shoplifting alarm went off.

   • He had not stolen anything.

   • The clerk had forgotten to remove the magnetic tag.

   • The tag was on a shirt Justin had bought.

   When Justin was leaving the store, the shoplifiting alarm went off, but he

   had not stolen anything. The clerk had forgotten to remove the magnetic

   tag on a shirt Justin had bought.

Revise by Beginning with a Special Opening Word or Phrase Among the special openers that can be used to start sentences are (1) *-ed* words, (2) *-ing* words, (3) *-ly* words, (4) *to* word groups, and (5) prepositional phrases. Here are examples of all five kinds of openers:

ESL NOTE
Nonnative speakers often confuse adjectives that end in -ed or -ing.

TEACHING TIP
Remind students that an opener might also be placed at the end of a sentence. For example, the sentence "Using a thick towel, Mel dried his hair quickly" might be written as "Mel dried his hair quickly using a thick towel."

-ed word

Tired from a long day of work, Phoebe fell asleep on the sofa.

-ing word

Using a thick towel, Ian dried his hair quickly.

-ly word

Reluctantly, I agreed to rewrite the paper.

to word group

To get to the church on time, you must leave now.

Prepositional phrase

With Luke's help, Monika planted the evergreen shrubs.

Combine the simple sentences into one sentence by using the opener shown in the margin and omitting repeated words. Use a comma to set off the opener from the rest of the sentence.

ACTIVITY 20

TEACHING TIP
You may want to do this activity with the entire class. Ask students to "talk out" their answers.

EXAMPLE

   • Jen found her car keys.

   • She searched through her purse.

   Searching through her purse, Jen found her car keys.

-ing word

1. • Raj studied for the anthropology exam.

   • He was determined to do well.

   Determined to do well, Raj studied for the anthropology exam

-ed word

-ing word

2. • The soldier volunteered for another tour of duty.

   • She knew the danger involved.

Knowing the danger involved, the soldier volunteered for another tour of duty.

-ly word

3. • I entered the online sweepstakes contest.

   • I was optimistic.

Optimistically, I entered the online sweepstakes contest.

---

to word group

4. • Gina worked out daily at the gym.

   • She wanted to build muscle and lose fat.

To build muscle and lose fat, Gina worked out daily at the gym.

Prepositional phrase

5. • Rick and I sought counseling.

   • We hoped to save our relationship.

With the hope of saving our relationship, Rick and I sought counseling.

ACTIVITY 21

Combine the simple sentences into one sentence by using the opener shown in the margin and omitting repeated words. Use a comma to set off the opener from the rest of the sentence.

-ed word

1. • We were exhausted from four hours of hiking.

   • We decided to stop for the day.

Exhausted from four hours of hiking, we decided to stop for the day.

-ing word

2. • Gus was staring out the window.

   • He didn't hear the instructor call on him.

Staring out the window, Gus didn't hear the instructor call on him.

-ly word

3. • Nobody saw the thieves steal our bikes.

   • This was unfortunate.

Unfortunately, nobody saw the thieves steal our bikes.

---

to word group

4. • Marcel rented a limousine for the night.

   • He wanted to make a good impression.

To make a good impression, Marcel rented a limousine for the night.

---

5. • Paige logs into Facebook to chat with her friends.

    • She does this during her lunch breaks.

      During her lunch breaks, Paige logs into Facebook to chat with her friends.

Prepositional phrase

Revise by Placing Adjectives or Verbs in a Series Various parts of a sentence may be placed in a series. Among these parts are adjectives (descriptive words) and verbs. Here are examples of both in a series.

Adjectives

The *black, smeary* newsprint rubbed off on my *new butcher-block* table.

Verbs

The quarterback *fumbled* the ball, *recovered* it, and *sighed* with relief.

Combine the simple sentences in each group into one sentence by using adjectives or verbs in a series and by omitting repeated words. In most cases, use a comma between the adjectives or verbs in a series.

ACTIVITY 22

ESL NOTE
When combining verbs, remind nonnative speakers to be consistent with verb tense.

TEACHING TIP
For the next two activities, read the sentences aloud so that students can "hear" the sound of choppy, simple sentences.

EXAMPLE

  • Before Christmas, I made fruitcakes.

  • I decorated the house.

  • I wrapped dozens of toys.

    Before Christmas, I made fruitcakes, decorated the house, and wrapped

    dozens of toys.

1. • Before going to bed, I locked all the doors.

    • I activated the burglar alarm.

    • I slipped a kitchen knife under my mattress.

      Before going to bed, I locked all the doors, activated the burglar alarm,

      and slipped a kitchen knife under my mattress.

2. • Jasmine picked sweater hairs off her coat.

    • The hairs were fuzzy.

    • The hairs were white.

    • The coat was brown.

    • The coat was suede.

      Jasmine picked fuzzy white sweater hairs off her brown suede coat.

3.   • The contact lens fell onto the floor.

• The contact lens was thin.

• The contact lens was slippery.

• The floor was dirty.

• The floor was tiled.

The thin, slippery contact lens fell onto the dirty tiled floor.

_____

ACTIVITY 23

TEACHING TIP
Point out to students that adjectives and verbs in a series need to be parallel.

ESL NOTE
Nonnative speakers require practice in the order of adjectives in English.

Combine the simple sentences in each group into one sentence by using adjectives or verbs in a series and by omitting repeated words. In most cases, use a comma between the adjectives or verbs in a series.

1. Jackie carefully looked into her rear view mirror before leaving the driveway.

   She locked her car door.

   She strapped on her seat belt.

   Jackie locked her car door, strapped on her seat belt, and carefully

   looked into her rear view mirror before leaving the driveway.

2. I downloaded several games to my laptop.

   The games were free.

   The games require role playing.

   The laptop is new.

   The laptop is a Dell.

   I downloaded several free role-playing games to my new Dell laptop.

   _____

3. Steve picked up the phone.

   He cleared his throat.

   He dialed Angelina's number.

   He cleared his throat again.

   He hung up before the first ring.

   Steve picked up the phone, cleared his throat, dialed Angelina's number,

   cleared his throat again, and then hung up before the first ring.

4. The applicant entered the room.

   She was confident.

   She was applying for a job.

The room was large.

The room was designated for the interview.

The confident job applicant entered the large interview room.

_____

5. The pasta was served with a sauce.

The pasta was freshly made.

The pasta was linguini.

The sauce was pesto.

The sauce was topped with roasted pine nuts.

The freshly made linguini pasta was served with a pesto sauce and
topped with roasted pine nuts.

Editing Sentences

After revising sentences in a paragraph so that they flow smoothly and clearly, you need to edit the paragraph for mistakes in grammar, punctuation, mechanics, usage, and spelling. Even if a paragraph is otherwise well-written, it will make an unfavorable impression on readers if it contains such mistakes. To edit a paragraph, check it against the agreed-upon rules or conventions of written English—simply called *sentence skills* in this book. Here are the most common of these conventions:

1. Write complete sentences rather than fragments.

2. Do not write run-ons.

3. Use verb forms correctly.

4. Make sure that subject, verbs, and pronouns agree.

5. Eliminate faulty modifiers.

6. Use pronoun forms correctly.

7. Use capital letters where needed.

8. Use the following marks of punctuation correctly: apostrophe, quotation marks, comma, semicolon, colon, hyphen, dash, parentheses.

9. Use correct manuscript form.

10. Eliminate slang, clichés, and pretentious words.

11. Check for possible spelling errors.

12. Eliminate careless errors.

These sentence skills are treated in detail in Part 6 of this book, and they can be referred to easily as needed. The list of sentence skills on the inside back cover includes chapter references so that you can turn quickly to any skill you want to check.

TEACHING TIP
Ask your students if first impressions matter. Provide examples, such as a job interview or a blind date. Then ask them to consider how errors in their writing might influence their readers.

TIP   Here are some tips that can help you edit the next-to-final draft of a paper for sentence-skills mistakes:

1. Have at hand two essential tools: a good dictionary and a grammar handbook (you can use Part 6 of this book).

2. Use a sheet of paper to cover your paragraph so that you will expose only one sentence at a time. Look for errors in grammar, spelling, and typing. It may help to read each sentence out loud. If a sentence does not read clearly and smoothly, chances are something is wrong.

3. Pay special attention to the kinds of errors you tend to make. For example, if you tend to write run-ons or fragments, be especially on the lookout for those errors.

4. Try to work on a printed draft, where you'll be able to see your writing more objectively than you can on a handwritten page; use a pen with colored ink so that your corrections will stand out.

A Note on Proofreading

Proofreading means checking the final, edited draft of your paragraph closely for typos and other careless errors. A helpful strategy is to read your paper backward, from the last sentence to the first. This helps keep you from getting caught up in the flow of the paper and missing small mistakes. Here are six helpful proofing symbols:

Proofing Symbol	Meaning	Example
∧	insert missing letter or word	*i* beleve ∧
✗	omit	in the the meantime
∽	reverse order of words or letters	once a upon time
#	add space	alltogether #
‿	close up space	foot ball
cap, lc	Add a capital (or a lowercase) letter ⓒᵃᵖ	My persian Cat ⓛᶜ

If you make too many corrections, type in the corrections and reprint the page.

ACTIVITY 24

In the spaces at the bottom of this paragraph, write the numbers of the ten word groups that contain fragments or run-ons. Then, in the spaces between the lines, edit by making the necessary corrections. One is done for you as an example.

> [1]Two groups of researchers have concluded that "getting cold" has little to do with "catching a cold." [2]When the experiment was

continued

done for the first time/,³R̂esearchers exposed more than four hundred people to the cold virus/,⁴T̂hen divided those people into three groups. ⁵One group, wearing winter coats, sat around in ten-degree temperatures. T̂he second group was placed in sixty-degree temperatures/,⁶Ŵith the third group staying in a room/,⁷Ŵhere it was eighty degrees. ⁸The number of people who actually caught colds was the same/,⁹în each group. ¹⁰Other researchers repeated this experiment ten years later. ¹¹This time they kept some subjects cozy and warm. T̂hey submerged others in a tank filled with water/, ¹²Ŵhose temperature had been lowered to seventy-five degrees. ¹³They made others sit around in their underwear in forty-degree temperatures. ¹⁴The results were the same/,T̂he subjects got sick at the same rate/,p̂roving that people who get cold do not always get colds.

1. __2__   2. __3__   3. __4__   4. __5__   5. __6__

6. __7__   7. __9__   8. __11__   9. __12__   10. __14__

EXPLORING WRITING ONLINE

Visit one of these Web sites and read a news article of your choice. As you read the article, think about how the writer uses transition signals to organize and connect evidence. Then, on a separate sheet of paper, list those transition signals.

CNN.com: http://www.cnn.com
ABC News: http://www.abcnews.go.com
FoxNews.com: http://www.foxnews.com
MSNBC: http://www.msnbc.msn.com

©Tetra Images/
Shutterstock

Four Bases for Revising Writing

No doctor would ever prescribe tobacco... so why do pharmacies sell it?

52% of all pharmacies in New York State still sell tobacco products. It's time to end this practice. Lend your support at BreatheFreely.org

Tobacco Action Coalition OF LONG ISLAND

©Ira Berger/Alamy Stock Photo

TEACHING TIP
Get students to talk about this ad before they complete this writing prompt.

RESPONDING TO IMAGES

Write a paragraph about this ad, answering the following questions: What statement is it trying to make? Do you believe it makes this statement effectively? Do you agree with the statement? Remember to support your topic sentence with specific evidence.

In the preceding chapters, you learned four essential steps in writing an effective paragraph. The box below shows how these steps lead to four standards, or bases, you can use in revising a paragraph.

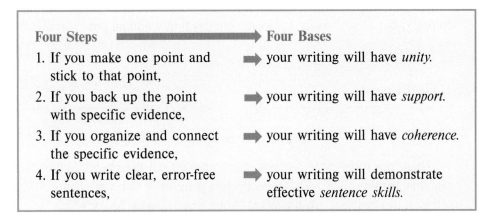

Four Steps ⟶	Four Bases
1. If you make one point and stick to that point,	⇒ your writing will have *unity*.
2. If you back up the point with specific evidence,	⇒ your writing will have *support*.
3. If you organize and connect the specific evidence,	⇒ your writing will have *coherence*.
4. If you write clear, error-free sentences,	⇒ your writing will demonstrate effective *sentence skills*.

TEACHING TIP
After you discuss the four bases, you may want to quiz your students on the meaning of unity, support, coherence, and sentence skills.

This chapter will discuss the four bases—unity, support, coherence, and sentence skills—and will show how these four bases can be used to evaluate and revise a paragraph.

Base 1: Unity

Understanding Unity

The following two paragraphs were written by students on the topic "Why Students Drop Out of College." Read them and decide which one makes its point more clearly and effectively, and why.

ESL NOTE
In English, it is not uncommon to digress while speaking. In some native languages, digression is also acceptable in written expression. Explain to nonnative students that all details should support the main point; otherwise, the reader will get confused.

PARAGRAPH A

Why Students Drop Out

Students drop out of college for many reasons. First of all, some students are bored in school. These students may enter college expecting nonstop fun or a series of fascinating courses. When they find out that college is often routine, they quickly lose interest. They do not want to take dull required courses or spend their nights studying, and so they drop out. Students also drop out of college because the work is harder than they thought it would be. These students may have made decent grades in high school simply by showing up for class. In college, however, they may have to prepare for two-hour exams, write fifteen-page term papers, or make detailed presentations to a class. The hard work comes as a shock, and students give up. Perhaps the most common reason students drop out is that they are having personal or emotional problems. Younger students, especially, may be attending college at an age when they are also feeling confused, lonely, or depressed. These

TEACHING TIP
Ask a volunteer to read these paragraphs aloud. Ask students to underline the topic sentence in each paragraph.

continued

students may have problems with roommates, family, boyfriends, or girlfriends. They become too unhappy to deal with both hard academic work and emotional troubles. For many types of students, dropping out seems to be the only solution they can imagine.

PARAGRAPH B

Student Dropouts

There are three main reasons students drop out of college. Some students, for one thing, are not really sure they want to be in school and lack the desire to do the work. When exams come up, or when a course requires a difficult project or term paper, these students will not do the required studying or research. Eventually, they may drop out because their grades are so poor they are about to flunk out anyway. Such students sometimes come back to school later with a completely different attitude about school. Other students drop out for financial reasons. The pressures of paying tuition, buying textbooks, and possibly having to support themselves can be overwhelming. These students can often be helped by the school because financial aid is available, and some schools offer work-study programs. Finally, students drop out because they have personal problems. They cannot concentrate on their courses because they are unhappy at home, they are lonely, or they are having trouble with boyfriends or girlfriends, or their husbands or wives. Instructors should suggest that such troubled students see counselors or join support groups. If instructors would take a more personal interest in their students, more students would make it through troubled times.

ACTIVITY 1

Fill in the blanks: Paragraph __A__ makes its point more clearly and effectively because it is unified. All the details support and develop a single main point.

_____

_____

EXPLANATION

Paragraph A is more effective because it is *unified.* All the details in paragraph A are *on target;* they support and develop the single point expressed in the first sentence—that there are many reasons students drop out of college.

continued

On the other hand, paragraph B contains some details irrelevant to the opening point—that there are three main reasons students drop out. These details should be omitted in the interest of paragraph unity. Go back to paragraph B and cross out the sections that are off target—the sections that do not support the opening idea.

You should have crossed out the following sections: "Such students sometimes . . . attitude about school"; "These students can often . . . work-study programs"; and "Instructors should suggest . . . through troubled times."

The difference between these two paragraphs leads us to the first base, or standard, of effective writing: *unity*. To achieve unity is to have all the details in your paper related to the single point expressed in the topic sentence, the first sentence. Each time you think of something to put in, ask yourself whether it relates to your main point. If it does not, leave it out. For example, if you were writing about a certain job as the worst job you ever had and then spent a couple of sentences talking about the interesting people that you met there, you would be missing the first and most essential base of good writing.

Checking for Unity

To check a paragraph for unity, ask yourself these questions:

1. Is there a clear, single point in the first sentence of the paragraph?

2. Does all the evidence support the opening point?

Evaluating Scratch Outlines for Unity

The best time to check a paragraph for unity is at the outline stage. A scratch outline, as explained in Chapter 2, is one of the best techniques for getting started with a paragraph.

Look at the following scratch outline that one student prepared and then corrected for unity:

Weekend was depressing

- hay fever bothered me
- had to pay seventy-seven-dollar car bill
- ~~felt bad~~
- boyfriend and I had a fight
- ~~did poorly in my math test today as a result~~
- my mother yelled at me unfairly

Four reasons support the opening statement that the writer was depressed over the weekend. The writer crossed out "felt bad" because it was not a reason for her depression. (Saying that she felt bad is only another way of saying that she was depressed.) She also crossed out the item about the math test because the point she is supporting is that she was depressed over the weekend.

ACTIVITY 2

In each scratch outline, cross out the two items that do not support the opening point. These items must be omitted in order to achieve paragraph unity.

TEACHING TIP
You may want to do this activity with the entire class.

Overweight dogs more likely to develop health problems
* dogs can develop arthritis
* dogs can develop diabetes
* ~~shouldn't be fed table scraps by owners~~
* heart disease another problem
* ~~overweight cats also at risk~~

Community shelter provides needed services
* emergency housing available
* ~~food bank located two blocks away~~
* medical care offered at no charge
* ~~receives funding from the government~~
* substance abuse counseling offered

Husband Tom takes several medications
* takes pills for hypertension
* takes insulin for type 2 diabetes
* ~~doctor wants him to exercise more~~
* takes pills for high cholesterol
* ~~started eating oatmeal for breakfast~~

Many opportunities for teens to volunteer
* can help at animal shelters
* ~~don't know how to help~~
* can start a recycling project
* can write letters to soldiers
* ~~don't have time to volunteer~~

Jena planned affordable birthday party for her daughter
* held the party in the city's beautiful garden pavilion
* ~~daughter's best friend came down with chickenpox~~
* baked cupcakes and had guests decorate them
* ~~bought an overpriced cake last year~~
* planned old-fashioned games

Evaluating Paragraphs for Unity

ACTIVITY 3

TEACHING TIP
Suggest that students create a scratch outline for each paragraph.

Each of the following three paragraphs contains sentences that are off target—sentences that do not support the opening point—and so the paragraphs are not unified. In the interest of paragraph unity, such sentences must be omitted.

Cross out the irrelevant sentences and write the numbers of those sentences in the spaces provided. The number of spaces will tell you the number of irrelevant sentences in each paragraph.

 TIP As you read each paragraph, underline the opening point so you can better detect which details support that point, and which do not.

1.

 Personal

Other Uses for Cars

¹Many people who own a car manage to turn the vehicle into a trash can, a clothes closet, or a storage room. ²People who use their cars as trash cans are easily recognized. ³Empty snack bags, hamburger wrappers, pizza cartons, soda cans, and doughnut boxes litter the floor. ⁴On the seats are old scratched CDs, blackened fruit skins, crumpled receipts, crushed cigarette packs, and used tissues. ⁵~~At least the trash stays in the car, instead of adding to the litter on our highways.~~ ⁶Other people use a car as a clothes closet. ⁷The car contains several pairs of shoes, pants, or shorts, along with a suit or dress that's been hanging on the car's clothes hanger for over a year. ⁸Sweaty, smelly gym clothes will also find a place in the car, a fact passengers quickly discover. ⁹~~The world would be better off if people showed more consideration of others.~~ ¹⁰Finally, some people use a car as a spare garage or basement. ¹¹In the backseats or trunks of these cars are bags of fertilizer, beach chairs, old textbooks, chainsaws, or window screens that have been there for months. ¹²The trunk may also contain an extra spare tire, a dented hubcap, an empty gallon container of window washer fluid, and discarded computer equipment. ¹³~~If apartments offered more storage space, probably fewer people would resort to using their cars for such storage purposes.~~ ¹⁴All in all, people get a lot more use out of their cars than simply the miles they travel on the road.

The numbers of the irrelevant sentences: _5_ _9_ _13_

2.

 Academic

Yoga

¹Many people start practicing yoga because they think it will help them lose weight, but they get more than just weight loss. ²For starters, the poses, or *asanas*, are specifically designed to stretch and bend

continued

in a writer's words
" *What lasts in the reader's mind is not the phrase but the effect the phrase created: laughter, tears, pain, joy. If the phrase is not affecting the reader, what's it doing there? Make it do its job or cut it without mercy or remorse.*"
            —Isaac Asimov

different parts of the body to increase blood flow and flexibility. ³This helps avoid injuries, stiff joints, arthritis, and other ailments that are brought on because of poor circulation. ⁴Another benefit that people discover is that they gain better daily focus. ⁵~~Many people struggle with concentration during the day, which affects work and relationships.~~ ⁶Many of the *asanas* require very specific movements and positions. ⁷~~Inverted positions are really difficult to do.~~ ⁸Moving into the proper stances takes practice, concentration, and patience. ⁹The first time getting into the proper pose can be frustrating; however, yoga emphasizes that people listen to their bodies. ¹⁰Some days the body might easily move into a beautiful *utkatasana* (chair pose), and other days it might be very difficult to hold the position. ¹¹~~It is often difficult to do positions right after eating a large meal.~~ ¹²With patience and focus, the *utkatasana* becomes a position that works the muscles while stimulating the heart without causing aggravation. ¹³People who practice yoga also find that they gain better overall health. ¹⁴Many inverted poses like the *salamba sarvangasana* (supported shoulder stand) require strength and stillness. ¹⁵While in a position like this, the blood flows better to the brain, helping nourish the brain and all the glands contained within the upper portion of the body. ¹⁶Such positions also stimulate the thyroid and digestive system and offer better peace of mind because they require meditation and deep breathing, especially when the pose is held for several minutes. ¹⁷People often feel better, have a stronger sense of self, and feel peaceful after a yoga session.

The numbers of the irrelevant sentences: 5   7   11

3.

Health Inspection Report: Main Street Grill

¹The following is a summary of the May 2018 report that recommends Main Street Grill be closed immediately:

²The entry of the restaurant is in need of dire repair. ³Several windows are broken, the front steps are missing a handrail, and the door does not close properly, allowing flies freedom to enter the establishment. ⁴~~The color of the door was a very ugly blue.~~ ⁵~~The flowers in the flower boxes and the grass needed watering.~~ ⁶Immediately inside the entryway, sections of flooring are missing, but have been temporarily covered with loose boards. ⁷The interior of the restaurant does not appear to have been cleaned in several years. ⁸Layers of dust and grease were visible on the lighting fixtures and window sills. ⁹The floor, where it wasn't broken, was a dingy gray that upon further inspection should have been white. ¹⁰The kitchen contains several nonworking appliances. ¹¹Fifteen extension cords were being used to connect appliances to one

continued

outlet. [12]Foods were not being stored at the proper temperatures. [13]Tests showed meats at 105 degrees Fahrenheit and showed milk at 52 degrees Fahrenheit. [14]~~The meals that the kitchen staff were preparing were burgers and fries, even though the restaurant does not have these meals on the menu.~~ [15]Workers were not wearing hair nets, nor did any of them wash their hands during the inspection. [16]This is the third time that Main Street Grill has failed a health inspection; no improvements have been made since the last visit. [17]The restaurant must be closed immediately.

The number of irrelevant sentences: 4   5   14

Base 2: Support

Understanding Support

The following student paragraphs were written on the topic "A Quality of Some Person You Know." Both are unified, but one communicates more clearly and effectively. Which one, and why?

PARAGRAPH A

My Quick-Tempered Father

My father is easily angered by normal everyday mistakes. For example, one day my father told me to wash the car and cut the grass. I did not hear exactly what he said, and so I asked him to repeat it. Then he became hysterical and shouted, "Can't you hear?" Another time he asked my mother to go to the store and buy groceries with a fifty-dollar bill, and he told her to spend no more than twenty dollars. She spent twenty-two dollars. As soon as he found out, he immediately took the change from her and told her not to go anywhere else for him; he did not speak to her the rest of the day. My father even gives my older brothers a hard time with his irritable moods. One day he told them to be home from their dates by midnight; they came home at 12:15. He informed them that they were grounded for three weeks. To my father, making a simple mistake is like committing a crime.

TEACHING TIP
Ask a volunteer to read these paragraphs aloud. Ask students to underline the topic sentences and specific examples.

PARAGRAPH B

My Generous Grandfather

My grandfather is the most generous person I know. He gave up a life of his own in order to give his children everything they wanted. Not only did he give up many years of his life to raise his

continued

children properly, but he is now sacrificing many more years to his grandchildren. His generosity is also evident in his relationship with his neighbors, his friends, and the members of his church. He has been responsible for many good deeds and has always been there to help all the people around him in times of trouble. Everyone knows that he will gladly lend a helping hand. He is so generous that you almost have to feel sorry for him. If one day he suddenly became selfish, it would be earthshaking. That's my grandfather.

ACTIVITY 4

Fill in the blanks: Paragraph __A__ makes its point more clearly and effectively because it offers vivid, specific examples of the main point.

EXPLANATION

Paragraph A is more effective, because it offers specific examples that show us the father in action. We see for ourselves why the writer describes the father as quick-tempered.

Paragraph B, on the other hand, gives us no specific evidence. The writer of paragraph B tells us repeatedly that the grandfather is generous but never shows us examples of that generosity. Just how, for instance, did the grandfather sacrifice his life for his children and grandchildren? Did he hold two jobs so that his son could go to college, or so that his daughter could have her own car? Does he give up time with his wife and friends to travel every day to his daughter's house to babysit, go to the store, and help with the dishes? Does he wear threadbare suits and coats and eat frozen dinners and other inexpensive meals (with no desserts) so that he can give money to his children and toys to his grandchildren? We want to see and judge for ourselves whether the writer is making a valid point about the grandfather, but without specific details we cannot do so. In fact, we have almost no picture of him at all.

Consideration of these two paragraphs leads us to the second base of effective writing: *support.* After realizing the importance of specific supporting details, one student writer revised a paper she had done on a restaurant job as the worst job she ever had. In the revised paper, instead of talking about "unsanitary conditions in the kitchen," she referred to such specifics as "green mold on the bacon" and "ants in the potato salad." All your papers should include many vivid details!

Checking for Support

To check a paragraph for support, ask yourself these questions:

1. Is there *specific* evidence to support the opening point?
2. Is there *enough* specific evidence?

Evaluating Paragraphs for Support

The three paragraphs that follow lack sufficient supporting details. In each paragraph, identify the spot or spots where more specific details are needed.

TEACHING TIP
After students complete this activity, suggest that they provide the needed details for each paragraph.

1.

Chicken: Our Best Friend

[1]Chicken is the best-selling meat today for a number of good reasons. [2]First of all, its reasonable cost puts it within everyone's reach. [3]Chicken is popular, too, because it can be prepared in so many different ways. [4]It can, for example, be cooked by itself, in spaghetti sauce, or with noodles and gravy. [5]It can be baked, boiled, broiled, or fried. [6]Chicken is also convenient. [7]Last and most important, chicken has a high nutritional value. [8]Four ounces of chicken contain twenty-eight grams of protein, which is almost half the recommended daily dietary allowance.

Fill in the blanks: The first spot where supporting details are needed occurs after sentence number ___2___ . The second spot occurs after sentence number ___6___ .

2.

Controversial Adventures

[1]*The Adventures of Huckleberry Finn* by Mark Twain has been causing controversy since it was first written. [2]When first printed in 1885, Twain's book was considered as nothing more than garbage with absolutely no moral or literary value. [3]In fact, the Concord Public Library refused to shelve the book after the library committee met and agreed that "it contain[ed] but little humor . . . of a very coarse type . . . being more suited to the slums than to intelligent, respectable people." [4]Later, many claimed that the book glamorized juvenile delinquency. [5]Huckleberry Finn is a runaway who engages in many questionable activities while harboring a fugitive. [6]Since the 1960s, however, most people have been offended by the language in *Huckleberry Finn*. [7]Regardless of the controversy, *The Adventures of Huckleberry Finn* will continue to be read by future generations.

Fill in the blank: The point where details are needed occurs after sentence number ___6___ .

3.

> **Being on TV**
>
> ¹People act a little strangely when a television camera comes their way. ²Some people behave as if a crazy puppeteer were pulling their strings. ³Their arms jerk wildly about, and they begin jumping up and down for no apparent reason. ⁴Often they accompany their body movements with loud screams, squeals, and yelps. ⁵Another group of people engage in an activity known as the cover-up. ⁶They will be calmly watching a sports game or other televised event when they realize the camera is focused on them. ⁷The camera operator can't resist zooming in for a close-up of these people. ⁸Then there are those who practice their funny faces on the unsuspecting public. ⁹They take advantage of the television time to show off their talents, hoping to get that big break that will carry them to stardom. ¹⁰Finally, there are those who pretend they are above reacting for the camera. ¹¹They wipe an expression from their faces and appear to be interested in something else. ¹²Yet if the camera stays on them long enough, they will slyly check to see if they are still being watched. ¹³Everybody's behavior seems to be slightly strange in front of a TV camera.

Fill in the blanks: The first spot where supporting details are needed occurs after sentence number ___6___ . The second spot occurs after sentence number ___8___ .

Base 3: Coherence

Understanding Coherence

The following two paragraphs were written on the topic "The Best or Worst Job You Ever Had." Both are unified and both are supported. However, one communicates more clearly and effectively. Which one, and why?

PARAGRAPH A

TEACHING TIP
Ask a volunteer to read these paragraphs aloud. Ask students to underline the topic sentences, specific examples, and transitions.

> **Pantry Helper**
>
> My worst job was as a pantry helper in one of San Diego's well-known restaurants. I had an assistant from three to six in the afternoon who did little but stand around and eat the whole time she was there. She would listen for the sound of the back door opening, which was a sure sign our boss was coming in. The boss would testily say to me, "You've got a lot of things to do here, Meghan. Try to get a move on." I would come in at two o'clock to relieve the woman on the morning shift. If her day was busy, that meant I would have to prepare salads, slice meat and cheese, and so on. Orders for sandwiches and

continued

cold platters would come in and have to be prepared. The worst thing about the job was that the heat in the kitchen, combined with my nerves, would give me an upset stomach by seven o'clock almost every night. I might be going to the storeroom to get some supplies, and one of the waitresses would tell me she wanted a bacon, lettuce, and tomato sandwich on white toast. I would put the toast in and head for the supply room, and a waitress would holler out that her customer was in a hurry. Green flies would come in through the torn screen in the kitchen window and sting me. I was getting paid only $8.00 an hour. At five o'clock, when the dinner rush began, I would be dead tired. Roaches scurried in all directions whenever I moved a box or picked up a head of lettuce to cut.

PARAGRAPH B

My Worst Job

The worst job I ever had was as a waiter at the Westside Inn. First of all, many of the people I waited on were rude. When a baked potato was hard inside or a salad was flat or their steak wasn't just the way they wanted it, they blamed me, rather than the kitchen. Or they would ask me to light their cigarettes, or chase flies from their tables, or even take their children to the bathroom. Also, I had to contend not only with the customers but with the kitchen staff as well. The cooks and busboys were often undependable and surly. If I didn't treat them just right, I would wind up having to apologize to customers because their meals came late or their water glasses weren't filled. Another reason I didn't like the job was that I was always moving. Because of the constant line at the door, as soon as one group left, another would take its place. I usually had only a twenty-minute lunch break and another ten-minute break in almost nine hours of work. I think I could have put up with the job if I had been able to pause and rest more often. The last and most important reason I hated the job was my boss. She played favorites, giving some of the waiters and waitresses the best-tipping repeat customers and preferences on holidays. She would hover around during my break to make sure I didn't take a second more than the allotted time. And even when I helped out by working through a break, she never had an appreciative word but would just tell me not to be late for work the next day.

Fill in the blanks: **Paragraph** __B__ **makes its point more clearly and effectively because** its points, details, and examples are organized more clearly and logically.

ACTIVITY 6

EXPLANATION

Paragraph B is more effective because the material is organized clearly and logically. Using emphatic order, the writer gives us a list of four reasons why the job was so bad: rude customers, an unreliable kitchen staff, constant motion, and—most of all—an unfair boss. Further, the writer includes transitional words that act as signposts, making movement from one idea to the next easy to follow. The major transitions are *First of all, Also, Another reason,* and *The last and most important reason.*

While paragraph A focuses on one main topic and has support, the writer does not have any clear and consistent way of organizing the material. Partly, emphatic order is used, but this is not made clear by transitions or by saving the most important reason for last. Partly, time order is used, but it moves inconsistently from two to seven to five o'clock.

These two paragraphs lead us to the third base of effective writing: *coherence.* The supporting ideas and sentences in a composition must be organized so that they cohere, or "stick together." As has already been mentioned, key techniques for tying material together are a clear method of organization (such as time order or emphatic order), transitions, and other connecting words.

Checking for Coherence

To check a paragraph for coherence, ask yourself these questions:

1. Does the paragraph have a clear method of organization?

2. Are transitions and other connecting words used to tie the material together?

Evaluating Paragraphs for Coherence

ACTIVITY 7   Answer the questions about coherence that follow the paragraph below.

TEACHING TIP
Read this paragraph aloud. Ask students to underline the topic sentence, specific examples, and transitions before answering the questions.

Apartment Hunting

[1]Apartment hunting is a several-step process that all potential renters should follow. [2]They should visit and carefully inspect the most promising apartments. [3]They should check each place for signs of unwanted guests such as roaches or mice. [4]Making sure that light switches and appliances work and that there are enough electrical outlets are also important steps. [5]Turning faucets on and off and flushing the toilet will help potential renters be sure that the plumbing works smoothly. [6]Talking to the landlord for a bit can help develop a feeling for the kind of person he or she is. [7]If a problem develops after renters move in, they will want to know that a decent and capable person will be there to handle the matter. [8]People

continued

should find out what's available that matches their interests. ⁹The town newspaper and local real estate offices can provide lists of apartments for rent. ¹⁰Family and friends may be able to give leads. ¹¹And local schools may have a housing office that keeps a list of approved apartments for rent. ¹²Potential renters should decide what they want in an apartment. ¹³If they can afford no more than $700 a month, they need to find a place that will cost no more than that. ¹⁴If location near work or school is important, these factors should be considered. ¹⁵For those who plan to cook, a workable kitchen is important. ¹⁶By taking these steps, anyone should be ready to select the apartment that is best for him or her.

a. The paragraph should use time order. Write 1 before the step that should come first, 2 before the intermediate step, and 3 before the final step.

  3   Visit and carefully inspect the most promising apartments.

  1   Decide what one needs in an apartment.

  2   Find out what's available that matches interests.

b. Before which of the three steps could the transitional words *The first step is to* be added? step 1

c. Before which step could the transitional words *After a person has decided what he or she is looking for, the next step is to* be added? step 2

d. Before which step could the transitional words *The final step is to* be added? step 3

e. To whom does the pronoun *him or her* in sentence 6 refer to? the landlord

f. What is a synonym for *landlord* in sentence 7? person

g. What is a synonym for *apartment* in sentence 13? place

Revising Paragraphs for Coherence

The two paragraphs in this section begin with a clear point, but in each case the supporting material that follows the point is not coherent. Read each paragraph and the comments that follow it on how to organize and connect the supporting material. Then do the activity for the paragraph.

PARAGRAPH 1

A Difficult Period

Since I arrived in the Bay Area in midsummer, I have had the most difficult period of my life. I had to look for an apartment. I found only one place that I could afford, but the landlord said I could not move in until it was painted. When I first arrived in San Francisco, my thoughts were to stay with my father and stepmother. I had to set out looking for a job so that I could afford my own place, for I soon realized that my stepmother was not at all happy

TEACHING TIP
Read these paragraphs aloud to your students.

continued

having me live with them. A three-week search led to a job shampooing rugs for a housecleaning company. I painted the apartment myself, and at least that problem was ended. I was in a hurry to get settled because I was starting school at the University of San Francisco in September. A transportation problem developed because my stepmother insisted that I return my father's bike, which I was using at first to get to school. I had to rely on a bus that often arrived late, with the result that I missed some classes and was late for others. I had already had a problem with registration in early September. My counselor had made a mistake with my classes, and I had to register all over again. This meant that I was one week late for class. Now I'm riding to school with a classmate and no longer have to depend on the bus. My life is starting to order itself, but I must admit that at first I thought it was hopeless to stay here.

COMMENTS ON PARAGRAPH 1

The writer of this paragraph has provided a good deal of specific evidence to support the opening point. The evidence, however, needs to be organized. Before starting the paragraph, the writer should have decided to arrange the details by using time order. He or she could then have listed in a scratch outline the exact sequence of events that made for such a difficult period.

ACTIVITY 8	Here is a list of the various events described by the writer of paragraph 1. Number the events in the correct time sequence by writing 1 in front of the first event that occurred, 2 in front of the second event, and so on.

Since I arrived in the Bay Area in midsummer, I have had the most difficult period of my life.

___3___ I had to search for an apartment I could afford.

___2___ I had to find a job so that I could afford my own place.

___1___ My stepmother objected to my living with her and my father.

___4___ I had to paint the apartment before I could move in.

___6___ I had to find an alternative to unreliable bus transportation.

___5___ I had to register again for my college courses because of a counselor's mistake.

Your instructor may now have you rewrite the paragraph on separate paper. If so, be sure to use time signals such as *first, next, then, during, when, after,* and *now* to help guide your reader from one event to the next.

PARAGRAPH 2

Childhood Cruelty

When I was in grade school, my classmates and I found a number of excuses for being cruel to a boy named Andy Poppovian. Sometimes Andy gave off a strong body odor, and we knew that several days had passed since he had taken a bath. Andy was very slow in speaking, as well as very careless in personal hygiene. The teacher would call on him during a math or grammar drill. He would sit there silently for so long before answering that she sometimes said, "Are you awake, Andy?" Andy had long fingernails that he never seemed to cut, with black dirt caked under them. We called him "Poppy," or we accented the first syllable in his name and mispronounced the rest of it and said to him, "How are you today, POP-o-van?" His name was funny. Other times we called him "Popeye," and we would shout at him. "Where's your spinach today, Popeye?" Andy always had sand in the corners of his eyes. When we played tag at recess, Andy was always "it" or the first one who was caught. He was so physically slow that five guys could dance around him and he wouldn't be able to touch any of them. Even when we tried to hold a regular conversation with him about sports or a teacher, he was so slow in responding to a question that we got bored talking with him. Andy's hair was always uncombed, and it was often full of white flakes of dandruff. Only when Andy died suddenly of spinal meningitis in seventh grade did some of us begin to realize and regret our cruelty toward him.

COMMENTS ON PARAGRAPH 2

The writer of this paragraph provides a number of specifics that support the opening point. However, the supporting material has not been organized clearly. Before writing this paragraph, the author should have (1) decided to arrange the supporting evidence by using emphatic order and (2) listed in an outline the reasons for the cruelty to Andy Poppovian and the supporting details for each reason. The writer could also have determined which reason to use in the emphatic final position of the paragraph.

Create a clear outline for paragraph 2 by filling in the scheme below. The outline is partially completed.

ACTIVITY 9

When I was in grade school, my classmates and I found a number of excuses for being cruel to a boy named Andy Poppovian.

1. Funny name   Reason

    a. Called him "Poppy"   Details

    b. Called him "POP-o-van"

    c. Called him "Popeye"

Reason

Details

2. Physically slow

   a. First one caught in tag games

   b. Five guys could dance around him

Reason

Details

3. Verbally slow

   a. In class

   b. In regular conversation

Reason

Details

4. Carelessness in personal hygiene

   a. Strong body odor

   b. Sand in eyes

   c. Long, dirty fingernails

   d. Uncombed, dandruff-flaked hair

ESL NOTE
While nonnative speakers may struggle with unity, their greatest weakness is in the area of sentence skills. Many of the areas are global and need to be addressed. Nonnative speakers may require a lot of additional practice in: correct verb forms and tenses, subject–verb agreement, faulty pronouns, faulty parallelism, and modifiers.

Your instructor may have you rewrite the paragraph on separate paper. If so, be sure to introduce each of the four reasons with transitions such as *First, Second, Another reason,* and *Finally.* You may also want to use repeated words, pronouns, and synonyms to help tie your sentences together.

Base 4: Sentence Skills

Understanding Sentence Skills

Two versions of a paragraph are given below. Both are unified, supported, and organized, but one version communicates more clearly and effectively. Which one, and why?

PARAGRAPH A

TEACHING TIP
Slowly read these paragraphs. Allow students to "hear" many of the errors in Paragraph B.

Falling Asleep Anywhere

[1]There are times when people are so tired that they fall asleep almost anywhere. [2]For example, there is a lot of sleeping on the bus or train on the way home from work in the evenings. [3]A man will be reading the newspaper, and seconds later it appears as if he is trying to eat it. [4]Or he will fall asleep on the shoulder of the stranger sitting next to him. [5]Another place where unplanned naps go on is the lecture hall. [6]In some classes, a student will start snoring so loudly that the professor has to ask another student to shake the sleeper awake. [7]A more embarrassing situation occurs when a student leans on one elbow and starts drifting off to sleep. [8]The weight of the head pushes the elbow off the desk, and this momentum carries the rest of the body along. [9]The student wakes up on the floor with no memory of getting there. [10]The worst place to fall asleep is at the wheel of a car. [11]Police reports are full of accidents that occur when people lose consciousness and go off the road. [12]If the drivers are

---

continued

lucky, they are not seriously hurt. [13]One woman's car, for instance, went into a river. [14]She woke up in four feet of water and thought it was raining. [15]When people are really tired, nothing will stop them from falling asleep—no matter where they are.

PARAGRAPH B

"Falling Asleep Anywhere"

[1]There are times when people are so tired that they fall asleep almost anywhere. [2]For example, on the bus or train on the way home from work. [3]A man will be reading the newspaper, seconds later it appears as if he is trying to eat it. [4]Or he will fall asleep on the shoulder of the stranger sitting next to him. [5]Another place where unplanned naps go on are in the lecture hall. [6]In some classes, a student will start snoring so loudly that the professor has to ask another student to shake the sleeper awake. [7]A more embarrassing situation occurs when a student leans on one elbow and starting to drift off to sleep. [8]The weight of the head push the elbow off the desk, and this momentum carries the rest of the body along. [9]The student wakes up on the floor with no memory of getting there. [10]The worst time to fall asleep is when driving a car. [11]Police reports are full of accidents that occur when people conk out and go off the road. [12]If the drivers are lucky they are not seriously hurt. [13]One womans car, for instance, went into a river. [14]She woke up in four feet of water. [15]And thought it was raining. [16]When people are really tired, nothing will stop them from falling asleep—no matter where they are.

Fill in the blanks: Paragraph ___A___ makes its point more clearly and effectively because it demonstrates effective sentence skills. _____

_____

_____

ACTIVITY 10

EXPLANATION

Paragraph A is more effective because it incorporates *sentence skills,* the fourth base of competent writing.

See if you can identify the ten sentence-skills mistakes in paragraph B. Do this, first of all, by going back and underlining the ten spots in paragraph B that differ in wording or punctuation from paragraph A. Then try to identify the ten sentence-skills mistakes by circling what you feel is the correct answer in each of the ten statements on the following page.

ACTIVITY 11

> **TIP** Comparing paragraph B with the correct version may help you guess correct answers even if you are not familiar with the names of certain skills.

TEACHING TIP
You may want to review
these sentence skills.

1. The title should not be set off with
   a. capital letters.
   b. quotation marks. ⟵
2. In word group 2, there is a
   a. missing comma.
   b. missing apostrophe.
   c. sentence fragment. ⟵
   d. dangling modifier.
3. In word group 3, there is a
   a. run-on. ⟵
   b. sentence fragment.
   c. mistake in subject–verb agreement.
   d. mistake involving an irregular verb.
4. In word group 5, there is a
   a. sentence fragment.
   b. spelling error.
   c. run-on.
   d. mistake in subject–verb agreement. ⟵
5. In word group 7, there is a
   a. misplaced modifier.
   b. dangling modifier.
   c. mistake in parallelism. ⟵
   d. run-on.

6. In word group 8, there is a(n)
   a. incorrect subject–verb agreement. ⟵
   b. run-on.
   c. comma mistake.
   d. missing capital letter.
7. In word group 11, there is a
   a. mistake involving an irregular verb.
   b. sentence fragment.
   c. slang phrase. ⟵
   d. mistake in subject–verb agreement.
8. In word group 12, there is a
   a. missing apostrophe.
   b. missing comma. ⟵
   c. mistake involving an irregular verb.
   d. sentence fragment.
9. In word group 13, there is a
   a. mistake in parallelism.
   b. mistake involving an irregular verb.
   c. missing apostrophe. ⟵
   d. missing capital letter.
10. In word group 15, there is a
   a. missing quotation mark.
   b. mistake involving an irregular verb.
   c. sentence fragment. ⟵
   d. mistake in pronoun point of view.

You should have chosen the following answers:

1. b	2. c	3. a	4. d	5. c
6. a	7. c	8. b	9. c	10. c

Part 6 of this book explains these and other sentence skills. You should review all the skills carefully. Doing so will ensure that you know the most important rules of grammar, punctuation, and usage—rules needed to write clear, error-free sentences.

Checking for Sentence Skills

Sentence skills and the other bases of effective writing are summarized in the following chart and on the inside back cover of the book.

A SUMMARY OF THE FOUR BASES OF EFFECTIVE WRITING

TEACHING TIP
Draw this chart on the board, omitting the numbers 1 through 4. Ask students to number the four bases.

- Fragments eliminated? (Chapter 24)
- Run-ons eliminated? (Chapter 25)
- Correct verb forms? (Chapter 26)
- Subject and verb agreement? (Chapter 27)
- Faulty parallelism and faulty modifiers eliminated? (Chapters 4 and 32)
- Faulty pronouns eliminated? (Chapter 29)
- Capital letters used correctly? (Chapter 33)
- Punctuation marks where needed?

  (a) Apostrophe (Chapter 35)   (d) Semicolon; colon (Chapter 38)

  (b) Quotation marks (Chapter 36) (e) Hyphen; dash (Chapter 38)

  (c) Comma (Chapter 37)   (f) Parentheses (Chapter 38)

- Correct paper format? (Chapter 1)
- Needless words eliminated? (Chapter 4)
- Effective word choices? (Chapter 40)
- Possible spelling errors checked? (Chapter 4)
- Careless errors eliminated through proofreading? (Chapters 1, 2, and 4)
- Sentences varied? (Chapter 4)

Evaluating Paragraphs for All Four Bases: Unity, Support, Coherence, and Sentence Skills

In this activity, you will evaluate paragraphs in terms of all four bases: unity, support, coherence, and sentence skills. Evaluative comments follow each paragraph below. Circle the letter of the statement that best applies in each case.

1.

Worst Presidents

Over the years, the United States has had some terrible presidents. Andrew Jackson was president from 1829 to1837 and was responsible for the Trail of Tears with his support of the 1830 Indian Removal Act. He also was a gambler and had no problems breaking laws. Warren G. Harding, who was president from 1921 to 1923, had one of the most corrupt administrations. One example of the corruption is the Teapot Dome Scandal. Richard M. Nixon is considered by many to be the worst president. During his time in office, 1969 to 1974, he engaged in criminal behavior, most notably known as the Watergate Scandal, that led to impending impeachment and, ultimately, his resignation.

---

a.   The paragraph is not unified.
b.   The paragraph is not adequately supported.
c.   The paragraph is not well organized.
d.   The paragraph does not show a command of sentence skills.
e.   The paragraph is well written in terms of the four bases.

2.

Pop-Up Restaurants

Foodies don't just like to eat. They live to have that next outstanding food experience. And modern technology has provided a new way to link foodies and chefs. Lacking the funds to open their own establishments, chefs worldwide are beginning to follow Chef Ludo Lefebvre's. Lead in creating dining experiences at different locations and using technology to spread the word. Former executive chef at the famous L'Orangerie in Los Angeles. Seeking establishments that they can use for a limited period—anywhere from 72 hours to three weeks—chefs set up house in these locations and create original and creative meals. But how do the foodies find out? Twitter, Facebook, e-mail, blogs. All of these outlets for advertising are free to the chef, but far more effective than mainstream advertising, in fact, according to National Public Radio, whenever Chef Lefebvre announces his next location, "within seven hours, all reservations are snapped up." Finding that next great restaurant no longer requires a perusal through the yellow pages. But a faithful following on Twitter.

a. The paragraph is not unified.
b. The paragraph is not adequately supported.
c. The paragraph is not well organized.
d.⃝ The paragraph does not show a command of sentence skills.
e. The paragraph is well written in terms of the four bases.

3.

Becoming a Volunteer to Fight Cyberbullying

When I was in school, cyberbullying incidents had a big impact on why I now volunteer with an anti-cyberbullying group. Eric's ex-girlfriend, Marie, bullied Dianne at school, vandalized her car, and posted some horrible things online. The online bullying became so bad that Dianne tried to commit suicide, and Dianne's parents filed a police report against Marie. Sometimes Kaylie would show up to school in clothes that were smelly and dirty. Some of the other girls in school decided to take a bunch of pictures of Kaylie and posted them online, so they could make fun of her. Within a day, a large group of kids was involved in making online rude comments about Kaylie. This hurt her so badly that she ended up going to counseling and transferring to another school. A senior found out that John was gay and posted the information online. Not only did several students start calling him names online and in-person but his family found out. They were so hurt and angry that John actually ran away for several weeks. Because of these incidents, I made a decision to be part of the solution rather than part of the problem.

a. The paragraph is not unified.
b. The paragraph is not adequately supported.
c.⃝ The paragraph is not well organized.
d. The paragraph does not show a command of sentence skills.
e. The paragraph is well written in terms of the four bases.

4.

Linguists Beware!

Entertainment in the twenty-first century has been a catalyst for the invention of new words. J. K. Rowling's fantasy world of *Harry Potter* introduced millions of readers to "Muggles, Mudbloods, and Quidditch," and when the books became movies, millions more laid claim to the language of Harry Potter. James Cameron's screen sensation, *Avatar*, introduced viewers to the Na'vi tribe and its made-up language. Additionally, Cameron's movie is credited for the term "Pandora Effect," a feeling of being confused, wistful, and disappointed all at the same time. Furthermore, viewers of *Inception* now regularly "check their

continued

totems" to determine the reality of situations. Like movies, TV has affected language. In 2010, the word "Gleeks," referring to those who watch *Glee*, became a mainstream term. Snooki and her friends introduced viewers of *Jersey Shore* to the problem of "tanorexia" (not being tan enough) and being "Snookied" (punched in the face). *The "A" List* introduced its viewers to a "mantrum" (tantrum by a man). Of course, no TV viewing is complete without a good old fashioned Zitcom (a comedy for a teenage audience) with teenage characters. The Internet, with its endless entertainment possibilities, has given rise to "Mouse Potatoes" who become so glued to the latest online sensations, they often slip into "Internet comas." As entertainment continues to influence the development of language, maybe one day "Shatner commas" and their odd, purposeless positions will become mainstream and the fear of overusing commas will be "refudiated," just "like, like Valley Girls."

a.   The paragraph is not unified.
b.   The paragraph is not adequately supported.
c.   The paragraph is not well organized.
d.   The paragraph does not show a command of sentence skills.
(e.) The paragraph is well written in terms of the four bases.

5.

Velcro: Sticky Results

Velcro has ruined the world. Before Velcro was invented, children had to learn to tie shoes, but now they only have to stick one strap onto another. Learning to tie shoes is a problem-solving activity and can be hard, but sticking one strap to another is easy. There are two popular ways to learn to tie shoes: the bunny ears or the squirrel and the tree. The bunny ears method is probably the most popular. Problem-solving activities are important because they teach critical thinking. Without critical-thinking skills, people often have a hard time getting through college. College classes can be very difficult if students don't study properly. Getting a college degree is really important because it means a better job and better future.

(a.) The paragraph is not unified.
b.   The paragraph is not adequately supported.
c.   The paragraph is not well organized.
d.   The paragraph does not show a command of sentence skills.
e.   The paragraph is well written in terms of the four bases.

1. Look back at the paragraph that you wrote at the end of Chapter 3. Does your paragraph cover all four bases of effective writing?

2. Afterward, you and your classmates, perhaps working in small groups, should read your paragraphs aloud. Pay attention to spots where you see problems with unity, support, coherence, and sentence skills.

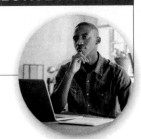

©mavo/Shutterstock

Visit one of these Web sites to read a movie review of your choice. As you read the movie review, look at how the critic uses specific categories—such as plot, actors, and special effects—to evaluate the movie. Then use the four bases of effective writing to evaluate the movie review itself for unity, support, coherence, and sentence skills.

Movie Review Query Engine: **www.mrqe.com**

FilmCritic.com: **www.filmcritic.com**

RottenTomatoes.com: **www.rottentomatoes.com/critics/**

©Tetra Images/
Shutterstock

The Writing Process in Action

In Chapters 1 through 5, you learned about the importance of supporting a point in writing, the structure of a traditional paragraph, and the writing process. You also practiced prewriting, creating thesis statements, developing good support, organizing your ideas, and creating effective introductions and conclusions. Finally, you learned the benefits of effective revision. The following pages illustrate the entire writing process—the complete development of a paragraph from prewriting through planning, drafting, peer review, revision, and final draft.

A Sample Paragraph

Mico created the following paragraph on the topic of "self-compassion" for her developmental writing class.

| The first thing Mico did was prewrite. She used listing

for her prewriting:

- dreams, goals, self-esteem

- what made you who you are today

- loving yourself

- self-esteem

- making yourself happy

- loving others/making them happy
- accepting others for who they are
- self-compassion vs. adversity
- self-image
- true to yourself
- personal growth
- self-love
- being able to say no
- honesty
- knowing limits
- not giving up
- self-confidence
- goals—set and follow through
- ok to make mistakes

Once Mico was done with her first listing exercise, she then looked to see what types of categories her ideas fell into. She came up with:

✓ Definition
✓ Treating Yourself Well
✓ Being True to Yourself
✓ Challenges

She then organized her list into her categories. While organizing, she was able to add a few more ideas. She also realized that she had some ideas like "loving yourself" and "self-love" that were actually the same idea.

✓ Definition
✓ Treating Yourself Well
✓ Being True to Yourself
✓ Challenges

- dreams, goals, self-esteem
- what made you who you are today
- loving yourself
- self-esteem
- making yourself happy
- loving others/making them happy
- accepting others for who they are

- self-compassion vs. adversity
- self-image
- true to yourself
- personal growth
- self-love
- being able to say no
- honesty
- knowing limits
- not giving up
- self-confidence
- goals—set and follow through
- ok to make mistakes

✓ Definition
- self-image
- self-esteem
- self-love
- honesty

✓ Treating Yourself Well
- making yourself happy
- loving others
- making others happy
- living essentials
- accomplishments
- being positive
- loving yourself
- personal growth, sponsorship/mentoring

✓ Being True to Yourself
- able to say no
- confidence
- trusting yourself
- staying true to yourself
- knowing limits
- never giving up
- self-confidence
- goals—setting and follow through
- ok to make mistakes

✓   Challenge

•   adversity

•   accepting others for who they are

•   forgiveness

•   staying true vs other perception

2 **II** **Once Mico had her ideas grouped into categories, she worked on a topic sentence.** She started by asking herself the following questions. As she answered the questions, she began to formulate ideas for a potential topic sentence.

•   What is self-compassion? Self-compassion is finding ways to be true to yourself and to love yourself.

•   What does it mean to use self-compassion? Self-compassion is showing compassion to your own self, which sounds obvious, but isn't easy.

•   How can one achieve self-compassion? One can achieve self-compassion by setting goals and noticing conflicts will happen.

•   How easy is self-compassion? Some people find it difficult to have self-compassion, because they are always trying to please others.

•   Why is self-compassion important? Self-compassion is important because it forms your self-identity.

•   How does self-compassion relate to our daily activities? Being nice to ourselves impacts how we do things.

•   Self-compassion is often described as being true to yourself. I've met many people that often offer that up as advice to me, but just how easy is it, and what exactly does it mean to be true to yourself, and to have self-compassion? It means doing what is right in my heart, but that seems difficult.

Mico then looked back over her prewriting and guiding questions to come up with several possible topic sentences:

•   Self-compassion is often described as being true to yourself; however, that is not a simple things to do.

- Self-compassion is important because it forms a person's self-identity while practicing moral values.
- Self-compassion is important because it varies from person to person and shows each person's individuality/identity.
- To be self-compassionate, a person has to be prepared to face the challenges of self-kindness, self-improvement, and sticking to personal values.
- Self-compassion relates to our daily lives by being able to say no, trusting ourselves, and not giving up.
- Self-compassion is finding ways to be true to and love oneself. However it is difficult for people to have self-compassion because they are always trying to please others.

She then went through her possible topic sentences and eliminated those that were too broad, too narrow, or tried to cover too many things:

- Self-compassion is often described as being true to yourself; however, that is not a simple things to do. (I like this one, but I don't think it is the best)
- Self-compassion is important because it forms a person's self-identity ~~while practicing moral values~~. (I like this one, but the moral values part doesn't seem to fit)
- ~~Self-compassion is important because it varies from person to person and shows each person's individuality/identity~~. (too broad)
- To be self-compassionate, a person has to be prepared to face the challenges of self-kindness, self-improvement, and sticking to personal values. (I like this one a lot.)
- Self-compassion relates to our daily lives by being able to say no, trusting ourselves, and not giving up. (this one is ok, but not great)
- ~~Self-compassion is finding ways to be true to and love oneself. However it is difficult for people to have self-compassion because they are always trying to please others~~. (this one covers too many ideas)

3

III   Mico selected one statement from her list and developed support points based on her categories.

Topic Sentence: "To be self-compassionate, a person has to be prepared to face the challenges of self-kindness, self-improvement, and sticking to personal values."

Definition: What is self-compassion?

> Showing compassion means showing love, forgiveness, and kindness. Self-compassion means to stay true to yourself and to your personal values. When someone begins to reach self-compassion, they are one step closer to personal growth. Self-compassion is important because it forms a person's self-identity.

Support Point 1: Challenges

> Self-compassion means self-forgiveness and self-kindness. We have to start forgiving ourselves before we can truly forgive others in order to reach a level of self-compassion. Forgiveness is not an easy thing to give or receive. Practicing forgiveness daily on small things (maybe give an example?) will eventually help you to forgive the bigger things that happen to you.

Support Point 2: Treating Yourself Well

> Improving yourself is an important aspect of practicing self-compassion. In order to truly practice self-compassion, you must be able to recognize your strengths and weaknesses and set yourself on a path for personal growth.

Support Point 3: Being True to Yourself

> First, everyone has their own values that stem from their beliefs and religion, but it's up to each individual to form their self-identity out of those values. People shouldn't let others talk them into things. It's important to respect other people's values. It's ok to make mistakes, good things can come from mistakes. Don't let it shake your confidence.

Concluding Sentence: A person has to demonstrate self-kindness, self-improvement, and sticking to personal values in order to be self-compassionate.

IV During peer review, Mico received numerous comments
to help her improve her paragraph.

4

Mico's Draft

Don't forget MLA format.

Steps to Self-Compassion

Seems like you got inspired to start with an interesting quote but this is not a topic sentence

Anna Quindlen has been quoted as saying "The thing that is really hard, and really amazing, is giving up on being perfect and beginning the work of becoming yourself." Self-compassion means showing compassion to yourself. To understand self-compassion, you have to be prepared to face the challenges. Practicing self-compassion is hard. For instance, women are often hard on themselves. They tend to be judgmental. I am often really hard on myself when I try on new clothes. Improving oneself is another important aspect of practicing self-compassion. To do this, you must be able to recognize your strengths and weaknesses and set yourself on a path for personal growth. Setting positive goals and taking time to reflect on triumphs and failures. You can learn to practice self-compassion. Finally, in order to be self-compassionate you needs to be true to yourself. Everyone has their own standards that stem from their beliefs and religions, but it is up to each individual to form a self-identity out of those values. You need to be skeptical of letting others talk them you out of what you believe. As well as also important to learn to respect others' opinions, boundaries, and limitations. Not giving in and loving oneself enough to stick to personal values while not demeaning others' values. Becoming self-compassionate is an important step, and you have to be prepared to face the challenges of demonstrating self-kindness, focusing on self-improvement, and sticking to personal values.

What do you think should be your topic sentence?

synonyms?

this doesn't fit the topic

revise out you

fragment

I wouldn't use religions

people? family? friends?

fragments

What kinds of challenges?

Your fragments create confusing sections. what are you trying to say?

5

V. After peer review, Mico looked over her rough draft and made additional comments based on her reviewers' feedback:

Steps to Self-Compassion

eliminate quote ~~Anna Quindlen has been quoted as saying "The thing that is really hard, and really amazing, is giving up on being perfect and beginning the work of becoming yourself."~~ Self- *✓ topic sentence* compassion means showing compassion ~~to yourself.~~ *how to become* *to oneself* To understand self-compassion, you have *compassionate* to be prepared to face the challenges. Practicing self-compassion is hard. For instance, women *add here* *add* are often hard on themselves. ~~They tend to be judgmental.~~ ~~I am often really hard on myself when I try on new clothes.~~ Improving oneself is another important aspect of practicing self- compassion. To do this, you must be able to recognize your strengths and weaknesses and set yourself on a path for personal growth. Setting positive goals and taking time to reflect on *> fix* triumphs and failures. You can learn to practice self-compassion. Finally, in order to be self- *his or her* compassionate you needs to be true to yourself. Everyone has their own standards that stem *personal* from their beliefs ~~and religions,~~ but it is up to each individual to form a self-identity out of those *People* values. You need to be skeptical of letting others talk them you out of what you believe. As well *fix fragments* as also important to learn to respect others' opinions, boundaries, and limitations. Not giving in and loving oneself enough to stick to personal values while not demeaning others' values.

Becoming self-compassionate is an important step, and you have to be prepared to face the challenges of demonstrating self-kindness, focusing on self-improvement, and sticking to personal values.

VI. Mico then incorporated the feedback and revised and edited her paragraph. She submitted the following paper to her professor:

6

Royce 1

Mico Royce

Professor Smith

English 90 9:30

September 20, 2019

Steps to Self-Compassion

To understand how to become self-compassionate, a person has to be prepared to face the challenges of demonstrating self-kindness, focusing on self-improvement, and sticking to personal values. Self-compassion means showing compassion – love, forgiveness, kindness – to one's self. Part of practicing self-compassion means practicing forgiveness. For instance, women are often hard on themselves when they don't fit society's ideal of beauty and often go to drastic measures to try and meet that ideal. Learning to love themselves for whom they are and ignoring outside standards will lead them to self-compassion. Improving oneself is another important aspect of practicing self-compassion. To do this, a person must be able to recognize his or her strengths and weaknesses and maintain a positive, forgiving attitude. By setting goals and taking time to reflect on how triumphs and failures, both large and small, have led toward self-improvement, a person learns to practice self-compassion. Finally, in order to be self-compassionate a person needs to be true to himself or herself. Everyone has his or her own standards that stem from personal beliefs, but it is up to each individual to form a self-identity out of those values. People need to be skeptical of letting others talk them out of what they believe, but it is also important to learn to respect others' opinions, boundaries, and limitations. Not giving in and loving oneself enough to stick to personal values while not demeaning others' values is a way to practice self-compassion. Becoming self-compassionate is an important step

Royce 2

for everyone, and a person has to be prepared to face the challenges of demonstrating self-

kindness, focusing on self-improvement, and sticking to personal values.

Mico submitted her paper on self-compassion because it was due, but she knew there were still areas that could have been improved. Either on your own or in a group, go through Mico's paragraph and look for weak spots. Like Mico's peer reviewers, you should focus on helping Mico improve her paragraph by examining the important areas first. To start, look at her topic sentence and decide whether it needs to be made stronger. If so, revise the topic sentence to make it as strong and clear a statement as possible. Then look at the support points to see if they still work well with your revised topic sentence. If not, make the changes necessary.

The next step is to read through the support points to make sure they are unified, coherent, and do support the topic sentence. Any information that doesn't support the topic sentence should be eliminated and replaced with ideas that advance the main idea of the paragraph.

Once you have revised the paragraph, read through it again to determine whether or not it now meets the four bases of effective writing. If not, decide how you can improve it. Finally, go back through to make sure the sentence skills are correct.

ACTIVITY 13

In college, you may want to ask your classmates to give you feedback on your writing, and you may want to help them with their writing. As you are reading the following paragraph written by Jakeem for a geology class, think about what advice you would offer him as he prepares to write his final draft. Does his paragraph cover all four bases of effective writing? To be sure, use the checklist that follows.

Types of Natural Resources

[1]Natural resources can be classified as either renewable or nonrenewable. [2]On the one hand, coal, oil, and gas are nonrenewable. [3]They take millions of years to form. [4]Some scientists predicts that we will run out of oil and gas in fifty to a hundred years. [5]Coal is more plentiful. [6]As a result, they may last for hundreds of years. [7]On the other hand, resources such as wood and water are renewable because they can be grown or recycled naturally.

A WRITER'S CHECKLIST

Unity

✔ Is there a clear topic sentence in this paragraph? __Yes__

✔ Does all the material work to support the topic sentence? __Yes__

Support

✔ Does Jakeem provide specific evidence to support his topic sentence? __Yes__

✔ Are there enough supporting details? __No__ If not, where would you recommend adding more

supporting details? __after sentence 7__

Coherence

✔ Does Jakeem use transitions and other connective devices? __Yes__ List them here:

On the one hand, On the other hand

Sentence Skills

✔ Is there a fragment in the paragraph? __No__

Is there a problem with subject and verb agreement in the paragraph?

Yes, sentence 4

✔ Can you find any other sentence skills mistakes, as listed on the back inside cover of the book? If

you can find a mistake, what type of mistake is it?

Yes, sentence 6 has a faulty pronoun

©Jacob Lund/
Shutterstock

Collaborative Activity

Work together as a group or class to make an outline of Jakeem's paragraph. Looking at the outline, can you think of any additional supporting details that could be added to make this paragraph more effective?

PART THREE GIVES YOU PRACTICE

- providing a series of examples to support a point

- telling a story that illustrates or explains a point

- describing a person, place, or thing by using words rich in sensory details

- explaining how to do or make something or how something works

- explaining the causes and/or effects of something

- explaining how things are similar and/or different

- illustrating the meaning of something with a series of examples or a story

- breaking one thing down into parts or sorting a group of things into categories according to a single principle

- arguing a position and defending it with a series of solid reasons

EXPLORING WRITING PROMPT:

In our everyday lives, we write to inform, persuade, and entertain. Think about the last time you wrote something—what was the purpose of that message? What did you hope to accomplish? Take a few minutes to freewrite about how you've used your writing recently.

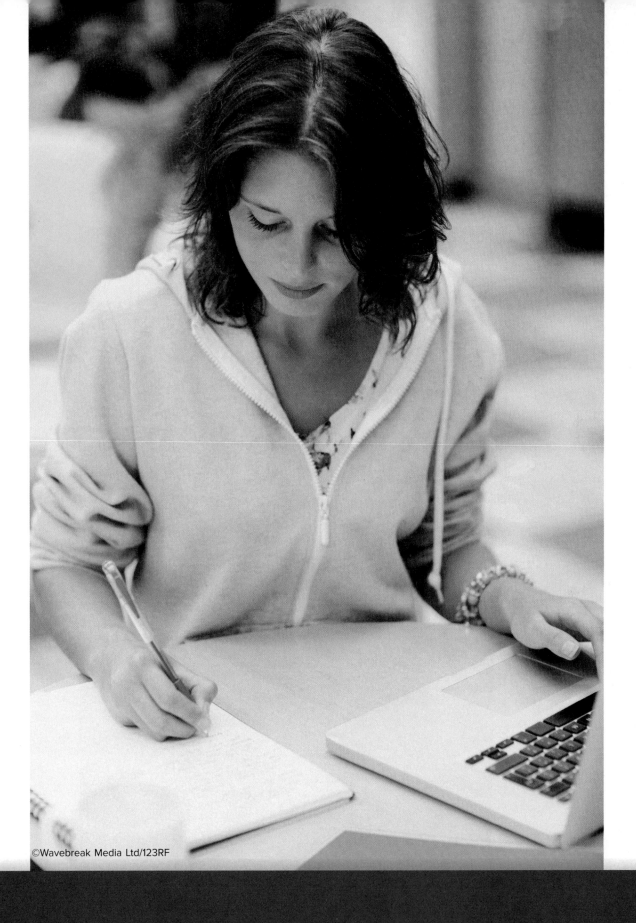

Exemplification

TEACHING TIP
Ask students to complete this writing prompt in class.

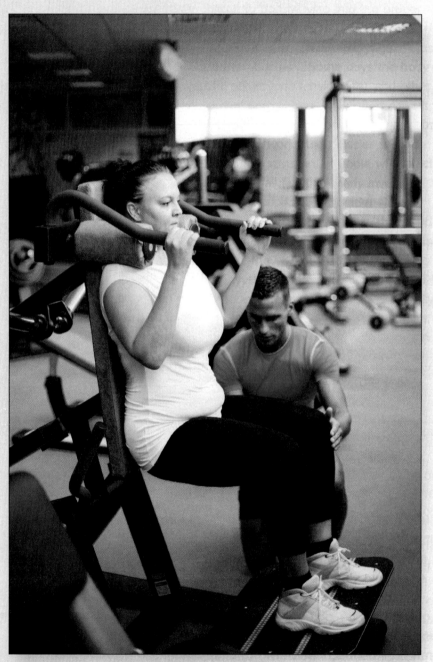

©Peter Bernik/Shutterstock

RESPONDING TO IMAGES

Most of us have gone on a diet or intended to do so. Are we as a nation obsessed with losing weight? Write a paragraph in which you answer this question. To support your point, use examples from what you have seen on TV, read in magazines and on Web sites, and experienced in your own life.

In our daily conversations, we often provide *examples*—that is, details, particulars, specific instances—to explain statements that we make. Consider the several statements and supporting examples in the box that follows:

Statement	Examples
Wal-Mart was crowded today.	There were at least four carts waiting at each of the checkout counters, and it took me forty-five minutes to get through a line.
The new shirt I bought is poorly made.	When I washed it, the colors began to fade, one button cracked and another fell off, a shoulder seam opened, and the sleeves shrank almost two inches.
My son Peter is unreliable.	If I depend on him to turn off a pot of beans in ten minutes, the family is likely to eat burned beans. If I ask him to turn down the thermostat before he goes to bed, the heat is likely to stay on all night.

In each case, the examples help us *see for ourselves* the truth of the statement that has been made. In paragraphs, too, explanatory examples help the audience fully understand a point. Lively, specific examples also add interest to a paper.

In this chapter, you will be asked to provide a series of examples to support a topic sentence. Providing examples to support a point is one of the most common and simplest methods of paragraph development. First read the paragraphs, they both use examples to develop their points. Then answer the questions that follow.

Paragraphs to Consider

World Cup Traveling Woes

¹Every four years, the world's largest sporting event, the FIFA World Cup, takes place, and when it does, tourists need to be aware of the changes that overcome the football-crazed countries. ²Countries like England and Spain, which don't have many World Cup Championship wins, witness their citizens temporarily leaving their jobs and homes to fly all over the world, cheering on their teams to hopeful victories. ³Although it may not seem like a big problem, this can often lead to limited services, flight cost increases, and crowded airports. ⁴Other countries that didn't make it into the tournament have citizens who become focused on cheering for befriended countries and cheering against rival countries, often causing crowding in the streets. ⁵During the 2010 World Cup tournament, the Czech Republic and Austria were busy watching how neighboring Germany's standing was affected, leading to very crowded streets and bars during each match that affected Germany's standing. ⁶This severely affected

continued

tourists' abilities to get around town during these time periods. [7]Countries like Germany, which has been in the top four eleven time, (four as a unified country), also set up large Jumbotrons in city squares, pub parking lots, and in front of historic castles to provide all citizens the opportunity to watch their countries represented on the field. [8]Although these mass viewings can be quite an experience for tourists, they can make it extremely difficult to visit the castles, museums, and sites that are on the planned itineraries. [9]The large TV screens are often ugly and don't fit in with the surrounding architecture. [10]Finally, countries like Italy, which has won the cup four times, become so focused during matches that businesses will close down or just refuse to serve customers until the match is over. [11]Regardless of how much tourists are willing to pay, they are not going to be able to make their purchase or visit the site while the match is on. [12]Tourists who are traveling during the World Cup have two choices: join in the festivities with the locals or be met with closed amenities and refused service for the duration of the matches.

Office Politics

[1]Office politics is a destructive game played by several types of people. [2]For instance, two supervisors may get into a conflict over how to do a certain job. [3]Instead of working out an agreement like adults, they carry on a power struggle that turns the poor employees under them into human Ping-Pong balls being swatted between two angry players. [4]Another common example of office politics is the ambitious worker who takes credit for other people's ideas. [5]He or she will chat in a "friendly" fashion with inexperienced employees, getting their ideas about how to run the office more smoothly. [6]Within minutes, Mr. or Ms. Idea-Stealer is having a closed-door session with the boss and getting promotion points for his or her "wonderful creativity." [7]Yet another illustration of office politics is the spy. [8]This employee acts very buddy-buddy with other workers, often dropping little comments about things he or she doesn't like in the workplace. [9]The spy encourages people to talk about their problems at work, how they don't like their boss, the pay, and the working conditions. [10]Then the spy goes straight back and repeats all he or she has heard to the boss, and the employees get blamed for their "poor attitude." [11]A final example of office politics is people who gossip. [12]Too often, office politics can turn a perfectly fine work situation into a stressful one.

QUESTIONS

About Unity

1. Which sentence in "World Cup Traveling Woes" is irrelevant to the point that tourists should be aware of the changes in countries during the World Cup?   8

About Support

2. In "World Cup Traveling Woes," what are some of the specific examples of changes tourists should be aware of?

Answers will vary

3. After which sentence in "Office Politics" are specific details needed?

11

About Coherence

4. What are the four transition words or phrases that are used to introduce each new example in "Office Politics"?

For instance   Another   Yet another   A final example

5. Which paragraph clearly uses emphatic order to organize its details, saving for last what the writer regards as the most important example?

"World Cup Traveling Woes"

Developing an Exemplification Paragraph

Development through Prewriting

Backing up your statements with clear, specific illustrations is the key to a successful exemplification paragraph. When Isabella, the writer of "Office Politics," was assigned an exemplification paragraph, she at first did not know what to write about.

Then her teacher made a suggestion. "Imagine yourself having lunch with some friends," the teacher said. "You're telling them *how* you feel about something and *why*. Maybe you're saying, 'I am so mad at my boyfriend!' or 'My new apartment is really great.' You wouldn't stop there—you'd continue by saying what your boyfriend does that is annoying, or in what way your apartment is nice. In other words, you'd be making a general point and backing it up with examples. That's what you need to do in this paper."

That night, Isabella was on the phone with her brother. She was complaining about the office where she worked. "Suddenly I realized what I was doing," Isabella said. "I was making a statement—I hate the politics in my office—and giving examples of those politics. I knew what I could write about!"

Isabella began preparing to write her paragraph by freewriting. She gave herself ten minutes to write down everything she could think of on the subject of politics in her office. This is what she wrote:

> Of all the places I've ever worked this one is the worst that way. Cant trust anybody there-everybody's playing some sort of game. Worst one of all is Bradley and the way he pretends to be friendly with people. Gets them to complain about Ms. Bennett and Mr. Hankins and then runs back to them

TEACHING TIP
You may want to provide a supplemental activity. First, ask students to freewrite for ten minutes about the politics in your classroom.

continued

and reports everything. He should realize that people are catching on to his game and figureing out what a jerk he is. Melissa steals people's ideas and then takes credit for them. Anything to get brownie points. She's always out for herself first you can tell. Then there's all the gossip that goes on. You think you're in a soap opera or something, and its kind of fun in a way but it also is very distracting people always talking about each other and worrying about what they say about you. And people talk about our bosses a lot. Nobody knows why Ms. Bennett and Mr. Hankins hate each other so much but they each want the workers on their sides. You do something one boss's way, but then the other boss appears and is angry that you're not doing it another way. You don't know what to do at times to keep people happy.

TEACHING TIP
Now ask students to create a scratch outline.

Isabella read over her freewriting and then spent some time asking questions about her paragraph. "Exactly what do I want my point to be?" she asked. "And exactly how am I going to support that point?" Keeping those points in mind, she worked on several scratch outlines and wound up with the following:

Office politics ruining the office
- Bradley reports people's complaints
- Melissa steals ideas
- people gossip
- Ms. Bennett and Mr. Hankins make workers choose sides

Working from this outline, she then wrote the following first draft:

TEACHING TIP
Next, ask students to write a draft.

My office is being ruined by office politics. It seems like everybody is trying to play some sort of game to get ahead and don't care what it does to anybody else. One example is Bradley. Although he pretends to be friendly with people he isn't sincere. What he is trying to do is get them to complain

continued

about their bosses. Once they do, he goes back to the bosses and tells them what's been said and gets the worker in trouble. I've seen the same kind of thing happen at two other offices where I've worked. Melissa is another example of someone who plays office politics games. She steals other people's ideas and takes the credit for them. I had a good idea about a new piece of software I thought could save employees time. She went to Ms. Bennett and pretended the idea was hers. I guess I was partly to blame for not acting on the idea myself. And Ms. Bennett and Mr. Hankins hate each other and try to get us to take sides in their conflict. Then there is all the gossip that goes on. People do a lot of backbiting, and you have to be very careful about your behavior or people will start talking about you. All in all, office politics is really a problem where I work.

TEACHING TIP
Ask students to read their drafts to a partner and discuss how their drafts might be revised.

Development through Revising

After completing her first draft, Isabella put it aside until the next day. When she reread it, this was her response:

> "I think the paragraph would be stronger if I made it about office politics in general instead of just politics in my office. The things I was writing about happen in many offices, not just in mine. And our instructor wants us to try some third-person writing. Also, I need to make better use of transitions to help the reader follow as I move from one example to another."

With these thoughts in mind, Isabella began revising her paper, and after several drafts she produced the paragraph that appears at the beginning of this chapter.

Writing an Exemplification Paragraph

DESCRIBING AN INDIVIDUAL

WRITING ASSIGNMENT 1

Write an exemplification paragraph about one quality of a person you know well. The person might be a member of your family, a friend, a roommate, a boss or supervisor, a neighbor, an instructor, or someone else. Here is a list of descriptions that you might consider choosing from. Feel free to choose another description that does not appear here.

Honest	Hardworking	Jealous
Bad-tempered	Supportive	Materialistic
Ambitious	Suspicious	Sarcastic
Prejudiced	Open-minded	Self-centered
Considerate	Lazy	Spineless
Argumentative	Independent	Good-humored
Softhearted	Stubborn	Cooperative
Energetic	Flirtatious	Self-disciplined
Patient	Irresponsible	Sentimental
Reliable	Stingy	Defensive
Generous	Trustworthy	Dishonest
Persistent	Aggressive	Insensitive
Shy	Courageous	Unpretentious
Sloppy	Compulsive	Tidy

PREWRITING

a.   Select the individual you will write about and the quality of this person that you will focus on. For example, you might choose a self-disciplined cousin. Her quality of self-discipline will then be the point of your paragraph.

b.   Decide if you want your paragraph to be informative, persuasive, or entertaining. Here are some questions to consider: Do you want your readers to understand the person better? Do you want to convince your readers to agree with you? Do you want to amuse them by providing humorous details? Keep in mind that your paragraph can combine purposes.

c.   Make a list of examples that will support your point. A list for the self-disciplined cousin might look like this:

   Exercises every day for forty-five minutes

   Never lets herself watch TV until homework is done

   Keeps herself on a strict budget

   Organizes her school papers in color-coordinated notebooks

   Eats no more than one dessert every week

   Balances her checkbook the day her statement arrives

d.   Read over your list and see how you might group the items into categories. The list above, for example, could be broken into three categories: schoolwork, fitness, and money.

   Exercises every day for forty-five minutes (fitness)

Never lets herself watch TV until homework is done (schoolwork)

Keeps herself on a strict budget (money)

Organizes her school papers in color-coordinated notebooks (schoolwork)

Eats no more than one dessert every week (fitness)

Balances her checkbook the day her bank statement arrives (money)

e. Prepare an outline made up of the details you've generated, with those details grouped into appropriate categories.

1. <u>Self-disciplined about fitness</u>
   A. Exercises every day for forty-five minutes
   B. Eats no more than one dessert every week
2. <u>Self-disciplined about schoolwork</u>
   A. Never lets herself watch TV until homework is done
   B. Organizes her school papers in color-coordinated notebooks
3. <u>Self-disciplined about money</u>
   A. Keeps herself on a strict budget
   B. Balances her checkbook the day her bank statement arrives

f. Write the topic sentence of your paragraph. You should include the name of the person you're writing about, your relationship to that person, and the specific quality you are focusing on. For example, you might write, "Keisha, a schoolmate of mine, is very flirtatious," or "Stubbornness is Uncle Carl's outstanding characteristic." And a topic sentence for the paragraph about the self-disciplined cousin might be "My cousin Mari is extremely self-disciplined."

   Remember to focus on only *one* characteristic. Also remember to focus on a *specific* quality, not a vague, general quality. For instance, "My English instructor is a nice person" is too general.

g. Now you have a topic sentence and an outline and are ready to write the first draft of your paragraph. Remember, as you flesh out the examples, your goal is not just to *tell* us about the person but to *show* us the person by detailing his or her words, actions, or both.

in a writer's words

" *Don't tell me the moon is shining; show me the glint of light on broken glass.* "

—Anton Chekhov

REVISING: PEER REVIEW

It's hard to criticize your own work honestly, especially just after you've finished writing. If at all possible, put your paragraph away for a day or so and then return to it. Better yet, wait a day and then read it aloud to a friend or classmate whose judgment you trust and ask that person to comment on your work using the FOUR BASES Checklist provided at the end of the chapter. Continue revising your work until you and your reader can answer "yes" to all the checklist questions.

©Jacob Lund/ Shutterstock

ASSIGNMENT 2

TEACHING TIP
For the following writing
assignments, encourage
your students to use the
prewriting and revising
ideas mentioned in Writing
Assignment 1.

SUPPORTING A STATEMENT

Write a paragraph that uses examples to develop one of the following statements or a related statement of your own.

1. The daily life of a college student is filled with conflicts.
2. The Internet cannot always be a trusted source of information.
3. Every student needs to have good computer skills in college.
4. Students attend college for various reasons.
5. One of my instructors, _____, has some good (*or* unusual) teaching techniques.
6. Travel is a great way to broaden someone's way of thinking.
7. Colleges have resources to help students succeed.
8. Apple and Microsoft should offer their products for free.
9. Dating in the workplace can be difficult.
10. Some students at _____ do not care about learning (*or* are overly concerned about grades).

Be sure to choose examples that truly support your topic sentence. They should be relevant facts, statistics, personal experiences, or incidents you have heard or read about. Organize your paragraph by listing several examples that support your point. Save the most vivid, most convincing, or most important example for last.

WRITING
ASSIGNMENT 3

PLANNING YOUR FUTURE

Write a paragraph that tells what you are majoring in and what you plan to do in your chosen field. In your paragraph you should include details that explain how you decided to enter this field and major influences on your decision. In order to provide added interest to your paragraph, you may want to refer to Chapter 7, "Narration," to read how to incorporate anecdotes into your support. Your topic sentence should include what it is you are majoring in and what you plan to go into.

"I am studying to get a B.S. in Civil Engineering, so I can become a highway designer."

"I am going to college to get a bachelor's degree in nursing because I want to become an emergency room nurse."

WRITING
ASSIGNMENT 4

EXPLAINING POOR CHOICES

The diet of many Americans is not healthy. We eat too much junk food and consume far too much cholesterol. Write a paragraph with a topic sentence like one of the following:

The diet of the average American is unhealthy.

The diet of many American families is unhealthy.

Many schoolchildren in America do not have a healthy diet.

Using strategies described in Chapter 21, "Writing a Research Paper," research the topic with keywords such as "unhealthy American diets." Combine information you find with your own observations to provide a series of examples that support your point.

REFLECTIVE ACTIVITY

©mavo/Shutterstock

1. Review the exemplification paragraph you wrote for Writing Assignment 2. Do you have a clear topic sentence? What is the point you are making in this sentence?

2. Now that you are rereading the paragraph, do you find that it is easy to follow? In other words, have you maintained unity and coherence? What might you add to improve unity and coherence, as explained in this chapter?

3. Check the paragraph's sentences. Are the words they contain specific and clear, or are they general and vague? What can you do to add more specific detail?

4. Are you being wordy? Are there words you can remove without changing the meaning of the paragraph or reducing its effectiveness?

BEYOND THE CLASSROOM

Exemplification

Work

ESL NOTE
Provide several topics that will enable nonnative speakers to explore their own experiences about their culture or native country.

Beyond the classroom, you will find yourself and others providing specific examples to illustrate a point that you have made. A supervisor who is working on a promotion recommendation for a loyal and diligent employee might cite examples of that employee's ability to solve problems or of her willingness to cooperate with others in a team effort. A plant manager might issue safety instructions that list examples of the kinds of behavior or work habits that cause injuries. A doctor might use examples to warn a patient about the various side effects he or she could experience after taking a drug.

For this writing assignment, you will write an exemplification paragraph with a specific purpose and for a specific audience.

Imagine that you are working as a certified nursing assistant in a hospital. A patient will go home in a few days, and you need to provide his or her family with follow-up instructions. Some areas you might consider are diet, medications, and hygiene. What point do you want to emphasize, and what examples will you use to help the patient's family understand the importance of proper care at home? Write your instructions in a paragraph.

EXPLORING WRITING ONLINE

©Tetra Images/
Shutterstock

Visit *This Day in History* at http://www.history.com/this-day-in-history.do to find out what happened on the day you were born. As you learn more about these events in history, think about how you would describe this day to someone. Then write a paragraph in which you make a point about this day and provide three examples. For example, your topic sentence might say, "Famous people were born on March 6."

OR

Visit *StopBullying.gov* at https://www.stopbullying.gov/ to learn about what the government has defined as bullying, how to prevent it, and what resources are available to help. Then write a paragraph in which you explain what you have learned.

EXEMPLIFICATION CHECKLIST: THE FOUR BASES

UNITY

✔ Have I included a topic sentence that illustrates the topic I am going to discuss?

✔ Do the examples support my topic sentence? Are there any that should be eliminated or rewritten?

SUPPORT

✔ Have I included enough vivid details that will help my readers understand the point I am trying to make?

✔ Does my concluding sentence clearly tie up the paragraph and explain why my topic is significant?

COHERENCE

✔ Are my details organized into clearly defined categories?

✔ Have I used transitional words such as *also*, *in addition*, *for example*, and *for instance* to help my reader follow my train of thought?

SENTENCE SKILLS

✔ Have I used a consistent point of view throughout my paragraph?

✔ Have I used specific rather than general words?

✔ Have I avoided wordiness and been concise?

✔ Are my sentences varied?

✔ Have I edited for spelling and other sentence skills errors, as listed on the inside back cover of the book?

Narration

©Al Bello/Getty Images

Paragraphs to Consider

Developing a Narrative Paragraph

Writing a Narrative Paragraph

RESPONDING TO IMAGES

When we watch an athlete win, we share in that person's victory. Look at this photo and write a paragraph about a time you experienced triumph in sports or some other area. How did the experience make you feel? In telling your story, be sure to provide vivid details so that your readers can see and understand why you felt the way you did.

TEACHING TIP
Ask students to complete this writing prompt in class.

At times we make a statement clear by relating in detail something that has happened. In the story we tell, we present the details in the order in which they happened. A person might say, for example, "I was embarrassed yesterday," and then go on to illustrate the statement with the following narrative:

> I was hurrying across campus to get to a class. It had rained heavily all morning, so I was hopscotching my way around puddles in the pathway. I called to two friends ahead to wait for me, and right before I caught up to them, I came to a large puddle that covered the entire path. I had to make a quick choice of either stepping into the puddle or trying to jump over it. I jumped, wanting to seem cool, since my friends were watching, but didn't clear the puddle. Water splashed everywhere, drenching my shoe, sock, and pants cuff, and spraying the pants of my friends as well. "Well done, Dave!" they said. My embarrassment was all the greater because I had tried to look so casual.

Narrative writing is enhanced by the inclusion of *dialogue* (the words that characters speak) and vivid *description*. In this paragraph, the author uses both dialogue and detailed description to help make his moment of embarrassment intense and real for us, allowing us to see and understand just why he felt as he did. For example, instead of saying he was walking around puddles, he describes his actions as "hopscotching" to provide extra context for his decision to jump over rather than step around the large puddle. He also describes exactly how wet he and his friends got by using the word *drenching* and pointing out explicitly how many pieces of clothing got splashed. Both dialogue and detailed descriptions can help create a dynamic narrative story that will interest your reader.

In this section, you will be asked to tell a story that illustrates or explains some point. The paragraphs below present narrative experiences that support a point. Read them and then answer the questions that follow.

Paragraphs to Consider

Heartbreak

¹Emily and I had gotten engaged in August, just before she left for college at Penn State. ²A week before Thanksgiving, I drove up to see her as a surprise. ³When I knocked on the door of her dorm room, she was indeed surprised, but not in a pleasant way. ⁴She introduced me to her roommate, who looked uncomfortable and quickly left. ⁵I asked Emily how classes were going, and at the same time I tugged on the sleeve of my heavy sweater in order to pull it off. ⁶As I was slipping it over my head, I noticed a large photo on the wall—of Emily and a tall guy laughing together. ⁷It was decorated with paper flowers and a yellow ribbon, and on the ribbon was written "Emily and Blake." ⁸"What's going on?" I said. ⁹I stood there stunned and then felt anger that grew rapidly. ¹⁰"Who is Blake?"

continued

ESL NOTE
In some cultures, digressions are acceptable in written expression. In a narrative, some nonnative speakers may add a lot of unrelated events that are not relevant to the development of a narrative. To achieve unity, suggest that students review their writing and eliminate details that don't explain or illustrate the point of the story or experience.

I asked. [11]Emily laughed nervously and said, "What do you want to hear about—my classes or Blake?" [12]I don't really remember what she then told me, except that Blake was a sophomore computer science major. [13]I felt a terrible pain in the pit of my stomach, and I wanted to rest my head on someone's shoulder and cry. [14]I wanted to tear down the sign and run out, but I did nothing. [15]Clumsily I pulled on my sweater again. [16]My knees felt weak, and I barely had control of my body. [17]I opened the room door, and suddenly more than anything I wanted to slam the door shut so hard that the dorm walls would collapse. [18]Instead, I managed to close the door quietly. [19]I walked away understanding what was meant by a broken heart.

Losing My Father

[1]Although my father died ten years ago, I felt that he'd been lost to me four years earlier. [2]Dad had been diagnosed with Alzheimer's disease, an illness that destroys the memory. [3]He couldn't work any longer, but in his own home he got along pretty well. [4]I lived hundreds of miles away and wasn't able to see my parents often. [5]So when my first child was a few weeks old, I flew home with the baby to visit them. [6]After Mom met us at the airport, we picked up Dad and went to their favorite local restaurant. [7]Dad was quiet, but kind and gentle as always, and he seemed glad to see me and his new little grandson. [8]Everyone went to bed early. [9]In the morning, Mom left for work. [10]I puttered happily around in my old bedroom. [11]I heard Dad shuffling around in the kitchen, making coffee. [12]Eventually I realized that he was pacing back and forth at the foot of the stairs as if he were uneasy. [13]I called down to him, "Everything all right there? [14]I'll be down in a minute." [15]"Fine!" he called back, with forced-sounding cheerfulness. [16]Then he stopped pacing and called up to me, "I must be getting old and forgetful. [17]When did you get here?" [18]I was surprised, but made myself answer calmly. [19]"Yesterday afternoon. [20]Remember, Mom met us at the airport, and then we went to The Skillet for dinner." [21]"Oh, yes," he said. [22]"I had roast beef." [23]I began to relax. [24]But then he continued, hesitantly, "And ... who are you?" [25]My breath stopped as if I'd been punched in the stomach. [26]When I could steady my voice, I answered, "I'm Laura; I'm your daughter. [27]I'm here with my baby son, Max." [28]"Oh," is all he said. [29]"Oh." [30]And he wandered into the living room and sat down. [31]In a few minutes I joined him and found him staring blankly out the window. [32]He was a polite host, asking if I wanted anything to eat, and if the room was too cold. [33]I answered with an aching heart, mourning for his loss and for mine.

in a writer's words

" The idea is to write it so that people hear it and it slides right through the brain and goes straight to the heart."

—Maya Angelou

QUESTIONS

About Unity

1. Which paragraph lacks a topic sentence?

   "Heartbreak"

   Write a topic sentence for the paragraph.

   One possibility: "Finding out that my girlfriend didn't love me was a

   heartbreaking experience."

Answers will vary.

TEACHING TIP
Ask students to explain how or why these details tugged at their emotions. If they can examine how powerful words can be, they are more likely to use those strategies.

About Support

2. What is for you the best (most real and vivid) detail or image in the paragraph "Heartbreak"?

   _____

   _____

3. What is the best detail or image in "Losing My Father"?

   _____

   _____

About Coherence

4. Do the two paragraphs use time order or emphatic order to organize details?

   Time order

Developing a Narrative Paragraph

Development through Prewriting

TEACHING TIP
You may want to provide a supplemental activity. Have students narrate an incident in college that made them feel either proud or ashamed. First, ask them to do some freewriting.

Tristan's instructor was helping her students think of topics for their narrative paragraphs. "A narrative is simply a story that illustrates a point," she said. "That point is often about an emotion you felt. Looking at a list of emotions may help you think of a topic. Ask yourself what incident in your life has made you feel any of these emotions."

The instructor then jotted these feelings on the board:

Anger	Thankfulness
Embarrassment	Loneliness
Jealousy	Sadness
Amusement	Terror
Confusion	Relief

As Tristan looked over the list, he thought of several experiences in his life. "The word 'angry' made me think about a time when I was a kid. My brother took my skateboard without permission and left it in the park, where it got stolen. 'Amused' made me think of when I watched my roommate, who claimed he spoke Spanish, try to bargain with a street vendor in Mexico. He got so flustered that he ended up paying even more than the vendor had originally asked for. When I got to 'sad,' though, I thought about when I visited Emily and found out she was dating someone else. 'Sad' wasn't a strong enough word, though—I was heartbroken. So I decided to write about heartbreak."

Tristan's first step was to do some freewriting. Without worrying about spelling or grammar, he simply wrote down everything that came into his mind concerning his visit with Emily. Here is what he came up with:

> I hadn't expected to see Emily until Christmas. We'd got engaged just before she went off to college. The drive to penn state took ten hours each way and that seemed like to much driving for just a weekend visit. But I realized I had a long weekend over thanksgiving I decided to surprise her. I think down deep I knew something was wrong. She had sounded sort of cool on the phone and she hadn't been writing as often. I guess I wanted to convince myself that everything was OK. We'd been dating since we were 16 and I couldn't imagine not being with her. When I knocked at her dorm door I remember how she was smiling when she opened the door. Her expresion changed to one of surprise. Not happy surprise. I hugged her and she sort of hugged me back but like you'd hug your brother. Another girl was in the room. Emily said, "This is Eva," and Eva shot out of the room like I had a disease. Everything seemed wrong and confused. I started taking off my sweater and then I saw it. On a bulletin board was this photo of Emily with Blake, the guy she had been messing around with. They broke up about a year later, but by then I never wanted to see Emily again. I couldn't believe Emily would start seeing somebody else when we were planing to get married. It had even been her idea to get engaged. Before she left for college. Later on I realized that wasn't the first dishonest thing she'd done. I got out of there as quick as I could.

TEACHING TIP
Next, ask them to write their first draft.

Development through Revising

Tristan knew that the first, freewritten version of his paragraph needed work. Here are the comments he made after he reread it the following day:

"Although my point is supposed to be that my visit to Emily was heartbreaking, I didn't really get that across. I need to say more about how the experience felt.

"I've included some information that doesn't really support my point. For instance, what happened to Emily and Blake later isn't important here. Also, I think I spend too much time explaining the

TEACHING TIP
Ask students to read their drafts to a partner and discuss how their draft might be revised.

ESL NOTE
Nonnative speakers may benefit from reviewing grammatical structures that help them achieve coherence and grammatical accuracy in writing (e.g., the simple present and past verb tenses, adverbials of time and sequence, and prepositions in time expressions).

WRITING ASSIGNMENT 1

TEACHING TIP
You may want to discuss third-person point of view in preparation for this writing activity.

TEACHING TIP
You may want to model the writing process for your students by doing this assignment along with them. Go through all the stages, including prewriting and revising, and seek feedback from them. They will appreciate your efforts to create a writing community.

circumstances of the visit. I need to get more quickly to the point where I arrived at Emily's dorm.

"I think I should include more dialogue, too. That would make the reader feel more like a witness to what really happened."

With this self-critique in mind, Tristan revised his paragraph until he had produced the version that appears at the beginning of this chapter.

Writing a Narrative Paragraph

OBSERVING EVENTS

Narrate a real-life event you have witnessed. Listed below are some places where interesting personal interactions often happen. Think of an event that you saw happen at one of these places, or visit one of them and take notes on an incident to write about.

The traffic court or small-claims court in your area

The dinner table at your or someone else's home

A waiting line at a supermarket, unemployment office, ticket counter, movie theater, or cafeteria

A doctor's office

An audience at a movie, concert, or sports event

A classroom

A restaurant

A student lounge

PREWRITING

a.   Decide what point you will make about the incident. What one word or phrase characterizes the scene you witnessed? Your narration of the incident will emphasize that characteristic.

b.   Write your topic sentence. The topic sentence should state where the incident happened as well as your point about it. Here are some possibilities:

I witnessed a *heartwarming* incident at Taco Bell yesterday.

Two fans at last week's baseball game got into a *hilarious* argument.

The scene at our family dinner table Monday was one of complete *confusion.*

A *painful* dispute went on in Atlantic County small-claims court yesterday.

c.   Use the questioning technique to remind yourself of details that will make your narrative come alive. Ask yourself questions like these and write down your answers:

Whom was I observing?

How were they dressed?

What were their facial expressions like?

What tones of voice did they use?

What did I hear them say?

d. Drawing details from the notes you have written, write the first draft of your paragraph. Remember to use time signals such as *then, after that, during, meanwhile,* and *finally* to connect one sentence to another.

REVISING: PEER REVIEW

After you have put your paragraph away for a day, read it to a friend or classmate who will give you honest feedback. You and your reader should then consider the questions in the FOUR BASES Checklist at the end of the chapter. Continue revising your work until you and your reader can answer "yes" to all the questions in the Checklist.

©Jacob Lund/
Shutterstock

EXPLAINING AN INCIDENT

In a story, something happens. Stories are often written in first person, from the point of view of the narrator. For this assignment, tell a story about something that happened to you.

Make sure that your story has a point, expressed in the first sentence of the paragraph. If necessary, tailor your narrative to fit your purpose. Use time order to organize your details (*first* this happened; *then* this; *after* that, this; *next*, this; and so on). Concentrate on providing as many specific details as possible so that the reader can really share your experience. Try to make it as vivid for the reader as it was for you when you first experienced it.

Choose one of the topics below. Whichever topic you choose, remember that your story must illustrate or support a point stated in the first sentence of your paragraph.

a. Think of a time when you achieved a personal goal. Some ideas might include being accepted into college, gaining employment at your dream job, or purchasing your first home. Tell the story of why this was an important goal and how you achieved it.

b. Think of a time when you disagreed with someone else's decision and decided to speak up against it. Some ideas might include a time a teacher gave you a grade you disagreed with, when a city implemented a new law you didn't like, or a neighbor painted his or her house in an unbearable color. In your story, explain how the decision was made, why you disagreed with it, how you stood up against it, and why it was important for you.

c. Think of a time when you stood up for yourself and/or your beliefs. Some ideas might be supporting a political candidate you like by canvassing neighborhoods, rallying support for someone being persecuted, or participating in an organized protest. In your story show why it was important for you to make the stand and how it affected you afterward.

d. Think of a time when you taught a skill, idea, or subject to another person. Some ideas might be teaching a child how to read or write, explaining a church tradition to a new parishioner, or teaching a friend about a class you are taking. Tell the story of what you taught, how you taught it, and why it needed to be taught.

WRITING ASSIGNMENT 2

Personal

TEACHING TIP
You may want to discuss first-person point of view in preparation for this writing activity.

WRITING ASSIGNMENT 3

TEACHING TIP
Encourage students to use the prewriting and revising ideas mentioned in Writing Assignment 1.

SUGGESTING A SOLUTION

Write a one-paragraph e-mail to your boss describing how something at the company could be done better. In your paragraph identify the problem, support it with a story that demonstrates the problem, and then suggest a possible solution. You must explain why your solution will work, so you will want to read Chapter 14, "Argument," to help you create a persuasive tone for both your story and solution. Keep in mind that writing to a boss requires formal language and detailed support. A formal e-mail also requires proper formatting that includes the sender, addressee, date, and subject matter. A sample has been provided for you in Chapter 1; refer to this e-mail for proper formatting.

BEYOND THE CLASSROOM

Narration

Beyond the classroom, there are many instances where narrative writing would be used. For example, a lifeguard might need to provide a narrative account of a swimming accident that he or she witnessed, or a sports reporter might need to narrate the key events of a sporting event.

For this writing assignment, you will write a narrative paragraph with a specific purpose and for a specific audience. You have two options.

OPTION 1 Imagine that you are a law enforcement officer at the scene of an accident or crime. You spoke to an eyewitness who saw the event, and now you must write up this person's statement. Write a paragraph in which you recount his or her story, presenting details in the order in which they happened. Begin your paragraph with a clear topic sentence that states whom you interviewed and what that person witnessed.

OPTION 2 Alternatively, imagine that you saw the accident or crime. The law enforcement officer has asked you to write a witness statement.

REFLECTIVE ACTIVITY

©mavo/Shutterstock

Review the paragraph that you wrote for Writing Assignment 1. Can you include additional descriptions to make your story more interesting? Can you add more details to support your story's topic sentence? Refer to Chapter 6 for information on examples and Chapter 8 for information on description.

EXPLORING WRITING ONLINE

©Tetra Images/Shutterstock

Visit one of these Web sites to watch a movie trailer of your choice. As you watch, think about what the movie's main point is. Then write a narration paragraph in which you state the movie's main point and include relevant details from the trailer.

Movie.com: http://www.movies.com/movie-trailers

ComingSoon.net: http://www.comingsoon.net/trailers

The Internet Movie Database: http://www.imdb.com/trailers

continued

OR

Visit the Smithsonian Institution at https://www.si.edu/ museums and explore one of the museums of your choice. Choose a piece of artwork or an artifact, such as the stamp shown in this picture, from the "Collections Sampler" and write a story about what you see happening in that artwork or artifact.

©Blank Archives/Getty Images

NARRATION CHECKLIST: THE FOUR BASES

UNITY

✔ Does my paragraph have a strongly stated topic sentence that clearly identifies a single experience or story that I am going to recount?

✔ Does each sentence help either to keep the action moving or to reveal important things about the characters?

✔ Are there sentences or details that do not support my topic sentence and therefore should be eliminated or rewritten?

SUPPORT

✔ Have I included enough vivid, exact details that will help my readers experience the event as it actually happened?

✔ Does my concluding sentence clearly tie up the story and explain why it is significant?

✔ Have I introduced one or more major characters?

COHERENCE

✔ Do transitional words and phrases—such as *first*, *later*, and *then*—help make the sequence of events clear?

SENTENCE SKILLS

✔ Have I used a consistent point of view throughout my paragraph?

✔ Have I used specific rather than general words?

✔ Have I avoided wordiness and been concise?

✔ Are my sentences varied?

✔ Have I edited for spelling and other sentence skills errors, as listed on the inside back cover of the book?

Description

TEACHING TIP
Ask students to complete this writing prompt in class.

©chrisdorney/Shutterstock

RESPONDING TO IMAGES

Imagine that you have subscribed to an online dating service, such as Bumble.com, Tinder.com, Match.com, Zoosk, eHarmony, or OurTime.com. Write a paragraph in which you describe yourself. Your goal is to give interested members of the dating service a good idea of who you are.

When you describe something or someone, you give your readers a picture in words. To make this "word picture" as vivid and real as possible, you must observe and record specific details that appeal to your readers' senses (sight, hearing, taste, smell, and touch). More than any other type of writing, a descriptive paragraph needs sharp, colorful details.

Here is a description in which only the sense of sight is used:

A rug covers the living-room floor.

In contrast, here is a description rich in sense impressions:

A thick, reddish-brown shag rug is laid wall to wall across the living-room floor. The long, curled fibers of the shag seem to whisper as you walk through them in your bare feet, and when you squeeze your toes into the deep covering, the soft fibers push back at you with a spongy resilience.

Sense impressions include sight (*thick, reddish-brown shag rug; laid wall to wall; walk through them in your bare feet; squeeze your toes into the deep covering; push back*), hearing (*whisper*), and touch (*bare feet, soft fibers, spongy resilience*). The sharp, vivid images provided by the sensory details give us a clear picture of the rug and enable us to share the writer's experience.

In this section, you will be asked to describe a person, place, or thing for your readers by using words rich in sensory details. To prepare for the assignment, first read the two paragraphs below and then answer the questions that follow.

Paragraphs to Consider

A Depressing Place

[1]The pet shop in the mall is a depressing place. [2]A display window attracts passersby who stare at the prisoners penned inside. [3]In the right-hand side of the window, two puppies press their forepaws against the glass and attempt to lick the human hands that press from the outside. [4]A cardboard barrier separates the dogs from several black-and-white kittens piled together in the opposite end of the window. [5]Inside the shop, rows of wire cages line one wall from top to bottom. [6]At first, it is hard to tell whether a bird, hamster, gerbil, cat, or dog is locked inside each cage. [7]Only an occasional movement or a clawing, shuffling sound tells visitors that living creatures are inside. [8]Running down the center of the store is a line of large wooden perches that look like coatracks. [9]When customers pass by, the parrots and mynahs chained to these perches flutter their clipped wings in a useless attempt to escape. [10]At the end of this center aisle is a large plastic tub of dirty, stagnant-looking water containing a few motionless turtles. [11]The shelves against the left-hand wall are packed with all kinds of pet-related items. [12]The smell inside the entire shop is an unpleasant mixture of strong chemical deodorizers, urine-soaked newspapers, and musty sawdust. [13]Because so many animals are crammed together, the normally pleasant, slightly milky smell of the puppies

---

continued

TEACHING TIP
Bring to class examples of descriptive writing. These examples might be found in novels, magazines, and other published sources. If your classroom has online access, find examples from Web sites. Help your students make connections.

in a writer's words

" *You can take for granted that people know more or less what a street, a shop, a beach, a sky, an oak tree look like. Tell them what makes this one different.* "

—Neil Gaiman

Academic

TEACHING TIP
Read these paragraphs aloud. Ask students to underline the topic sentence, specific examples, and transitions in each paragraph before answering the questions.

TEACHING TIP
Mixing Modes of Writing
Explain to students that this is a descriptive paragraph, but the author also creates an argument; his claim is that the pet shop is depressing, and he provides details to persuade the reader to agree.

and kittens is sour and strong. [14]The droppings inside the uncleaned birdcages give off a dry, stinging odor. [15]Visitors hurry out of the shop, anxious to feel fresh air and sunlight. [16]The animals stay on.

House for Sale!

[1]The wide porch encourages visitors to come into this awe-inspiring Craftsman-style home that was built in 2012 and is filled with details and characteristics that every new home owner should have. [2]Upon opening the front door, buyers will be greeted by a two-story foyer that opens into a formal dining room, featuring a boxed ceiling and hardwood wainscoting. [3]Off the dining room is the eat-in kitchen that boasts double-ovens, professional-grade appliances, a combined built-in buffet and wine cabinet, antiqued ceiling, and large oak table. [4]The kitchen opens into the cozy living room, which is accentuated by large French doors and a magnificent stone fireplace. [5]The master suite is also located on the main floor across from a uniquely designed half-bath. [6]A lot of people like having the master suite on the main level. [7]Bothrooms boast high ceilings and vibrantly warm colors that maintain the magnificence of this home. [8]The highlight of the home is the upstairs "kid zone." [9]A large playroom is the centerpiece, and the children's rooms all lead off this area. [10]Each of the rooms has been decorated to satisfy the whimsy of every child. [11]With lofts, hidden rooms, and undersea adventure murals, this child-focused area is a masterpiece of creativity and originality. [12]Not to be missed, the lower level of the house includes a home office, bar, media room equipped with a 70" television, and an additional play area for the children. [13]A final unique feature of this home is the carriage house located over the detached three-car garage and accessed through a beautifully designed breezeway, overlooking a little fountain bubbling in the backyard. [14]Boasting the same quality cabinetry and appliances that the main home has, the carriage house's one-bedroom apartment is a perfect getaway for guests and a perfect complement to the home.

QUESTIONS

About Unity

1. Which sentence in the paragraph about the house should be omitted in the interest of paragraph unity? (*Write the sentence number here.*)   6

About Support

2. Label as *sight, touch, hearing,* or *smell* all the sensory details in the following sentences taken from the two paragraphs. The first sentence is done for you as an example.

                    sight   hearing
   a. Only an occasional movement, or a clawing, shuffling sound tells visitors that living creatures are inside.

b. Because so many animals are crammed together, the normally pleasant, slightly milky smell of the puppies and kittens is sour and strong.
sight smell sight smell

c. The droppings inside the uncleaned birdcages give off a dry, stinging odor.
sight sight smell

d. A final unique feature of this home is the carriage house located over
the three-car garage and accessed through a beautifully designed
breezeway, overlooking a little fountain bubbling in the backyard.
sight sight sound

3. After which sentence in "A Depressing Place" are specific details
needed?   _11_

About Coherence

4. The writer of "House for Sale!" organizes the details by observing the
house in an orderly fashion. Which of the house's features is described
first? The front porch Which of the house's features is described last?
The carriage house Check the method of spatial organization that best
describes the paragraph:

_____✓_____ Exterior to interior

_____ Near to far

_____ Top to bottom

Developing a Descriptive Paragraph

Development through Prewriting

When Anthony was assigned a descriptive paragraph, he thought at first of
describing his own office at work. He began by making a list of details he
noticed while looking around the office:

adjustable black chair	computer
beige desk	pictures of Marie and kids on desk
piles of papers	desk calendar

But Anthony quickly became bored. Here is how he describes what happened
next:

"As I wrote down what I saw in my office, I was thinking, 'What a
drag.' I gave up and worked on something else. Later that evening I
told my wife that I was going to write a boring paragraph about my
boring office. She started laughing at me. I said, 'What's so funny?' and
she said, 'You're so certain that a writing assignment has to be boring
that you deliberately chose a subject that bores you. How about writing about something you care about?' At first I was annoyed, but then
I realized she was right. When I hear 'assignment' I automatically think
'pain in the neck' and just want to get it over with."

Anthony's attitude is not uncommon. Many students who are not experienced writers don't take the time to find a topic that interests them. They grab the one closest at hand and force themselves to write about it just for the sake of completing the assignment. Like Anthony they ensure that they (and probably their instructors as well) will be bored with the task.

In Anthony's case, he decided that this assignment would be different. That evening as he talked with his son, Mike, he remembered a visit the two had made to a mall a few days earlier. Mike had asked Anthony to take him to the pet store. Anthony had found the store a very unpleasant place. "As I remembered the store, I recalled a lot of descriptive details—sounds, smells, sights," Anthony said. "I realized not only that it would be easier to describe a place like that than my bland, boring office, but that I would actually find it an interesting challenge to make a reader see it through my words. For me to realize writing could be enjoyable was a real shock!"

Now that Anthony had his subject, he began making a list of details about the pet shop. Here is what he wrote:

Sawdust, animal droppings on floor

Unhappy-looking puppies and kittens

Dead fish floating in tanks

Screech of birds

Chained parrots

Tanks full of dirty water

Strong urine smell

No place for animals to play

Bored-looking clerks

Animals scratching cages for attention

As he looked over his list of details, the word that came to mind was "depressing." He decided his topic sentence would be "The pet store in the mall is depressing." He then wrote this first draft:

TEACHING TIP
Next, ask them to write their first draft.

The pet store in the mall is depressing. There are sawdust and animal droppings all over the floor. Sad-looking puppies and kittens scratch on their cages for attention. Dead fish and motionless turtles float in tanks of stagnant water. The loud screeching of birds is everywhere, and parrots with clipped wings try to escape when customers walk too near. Everywhere there is the

continued

> smell of animal urine that has soaked the sawdust and newspapers. The clerks, who should be cleaning the cages, stand around talking to each other and ignoring the animals.

Development through Revising

The next day Anthony's instructor asked to see the students' first drafts. This is what she wrote in response to Anthony's:

> This is a very good beginning. You have provided some strong details that appeal to the reader's senses of smell, hearing, and sight.
>
> In your next draft, organize your paragraph by using spatial order. In other words, describe the room in some logical physical order— maybe from left to right, or from the front of the store to its back. Such an organization mirrors the way a visitor might move through the store.
>
> I encourage you to become even more specific in your details. For instance, in what way did the puppies and kittens seem sad? As you work on each sentence, ask yourself if you can add more descriptive details to paint a more vivid picture in words.

TEACHING TIP
Ask students to read their drafts to a partner and discuss how their draft might be revised.

In response to his teacher's suggestion about a spatial method of organization, Anthony rewrote the paragraph, beginning with the display window that attracts visitors, then going on to the store's right-hand wall, the center aisle, and the left-hand wall. He ended the paragraph with a sentence that brought the reader back outside the shop. Thinking about the shop in this way enabled Anthony to remember and add a number of new specific details as well. He then wrote the version of "A Depressing Place" that appears at the beginning of this chapter.

Writing a Descriptive Paragraph

WRITING A CHARACTERIZATION

WRITING ASSIGNMENT 1

Write a paragraph describing a specific person. Select a dominant impression of the person, and use only details that will convey that impression. You might want to write about someone who falls into one of these categories.

TV or movie personality	Coworker
Instructor	Clergyman or clergywoman
Employer	Police officer
Child	Store owner or manager
Older person	Bartender
Close friend	Politician
Rival	Neighbor

TEACHING TIP
You may want to model the writing process for your students by doing this assignment along with them. Go through all the stages, including prewriting and revising, and seek feedback from them. They will appreciate your efforts to create a writing community.

PREWRITING

a. Reread the paragraph about the pet shop that appears earlier in this chapter. Note the dominant impression that the writer wanted to convey: that the pet shop is a depressing place. Having decided to focus on that impression, the writer included only details that contributed to his point. Profiling a person requires similar unity; instead of trying to tell everything about that person, you should focus on one dominant aspect of your subject's appearance, personality, or behavior.

Once you have chosen the person you will write about and the impression you plan to portray, put that information into a topic sentence. Here are some examples of topic sentences that mention a particular person and the dominant impression of that person:

Kate gives the impression of being permanently nervous.

The old man was as faded and brittle as a dying leaf.

The child was an angelic little figure.

Our high school principal resembled a cartoon character.

The TV newscaster seems as synthetic as a piece of Styrofoam.

Our neighbor is a fussy person.

The rock singer seemed to be plugged into some special kind of energy source.

The drug addict looked as lifeless as a corpse.

My friend Jeffrey is a slow, deliberate person.

The owner of that grocery store seems burdened with troubles.

b. Make a list of the person's qualities that support your topic sentence. Write quickly; don't worry if you find yourself writing down something that doesn't quite fit. You can always edit the list later. For now, just write down all the details that occur to you that support the dominant impression you want to convey. Include details that involve as many senses as possible (sight, sound, hearing, touch, smell). For instance, here's a list one writer jotted down to support the sentence "Our high school principal resembled a cartoon character":

tall with long spindly legs and arms

wore an eye-patch even though his vision was perfect

carried a briefcase

dashed everywhere, leaving a cloud of dust behind him

had a red moustache and a head of thick red curls

made a sound like a hyena when he laughed

wore lots of purple and smelled like patchouli

c. Edit your list, striking out details that don't support your topic sentence and adding others that do. The author of the paragraph on the high school principal crossed out one detail from the original list and added a new one:

tall with long spindly legs and arms

wore an eye-patch even though his vision was perfect

~~carried a briefcase~~

> dashed everywhere, leaving a cloud of dust behind him
>
> had a red moustache and a head of thick red curls
>
> made a sound like a hyena when he laughed
>
> wore lots of purple and smelled like patchouli
>
> had a huge forehead and exaggerated features

d. Decide on a spatial order of organization. In the example above, the writer ultimately decided to describe the principal from head to toe.

e. Make a scratch outline for your paragraph, based on the organization you have chosen.

f. Then proceed to write a first draft of your paragraph.

REVISING: PEER REVIEW

Put your paragraph away for a day or so if at all possible. When you return to it, read the paragraph aloud—ideally to a friend or classmate whose judgment you trust. Then work with your reader to answer the questions in the FOUR BASES Checklist at the end of the chapter. Continue revising your work until you and your reader can answer "yes" to all the questions in the Checklist.

©Jacob Lund/ Shutterstock

WRITING ABOUT MUSIC

As the picture shown here suggests, artists take great care to create an image that reflects their music. From the clothes they wear during concerts to the design of their album covers to their official Web sites, artists pay attention to every detail. In this assignment, you are to choose a music group that you enjoy and

©DWD-photo/Alamy Stock Photo

using details like those above, explain to your reader what type of music the group plays, why you relate to the music, how the music makes you feel, and when you most like to listen to that group. For added detail and interest, you may want to incorporate short stories to support your descriptive details. The purpose of this assignment is to help your reader gain a full understanding of the experience he or she would have by listening to this music group.

MARKETING A PRODUCT

Imagine that you work for a marketing firm and have to create an advertising campaign. Choose an object that you would like to sell, and then write a paragraph describing that object, how it is used, and why it would make a good purchase. Include as many sensory details as possible that will emotionally connect the buyer to the product. Once you decide on the impression you want to convey, compose a topic sentence like the one below that summarizes the details:

> Every household should not be without the amazing, all-purpose, environmentally friendly, lawn care system known as "The Goat."

Remember to provide colorful, detailed descriptions to help your readers picture the image you are writing about. Note the contrast in the two items below:

Lacks rich descriptive details: Our lawn looked really nice after it had been cut.

Includes rich descriptive details: After using "The Goat" for the first time, our lawn was only one-inch high and had a beautiful dark green color from all the natural fertilizer.

PROFILING A PLACE

Visit a place you have never gone to before and write a paragraph describing it. You may want to visit:

A restaurant

A classroom, a laboratory, an office, a workroom, or some other room in your school

A kind of store you ordinarily don't visit: for example, a hardware store, toy store, record shop, sports shop, or a particular men's or women's clothing store

A bus terminal, train station, or airport

A place of worship

A park, vacant lot, or street corner

You may want to jot down details about the place while you are there or very soon after you leave. Again, decide on a dominant impression you want to convey of the place, and use only those details that will support that impression. Follow the notes on "Prewriting" and "Revising" for Writing Assignment 1.

TEACHING TIP
Encourage students to use the prewriting and revising ideas mentioned in Writing Assignment 1.

REFLECTIVE ACTIVITY

©mavo/Shutterstock

1. Chapters 7 and 8 cover methods for narration and description, two types of writing that are related. Read each of the paragraphs you wrote for those chapters.

2. What do these paragraphs have in common? Does description appear in the narrative paragraph? Does narration appear in the descriptive paragraph? If not, find a way to include descriptive details in the narrative paragraph and narrative details in the descriptive paragraph.

Beyond the classroom, there are many circumstances that call for descriptive writing. For example, a journalist may need to use vivid, descriptive details to give his or her readers a clear mental picture of an event.

For this writing assignment, you will write a description paragraph with a specific purpose and for a specific audience. You have two options.

OPTION 1 Imagine that you are an interior designer. A new affordable-housing complex is going to be built, and you have been asked by the developers to stage the layout for a sample studio apartment. Write a paragraph describing your theme and overall concept, telling what it would include and how specific items would be arranged. You might list all the relevant needs you can think of, such as storage space, appropriate lighting, and a separate kitchen. Then put all the parts together to describe the floor plan. Use a spatial order in your paragraph to help the developers "see" the apartment. Begin your topic sentence with the words, "My design for the studio apartment offers…".

OPTION 2 As an alternative, write a paragraph describing your design for a public space. You might want to focus on a restaurant, coffee shop, night club, convenience store, preschool, playground, skate park, fitness center, or any public area of your choice.

BEYOND THE CLASSROOM

Description

Work

EXPLORING WRITING ONLINE

Visit the United States National Park Service at https://www.nps.gov/index.htm and find a park that is either located near you or one that you have always wanted to visit. Read the section dedicated to that park and view the pictures and webcams. Using the visual aids, write a description of the park from the perspective of a parks employee who is trying to bring in more visitors.

OR

Visit your favorite news site—perhaps BBC News at http://www.bbc.com/news, Fox News at http://www.foxnews.com/, or CBS News at https://www.cbsnews.com/. Find a news story that includes a visual (or visuals). Using only the visual(s), write a description from the perspective of a reporter who is explaining to the audience what is happening.

©Tetra Images/Shutterstock

DESCRIPTION CHECKLIST: THE FOUR BASES

UNITY

✔ Does my paragraph have a strongly stated topic sentence that clearly includes a dominant impression of the subject?

✔ Are there sentences or details that do not support my topic sentence and therefore should be eliminated or rewritten?

SUPPORT

✔ Have I included enough rich, specific details that appeal to a variety of senses (sight, hearing, smell, taste, touch)?

✔ Have I chosen dynamic and vibrant words that will enhance my description?

COHERENCE

✔ Do transitional words and phrases between sentences help make the description clear?

✔ Does my concluding sentence clearly tie up the paragraph and explain why this topic was significant enough to describe?

SENTENCE SKILLS

✔ Have I used a consistent point of view throughout my paragraph?

✔ Have I used specific rather than general words?

✔ Have I avoided wordiness and used concise wording?

✔ Are my sentences varied?

✔ Have I edited for spelling and other sentence skills errors, as listed on the inside back cover of the book?

Process

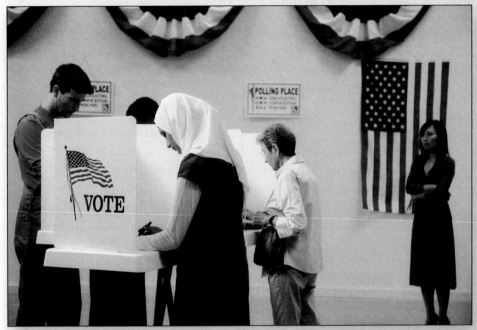

©Hill Street Studios/Getty Images

RESPONDING TO IMAGES

Every four years, a president and a vice president are elected in the United States. Each state, however, determines its own voting process. Some use paper ballots; others use electronic devices. Some provide absentee and early voting. Write a paragraph in which you explain how the voting process works—or how you think it should work—in your state.

TEACHING TIP
Ask students to complete this writing prompt in class.

TEACHING TIP
Find everyday examples of
process writing. Bring to
class several household
items, such as a shampoo
bottle, a tube of
toothpaste, and laundry
detergent. Read aloud the
directions included on
these products. Help
students make
connections.

Every day we perform many activities that are *processes*—that is, series of steps carried out in a definite order. Many of these processes are now familiar and automatic, but we first had to learn them: for example, tying shoelaces, changing bed linens, using a vending machine, and driving a car. In other cases, such as when we begin a new job, we may be painfully conscious of the whole series of steps involved in the process, and we may need to check and recheck each step that needs to be followed before we become comfortable with the process. However, once we learn the process, we are seldom aware of the sequence of steps making up each activity.

In this section, you will be asked to write a process paragraph—one that explains clearly how to do or make something. To prepare for this assignment, you should first read the student process paragraphs below and then respond to the questions that follow.

> **TIP** In process writing, you are often giving instruction to the reader, and so the pronoun *you* can appropriately be used. One of the model paragraphs here uses *you*—as indeed does much of this book, which gives instruction on how to write effectively. As a general rule, though, do not use *you* in your writing.

Paragraphs to Consider

TEACHING TIP
Read these
paragraphs aloud.
Ask students to underline
the topic sentence, specific
examples, and transitions
in each paragraph before
answering the questions.

TEACHING TIP
Mixing Modes of Writing:
Point out to students that
this process paragraph is
also a narrative.

My First Time Voting

[1]I took this more seriously than anything else I had done in my life until then. [2]I read up on the candidates and tried to see both sides of every argument. [3]I categorized how each candidate responded to my own views, especially in terms of education, the environment, and world affairs. [4]But there were other preparations to think about. [5]I made sure I had registered and that all the information on my card was accurate. [6]I also located my local precinct weeks before, to make sure I knew how to get there on Election Day. [7]I listened to the debates and the political analyses on television. [8]I discussed with my college professors and peers, all the while constructing my own arguments. [9]When Election Day finally came, I arrived at the location early. [10]Once I approached the identification table, an older woman searched for my name and verified my identity with my driver's license. [11]Once she located me on the roll, I was given instructions and a ballot. [12]Next, I was escorted to my booth. [13]I took a deep breath and began reading every line carefully and punching in my selections. [14]Before I knew it, I had gone through all the questions. [15]I reviewed all of my selections one more time before I cast my vote. [16]I've always wanted to do what was right. [17]I did very well in school and sports, and always made my parents proud. [18]After exiting the voting booth, a sticker was placed on my blouse. [19]It read, "I voted today." [20]I proudly wore that sticker all day. [21]I had voted, and no matter the outcome of the election, I truly felt like an American that day.

Dealing with Verbal Abuse

[1]If you are living with a significant other who abuses you verbally with criticism, complaints, and insults, you should take steps to change your situation. [2]First, realize that you are not to blame for the other person's abusive behavior. [3]This may be difficult for you to believe. [4]Years of verbal abuse have probably convinced you that you're responsible for everything that's wrong with the relationship. [5]But that is a lie. [6]If your partner is verbally abusive, it is his or her responsibility to learn why he or she chooses to deal with problems by saying nasty things. [7]Perhaps he observed his father treating his mother that same way. [8]Maybe she never learned positive ways to deal with negative emotions like anger, fear, or disappointment. [9]Steps two and three need to be done one right after the other. [10]Step two is for you to announce that being verbally abused will no longer be tolerated. [11]State that you are a person who deserves respect and civil behavior and that you will accept no less. [12]Next, offer to go with your partner to talk to a counselor who will help both partners learn new ways to communicate. [13]While the abuser learns to express feelings without attacking you, you can learn to stand up for yourself and express your feelings clearly. [14]If the significant other refuses to take responsibility for changing his or her abusive behavior, then you must consider step four: to leave. [15]You were not put here on earth to have your self-concept demolished by serving as someone else's verbal punching bag. [16]Getting out of an abusive relationship is not easy, but these four steps can help make it possible.

About Unity

1. Which paragraph lacks an opening topic sentence?

   "My First Time Voting"

2. Which two sentences in "My First Time Voting" should be eliminated in the interest of paragraph unity? (*Write the sentence numbers here.*)

   __16__   __17__

About Support

3. Summarize the four steps in the process of dealing with verbal abuse.

   a. Realize you are not to blame.

   b. Announce that you will no longer tolerate abuse.

   c. Offer to go with him or her to talk to a counselor.

   d. Leave him or her.

About Coherence

4. Do these paragraphs use time order or emphatic order?

   Time order

An Additional Paragraph to Consider

Learning a New Job

[1]When I began my first teaching job, it took me several months before I was able to do everything without constantly consulting my daily checklist. [2]The first thing I had to do every morning was get my classroom ready. [3]I would turn on the lights, start my computer, and check to make sure the desks were arranged properly. [4]I would consult my daily lesson plan and then make sure all the materials my class would need that day were ready and organized. [5]Then I would check my e-mail for any important messages from my principal, students, or students' parents. [6]After responding to those that required a timely response, I would then review the school schedule to remind myself what duties I had that day. [7]If I was on morning bus duty, I knew I would need to finish my tasks quickly in order to be at my station on time. [8]Once school was in session, I had to remember to take attendance, collect any parent notes and deliver them to the appropriate person, and answer the twenty questions my first-graders would ask each morning. [9]During the day, I would consult my lesson plan to be certain we were completing all the activities I had planned. [10]As we would complete one, I would check it off, so I knew we hadn't skipped it. [11]I liked using different colors on my checklist to help organize my topics. [12]Finally, in the afternoon, I had to make sure all students had their backpacks and coats, consult my transportation list so I could send each student to the proper line, and then sit down to answer more e-mails, grade students' assignments, and prepare for the next day's lessons. [13]Once I became more familiar with the daily procedures, I didn't need to constantly check my list to remind myself of my tasks.

QUESTIONS

About Unity

1. Which sentence should be eliminated in the interest of paragraph unity? (*Write the sentence number here.*)

   11

About Support

2. Summarize the tasks the teacher did before school, during school, and after school.

   a. Get classroom ready: turn on lights, start computer, check desks, ready materials, check/respond to e-mail, check daily duties

   b. Take attendance, collect/deliver parent notes, answer student questions, consult and teach lesson plans

   c. Help students get ready, consult transportation lists, answer e-mails, grade assignments, prepare for the next day

About Coherence

3. Does this paragraph use time order or emphatic order?

<u>Time order</u>

Developing a Process Paragraph

Development through Prewriting

To be successful, a process paragraph must explain clearly each step of an activity. The key to preparing to write such a paragraph is thinking through the activity as though you're doing it for the first time. Selma is the author of "Dealing with Verbal Abuse." As she considered possible topics for her paper, she soon focused on a situation in her own life: living with an abusive partner. Selma had not known how to change her situation. But with the help of a counselor, she realized there were steps she could take—a process she could follow. She carried out that process and finally left her abusive partner. Remembering this, Selma decided to write about how to deal with abuse.

TEACHING TIP
You may want to provide a supplemental activity. First, ask students to list all the steps needed to deal with a verbally abusive partner. Then ask them to use this list to create a scratch outline.

　　She began by making a list of the steps she followed in coping with her own abusive relationship. This is what she wrote:

> Tell him or her you won't accept any more abuse.
>
> Open your own checking account.
>
> Apply for credit cards in your own name.
>
> Offer to go with your partner to counseling.
>
> Realize you're not to blame.
>
> Learn to stand up for yourself.
>
> Go into counseling yourself if he or she won't do it.
>
> Call the police if he or she ever becomes violent.
>
> Leave if your partner refuses to change.

Next, she numbered the steps in the order in which she had performed them. She crossed out some items she realized weren't really part of the process of dealing with verbal abuse.

> 2　Tell him or her you won't accept any more abuse.
>
> ~~Open your own checking account.~~
>
> ~~Apply for credit cards in your own name.~~

continued

> 3 Offer to go with your partner to counseling.
>
> 1 Realize you're not to blame.
>
> 5 Learn to stand up for yourself.
>
> 4 Go into counseling yourself if he or she won't do it.
>
> ~~Call the police if he ever becomes violent.~~
>
> 6 Leave if your partner refuses to change.

Then Selma grouped her items into four steps. Those steps were (1) realize you're not to blame; (2) tell the abuser you won't accept more abuse; (3) get into counseling, preferably with him or her; and (4) if necessary, leave.

Selma was ready to write her first draft. Here it is:

TEACHING TIP
Next, ask students to write a draft.

> Some people think that "abuse" has to mean getting punched and kicked, but that's not so. Verbal abuse can be as painful inside as physical abuse is on the outside. It can make you feel worthless and sad. I know because I lived with a verbally abusive man for years. Finally I found the courage to deal with the situation. Here is what I did. With the help of friends, I finally figured out that I wasn't to blame. I thought it was my fault because that's what he always told me—that if I wasn't so stupid, he wouldn't criticize and insult me. When I told him I wanted him to stop insulting and criticizing me, he just laughed at me and told me I was a crybaby. One of my friends suggested a counselor, and I asked Harry to go talk to him with me. We went together once but Harry wouldn't go back. He said he didn't need anyone to tell him how to treat his woman. I wasn't that surprised because Harry grew up with a father who treated his mother like dirt and his mom just accepts it to this day. Even after Harry refused to go see the counselor, though, I kept going. The counselor helped me see that I couldn't make Harry change, but I was still free to make my own choices. If I didn't want to live my life being Harry's verbal punching bag, and if he didn't want to change, then I would have to. I told Harry that I wasn't going to live that way anymore. I told him if he wanted to work together on better ways to communicate, I'd work with him. But otherwise, I would leave. He gave me his

continued

usual talk about "Oh, you know I don't really mean half the stuff I say when I'm mad." I said that wasn't a good enough excuse, and that I did mean what I was saying. He got mad all over again and called me every name in the book. I stuck around for a little while after that but then realized "This is it. I can stay here and take this or I can do what I know is right for me." So I left. It was a really hard decision but it was the right one. Harry may be angry at me forever but I know now that his anger and his verbal abuse are his problem, not mine.

Development through Revising

After Selma had written her first draft, she showed it to a classmate for her comments. Here is what the classmate wrote in response:

> In order for this to be a good process essay, I think you need to do a couple of things.
>
> First, although the essay is based on what you went through, I think it's too much about your own experience. I'd suggest you take yourself out of it and just write about how any person could deal with any verbally abusive situation. Otherwise this paper is about you and Harry, not the process.
>
> Second, you need a clear topic sentence that tells the reader what process you're going to explain.
>
> Third, I'd use transitions like "first" and "next" to make the steps in the process clearer. I think the steps are all there, but they get lost in all the details about you and Harry.

TEACHING TIP
Ask students to read their drafts to a partner and discuss how their draft might be revised.

When Selma reread her first draft, she agreed with her classmate's suggestions. She then wrote the version of "Dealing with Verbal Abuse" that appears at the beginning of this chapter.

Writing a Process Paragraph

EXPLAINING HOW

Write a paragraph about one of the following processes. For this assignment, many of the topics are so broad that entire books have been written about them. A big part of your task, then, will be to narrow the topic down enough so that it can be covered in one paragraph. Then you'll have to invent your own steps for the process. In addition, you'll need to make decisions about how many steps to include and the order in which to present them.

- How to encourage someone's forgiveness
- How to gather information on a company in preparation for a job interview
- How to get along with a professor
- How to get over a broken relationship

WRITING
ASSIGNMENT 1

ESL NOTE
Additional topics for nonnative students:

- How to get a driver's license
- How to prepare for a natural disaster (flood, storm)
- How to adapt to a new country/culture

- How to improve a course you have taken
- How to improve the place where you work
- How to make someone happy
- How to procrastinate
- How to properly/improperly answer a phone at a place of business
- How to properly/improperly write an e-mail to a boss or professor
- How to show appreciation to others

PREWRITING

a. Choose a topic that appeals to you.

b. Decide if you want your paragraph to be informative, persuasive, or entertaining. Here are some questions to consider: Do you want your readers to understand this process better? Do you want to convince your readers to agree with your steps? Do you want to amuse them by providing humorous details? Keep in mind that your paragraph can combine purposes.

c. Ask yourself, "How can I make this broad, general topic narrow enough to be covered in a particular paragraph?" A logical way to proceed would be to think of a particular time you have gone through this process.

d. Make a list of as many different items as you can think of that concern your topic. Don't worry about repeating yourself, about putting the items in order, about whether details are major or minor, or about spelling. Simply make a list of everything about your topic that occurs to you. Here, for instance, is a list of items generated by a student writing about decorating her apartment on a budget:

Bought towels and used them as wall hangings

Trimmed overgrown shrubs in front yard

Used old mayonnaise jars for vases to hold flowers picked in the yard

Found an old oriental rug at a yard sale

Painted mismatched kitchen chairs in bright colors

Kept dishes washed and put away

Bought a slipcover for a battered couch

Used energy-saver lightbulbs

Hung colored sheets over the windows

e. Next, decide what order you will present your items in and number them. (As in the example of "decorating an apartment," there may not be an order that the steps *must* be done in. If that is the case, you'll need to make a decision about a sequence that makes sense, or that you followed yourself.) As you number your items, strike out items that do not fit in the list and add others that you think of, like this:

6   Bought towels and used them as wall hangings

~~Trimmed overgrown shrubs in front yard~~

7   Used old mayonnaise jars for vases to hold flowers picked in the yard

4   Found an old oriental rug at a yard sale

2   Painted mismatched kitchen chairs in bright colors

~~Kept dishes washed and put away~~

1   Bought a slipcover for a battered couch

8   Used energy-saver lightbulbs

5   Hung colored sheets over the windows

3   Built bookshelves out of cinder blocks and boards

f.   Referring to your list of steps, write the first draft of your paper. Add additional steps as they occur to you.

REVISING: PEER REVIEW

If you can, put your first draft away for a day or so and then return to it. Read it out loud to yourself or, better yet, to a friend or classmate who will give you honest feedback. Ask that person to comment on your work using the questions in the FOUR BASES Checklist at the end of this chapter as a guide. Continue revising your work until you and your reader can answer "yes" to all the questions.

©Jacob Lund/ Shutterstock

WRITING ABOUT WEIGHT GAIN

WRITING ASSIGNMENT 2

Every year, people are bombarded by advertisements promising incredible weight loss with very little effort. In this assignment, you are going to take the opposite view and write a paragraph describing how to gain weight. As the author, you could have a humorous tone and include steps like "eating until there is no food left in the fridge," or you could have a more serious tone and include steps like "ignoring the sensation of being full."

TEACHING TIP
Encourage students to use the prewriting and revising ideas mentioned in Writing Assignment 1.

ANALYZING YOUR JOB PERFORMANCE

WRITING ASSIGNMENT 3

Many employers require their employees to be reviewed each year. This often includes a self-evaluation of the employees' work over the past year. In this assignment, you are going to pretend that you are being required to assess your work over the course of the past year, focusing specifically on a new skill or task that you learned. Write a paragraph in which you discuss the steps involved in learning the new skill or task. It may be that your company introduced a new e-mail system and you had to learn how to use it, or it may be that you were promoted to a new position and had to learn some specific tasks related to that position.

REFLECTIVE ACTIVITY

Reread the process paragraph that you wrote for Writing Assignment 1. Have you explained your process enough that anyone reading your paragraph could understand each step? Can you add additional details and descriptions (Chapter 8) to make your process more clear? Is your process convincing (Chapter 14)? Could your process be enhanced by anecdotes (Chapter 7)?

©mavo/Shutterstock

BEYOND THE CLASSROOM

Process

Beyond the classroom, there are many instances where process writing is used. For example, a salesperson may need to explain to a customer how to install computer software or set up the wiring for a new TV.

For this writing assignment, you will write a process paragraph with a specific purpose and for a specific audience. You have two options.

OPTION 1 Imagine that you have a job helping out at a day-care center. The director, who is pleased with your work and wants to give you more responsibility, has put you in charge of a group activity (for example, an alphabet lesson, a playground game, or an art project). Before you actually begin the activity, the director wants to see a summary of how you would go about it. What advance preparation would be needed, and what exactly would you be doing throughout the project? Write a paragraph explaining the steps you would follow in conducting the activity.

OPTION 2 Alternatively, write an explanation you might give to the children on how to do a simple classroom task—getting ready for nap time, watering a plant, putting toys or other classroom materials away, or any task of your choice. Explain each step in a way that a child would understand.

EXPLORING WRITING ONLINE

Go to *Google Maps* at http://maps.google.com and find the directions from your home to your school. Notice the words used—such as *start, turn, merge*, and *make*—to describe specific steps. Then write a paragraph in which you write a new set of directions that provide an alternate route, one that might be quicker or more direct.

OR

Go to the *Food Network* at http://www.foodnetwork.com/recipes and find a recipe of a familiar dish. Notice the words used—such as *chop, sauté*, and *simmer*—to describe specific steps. Then write a paragraph in which you write a new set of directions for a new-and-improved recipe, one that might call for different ingredients or cooking steps.

©Tetra Images/ Shutterstock

PROCESS CHECKLIST: THE FOUR BASES

UNITY

✔ Have I included a topic sentence that clearly identifies the process I am going to discuss?

✔ Does my paragraph describe the steps in a clear, logical way?

✔ Are there sentences or details that do not support my topic sentence and therefore should be eliminated or rewritten?

SUPPORT

✔ Does my paragraph describe the necessary steps so that a reader could perform the task described?

✔ Is essential information missing that could help the reader understand the process?

COHERENCE

✔ Have I organized my paragraph in a consistent manner that is appropriate to my subject?

✔ Have I made the sequence of steps easy to follow by using transitions like *first*, *second*, *then*, *next*, *during*, and *finally*?

SENTENCE SKILLS

✔ Have I used a consistent point of view throughout my paragraph?

✔ Have I used specific rather than general words?

✔ Have I avoided wordiness and been concise?

✔ Are my sentences varied?

✔ Have I edited for spelling and other sentence skills errors, as listed on the inside back cover of the book?

CHAPTER 10

Cause and/or Effect

CHAPTER PREVIEW

Paragraphs to Consider

Developing a Cause and/or Effect Paragraph

Writing a Cause and/or Effect Paragraph

©Karl Spencer/Getty Images

RESPONDING TO IMAGES

In 2017, Hurricane Harvey devastated the Houston area, causing billions of dollars of damage and a great deal of human suffering. Write a paragraph in which you discuss the causes and/or effects of a natural disaster like a hurricane, tsunami, earthquake, or tornado. Consider such aspects as population growth and new development of previously uninhabited land, climate changes, and availability of state and federal aid.

TEACHING TIP
Ask students to complete this writing prompt in class.

What caused Todd to drop out of school? Why are soap operas so popular? Why does our football team do so poorly each year? How has retirement affected Mom and Dad? What effects does divorce have on children? Every day we ask such questions and look for answers. We realize that situations have causes and also effects—good or bad. By examining causes and effects, we seek to understand and explain things.

In this section, you will be asked to do some detective work by examining the causes of something or the effects of something. First read the two paragraphs that follow and answer the questions about them. Both paragraphs support their opening points by explaining a series of causes and/or or a series of effects.

Paragraphs to Consider

Treatment of American Indians

[1]Two major policies, the Indian Removal Act of 1830 and the Dawes Severalty Act of 1887, had profound and lasting effects on American Indians. [2]In 1830, President Andrew Jackson signed the act that authorized the United States government to transfer eastern American Indians like the Cherokee into unclaimed western territories. [3]After several years of court battles, what followed was one of the most heartbreaking events in early American history— The Trail of Tears. [4]Thousands of Cherokee men, women, and children were forced to march more than a thousand miles to Oklahoma. [5]Estimates say that at least four thousand died on the journey. [6]Then, in 1887, the Dawes Act allowed the United States government the right to divide reservation lands among individual American Indians and their families. [7]In other words, it gave plots of land to those who were willing to sign a registry, anglicize their name, and renounce allegiance to their tribe. [8]Reservations were broken up, tribes fought among themselves, and the unity that was central to tribes' survival disappeared. [9]Today, there are about three hundred reservations in the United States, but there are over five hundred recognized tribes. [10]Most reservations are located in the western portion of the United States in areas that often lack natural resources, and many have high rates of poverty and unemployment.

Why I Stopped Smoking

[1]For one thing, I realized that my cigarette smoke bothered others, irritating people's eyes and causing them to cough and sneeze. [2]They also had to put up with my stinking smoker's breath. [3]Also, cigarettes are a messy habit. [4]Our house was littered with ashtrays piled high with butts, matchsticks, and ashes, and the children were always knocking them over. [5]Cigarettes are expensive,

continued

TEACHING TIP
Bring to class everyday examples of cause and/or effect writing. These examples might be found in magazines, newspapers, and other published sources. If your classroom has online access, find examples from Web sites. Help your students make connections.

TEACHING TIP
Read these paragraphs aloud. Ask students to underline the topic sentence, specific examples, and transitions before answering the questions.

and I estimated that the carton a week that I was smoking cost me about $2,000 a year. [6]Another reason I stopped was because I felt exploited. [7]I hated the thought of wealthy, greedy corporations making money off my sweat and blood. [8]The rich may keep getting richer, but—at least as regards cigarettes—with no thanks to me. [9]Cigarettes were also inconvenient. [10]Whenever I smoked, I would have to drink something to wet my dry throat, and that meant I had to keep going to the bathroom all the time. [11]I sometimes seemed to spend whole weekends doing nothing but smoking, drinking, and going to the bathroom. [12]Most of all I resolved to stop smoking when the message about cigarettes being harmful to health finally got through to me. [13]I'd known they could hurt the smoker—in fact, a heavy smoker I know from work is in Eagleville Hospital now with lung cancer. [14]But when I realized what secondhand smoke could do to my wife and children, causing them bronchial problems and even increasing their risk of cancer, it really bothered me.

About Unity

1. Which of the above paragraphs lacks a topic sentence?

   "Why I Stopped Smoking"

About Support

2. What pieces of evidence does the author use to support the point that the Indian Removal Act and Dawes Severalty Act had lasting effects on American Indians?

   Trail of Tears and relocation

   Reservations breaking up

   Tribes fighting among themselves

   Current reservations have high rates of poverty and unemployment

3. How many separate causes are given in "Why I Stopped Smoking"?

   _____ four   _____ five   X six   _____ seven

About Coherence

4. Which sentences in "Treatment of American Indians" contain transition words or phrases? (Write the sentence numbers here.)

   3, 6, 7, 9

Developing a Cause and/or Effect Paragraph

Development through Prewriting

In order to write a good cause and/or effect paragraph, you must clearly define an effect (*what* happened) and the contributing causes (*why* it happened). In addition, you will need to provide details that support the causes and effects you're writing about.

Jackson is the student author of "Why I Stopped Smoking." As soon as the topic occurred to him, he knew he had his *effect* (he had stopped smoking). His next task was to come up with a list of *causes* (reasons he had stopped). He decided to make a list of all the reasons for his quitting smoking that he could think of. This is what he came up with:

Annoyed others	Bad for health
Messy	Expensive

Taking his list, Jackson then jotted down details that supported each of those reasons:

Annoyed others

Bad breath

Irritates eyes

Makes other people cough

People hate the smell

Messy

Ashtrays, ashes, butts everywhere

Messes up my car interior

Bad for health

Marco in hospital with lung cancer

Secondhand smoke dangerous to family

My morning cough

Expensive

Carton a week costs more than $2,000 a year

Tobacco companies getting rich off me

Jackson then had an effect and four causes with details to support them. On the basis of this list, he wrote a first draft:

My smoking annoyed other people, making them cough and burning their eyes. I bothered them with my smoker's breath. Nonsmokers usually hate the smell of

continued

TEACHING TIP
Next, ask students to write a draft.

cigarettes and I got embarrassed when nonsmokers visited my house. I saw them wrinkle their noses in disgust at the smell. It is a messy habit. My house was full of loaded ashtrays that the kids were always knocking over. My car was messy too. The price of cigarettes keeps going up and I was spending too much on smokes. When I see things in the paper about tobacco companies and their huge profits it made me mad. A guy from work, Marco, who has smoked for years, is in the hospital now with lung cancer. It doesn't look as though he's going to make it. Secondhand smoke is bad for people too and I worried it would hurt my wife and kids. Also I realized I was coughing once in a while.

Development through Revising

The next day, Jackson traded first drafts with his classmate Aiden. This is what Aiden had to say about Jackson's work:

> The biggest criticism I have is that you haven't used many transitions to tie your sentences together. Without them, the paragraph sounds like a list, not a unified piece of writing.
>
> Is one of your reasons more important than the others? If so, it would be good if you indicated that.
>
> You could add a little more detail in several places. For instance, how could secondhand smoke hurt your family? And how much were you spending on cigarettes?

As Jackson read his own paper, he realized he wanted to add one more reason to his paragraph: the inconvenience to himself. "Maybe it sounds silly to write about always getting drinks and going to the bathroom, but that's one of the ways that smoking takes over your life that you never think about when you start," he said. Jackson decided that the most important reason for quitting was health—both his family's and his own. Using Aiden's comments and his own new idea, he produced the paragraph that appears at the beginning of this chapter.

TEACHING TIP
Ask students to read their drafts to a partner and discuss how their draft might be revised.

Writing a Cause and/or Effect Paragraph

WRITING ASSIGNMENT 1

GIVING PRAISE

Most of us find it easy to criticize other people, but we may find it harder to give compliments. In this assignment, you will be asked to write a one-paragraph letter praising someone. The letter may be to a person you know (for instance, a parent, relative, or friend); to a public figure (an actor, politician, religious leader, sports star, and so on); or to a company or organization (for example, a newspaper, a government agency, a store where you shop, or the manufacturer of a product you own).

PREWRITING

a. The fact that you are writing this letter indicates that its recipient has had an *effect* on you: you like, admire, or appreciate the person or organization. Your job will be to put into words the *causes,* or reasons, for this good feeling. Begin by making a list of reasons for your admiration. Here, for example, are a few reasons a person might praise an automobile manufacturer:

> My car is dependable.
>
> The price was reasonable.
>
> I received prompt action on a complaint.
>
> The car is well designed.
>
> The car dealer was honest and friendly.
>
> The car has needed little maintenance.

Reasons for admiring a parent might include these:

> You are patient with me.
>
> You are fair.
>
> You have a great sense of humor.
>
> You encourage me in several ways.
>
> I know you have made sacrifices for me.

Develop your own list of reasons for admiring the person or organization you've chosen.

b. Now that you have a list of reasons, you need details to back up each reason. Jot down as many supporting details as you can for each reason. Here is what the writer of a letter to the car manufacturer might do:

My car is dependable.

Started during last winter's coldest days when neighbors' cars wouldn't start

Has never stranded me anywhere

The price was reasonable.

Costs less than other cars in its class

Came standard with more options than other cars of the same price

I received prompt action on a complaint.

When I complained about rattle in door, manufacturer arranged for a part to be replaced at no charge

The car is well designed.

Controls are easy to reach

Dashboard gauges are easy to read

in a writer's words

" *Write freely and as rapidly as possible and throw the whole thing on paper. Never correct or rewrite until the whole thing is down. Rewrite in process is usually found to be an excuse for not going on.* "

—John Steinbeck

The car dealer was honest and friendly.

No pressure, no fake "special deal only today"

The car has needed little maintenance.

Haven't done anything but regular tune-ups and oil changes

c. Next, select from your list the three or four reasons that you can best support with effective details. These will make up the body of your letter.

d. Now number these three or four reasons by order of importance (1 as most important). Save your most important point for last.

e. For your topic sentence, make the positive statement you wish to support. For example, the writer of the letter to the car manufacturer might begin like this: "I am a very satisfied owner of a 2012 Chevy Impala."

f. Now combine your topic sentence, reasons, and supporting details, and write a draft of your letter.

REVISING: PEER REVIEW

If possible, put your letter aside for a day. Then read it aloud to a friend or classmate. Once you have finished reading, you should both refer to the FOUR BASES Checklist at the end of this chapter for questions to consider for revision. Continue revising your work until you and your reader can answer "yes" to all the questions.

©Jacob Lund/
Shutterstock

WRITING ABOUT ADDICTION

©dolgachov/123RF

What does this picture suggest? Look at the image and write a paragraph about a particular addiction or risky behavior. You might write about someone you know who is addicted to soda, shopping, watching TV, online gambling, or thrill seeking. In your paragraph, discuss several possible reasons for this addiction, or discuss several effects on the person's life. To create a persuasive tone to your paragraph, refer to Chapter 14, "Argument," and to add support using stories, refer to Chapter 7, "Narration."

Here are some sample topic sentences for this assignment:

My cousin is addicted to overeating, and her addiction is harming her in a number of ways.

There were at least three reasons why I became addicted to cigarettes.

ANALYZING AN EVENT

Investigate the reasons behind a current news event. For example, you may want to discover the causes of one of the following:

A civilian protest against a governmental decision

A new law, policy, or tax

A traffic accident, a fire, a plane crash, or some other disaster

The popularity of a new phone, car, or other gadget

Research the reasons for the event by reading current newspapers (especially big-city dailies that are covering the story in detail) or weekly news magazines (such as *Time* and *Newsweek*), watching television shows and specials, or consulting an Internet news source.

Decide on the major cause or causes of the event and their specific effects. Then write a paragraph explaining in detail the causes and effects. To avoid any possible plagiarism, you may want to read Chapters 20 and 21 to help you properly incorporate your research material. Below is a sample topic sentence for this assignment.

The rape and murder that occurred recently on Willow Street have caused much fear and caution throughout the neighborhood.

Note how this topic sentence uses general words (*fear, caution*) that can summarize specific supporting details. Support for the word *caution,* for example, might include specific ways in which people in the neighborhood are doing a better job of protecting themselves.

WRITING ASSIGNMENT 3

ESL NOTE
This writing assignment could allow nonnative speakers to explore a current news event in their native country.

REFLECTIVE ACTIVITY

Reread the cause and/or effect paragraph you chose to write for Writing Assignment 3. Did your paragraph need only causes, effects, or both? Could you strengthen your paper by adding a mix of causes and effects or by focusing on one or the other? Would your paragraph benefit from added details like anecdotes (Chapter 7), some comparisons (Chapter 11), or more persuasive language (Chapter 14)? Choose what types of evidence will create a stronger paragraph and make the necessary revisions.

©mavo/Shutterstock

BEYOND THE CLASSROOM

Cause and/or Effect

Beyond the classroom, there are many instances where cause and/or effect writing would be used. For example, a nutritionist may have to explain to a patient the dietary causes of hypertension, or a pharmacist may have to explain the effects that a particular drug has on someone with diabetes.

For this writing assignment, you will write a cause and/or effect paragraph with a specific purpose and for a specific audience. You have two options.

OPTION 1 Assume that your boss has asked you to prepare a report about an issue that is affecting your career field. In your report, you should write what has caused this issue. For instance, nurses might be affected by a rise in workloads because of a lack of qualified nurses, budget cuts, or an increase in patients.

OPTION 2 Alternatively, think about the effects that this issue might have on your career field. Write a report to your boss indicating what the impact of this issue will be on you. For instance, nurses who have bigger workloads may be suffering exhaustion that leads to mistakes being made on the job.

EXPLORING WRITING ONLINE

©Tetra Images/
Shutterstock

Visit *The Why Files* at http://whyfiles.org/ and find an article to read. Then write a short paragraph that summarizes the causes and effects examined in your article. (For example, an article about Puerto Rico's devastation after Hurricane Maria in 2017 might attempt to explain why one of the world's largest blackouts in history occurred.)

OR

Visit *WebMD* at https://www.webmd.com/ and explore the everyday health topics discussed there. Choose a common condition and read about its causes and potential effects on the body. Then write a short paragraph that summarizes the causes and effects.

CAUSE AND/OR EFFECT CHECKLIST: THE FOUR BASES

UNITY

✔ Do I have a topic sentence that is narrow and focused and contains a claim about the causes and/or effects of my topic?

✔ Are there sentences or details that do not support my topic sentence and therefore should be eliminated or rewritten?

SUPPORT

✔ Have I backed up my main point with one extended example or several shorter examples?

✔ Do my examples clearly support the cause, effect, or both?

✔ Are there any repetitive areas that need to be revised?

COHERENCE

✔ Have I organized my paragraph in a manner that clearly expresses whether this is a cause, an effect, or both?

✔ Are my sentences linked by transitional words and phrases?

✔ Does my conclusion clearly tie up the essay and explain why this topic was significant enough to discuss?

SENTENCE SKILLS

✔ Have I used a consistent point of view throughout my paragraph?

✔ Have I used specific rather than general words?

✔ Have I avoided wordiness and been concise?

✔ Are my sentences varied?

✔ Have I edited for spelling and other sentence skills errors, as listed on the inside back cover of the book?

Comparison and/or Contrast

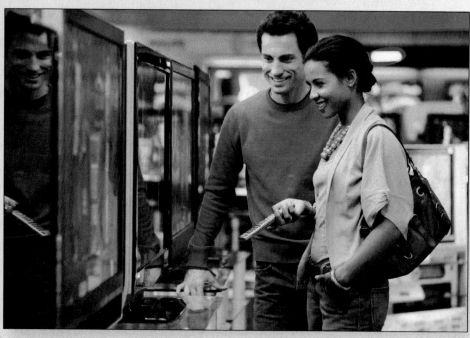

©Juice Images/Getty Images

TEACHING TIP
Ask students to complete this writing prompt in class.

RESPONDING TO IMAGES

Before you make a household purchase, you might compare brands, models, prices, and features. You might even look at consumer ratings. Write a paragraph in which you compare two products, such as two child car seats, two TVs, or two gaming consoles. Think about the categories and criteria that you use to help you make your decision.

Comparison and contrast are two everyday thought processes. When we *compare* two things, we show how they are similar; when we *contrast* two things, we show how they are different. We might compare and/or contrast two brand-name products (for example, Nike versus Adidas running shoes), two television shows, two instructors, two jobs, two friends, or two courses of action we could take in a given situation. The purpose of comparing or contrasting is to understand each of the two things more clearly and, at times, to make judgments about them.

In this chapter, you will be asked to write a paragraph that compares and/or contrasts. First, however, you must learn the two common methods of developing a comparison or contrast paragraph. Read the two paragraphs that follow and try to explain the difference in the two methods of development.

Paragraphs to Consider

My Senior Prom

¹My senior prom was nothing like what I expected it to be. ²From the start of my senior year, I had pictured putting on a sleek silvery slip dress that my aunt would make and that would cost more than $500 in any store. ³No one else would have a gown as attractive as mine. ⁴I imagined my boyfriend coming to the door with a lovely deep-red corsage, and I pictured myself happily inhaling its perfume all evening long. ⁵I saw us setting off for the evening in his brother's BMW convertible. ⁶We would make a flourish as we swept in and out of a series of parties before the prom. ⁷Our evening would be capped by a delicious shrimp dinner at the prom and by dancing close together into the early morning hours. ⁸The prom was held on May 15, 2005, at the Pony Club on Black Horse Pike. ⁹However, because of an illness in her family, my aunt had no time to finish my gown and I had to buy the only dress I could find in my size at such short notice. ¹⁰Not only was it ugly, but it was my least favorite color, pink. ¹¹My corsage of red roses looked terrible on my pink gown, and I do not remember its having any scent. ¹²My boyfriend's brother was out of town, and I stepped outside and saw the stripped-down Chevy that he used at the races on weekends. ¹³We went to one party where I drank a lot of wine that made me sleepy and upset my stomach. ¹⁴After we arrived at the prom, I did not have much more to eat than a roll and some celery sticks. ¹⁵Worst of all, we left early without dancing because my boyfriend and I had had a fight several days before, and at the time we did not really want to be with each other.

Keys to Success in College

¹College is very different from high school, and in order to succeed, students should practice good organizational skills that aren't commonly needed in high school. ²First of all, instead of going to class

continued

TEACHING TIP
Bring to class everyday examples of comparison and/or contrast writing. These examples might be found in magazines, newspapers, and other published sources. If your classroom has online access, find examples from Web sites. Help your students make connections.

TEACHING TIP
Mixing Modes of Writing: Explain to students that this comparison and/or contrast paragraph is written in narrative form.

every day, students may attend college classes only one day a week, three days a week, or even at night. [3]With this flexibility, students need to schedule blocks of study time in order to make sure they are getting their work done on time because it can be very tempting not to study until the last minute. [4]In high school, students are in class for at least six hours a day, and teachers often schedule time in class to work on assignments. [5]Conversely, in college, students may spend as little as two hours a day in class, and professors rarely allow in-class time to work on assignments. [6]In high school, students may need to spend an hour or two each evening on homework, but in college, students are expected to work on homework for at least two hours for each hour they are in class. [7]High school teachers and college professors have very different attitudes toward students' social lives. [8]High school teachers often accommodate students' activities like prom, sports, and school plays by assigning less homework, so students can participate in the activities. [9]On the other hand, college professors aren't concerned about activities outside of the classroom; regardless of students' schedules, they must complete the assignments on time. [10]Finally, in high school, teachers don't always use syllabi with course schedules, and they spend a lot of time reminding students about due dates. [11]College professors, however, hand out the syllabi at the beginning of the semester and expect students to complete the assignments by the due dates with few or no reminders. [12]Students who are new to college may find it difficult at first, but with good organization and planning, students can succeed.

Complete this comment: The difference in the methods of contrast in the two paragraphs is that

"My Senior Prom" discusses one side fully before addressing the other side. "Keys

to Success in College" switches back and forth between the two sides in a

point-by-point manner.

Compare your answer with the following explanation of the two methods of development used in comparison or contrast paragraphs.

Methods of Development

There are two common methods, or formats, of development in a comparison and/or contrast paper. One format presents the details *one side at a time.* The other presents the details *point by point.* Each format is explained next.

One Side at a Time

Look at the outline of "My Senior Prom":

Topic sentence: My senior prom was nothing like what I had expected it to be.

A. Expectations (first half of paragraph)

　　1. Dress (expensive, silver)

　　2. Corsage (deep red, fragrant)

　　3. Car (BMW convertible)

　　4. Parties (many)

　　5. Dinner (shrimp)

　　6. Dancing (all night)

B. Reality (second half of paragraph)

　　1. Dress (ugly, pink)

　　2. Corsage (wrong color, no scent)

　　3. Car (stripped-down Chevy)

　　4. Parties (only one)

　　5. Dinner (roll and celery)

　　6. Dancing (none because of quarrel)

When you use the one-side-at-a-time method, follow the same order of points of contrast or comparison for each side, as in the outline above. For example, both the first half of the paragraph and the second half begin with the same idea: what dress would be worn. Then both sides go on to the corsage, the car, and so on.

Point by Point

Now look at the outline of "Keys to Success in College":

Topic sentence: College is very different from high school, and in order to succeed students should practice good organizational skills that aren't commonly needed in high school.

A. Class schedules

　　1. High school students go to school every day.

　　2. College students have varied schedules.

　　3. High school students go to school at least six hours a day.

　　4. College students may be in class as little as two hours a day.

B. Homework

　　1. High school students may have only an hour or two of homework.

　　2. College students need to spend at least two hours on homework for each hour of class.

C. Attitudes toward social activities

　　1. High school teachers accommodate student activities by adjusting assignments and homework.

　　2. College professors expect students to meet assignment deadlines regardless of extracurricular activities.

D. Syllabus and deadline reminders

1. High school teachers don't always use syllabi with schedules and they remind students of due dates.

2. College professors hand out syllabi with due dates at the beginning of the semester and rarely remind students of the deadlines.

The outline shows how the two experiences are contrasted point by point. First, the writer contrasts the schedule differences between high school and college. Next, the writer contrasts the homework differences between high school and college. Then the writer contrasts the attitudes between high school teachers and college professors. Finally, the writer contrasts how teachers and college professors tell students about due dates.

When you begin a comparison or contrast paper, you should decide right away which format you are going to use: one side at a time or point by point. An outline is an essential step in helping you decide which format will be more workable for your topic. Keep in mind, however, that an outline is just a guide, not a permanent commitment. If you later feel that you've chosen the wrong format, you can reshape your outline to the other format.

TEACHING TIP
Stress to students that they must decide on the format of their comparison or contrast paper ahead of time.

ACTIVITY 1   Complete the partial outlines provided for the two paragraphs that follow.

1.

TEACHING TIP
You may want to do this activity as an entire class.

Reorganization Summary Report for Smith Family

In order to instill a sense of calm inside the main floor of the Smith home, the team from Organize It! reorganized, discarded, and repurposed items within the home. Before the reorganization took place, the owners' home was confined, dark, and crowded. The kitchen counters were covered with appliances and nonperishable food items. Many of the drawers were stuffed and didn't close properly. Several cupboards contained both food items and dishes. The living room had two couches, three chairs, and four tables crammed around a large television. The floor space of the living room was eaten up by toys, DVDs, and books. The dining room contained a table and four chairs, but all surface space, including the floor, was covered in toys, projects, and outdated mail. The final room of the main floor, the bathroom, was overfilled with towels, soap products, and toilet paper. After the organization team worked for three days, the differences were obvious. Many of the appliances in the kitchen were no longer working, so they were properly discarded, opening space on the counters. Cupboards were organized by purpose—food was with food, dishes with dishes, and glasses with glasses. Organization was created in the drawers by using dividers and baskets. Nonworking and duplicate items were discarded and multiple items were sorted; some were

continued

kept and others were donated. Similar organization occurred in the living and dining areas. All items were pulled out of the rooms and then sorted into keep, donate, and discard. The furniture in the living room was rearranged to provide more space, and a specific area was set aside for a play area. Toys were sorted and stored in large baskets to provide easy access and easy cleanup. DVDs and books were organized and put into a new bookcase. One of the tables from the living room was repurposed into a desk in the dining room. On this desk, several baskets were placed to help the owner organize mail and keep track of bills. The bathroom went through a similar process as all items were removed; only necessary items like spare rolls of toilet paper and a couple of extra hand towels were put back. Afterward, the team demonstrated how the owners could work to maintain the new sense of calm on the main level and create the same sense of calm on the upper levels.

Topic sentence: In order to instill a sense of calm inside the main floor of the Smith home, the team from Organize It! reorganized, discarded, and repurposed items within the home.

A. Before the reorganization

    1. Kitchen counters were overflowing.

    2. Living room was crowded with furniture and toys.

    3. Dining room was crowded with toys and mail.

    4. Bathroom was filled with too many extras.

B. After the reorganization

    1. Kitchen drawers and cupboards were organized; counters were cleared; nonworking appliances and duplicate items were discarded or donated.

    2. Living room furniture was arranged to create areas; storage was added.

    3. Dining room was cleaned and a desk was added; organizers for mail were placed on desk.

    4. Bathroom was emptied of all but necessities.

Complete the following statement: Paragraph 1 uses the one-side-at-a-time method of development.

2.

Good and Bad Horror Movies

A good horror movie is easily distinguishable from a bad one. A good horror movie, first of all, has both male and female victims. Both sexes suffer terrible fates at the hands of monsters and

continued

maniacs. Therefore, everyone in the audience has a chance to identify with the victim. Bad horror movies, on the other hand, tend to concentrate on women, especially half-dressed ones. These movies are obviously prejudiced against half the human race. Second, a good horror movie inspires compassion for its characters. For example, the audience will feel sympathy for the victims in the horror classics about the Wolfman, played by Lon Chaney, Jr., and also for the Wolfman himself, who is shown to be a sad victim of fate. In contrast, a bad horror movie encourages feelings of aggression and violence in viewers. For instance, in the *Halloween* films, the murders are seen from the murderer's point of view. The effect is that the audience stalks the victims along with the killer and feels the same thrill he does. Finally, every good horror movie has a sense of humor. In *Alien*, as a crew member is coughing and choking just before the horrible thing bursts out of his chest, a colleague chides him, "The food ain't *that* bad, man." Humor provides relief from the horror and makes the characters more human. A bad horror movie, though, is humorless and boring. One murder is piled on top of another, and the characters are just cardboard figures. Bad horror movies may provide cheap thrills, but the good ones touch our emotions and live forever.

Topic sentence: A good horror movie is easily distinguished from a bad one.

A. Kinds of victims

   1. Male and female

   2. Women only

B. Effect on audience

   1. Feeling of sympathy

   2. Feelings of aggression and violence

C. Tone

   1. Sense of humor

   2. Humorless

Complete the following statement: Paragraph 2 uses the point-by-point method of development.

Additional Paragraph to Consider

Read this additional paragraph of comparison and/or contrast and then answer the questions that follow.

My Broken Dream

¹When I finally became a broadcast journalist, the job was not as I had dreamed it would be. ²I began to dream about becoming a news anchor on a show like *The Today Show* when I was about ten. ³I could picture myself in fabulous outfits and perfectly styled hair. ⁴I could also picture myself delivering breaking news and changing people's lives. ⁵But most of all, I dreamed of being on TV and being adored by my millions of fans. ⁶My favorite news anchor is Savannah Guthrie. ⁷I knew everyone would be proud and envious of me. ⁸I could almost hear my classmates saying, "Courtney sure made it big. ⁹Did you hear she is a news anchor on *The Today Show*?" ¹⁰I dreamed of leading an exciting life, jetsetting around the country, and meeting lots of people. ¹¹I knew that if I made it on TV, everyone in town would be impressed. ¹²However, when I actually did get started in broadcast journalism, I soon found out the reality was different. ¹³First off, most new young journalists don't start out in big markets like New York or Los Angeles. ¹⁴Instead, I got my first job in Joplin, Missouri, a very small market. ¹⁵My disappointment continued when I was not offered a news anchor position but instead was given a part-time social media manager position. ¹⁶Not only was I working part-time, but my hours were weekend evenings. ¹⁷Disappointment seemed to continue. ¹⁸I soon found out that I was not the envy of all my friends. ¹⁹My job was not as exciting as I had dreamed it would be, either. ²⁰Instead of breaking stories to the public on camera, I found that I spent a great deal of time alone, in a quiet office, writing and posting information to help promote the careers of the news anchors.

TEACHING TIP
Read this paragraph aloud. Ask students to underline the topic sentence, specific examples, and transitions before answering the questions.

QUESTIONS

About Unity

1. Which sentence in "My Broken Dream" should be eliminated in the interest of paragraph unity? (*Write the sentence number here.*)   6

About Support

2. After which sentence are supporting details needed?   18

About Coherence

3. What method of development (one side at a time or point by point) is used in "My Broken Dream"?

   One side at a time

Developing a Comparison and/or Contrast Paragraph

Development through Prewriting

Sophia, the author of "My Senior Prom," had little trouble thinking of a topic for her comparison or contrast paragraph.

TEACHING TIP
You may want to provide a supplemental activity. First, have students compare or contrast their experiences in high school and in college. Ask them to cluster their ideas. Then ask them to choose a point-by-point or one-side-at-a-time format to write their first draft.

"My instructor said, 'You might compare or contrast two individuals, jobs you've had, or places you've lived,'" Sophia said. "Then he added, 'Or you might compare or contrast your expectations of a situation with the reality.' I immediately thought of my prom—boy, were my expectations different from the reality! I had thought it would be the high point of my senior year, but instead it was a total disaster."

Because she is a person who likes to think visually, Sophia started her preparations for her paragraph by clustering. She found this a helpful way to "see" the relationships between the points she was developing. Her diagram is shown here:

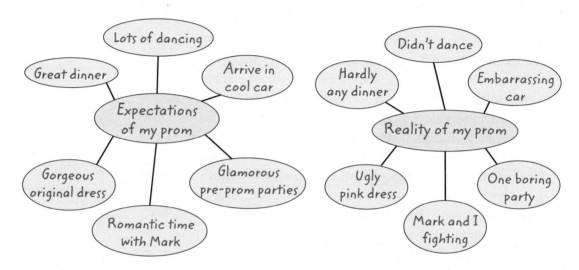

Taking a detail first from the "Expectations" part of the diagram, then one from the "Reality" portion, then another from "Expectations," and so on, Sophia began to write her paragraph using a point-by-point format:

> My senior prom was nothing like what I expected. First of all, I expected to be wearing a beautiful dress that my aunt would make for me. But because she couldn't finish it in time, I had to buy an ugly one at the last minute. Second, I thought I'd have a wonderful romantic evening with my boyfriend. But we'd been fighting that week and by the time the prom came around we were barely speaking. I thought we'd have a great time stopping in at lots of parties before the prom, but we went to only one and I left with an upset stomach.

Sophia stopped here, because she wasn't satisfied with the way the paragraph was developing. "I wanted the reader to picture the way I had imagined my prom, and I didn't like interrupting that picture with the reality of the evening.

So I decided to try the one-side-at-a-time approach instead." Here is Sophia's first draft:

> My senior prom was nothing like what I expected. I imagined myself wearing a beautiful, expensive-looking dress that my aunt would make. I thought my boyfriend and I would have a wonderful romantic evening together. We'd dance all through the night and we would cruise around in my boyfriend's brother's hot car. We would stop in at a lot of fun pre-prom parties, I thought, and we'd have a delicious shrimp dinner at the prom itself. But instead my uncle had a gallbladder attack that the doctor thought might be a heart attack and my aunt went to the hospital with him instead of finishing my dress. I had to go to the mall at the last minute and buy an ugly dress that nobody else had wanted. Mark and I had been fighting all week. Because he's in track and has a part-time job too we don't have much time together and still he wants to go out on Saturdays with his guy friends. So by the night of the prom we were hardly speaking to each other. We went to only one party before the prom and I left it feeling sick. And the restaurant was so crowded and noisy that I hardly got anything to eat. Because we were angry at each other, we didn't dance at all. And instead of his brother's luxury car, we had to use a stripped-down racing car.

Development through Revising

Sophia's instructor reviewed her first draft. Here are his comments:

> All this is very promising, but some of your details are out of order—for example, you mention the pre-prom parties after the dance itself. Be sure to follow the evening's sequence of events.
>
> More descriptive details are needed! For instance, what was your "beautiful" dress supposed to look like, and what did the "ugly" one you ended up with look like?
>
> You include some unnecessary information: for example, the details of your uncle's illness. Everything in your paragraph should support your topic sentence.

Following her instructor's suggestions (and remembering a few more details she wanted to include), Sophia created the outline shown in the "One Side at a Time" section in this chapter. She then wrote the version of her paragraph that appears at the beginning of the chapter.

TEACHING TIP
Ask students to read their drafts to a partner and discuss how their draft might be revised.

Writing a Comparison and/or Contrast Paragraph

LOOKING AT LIFE

Write a paragraph in which you compare and/or contrast your life in the real world with your life in an imagined "perfect world." If the purpose of your writing is to inform, your paragraph will be serious. If your purpose is to entertain, your paragraph will be humorous.

PREWRITING

ESL NOTE
Encourage nonnative
students to explore topics
about their own culture or
native country.

a.   As your "real life" and "ideal life" are too broad for a paragraph, choose three specific areas to focus on. You might select any of the areas below, or think of a specific area yourself.

Work	Friends
Money	Possessions
Romance	Housing
Physical location	Talents
Personal appearance	

TEACHING TIP
You may want to model
the writing process for
your students by doing this
assignment along with
them. Go through all the
stages, including prewriting
and revising, and seek
feedback from them. They
will appreciate your efforts
to create a writing
community.

b.   Write the name of one of your three areas (for example, "Work"), across the top of a page. Divide the page into two columns. Label one column "real world" and the other "perfect world." Under "real world," write down as many details as you can think of describing your real-life work situation. Under "perfect world," write down details describing what your perfect work life would be like. Repeat the process on separate pages for your other two major areas.

c.   Write a topic sentence for your paragraph. Here's an example: "In my perfect world, my life would be quite different in the areas of work, money, and housing."

d.   Decide which approach you will take: one side at a time or point by point.

e.   Write a scratch outline that reflects the format you have selected. The outline for a point-by-point format would look like this:

Topic sentence: In my perfect world, my life would be quite different in the areas of work, money, and housing.

- work
  - real-life work
  - perfect-world work
- money
  - real-life money
  - perfect-world money
- housing
  - real-life housing
  - perfect-world housing

The scratch outline for a one-side-at-a-time format would look like this:

Topic sentence: In my perfect world, my life would be quite different in the areas of work, money, and housing.

- real life
  - work
  - money
  - housing
- perfect world
  - work
  - money
  - housing

f. Drawing from the three pages of details you generated in step *b,* complete your outline by jotting down your strongest supporting details for each point.

g. Write the first draft of your paragraph.

REVISING: PEER REVIEW

Reread your paragraph, and then show it to a friend or classmate who will give you honest feedback. You should both review it, keeping in mind the questions in the FOUR BASES Checklist at the end of the chapter. Continue revising your work until you and your reader can answer "yes" to all the questions.

©Jacob Lund/ Shutterstock

CONSIDERING ALTERNATIVES

Write a comparison and/or contrast paragraph on one of the topics listed below. Once you choose a topic, you will need to decide if you want to emphasize comparisons, contrasting details, or a mixture of both. Some of these topics may require you to use research (Chapters 20 and 21) or incorporate other modes of writing like description (Chapter 8) and exemplification (Chapter 6).

Here is an example of a possible topic sentence for a paper that contrasts a dream vacation and a real vacation:

I have always wanted to take a luxury cruise around the world, but my budget only allows road trips through my home state.

- A used car versus a new one
- An ad on television versus an ad for the same product in a magazine
- Different ways to lose weight
- News in a newspaper versus news on the Internet
- *People* versus *OK!* (or any other two popular magazines)
- People who love their jobs versus people who hate their jobs
- Two historical events
- Two or more stages in a person's life
- Two poems, two short stories, or two books
- Two political candidates
- Working parents versus stay-at-home parents

WRITING ASSIGNMENT 2

Academic

ESL NOTE
Additional topics for ESL students:
- English versus native language
- US versus native country
- American food versus food from native country

These topics should be narrowed down. For example, US versus native country could be discussed in terms of punctuality expectations.

TEACHING TIP
Encourage students to use the prewriting and revising ideas mentioned in Writing Assignment 1.

**WRITING
ASSIGNMENT 3**

ANALYZING FAVORITE FOODS

Dave Zinczenko uses comparison and contrast in his popular weight-loss book, *Eat This, Not That!* by comparing two food items—cheeseburgers, pizza, or chicken meals, for example—and then contrasting calories and grams of fat.

Write a paragraph in which you compare two food items that are familiar to you, and then contrast at least two qualities that both items share. Zinczenko focuses on calories and fat, but you can focus on flavor, spiciness, authenticity, or whatever qualities seem appropriate. Here are some suggestions:

Grandma's fried chicken and KFC fried chicken

homemade burritos and Taco Bell burritos

organic strawberries and nonorganic strawberries

New York–style pizza and Chicago-style pizza

chocolate ice cream and chocolate frozen yogurt

**BEYOND THE
CLASSROOM**

**Comparison and/or
Contrast**

Beyond the classroom, you will find yourself and others comparing and contrasting people, places, and things. Sales representatives contrast their products with those of competitors. Historians compare and contrast events, circumstances, and problems that have occurred in different ages. Politicians contrast their voting records with those of their opponents during election campaigns. Consumer advocates compare and contrast different makes or brands of a product to help consumers make appropriate decisions. Automotive engineers use contrast to explain the workings of two different fuel or braking systems.

For this writing assignment, you will write a comparison or contrast paragraph with a specific purpose and for a specific audience.

Imagine that you are living in an apartment building in which new tenants are making life unpleasant for you. Write a letter of complaint to your landlord comparing and contrasting life before and after these neighbors arrived. You might want to focus on one or more of the following:

Noise

Guests

Trash

Safety hazards

Parking situation

Visit *AllSides* at https://www.allsides.com/unbiased-balanced-news. Choose a story that interests you and read the three different points of view. Then write a paragraph in which you compare and/or contrast each news story's perspective.

OR

Many students enter college with an idea of what type of job they want and what that job will entail. Visit the *Occupational Outlook Handbook* at https://www.bls.gov/ooh/ and search the handbook for the career you think might be right for you. After reading through the detailed descriptions provided for that career, write a paragraph comparing what you have learned about the career with what you had originally thought the career might be like.

©Tetra Images/
Shutterstock

COMPARISON AND/OR CONTRAST CHECKLIST: THE FOUR BASES

UNITY

✔ Does my paragraph have a strongly stated topic sentence that presents the main idea and clearly identifies whether I am comparing, contrasting, or using both processes to discuss my subject?

✔ Are there sentences or details that do not support my topic sentence and therefore should be eliminated or rewritten?

SUPPORT

✔ Does my paragraph include strong details that help the reader understand my claim?

COHERENCE

✔ Is my paragraph organized as point by point or one side at a time?

✔ Is the current organization the most effective choice?

✔ Do I use logical transitions to make points of comparison and/or contrast clear?

✔ Do I have a concluding sentence that supports my overall paragraph?

SENTENCE SKILLS

✔ Have I used a consistent point of view throughout my paragraph?

✔ Have I used specific rather than general words?

✔ Have I avoided wordiness and used concise wording?

✔ Are my sentences varied?

✔ Have I edited for spelling and other sentence skills errors, as listed on the inside back cover of the book?

Definition

©Hill Street Studios/Getty Images

TEACHING TIP
Ask students to complete this writing prompt in class.

RESPONDING TO IMAGES

What are some words that come to mind as you look at this photo of art students learning to sculpt? Write a paragraph in which you define one of those words. For example, you may look at the photograph and think persistence, skill, concentration, or talent.

In talking with other people, we sometimes offer informal definitions to explain just what we mean by a particular term. Suppose, for example, we say to a friend, "Oliver can be so clingy." We might then expand on our idea of "clingy" by saying, "You know, a clingy person needs to be with someone every single minute. If Oliver's best friend makes plans that don't include him, he becomes hurt. And when he dates someone, he calls her several times a day and gets upset if she even goes to the grocery store without him. He hangs on to people too tightly." In a written definition, we make clear in a more complete and formal way our own personal understanding of a term. Such a definition typically starts with one meaning of a term. The meaning is then illustrated with a series of examples or a story.

In this section, you will be asked to write a paragraph that begins with a one-sentence definition; that sentence will be the topic sentence. The two student papers below are both examples of definition paragraphs. Read them and then answer the questions that follow.

TEACHING TIP
Bring in examples of written definitions. These examples might be found in magazines, newspapers, and other published sources. If your classroom has online access, find examples from Web sites. Help your students make connections.

Paragraphs to Consider

Disillusionment

[1]Disillusionment is the feeling we have when one of our most cherished beliefs is stolen from us. [2]I learned about disillusionment firsthand the day Mr. Keller, our eighth-grade teacher, handed out the grades for our class biology projects. [3]I had worked hard to assemble what I thought was the best insect collection any school had ever seen. [4]For weeks, I had set up homemade traps around our house, in the woods, and in vacant lots. [5]At night, I would stretch a white sheet between two trees, shine a lantern on it, and collect the night-flying insects that gathered there. [6]With my own money, I had bought killing jars, insect pins, gummed labels, and display boxes. [7]I carefully arranged related insects together, with labels listing each scientific name and the place and date of capture. [8]Slowly and painfully, I wrote and typed the report that accompanied my project at the school science fair. [9]In contrast, my friend Dylan did almost nothing for his project. [10]He had his father, a psychologist, build an impressive maze complete with live rats and a sign that read, "You are the trainer." [11]A person could lift a little plastic door, send a rat running through the maze, and then hit a button to release a pellet of rat food as a reward. [12]This exhibit turned out to be the most popular one at the fair. [13]I felt sure that our teacher would know that Dylan could not have built it, and I was certain that my hard work would be recognized and rewarded. [14]Then the grades were finally handed out, and I was crushed. [15]Dylan had gotten an A+, but my grade was a B. [16]I suddenly realized that honesty and hard work don't always pay off in the end. [17]The idea that life is not fair, that sometimes it pays to cheat, hit me with such force that I felt sick. [18]I will never forget that moment.

TEACHING TIP
Read each paragraph aloud. Ask students to underline the topic sentence, specific examples, and transitions before answering the questions.

Classroom Ringmasters

¹Elementary teachers should not be self-important experts, but enthusiastic ringmasters. ²Like ringmasters in circuses, teachers need to organize, introduce, and guide, but instead of circus acts and performers, teachers work with information and students. ³Many ringmasters participate in the planning and organizing of the show; if they weren't involved, performers wouldn't know their cues, stagehands wouldn't know when to set up, and the show would not become a unified experience. ⁴Teachers are also in charge of planning and organizing their lessons, but some teachers fail to do this and, like a bad circus, create a disjointed and choppy experience. ⁵My sixth-grade language arts teacher rarely had any plan for what was going to occur each day. ⁶As a result, our class spent many days repeating lessons or skipping over information, which led to frustration and poor learning. ⁷I hated the reading selections that we were assigned for language arts. ⁸Another job of circus ringmasters is to introduce the acts that are coming up. ⁹Teachers also prepare students for and introduce students to new information. ¹⁰For a new math unit on subtraction, a second-grade teacher brought in clusters of grapes. ¹¹She passed out filled bowls to the students and had them count the individual grapes. ¹²Once they knew how many grapes they had, the teacher invited the students to eat some of the grapes. ¹³She then had the students count up their new totals. ¹⁴Within a very short period, the students were excited about the new topic of subtraction and already had a strong understanding of what it meant, as well as a nice snack. ¹⁵Like a good ringmaster, a good teacher has to make sure that each "act" runs smoothly into another without any major breaks, overlaps, or mishaps. ¹⁶My son's first-grade teacher was the ultimate ringmaster. ¹⁷He was full of enthusiasm for his subject, and students responded. ¹⁸It was hard for six-year-olds not to get excited about spelling when the teacher was standing on his desk leading the class in a spelling cheer. ¹⁹But like a good ringmaster, the teacher never let the lesson get out of hand; instead, he transitioned the students from spelling cheers to quiet reading time with the precision of a veteran director. ²⁰There are many types of teachers, but the best recognize that their jobs are to keep the show running, not be the star of the show.

QUESTIONS

About Unity

1. Which sentence in "Classroom Ringmasters" should be omitted in the interest of paragraph unity? (*Write the sentence number here.*)

___7___

About Support

2. Which paragraph develops its definitions through a series of short narrative examples?

"Classroom Ringmasters"

_____

3. Which paragraph develops its definition through a single extended example?

"Disillusionment"

About Coherence

4. Which paragraph uses time order to organize its details?

"Disillusionment"

Developing a Definition Paragraph

Development through Prewriting

When Mateo, the author of "Disillusionment," started working on his assignment, he did not know what he wanted to write about. He looked around the house for inspiration. His two-year-old twins racing around the room made him think about defining "energy." The fat cat asleep on a sunny windowsill suggested that he might write about "laziness" or "relaxation." Still not sure of a topic, he looked over his notes from that day's class. His instructor had jotted a list of terms on the blackboard, saying, "Maybe you could focus on what one of these words has meant in your own life." Mateo looked over the words he had copied down: *honesty, willpower, faith, betrayal, disillusionment.* "When I got to the word 'disillusionment,' the eighth-grade science fair flashed into my mind," Mateo said. "That was a bitter experience that definitely taught me what disillusionment was all about."

Because the science fair had occurred many years before, Mateo had to work to remember it well. He decided to try the technique of questioning himself to come up with the details of what had happened. Here are the questions Mateo asked himself and the answers he wrote:

When did I learn about disillusionment?

When I was in eighth grade

Where did it happen?

At the school science fair

Who was involved?

Me, Dylan Loomis and his father, and Mr. Keller

continued

in a writer's words

" *New writers are often told, 'Write what you know.' I would broaden that by saying, 'Write what you know emotionally.'*"

—Marjorie Franco

TEACHING TIP
You may want to provide a supplemental activity. Have students define the term "successful student." Ask students to use the technique of questioning. Then ask them to write their first draft.

<u>What happened?</u>

I had worked very hard on my insect collection. Dylan had done almost nothing but he had a rat maze that his father had built. I got a B on my project while Dylan got an A+.

<u>Why was the experience so disillusioning?</u>

I thought my hard work would be rewarded. I was sure Mr. Keller would recognize that I had put far more effort into my project than Dylan had. When Dylan won, I learned that cheating can pay off and that honest work isn't always rewarded.

<u>How did I react?</u>

I felt sick to my stomach. I wanted to confront Mr. Keller and Dylan and make them see how unfair the grades were. But I knew I'd just look like a poor loser, so I didn't do anything.

<u>On the basis of this experience, how would I define "disillusionment"?</u>

It's finding out that something you really believed in isn't true.

Drawing from the ideas generated by his self-questioning, Mateo wrote the following draft of his paragraph:

Disillusionment is finding out that one of your most important beliefs isn't true. I learned about disillusionment at my eighth-grade science fair. I had worked very hard on my project, an insect collection. I was sure it would get an A. I had worked so hard on it, even spending nights outside making sure it was very good. My friend Dylan also did a project, but he barely worked on his at all. Instead, he had his father build a maze for a rat to run through. The trainer lifted a little plastic door to let the rat into the maze, and if it completed the maze, the trainer could release a pellet of food for it to eat. It was a nice project, but the point is that Dylan hadn't made it. He just made things like the banner that hung over it. Mr. Keller was our science teacher. He gave Dylan an A+ and me just a B. So that really taught me about disillusionment.

Development through Revising

The next day, Mateo's teacher divided the class into peer-review groups of three. The groups reviewed each member's paragraph. Mateo was grouped with Curtis and Jocelyn. After reading through Mateo's paper several times, the group had the following discussion:

> Jocelyn: "My first reaction is that I want to know more about your project. You give details about Dylan's, but not many about your own. What was so good about it? You need to show us, not just tell us. Also, you said that you worked very hard, but you didn't show us how hard."
>
> Mateo: "Yeah. I remember my project clearly, but I guess the reader has to know what it was like and how much effort went into it."
>
> Curtis: "I like your topic sentence, but when I finished the paragraph I wasn't sure what 'important belief' you'd learned wasn't true. What would you say that belief was?"
>
> Mateo: "I'd believed that honest hard work would always be rewarded. I found out that it doesn't always happen that way, and that cheating can actually win."
>
> Curtis: "I think you need to include that in your paragraph."
>
> Jocelyn: "I'd like to read how you felt or reacted after you saw your grade, too. If you don't explain that, the paragraph ends sort of abruptly."

Mateo agreed with his classmates' suggestions. After he had gone through several revisions, he produced the version that appears at the beginning of this chapter.

Writing a Definition Paragraph

PORTRAYING A PERSON

Write a paragraph that defines one of the following terms. Each term refers to a certain kind of person.

Artist	Geek	Pack rat
Beauty	Genius	Pessimist
Bubba	Good neighbor	Philanthropist
Charmer	Good sport	Pushover
Con-artist	Idealist	Romantic
Control freak	Intellect	Self-promoter
Coward	Introvert	Showoff
Darwin Award winner	Know-it-all	Slacker
Fair-weather friend	Leader	Snob
Feminist	Manipulator	Visionary
Flirt	Optimist	Workaholic

PREWRITING

a. Write a topic sentence for your definition paragraph. This is a two-part process:

- *First,* place the term in a class, or category. For example, if you are writing about a certain kind of person, the general category is *person.* If you are describing a type of friend, the general category is *friend.*

- *Second,* describe what you consider the special feature or features that set your term apart from other members of its class. For instance, say what *kind* of person you are writing about or what *type* of friend.

In the following topic sentence, try to identify three things: the term being defined, the class it belongs to, and the special feature that sets the term apart from other members of the class.

A chocoholic is a person who craves chocolate.

The term being defined is *chocoholic.* The category it belongs to is *person.* The words that set *chocoholic* apart from any other person are *craves chocolate.*

Below is another example of a topic sentence for this assignment. It is a definition of *whiner.* The class, or category, is underlined: A whiner is a type of person. The words that set the term *whiner* apart from other members of the class are double-underlined.

A whiner is a <u>person</u> who <u><u>feels wronged by life.</u></u>

In the following sample topic sentences, underline the class and double-underline the special features.

A clotheshorse is a <u>person</u> who <u><u>needs new clothes to be happy.</u></u>

The class clown is a <u>student</u> who <u><u>gets attention through silly behavior.</u></u>

A worrywart is a <u>person</u> who <u><u>sees danger everywhere.</u></u>

b. Develop your definition by using one of the following methods:

Examples. Give several examples that support your topic sentence.

Extended example. Use one longer example to support your topic sentence.

Contrast. Support your topic sentence by contrasting what your term *is* with what it is *not.* For instance, you may want to define a *fair-weather friend* by contrasting his or her actions with those of a true friend.

c. Once you have created a topic sentence and decided how to develop your paragraph, make a scratch outline. If you are using a contrast method of development, remember to present the details one side at a time or point by point (see Chapter 11).

d. Write a first draft of your paragraph.

REVISING: PEER REVIEW

Before revising, have a friend or classmate read your paragraph. Together, you should respond to the questions in the FOUR BASES Checklist at the end of this chapter. Continue revising your work until you and your reader can answer "yes" to all the questions.

©Jacob Lund/ Shutterstock

DESCRIBING IN FIVE

Many times during job interviews, people are asked to describe themselves in five adjectives; in essence, they are being asked to define themselves. For this assignment, you are to pretend that you are preparing for a job interview and write a paragraph that answers the question, "What five adjectives would you use to describe yourself and why?"

As a guide in writing your paragraph, use the suggestions for "Prewriting" and "Revising" in Writing Assignment 1. Also, to add support and detail to your paragraph, you will need to offer examples that demonstrate your definition of the adjectives you are using to describe yourself. Read Chapter 7, "Narration," for ways to incorporate stories as part of your definition. Read Chapter 8, "Description," for ways to improve your specific details to better support your definition. Read Chapter 14, "Argument," for ways to create a persuasive tone to help you convince your audience that the adjectives you have chosen really do define you.

Here are some sample topic sentences:

- I will make a great nurse because I am honest, compassionate, intelligent, independent, and confident.

- The five words that describe me are dedicated, funny, bold, logical, and thoughtful.

- Good teachers should be intelligent, creative, compassionate, funny, and understanding, which are five words that describe me.

WRITING ASSIGNMENT 2

Personal

TEACHING TIP
Encourage students to use the prewriting and revising ideas mentioned in Writing Assignment 1.

EXPLORING STRESS

Since stress affects all of us to some degree—in the workplace (as shown in the cartoon here), in school, in our families, and in our everyday lives—it is a useful term to explore. Write a paragraph defining *stress*. Organize your paragraph in one of these ways:

- Use a series of examples (see Chapter 6) of stress.

- Use narration (see Chapter 7) to provide one longer example of stress: Create a hypothetical person (or use a real person) and show how this person's typical morning or day illustrates your definition of *stress*.

Using strategies described in Chapters 19, 20, and 21, do some research on stress. Your reading will help you think about how to proceed with the paper.

TIP Do not simply write a series of general, abstract sentences that repeat and reword your definition. If you concentrate on providing specific support, you will avoid the common trap of getting lost in a maze of generalities.

WRITING ASSIGNMENT 3

Academic

© Mike Baldwin/Cornered
"You win some, you lose some. Don't worry about it. No one's keeping score."

Make sure your paragraph is set firmly on the four bases: unity, support, coherence, and sentence skills. Edit the next-to-final draft of the paragraph carefully for sentence-skills errors, including spelling.

BEYOND THE CLASSROOM
Definition

TEACHING TIP
An alternate assignment could be to ask students to imagine their boss has asked them to explain "teamwork" to a new employee. Have them write a paragraph that defines in detail what their boss means by "teamwork."

Beyond the classroom, there are many instances where definition writing would be used. For example, a restaurant manager may have to define the job requirements for a newly hired food server, or a zookeeper may need to provide a descriptive definition of an animal for the signage of a new exhibit. Attorneys often define legal terms or complicated legal procedures to clients, and computer technicians and instructors sometimes need to explain terms such as *flash drive* or *spyware*. A health professional might have to explain CAT or MRI to a patient, and an investment counselor or banker might be asked to define terms like *hedge fund* or *ARM* (*adjustable-rate mortgage*).

For this writing assignment, you will write a definition paragraph with a specific purpose and for a specific audience.

Imagine that one of your coworkers has just quit, creating a new job opening. Since you have been working there for a while, your boss has asked you to write a description of the position. That description—a detailed definition of the job—will be sent to employment agencies. These agencies will be responsible for interviewing candidates. Choose any position you know about, and write a paragraph defining it. First state the purpose of the job, and then list its duties and responsibilities. Finally, describe the qualifications for the position. Below is a sample topic sentence for this assignment:

Purchasing clerk is a position in which someone provides a variety of services to suppliers and contractors.

In a paragraph with this topic sentence, the writer would go on to list and describe the various services the purchasing clerk must provide.

EXPLORING WRITING ONLINE

©Tetra Images/ Shutterstock

Think of a word used as slang that has a separate formal meaning (for example *chill, sweet, tight, cheesy,* etc.). Visit https://www.urbandictionary.com/ to look at the slang definitions and uses. Then, visit http://www.dictionary.com and find the word's formal meaning. Write a paragraph that discusses the differences in meanings, when they would be used, and how listeners know the difference. Review Chapter 11, "Comparison and/ or Contrast," to help organize your paragraph.

OR

Visit *Political Dictionary* at http://politicaldictionary.com/ and find a term you are unfamiliar with. Notice that some of the terms are more unusual than others—such as *snollygoster, frugging, mugwump,* and *turkey farm*. Then write a paragraph that explains that term by using an extended definition with examples.

DEFINITION CHECKLIST: THE FOUR BASES

UNITY

✔ Does my topic sentence indicate why the term is important and how I define the term?

✔ Are there sentences or details that do not support my topic sentence and therefore should be eliminated or rewritten?

SUPPORT

✔ Have I supported my definition by providing several examples, one extended example, or contrast?

✔ Should I support my definition through another method?

✔ Do my details help explain my definition of the term?

COHERENCE

✔ If I supported my definition through contrast, have I consistently followed either a point-by-point or a one-side-at-a-time format?

✔ Have I used appropriate transitions (*another*, *in addition*, *in contrast*, *for example*) to tie my thoughts together?

SENTENCE SKILLS

✔ Have I used a consistent point of view throughout my paragraph?

✔ Have I used specific rather than general words?

✔ Have I avoided wordiness and used concise wording?

✔ Are my sentences varied?

✔ Have I edited for spelling and other sentence skills errors, as listed on the inside back cover of the book?

Division-Classification

©LeoPatrizi/Getty Images

RESPONDING TO IMAGES

Modern technology allows us to communicate in so many ways. In the span of a few minutes, we might make a call to the babysitter, send a text message to our friend, and e-mail our teacher about a quiz. Write a paragraph in which you classify three different means of communication and explain how each one is used.

If you were doing the laundry, you might begin by separating the clothing into piles. You would then put all the whites in one pile and all the colors in another. Or you might classify the laundry not according to color, but according to fabric—putting all cottons in one pile, polyesters in another, and so on. *Classifying* is the process of taking many things and separating them into categories. We generally classify to better manage or understand many things. Librarians classify books into groups (novels, travel, health, etc.) to make them easier to find. A scientist sheds light on the world by classifying all living things into two main groups: animals and plants.

Dividing, in contrast, is taking one thing and breaking it down into parts. We often divide, or analyze, to better understand, teach, or evaluate something. For instance, a tinkerer might take apart a clock to see how it works; a science text might divide a tree into its parts to explain their functions. A music reviewer may analyze the elements of a band's performance—for example, the skill of the various players, rapport with the audience, selections, and so on.

In short, if you are classifying, you are sorting *numbers of things* into categories. If you are dividing, you are breaking *one thing* into parts. It all depends on your purpose—you might classify flowers into various types or divide a single flower into its parts.

In this section, you will be asked to write a paragraph in which you classify a group of things into categories according to a single principle. To prepare for this assignment, first read the paragraphs below, and then work through the questions and the activity that follows.

TEACHING TIP
Bring to class everyday examples of division or classification writing. These examples might be found in magazines, newspapers, and other published sources. If your classroom has online access, find examples from Web sites. Help your students make connections.

Paragraphs to Consider

Three Little Dumplings

[1]First, there are the light, fluffy dumplings that are found in England and the United States. [2]These dumplings are generally half-boiled or half-steamed and usually incorporated into soups and stews. [3]In the United States, the most well-known dish is "Chicken and Dumplings." [4]Jamaica has a fluffy dumpling. [5]The second type of dumpling is the filled pocket of pasta. [6]Italy's ravioli and tortellini are often filled with cheeses, vegetables, fish, and/or meats, depending on the region. [7]Preparation also varies from region to region; pastas can be boiled, baked, fried, or poached. [8]Chinese potstickers are similar to ravioli and tortellini as they are also both steamed and then fried until they "stick to the pot." [9]In Latin America, empanadas are often filled with pork, chicken, cheese, and vegetables. [10]Although they are larger than ravioli or potstickers, they contain many of the same basic ingredients. [11]The third type of dumpling is the sweet dessert dumpling. [12]In countries like Poland, the sweet filled pierogi are often boiled and then fried and served with butter or sour cream. [13]In Germany and Hungary, sweet dumplings are wrapped around plums or apricots. [14]In Japan, kushi-dango are small sweet dumplings made out of rice flour, skewered on a stick, and then grilled. [15]Attempting to taste every type of dumpling in the world will be a treat for the taste buds.

TEACHING TIP
Mixing Modes of Writing: Point out to students that this classification paragraph uses a good deal of description.

TEACHING TIP
Read these paragraphs aloud. Ask students to underline the topic sentence, specific examples, and transitions in each paragraph before answering the questions.

Three Kinds of Dogs

[1]A city walker will notice that most dogs fall into one of three categories. [2]First there are the big dogs, which are generally harmless and often downright friendly. [3]They walk along peacefully with their masters, their tongues hanging out and big goofy grins on their faces. [4]Apparently they know they're too big to have anything to worry about, so why not be nice? [5]Second are the spunky medium-sized dogs. [6]When they see a stranger approaching, they go on alert. [7]They prick up their ears, they raise their hackles, and they may growl a little deep in their throats. [8]"I could tear you up," they seem to be saying, "but I won't if you behave yourself." [9]Unless the walker leaps for their master's throat, these dogs usually won't do anything more than threaten. [10]The third category is made up of the shivering neurotic little yappers whose shrill barks could shatter glass and whose needle-like little teeth are eager to sink into a friendly outstretched hand. [11]Walkers always wonder about these dogs—don't they know that people who really wanted to could squash them under their feet like bugs? [12]Apparently not, because of all the dogs a walker meets, these provide the most irritation. [13]Such dogs are only one of the potential hazards that the city walker encounters.

QUESTIONS

About Unity

1. Which paragraph lacks a topic sentence?

   "Three Little Dumplings"

2. Which sentence in "Three Kinds of Dogs" should be eliminated in the interest of paragraph unity? (*Write the sentence number here.*) __13__

About Support

3. Which of the examples in "Three Little Dumplings" lacks specific details?

   Jamaican dumplings

About Coherence

4. Which sentences in "Three Kinds of Dogs" contain transition words or phrases? (*Write the sentence numbers here.*)

   __2__   __5__   __10__

ACTIVITY 1

This activity will sharpen your sense of the classifying process. In each of the ten groups, cross out the one item that has not been classified on the same basis as the other three. Also, indicate in the space provided the single principle of classification used for the remaining three items. Note the examples.

TEACHING TIP
You may want to do this
activity with the entire
class.

EXAMPLES

Water

a. Cold

b. ~~Lake~~

c. Hot

d. Lukewarm

Unifying principle:

Temperatures

1. Eyes

a. Blue

b. ~~Nearsighted~~

c. Brown

d. Hazel

Unifying principle:

Colors

2. Mattresses

a. Double

b. Twin

c. Queen

d. ~~Firm~~

Unifying principle:

Sizes

3. Zoo animals

a. Flamingo

b. Peacock

c. ~~Polar bear~~

d. Ostrich

Unifying principle:

Birds

4. Vacation

a. Summer

b. Holiday

c. ~~Seashore~~

d. Weekend

Unifying principle:

Times for vacation

Household pests

a. ~~Mice~~

b. Ants

c. Roaches

d. Flies

Unifying principle:

Insects

5. Books

a. Novels

b. Biographies

c. ~~Boring~~

d. Short stories

Unifying principle:

Types of genres

6. Wallets

a. Leather

b. Plastic

c. ~~Stolen~~

d. Fabric

Unifying principle:

Materials

7. Newspaper

a. Wrapping fragile shipping items

b. ~~Editorials~~

c. Making paper planes

d. Covering floor while painting

Unifying principle:

Uses for newspapers

8. Students

a. First-year

b. ~~Transfer~~

c. Junior

d. Sophomore

Unifying principle:

Grades or classes

9. Exercise
   a. Running
   b. Swimming
   c. Gymnastics
   d. ~~Fatigue~~
   Unifying principle:
   Kinds of exercise

10. Leftovers
   a. ~~Cold chicken~~
   b. Feed to dog
   c. Reheat
   d. Use in a stew
   Unifying principle:
   Uses for leftovers

Developing a Division-Classification Paragraph

Development through Prewriting

TEACHING TIP
You may want to provide a supplemental activity. Have students classify types of students. First, ask them to create categories, and then ask them to jot down characteristics for each category.

Malik walked home from campus to his apartment, thinking about the assignment to write a division-classification paragraph. As he strolled along his familiar route, his observations made him think of several possibilities. "First I thought of writing about the businesses in my neighborhood, dividing them into the ones run by Hispanics, Asians, and African Americans," he said. "When I stopped in at my favorite coffee shop, I thought about dividing the people who hang out there. There is a group of old men who meet to drink coffee and play cards, and there are students like me, but there didn't seem to be a third category and I wasn't sure two was enough. As I continued walking home, though, I saw Mr. Enriquez and his big golden retriever, and a woman with two nervous little dogs that acted as if they wanted to eat me, and the newsstand guy with his mutt that's always guarding the place, and I thought 'Dogs! I can classify types of dogs.'"

But how would he classify them? Thinking further, Malik realized that he thought of dogs as having certain personalities depending on their size. "I know there are exceptions, of course, but since this was going to be a light-hearted, even comical paragraph, I thought it would be OK if I exaggerated a bit." He wrote down his three categories:

Big dogs

Medium-sized dogs

Small dogs

Under each division, then, he wrote down as many characteristics as he could think of:

Big dogs   good-natured

calm   dumb

friendly   lazy

continued

Small dogs	Medium-sized dogs
nervous	spunky
trembling	energetic
noisy	ready to fight
yappy	protective
snappy	friendly if they know you
annoying	

Malik then wrote a topic sentence: "Dogs seem to fall into three categories." Using that topic sentence and the scratch outline he'd just produced, he wrote the following paragraph:

TEACHING TIP
Next, ask them to write their first draft.

Most dogs seem to fall into three categories. First there are the big dumb friendly dogs. They give the impression of being sweet but not real bright. One example of this kind of dog is Lucy. She's a golden retriever belonging to a man in my neighborhood. Lucy goes everywhere with Mr. Enriquez. She doesn't even need a leash but just follows him. Dogs like Lucy never bother anybody. She just lies at Mr. Enriquez's feet when he stops to talk to anyone. The guy who runs the corner newsstand I pass every day has a spunky medium-sized dog. Once the dog knows you he's friendly and even playful. But he's always on the lookout for a stranger who might mean trouble. For a dog who's not very big he can make himself look pretty fierce if he wants to. Then there are my least favorite kind of dogs. Little nervous yappy ones. My aunt used to have a Chihuahua like that. It knew me for nine years and still went crazy shaking and yipping at me every time we met. She loved that dog but I can't imagine why. If I had a dog it would definitely come from category 1 or 2.

TEACHING TIP
Ask students to read their
drafts to a partner and
discuss how their draft
might be revised.

Development through Revising

Malik traded his first draft with a fellow student, Rachel, and asked her to give him feedback. Here are the comments Rachel wrote on his paper:

Most dogs seem to fall into one of three categories. First there are the big dumb friendly dogs. They give the impression of being sweet but not real bright. One example of this kind of dog is Lucy, a golden retriever belonging to a man in my neighborhood. Lucy goes everywhere with Mr. Enriquez. She doesn't even need a leash but just follows him everywhere. Lucy never bothers you. She just lies at Mr. Enriquez's feet when he stops to talk to anyone. The guy who runs the corner newsstand I pass every day has a spunky medium-sized dog. Once the dog knows you he's friendly and even playful. But he's always on the lookout for a stranger who might mean trouble. For a dog who's not very big he can make himself look pretty fierce if he wants to scare you. Then there are my least favorite kind of dogs. Little nervous yappy ones. My aunt used to have a Chihuahua like that. It knew me for nine years and still went crazy shaking and yipping at me every time we met. She loved that dog but I can't imagine why. If I had a dog it would definitely come from category 1 or 2.

This is a change in point of view—you haven't been using "you" before.

Is this the beginning of a second category? That's not clear.

Not a complete sentence.

Another change in point of view—you've gone from writing in the third person to "you" to "me."

Rachel also provided Malik with the following helpful feedback:

Malik—I think you need to make your three categories clearer. Your first one is OK—"big dogs," which you say are friendly—but categories 2 and 3 aren't stated as clearly.

It's distracting to have your point of view change from third person to "you" to "me."

Since you're trying to divide and classify all dogs, I'm not sure it's a good idea to talk only about three individual dogs. This way it sounds as if you're just describing those three dogs instead of putting them into three groups.

When Malik considered Rachel's comments and reread his paragraph, he agreed with what she had written. "I realized it was too much about three particular dogs and not enough about the categories of dogs," he said. "I decided to revise it and focus on the three classes of dogs."

Malik then wrote the version that appears at the beginning of this chapter.

Writing a Division-Classification Paragraph

ORGANIZING IDEAS

Write a classification paragraph on one of the following topics:

Attitudes toward life	Houseguests
Commercials	Reasons for attending college
Employers	Ways to get a new job
Jobs	Types of political candidates
First dates	Ways to save money
Parents	Ways to protect/destroy the environment
Neighbors	Types of characters in a favorite novel, TV show, or movie
Preferred Pandora stations	

PREWRITING

a. Decide if you want your paragraph to be informative, persuasive, or entertaining. Here are some questions to consider: Do you want your readers to understand your topic and categories better? Do you want to convince your readers to agree with your method of classification? Do you want to amuse them by providing humorous details for each category? Keep in mind that your paragraph can combine purposes.

b. Classify members of the group you are considering writing about into three categories. Remember: *You must use a single principle of division when you create your three categories.* For example, if your topic is "school courses" and you classify them into easy, moderate, and challenging, your basis for classification is "degree of difficulty." It would not make sense to have as a fourth type "foreign language" (the basis of such a categorization would be "subject matter") or "early morning" (the basis of that classification would be "time of day the classes meet"). You *could* categorize school courses on the basis of subject matter or time of day they meet, for almost any subject can be classified in more than one way. In a single paper, however, you must choose *one* basis for classification and stick to it.

c. Once you have a satisfactory three-part division, spend at least five minutes freewriting about each of your three points. Don't be concerned yet with grammar, spelling, or organization. Just write whatever comes into your mind about each of the three points.

d. Expand your topic into a fully stated topic sentence.

e. At this point, you have all three elements of your paragraph: the topic sentence, the three main points, and the details needed to support each point. Now weave them all together in one paragraph.

WRITING ASSIGNMENT 1

Academic

TEACHING TIP
You may want to model the writing process for your students by doing this assignment along with them. Go through all the stages, including prewriting and revising, and seek feedback from them. They will appreciate your efforts to create a writing community.

©Jacob Lund/
Shutterstock

REVISING: PEER REVIEW

Do not attempt to revise your paragraph right away. Put it away for a while, if possible until the next day. When you reread it, try to be as critical of it as you would be if someone else had written it. Have a friend or classmate read your paragraph as well, and as you both go over your work, refer to the questions in the FOUR BASES Checklist at the end of this chapter. Continue revising your work until you and your reader can answer "yes" to all the questions.

WRITING ASSIGNMENT 2

Personal

ESL NOTE
Nonnative speakers might also consider the following topics, which tap into their experience:
• Attitude toward instructor
• Proficiency in English
• Diversity

TEACHING TIP
Encourage students to use the prewriting and revising ideas mentioned in Writing Assignment 1.

ANALYZING CLASSMATES

There are many ways you could classify your fellow students. Pick out one of your courses and write a paragraph in which you classify the students in that class according to one underlying principle. You may wish to choose one of the classification principles below.

Attitude toward the class

Participation in the class

Method of taking notes in class

Performance during oral reports, speeches, presentations, lab sessions

Punctuality

Attendance

Level of confidence

If you decide, for instance, to classify students according to their attitude toward class, you might come up with these three categories:

Students actually interested in learning the material

Students who know they need to learn the material, but don't want to overdo it

Students who find the class a good opportunity to catch up with lost sleep

Of course, you may use any other principle of classification that seems appropriate. Follow the steps listed under "Prewriting" and "Revising" for Writing Assignment 1.

WRITING ASSIGNMENT 3

Personal

REVIEWING A RESTAURANT

When we go to a restaurant, we probably hope that the service will be helpful, the atmosphere will be pleasant, and the food will be tasty. But as the cartoon shown here suggests, restaurants that are good in all three respects may be hard to find. Write a review of a restaurant, analyzing its (1) service, (2) food, and (3) atmosphere. Visit a restaurant for this assignment, or draw on an experience you have had recently. Freewrite or make a list of observations about such elements as:

Quantity of food you receive

Taste of the food

Temperature of the food

Freshness of the ingredients

How the food is presented
(garnishes, dishes, and so on)

Attitude of the servers

Efficiency of the servers

Décor

Level of cleanliness

Noise level and music, if any

Feel free to write about details other than those listed above. Just be sure each detail fits into one of your three categories: food, service, or atmosphere.

For your topic sentence, rate the restaurant by giving it from one to five stars, on the basis of your overall impression. Include the restaurant's name and location in your topic sentence. Here are some examples:

Guido's, an Italian restaurant downtown, deserves three stars.

The McDonald's on Route 70 merits a four-star rating.

The Circle Diner in Westfield barely earns a one-star rating.

Used with permission of Brad Fitzpatrick, Fitzillo Incorporated.

REFLECTIVE ACTIVITY

1. Reread the paragraph you wrote for Writing Assignment 1. Does your paragraph contain enough detail to support the main point made in your topic sentence? Is all of the information in the paragraph directly related to the topic sentence?

2. Can you think of a way to incorporate another mode of writing, like narration (Chapter 7) or argument (Chapter 14)? If so, revise the paragraph to incorporate the added support by using an additional mode(s) of writing.

©mavo/Shutterstock

BEYOND THE CLASSROOM

Division-Classification

Work

Beyond the classroom, you will find yourself and others dividing or classifying objects and concepts. Scientists classify plants and animals in order to study them more effectively. Medical researchers use this method to organize information about related diseases or drugs. Educators sometimes classify students into groups based on placement-test scores in order to design and deliver effective programs of study. Psychiatrists use classification to organize information about various emotional disorders, and marketing researchers use classification to determine which age, ethnic, or income group might be more interested in a product than another group.

For this writing assignment, you will write a division or classification paragraph with a specific purpose and for a specific audience.

Imagine that you are a travel agent and several clients have asked you for suggestions about affordable family vacations. Write a paragraph classifying vacations for families into three or more types—for example, vacations in amusement parks, on cruises, at resorts, or in the outdoors. For each type, include an explanation with one or more examples. Keep in mind that all these suggestions should be affordable.

EXPLORING WRITING ONLINE

©Tetra Images/
Shutterstock

Visit an online music store and browse through the categories of music. You may want to visit *iTunes* at https://www.apple.com/itunes/music/ or *Pandora* at https://www.pandora.com/ or *Spotify* at https://www.spotify.com/us/. Then write a paragraph that explains what categories of music you listen to, why you listen to that type of music, and what makes each category special.

OR

Visit *Amazon* at https://www.amazon.com/ and browse the departments. Choose three departments that you could use to categorize your interests. Then write a paragraph explaining why and how the categories apply to your life.

DIVISION-CLASSIFICATION CHECKLIST: THE FOUR BASES

UNITY

✔ Have I divided or classified my topic into three distinct parts?

✔ Is each of those parts based on the same principle of division?

✔ Does my paragraph describe the classification in a clear, logical way?

✔ Are there portions in my paragraph that do not support my thesis and therefore should be eliminated or rewritten?

SUPPORT

✔ Have I backed up my topic sentence with specific examples that support the divisions I am discussing?

✔ Have each of the three points been given approximately equal weight? Have I spent about the same amount of time discussing each part?

✔ Is essential information missing that could help the reader understand my point?

COHERENCE

✔ Do transitional words and phrases help make the divisions and my point clear?

✔ Does my concluding sentence clearly tie up the paragraph and explain why this topic was significant enough to discuss?

SENTENCE SKILLS

✔ Have I used a consistent point of view throughout my paragraph?

✔ Have I used specific rather than general words?

✔ Have I avoided wordiness and used concise wording?

✔ Are my sentences varied?

✔ Have I edited for spelling and other sentence skills errors, as listed on the inside back cover of the book?

Argument

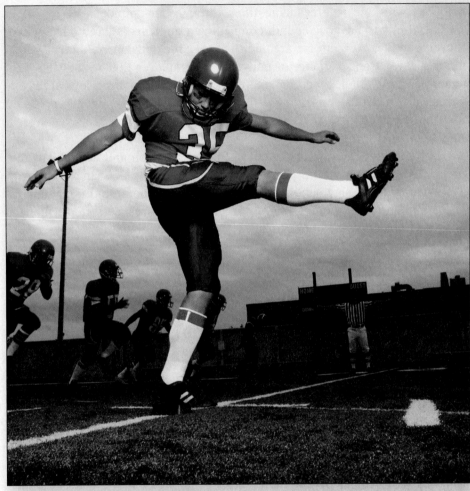

©Radius Images/Alamy Stock Photo

RESPONDING TO IMAGES

A large number of high school and college football players have experienced numerous concussions despite rules and new equipment standards. Write a paragraph in which you argue what more might be done to protect young football players' health or whether enough has already been done. Include at least three specific reasons to support your position.

TEACHING TIP
Ask students to complete
this writing prompt in class.

Most of us know someone who enjoys a good argument. Such a person usually challenges any sweeping statement we might make. "Why do you say that?" he or she will ask. "Give your reasons." Our questioner then listens carefully as we cite our reasons, waiting to see if we really do have solid evidence to support our point of view.

In an argument, each party must present his or her supporting evidence. The goal is to determine who has the more solid evidence to support his or her point of view. Having someone question us and ask for evidence may make us feel nervous, but it forces us to think through our opinions.

The ability to advance sound, compelling arguments is an important skill in everyday life. We can use argument to get an extension on a term paper, obtain a favor from a friend, or convince an employer that we are the right person for a job. Understanding argumentation based on clear, logical reasoning can also help us see through the sometimes faulty arguments advanced by advertisers, editors, politicians, and others who try to bring us over to their side.

In this section, you will be asked to argue a position and defend it with a series of solid reasons. In a general way, you are doing the same thing with all the paragraph assignments in the book: making a point and then supporting it. The difference here is that an argument advances a *debatable* point, a point that at least some of your readers will not be inclined to accept, so you must consider their objections. To prepare for this assignment, first read about seven strategies you can use in advancing an argument and work through the accompanying activities. Then read two student paragraphs and work through the questions that follow.

TEACHING TIP
Bring to class examples of argumentative writing. These examples might be found in newspaper editorials and other published sources. If your classroom has access to the Internet, find examples from Web sites. Help your students make connections.

ESL NOTE
Students from other cultures may not be accustomed to arguing a point or stating an opinion.

Strategies for Arguments

Because an argument assumes controversy, you have to work especially hard to convince readers of the validity of your position. Here are seven strategies to help you deal with readers whose viewpoints may differ from yours.

Use Tactful, Courteous Language

In an argument paragraph, you are attempting to persuade readers to see the merit of your viewpoint. It is important, then, not to anger them by referring to them or their opinions in rude terms. Don't write, "People who talk on the phone while driving are stupid." Also, stay away from sweeping statements like "Everyone knows that Internet dating is dangerous." Also, keep the focus on the issue you are discussing, not on the people involved in the debate. Don't write, "My opponents say that vaccines don't cause autism." Instead, write, "Supporters of vaccines say that vaccines don't cause autism," which suggests that those who don't agree with you are still reasonable people who are willing to consider differing opinions.

Establish Your Credibility

Another important requirement for arguing persuasively is establishing your credibility. In other words, you will need to convince your readers that you know what you are talking about and that your opinion is sound.

For instance, if you have been hit by a driver who was texting and you write an argument that texting and driving is dangerous, your personal experience would establish your credibility. You can also establish your credibility through researching your topic and using that research to support your points. Using research will be discussed in more detail in Chapters 20 and 21.

Point Out Common Ground

Another way to persuade readers to consider your opinion is to point out common ground—opinions that you share. Find points on which people on all sides of the argument can agree. Perhaps you are arguing that soda machines should be banned in schools. Before going into detail about your proposal, remind readers who oppose such a ban that you and they share certain goals: the importance of proper nutrition and a lower obesity rate for children and teens. Readers will be more receptive to your idea once they have considered the ways in which you and they think alike.

Provide Logical Support

A fourth way to persuade your readers is to provide logical support for your position. Thus, if you were trying to persuade the president of your college to hire more librarians, you might start by explaining that you have had to wait more than an hour to get help with research skills on several occasions. Instead of becoming emotional about it, you might then present logical reasons that these delays are hurting your experience as a student. For instance, you might point out that every time you have to wait for more than an hour, it stalls your progress and hurts your ability to finish the project on time. You might also survey other students to find out how many have had similar experiences. Finally, you might find out how many students use the library each semester and how many research papers are assigned each term. You could then present all this evidence as support to demonstrate why librarians are important to students' success and why more librarians should be available.

Acknowledge Differing Viewpoints

It's also important to acknowledge other viewpoints, rather than simply ignoring those that conflict with your own. Readers are more likely to consider your point of view if you indicate a willingness to consider theirs. One effective technique is to cite the opposing viewpoint in your topic sentence. For example, you might say, "Although some students believe that studying a foreign language is a waste of time, two years of foreign-language study should be required of all college graduates." In the first part, you acknowledge the other side's point of view; in the second, you state your opinion, suggesting that yours is the stronger viewpoint. Another effective technique is to include a separate sentence before your topic sentence to acknowledge the opposing viewpoint. If you oppose workplace discrimination, you might first say, "Some employers believe that male employees shouldn't wear earrings."

When Appropriate, Grant the Merits of Differing Viewpoints

Sometimes an opposing viewpoint contains a point whose validity you cannot deny. The strongest strategy, then, is to admit that the point is a good one. Admit the merit of one aspect of the other argument while making it clear that you still believe your argument to be stronger overall. Suppose that you oppose mandatory curbside recycling. You might start with a statement admitting that the other side has a valid point, but you could quickly follow this admission with a statement making your own viewpoint clear: "Granted, recycling reduces landfill waste and conserves natural resources, but mandatory curbside recycling will cost taxpayers too much and, therefore, curbside recycling should be voluntary."

Rebut Differing Viewpoints

Sometimes simply acknowledging a differing viewpoint and presenting your own may not be enough. When you are dealing with an issue that your readers feel strongly about, you may need to rebut an opposing viewpoint by pointing out problems with that viewpoint. You can use this strategy at any point in your paragraph. Imagine, for instance, that you oppose a sex offender registry, but you know that many supporters believe that a registry reduces crimes of this nature. You might rebut that point by citing that only offenders who comply with the law register, so the registry offers a false sense of security.

ACTIVITY 1

The box below summarizes the seven strategies for arguments. Read the statements that follow it, and in the space provided, write the letter of the kind of strategy used in each case.

A. Use Tactful, Courteous Language

B. Establish Your Credibility

C. Point Out Common Ground

D. Provide Logical Support

E. Acknowledge Differing Viewpoints

F. Grant the Merits of Differing Viewpoints

G. Rebut Differing Viewpoints

_____E_____ 1. While homeless shelters are one answer to helping the homeless population, a better answer is providing needy families with more affordable housing, job training, and subsidized child care.

_____F_____ 2. Granted, online classes are an excellent option for college courses, but they work primarily for students who are self-motivated and not for students who lack time-management skills.

_____A_____ 3. Supporters of closed or confidential adoption value the privacy of the birth mother.

<u> C </u> 4. We all want what is best for our children and believe that they should be protected.

<u> G </u> 5. The new athletic center sounds like a good idea, but college students, already financially strapped, would have trouble paying the proposed tuition increase to cover the cost of building it.

<u> D </u> 6. Students who are struggling in classes often need the extra help that tutors can provide, so the college should open a tutoring center.

<u> B </u> 7. Having lived alone for ten years, I can say with certainty that there are some benefits to not having roommates.

ACTIVITY 2

This activity will give you practice in stating a clear position and acknowledging an opposing viewpoint. In each item, you will see a statement and then a question related to that statement. Write *two* answers to each question. Your first will answer "yes" to the question and briefly explain why. The other will answer "no" to the question and also state why.

 TIP Use words such as *should* (*not*), *must* (*not*), and *ought* (*not*) to make your position clear.

EXAMPLE

Cigarette smoking has been proven to be harmful. Should it therefore be made illegal?

Answers will vary.

"**Yes**": Because smoking has been shown to have so many harmful health effects, the sale of cigarettes should be made illegal.

"**No**": Although smoking has been linked to various health problems, adults should have the right to make their own decision about whether or not to smoke. Smoking, therefore, should not be made illegal.

1. Animals feel pain when they are killed for food. Is eating animals therefore immoral?

   "**Yes**": When animals are slaughtered, these animals feel real pain, therefore killing animals for food is immoral.

   "**No**": Humane devices are used to slaughter animals for food, so eating those animals is not morally wrong.

2. Professional boxing often leads to serious injury. Should this sport be outlawed?

"Yes": Because professional boxers suffer serious injuries such as Parkinson's disease, this brutal sport should be outlawed.

"No": Although some professional boxers suffer injuries, the majority of boxers don't. Professional boxing, therefore, is generally a safe sport that should not be outlawed.

3. The obesity rate among children and teenagers is rising. Should schools ban the sale of soda and junk food?

"Yes": Because the obesity rate among children and teenagers is rising, schools have a responsibility to teach students about proper nutrition. One way schools ought to do this is by banning the sale of soda and junk food on campus.

"No": If the sale of soda and junk food are banned on campus, students will go elsewhere to purchase these items, taking with them revenue currently used for school functions. Vending machines, therefore, should not be removed from campuses.

4. Some teenagers commit violent crimes, such as rape and murder. Should they be tried in court as adults?

"Yes": Teenagers who commit violent crimes such as rape and murder should be tried in court as adults because they should be in control of and responsible for their own actions.

"No": Although teenagers do commit violent crimes, these youth are still minors with their whole lives ahead of them, and therefore should be tried in court as juveniles rather than as adults.

5. Studies show that boys and girls learn differently. Should single-sex education be encouraged?

"Yes": Because studies show that boys and girls learn differently, single-sex education should be encouraged to accommodate each group's specific learning needs.

"No": Because boys and girls learn differently, they can benefit from being in the same learning environment. Single-sex education, therefore, should not be encouraged.

Part of arguing persuasively is being able to acknowledge, grant the merits of, and/ or rebuff differing viewpoints. To do this successfully, you must be able to critically evaluate another person's argument. This activity will give you practice in evaluating other people's arguments.

1. First, select a reading from the anthology in the back of the text or use a reading assigned to you by your instructor.

2. List the author's main argument and supporting points.

3. Evaluate how the author supports his or her argument and whether, even if you disagree with the position, the argument is shown to have validity.

4. Discuss whether you personally agree or disagree with the author. Explain why.

5. Explain how the author's argument could be made stronger or which points you would most strongly rebuff.

Paragraphs to Consider

Mandatory Attendance Isn't the Answer

[1]Teachers want students to learn, and students want this, too. [2]They both know that one of the best places to learn is the classroom. [3]In college, however, class attendance shouldn't be mandatory. [4]First of all, mandatory attendance has its flaws. [5]Even if students are in class, they may not be learning. [6]A student may be so tired from pulling a double shift at work that he dozes off in class, and another student may be preoccupied because her daughter is sick. [7]Some teachers are too nice, so they don't enforce the attendance policy. [8]If a student begs or gives a sob story, a teacher might make an exception. [9]Teachers sometimes forget to take attendance, so those who weren't in class get a free pass, which is unfair. [10]Another reason attendance shouldn't be mandatory is because college students have valid reasons for their absences. [11]Many students have jobs, and sometimes a boss may be inflexible about a work schedule. [12]Plus, students often cannot afford to miss work. [13]Many students have a family, which is just as important as school. [14]A child might be sick, or a babysitter might cancel at the last minute, causing a student to miss class. [15]Students might also miss class because they are sick and don't want to make anyone else sick. [16]The most important reason against a mandatory attendance is that college students are responsible for their own learning. [17]Although some students may be recent high school graduates, in college they are considered adults. [18]If students miss

continued

ACTIVITY 3

TEACHING TIP
Multiple essays in the anthology present arguments that students can analyze. Use the "Readings Listed by Rhetorical Mode" at the beginning of the book to assign readings, or allow students to make their own choices.

TEACHING TIP
Read these paragraphs aloud. Ask students to underline the topic sentence, specific examples, and transitions in each paragraph before answering the questions.

class, they can catch up by asking classmates for lecture notes or emailing instructors about their absence. [19]When a student simply "blows off" class, that student should accept the consequences. [20]Some supporters of mandatory attendance worry that students will think that class is optional if attendance is no longer required. [21]However, teachers can emphasize its importance and promote attendance by having in-class activities that can't be made up later. [22]For all these reasons, mandatory attendance has no place in college.

Bring Back Public Humiliation!

[1]Society has gotten lazy about manners, and in order to get people back on track, public humiliation should be reinstated. [2]One offense that many people are guilty of is forgetting to say "please" or "thank you." [3]Using words like "please" and "thank you" shows gratitude to others for their actions, but omitting these words shows a lack of concern for how others may feel. [4]Those who are found guilty of this offense should be required to stand outside of the location where they committed the offense and wear a board that announces, "I don't know how to use 'please' and 'thank you.' Please help me practice." [5]They should be required to do this exercise for one hour per offense. [6]In order to be good parents, people should teach their children to use "please" and "thank you." [7]Another offense that many people are guilty of is talking on cell phones at inappropriate times. [8]When people are found guilty, they should be subjected to *The Scarlet Letter* punishment and be forced to wear a large letter "R" for one month. [9]This letter would alert others that the person is guilty of being rude. [10]Restaurants could refuse service to or have a special section for people bearing the letter "R"; stores could force people with the letter "R" to use one specific check-out line. [11]In this way, people in general would know that the offender had treated others disrespectfully. [12]A final rude offense that many people are guilty of is aggressive driving like tailgating, cutting off other cars, or failing to stay in one lane. [13]People who are found guilty should be required to turn in their car for a period of a month and drive a punishment car. [14]Punishment cars would be painted in obnoxious colors and announce that the driver had "committed rudeness." [15]Using public humiliation to deter social misbehavior has a long history of working and should be brought back in full force before society's rudeness gets out of hand.

About Unity

1. Which sentence in "Bring Back Public Humiliation!" should be eliminated in the interest of paragraph unity? (*Write the sentence number here.*)   6

About Support

2. How many reasons are given to support the topic sentence in each paragraph?

   a. In "Mandatory Attendance Isn't the Answer" ___ one ___ two

       √ three ___ four

   b. In "Bring Back Public Humiliation!" ___ one ___ two √ three

       ___ four

3. Which sentences in "Mandatory Attendance Isn't the Answer" point out common ground?   1   and   2

4. Which paragraph rebuts differing viewpoints? "Mandatory Attendance Isn't the Answer"

About Coherence

5. What transition words or phrases are used to introduce the three reasons listed in "Mandatory Attendance Isn't the Answer"?

   First of all   Another reason   The most important reason

QUESTIONS

ESL NOTE
To achieve coherence and grammatical accuracy in their writing, nonnative students would benefit from instruction in the context of an argumentative paragraph. Among Spanish-speaking students, a typical error is "I am agree," which is a direct translation. A review of connectors that show adding information would be helpful, too.

Developing an Argument Paragraph

Development through Prewriting

Lily is the author of "Mandatory Attendance Isn't the Answer." She was stumped when her instructor told her to choose a topic for the argument paragraph. She first thought of topics that she thought she *should* write about—death penalty, abortion, gun control, cloning, medical marijuana, drinking age, mercy killing—but worried that she wouldn't have enough evidence. Lily also worried that her topic wouldn't be good enough because, as she said, she "just didn't feel it."

She decided on her topic after her classmate Nate said, "Think of an issue that gets you all riled up, one that makes you clench your jaw just thinking about it." That morning, her classmate Zach slept through most of class but received credit for being there, yet the week before Lily missed class to take her daughter to the doctor's and, as a result, lost points for attendance. "That's so unfair," she told Nate. "Attendance shouldn't be mandatory. We're in college after all, not high school."

TEACHING TIP
You may want to provide a supplemental activity. Have students choose another topic related to college life, such as cell-phone use and texting during class. Next, ask them to make a list of their ideas, which they can then use to create a scratch outline.

Lily began by making a list of all the negative aspects of mandatory attendance. This is what she came up with:

---

college students are adults!

college is not high school

we're responsible for our own learning

we should accept the consequences

teachers should make classes more fun

valid reasons for missing classes

work conflicts

family is just as important

not want to make others sick

mandatory classroom participation doesn't work

able to catch up

not always learning even if in class

some teachers are too nice and don't enforce the policy

Prof. Cummins is too strict about everything

some teachers forget to take attendance

teachers have different tardiness rules

After Lily wrote her list, she thought about how she could organize her ideas. She came up with three supporting reasons: (1) flaws in the current policy, (2) valid reasons for absences, and (3) students' own responsibility. She went back to her list, struck out items that didn't fit, and numbered items according to her three reasons:

---

3 college students are adults!

3 college is not high school

3 we're responsible for our own learning

3 we should accept the consequences

~~teachers should make classes more fun~~

---

continued

2 valid reasons for missing classes

2 work conflicts

2 family is just as important

2 not want to make others sick

~~mandatory classroom participation doesn't work~~

3 able to catch up

1 not always learning even if in class

1 some teachers are too nice and don't enforce the policy

~~Prof. Cummins is too strict about everything~~

1 some teachers forget to take attendance

~~teachers have different tardiness rules~~

Lily then prepared a scratch outline:

Class attendance shouldn't be mandatory in college

- mandatory attendance has flaws
- valid reasons for students' absences
- students responsible for their own learning

Lily knew that some of her readers might not share her opinions, so she needed to consider their viewpoints. She jotted down three reasons in favor of mandatory attendance, and then thought about how she might address those points:

recent high school graduates are used to this being the policy (they're not in high school anymore)

students will think that class is optional (need to promote, not require, attendance)

~~rewards those who regularly attend class~~ (this point is weak)

Using the material she created, Lily wrote the following first draft of her paragraph:

In my own opinion, class attendance shouldn't be mandatory in college. First, mandatory attendance has its flaws. Even if students are in class, they may not be learning. Some teachers are too nice, so they don't enforce the attendance policy. If a student begs or gives a sob story, a teacher might make an exception. Teachers sometimes forget to take attendance, so those who weren't in class get a free pass. I think that that's so unfair! Second, college students have valid reasons for their absences. Many students have jobs. Many students in this day and age also have a family. A student might also miss class because he or she is sick and doesn't want to make anyone else sick. Third, I'm against a mandatory attendance policy because we are responsible for our own learning. Although some students may be used to such a policy having just come from high school, college students are adults. If a student misses class, he or she should be able to catch up by asking a classmate for the lecture notes or emailing the instructor. When a student simply blows off class, that student should accept the consequences. My opponents worry that students will think that class is optional if attendance is no longer required. However, teachers can emphasize its importance and promote attendance by having in-class activities that can't be made up later.

Development through Revising

Lily's instructor asked her to pair up with another student, so she turned to her classmate Nate. He read her paper aloud while she listened. As Nate read, they listened for spots where her paper didn't read clearly. Then Nate wrote several comments on Lily's draft:

Given how many times *I've* been absent, you know I support your position! Seriously, I like how you consider other viewpoints but don't let those points weaken yours. In fact, this strategy makes your argument stronger. Also, you found a topic that you care about, and this shows. As a reader, I know exactly what your position is.

Okay, you know I hate pointing out what's wrong, but I want to help you, so here goes. You use transitions—*first, second, third*—but I'm wondering why you organized your ideas in this way. I'm thinking that the last point is the most important. Also, I found myself wanting to see more details about work and family. There's so much more

CHAPTER 14   Argument   263

you could say. You could also end on a stronger note by adding one last sentence.

  If you still want to revise your paragraph, think about what our instructor said regarding point of view and concise wording.

With these comments in mind, Lily revised her paragraph until she produced the version that appears at the beginning of this chapter.

©tonioyumui/Getty Images

RESPONDING TO IMAGES

Images can make effective arguments as well. What visual argument does the poster shown here make?

Writing an Argument Paragraph

ARGUING YOUR OPINION

Choose one of the topics below and follow the directions. The purpose is to take a strong stand, and you must support your claim with at least three reasons.

- Write a letter to the editor arguing against or supporting the banning of a specific book like *To Kill a Mockingbird*, *Slaughter-house Five*, *The Adventures of Huckleberry Finn*, or a book of your choosing.

- Your college has just announced that the grading scale is going to be changed from a 10-point scale (79–89, 90–100) to a 7-point scale (85–92, 93–100). Write a paragraph in which you support or oppose this decision.

- Your local school district is going to require all students to wear school uniforms. Write a paragraph (either as a student attending or as a parent) in which you support or oppose this decision.

- As you are applying for a new job, your potential employer requests to see your social networking profiles. Write a letter expressing why you don't think this is a valid way to check a potential employee's background.

- As you are starting your new job, you are informed that you get eight days of holiday and vacation time a year. Write a paragraph explaining why you should get more holidays and longer vacations.

- Since the current age for a person to get his or her own credit card is eighteen, many credit card companies canvas college campuses getting college students to sign up for multiple cards. Write a paragraph arguing that the minimum age for a credit card should be raised from eighteen to twenty-one years.

TEACHING TIP
You may want to model
the writing process for
your students by doing this
assignment along with
them. Go through all the
stages, including prewriting
and revising, and seek
feedback from them. They
will appreciate your efforts
to create a writing
community.

PREWRITING

a. As a useful exercise to help you begin developing your argument, your instructor might give class members a chance to "stand up" for what they believe in. One side of the front of the room should be designated *strong agreement* and the other side *strong disagreement*, with an imaginary line representing varying degrees of agreement or disagreement in between. As the class stands in front of the room, the instructor will read one value statement at a time from the list above, and students will move to the appropriate spot, depending on their degree of agreement or disagreement. Some time will be allowed for students, first, to discuss with those near them the reasons they are standing where they are; and, second, to state to those at the other end of the scale the reasons for their position.

b. Begin your paragraph by writing a sentence that expresses your attitude toward one of the value statements above, for example, "I feel that the minimum age to apply for a credit card should be raised from eighteen to twenty-one years."

c. Outline the reason or reasons you hold the opinion that you do. Your support may be based on your own experience, the experience of someone you know, or logic. For example, an outline of a paragraph based on one student's logic looked like this:

> I feel that the minimum age to apply for a credit card should be raised from eighteen to twenty-one years for the following reasons:
> 1. Eighteen-year-olds may be inexperienced handling their finances.
> 2. Eighteen-year-olds may not have the income to make credit card payments.
> 3. Most of all, given that so many young adults are in financial debt, they should avoid ruining their credit history.

Another outline, based on experience, proceeded as follows:

> The experiences of a twenty-one-year-old I know show that the minimum age to apply for a credit card should be raised from eighteen to twenty-one years.
> 1. At eighteen, this person had a credit card but did not even have a checking account.
> 2. At eighteen, this person was earning minimum wage at a part-time, temporary job and was unable to make monthly credit card payments.
> 3. This person didn't realize until he was twenty-one that a few missed payments would ruin his credit history.

d. Write a first draft of your paragraph, providing specific details to back up each point in your outline.

REVISING: PEER REVIEW

Put your paragraph away for a while, ideally at least a day. Ask a friend or classmate whose judgment you trust to read and critique it. Your reader should refer to the FOUR BASES Checklist provided at the end of this chapter for questions to consider. Continue revising your work until you and your reader can answer "yes" to all the questions.

©Jacob Lund/ Shutterstock

Requiring Civil Service

Currently, when high school students in America graduate, they have the option of continuing their education or working, in contrast to countries like Switzerland and Israel that require either military or civilian service for a minimum period of time. Some countries, like Austria, allow conscientious objectors to participate in a civilian corps instead of military service. In this assignment, you are to argue that all high school graduates must participate in AmeriCorps for a minimum of twelve months. Your argument will require you to visit the AmeriCorps Web site (https://www.nationalservice.gov/programs/americorps) to learn about the three different programs and their projects and benefits. Use the following, or something similar, for your topic sentence:

> Upon graduating from high school, all American students should be required to participate in AmeriCorps for a minimum period of twelve months, after which they can enter college, enter the working force, or re-enter AmeriCorps.

> For each reason you advance, include at least one persuasive example. Support can be presented as researched facts (Chapters 20 and 21), as anecdotes (Chapter 7), as contrasts (Chapter 11), and/or as processes (Chapter 9). After deciding on your points of support, arrange them in a brief outline, saving your strongest point for last. In your paragraph, introduce each of your reasons with an additional transition, such as *first of all, another, also,* and *finally.*

WRITING ASSIGNMENT 2

Academic

TEACHING TIP
Encourage students to use the prewriting and revising ideas mentioned in Writing Assignment 1.

Using Research for Support

Write a paragraph in which you use research findings to help support one of the points below.

- Cigarettes should be illegal.

- Any person convicted of drunken driving should be required to spend time in jail.

- Drivers should not be permitted to text while driving.

- High schools should (or should not) pass out birth control devices and information to students.

- Schools should be in session year round.

- Advertising should not be permitted on young children's TV shows.

WRITING ASSIGNMENT 3

Academic

- All college students should be required to take four years of a foreign language.

- All students (K–12) and all college students should be required to take a physical education course every day.

- To save money, all high schools should require every student to take at least four online courses.

See if you can organize your paragraph in the form of three separate and distinct reasons that support the topic. Put these reasons into a scratch outline and use it as a guide in writing your paragraph. Part 4 will show you how to use keywords and the Internet to think about your topic and do research.

REFLECTIVE ACTIVITY

1. Exchange argument paragraphs with a classmate. Ask him or her to explain whether your paragraph is convincing. If not, ask your partner to offer suggestions to strengthen it. Do the same for him or her.
2. Think about the suggestions your partner has made. Do you agree with all of them? Are there any that you might reject?

©mavo/Shutterstock

BEYOND THE CLASSROOM

Argument

Beyond the classroom, you will find yourself taking a stand on an issue and providing solid evidence to support that position. Attorneys use arguments in courts, both criminal and civil. Legislators, meeting in bodies such as city councils, state assemblies, and the U.S. Congress, argue for the passage of bills and resolutions. Advertisers use argumentative techniques to get consumers to buy products or use services. Fundraisers use argumentation to persuade people to donate to charities, building funds, and other worthy causes.

For this writing assignment, you will write an argument paragraph with a specific purpose and for a specific audience. Imagine that, for various reasons, you experienced financial hardship and had to use your credit card to help you "make ends meet." Now you are having a difficult time making minimum monthly payments. Write a letter to the credit card company in which you explain your situation and negotiate a new payment plan. Be sure to address any doubts that the company may have about your ability to honor the agreement.

Visit the *US Newspaper List* at http://www.usnpl.com and click on the link to your state. From the listing, select a newspaper in your area, and then scroll to that paper's Opinion or Op-Ed section. Read one of the articles posted and write a paragraph in which you identify the author's main point and supporting reasons.

OR

Go to https://www.pinterest.com/ and put the following terms into the search box: visual rhetoric social justice OR activist art social justice. Choose an image from the search results and explain what argument the image creator is making and how the argument is being made.

©Tetra Images/
Shutterstock

ARGUMENT CHECKLIST: THE FOUR BASES

UNITY

✔ Does my paragraph have a stated topic sentence that clearly asserts an argument?

✔ Are there sentences or details that do not support my topic sentence and therefore should be eliminated or rewritten?

SUPPORT

✔ Have I provided persuasive details to support my argument?

✔ Have I included enough specific details to persuade my reader to agree with my argument?

COHERENCE

✔ Have I acknowledged the opposing point of view, to demonstrate I have considered other arguments?

✔ Has the most powerful reason been saved for last?

✔ Do transitional words and phrases help make the paragraph clear?

✔ Does my concluding sentence clearly tie up the paragraph and add a final persuasive touch?

SENTENCE SKILLS

✔ Have I used a consistent point of view throughout my paragraph?

✔ Have I used specific rather than general words?

✔ Have I avoided wordiness and used concise wording?

✔ Are my sentences varied?

✔ Have I edited for spelling and other sentence skills errors, as listed on the inside back cover of the book?

A WRITER'S TEMPLATE: Across Disciplines

As you are reading the following paragraph written by Sarah for her English class, think about what advice you would offer her as she prepares to write the final draft. Does her paragraph cover all four bases of effective writing? In order to be sure, review each question in the checklist that follows and write your answers on the lines provided.

TEACHING TIP
In pairs, ask students to discuss what advice they would give this writer.

Shania Ralston's Remarkable Career

[1]Until her recent retirement, Shania Ralston was a partner and highly successful attorney at Hoffman, Hardy & Brooks. [2]For more than thirty-five years, her practice focused exclusively on environmental litigation, environmental and natural resources, and chemical manufacturing. [3]Before coming to Hoffman, Hardy & Brooks, Ralston received her bachelor's degree in philosophy and political science from Washington University in St. Louis. [4]In 1989, Ralston graduated from Harvard Law School, earning a J.D. in Law and Social Change. [5]In her many years at Hoffman, Hardy & Brooks, Ralston became known for litigation concerning the endangered species act, natural resource damages, and class action suits against chemical companies. [6]She regularly represented clients in environmental cases in which individual plaintiffs sought statutory and/or punitive damages on behalf of themselves and a class. [7]Over the years, Ralston successfully litigated several lawsuits that were worth millions. [8]For example, she represented farming operations that faced polluted water from regional factories. [9]She made frequent trips to meet with the farmers in those regions. [10]In 2014, she testified in the congressional hearing for the new Environmental Protection Agency (EPA) standards, her testimony was key to the passage of the new standards. [11]At her retirement party last month, several clients spoke warmly and appreciatively about her tireless work on their behalf, and the firm presented her with a special plaque commemorating her many achievements.

A WRITER'S CHECKLIST

Unity

✔ Does the writer give a clear, direct topic sentence stating the main point of the paragraph? _Yes_

✔ Is all the material on target and in support of the topic sentence? If not, which sentences should be deleted in the interest of unity? _No, sentences 7 and 9 are irrelevant to the overall purpose of the paragraph and should be deleted in the interest of unity._

Support

✔ Does Sarah provide specific evidence to support her topic sentence? _Yes_

✔ Are there enough supporting details? _Yes_

Coherence

✔ Does the writer use transitions and other connective devices? _Yes_ List at least two here: _until, for more than, before coming, for example_

Sentence Skills

✔ Are sentences varied? _Yes_

✔ Can you find any other sentence skills mistakes, as listed on the back inside cover of the book? If you can find a mistake, what type of mistake is it? _Yes, sentence 10 is a comma splice._

Collaborative Activity

In your group or class, make an outline of Sarah's paragraph. Looking at the outline, can you think of any additional supporting details that could be added to make this paragraph more effective?

©Jacob Lund/
Shutterstock
TEACHING TIP
Encourage everyone in the
class to participate in this
collaborative activity.

4 Essay Development

PART FOUR SHOWS YOU HOW TO

- differentiate between an essay and a paragraph

- structure a traditional essay

- determine your point of view

- do a personal review

PART FOUR ALSO GIVES YOU PRACTICE

- beginning an essay with a point, or thesis

- revising essays for unity, support, coherence, and sentence skills

- writing introductory and concluding paragraphs

- developing nine different patterns of essay development

EXPLORING WRITING PROMPT:

In college, you will be asked to write essays. In Part 4, you will learn how to write them, but before you start, take a few minutes to explore what you think—and how you feel—about essays. Freewrite, brainstorm, or diagram your thoughts on this topic.

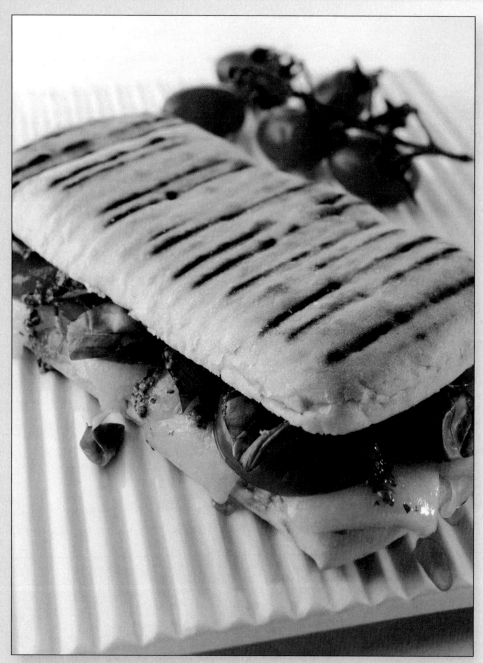

©Ingram Publishing/Superstock

TEACHING TIP
Ask students to complete this writing prompt in class.

RESPONDING TO IMAGES

Everyone knows how to fix a sandwich. No matter what we use for its filling—a hamburger patty, egg salad, peanut butter and jelly, cold cuts—we always start with two pieces of bread. An essay is like a sandwich in that it has a "top" and "bottom" bun; namely, an introduction and a conclusion. Think about how else a sandwich resembles an essay. Using this food metaphor, what are paragraphs and transitions?

What Is an Essay?

Differences between an Essay and a Paragraph

An essay is simply a paper of several paragraphs, rather than one paragraph, that supports a single point. In an essay, subjects can and should be treated more fully than they would in a single-paragraph paper. Unlike paragraphs that are usually developed using one mode of writing, like description, essays are usually developed using several modes of writing to support the single point.

The main idea or point developed in an essay is called the *thesis statement* or *thesis sentence* (rather than, as in a paragraph, the *topic sentence*). The thesis statement appears in the introductory paragraph, and it is then developed in the supporting paragraphs that follow. A concluding paragraph closes the essay.

TEACHING TIP
You may want to point out the similarities between an essay and a paragraph.

Structure of the Traditional Essay

A Model Essay

The following model will help you understand the form of an essay. Diane Woods, the writer of the paragraph on moviegoing in Chapter 1, later decided to develop her subject more fully. Here is the essay that resulted.

The Hazards of Moviegoing

I am a movie fanatic. My friends count on me to know movie trivia (who was the pigtailed little girl in *E.T.: The Extra-Terrestrial*? Drew Barrymore) and to remember every big Oscar awarded since I was in grade school (Best picture 1994? *Forrest Gump*). My friends, though, have stopped asking me if I want to go out to the movies. While I love movies as much as ever, the inconvenience of going out, the temptations of the theater, and the behavior of some patrons are reasons for me to wait and rent the DVD.

To begin with, I just don't enjoy the general hassle of the evening. Since small local movie theaters are a thing of the past, I have to drive for fifteen minutes to get to the nearest multiplex. The parking lot is shared with several restaurants and a giant supermarket, so it's always jammed. I have to drive around at a snail's pace until I spot another driver backing out. Then it's time to stand in an endless line, with the constant threat that tickets for the show I want will sell out. If we do get tickets, the theater will be so crowded that I won't be able to sit with my friends, or we'll have to sit in a front row gaping up at a giant screen. I have to shell out a

Introductory paragraph

TEACHING TIP
Mention that an essay may contain more than one introductory paragraph.

First supporting paragraph

continued

Second supporting
paragraph

TEACHING TIP
Mixing Modes of Writing:
Point out to students the
different modes of writing
used in this essay. You
might discuss with them
why the author chose
these modes to support
the essay and what other
modes might have been
used.

Third supporting paragraph

Concluding paragraph

ridiculous amount of money—up to $11—for a ticket. That entitles me
to sit while my shoes seal themselves to a sticky floor coated with
spilled soda, bubble gum, and crushed Raisinets.

Second, the theater offers tempting snacks that I really don't
need. Like most of us, I have to battle an expanding waistline. At
home I do pretty well by simply not buying stuff that is bad for me.
I can make do with snacks like celery and carrot sticks because
there is no ice cream in the freezer. Going to the theater, however,
is like spending my evening in a 7-Eleven that's been equipped with
a movie screen and comfortable seats. As I try to persuade myself
to just have a diet Coke, the smell of fresh popcorn dripping with
butter soon overcomes me. Chocolate bars the size of small
automobiles seem to jump into my hands. I risk putting on the
pounds as I chew enormous mouthfuls of Milk Duds. By the time I
leave the theater, I feel disgusted with myself.

Many of the other patrons are even more of a problem than the
concession stand. Little kids race up and down the aisles, usually in
giggling packs. Teenagers try to impress their friends by talking
back to the screen, whistling, and making what they consider to be
hilarious noises. Adults act as if they were at home in their own
living room. They comment loudly on the ages of the stars and
reveal plot twists that are supposed to be a secret until the film's
end. Additionally, people of all ages create disgusting messes and
rude distractions. They leave tacky remnants of candy on the hand
rests, stick gum on their seats, and drop popcorn tubs or cups of
crushed ice and soda on the floor. They also cough and burp,
squirm endlessly in their seats, file out for repeated trips to the
restrooms or concession stands, and elbow me out of the armrest
on either side of my seat.

After arriving home from the movies one night, I decided that I
was not going to be a moviegoer anymore. I was tired of the
problems involved in getting to the theater, resisting unhealthy
snacks, and dealing with the patrons. The next day, I arranged to
have premium movie channels added to my cable TV service, and I
also subscribed to Netflix. I may now see movies a bit later than
other people, but I'll be more relaxed watching box office hits in the
comfort of my own living room.

Parts of an Essay

"The Hazards of Moviegoing" is a good example of the standard short essay you will write in college English. It is a composition of over five hundred words that consists of an introduction, conclusion, and body. The introduction and conclusion are usually only one paragraph each, and the body of the essay is at least three paragraphs, but can often be more.

Introductory Paragraph

The introductory paragraph of an essay should start with several sentences that attract the reader's interest. It should then advance the central idea, or *thesis,* that will be developed in the essay. The thesis often includes a *plan of development*—a "preview" of the major points that will support the thesis. These supporting points should be listed in the order in which they will appear in the essay. Such a thesis might assert, "Winter is my favorite season because I like the weather, the holidays, and the sports," leading to an essay that has a paragraph about weather, followed by a paragraph about the holidays, and so forth. In some cases, however, the plan of development is omitted. For example, a thesis that claims, "Education can be a key to socioeconomic security" doesn't state how the essay will be developed, but still advances a central idea.

ESL NOTE
The development of an essay may be different in other countries, so direct instruction about the parts of an essay will be helpful for nonnative speakers, especially the introductory and concluding paragraphs.

TEACHING TIP
The introductory paragraph serves as the "movie trailer" for the actual "film."

ACTIVITY 1

1. In "The Hazards of Moviegoing," which sentence or sentences are used to attract the reader's interest?

   a. First sentence

   b. First two sentences

   c. First three sentences

2. In which sentence is the thesis of the essay presented?

   a. Third sentence

   b. Fourth sentence

3. Does the thesis include a plan of development?

   a. Yes

   b. No

4. Write the words in the thesis that announce the three major supporting points in the essay:

   a.   inconvenience of going out

   b.   temptations of the theater

   c.   behavior of some patrons

TEACHING TIP
Stress to students that not all essays have three body paragraphs.

Body: Supporting Paragraphs

Many essays have three supporting points, developed at length over three separate paragraphs. However, more developed essays require four or more body paragraphs to support the thesis. This is very common in essays with thesis statements that omit a plan of development. Each of the supporting paragraphs should begin with a *topic sentence* that states the point to be detailed in that paragraph. Just as a thesis provides a focus for the entire essay, the topic sentence provides a focus for a supporting paragraph.

ACTIVITY 2

TEACHING TIP
Remind students to avoid announcing their topic.

1. What is the topic sentence for the first supporting paragraph of the model essay?

   To begin with, I just don't enjoy the general hassle of the evening.

   _____

2. The first topic sentence is then supported by the following details (fill in the missing details):

   a. Have to drive fifteen minutes

   b. Parking lot is always jammed.

   c. Endless ticket line

   d. Tickets may sell out, and theater is crowded.

   e. Tickets cost up to $11 each.

   f. Sticky floor

3. What is the topic sentence for the second supporting paragraph of the essay?

   Second, the theater offers tempting snacks that I really don't need.

   _____

4. The second topic sentence is then supported by the following details:

   a. At home, only snacks are celery and carrot sticks.

   b. Theater is like a 7-Eleven with seats.

      (1) fresh popcorn

      (2) chocolate bars

      (3) Milk Duds

5. What is the topic sentence for the third supporting paragraph of the essay?

Many of the other patrons are even more of a problem than the concession stand.

6. The third topic sentence is then supported by the following details:

a. Little kids race up and down the aisles.

b. Teenagers talk back to the screen, whistle, make funny noises.

c. Adults talk loudly and reveal plot twists.

d. People of all ages create disgusting messes and rude distractions.

Concluding Paragraph

The concluding paragraph often summarizes the essay by briefly restating the thesis and, at times, the main supporting points. In addition, the writer often presents a concluding thought about the subject of the paper.

TEACHING TIP
The concluding paragraph serves as the "ending" to a "movie." Unlike a movie, though, writers should avoid cliffhanger endings.

1. Which two sentences in the concluding paragraph restate the thesis and supporting points of the essay?

(a.) First and second

b. Second and third

c. Third and fourth

ACTIVITY 3

2. Which sentence in the concluding paragraph contains the final thought of the essay?

a. Second

b. Third

(c.) Fourth

Diagram of an Essay

Introduction

Introductory Paragraph

Introduction

Thesis statement

Plan of development

Points 1,2,3

The *introduction* attracts the reader's interest.

The *thesis statement* (or *thesis sentence*) states the main idea advanced in the paper.

The *plan of development* is a list of points that support the thesis. The points are presented in the order in which they will be developed in the paper.

Body

First Supporting Paragraph

Topic sentence (point 1)

Specific evidence

The *topic sentence* advances the first supporting point for the thesis, and the *specific evidence* in the rest of the paragraph develops that first point.

Second Supporting Paragraph

Topic sentence (point 2)

Specific evidence

The *topic sentence* advances the second supporting point for the thesis, and the *specific evidence* in the rest of the paragraph develops that second point.

Third Supporting Paragraph

Topic sentence (point 3)

Specific evidence

The *topic sentence* advances the third supporting point for the thesis, and the *specific evidence* in the rest of the paragraph develops that third point.

Conclusion

Concluding Paragraph

Summary,

conclusion,

or both

A *summary* is a brief restatement of the thesis and its main points. A *conclusion* is a final thought or two stemming from the subject of the paper.

TEACHING TIP
Remind students that this diagram shows one basic model. Some essays do not include a "plan of development" and many include more than three supporting paragraphs.

TEACHING TIP
Encourage students to refer to this diagram when working on an essay.

The Only Thing We Have to Fear

Introduction

During the Great Depression, President Roosevelt claimed, "The only thing we have to fear is fear itself." He wanted to inspire citizens as a way to spur the economy. In his Nobel Prize acceptance speech delivered in December 1950, William Faulkner, the great American novelist, said, "The basest of all things is to be afraid." Uttered many decades ago, both these ideas still have relevance. Some young people make important life decisions based on deep-seated anxieties. They fear that they won't be accepted by others, that they won't find a mate, or that they just aren't living life to the fullest.

Thesis with plan of development

Body

Many people are frightened they won't fit in. To try and fit in, they spend money on things like expensive boats, cars, and clothes they feel will secure friendships. Deep in the pits of their stomachs is the gnawing fear that, without such material objects, their friends will abandon them. Then they will have to sit home alone on the weekends. They have forgotten that, to those of character, possessions and image are far less important than integrity, honesty, and compassion.

Topic sentence that connects to thesis with first point

Some individuals—both men and women—fear they will never be able to attract and keep a lifelong partner. Therefore, they make enormous efforts to re-create themselves. For example, they follow ludicrous diets and exercise for hours each day. Some even drink expensive commercial concoctions to curb their appetites and lose weight. Others, looking ahead to their more mature years, plan to get collagen injections, face lifts, and even breast implants.

Topic sentence that connects to thesis with second point

However, the fear that causes the greatest damage to the human spirit is the one that makes people question the value and fullness of their own lives. Too many—young and old alike—are afraid that they might miss out on "the good life," which people equate as owning the best of everything. So, they take a second and even a third job to afford the things they believe will make their lives good. This is the worst perversion of all because it turns human beings into slaves. They are owned by the possessions. The irony is, of course, that, in seeking the good life, people have lost the good life. Instead of having the luxury to relax at home, talk to family, enjoy dinner, go for long walks, or watch the sun set, too many men and women are rushing off to an evening of more work to pay off the bills.

Topic sentence that connects to thesis with third point

Conclusion

Cowering to silly fears, spending too much, or changing to fit in with the ridiculous images created by a plastic society is harmful. It is blurring Americans' moral vision. People need to realize once more that the true source of happiness, the measure of a life fulfilled, is the ability to see eternal beauty in the night sky, to become inspired by gently falling snow, and to make those ever important human connections.

Restatement of thesis/ summary

| ACTIVITY 4 | Each cluster below contains one topic, one thesis statement, and two supporting sentences. In the space provided, label each item as follows: |

> T   topic
> TH   thesis statement
> S   supporting sentence

TEACHING TIP
You may want to ask your students to come up with an additional support sentence for each cluster.

GROUP 1

___S___   a. People listen to audiobooks while doing other tasks, such as commuting or exercising.

___TH___   b. Audiobooks are more convenient than printed books for several reasons.

___S___   c. Listeners hear a dramatization of a printed book by the actual author or an actor.

___T___   d. Audiobooks

GROUP 2

___S___   a. A radiologic technology degree allows a person to work in medical settings where x-rays, CT scans, MRIs, sonograms, and other diagnostic imaging are needed.

___TH___   b. There are many career opportunities for those in the medical sciences.

___T___   c. Medical sciences

___S___   d. A person who obtains a degree in phlebotomy is able to work as a clinical laboratory technician.

GROUP 3

___T___   a. Study skills

___S___   b. Time management is essential when juggling deadlines and other responsibilities.

___TH___   c. Strong study skills are needed if a student wants to be successful in college.

___S___   d. Notetaking provides a student with the opportunity to review information later.

GROUP 4

___T___   a. Shingles

___TH___   b. People should be aware of the symptoms of shingles, a neurological disease.

___S___   c. Burning pain is one of the first symptoms of shingles.

___S___   d. Painful skin rash and blisters often follow the burning pain.

GROUP 5

<u>TH</u>   a. Dogs should be trained at an early age.

<u>S</u>   b. A puppy can be housebroken as soon as he or she is brought home.

<u>T</u>   c. Dogs

<u>S</u>   d. A puppy should be trained not to bite or "mouth" people, especially children.

ACTIVITY 5

This activity will sharpen your sense of the parts of an essay. "Coping with Old Age" has no indentations starting new paragraphs. Read this essay carefully, and then <u>double-underline</u> the thesis and <u>single-underline</u> the topic sentence for each of the three supporting paragraphs and the first sentence of the conclusion. Write the numbers of those sentences in the spaces provided at the end.

Coping with Old Age

[1]I recently read about an area of the former Soviet Union where many people live to be well over a hundred years old. [2]Being 115 or even 125 isn't considered unusual there, and these old people continue to do productive work right up until they die. [3]The United States, however, isn't such a healthy place for older people. [4]<u>Since I retired from my job, I've had to cope with the physical, mental, and emotional stresses of being "old."</u> [5]<u>For one thing, I've had to adjust to physical changes.</u> [6]Now that I'm over sixty-five, the trusty body that carried me around for years has turned traitor. [7]Aside from the deepening wrinkles on my face and neck, and the wiry gray hairs that have replaced my brown hair, I face more frightening changes. [8]I don't have the energy I used to. [9]My eyes get tired. [10]Once in a while, I miss something that's said to me. [11]My once faithful feet seem to have lost their comfortable soles, and I sometimes feel I'm walking on marbles. [12]In order to fight against this slow decay, I exercise whenever I can. [13]I walk, I stretch, and I climb stairs. [14]I battle constantly to keep as fit as possible. [15]<u>I'm also trying to cope with mental changes.</u> [16]My mind was once as quick and sure as a champion gymnast. [17]I never found it difficult to memorize answers in school or to remember the names of people I met. [18]Now, I occasionally have to search my mind for the name of a close neighbor or favorite television show. [19]Because my mind needs exercise, too, I challenge it as much as I can. [20]Taking a college course like this English class, for example, forces me to concentrate. [21]The mental gymnast may be a little slow and out of shape, but he can still do a back flip or turn a somersault when he has to.

continued

²²Finally, I must deal with the emotional impact of being old. ²³Our society typecasts old people. ²⁴We're supposed to be unattractive, senile, useless leftovers. ²⁵We're supposed to be the crazy drivers and the cranky customers. ²⁶At first, I was angry and frustrated that I was considered old at all. ²⁷And I knew that people were wrong to stereotype me. ²⁸Then I got depressed. ²⁹I even started to think that maybe I was a cast-off, one of those old animals that slow down the rest of the herd. ³⁰But I have now decided to rebel against these negative feelings. ³¹I try to have friends of all ages and to keep up with what's going on in the world. ³²I try to remember that I'm still the same person who sat at a first-grade desk, who fell in love, who comforted a child, who got a raise at work. ³³I'm not "just" an old person. ³⁴Coping with the changes of old age has become my latest full-time job. ³⁵Even though it's a job I never applied for, and one for which I had no experience, I'm trying to do the best I can.

Thesis statement in "Coping with Old Age":   4

Topic sentence of first supporting paragraph: 5

Topic sentence of second supporting paragraph: 15

Topic sentence of third supporting paragraph: 22

Topic sentence of the conclusion: 34

TEACHING TIP
Bring to class examples of writing expressing different points of view. These examples might be found in magazine articles, advertisements, and other published sources. If your classroom has online access, find examples from Web sites. Help your students make connections.

Important Considerations in Essay Development

Determining Your Point of View

When you write, you can take any of three approaches, or points of view: first person, second person, or third person.

First-Person Approach

In the first-person approach—a strongly individualized point of view—you draw on your own experience and speak to your audience in your own voice, using pronouns like *I, me, mine, we, our,* and *us.*

The first-person approach is most common in narrative essays based on personal experience. It also suits other essays where most of the evidence presented consists of personal observation.

Here is a first-person supporting paragraph from an essay on camping:

> First of all, I like comfort when I'm camping. My Airstream motor home, with its completely equipped kitchen, shower stall, toilet, double bed, and television, resembles a mobile motel room. I can sleep on a real mattress, clean sheets, and fluffy pillows. Next to my bed are devices that make me feel at home: a radio, an alarm clock, and a TV remote-control unit. Unlike the poor campers huddled in tents, I don't have to worry about cold, rain, heat, or annoying insects. After a hot shower, I can slide into my best nightgown, sit comfortably on my down-filled quilt, and read the latest mystery novel while a thunderstorm booms outside.

Second-Person Approach

In the second-person approach, the writer speaks directly to the reader, using the pronoun *you.* The second-person approach is considered appropriate for giving direct instructions and explanations to the reader. That is why *you* is used throughout this book.

You should plan to use the second-person approach only when writing a process essay, though a better approach would be third-person. As a general rule, never use the word *you* in academic writing. (If doing so has been a common mistake in your writing, you should review the rule about pronoun point of view in Chapter 4.)

Third-Person Approach

The third-person approach is by far the most common point of view in academic writing. In the third person, the writer includes no direct references to the reader (*you*) or the self (*I, me*). Third person gets its name from the stance it suggests—that of an outsider or "third person" observing and reporting on matters of public rather than private importance. In this approach, you draw on information that you have gotten through observation, thinking, or reading.

Here is the paragraph on camping, recast in the third person. Note the third-person pronouns *their, them,* and *they,* which all refer to *campers* in the first sentence.

> First of all, modern campers bring complete bedrooms with them. Winnebagos, Airstream motor homes, and Fleetwood recreational vehicles lumber into America's campgrounds every summer like mobile motel rooms. All the comforts of home are provided inside. Campers sleep on real mattresses with clean sheets and fluffy pillows. Next to their beds are the same gadgets that litter their night tables at home—radios, alarm clocks, and TV remote-control units. It's not necessary for them to worry about annoyances like cold, heat, rain, or buzzing insects, either. They can sit comfortably in bed and read the latest mystery novels while a thunderstorm booms outside.

in a writer's words

" *Good writing is rewriting.*"

—Truman Capote

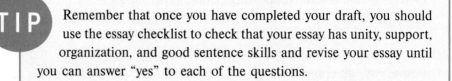

TIP Remember that once you have completed your draft, you should use the essay checklist to check that your essay has unity, support, organization, and good sentence skills and revise your essay until you can answer "yes" to each of the questions.

TEACHING TIP
You may want to use this checklist to evaluate your students' essays.

ESSAY CHECKLIST: THE FOUR BASES

UNITY

✔ Do I have a clearly stated thesis that is narrow and focused and is located at the beginning of my introduction?

✔ Do all the supporting paragraphs have topic sentences that help advance the thesis?

✔ Are there portions of the essay that do not support my thesis and therefore should be eliminated or rewritten?

SUPPORT

✔ Do I have at least three separate supporting points for my thesis?

✔ Have I backed up each main point with *specific* and detailed evidence?

✔ Have I provided enough evidence to support my points?

✔ Do have any repetitive areas that need to be revised?

COHERENCE

✔ Have I organized my essay by using a clear method?

✔ Do I use strong transitions and other connecting words?

✔ Do I have an introduction that is effective and engages the reader?

✔ Do I have a concluding paragraph that effectively supports and completes my essay?

SENTENCE SKILLS

✔ Have I used a consistent point of view throughout my essay?

✔ Have I used specific rather than general words?

✔ Have I avoided wordiness and been concise?

✔ Are my sentences varied?

✔ Have I edited for spelling and other sentence skills errors, as listed on the inside back cover of the book?

Writing the Essay

©topdeq/123RF

CHAPTER PREVIEW

Step 1: Begin with a Point, or Thesis

Step 2: Support the Thesis with Specific Evidence

Step 3: Organize and Connect the Specific Evidence

Step 4: Write Clear, Error-Free Sentences

Revising Essays for All Four Bases: Unity, Support, Coherence, and Sentence Skills

RESPONDING TO IMAGES

In 2012, the Costa Concordia struck a rock and capsized off the coast of Italy, killing thirty-two people. This photo shows the magnitude of the damage caused by what was determined to be the captain's carelessness. Write an essay about a tragedy you experienced in your own life. What was the experience like and how did it change you—for better or worse?

TEACHING TIP
Ask students to complete the chapter opening writing prompt in class.

The four steps in writing an effective essay are the same steps you have been using to write effective paragraphs:

1. Begin with a point, or thesis.

2. Support the thesis with specific evidence.

3. Organize and connect the specific evidence.

4. Write clear, error-free sentences.

Much of this chapter, then, will be familiar, as we walk through how these steps can be applied to writing the essay as well.

Step 1: Begin with a Point, or Thesis

You already know from your work on the paragraph that your first step in writing is to discover what point you want to make and to write that point out as a single sentence. There are two reasons for doing this. You want to know right from the start if you have a clear and workable thesis. Also, you will be able to use the thesis as a guide while writing your essay. At any stage you can ask yourself, "Does this support my thesis?" With the thesis as a guide, the danger of drifting away from the point of the essay is greatly reduced.

TEACHING TIP
Point out the similarities between a thesis statement and a topic sentence.

Understanding Thesis Statements

In Chapter 15, you learned that effective essays center around a thesis, or main point, that a writer wishes to express. This central idea is usually presented as a *thesis statement* in an essay's introductory paragraph.

Just like the topic sentence of a paragraph, a good thesis statement does two things. First, it tells readers an essay's *topic*. Second, it presents the writer's *attitude, opinion, idea*, or *point* about that topic. For example, look at the following thesis statement:

> Owning a pet has several important benefits.

In this thesis statement, the topic is *owning a pet;* the writer's main point is that owning a pet *has several important benefits.*

Preparing to Write a Good Thesis

TEACHING TIP
You may want to provide your students with other examples of general topics. Ask your students to limit these subjects and create thesis statements.

Now that you know how thesis statements work, you can prepare to begin writing your own. To start, you need a topic that is neither too broad nor too narrow. Suppose, for example, that an instructor asks you to write a paper on marriage. Such a subject is too broad to cover in a five-hundred-word essay. You would have to write a book to support adequately any point you might make about the general subject of marriage. What you need to do, then, is limit your subject. Narrow it down until you have a thesis that you can deal with specifically in about five hundred words. In the box that follows are (1) several general subjects, (2) a limited version of each general subject, and (3) a thesis statement about each limited subject.

General Subject	Limited Subject	Thesis
Marriage	Honeymoon	A honeymoon is perhaps the worst way to begin a marriage.
Family	Older sister	My older sister helped me overcome my shyness.
Television	TV preachers	TV evangelists use sales techniques to promote their messages.
Children	Disciplining of children	My husband and I have several effective ways of disciplining our children.
Sports	Players' salaries	Players' high salaries are bad for the game, for the fans, and for the values our children are developing.

ACTIVITY 1

Sometimes a subject must go through several stages of limiting before it is narrow enough to write about. Below are four lists reflecting several stages that writers went through in moving from a general subject to a narrow thesis statement. Number the stages in each list from 1 to 5, with 1 marking the broadest stage and 5 marking the thesis.

LIST 1

2 Teachers
1 Education
3 Math teacher
5 My high school math teacher was incompetent.
4 High school math teacher

LIST 2

3 Bicycles
4 Dangers of bike riding
1 Recreation
2 Recreational vehicles
5 Bike riding in the city is a dangerous activity.

LIST 3

1 Retail companies
2 Supermarkets
4 Dealing with customers
3 Working in a supermarket
5 I've learned how to handle unpleasant supermarket customers.

LIST 4

3 Camping
4 First camping trip
2 Summer vacation
5 My first camping trip was a disastrous experience.
1 Vacations

Later in this chapter you will get more practice in narrowing general subjects to thesis statements.

Writing a Good Thesis

When writing thesis statements, you want to avoid making the same mistakes we discussed when writing topic sentences for your paragraphs. One mistake is to simply announce the subject rather than state a true thesis. A second mistake is to write a thesis that is too broad, and a third is to write a thesis that is too narrow. An additional mistake is to write a thesis containing more than one idea. The following activities will give you practice in avoiding such mistakes and writing good thesis statements.

Write Statements, Not Announcements

ACTIVITY 2

Write A beside each sentence that is an announcement rather than a thesis statement. Write OK beside the statement in each pair that is a clear, limited point that could be developed in an essay.

1. __A__ a. This essay will discuss the fitness classes offered at my gym.

   __OK__ b. My gym offers spinning, kick boxing, and yoga classes.

2. __OK__ a. I learned the hard way that online gambling is very addictive.

   __A__ b. My thesis in this paper is the very addictive nature of online gambling.

3. __OK__ a. The Korean *jeon*, the French crêpe, and the American hotcake are variations of the pancake.

   __A__ b. Variations of the pancake is the subject of this paper.

4. __A__ a. This paper will be about the toys my cat prefers.

   __OK__ b. My cat snubs store-bought toys in favor of toilet paper rolls, twist ties, and paper bags.

5. __A__ a. My concern here is to discuss the rising fuel costs in the U.S. today.

   __OK__ b. There are several possible explanations for the rising fuel costs in the U.S. today.

Avoid Statements That Are Too Broad

ACTIVITY 3

Write TB beside each statement that is too broad to be developed in an essay. Write OK beside the statement in each pair that is a clear, limited point.

1. __TB__ a. In many ways, sports are an important part of American life.

   __OK__ b. Widespread gambling has changed professional football for the worse.

2. __TB__ a. Modern life makes people suspicious and unfriendly.

   __OK__ b. A frightening experience in my neighborhood has caused me to be a much more cautious person in several ways.

3. __OK__ a. Toy ads on television teach children to be greedy, competitive, and snobbish.

   __TB__ b. Advertising has bad effects on all of society.

4. __TB__ a. Learning new skills can be difficult and frustrating.

   __OK__ b. Learning to write takes work, patience, and a sense of humor.

5. __TB__ a. I didn't get along with my family, so I did many foolish things.

   __OK__ b. Running away from home taught me that my parents weren't as terrible as I thought.

Avoid Statements That Are Too Narrow

> Write TN beside each statement that is too narrow to be developed in an essay. Write OK beside the statement in each pair that is a clear, limited point.

ACTIVITY 4

TEACHING TIP
For added practice, ask students to rewrite sentences that are too narrow ("TN").

1. __TN__ a. I had squash, tomatoes, and corn in my garden last summer.

   __OK__ b. Vegetable gardening can be a frustrating hobby.

2. __TN__ a. The main road into our town is lined with billboards.

   __OK__ b. For several reasons, billboards should be abolished.

3. __TN__ a. There are now more single-parent households in our country than ever before.

   __OK__ b. Organization is the key to being a successful single parent.

4. __OK__ a. My first job taught me that I had several bad work habits.

   __TN__ b. Because I was late for work yesterday, I lost an hour's pay and was called in to see the boss.

5. __OK__ a. Americans abuse alcohol because it has become such an important part of their personal and public celebrations.

   __TN__ b. Consumption of wine, beer, and hard liquor increases in the United States every year.

Make Sure Statements Develop Only One Idea

Here are three statements that contain more than one idea:

> One of the most serious problems affecting young people today is bullying, and it is time more kids learned the value of helping others.

> Studying with others has several benefits, but it also has drawbacks and can be difficult to schedule.

> Teachers have played an important role in my life, but they were not as important as my parents.

In this group, each statement contains more than one idea. For instance, "One of the most serious problems affecting young people today is bullying, and it is time more kids learned the value of helping others" clearly has two separate ideas ("One of the most serious problems affecting young people today is bullying" *and* "it is time more kids learned the value of helping others"). The reader is asked to focus on two separate points, each of which more logically belongs in an essay of its own. Remember, the point of an essay is to communicate a *single* main idea to readers. To be as clear as possible, then, try to limit your thesis statement to the single key idea you want your readers to know. Revised thesis statements based on each of the examples above are as follows:

One of the most serious problems affecting young people today is bullying.

Studying with others has several benefits.

Teachers have played an important role in my life.

ACTIVITY 5

For each pair, write 2 beside the statement that contains more than one idea. Write OK beside the statement that is a clear, limited point.

1. __2__ a. The firefighters in our town do their jobs very well and the fire chief is extremely nice.

   __OK__ b. Our town's fire department is responsive, professional, and charitable.

2. __OK__ a. My oldest daughter has her own unique system for getting ready for school.

   __2__ b. My daughters get along most of the time, but they still have serious conflicts once in a while.

3. __2__ a. School buildings in America need to be improved and more teachers need to be hired.

   __OK__ b. Schools in America need more teachers, better facilities, and better technology.

4. __OK__ a. Working with at-risk youth changed my stereotypical ideas about teens who attend alternative high schools.

   __2__ b. My life has taken an exciting new direction because I learned so much from the job I had working with at-risk youth last summer.

5. __OK__ a. The sights, sounds, and smells of the amusement park made the visit very interesting.

   __2__ b. The amusement park was uncomfortably crowded and my brother made himself ill eating all the available fried food.

Make Sure Thesis Statements Show a Logical Relationship between the Thesis and the Supporting Points

---

ACTIVITY 6

Complete the following thesis statements by adding a third supporting point that will parallel the two already provided. You might first want to revisit the section on parallelism in Chapter 4 to make sure you understand parallel form.

TEACHING TIP
You may want to review parallelism with your students.

Answers will vary; examples are given.

1. Because I never took college preparatory courses in high school, I entered college deficient in mathematics, study skills, and science_____.

2. A good salesperson needs to like people, to be aggressive, and to be enthusiastic_____.

3. Rather than blame myself for failing the course, I blamed the instructor, my adviser, and even <u>my boyfriend</u>   .

4. Anyone who buys an old house planning to fix it up should be prepared to put in a lot of time, hard work, and <u>money</u>   .

5. Our old car eats gas, makes funny noises, and <u>fails to start on cold mornings</u>   .

6. My mother, my boss, and my <u>   coach   </u> are three people who are very important in my life right now.

7. Getting married too young was a mistake because we hadn't finished our education, we weren't ready for children, and <u>we weren't able to commit ourselves to each other</u>   .

8. Some restaurant patrons seem to leave their honesty, their cleanliness, and their <u>manners</u>   at home.

9. During my first semester at college, I had to learn how to manage my time, my diet, and <u>my relationships with others</u>   .

10. Three experiences I wish I could forget are the time I fell off a ladder, the time I tried to fix my parents' lawn mower, and <u>the time I performed in a piano recital</u>   .

Working with a partner, write a thesis for each group of supporting statements. This activity will give you practice in writing an effective essay thesis—one that is neither too broad nor too narrow. It will also help you understand the logical relationship between a thesis and its supporting details.

ACTIVITY 7

©Jacob Lund/
Shutterstock

Wording of thesis may vary.

1. Thesis: <u>My cars have reflected stages in my life</u>   .

   a. My first car was a rebellious-looking one that matched the way I felt and acted as a teenager.

   b. My next car reflected my more mature and practical adult self.

   c. My latest car seems to tell me that I'm aging; it shows my growing concern with comfort and safety.

2. Thesis: <u>A two-year college has certain advantages</u>   .

   a. All the course credits that are accumulated can be transferred to a four-year school.

   b. Going to a two-year college can save a great deal of money in tuition and other fees.

   c. If the college is nearby, there are also significant savings in everyday living expenses.

3. Thesis: I have tried several ways to give up snacks   .

   a. First, I tried simply avoiding the snacks aisle of the supermarket.

   b. Then I started limiting myself to only one serving of any given snack.

   c. Finally, in desperation, I began keeping the bags of snacks in a pad-locked cupboard.

4. Thesis: Halloween is not all fun   .

   a. The holiday can be very frightening for little children.

   b. Children can be struck by cars while wearing vision-obstructing masks and dark costumes.

   c. There are always incidents involving deadly treats: fruits, cookies, and candies that contain razor blades or even poison.

5. Thesis: Three factors contributed to my heart attack   .

   a. First of all, I was a typical "type A" personality: anxious, impatient, and hard-driving.

   b. I also had a family history of relatives with heart trouble.

   c. My unhealthy lifestyle, though, was probably the major factor.

The following activity will give you practice in distinguishing general from limited subjects and in writing a thesis.

ACTIVITY 8

©Jacob Lund/
Shutterstock

Answers will vary;
examples are given.

Here is a list of ten general subjects. Working in pairs with a fellow classmate, limit five of the subjects. Then write a thesis statement about each of the five limited subjects.

> **TIP** To create a thesis statement for a limited subject, ask yourself, "What point do I want to make about _____ (*my limited subject*)?"

GENERAL SUBJECT	LIMITED SUBJECT
1. Pets	Beagles
2. Teens	Teen motherhood
3. Internet	Search engines
4. Work	Working at home
5. College	The first week at college
6. Doctors	Our family doctor
7. Vacations	Disastrous vacations
8. Cooking	Cooking for one
9. Money	Unusual things used as money
10. Shopping	Shopping for a wedding gown

Thesis statements for five of the limited subjects:

1. Beagles make great pets because they are loving, cheerful, and sturdy.

2. Teen motherhood can be harmful to the mother herself, to her child, and to society.

4. Working at home is a sensible alternative for many people, including parents of young children, older people, and technology wizards.

5. A few simple tips will help any college student survive the first week at college.

8. Cooking for one person can be remarkably pleasant.

Answers will vary; examples are given.

Step 2: Support the Thesis with Specific Evidence

The first essential step in writing a successful essay is to formulate a clearly stated thesis. The second basic step is to support the thesis with specific reasons or details, just as you would support the topic sentence of your paragraph.

To ensure that your essay will have adequate support, you may find an informal outline very helpful. Write down a brief version of your thesis idea, and then work out and jot down three or more points that will support the thesis.

Here is the scratch outline that was prepared by the author of the essay on moviegoing in Chapter 15:

Moviegoing a problem

- inconvenience of going out

- tempting snacks

- other moviegoers

A scratch outline like this one looks simple, but developing it requires a great deal of careful thinking. The time spent on developing a logical outline is invaluable, though. Once you have planned the steps that logically support your thesis, you will be in an excellent position to go on to write an effective essay.

Activities in this section will give you practice in the crucial skill of planning an essay clearly.

Following are ten informal outlines. Complete any five of them by adding a third logical supporting point (*c*) that will parallel the two already provided (*a* and *b*).

ACTIVITY 9

TEACHING TIP
Students can do this activity alone or in pairs.

Answers will vary; examples are shown.

1. College registration can be a confusing process.

    a. Some classes fill quickly.

    b. Several placement tests are needed.

    c. Everything is done online.

2. People seek out comfort food at roadside diners.

   a. Meatloaf sandwich

   b. Baked macaroni and cheese

   c. Hot fudge sundae

3. Online shopping is more convenient than going to a brick-and-mortar store.

   a. Online stores never close

   b. Don't have to leave the house

   c. Don't have to go to multiple stores to find specific items

4. Back-to-school shopping can be expensive.

   a. Backpack

   b. Textbooks

   c. Clothes

5. HGTV produces the best DIY home improvement shows on cable television.

   a. *Fixer Upper*

   b. *Property Brothers*

   c. *Rehab Addict*

6. Ian moved to Southern California to enjoy water sports.

   a. He surfs.

   b. He scuba dives.

   c. He kayaks.

7. Charleston, a city in South Carolina, is the best place to live.

   a. It is a historical city.

   b. It has great award-winning restaurants.

   c. It is on the Atlantic coast.

8. Technology makes handling finances so much easier.

   a. Automatic bill payments

   b. Online banking services

   c. Personal finance software

9. My boss has three qualities I admire.

   a. Shrewdness

   b. Intelligence

   c. Ambition

10. Traveling by air is stressful.

    a. Security restrictions

    b. Delayed flights

    c. <u>Crowded seats</u>

The Importance of *Specific* Details

Just as a thesis must be developed with at least three supporting points, each supporting point must be developed with specific details.

All too often, the body paragraphs in essays contain only vague generalities, rather than the specific supporting details that are needed to engage and convince a reader. Here is what one of the paragraphs in "The Hazards of Moviegoing" (see Chapter 15) would have looked like if the writer had not detailed her supporting evidence vividly:

TEACHING TIP
You may want to point out to students the shifts in point of view in these samples and show how the author revised the shifts to a single point of view in the final piece.

> Some of the other patrons are even more of a problem than the theater itself. Many people in the theater often show themselves to be inconsiderate. They make noises and create disturbances at their seats. Included are people in every age group, from the young to the old. Some act as if they were at home in their own living room watching TV. And people are often messy, so that you're constantly aware of all the food they're eating. People are also always moving around near you, creating a disturbance and interrupting your enjoyment of the movie.

The following box contrasts the vague support in the preceding paragraph with the specific support in the essay.

Vague Support	Specific Support
1. Many people in the theater show themselves to be inconsiderate. They make noises and create disturbances at their seats. Included are people in every age group, from the young to the old. Some act as if they were at home in their own living room watching TV.	1. Little kids race up and down the aisles, usually in giggling packs. Teenagers try to impress their friends by talking back to the screen, whistling, and making what they consider to be hilarious noises. Adults act as if they were at home in their own living room. They comment loudly on the ages of the stars and reveal plot twists that are supposed to be a secret.
2. And people are often messy, so that you're constantly aware of all the food they're eating.	2. And people of all ages leave tacky remnants of candy on the hand rests, stick gum on their seats, and drop popcorn tubs or cups of crushed ice and soda on the floor.
3. People are also always moving around near you, creating a disturbance and interrupting your enjoyment of the movie.	3. They also cough and burp, squirm endlessly in their seats, file out for repeated trips to the rest rooms or concession stands, and elbow me out of the armrest on either side of my seat.

The effective paragraph from the essay provides details that make vividly clear the statement that patrons are a problem in the theater. The writer specifies the exact age groups (little kids, teenagers, and adults) and the offenses of each (giggling, talking and whistling, and loud comments). She specifies the various food excesses (tacky remnants of candy, gum on seats, dropped popcorn and soda containers). Finally, she provides concrete details that enable us to see and hear other disturbances (coughs and burps, squirming, constant trips to rest rooms, jostling for elbow room). The ineffective paragraph asks us to guess about these details; the effective paragraph describes the details in a specific and lively way.

In the strong paragraph, then, sharp details capture our interest and enable us to share the writer's experience. They provide pictures that make each of us feel, "I am there." The particulars also enable us to understand clearly the writer's point that patrons are a problem. Aim to make your own writing equally convincing by providing detailed support.

TEACHING TIP
You may want to provide students with other examples of vague support. Ask them to provide specific support for each example.

The Importance of *Adequate* Details

You must provide *enough* specific details to fully support the point in a body paragraph of an essay. You could not, for example, include a paragraph about a friend's unreliability and provide only a one- or two-sentence example. You know from your previous work on writing paragraphs that you would have to extend the example or add several other examples showing your friend as an unreliable person. Without such additional support, your paragraph would be underdeveloped.

ACTIVITY 10

©Jacob Lund/
Shutterstock

Take a few minutes to write a paragraph supporting the point "My _____ is (are) a mess." You might write about your backpack, your bedroom, your desk, your finances, your personal life, even your life as a whole. If you want, be humorous. Afterward, you and your classmates, working in small groups, should read your paragraphs aloud. The best-received paragraphs are almost sure to be those with plenty of specific details.

Adding Details to Complete an Essay

ACTIVITY 11

Answers will vary.

TEACHING TIP
Suggest that students work in pairs to complete this activity.

Introduction

The following essay needs specific details to back up the ideas in the supporting paragraphs. Using the spaces provided, add a sentence or two of clear, convincing details for each supporting idea. This activity will give you practice at supplying specific details and an initial feel for writing an essay.

Life Off-Line

When my family's Internet provider had some mechanical problems that interrupted our service for a week, my parents, my sister, and I thought we would never make it. Getting through long evenings without streaming movies, e-mails, Twitter updates, and Internet searches seemed impossible. We soon realized, though,

continued

that living off-line for a while was a stroke of good fortune. It became easy for each of us to enjoy some activities alone, to complete some postponed chores, and to spend rewarding time with each other and friends.

First supporting paragraph

First of all, now that we were disconnected, we found plenty of hours for personal interests. We all read more that week than we had read during the six months before. _____

_____

_____

We each also enjoyed some hobbies we had ignored for ages. _____

_____

_____

In addition, my sister and I both stopped procrastinating with our homework. _____

_____

_____

Second supporting paragraph

Second, we did chores that had been hanging over our heads for too long. There were many jobs around the house that had needed attention for some time. _____

_____

_____

We had a chance to do some long-postponed shopping. _____

_____

_____

Also, each of us did some paperwork that was long overdue. _____

_____

_____

Third supporting paragraph

Finally, and probably most important, we spent time with each other. Instead of just being in the same room together while we stared at different screens, we actually talked for many pleasant hours. _____

_____

_____

continued

Moreover, for the first time in years my family played some card games and board games together. _____

_____

_____

Because we couldn't keep up with everyone electronically, we had some family friends over one evening and spent an enjoyable time with them.

_____

_____

_____

Conclusion

Once our Internet provider got the problems fixed, we were not prepared to go back to our previous ways. We had gained a sense of how our online activities had not only taken over our lives, but had interrupted our family's life. We still spend time streaming movies, gaming, e-mailing, and tweeting, but we make sure to spend at least two evenings a week focusing on each other. As a result, we have found that we can enjoy our virtual lives and still have time left over for our real lives!

Step 3: Organize and Connect the Specific Evidence

As you are generating the specific details needed to support a thesis, you should be thinking about ways to organize and connect those details. All the details in your essay must *cohere*, or stick together, so that your reader will be able to move smoothly from one bit of supporting information to the next. This section shows you how to organize and connect supporting details by using (1) common methods of organization, (2) transitions, and (3) other connecting words.

TEACHING TIP
You may want to review with your students what they have learned about organization with the paragraph.

Common Methods of Organization

You are already familiar with the two common methods used to organize the supporting material in an essay: *time order* and *emphatic order.*

As you'll recall *time,* or *chronological, order* simply means that details are listed as they occur in time. *First* this is done; *next* this; *then* this; *after* that, this; and so on. Here is an outline of an essay in which time order is used:

> To exercise successfully, a person should follow a simple plan consisting of arranging time, making preparations, and warming up properly.
>
> 1. The first thing that should be done is to set aside a regular hour for exercise.
>
> 2. Next, preparations for the exercise session should be made.
>
> 3. Finally, a series of warm-up activities should be completed.

Thesis

Fill in the missing words: The topic sentences in the essay use the words The first thing, ___Next___, and ___Finally___ to help show time order.

Emphatic order is a way to put *emphasis* on the most interesting or important detail by placing it in the last part of a paragraph or in the final supporting paragraph of an essay. *Finally, last of all,* and *most important* are typical words or phrases showing emphasis. Here is an outline of an essay that uses emphatic order:

> Celebrities lead very stressful lives.
>
> 1. For one thing, celebrities don't have the privacy an ordinary person does.
>
> 2. In addition, celebrities are under constant pressure.
>
> 3. Most important, celebrities must deal with the stress of being in constant danger.

Thesis

Fill in the missing words: The topic sentences in the essay use the words ___For one thing___, ___In addition___, and ___Most important___ to help show emphatic order.

Some essays use a combination of time order and emphatic order. For example, the essay on moviegoing in Chapter 15 includes time order: the writer first describes getting to the theater, then her experiences in the theater itself, and finally what happens when she arrives home one night. At the same time, the writer uses emphatic order, ending with the most important reason for her dislike of moviegoing—the behavior of the other patrons during the movie.

Transitions

Transitional Words

TEACHING TIP
You may want to review
with your students what
they have learned about
transitions.

Transitions signal the direction of a writer's thought. They are like the road signs that guide travelers. In the box that follows are some common transitions you have already been using in writing your paragraphs. They are grouped according to the kind of signal they give to readers. Note that certain words provide more than one kind of signal.

Addition signals: one, first of all, second, the third reason, also, next, another, and, in addition, moreover, furthermore, finally, last of all

Time signals: first, then, next, after, as, before, while, meanwhile, soon, now, during, finally

Space signals: next to, across, on the opposite side, to the left, to the right, above, below, near, nearby

Change-of-direction signals: but, however, yet, in contrast, although, otherwise, still, on the contrary, on the other hand

Illustration signals: for example, for instance, specifically, as an illustration, once, such as

Conclusion signals: therefore, consequently, thus, then, as a result, in summary, to conclude, last of all, finally

---

ACTIVITY 12   Work together with a fellow classmate to complete the following activity.

©Jacob Lund/
Shutterstock

1.   Underline the two *illustration* signals in the following selection:

   Supermarkets also use psychology to encourage people to buy. <u>For example</u>, in most supermarkets, the milk and the bread are either at opposite ends of the store or located far away from the first aisle. Even if shoppers have stopped at the market only for staples like these, they must pass hundreds of items in order to reach them. The odds are that instead of leaving with just a quart of milk, they will leave with additional purchases as well. Special displays, <u>such as</u> a pyramid of canned green beans in an aisle and a large end display of cartons of paper towels, also increase sales. Because shoppers assume that these items are a good buy, they may pick them up. However, the items may not even be on sale! Store managers know that customers are automatically attracted to a display like this, and they will use it to move an overstocked product.

2.   Underline the two conclusion signals in the following selection:

   <u>Finally</u>, the works of Joanne Fluke represent entertaining, regional writing that appeals to a wide audience. Her Hannah Swensen series stars a bubbly, mystery-solving cookie baker in a small town in Minnesota, a town much like the one that Fluke grew up in. Although the stories often feature plots that include dealing with the cold of Minnesota winters or the bugs and heat of Minnesota summers, the books are so well written, even readers in southern Florida or coastal Oregon can enjoy the stories. <u>As a result</u>, Fluke has gained a wide following that has led to a miniseries deal with the Hallmark channel.

3. Underline the three *addition* signals in the following selection:

To create the time a student needs to pass each semester, he or she should incorporate different types of courses. Mixing course types allows students to access different parts of their brains to avoid overload. <u>One</u> way a student can mix courses is to take a course that keeps him or her active—for example, a physical education course. Hours of studying can be exhausting, but exercise has been shown to be a positive cure. After studying anatomy facts like the muscular system, a student could work out those very muscles, creating a hands-on review. <u>Another</u> way a student can mix courses is to take a literature course during the same semester as a math course. Math homework can often be repetitive and lengthy, but breaking it up by reading a story about growing up during the Industrial Age can offer the mental break needed. A <u>final</u> way a student can add variety to his or her schedule is to take a "fun" course each semester. For one student, a fun course might be a photography course, but for another student computer programming would be more fun. Fun courses are not necessarily easy, but they are courses that a student chooses based upon his or her personal interest.

4. Underline the four *time* signals in the following selection:

<u>After</u> a person has acquired the job of TV sports reporter, it is important to begin working on the details of his or her image, so viewers connect. <u>First</u>, it is important that a new sports reporter invests in two or three versatile suit jackets. They should be made from fabrics that are neutral in color, so the reporter can mix-and-match a variety of shirts and ties. The best colors would be basic neutrals like black, navy, and beige. <u>Next</u>, a new sports reporter should invest in a variety of ties. Everyday ties should include basic stripes and muted patterns. However, since a reporter is on TV daily, it is also important to have one or two unique ties that viewers will enjoy seeing occasionally. It is also good to have a few holiday ties that will bring smiles to the viewers. <u>Finally</u>, it is important that a new sportscaster create a personality that viewers will respond to. Supporting the home team is always important, and a good reporter will find ways to describe both wins and losses in a positive manner. His or her tone should always show that despite the home team's performance, the fans will remain loyal.

5. Underline the four *change-of-direction* signals in the following selection:

Last year, my mom and dad decided to quit their corporate jobs and start farming. Both had had very successful careers, <u>but</u> they decided that the stress and hours weren't worth it anymore. They decided they wanted to become urban farmers and sell fresh, local meats and produce. The first thing they did was sell our house and buy a small farm on the outskirts of our city. The farm came with some cows and farming equipment; <u>however</u>, my parents decided that they didn't want to raise cows, so they sold them and purchased sheep and goats instead. They also purchased a bunch of hens and baby chicks. I thought having chickens was going to be awful, <u>yet</u> I quickly fell in love with all our ladies and pleaded with my parents to let me be in charge of caring for the flock. Now, every morning I have to get up early to collect the eggs, feed and water the hens, and open the coop, so they can roam the farm. <u>Although</u> I was not initially excited about moving to a farm with my parents, I have loved everything about our new life, including the hard work.

6. Underline the six *space* signals in the following selection:

To get the help they need, students should be aware of the services offered at the student success center. Upon entering, students will see the help desk. Students who are unfamiliar with the layout of the center or unsure of where they need to go should ask at the desk for help. Students who do know what service they are looking for should keep the following information in mind. <u>To the right</u> of the desk is the math lab, a large room with tables <u>on one side</u>. <u>On the opposite side</u> of the room is a computer lab. The computers in this lab have all the special programs necessary for any of the math classes on campus. <u>To the left</u> of the help desk is the writing center, which is a series of smaller, private rooms for individualized writing tutoring. Each room has its own computer, so students don't need to bring their own. <u>Behind</u> the help desk is a hallway that leads to the counselors' and advisers' offices. Their offices are <u>across</u> from each other and offer different services. The counselors specialize in helping with personal problems like stress, depression, and family issues, while the advisers specialize in helping students plan their course schedules, register for classes, and pick majors. Knowing the layout and services of the student success center should make it easier for students to get support and assistance when they need it.

Transitional Sentences

Transitional, or *linking, sentences* are used between paragraphs to help tie together the supporting paragraphs in an essay. They enable the reader to move smoothly from the idea in one paragraph to the idea in the next paragraph.

Here is the linking sentence used in the essay on moviegoing:

> Many of the other patrons are even more of a problem than the concession stand.

The words *concession stand* remind us of the point of the first supporting paragraph, while *Many of the other patrons* presents the point to be developed in the second supporting paragraph.

ACTIVITY 13 ©Jacob Lund/Shutterstock **Thesis 1** First supporting paragraph	Following are brief sentence outlines from two essays. In each outline, the second and third topic sentences serve as transitional, or linking, sentences. Each reminds us of the point in the preceding paragraph and announces the point to be developed in the current paragraph. Working in groups of two or three, use the spaces provided to add the words needed to complete the second and third topic sentences. In order to set up an in-home day-care center, a person must be sure the house conforms to state regulations, the necessary legal permits are in place, and services are advertised in the right places. First of all, a potential operator of an in-home day-care center must make sure the house conforms to state regulations. . . .

After making certain that ___the house conforms to regulations___

_____,

the potential operator must obtain ___legal permits___ . . . .

Second supporting paragraph

Finally, once the necessary ___legal permits have been obtained,___

the potential operator can begin to ___advertise___ .

Third supporting paragraph

Cheaper cost, greater comfort, and superior electronic technology make watching football at home more enjoyable than attending a game at the stadium.

Thesis 2

For one thing, watching the game on TV eliminates the cost of attending the game. . . .

First supporting paragraph

In addition to saving me money, watching the game at home is more ___comfortable___ than sitting in a stadium. . . .

Second supporting paragraph

Even more important than ___cost___ and ___comfort___ , though, is the ___technology___ that makes a televised game better than the "real thing.". . . .

Third supporting paragraph

Other Connecting Words

In addition to transitions, there are three other kinds of connecting words that help tie together the specific evidence in a paper: _repeated words, pronouns,_ and _synonyms._ For a description of each, revisit "Other Connecting Words" in Chapter 4.

Identifying Transitions and Other Connecting Words

The following items use connecting words to help tie ideas together. The connecting words you are to identify are set off in italics. In the space, write T for _transition,_ RW for _repeated word,_ S for _synonym,_ or P for _pronoun._

ACTIVITY 14

___S___   1. The family watched helplessly as the firefighters rushed into their home. Their *house* was engulfed in flames.

___P___   2. Aashi's dream is to become a computer software engineer. *That* is why she is going to college.

___T___   3. Fiji is located between New Caledonia and Tonga. *Nearby* in the Pacific Ocean is Samoa.

___S___   4. Elan donated his Lunar Epic Flyknits to the Nike Reuse-A-Shoe Program. His *shoes* will be recycled to build the turf for playgrounds and basketball courts.

___P___   5. Grant's daughter Violet was adopted from an orphanage in Sichuan Province, China. At seven years of age, *she* is now eager to have a younger sibling.

___RW___   6. Mia is taking classes to learn American Sign Language. Once she masters this *language*, she wants to become an interpreter.

___P___   7. Ethan completed his ten weeks of basic training for the Army National Guard. After *he* was done, he said that he felt like a changed person.

___P___   8. The nurse advised his patient to prepare a living will before the surgery. *He* also told his patient that everything would be okay.

___T___   9. My son is constantly texting his friends. *On the other hand*, his sister spends all her time communicating through social media.

___RW___   10. The Lululemon yoga pants that I bought are a relaxed fit. When I wear them, I feel *relaxed*.

___S___   11. I'm so lucky that my apartment has a full-sized washer and dryer. These *appliances* are fairly new.

___T___   12. During deforestation, trees are cut down. *As a result*, more carbon dioxide remains in the air.

___RW___   13. Grace works part time as an accounting clerk. She plans to earn an *accounting* degree so that she can secure a full-time job.

___S___   14. During the winter, I constantly tell my kids to put on winter clothes before going out. Predictably, one always forgets to put on a *coat*.

___T___   15. The library is located near the admissions office. *On the opposite side* of campus, there is a computer lab and a tutoring center.

Step 4: Write Clear, Error-Free Sentences

You have now seen how the first three goals in effective writing, unity, support, and coherence, can be applied to writing the essay. This section focuses on the fourth goal of writing effectively: sentence skills. When writing essays, you should continue to revise your sentences using the following strategies:

- parallelism
- a consistent point of view
- specific words
- concise words
- varied sentences

An additional strategy, which will be discussed below, is to use active verbs.

Use Active Verbs

When the subject of a sentence performs the action of the verb, the verb is in the *active voice.* When the subject of a sentence receives the action of a verb, the verb is in the *passive voice.*

The passive form of a verb consists of a form of the verb *to be (am, is, are, was, were)* plus the past participle of the main verb (which is usually the same as its past tense form). Look at the following active and passive forms.

Passive

The computer was *turned on* by Hakim.

The car's air conditioner *was fixed* by the mechanic.

Active

Hakim *turned on* the computer.

The mechanic *fixed* the car's air conditioner.

In general, active verbs are more effective than passive verbs. Active verbs give your writing a simpler and more vigorous style.

Revise the following sentences, changing verbs from the passive to the active voice and making any other word changes necessary.

ACTIVITY 15

TEACHING TIP
You may want to mention that passive verbs are encouraged in certain contexts, such as scientific writing.

EXAMPLE

Fruits and vegetables are painted often by artists.

Artists often paint fruits and vegetables.

1. Many unhealthy foods are included in the typical American diet.

   The typical American diet includes many unhealthy foods.

2. The family picnic was invaded by hundreds of biting ants.

   Hundreds of biting ants invaded the family picnic.

3. Antibiotics are used by doctors to treat many infections.

   Doctors use antibiotics to treat many infections.

4. The fatal traffic accident was caused by a drunk driver.

   A drunk driver caused the fatal traffic accident.

5. Final grades will be determined by the instructor on the basis of class performance.

> The instructor will determine final grades . . .

Practice in Revising Sentences

You are already aware that practice in *editing* sentences is best undertaken after you have worked through the sentence skills in Part Five. The focus in this section, then, will be a review on revising sentences—using a variety of methods to ensure that your sentences flow smoothly and are clear and interesting. You will work through the following series of Review Activities:

1. Using parallelism

2. Using a consistent point of view

3. Using specific words

4. Using active verbs

5. Using concise words

6. Varying your sentences

Using Parallelism

REVIEW ACTIVITY 1

Cross out the unbalanced part of each sentence. In the space provided, revise the unbalanced part so that it matches the other item or items in the sentence.

EXAMPLE

Microwavable pizza is convenient, cheap, and ~~it tastes good~~.

tasty

1. Before I do my homework, I need to prepare dinner, ~~bathing~~ the kids, and pay bills.

bathe

2. Features I look for in a new car are ~~seats that get warm and toasty~~, a backup camera, and a five-year warranty.

heated seats

3. Whenever I clean my bathroom, I scrub the toilet first, then clean the shower, and finally ~~mopping the floor~~.

mop the floor

4. On the weekends, Kurt enjoys playing basketball, ~~TV~~, and hanging out with his friends.

watching TV

5. My ideal mate would be attractive, wealthy, and ~~have a great personality~~.

personable

Using a Consistent Point of View

Change verbs as needed in the following selection so that they are consistently in the past tense. Cross out each incorrect verb and write the correct form above it, as shown in the example. You will need to make ten corrections.

My uncle's shopping trip last Thursday was discouraging to him. First of all, he had to drive around for fifteen minutes until he ~~finds~~ *found* a parking space. There was a half-price special on paper products in the supermarket, and every spot ~~is~~ *was* taken. Then, when he finally got inside, many of the items on his list were not where he expected. For example, the pickles he wanted ~~are~~ *were* not on the same shelf as all the other pickles. Instead, they were in a refrigerated case next to the bacon. And the granola was not on the cereal shelves but in the health-food section. Shopping thus ~~proceeds~~ *proceeded* slowly. About halfway through his list, he knew there would not be time to cook dinner and ~~decides~~ *decided* to pick up a barbecued chicken. The chicken, he learned, was available at the end of the store he had already passed. So he ~~parks~~ *parked* his shopping cart in an aisle, ~~gets~~ *got* the chicken, and came back. After adding half a dozen more items to his cart, he suddenly ~~realizes~~ *realized* it contained someone else's food. So he retraced his steps, found his own cart, ~~transfers~~ *transferred* the groceries, and continued to shop. Later, when he began loading items onto the checkout counter, he ~~notices~~ *noticed* that the barbecued chicken was missing. He must have left it in the other cart, certainly gone by now. Feeling totally defeated, he returned to the deli counter and ~~says~~ *said* to the clerk, "Give me another chicken. I lost the first one." My uncle told me that when he saw the look on the clerk's face, he felt as if he'd flunked Food Shopping.

Using Specific Words

Revise the following sentences, changing vague, indefinite words into sharp, specific ones.

EXAMPLE

My roommate Marcelo listens to a *variety of music*.

. . . hip-hop, heavy metal, and reggae.

1. When my marriage broke up, I felt *various emotions*.

   . . . I felt sad, angry, and worried.

2. The *food choices* in the cafeteria were unappetizing.

   The lukewarm soup, stale sandwiches, and limp salads . . .

3. *Bugs* invaded our kitchen and pantry this summer.

   Ants, moths, and spiders . . .

4. All last week, *the weather was terrible*.

   . . . it rained nonstop, with a bone-chilling wind.

5. In the car accident, our teacher suffered *a number of injuries*.

   . . . a broken arm, two broken ribs, and a concussion.

Using Active Verbs

REVIEW ACTIVITY 4

Revise the following sentences, changing verbs from the passive to the active voice and making any other necessary word changes.

EXAMPLE

Soccer is played by children all over the world.

Children all over the world play soccer.

1. The pizza restaurant was closed by the health inspector.

   The health inspector closed the pizza restaurant.

2. Huge stacks of donated books were sorted by the workers in the library.

The workers in the library sorted huge stacks of donated books.

3. My computer was infected by a virus.

A virus infected my computer.

4. Gasoline prices will not be increased by oil companies this winter.

Oil companies will not increase gasoline prices this winter.

5. High-powered bombs were dropped by drones onto enemy bases.

Our drones dropped high-powered bombs onto enemy bases.

6. An additional charge was placed on our bill by the cell phone company.

The cell phone company placed an additional charge on our bill.

7. The community center was damaged by a group of vandals.

A group of vandals damaged the community center.

8. Stress is relieved by physical activity, meditation, and relaxation.

Physical activity, meditation, and relaxation relieve stress.

9. Taxes will be raised by the federal government to pay for highway improvements.

The federal government will raise taxes to pay . . .

10. Studies show that violent behavior among young children is increased by watching violent TV programs.

Studies show that watching violent TV programs increases violent behavior.

Using Concise Words

REVIEW ACTIVITY 5

Revise the following sentences, omitting needless words.

EXAMPLE

The ground beef patties that are manufactured at Wendy's are square in size.

The burgers at Wendy's are square.

Answers may vary; examples are given.

1. Gio at this point in time does not know the answer owing to the fact that he was not in attendance at class last week.

Gio does not know the answer because he missed class last week.

2. The oval in shape pendant that I chose holds a large in size and blue in color sapphire stone.

The oval pendant that I chose holds a large blue sapphire stone.

3. You are informed that your line of credit has been increased due to the fact that you made payments by the deadlines.

Your line of credit has been increased because you made timely payments.

4. Professor Lee is of the opinion that students enrolled in his class should turn off their cellular phone devices before the beginning of a class session.

Professor Lee wants his students to turn off their phones before class.

5. Alberta has a personal preference for a writing instrument that is a pencil over a writing instrument that is a pen, which, in her honest and humble opinion, is preferable because her handwritten mistakes can be removed with a rubber eraser.

Alberta prefers a pencil to a pen because she can erase her mistakes.

Varying Your Sentences

REVIEW ACTIVITY 6

Combine each of the following groups of simple sentences into one longer sentence. Omit repeated words. Various combinations are often possible, so try to find a combination in each group that flows most smoothly and clearly.

Answers will vary; examples are shown.

EXAMPLE

The technician arrived at the scene.
The technician worked for a crime lab.
The technician needed to dust for fingerprints.

The crime lab technician arrived at the scene to dust for fingerprints.

1. Sadie had repaired her broken watchband with a paper clip.
The clip snapped.
The watch slid off her wrist.

. . . with a paper clip, but the clip snapped and the watch slid . . .

2. The physical therapist watched.
Ashley tried to stand on her weakened legs.
They crumpled under her.

. . . watched as Ashley tried to stand on her weakened legs and they crumpled under her.

3. There were parking spaces on the street.
Albus pulled into an expensive garage.
He did not want to risk damage to his new car.

Although there were parking spaces on the street, Albus pulled . . . garage because he did not want . . .

4. The truck was speeding.
    The truck was brown.
    The truck skidded on some ice.
    The truck almost hit a police officer.
    The police officer was startled.
    The police officer was young.

    Speeding, the brown truck skidded on some ice and almost hit a startled young police officer.

5. The rainstorm flooded our basement.
    The rainstorm was sudden.
    The rainstorm was terrible.
    It knocked slates off the roof.
    It uprooted a young tree.

    A sudden terrible rainstorm flooded our basement, knocked slates off the roof, and uprooted a young tree.

Revising Essays for All Four Bases: Unity, Support, Coherence, and Sentence Skills

In this activity, you will evaluate and revise two essays in terms of all four bases: unity, support, coherence, and sentence skills. Comments follow each supporting paragraph. Circle the letter of the *one* statement that applies in each case.

ACTIVITY 16

TEACHING TIP
Consider having students do this activity with a partner. Ask them to discuss their answers.

Essay 1

1

2

Chiggers

I had lived my whole life not knowing what chiggers are. I thought they were probably a type of insect Humphrey Bogart encountered in *The African Queen*. I never had any real reason to care, until one day last summer. Within twenty-four hours, I had vividly experienced what chigger bites are, learned how to treat them, and learned how to prevent them.

First of all, I learned that chiggers are the larvae of tiny mites found in the woods and that their bites are always multiple and cause intense itching. A beautiful summer day seemed perfect for a walk in the woods. I am definitely not a city person, for I couldn't stand to be surrounded by people, noise, and concrete. As I walked through the ferns and pines, I noticed what appeared to be a dusting of reddish seeds or pollen on my slacks. Looking more closely, I realized that each speck was a tiny insect. I casually brushed off a few and gave them no further thought. I woke up the next morning feeling like a victim staked to an anthill by an enemy wise in the

continued

ways of torture. Most of my body was speckled with measlelike bumps that at the slightest touch burned and itched like a mosquito bite raised to the twentieth power. When antiseptics and calamine lotion failed to help, I raced to my doctor for emergency aid.

(a.) Paragraph 2 contains an irrelevant sentence.

b. Paragraph 2 lacks supporting details at one key spot.

c. Time order in paragraph 2 is confused.

d. Paragraph 2 contains two run-ons.

3

Healing the bites of chiggers, as the doctor diagnosed them to be, is not a simple procedure. It seems that there is really no wonder drug or commercial product to help. The victim must rely on a harsh and primitive home remedy and mostly wait out the course of the painful bites. First, the doctor explained, the skin must be bathed carefully in alcohol. An antihistamine spray applied several hours later will soothe the intense itching and help prevent infection. Before using the spray, I had to saturate each bite with gasoline or nail polish remover to kill any remaining chiggers. A few days after the treatment, the bites finally healed. Although I was still in pain, and desperate for relief, I followed the doctor's instructions. I carefully applied gasoline to the bites and walked around for an hour smelling like a filling station.

a. Paragraph 3 contains an irrelevant sentence.

b. Paragraph 3 lacks supporting details at one key spot.

(c.) Time order in paragraph 3 is confused.

d. Paragraph 3 contains one fragment.

4

Most important of all, I learned what to do to prevent getting chigger bites in the future. Mainly, of course, stay out of the woods in the summertime. But if the temptation is too great on an especially beautiful day, I'll be sure to wear the right type of clothing, like a long-sleeved shirt, long pants, knee socks, and closed shoes. In addition, I'll cover myself with clouds of superstrength insect repellent. I will then shower thoroughly as soon as I get home, I also will probably burn all my clothes if I notice even one suspicious red speck.

a.   Paragraph 4 contains an irrelevant sentence.

b.   Paragraph 4 lacks supporting details at one key spot.

c.   Paragraph 4 lacks transitional words.

(d.) Paragraph 4 contains a run-on and a fragment.

I will never forget my lessons on the cause, cure, and prevention of chigger bites. I'd gladly accept the challenge of rattlesnakes and scorpions in the wilds of the West but will never again confront a siege of chiggers in the pinewoods.

5

The Hazards of Being an Only Child

Essay 2

Many people who have grown up in multichild families think that being an only child is the best of all possible worlds. They point to such benefits as the only child's annual new wardrobe and the lack of competition for parental love. But single-child status isn't as good as people say it is. Instead of having everything they want, only children are sometimes denied certain basic human needs.

1

Only children lack companionship. An only child can have trouble making friends, since he or she isn't used to being around other children. Often, the only child comes home to an empty house; both parents are working, and there are no brothers or sisters to play with or to talk to about the day. At dinner, the single child can't tell jokes, giggle, or throw food while the adults discuss boring adult subjects. An only child always has his or her own room but never has anyone to whisper to half the night when sleep doesn't come. Some only children thrive on this isolation and channel their energies into creative activities like writing or drawing. Owing to this lack of companionship, an only child sometimes lacks the social ease and self-confidence that come from being part of a close-knit group of contemporaries.

2

(a.) Paragraph 2 contains an irrelevant sentence.

b.   Paragraph 2 lacks supporting details at one key spot.

c.   Paragraph 2 lacks transitional words.

d.   Paragraph 2 contains one fragment and one run-on.

3

Second, only children lack privacy. An only child is automatically the center of parental concern. There's never any doubt about which child tried to sneak in after midnight on a weekday. And who will get the lecture the next morning. Also, whenever an only child gives in to a bad mood, runs into his or her room, and slams the door, the door will open thirty seconds later, revealing an anxious parent. Parents of only children sometimes don't even understand the child's need for privacy. For example, they may not understand why a teen wants a lock on the door or a personal telephone. After all, the parents think, there are only the three of us, there's no need for secrets.

a. Paragraph 3 contains an irrelevant sentence.

b. Paragraph 3 lacks supporting details at one key spot.

c. Paragraph 3 lacks transitional words.

d. Paragraph 3 contains one fragment and one run-on.

4

Most important, only children lack power. They get all the love; but if something goes wrong, they also get all the punishment. When a bottle of perfume is knocked to the floor or the television is left on all night, there's no little sister or brother to blame it on. Moreover, an only child has no recourse when asking for a privilege of some kind, such as permission to stay out late or to take an overnight trip with friends. There are no other siblings to point to and say, "You let them do it. Why won't you let me?" With no allies their own age, only children are always outnumbered, two to one. An only child hasn't a chance of influencing any major family decisions, either.

a. Paragraph 4 contains an irrelevant sentence.

b. Paragraph 4 lacks supporting details at one key spot.

c. Paragraph 4 lacks transitional words.

d. Paragraph 4 contains one fragment and one run-on.

5

Being an only child isn't as special as some people think. It's no fun being without friends, without privacy, and without power in one's own home. But the child who can triumph over these hardships grows up self-reliant and strong. Perhaps for this reason alone, the hazards are worth it.

Introductions, Conclusions, and Titles

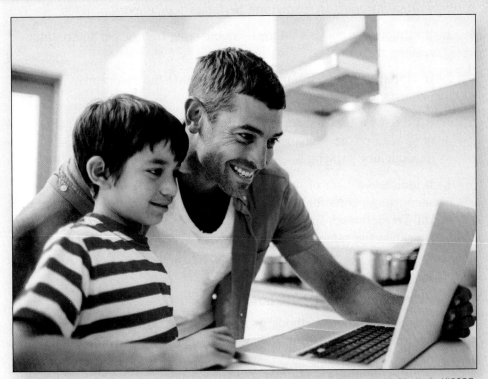

©Wavebreak Media Ltd/123RF

CHAPTER PREVIEW

Introductory Paragraph

Concluding Paragraph

Identifying Introductions and Conclusions

Titles

Essay Writing Assignments

RESPONDING TO IMAGES

What would you and your family or friends do without electronic media or online access? In the previous chapter, you helped complete one student's essay in response to a similar question. How would your own essay about life without electronic media and/or online access be different? Take some time to brainstorm, and then prepare a scratch outline before writing your first draft.

TEACHING TIP
Ask students to complete this writing prompt in class.

A well-organized essay also needs a strong introductory paragraph, an effective concluding paragraph, and a good title.

Introductory Paragraph

Functions of the Introduction

A well-written introductory paragraph performs four important roles:

1. It attracts the reader's interest, encouraging him or her to continue reading the essay.

2. It supplies any background information that the reader may need to understand the essay.

3. It presents a thesis statement. This clear, direct statement of the main idea of the essay usually appears near the end of the introductory paragraph.

4. It indicates a plan of development. In this "preview," the major supporting points for the thesis are listed in the order in which they will be presented. In some cases, the thesis and plan of development appear in the same sentence. However, writers sometimes choose not to describe the plan of development.

TEACHING TIP
Writers may want to write several introductions for the same topic, and then decide which introductory paragraph is most effective.

Common Methods of Introduction

Here are some common methods of introduction. Use any one method, or a combination of methods, to introduce your subject to the reader in an interesting way.

1. **Begin with a broad, general statement of your topic and narrow it down to your thesis statement.** Broad, general statements ease the reader into your thesis statement by first introducing the topic. In the example below, the writer talks generally about diets and then narrows down to comments on a specific diet.

> Bookstore shelves today are crammed with dozens of different diet books. The American public seems willing to try any sort of diet, especially the ones that promise instant, miraculous results. Authors are more than willing to invent new fad diets to cash in on this craze. Unfortunately, some of these fad diets are ineffective or even unsafe. One of the worst fad diets is the Cookie Diet. It is impractical, doesn't achieve the results it claims, and is a sure route to poor nutrition.

2. **Start with an idea or a situation that is the opposite of the one you will develop.** This approach works because your readers will be surprised, and then intrigued, by the contrast between the opening idea and the thesis that follows it.

When I decided to return to school at age thirty-five, I wasn't at all worried about my ability to do the work. After all, I was a grown woman who had raised a family, not a confused teenager fresh out of high school. But when I started classes, I realized that those "confused teenagers" sitting around me were in much better shape for college than I was. They still had all their classroom skills in bright, shiny condition, while mine had grown rusty from disuse. I had to learn how to use the library's databases, how to write a research paper, and even how to speak up in class discussions.

3. **Explain the importance of your topic to the reader.** If you can convince your readers that the subject in some way applies to them, or is something they should know more about, they will want to keep reading.

Diseases like scarlet fever and whooping cough used to kill more young children than any other cause. Today, however, child mortality due to disease has been almost completely eliminated by medical science. Instead, car accidents are the number-one killer of children and young adults under twenty-four. Most of the children fatally injured in car accidents were not protected by car seats, belts, or restraints of any kind. Several steps must be taken to reduce the serious dangers car accidents pose to our children.

TEACHING TIP
Consider introducing students to the idea of using rhetorical questions in their introductions. You may want to demonstrate a good example of incorporating a rhetorical question to help students avoid asking questions that use second-person point of view.

4. **Use an incident or a brief story.** Stories are naturally interesting. They appeal to a reader's curiosity. In your introduction, an anecdote will grab the reader's attention right away. The story should be brief and should be related to your main idea. The incident in the story can be something that happened to you, something you have heard about, or something you have read about in a newspaper, magazine, or online.

Early Sunday morning the young mother dressed her little girl warmly and gave her a candy bar, a picture book, and a well-worn stuffed rabbit. Together, they drove downtown to a Methodist church. There the mother told the little girl to wait on the stone steps until children began arriving for Sunday school. Then the young mother drove off, abandoning her five-year-old because she couldn't cope with being a parent anymore. This incident is one of thousands of cases of child neglect and abuse that occur annually. Perhaps the automatic right to become a parent should no longer exist. Would-be parents should be forced to apply for parental licenses for which they would have to meet three important conditions.

5. **Use a quotation.** A quotation can be something you have read in a book or an article. It can also be something that you have heard: a popular saying or proverb ("Never give advice to a friend"), a current or recent advertising slogan ("Just do it"), or a favorite expression used by friends or family ("My father always says …"). Using a quotation in your introductory paragraph lets you add someone else's voice to your own.

> "Fish and visitors," wrote Benjamin Franklin, "begin to smell after three days." Last summer, when my sister and her family came to spend their two-week vacation with us, I became convinced that Franklin was right. After only three days of my family's visit, I was thoroughly sick of my brother-in-law's corny jokes, my sister's endless complaints about her boss, and their children's constant invasions of our privacy.

6. **Include a startling statement and/or statistic.** Some essays start with statements or statistics (numerical data) that may shock readers and get them so intrigued that they want to read more. Some paragraphs use both statistics and a startling statement to capture readers' interest.

> The Spanish influenza (flu) was a pandemic that, between 1918 and 1920, reached every corner of the earth, including the Arctic and the most remote Pacific islands. Unlike most other flus, this one attacked healthy young men and women primarily, not the very old or the very young. Scientists estimate that the disease killed 50 to 100 million people worldwide. Even more significantly, the Spanish influenza was caused by a strain of the H1N1 virus that threatens the world today.

ACTIVITY 1	The box below summarizes the six kinds of introduction. Read the introductions that follow it and, in the space provided, write the letter of the kind of introduction used in each case.

TEACHING TIP
You may want to do this activity with the entire class.

A. General to narrow	D. Incident or story
B. Starting with an opposite	E. Quotation
C. Stating importance of topic	F. Startling statement or statistic

B 1. The ad, in full color on a glossy magazine page, shows a beautiful kitchen with gleaming counters. In the foreground, on one of the counters, stands a shiny new food processor. Usually, a feminine hand is touching it lovingly. Around the main picture are other, smaller shots. They show mounds of perfectly sliced onion rings, thin rounds of juicy tomatoes, heaps of matchstick-sized potatoes, and piles of golden, evenly grated cheese. The ad copy tells the reader how wonderful, how easy, food preparation will be with a processor. Don't believe it. My processor turned out to be expensive, difficult to operate, and very limited in its use.

E 2. My father stubbornly says, "You *can* often tell a book by its cover," and when it comes to certain paperbacks, he's right. Whenever a person is browsing in the drugstore or supermarket and he or she sees a paperback featuring an attractive young woman in a low-cut dress fleeing from a handsome dark figure in a shadowy castle, it is obvious what the book will be about. Every romance novel has the same elements: an innocent heroine, an exotic setting, and a cruel but fascinating hero.

A 3. Americans are incredibly lazy. Instead of cooking a simple, nourishing meal, they heat up a frozen dinner in the microwave. Instead of studying a daily newspaper, they are content with quick summaries on social media. Worst of all, instead of walking even a few blocks to the local convenience store, they jump into their cars. This dependence on the automobile, even for short trips, has robbed Americans of a valuable experience—walking. If Americans drove less and walked more, they would save money, become healthier, and discover fascinating things about their surroundings.

Concluding Paragraph

A concluding paragraph is your chance to remind the reader of your thesis idea and bring the paper to a natural and graceful end.

Common Methods of Conclusion

You may use any one of the methods below, or a combination of methods, to round off your paper.

1. **End with a summary and final thought.** When army instructors train new recruits, each of their lessons follows a three-step formula:
   a. Tell them what you're going to tell them.
   b. Tell them.
   c. Tell them what you've told them.

TEACHING TIP
Consider introducing students to the idea of posing questions in their conclusions. You may want to demonstrate a good example of incorporating a rhetorical question to help students avoid asking questions that use second-person point of view or are unrelated to the thesis, which is like "opening a can of worms."

An essay that ends with a summary is not very different. After you have stated your thesis ("Tell them what you're going to tell them") and supported it ("Tell them"), you restate the thesis and supporting points ("Tell them what you've told them"). However, don't use the exact wording you used before. Here is a summary conclusion:

> Catalog shopping at home, then, has several advantages. Such shopping is convenient, saves money, and saves time. It is not surprising that growing numbers of devoted catalog shoppers are welcoming those full-color mail brochures that offer everything from eggplant seeds to electronic devices.

Note that the summary is accompanied by a final comment that "rounds off" the paper and brings the discussion to a close. This combination of a summary and a final thought is the most common method of concluding an essay.

2. **Include a thought-provoking quotation.** A well-chosen quotation can be effective in re-emphasizing your point. Here is an example:

> Rude behavior has become commonplace and needs to stop. People no longer treat each other with the respect and courtesy they should. People talk on their cell phones at inappropriate times and places. Cutting off other drivers in order to save mere seconds happens more and more often. As the Dalai Lama said, "Love and kindness are the very basis of society. If we lose these feelings, society will face tremendous difficulties; the survival of humanity will be endangered."

3. **End with a prediction or recommendation.** Predictions and recommendations appeal to the reader to continue thinking about the essay.

A prediction states what may happen in the future:

> If people stopped to think before acquiring pets, there would be fewer instances of cruelty to animals. Many times, it is the people who adopt pets without considering the expense and responsibility involved who mistreat and neglect their animals. Pets are living creatures. They do not deserve to be treated as carelessly as one would treat a stuffed toy.

A recommendation suggests what should be done about a situation or problem:

> Stereotypes such as the helpless homemaker, harried executive, and dotty grandparent are insulting enough to begin with. In online ads or television commercials, they become even more insulting. Now these unfortunate characters are not just being laughed at; they are being turned into peddlers to sell products to an unsuspecting public. Consumers should boycott companies whose advertising continues to use such stereotypes.

In the space provided, identify each concluding paragraph. If the concluding paragraph is a summary and final thought, write S in the space; if it is a prediction or recommendation, write P/R; if it is a quotation, write Q.

ACTIVITY 2

___P/R___ 1. Even though tens of thousands of people die each year in the United States from lung cancer, there are steps that can be taken to reduce risk factors. Smokers should stop smoking. People should avoid being around smokers, ask those smoking to stop, or leave if others are smoking. Life is too valuable to have it ended by this disease.

___Q___ 2. My father spent thirty years smoking three packs of cigarettes a day, a habit that he thought was more harmful to his wallet than to his lungs. According to the American Society of Addiction Medicine, "[n]icotine dependence is the most common form of chemical dependence in the United States … and [in 1989] caused more than 400,000 premature deaths in the United States." My father was one of them.

___S___ 3. Lung cancer, then, can spread to the esophagus, the trachea, and the heart. Although an operation to remove the tumor is often unlikely, there are treatments available to control its spread. More research, however, is needed to find a cure.

Identifying Introductions and Conclusions

ACTIVITY 3	The following box lists six common kinds of introductions and three common kinds of conclusions. Read the three pairs of introductory and concluding paragraphs that follow. Then, in the space provided, write the letter of the kind of introduction and conclusion used in each paragraph.

TEACHING TIP
Consider making a game out of this activity. See how quickly your students can complete the activity correctly. You may want to ask them to create a set of game rules first.

Introductions	Conclusions
A. General to narrow	G. Summary and final thought
B. Starting with an opposite	H. Quotation
C. Stating importance of topic	I. Prediction or recommendation
D. Incident or story	
E. Quotation	
F. Startling statement and/or statistic	

PAIR 1

___D___   Shortly before Easter, a local elementary school sponsored a fund-raising event at which classroom pets and their babies—hamsters, guinea pigs, and chicks—were available for adoption. Afterward, a young boy found a guinea pig huddled by the side of the road. One of the parents must have taken the pet, regretted the decision, and decided to get rid of it. Many have never stopped to consider the several real obligations involved in owning a pet.

___I___   A pet cannot be thrown onto a trash heap when it is no longer wanted or tossed into a closet if it begins to bore its owner. A pet, like us, is a living thing that needs attention and care. Would-be owners, therefore, should think seriously about their responsibilities before they acquire a pet.

PAIR 2

___E___   "Few things are harder to put up with," said Mark Twain, "than the annoyance of a good example." Twain obviously knew the problems faced by siblings cursed with older brothers or sisters who are models of perfection. All our lives, my older sister Shelley and I have been compared. Unfortunately, in competition with my sister's virtues, my looks, talents, and accomplishments always ended up on the losing side.

___G___   Although I always lost in the sibling contests of looks, talents, and accomplishments, Shelley and I have somehow managed not to turn into deadly enemies. Feeling like the "dud" of the family, in fact, helped me to develop a drive to succeed and a sense of humor. In our sibling rivalry, we both managed to win.

PAIR 3

___E___   In 2011, the school board sent out a letter laying out all the changes that were going to occur for the future school year. In an effort to cut costs, music classes, physical education classes, art classes, and honors classes were no longer going to be offered. When Franklin D. Roosevelt was president, he stated that "[t]he school is the last expenditure upon which America should be willing to economize." Despite the budget crisis that the school district faces, FDR's words must be heeded and a better plan must be made in order not to put the education of our students at risk.

_____ Cutting classes like music and physical education is a mistake. Students should not be put at risk by taking away the very classes that create culture and focus on the health of the population. If the school board continues to cut funding from education, it is ensuring that the future for our children will be bleak.

Titles

A title is usually a very brief summary of what your essay is about. It is often no more than several words. You may find it easier to write the title *after* you have completed your essay.

Following are the introductory paragraphs for two of the essays in this text, along with the titles of the essays.

> I'm not just a consumer—I'm a victim. If I order a product, it is sure to arrive in the wrong color, size, or quantity. If I hire people to do repairs, they never arrive on the day scheduled. If I owe a bill, the computer is bound to overcharge me. Therefore, in self-defense, I have developed the following consumer's guide to complaining effectively.

Title: How to Complain

TEACHING TIP
Writers sometimes forget that a title should be a phrase, not a complete sentence.

Introductory Paragraph

> Schools divide people into categories. From first grade on up, students are labeled "advanced" or "deprived" or "remedial" or "antisocial." Students pigeonhole their fellow students, too. We've all known the "brain," the "jock," the "dummy," and the "teacher's pet." In most cases, these narrow labels are misleading and inaccurate. But there is one label for a certain type of college student that says it all: "zombie."

Title: Student Zombies

Introductory Paragraph

Note that you should not underline the title, put quotation marks around it, boldface it, or increase the font size. On the other hand, you should capitalize the first letter of all but the small connecting words in the title. For more information about formatting and positioning the title of a paper, see "MLA Format" in Chapter 1.

ACTIVITY 4	Write an appropriate title for each of the introductory paragraphs that follow.

Answers may vary.

1. It is a terrible time to be a teenager or even a teenager's parent. Television, news programs, and social media are all full of frightening stories about teenagers and families. They say that America's families are falling apart, that kids do not care about anything, and that parents have trouble doing anything about it. However, not all teens and families are lost and without values. While they struggle with problems, successful families are doing what they have always done: finding ways to protect and nurture their children. Families are fighting against the influence of the media, against the loss of quality family time, and against the loss of community.

    Title: Successful Families: Fighting for Their Kids

2. Some of my friends can't believe that my car still runs. Others laugh when they see it parked outside the house and ask if it's an antique. They aren't being fair to my twenty-year-old Subaru Outback. In fact, my "antique" has opened my eyes to the rewards of owning an old car.

    Title: The Joys of an Old Car

3. Regular exercise is something like the weather—we all talk about it, but we tend not to do anything about it. Exercise programs on TV and DVD and via apps and the Internet now make it easy to have a low-cost personal exercise program without leaving home. However, for success in exercise, we should follow a simple plan consisting of arranging time, making preparations, and starting off at a sensible place.

    Title: Successful Exercise

in a writer's words

" *It's important to try to write when you are in the wrong mood or the weather is wrong. Even if you don't succeed you'll be developing a muscle that may do it later on.*"

—John Ashbery

Essay Writing Assignments

 Keep the points below in mind when writing an essay on any of the topics that follow.

1. Your first step must be to plan your essay. Prepare both a scratch outline and a more detailed outline.
2. While writing your essay, use the checklist at the end of Chapter 15 to make sure that your essay touches all four bases of effective writing.
3. Each essay will require support that incorporates different modes of writing. The appropriate chapters are listed in each assignment. You will want to review those chapters as necessary.
4. Don't forget to give your essay a title.

ANALYZING YOUR HOME

WRITING ASSIGNMENT 1

Write an essay on the advantages or disadvantages (not both) of the house or apartment where you live. In your introductory paragraph, briefly describe the place you plan to write about. End the paragraph with your thesis statement and a plan of development. Here are some suggestions for thesis statements:

> The best features of my apartment are its large windows, roomy closets, and great location.

> The drawbacks of my house are its unreliable oil burner, tiny kitchen, and old-fashioned bathroom.

> An inquisitive landlord, sloppy neighbors, and platoons of cockroaches came along with our rented house.

> My apartment has several advantages, including friendly neighbors, lots of storage space, and a good security system.

Depending on your chosen plan, you will want to incorporate support that includes anecdotes (Chapter 7), vivid descriptions of the home (Chapter 8), and/or a tone that persuades your reader to agree with you (Chapter 14).

PROMOTING A CAMPAIGN

WRITING ASSIGNMENT 2

The yellow ribbon is used as a symbol for many things, including suicide prevention, support for our troops, and bone cancer awareness. In this assignment, you are to write an essay that creates a campaign, complete with a symbol, to improve something in your community. First, you will want to find out what issues are affecting your community, like teen suicide, homeless veterans, or decaying parks. After you have decided on your topic, you will want to explain what the problem is and why it is important, what your campaign will be like, and what you hope to accomplish with your campaign.

You will want to make sure you provide good examples (Chapter 6) that explain the causes of the problem and how your campaign can have a positive effect (Chapter 10).

DESCRIBING DEMANDS IN LIFE

WRITING ASSIGNMENT 3

College demands a lot. You must attend classes, take notes, read textbooks, study for quizzes, write papers—the list goes on. In addition to school, you probably have other demands in your life. What are those demands? Write an essay that focuses on three demands that compete for your time. To help you get started, here is a list of demands common to college students:

Job	Health conditions
Housing	Other family members
Children	Financial debt
Transportation	Living expenses
Spouse or significant other	Hobbies and leisure activities

In your thesis statement, let your readers know what your three demands are and how they affect your life. Each of these demands should be developed in a separate paragraph. Each paragraph should have its own detailed examples. To create a strong essay, you will want to review Chapter 14, "Argument"; Chapter 13, "Division-Classification"; Chapter 10, "Cause and/or Effect"; and Chapter 6, "Exemplification."

WRITING ASSIGNMENT 4

SELLING (OR NOT) THE SINGLE LIFE

Write an essay on the advantages or drawbacks of single life. To get started, make a list of all the advantages and drawbacks you can think of.

Advantages might include:

Fewer expenses

Fewer responsibilities

More personal freedom

More opportunities to move or travel

Drawbacks might include:

Parental disapproval

Being alone at social events

No companion for shopping, movies, and so on

Sadness at holiday time

After you make up two lists, select the thesis for which you feel you have more supporting material. Then organize your material into a scratch outline. Be sure to include an introduction, a clear topic sentence for each supporting paragraph, and a conclusion. Alternatively, write an essay on the advantages or drawbacks of married life. Follow the directions given above.

Good support should include exemplification (Chapter 6) and argument (Chapter 14).

WRITING ASSIGNMENT 5

ANALYZING LIVES

Write an essay that claims that students' lives are much more difficult than professors' lives (or vice versa). You will need to speak with both professors and students and ask questions like:

Daily life: What does a typical day look like for you? What are your responsibilities? Do you have time each day just for yourself?

Academic life: How much time do you spend preparing for class? How much time do you spend in class? How much time do you spend grading (professors only)?

Social life: How much time do you spend participating in social activities?

Personal life: Do you work outside of your academic life? Do you have added responsibilities you haven't addressed?

Once you have gathered information, you will want to write an essay that asserts one group has a tougher life than the other. One way to organize your essay would be creating a paragraph for each of the categories; another way to organize it would be to write all the information that supports the thesis about one group and then follow with information about the other group. You will want to review Chapter 11, "Comparison and/or Contrast"; Chapter 14, "Argument"; and the research chapters in Part 5 to help create a persuasive and effective essay.

EXAMINING THE EFFECTS OF ADVERSITY

We all experience adversity. Some believe that adversity—hardship, misfortune, bad luck, or suffering—makes a person stronger. Others believe that hardship wears a person down. What do you believe? Think about an adversity that you lived through and how that experience affected your life. Here are several categories to consider:

Relationships	Peer pressure
Employment	Finances
Physical health	Discrimination
Education	Housing
Mental health	

Then, write an essay on the effects—positive or negative—that this adversity has had on you. In your introduction, describe your adversity. Each of your body paragraphs should explain how this experience affected you in a specific way. You will need to review Chapter 7, "Narration"; Chapter 8, "Description"; and Chapter 10, "Cause and/or Effect."

EVALUATING A FILM OR TELEVISION SHOW

Write an essay about a television show or movie you have seen very recently. The thesis of your essay will be that the show (or movie) has both good and bad features. (If you are writing about a TV series, be sure that you evaluate only one episode.)

In your first supporting paragraph, briefly summarize the show or movie. Don't get bogged down in small details here; just describe the major characters briefly and give the highlights of the action.

In your second supporting paragraph, explain what you feel are the best features of the show or movie. Listed below are some examples of good features you might write about:

Suspenseful, ingenious, or realistic plot

Good acting

Good scenery or special effects

Surprise ending

Good music

Believable characters

In your third supporting paragraph, explain what you feel are the worst features of the show or movie. Here are some possibilities:

Far-fetched, confusing, or dull plot

Poor special effects

Bad acting

Cardboard characters

Unrealistic dialogue

Remember to cover only a few features in each paragraph; do not try to include everything. You will want to review Chapter 8, "Description" and Chapter 14, "Argument" to help you create a persuasive and detailed essay.

WRITING ASSIGNMENT 8

PROFILING A HISTORICAL PERSON

Write an essay in which you research an historical figure and come to a conclusion about that figure. The person you choose may be assigned by your instructor, or may require your instructor's approval. Options might include such figures as Mother Teresa, Malcolm X, Queen Elizabeth II, or Nelson Mandela.

After you choose your topic, you will want to research as much information as possible. Not only will you want to get a biographical understanding of your person but you will also want to learn about some of the more controversial ideas or actions that your person was known for. You will also want to come to a conclusion about that person. Was she unfairly maligned? Was he really as good as people thought? What you conclude should become the basis of your thesis statement.

You will want to review Chapter 14, "Argument"; Chapter 20, "Working with Sources"; and Chapter 21, "Writing a Research Paper," to help you create a persuasive and effective essay.

REFLECTIVE ACTIVITY

©mavo/Shutterstock

1. Reread an essay you wrote in response to one of the writing assignments in this chapter. Did you use any of the six common methods for writing introductions explained earlier in this chapter? If so, which one(s)? If not, which of those method(s) might you include when you rewrite this essay?

2. Do the same for the conclusion of your essay. Refer to the methods for writing conclusions explained earlier in this chapter.

3. Reread the essay yet again and consider the various methods for writing introductions and conclusions once more. Would methods other than the ones you chose have been useful as well? Explain.

Patterns of Essay Development

Source: Library of Congress, Prints & Photographs Division, Reproduction number LC-DIG-ppmsca-40824 (digital file from original print) LC-USZC4-1124 (color film copy transparency) LC-USZ62-42150 (b&w film copy neg.)

LT Rebecca "Badger" Smith
USS JOHN C. STENNIS (CVN 74)

She owes her success to trailblazers like LCDR Barbara Allen Rainey who paved the way for limitless opportunities.

Source: US Navy

CHAPTER PREVIEW

Developing an Essay with Emphasis on Exemplification

Developing an Essay with Emphasis on Narration

Developing an Essay with Emphasis on Description

Developing an Essay with Emphasis on Process

Developing an Essay with Emphasis on Cause and/or Effect

Developing an Essay with Emphasis on Comparison and/or Contrast

Developing an Essay with Emphasis on Definition

Developing an Essay with Emphasis on Division-Classification

Developing an Essay with Emphasis on Argument

TEACHING TIP
Ask students to complete this writing prompt in class.

RESPONDING TO IMAGES

These two recruiting posters are from the United States Navy. The first was used in 1917, and the second is from today. Think about different ways to write about these posters. What is the main point of each poster, and how would you support that point with examples? How would you compare or contrast the posters? How would you describe them? Using a specific pattern of development, write an essay about these posters.

The nine different patterns of paragraph writing you learned in Part 3—*exemplification, narration, description, process, cause and/or effect, comparison and/or contrast, definition, division-classification*, and *argument*—can also be used to write essays. Because essays are much longer works than paragraphs, it is common that multiple patterns are incorporated to fully support the thesis statement. A history student may need to employ exemplification, cause and/or effect, and argument in a class paper. A scientist preparing a report may need to employ description, definition, and argument to defend his or her hypothesis. A real estate agent may employ description and narration to write about a house for sale. Everyday writing involves determining which patterns to use and how best to organize them to effectively support your purpose. The rest of this chapter will show you how.

Developing an Essay with Emphasis on Exemplification

Considering Purpose and Audience

If you make a statement and someone says to you, "Prove it," what do you do? Most likely, if you can, you will provide an example or two to support your claim. An essay that emphasizes exemplification has the same purpose: to use specific instances or actual cases to convince an audience that a particular point is true.

TEACHING TIP
You may want to remind students that an academic audience may not share their beliefs and opinions.

In an essay that emphasizes exemplification, you support it by *illustrating* it with examples. These examples may range from facts that you have researched to personal accounts. If, for instance, you decide to write an essay that claims capital punishment is immoral, you might cite several cases in which an innocent person was executed. Keep in mind that your examples should connect clearly to your main point so that readers will see the truth of your claim.

The number of examples you choose to include in your essay may vary depending, in part, on your audience. For a group already opposed to the death penalty, you would not need detailed examples to support your belief that capital punishment is immoral. However, if you were writing to a group undecided about capital punishment, you would need more instances to get your point across—and even then, some would not believe you. Still, when used well, examples make writing more persuasive, increasing the chances readers will understand and believe your point.

Student Essay to Consider

Directions for Reading the Essay: As you read the following essay, circle areas that strike you as interesting or especially descriptive, underline areas that seem to be out of place or need work, place stars by any areas where you think additional information could be added, and mark the different modes of writing within this essay. Finally, respond to the claim made within the essay. Do you agree with the author about Americans' state of mind?

Altered States

Most Americans are not alcoholics. Most do not cruise seedy city streets looking to score crack cocaine or heroin. Relatively few try to con their doctors into prescribing unneeded mood-altering medications. And yet, many Americans are traveling through life with their minds slightly out of kilter. In its attempt to cope with modern life, the human mind seems to have evolved some defense strategies. Confronted with inventions like television, the shopping mall, and the Internet, the mind will slip—all by itself—into an altered state.

Never in the history of humanity have people been expected to sit passively for hours, staring at moving pictures emanating from an electronic box. Since too much exposure to flickering images of police officers, detectives, and talk-show hosts can be dangerous to human sanity, the mind automatically goes into a state of TV hypnosis. The eyes see the sitcom or the dog-food commercial, but the mind goes into a holding pattern. None of the televised images or sounds actually enters the brain. This is why, when questioned, people cannot remember commercials they have seen five seconds before or why the TV cops are chasing a certain suspect. In this hypnotic, trancelike state, the mind resembles an armored armadillo. It rolls up in self-defense, letting the stream of televised information pass by harmlessly.

If the TV watcher arises from the couch and goes to a shopping mall, he or she will again cope by slipping into an altered state. In the mall, the mind is bombarded with the sights, smells, and sounds of dozens of stores, restaurants, and movie theaters competing for its attention. There are hundreds of questions to be answered. Should I start with the upper or lower mall level? Which stores should I look in? Should I bother with the sweater sale at J. Crew? Should I eat fried chicken or try the healthier-sounding pita wrap? Where is my car parked? To combat this mental overload, the mind goes into a state resembling the whiteout experienced by mountain climbers trapped in a blinding snowstorm. Suddenly, everything looks the same. The shopper is unsure where to go next and cannot remember what he or she came for in the first place. The mind enters this state deliberately so that the shopper has no choice but to leave. Some kids can be in a shopping mall for hours, but they are exceptions to the rule.

But no part of everyday life so quickly triggers the mind's protective shutdown mode as that favorite pastime of the new millennium: Internet surfing. A computer user sits down with the intention of briefly checking his or her e-mail or looking up a fact for a research paper. But once tapped into the immense storehouse of information, entertainment, and seemingly intimate personal

continued

1

2

3

4

connections that the Internet offers, the user loses all sense of time and priorities. Prospects flood the mind: Should I explore the rise of Nazi Germany? Play a trivia game? Hear the life story of a lonely stranger in Duluth? With a mind dazed with information overload, the user numbly hits one key after another, leaping from topic to topic, from distraction to distraction. Hours fly by as he or she sits hunched over the terminal, unable to account for the time that has passed.

These poor victims are merely trying to cope with the mind-numbing inventions of modern life and are not responsible for their glazed eyes and robotic motions. People need to be aware of them and treat them with kindness and understanding. Going out of the way to bring these coma sufferers back to real life is the job of all those who have managed to avoid the side effects of television, shopping, and the Internet; otherwise, humanity will suffer.

5

QUESTIONS

ESL NOTE
To achieve coherence, nonnative students might review connectors that explain or emphasize, that give an example or explain a point, and that add information.

About the Main Idea and Author's Purpose

1. In your own words, write the main idea of the essay.

   The author is explaining that modern things like TV, malls, and the Internet have caused addiction-like behavior.

2. What is the author's purpose, and how can you determine this?

   To inform and entertain the reader. The author's purpose is to explain the effects of modern technology. The author uses adjectives and descriptions that relay humor.

About Unity

3. Which sentence in paragraph 3 of "Altered States" should be omitted in the interest of paragraph unity? (Write the opening words.)

   Some kids can be . . .

About Support

4. What three pieces of evidence does the writer offer to support the statement that the Internet is an "immense storehouse of information, entertainment, and seemingly intimate personal connections"?

   . . . the rise of Nazi Germany . . .

   . . . Play a trivia game . . .

   . . . Hear the life story of a lonely stranger . . .

About Coherence

5. What sentence indicates that the author has used emphatic order, saving his most important point for last? (Write the opening words.)

   But no part of everyday life . . .

6. Which sentence in paragraph 1 begins with a change-of-direction signal phrase? (Write the opening words.)

And yet, many Americans . . .

7. Which sentence in paragraph 2 begins with an illustration signal phrase? (Write the opening words.)

This is why, when questioned, . . .

About Mixed Modes

8. What are the different types of modes the author employs to create such a fluid and interesting essay?

The author uses exemplification and description.

About the Introduction and/or Conclusion

9. Which sentence in paragraph 5 begins with a concluding signal word? (Write the opening words.)

Therefore, the next time . . .

10. Which statement best describes the concluding paragraph?
    a. It contains a prediction.
    (b.) It combines a summary with a recommendation of how to treat people in an altered state.
    c. It refers to the point made in the introduction about alcohol and drugs.
    d. It contains thought-provoking questions about altered states.

Writing an Essay with Emphasis on Exemplification

RESPONDING TO STATEMENTS

Write an essay that uses examples to develop one of the following statements.

I would do anything for/to _____ .

There are many terrible jobs that people do, but the worst is _____

_____ .

I wouldn't _____ even if someone paid me a million dollars.

Be sure to choose examples that support your topic sentence. They should include relevant personal experiences (Chapter 7), examples you have researched and read about (Chapters 20 and 21), and as many descriptive details as possible (Chapter 8). Organize your paragraph so you save your most vivid, most convincing, or most important example for last.

WRITING ASSIGNMENT 1

Personal

TEACHING TIP
Encourage students to use the four steps, including prewriting and revision, to complete these assignments.

RESPONDING TO A READING

Write an essay that is based on an outside reading. It might be a selection recommended by your instructor, or it might be a piece by one of the following authors, all of whom have written short stories, books, or essays that should be available in your college library.

Willa Cather	Nelson Mandela
Winston Churchill	Toni Morrison
Sandra Cisneros	George Orwell
Annie Dillard	Ann Patchett
Ralph Waldo Emerson	Katherine Ann Porter
F. Scott Fitzgerald	John Steinbeck
Ellen Goodman	Amy Tan
Thomas Jefferson	Deborah Tannen
Maxine Hong Kingston	Calvin Trillin
Jhumpa Lahiri	Kurt Vonnegut
Sinclair Lewis	Walt Whitman

Base your essay on an idea in the selection you have chosen, and provide examples to back up your idea. You will want to review Chapter 6, "Exemplification" and Chapter 8, "Description" to help you provide the best examples for your essay. You will also want to review Chapter 20, "Working with Sources" and Chapter 21, "Writing a Research Paper" to help you use quotations and summaries from your chosen work to establish solid support for your thesis.

BEYOND THE CLASSROOM

Exemplification

In this essay that emphasizes exemplification, you will write with a specific purpose and for a specific audience.

EXPLAINING A DECISION Often when students are applying for grants or scholarships, they have to write an essay that demonstrates why they should receive the funds. Assume that you are writing an essay to receive a scholarship for "students who are new to college." The decision to receive the funds is based on your honesty about your reasons for attending college and your hopes of what a college degree will get you. You will want to incorporate stories and examples to support your claims. You will want to review Chapter 6, "Exemplification"; Chapter 7, "Narration"; and Chapter 8, "Description."

Developing an Essay with Emphasis on Narration

Considering Purpose and Audience

In an essay that emphasizes narration you make a point and incorporate one central story or several brief stories as support. Colorful details and interesting events that build up to a point make these essays enjoyable for readers and writers alike.

Life requires recalling events for different purposes. Students tell stories to teachers explaining why they didn't get their homework done. Witnesses recall events to police officers and juries. Boards and committees have to keep detailed minutes of all meetings. All of these examples require people to remember the events in order, provide details that affect meaning and understanding, and relay the information to others in a clear and coherent manner.

Unlike a narrative paragraph that only focuses on telling a story, an essay that emphasizes narration may also contain description, argument, cause and/or effect, and/or research. As you have seen in the paragraph development sections, different modes require different forms of writing, so it is important to use the specific modes and writing techniques where and when needed. The purpose of your essay will determine what events should be told, what events should be eliminated, and what strategies should be employed when writing.

Student Essay to Consider

Directions for Reading the Essay: As you read the following essay, circle areas that strike you as interesting or especially descriptive, underline areas that seem to be out of place or need work, place stars by any areas you think additional information could be added, and mark the different modes of writing within this essay. This essay remarks about several novels the student read; if you are familiar with any of the books, decide if you agree with the author's opinion. If you aren't familiar with the books, do the author's descriptions make you want to read any of the books? Be prepared to explain your decision.

Summer Read-a-thons

I remember when I was growing up that I spent many sunny afternoons in my backyard. I was fortunate to have a carefree, happy mother who enjoyed reading and helped books come alive. We would spread out a blanket on the long green grass and have read-a-thons together. Reading became a doorway into a new and exciting world that I have often chosen to enter. I fell in love with reading in my yard, where my kind mother helped me find my imagination, learn about the world, and learn more about myself.

At first my mother would bribe me with candy and popcorn, enticing me onto the reading blanket, but soon I would gladly assemble near her ready for the adventures to begin. She would ask me what book I wanted to hear for the day. Did I want to listen to a story of a little mouse that lived in a hotel and snuck around at night, flying through the hallways on his *real* toy-sized motorcycle? Or perhaps I would prefer finding myself in the middle of the Salem witch trials running for my life with Kit Tyler from *The Witch of Blackbird Pond*?

My mom would help me think about new ideas through books. We would read a story together and then discuss deep topics about what symbolism we found. My brother often liked to be part of these conversations. One of my favorite discussions we had sparked from the book *Mrs. Frisby and the Rats of Nimh*. It's about Mrs. Frisby, a

1 TEACHING TIP
Read this essay aloud. In tandem with having students follow the "Directions for Reading the Essay" above, ask them to underline the thesis statement, specific examples, and transitions before answering the
2 questions.

3

continued

mother field mouse, and her determination to protect her children, especially her young, ill son. She needs additional help from some neighbors who happen to be rats. The other animals had previously been afraid of the rats on this farm because they have strange ways and do strange things. Mrs. Frisby learns not to judge only by appearance. One young rat is especially notable as he gives his life for his fellow rats because it is the right thing to do. He became a hero of mine. As a young child I learned about service and sacrifice from this simple yet beautifully told story of rats and mice. I learned not to be as judgmental, and my imagination grew abundantly.

As I grew older, I developed a love for novels, biographies, and historical fiction. I especially enjoyed reading about World War II. In the book *The Hiding Place*, by Corrie ten Boom, I felt as if I knew Corrie and her sister Betsie, and was alongside them as they helped hide Jews from the Gestapo. They had tremendous courage and became symbols of bravery and tenacity. I learned much from these young girls as I read about the Nazis taking all of their possessions, locking them into a concentration camp, and enduring the indignities that they suffered. If I am ever feeling sorry for myself or that the world is out to get me, I think about Corrie ten Boom and her story, and I am humbled and grateful for my simple life.

Like the previous books, Catherine Clinton's book also inspired me. In *Harriet Tubman: The Road to Freedom*, a book about the Underground Railroad during the Civil War era, Harriet helps to free 300 slaves and guides them north to safety. I was in awe of the miracles that happened in her quest. No one was captured; again and again she found families to hide fleeing slaves. I found myself wishing I could meet her and talk with her about how she became so daring, so willing to sacrifice her own life for others. An enjoyment of history developed from these books, and I couldn't get enough of them. I wanted to immerse myself in them and learn about other leaders throughout history, what made them strong, what made them act! Harriet Tubman's story inspired me to do more, to not be as selfish, and to be more understanding of different cultures and different beliefs. I learned that it is good to have a strong opinion, but I should listen to others, and be compassionate in my judgments.

I am thankful my mother loves to read, and that she had the insight to hold those summer read-a-thons to help me develop a deep love of reading that has stayed with me throughout my life. I still think back to those summer days beside her in my yard, and the contentment I felt, hearing her laughter and gaining strength from her soft-spoken voice. I remember the encouragement she gave me, telling me that I could do anything I put my mind to, and that I was smart and capable. I am grateful my mother brought reading to life, and I discovered a part of me that I hadn't realized was there to find.

4

5

6

About the Main Idea and Author's Purpose

1. In your own words, write the main idea of the essay.

   The author describes how a simple summer activity turned into a lifetime love of reading.

2. What is the author's purpose and how can you determine this?

   To inform the reader. The author does not use persuasive words or a persuasive thesis, but is relaying information.

About Unity

3. Which sentence in paragraph 3 should be omitted and why?

   The sentence: "My brother often liked to be part of these conversations. . . ." This sentence is irrelevant to the purpose of the story. The brother may have been part of the conversations, but the focus of the story is how this activity affected the author.

About Support

4. The author uses a variety of descriptive words to help create strong images in the reader's mind. List some of the words and phrases and explain why you chose these specific examples.

   Answers will vary, but some answers could be as follows:

   . . . sunny afternoons . . . long green grass . . . in my yard—gives the reader a sense of what it was like during the read-a-thons

   . . . flying through the hallways on his real toy-sized motorcycle—gives a detailed image of the mouse hero

About Coherence

5. Which paragraph could be enhanced with stronger transitional words?

   Paragraph 6 needs to reflect back on the first paragraph and let the reader know that the author has taken the reader back into the present and is no longer in the past.

About Mixed Modes

6. What are the different types of modes the author employs in her paragraphs to create such a fluid and interesting essay?

   The author employs exemplification, narration, and description.

About the Introduction and/or Conclusion

7. What technique does the author use in her conclusion? Explain your answer.

The author summarizes the essay and makes some final remarks. She refers back to the introduction when she reminds the reader that the read-a-thons are what started her love for reading. She then emphasizes how important reading is for her, connecting her past to her present.

Writing an Essay with Emphasis on Narration

WRITING ASSIGNMENT 1

RECALLING AN IMPORTANT LEARNING MOMENT

In this assignment, you should recall a significant learning moment. This learning moment might be learning to read and/or write, learning to read and/or write music, teaching a child to read, or recalling a teacher who made a positive or negative impact. You will want to review Chapter 7, "Narration" and Chapter 8, "Description." If you choose to focus on someone who had a positive or negative impact on your learning, you should also review Chapter 10, "Cause and/or Effect."

WRITING ASSIGNMENT 2

TEACHING TIP
Encourage students to use the four steps to complete these assignments, including prewriting and revision.

WRITING YOUR OBITUARY

Many of us live in the here and now, not contemplating what our obituary will say when we die. Think about what your obituary might say if you were to die tomorrow. Then think about what you would like your obituary to say after you have lived a long life. Would you be proud of the things that are included? What would you like to change? Write an essay detailing what you would like your obituary to say about you after you have lived a long and fulfilled life. You will want to review Chapter 7, "Narration"; Chapter 8, "Description"; and Chapter 10, "Cause and/or Effect."

BEYOND THE CLASSROOM

Narration

In this essay that emphasizes narration, you will write with a specific purpose and for a specific audience.

BECOMING A TRAVEL WRITER In this assignment, you should pretend to be a travel writer and write about your hometown, making it sound like the ultimate destination. As many travel writers do, you will want to incorporate short vignettes, or stories, to demonstrate the excitement of visiting your hometown. You will want to review Chapter 7, "Narration"; Chapter 8, "Description"; and Chapter 14, "Argument."

Developing an Essay with Emphasis on Description

Considering Purpose and Audience

The main purpose of an essay with an emphasis on description is to make readers see—or hear, taste, smell, or feel—what you are writing about. Vivid details are the key to good descriptions, enabling your audience to picture and, in a way, experience what you describe.

Unlike a descriptive paragraph that focuses only on describing the topic, an essay that emphasizes description may also contain cause and/or effect, comparison and/or contrast, or narration. As you start to think about your own essay, choose a topic that will allow you to write descriptions that appeal strongly to at least one of your senses.

As you have seen in the paragraph development sections, different modes require different forms of writing, so it is important to use the specific modes and writing techniques where and when needed. The purpose of your essay will determine what events should be told, what events should be eliminated, and what strategies should be employed when writing. If your topic is a familiar one you can assume your audience already understands the general idea. However, if you are presenting something new or unfamiliar to your readers—perhaps a description of one of your relatives or a place where you've lived—you must provide background information.

Student Essay to Consider

Directions for Reading the Essay: As you read the following essay, circle areas that strike you as interesting or especially descriptive, underline areas that seem to be out of place or need work, place stars by any areas where you think additional information could be added, and mark the different modes of writing within this essay. Additionally, think about why the grandmother would have given her granddaughter the picture and whether or not it made a true difference for the granddaughter. Use words and images from the essay to support your opinion.

Family Portrait

My grandmother, who is ninety years old, recently sent me a photograph of herself that I had never seen before. While cleaning out the attic of her Florida home, she came across a studio portrait she had taken about a year before she married my grandfather. This picture of my grandmother as a twenty-year-old girl and the story behind it have fascinated me from the moment I began to consider it.

The young woman in the picture has a face that resembles my own in many ways. Her face is a bit more oval than mine, but the

1

2

continued

softly waving brown hair around it is identical. The small, straight nose is the same model I was born with. My grandmother's mouth is closed, yet there is just the slightest hint of a smile on her full lips. I know that if she had smiled, she would have shown the same wide grin and down-curving "smile lines" that appear in my own snapshots. The most haunting feature in the photo, however, is my grandmother's eyes. They are an exact duplicate of my own large, dark-brown ones. Her brows are plucked into thin lines, which are like two pencil strokes added to highlight those fine, luminous eyes.

3   I've also carefully studied the clothing and jewelry in the photograph. Although the photo was taken seventy years ago, my grandmother is wearing a blouse and skirt that could easily be worn today. The blouse is made of heavy eggshell-colored satin and reflects the light in its folds and hollows. It has a turned-down cowl collar and smocking on the shoulders and below the collar. The smocking (tiny rows of gathered material) looks hand-done. The skirt, which covers my grandmother's calves, is straight and made of light wool or flannel. My grandmother is wearing silver drop earrings. They are about two inches long and roughly shield-shaped. On her left wrist is a matching bracelet. My grandmother can't find this bracelet now, despite the fact that we spent hours searching through the attic for it. On the third finger of her left hand is a ring with a large, square-cut stone.

4   The story behind the picture is as interesting to me as the young woman it captures. Grandma, who was earning twenty-five dollars a week as a file clerk, decided to give her boyfriend (my grandfather) a picture of herself. She spent almost two weeks' salary on the skirt and blouse, which she bought at a fancy department store downtown. She borrowed the earrings and bracelet from her older sister, my Great-Aunt Dorothy. The ring she wore was a present from another young man she was dating at the time. Grandma spent another chunk of her salary to pay the portrait photographer for the hand-tinted print in old-fashioned tones of brown and tan. Just before giving the picture to my grandfather, she scrawled at the lower left, "Sincerely, Gloria."

5   When I study this picture, I react in many ways. I think about the trouble that Grandma went to in order to impress the young man who was to be my grandfather. I laugh when I look at the ring, which was probably worn to make my grandfather jealous. I smile at the serious, formal inscription my grandmother used at this stage of the budding relationship. Sometimes, I am filled with a mixture of pleasure and sadness when I look at this frozen long-ago moment. It is a moment of beauty, of love, and—in a way—of my own past.

About the Main Idea and Author's Purpose

1. In your own words, write the main idea of the essay.

   The author describes a portrait of her grandmother that was taken when her

   grandmother was a young woman. As she describes the portrait, the author

   makes connections between her grandmother and herself.

2. What is the author's purpose and how can you determine this?

   To inform the reader. The author uses descriptive words to help the reader get

   to know the grandmother.

About Unity

3. Which of the following sentences from paragraph 3 of "Family Portrait" should be omitted in the interest of paragraph unity?

   a. Although the photo was taken seventy years ago, my grandmother is wearing a blouse and skirt that could easily be worn today.

   b. It has a turned-down cowl collar and smocking on the shoulders and below the collar.

   (c.) My grandmother can't find this bracelet now, despite the fact that we spent hours searching the attic for it.

   d. On the third finger of her left hand is a ring with a large, square-cut stone.

ESL NOTE
Nonnative students may need to consult a dictionary to find colorful and vivid vocabulary.

About Support

4. How many separate items of clothing and jewelry are described in paragraph 3?

   a. four

   (b.) five

   c. seven

5. Label as sight, touch, hearing, or smell all the sensory details in the following sentences taken from the essay.

   a. "The blouse is made of heavy eggshell-colored satin and reflects the *touch*   *sight*
   light in its folds and hollows." *sight*   *sight*

   b. "Her brows are plucked into thin lines, which are like two pencil *touch*   *sight*   *sight*
   strokes added to highlight those fine, luminous eyes." *sight*

ESL NOTE
To improve coherence and grammatical accuracy when describing a place, nonnative speakers should review adverbs of place or prepositional expressions that indicate spatial organization.

About Coherence

6. Which method of organization does paragraph 2 use?

   a. Time order

   (b.) Emphatic order

7. Which sentence in paragraph 2 suggests the method of organization? (Write the opening words.)

   The most haunting . . .

QUESTIONS

About Mixed Modes

8. What are the different types of modes the author employs in the paragraphs to create such an interesting essay?

The author uses narration and description.

About the Introduction and/or Conclusion

9. Which statement best describes the introduction?

 a. It starts with an idea that is the opposite of the one that is developed.

 b. It explains the importance of the topic to its readers

 c. It begins with a general statement of the topic and narrows it down to a thesis statement.

 (d.) It begins with an anecdote.

Writing an Essay with Emphasis on Description

WRITING ASSIGNMENT 1

RECALLING AN IMPORTANT EXPERIENCE

In this assignment, you will write an essay that describes an experience that has significantly affected you. You will want to use specific details in addition to examples that support your purpose. You will want to review Chapter 6, "Exemplification"; Chapter 8, "Description"; and Chapter 10, "Cause and/or Effect."

WRITING ASSIGNMENT 2

WRITING A BIOGRAPHY

In this assignment, you should choose a person whom you would like to know more about. A good biographical profile will include information that is relevant to your purpose, which should describe why you think this person is important enough to profile. As you interview your person, you will want to take careful notes to ensure the material you write is accurate and to allow you to use direct quotes where needed. Your purpose will determine the information you need to include. You may need to write about your person's childhood, education, and/or work, or you may only need to focus on one specific aspect of his or her life. You will want to review Chapter 7, "Narration"; Chapter 8, "Description"; and the Part 5 chapters, which cover research.

WRITING ASSIGNMENT 3

REACTING TO A WORK OF ART

In this assignment, you will be required to choose a piece of art, like the *Mona Lisa* or Michelangelo's *David*, and explain why it is significant. You will need to describe the work so the reader fully understands what the piece looks like, and you will need to argue the work's importance. You will want to review Chapter 8, "Description" and Chapter 14, "Argument." If you need to research information about your chosen work of art, you will need to review the Part 5 chapters, which cover research.

TEACHING TIP
Encourage students to use the four steps to complete these assignments, including prewriting and revision.

In this essay that emphasizes description, you will write with a specific purpose and for a specific audience.

DESIGNING A BROCHURE Imagine that you work at your city's visitor's bureau and need to create a brochure for tourists describing your city's top attractions and "selling" your city as a top tourist destination. You will want to consider which sites should be highlighted, which hotels would offer different levels of accommodation, and why your city is the best choice. You will want to review Chapter 8, "Description" and Chapter 14, "Argument."

Developing an Essay with Emphasis on Process

Considering Purpose and Audience

Glance at a newsstand and you'll see magazine cover stories with titles such as "How to Impress Your Boss," "How to Add Romance to Your Life," or "How to Dress Like a Movie Star." These articles promise to give readers directions or information they can follow, and they are popular versions of essays that emphasize process.

In general, essays that emphasize process will explain the steps involved in a particular action, process, or event. Some of these essays focus on giving readers actual instructions, others focus on giving readers information, and still others focus on persuading readers. The type of essay you write depends on the specific topic and purpose you choose.

No matter what your main purpose, keep your audience in mind as you work. As with any essay, select a topic that will interest readers. A group of college students, for example, might be interested in reading an essay that explains how and why to get financial aid but bored by an essay on how and why to plan for retirement. In addition, consider how much your readers already know about your topic. An audience unfamiliar with financial aid may need background information and definitions in order to understand your essay. Finally, be sure that your organization is very logically organized so your readers can easily follow your ideas, thus supporting your purpose.

Student Essay to Consider

Directions for Reading the Essay: As you read the following essay, circle areas that strike you as interesting or especially descriptive, underline areas that seem to be out of place or need work, place stars by any areas where you think additional information could be added, and mark the different modes of writing within this essay. Finally, respond to the claim made within the essay. Do you agree or disagree with the author? Could the author have used better examples to support his or her claim? Be prepared to explain your opinion.

Successful Exercise

1 Regular exercise is something like the weather—we all talk about it, but we tend not to do anything about it. Fitness programs on TV and DVD and via apps and the Internet now make it easy to have a low cost personal exercise program without leaving home. However, for success in exercise, people should follow a simple plan consisting of arranging time, making preparations, and starting off at a sensible pace.

2 Most people who don't regularly exercise have excuses for not exercising: a heavy schedule at work or school; being rushed in the morning and exhausted at night; too many other responsibilities. However, one solution is simply to get up half an hour earlier in the morning. In this thirty-minute time period, a very effective workout can occur. Even without leaving the house, a person can complete a full-body workout using exercise videos, objects around the house, and his or her own body weight. To offset the excuse of not enough time in the morning, preparing ahead of time becomes a necessity. By laying out clothes for the work day, filling the coffee maker, and gathering books and materials for the day before going to bed, a person can wake up knowing that time has been arranged to allow for exercise.

3 The next step a person should follow is to prepare for the workout. Most people who exercise in the morning do so on an empty stomach. Because food takes a while to digest, it is unwise to attempt to exercise while the body is trying to break down food; plus, people who exercise on an empty stomach have the added benefit of tapping into the body's fat reserves during the thirty-minute session. Working out in the home has the added advantage of privacy, so a person doesn't need to invest in high-cost workout gear; usually a loose T-shirt and shorts are fine. Some people, to save time, will throw tennis shoes on with their pajamas, thus saving one extra step! Then people need to make sure their exercise materials are ready.

4 Finally, a person who is just beginning an exercise regime should use common sense in getting started. Common sense isn't so common, as anyone who reads newspapers and watches the world can attest. It has taken a while to get out of shape and getting back into shape is not going to be an overnight phenomenon. Starting too quickly can lead to injuries, which will delay the whole process. Whether a person starts with a DVD or with a written program, he or she should know that the first few times are often the hardest. It is not uncommon for someone starting to exercise not to be able to finish the whole program the first time, but it does get easier. After five or six sessions of exercise, most people find that they are able to complete most of the exercises without their muscles screaming in resistance.

continued

> Establishing an exercise program isn't difficult, but it can't be achieved by reading about it, talking about it, or watching models exercise on television. It happens only when a person decides to make the change and employs it. Through careful planning and good common sense, anyone can start exercising and start feeling the benefits of health. As doctors often like to say, "If you don't use it, you'll lose it."

5

About the Main Idea and Author's Purpose

1. In your own words, write the main idea of the essay.

   The author is explaining that with a few simple steps, anyone can successfully start an exercise routine.

2. What is the author's purpose, and how can you determine this?

   To inform and persuade. The author is persuading the reader that anyone can successfully start an exercise program. The author uses simple steps and examples that make following the program easy.

About Unity

3. The (*fill in the correct answer:* first, second, third) ___*first*___ supporting paragraph of "Successful Exercise" lacks a topic sentence. Write a topic sentence that expresses its main point: ___*First, arrange time for exercise.*___

4. Which of the following sentences from paragraph 4 should be omitted in the interest of paragraph unity and consistent point of view?

   a. "Starting too quickly can lead to injuries, which will delay the whole process."

   (b) "Common sense isn't so common, as anyone who reads newspapers and watches the world can attest."

   c. "Whether a person starts with a DVD or with a written program, he or she should know that the first few times are often the hardest.

About Support

5. Which sentence in paragraph 3 needs to be followed by more supporting details? (Write the opening words.)

   Then people need to . . .

About Coherence

6. List three transitional words that are used in "Successful Exercise."

   however

   the next step

   finally

About Mixed Modes

7. What are the different types of modes the author employs in the paragraphs to create such a fluid and interesting essay?

process and exemplification

About the Introduction and/or Conclusion

8. Which statement best describes the introduction?
   - (a.) It begins with a couple of general points about the topic and narrows down to the thesis.
   - b. It explains the importance of daily exercise to the reader.

Writing an Essay with Emphasis on Process

SHARING YOUR EXPERTISE

Everyone is an expert at something. Using your personal experiences and insights, write an essay with an emphasis on process. If you are a parent, you might write about how you taught your children to read. If you work as a sales representative, you might write about how monthly sales quotas are met. If you are a recovering addict, you might write about how the twelve-step recovery process works. As a college student, you might write about how the registration process works at your school. Each of these topics will require you to incorporate several modes of writing, such as narration (Chapter 7) and description (Chapter 8).

THINKING AS A SCIENTIST

The scientific method is a process that all scientists use. In this essay, you are to research the scientific method; then, using this method, write about an experiment. Possible experiments that could be described are dropping Mentos candies into Coca-Cola bottles, creating non-Newtonian oobleck, or turning needles into magnets. This essay will require you to read Chapter 21, "Writing a Research Paper"; Chapter 8, "Description"; and Chapter 9, "Process."

In this essay that emphasizes process, you will write with a specific purpose and for a specific audience.

PREPARING A HANDOUT Imagine that you are a job recruiter working at an employment agency. Your supervisor has asked you to help new clients understand the job-seeking process. You decide to create a handout on how to prepare for a job interview. What would be the first step that a job seeker should consider? What would be the next step? What about the final step? Select three steps and develop each in a separate paragraph. Some areas you might consider are these: dressing appropriately, arriving on time, offering a firm handshake, maintaining eye contact, staying positive throughout the interview, bringing a sense of humor, and being honest at all times. You will want to review Chapter 6, "Exemplification" and Chapter 9, "Process."

WRITING ASSIGNMENT 1

TEACHING TIP
Encourage students to use the four steps, including prewriting and revision, to complete these assignments.

WRITING ASSIGNMENT 2

BEYOND THE CLASSROOM

Process

Developing an Essay with Emphasis on Cause and/or Effect

Considering Purpose and Audience

The main purpose of an essay that emphasizes cause and/or effect is to support your purpose by using examples that explain (1) the causes of a particular event or situation; (2) the effects of an event or a situation; or, more rarely, (3) a combination of both.

The type of essay you write will depend on the topic you choose and the main point you wish to communicate. If, for example, your purpose is to profile a special person who has had a great impact on you, your essay would emphasize the effects of that person. However, if your purpose is to exemplify why you moved out of your family home, your essay would focus on the causes of your decision.

As with all essays, try to pick a topic that will appeal to your audience of readers. An essay on the negative effects of steroids and other drugs on professional athletes may be especially interesting to an audience of sports fans. On the other hand, this same topic might not be as appealing to people who dislike sports. In addition to selecting a lively topic, be sure to make your main point clear so that your audience can follow the cause-effect relationship you've chosen to develop. In the above instance, you might even announce specific causes or effects by signaling them to readers: "One effect drug use has on athletes is to . . . ."

Student Essay to Consider

Directions for Reading the Essay: As you read the following essay, circle areas that strike you as interesting or especially descriptive, underline areas that seem to be out of place or need work, place stars by any areas where you think additional information could be added, and mark the different modes of writing within this essay. Additionally, think about the student's experience with college and your own experience. What types of comparisons can you make? Be prepared to share your findings.

The Challenges of Going Back to School

When I first decided to go back to school, I wasn't sure about my ability to do the work. When I was in high school, I was a pretty good student. Once I graduated, I started working full-time for the clothing store where I had been employed part-time during high school. I loved the feeling of being an independent full-time employee, and I loved my job. I got married during this time and felt I was living a good life. However, after fifteen years of not getting promotions or new job opportunities because of my lack of a college degree, I finally decided to return to school. Little did I know that returning to school after a long period would bring me so many challenges.

First of all, my writing skills had really deteriorated. As a result of not having used my grammar skills in fifteen years, I tested into a developmental writing class. I was frustrated when I couldn't recognize a fragment, use commas correctly, or fix a dangling modifier.

1 TEACHING TIP
Read this essay aloud. In tandem with having students follow the "Directions for Reading the Essay" above, ask them to underline the thesis statement, specific examples, and transitions before answering the questions.

2

continued

My essays started off terribly, but eventually, with a lot of hard work and effort, the grades started to improve. My favorite essay assignment involved attending a campus rally and writing about it.

Second, math classes were another challenge for me. Even though both my husband and I worked, neither of our jobs paid very well, so I had to keep a pretty tight budget with groceries and expenses. I thought I had maintained my basic math skills, especially as my job as a salesclerk involved math. Was I wrong! That's when it really hit me. I really liked working, but was tired of struggling to make ends meet. My parents had tried to get me to see that my choices were going to be limited if I didn't go to college, but I thought I knew better. The choices I had made at eighteen came suddenly crashing before me.

3

I felt awkward socially as well. I didn't seem to have the leisure time some of my classmates had to socialize and study in groups. I once tried to study with a group in my American History class, but the time the group met conflicted with my job. I found myself studying mostly on my own. My husband was a great support, but he couldn't help me with some of my homework. After much time and effort, I completed all my coursework, including my paralegal courses, and was ready to start my new life.

4

Going back to school after so many years proved to be an enormous challenge. I am now working as a paralegal and feel that my life is back on track. I'm even thinking about applying for law school. I don't want to rush things, though. I am presently enjoying my job and learning many things about the law and society. My experience with going back to school changed my view of myself and my personal goals. I learned that decisions carry many consequences, and that I should look at all my options before I make an important, life-altering decision.

5

QUESTIONS

About the Main Idea and Author's Purpose

1. In your own words, write the main idea of the essay.

   The author explains her experience of going to college after being out of school for fifteen years.

2. What is the author's purpose, and how can you determine this?

   To inform and persuade. The author is sharing her personal experiences to demonstrate what happened to her educational abilities, what life was like before she returned to school, and what life was like when she finally finished school. The essay also has a secondary purpose of demonstrating how choices have consequences, and it is important to think before acting.

About Unity

3. Which sentence in paragraph 2 should be omitted in the interest of paragraph unity? (Write the opening words.)

My favorite essay assignment . . .

About Support

4. After which sentence in paragraph 3 is more support needed?

Was I wrong!

About Coherence

5. What are the two transition words or phrases that signal two major points of support for the thesis?

First of all   _Second_

Mixed Modes

6. What are the different types of modes the author employs in her paragraphs to create such an interesting essay?

Narration and Cause and/or Effect

About the Introduction and/or Conclusion

7. Which sentence best describes the opening paragraph?

   a. It begins with a general statement of the topic and narrows it down to a thesis statement.

   (b.) It uses an incident or brief story.

   c. It explains the importance of the topic to the reader.

   d. It starts with an idea that is the opposite of the one then developed.

8. Which method is used in the conclusion?

   (a.) Summary and final thoughts

   b. Recommendation

   c. Thought-provoking quotation

Writing an Essay with Emphasis on Cause and/or Effect

CONSIDERING THE STATE OF THE HUMAN RACE

If friendly aliens from a highly developed civilization decided to visit our planet, they would encounter a contradictory race of beings—us. We humans would have reasons to feel both proud and ashamed of the kind of society the aliens would encounter. Write an essay explaining whether you would be proud or ashamed of the state of the human race today. Good support may include narration (Chapter 7), description (Chapter 8), cause and/or effect (Chapter 10), argument (Chapter 14), and possibly some research (the Part 5 chapters).

WRITING ASSIGNMENT 1

Personal

TEACHING TIP
Encourage students to use the four steps to complete these assignments, including prewriting and revision.

WRITING ASSIGNMENT 2

ANALYZING A FAMOUS FIGURE

Write an essay about an author, a musician, or an actor who has had a positive or negative influence on society. To develop your idea, use reasons that demonstrate the effects of your chosen subject's actions. You may want to refer to Chapter 6, "Exemplification"; Chapter 10, "Cause and/or Effect"; and Chapter 14, "Argument." If you use ideas other than your own, refer to Chapter 20, "Working with Sources" and Chapter 21, "Writing a Research Paper" for proper documentation and citation.

BEYOND THE CLASSROOM

Cause and/or Effect

In this essay that emphasizes cause and/or effect, you will write with a specific purpose and for a specific audience.

REVIEWING AN EMPLOYEE Imagine that you are a retail store manager and must write a quarterly performance report for one of your employees. Not only is this person a top seller, but he or she has a positive attitude and shows leadership qualities. Write an essay in which you focus on how this person has brought about three positive changes in the company. Each change should be developed in a separate paragraph.

Although much of your essay will focus on the effects (Chapter 10) this person has had on the company, it should also incorporate examples (Chapter 6) and anecdotes (Chapter 7) that support the thesis.

Developing an Essay with Emphasis on Comparison and/or Contrast

Considering Purpose and Audience

TEACHING TIP
Ask students to consider what would happen if they did not consider the purpose and audience for an essay assignment.

The purpose of an essay that emphasizes comparison and/or contrast is to make a point by including examples that show how distinct items or people are either similar or different. Whether you choose to use comparison or contrast depends on the specific point you want to convey to readers. As you think about your own essay, ask yourself what type of essay would benefit from this type of support. Then determine whether you want to focus on the differences between the items or their similarities. You may even decide that you want to do both. If, say, you choose to persuade your reader that he or she should purchase a specific type of computer, you may include paragraphs on the similarities and differences between Mac and PC computers. Once you determine your purpose, be sure you keep your readers in mind when planning your essay as your audience will determine your tone and needed background information, definitions, and examples.

Unlike a comparison or contrast paragraph that focuses only on the similarities or differences of two or more subjects, an essay that emphasizes comparison and/or contrast may also contain description, narration, persuasion, and/or research. As you have seen in the paragraph development sections, different modes require different forms of writing, so it is important to look at your essay as a mix, using the specific modes and writing techniques where and when needed.

Student Essay to Consider

Directions for Reading the Essay: As you read the following essay, circle areas that strike you as interesting or especially descriptive, underline areas that seem to be out of place or need work, place stars by any areas where you think additional information could be added, and mark the different modes of writing within this essay. Additionally, compare the author's study habits, both in high school and college, to your own study habits, and be prepared to discuss them.

Studying: Then and Now

One June day, I staggered into a high school classroom to take my final exam in United States History IV. I had made my usual desperate effort to cram the night before, with the usual dismal results—I had gotten only to page seventy-five of a four-hundred-page textbook. My study habits in high school, obviously, were a mess. But in college, I've made an attempt to reform my note-taking, studying, and test-taking skills.   1

As I took notes in high school classes, I often lost interest and began doodling, drawing Martians, or seeing what my signature would look like if I married and took the last name of the cute guy in the second row. Now, however, I try not to let my mind wander, and I pull my thoughts back into focus when they begin to go fuzzy. In high school, my notes often looked like something written in hieroglyphics. In college, I've learned to use a semiprint writing style that makes my notes understandable. When I would look over my high school notes, I couldn't understand them. There would be a word like "Reconstruction," then a big blank, then the word "important." Weeks later, I had no idea what Reconstruction was or why it was important. I've since learned to write down connecting ideas, even if I have to take the time to do it after class. Taking notes is one thing I've really learned to do better since high school days.   2

Ordinary studying during the term is another area where I've made changes. In high school, I let reading assignments go. I told myself that I'd have no trouble catching up on two hundred pages during a fifteen-minute ride to school. College courses have taught me to keep pace with the work. Otherwise, I feel as though I'm sinking into a quicksand of unread material. When I finally read the high school assignment, my eyes would run over the words but my brain would be plotting how to get the car for Saturday night. Now, I use several techniques that force me to really concentrate on my reading.   3

In addition to learning how to cope with daily work, I've also learned to handle study sessions for big tests. My all-night study sessions in high school were experiments in self-torture. Around 2:00 A.M., my mind, like a soaked sponge, simply stopped absorbing things. Now, I space out exam study sessions over   4

continued

TEACHING TIP
Read this essay aloud. In tandem with having students follow the "Directions for Reading the Essay" above, ask them to underline the thesis statement, specific examples, and transitions before answering the questions.

several days. That way, the night before can be devoted to an overall review rather than raw memorizing. Most important, though, I've changed my attitude toward tests. In high school, I thought tests were mysterious things with completely unpredictable questions. Now, I ask instructors about the kinds of questions that will be on the exam, and I try to anticipate which areas or facts instructors are likely to ask about. These practices really work, and for me they've taken much of the fear and mystery out of tests.

Since I've reformed, note-taking and studying are not as tough as they once were. And I am beginning to reap the benefits. As time goes on, my college test sheets are going to look much different from the red-marked tests of my high school days.

5

QUESTIONS

ESL NOTE
To improve coherence and grammatical accuracy, nonnative speakers should review the comparative and superlative forms of adjectives and adverbs, especially the usage of *less* and *fewer*. They should also practice using adverbial clauses of comparison and contrast.

About the Main Idea and Author's Purpose

1. In your own words, write the main idea of the essay.

The author's purpose is to demonstrate how her study skills in college are better than in high school.

2. What is the author's purpose, and how can you determine this?

To inform. The author uses personal examples to explain how her studying changed from high school to college.

About Unity

3. In which supporting paragraph in "Studying: Then and Now" is the topic sentence at the end rather than at the beginning, where it generally belongs in student essays?

2 (the first supporting paragraph)

About Support

4. Which sentence in paragraph 3 needs to be followed by more supporting details? (Write the opening words.)

Now I use several techniques . . .

About Coherence

5. What method of development does the author use?

Point by point

About Mixed Modes

6. What are the different types of modes the author employs to support her purpose?

Comparison and/or contrast, exemplification, and narration

CHAPTER 18 Patterns of Essay Development 353

About the Introduction and/or Conclusion

7. Which sentence best describes the opening paragraph?

    a. It begins with a broad statement that narrows down to the thesis.

    b. It explains the importance of the topic to the reader.

    (c.) It uses an incident or a brief story.

RESPONDING TO IMAGES

Is there such a thing as a "typical family"? The Pritchetts, of the long-running TV show "Modern Family," resemble what many families of the twenty-first century now look like. What is your idea of a typical family? Write an essay comparing or contrasting your own family with your concept of a typical family.

©Splash News/Alamy Stock Photo

Writing an Essay with Emphasis on Comparison and/or Contrast

ANALYZING ATTITUDES

WRITING ASSIGNMENT 1

Personal

Write an essay in which you analyze two attitudes on a controversial subject. You may want to contrast your views with those of someone else, or contrast the way you felt about the subject in the past with the way you feel now. You will want to review Chapter 11, "Comparison or Contrast"; additionally, if you choose the first option, you may need to do research, so you will need to read Chapter 20, "Working with Sources" and Chapter 21, "Writing a Research Paper" in order to properly document and cite your information.

COMPARING VIEWPOINTS

WRITING ASSIGNMENT 2

Academic

Emily Dickinson is known for her poems about solitude. Write an essay that compares or contrasts Dickinson's view about solitude in two of the poems. Then discuss how your view of solitude is either similar to or different from that which is presented by the poems. To create good support, you will want to review Chapter 11, "Comparison or Contrast" and Chapter 6, "Exemplification." You may also want to review Chapter 12, "Definition" as this assignment may require you to compare your definition of solitude to Emily Dickinson's definition. Finally, if you use direct quotes or paraphrases of Dickinson's poems, you should review Chapter 20, "Working with Sources" and Chapter 21, "Writing a Research Paper" for proper citation and documentation.

TEACHING TIP
Encourage students to use the four steps to complete these assignments, including prewriting and revision.

BEYOND THE CLASSROOM

Comparison and/or Contrast

In this essay that emphasizes comparison and/or contrast, you will write with a specific purpose and for a specific audience.

REQUESTING A PROMOTION   Assume that there is a desirable job opening at your workplace. Write a letter in which you persuade your boss that you are the ideal candidate for this position. To support your point, you will want to compare your abilities with those of the ideal candidate for this position. Use the point-by-point method, discussing each desired qualification and then describing how well you measure up to it. Use the requirements of a job you are familiar with, ideally a job you would really like to apply for someday. Additional support should be given through actual examples (Chapter 6, "Exemplification" and Chapter 7, "Narration") of your abilities.

Developing an Essay with Emphasis on Definition

Considering Purpose and Audience

When you write an essay that emphasizes definition, your main purpose is to explain to readers your understanding of a key term or concept, while your secondary purpose is to persuade them that your definition is a legitimate one. Keep in mind that when you present a definition in your essay, you should not simply repeat a word's dictionary meaning. Instead, you should convey what a particular term means to you through persuasive examples. For example, if you were to write about the term "patriotism," you might begin by presenting your definition of the word. You might say patriotism means turning out for Fourth of July parades, displaying the flag, or supporting the government. Or perhaps you think patriotism is about becoming politically active and questioning government policy. Whatever definition you choose, be sure to provide specific instances so that readers can fully understand your meaning of the term. For example, in writing an essay on patriotism, you might describe three people whom you see as truly patriotic. Writing about each person will help ensure that readers see and understand the term as you do.

As with other essay forms, keep your audience in mind. If, for instance, you were proposing a new definition of "patriotism," an audience of war veterans might require different examples than would an audience of college students.

Student Essay to Consider

Directions for Reading the Essay: As you read the following essay, circle areas that strike you as interesting or especially descriptive, underline areas that seem to be out of place or need work, place stars by any areas where you think additional information could be added, and mark the different modes of writing within this essay. Do you agree or disagree with these labels? Can you think of a label the author left out? Be prepared to discuss your ideas.

Student Zombies

Schools divide people into categories. From first grade on up, students are labeled "advanced" or "deprived" or "remedial" or "antisocial." Students pigeonhole their fellow students, too. We've all known the "brain," the "jock," the "dummy," and the "teacher's pet." In most cases, these narrow labels are misleading and inaccurate. But there is one label for a certain type of college student that says it all: "zombie."

1

Zombies are the living dead. Most of us haven't known a lot of real zombies personally, but we do know how they act. We have horror movies to guide us. The special effects in horror movies are much better these days. Over the years, we've learned from the movies that zombies stalk around graveyards, their eyes glued open by Hollywood makeup artists, bumping like cheap toy robots into living people. Zombie students in college do just about the same thing. They stalk around campus, eyes glazed, staring off into space. When they do manage to wander into a classroom, they sit down mechanically and contemplate the ceiling. Zombie students rarely eat, talk, laugh, or toss Frisbees on campus lawns. Instead, they vanish when class is dismissed and return only when some mysterious zombie signal summons them back into a classroom. The signal may not occur for weeks.

2 TEACHING TIP
Read this essay aloud. In tandem with having students follow the "Directions for Reading the Essay" above, ask them to underline the thesis statement, specific examples, and transitions before answering the questions.

Zombies are controlled by some mysterious force. According to legend, real zombies are corpses that have been brought back to life to do the bidding of a voodoo master. Student zombies, too, seem directed by a strange power. They continue to attend school although they have no apparent desire to do so. They show no interest in college-related activities like tests, grades, papers, and projects. And yet some inner force compels them to wander through the halls of higher education.

3

An awful fate awaits all zombies unless something happens to break the spell they're under. In the movies, zombies are often shot, stabbed, drowned, electrocuted, and run over by large vehicles, all to no avail. Finally the hero or heroine realizes that a counterspell is needed. Once that spell is cast, with the appropriate props of chicken feet, human hair, and bats' eyeballs, the zombie-corpse can return peacefully to its coffin. The only hope for a student zombie to change is for him or her to undergo a similarly traumatic experience.

4

All college students know that it's not necessary to see *Night of the Living Dead* or *Land of the Dead* in order to see zombies in action—or nonaction. They can forget the campus film series or the late-late show. All they need to do is just sit in a classroom and wait. They know what they're looking for—the students who walk in without books or papers and sit in the very last row of seats. The ones plugged constantly into their smartphone earbuds don't count as zombies—that's a whole different category of "student." *Day of the Living Dead* is showing every day at a college nearby.

5

About the Main Idea and Author's Purpose

1. In your own words, write the main idea of the essay.

   The author is defining a type of college student that is found on every college campus.

2. What is the author's purpose, and how can you determine this?

   To entertain the reader with a definition of a type of college student. The author uses adjectives and descriptions that relay humor.

About Unity

3. Which sentence in paragraph 2 of "Student Zombies" should be omitted in the interest of paragraph unity? (Write the opening words.)

   The special effects . . .

4. What sentence in the final paragraph introduces a new topic and so should be eliminated? (Write the opening words.)

   The ones plugged constantly. . .

About Support

5. After which sentence in paragraph 4 is more support needed? (Write the opening words.)

   The only hope for a student zombie . . .

About Coherence

6. Which sentence in paragraph 2 begins with a change-of-direction transitional word? (Write the opening words.)

   Instead, they vanish . . .

About Mixed Modes

7. What are the different types of modes the author employs in the paragraphs to create such an entertaining and interesting essay?

   Definition, description, and comparison and contrast

About the Introduction and/or Conclusion

8. Which method of introduction is used in the opening paragraph? (Circle the letter of the answer.)

   a. Anecdote

   b. Idea that is the opposite of the one to be developed

   c. Quotation

   (d.) Broad, general statement narrowing to a thesis

Writing an Essay with Emphasis on Definition

DEFENDING A BOOK

Each year, the Young Adult Library Services Association puts out a list of the best books for young adults. The decisions are made by a committee. Pretend you are on the committee and you need to defend your choice of book. You will need to define what you think makes a great book, and then demonstrate how this book fits your definition. You will want to review Chapter 12, "Definition" and Chapter 14, "Argument" to help you present a solid essay that persuades the committee to include your book on the list. You may also need to review the three Part 5 chapters, which cover research, if you decide to visit the YALSA Web site, http://www.ala.org/yalsa/booklistsawards/booklistsbook, and/or incorporate direct quotations or summaries of your book.

WRITING ASSIGNMENT 1

Personal

TEACHING TIP
Encourage students to use the four steps including prewriting and revision, to complete these assignments.

DEFENDING A THEORY

Famous philosophers like Aristotle, Plato, and Friedrich Nietzsche spent their lives thinking about and trying to solve some of life's most difficult questions. In this assignment, you are to research a philosopher and learn about his or her most famous theory/theories. You could study Epicurus and his theory of happiness or G. E. Moore and his theory of truth. Then, you are to write an essay that explains why you agree or disagree with the ideas you have studied and why.

If your idea of happiness differs from that of Epicurus, give examples of the differences, or if your idea of truth is the same as that of Moore, explain why you have come to that idea. This essay will require you to define the term or theory (Chapter 12), compare and/or contrast your definition to the philosopher's definition (Chapter 11), and persuade your audience to believe why your definition is the correct one (Chapter 14).

WRITING ASSIGNMENT 2

Academic

In this essay that emphasizes definition, you will write with a specific purpose and for a specific audience.

PROMOTING A HEALTHY LIFESTYLE You work in a doctor's office and have been asked to write a brochure that will be placed in the waiting room. The brochure is intended to tell patients what a healthy lifestyle is. Write an essay that defines "healthy lifestyle" for your readers, using examples whenever appropriate. Your definition might focus on both mental and physical health and might include eating, sleeping, exercise, and recreational habits. You may want to look at Chapter 6, "Exemplification"; Chapter 7, "Narration"; and Chapter 12, "Definition" for help in developing solid support for your essay.

BEYOND THE CLASSROOM

Definition

Work

Developing an Essay with Emphasis on Division and Classification

Considering Purpose and Audience

When writing an essay that emphasizes division and classification, your purpose is to present your audience with your own unique way of dividing and classifying particular topics. In order to write a successful essay, you will need to first choose a topic that interests readers and lends itself to support that can be divided and classified. Once you pick your topic and decide on the support you will use, you will then have to come up with your own unique sorting system—one that readers will be able to understand.

For example, if your essay focuses on types of clothing, there are a number of ways to sort this topic into categories. You could divide clothing by the function it serves: shirts and jackets (to cover the upper body), pants and skirts (for the lower body), and shoes and socks (for the feet). Or you could divide clothes according to the materials they are made from: animal products, plant products, and synthetic materials. A more interesting, and potentially humorous, way to divide clothes is by fashion: clothes that are stylish, clothes that are going out of style, and clothes that are so unattractive that they never were in style. Notice that in all three of these cases, the broad topic of clothing has been divided into categories according to a particular principle (function, materials, and fashion).

Unlike a classification and division paragraph that focuses only on presenting the categories, an essay that emphasizes classification and division may also contain description and/or narration. As you have read in the paragraph development sections, different modes require different forms of writing, so it is important to use the specific modes and writing techniques where and when needed. Also, depending on the different categories that you include, you may need to research more information. Your audience and the purpose of your essay will determine the kinds of categorizations you will establish, if research is required, where extra description may be needed, and what strategies should be employed while writing.

Student Essay to Consider

Directions for Reading the Essay: As you read the following essay, circle areas that strike you as interesting or especially descriptive, underline areas that seem to be out of place or need work, place stars by any areas where you think additional information could be added, and mark the different modes of writing within this essay. Additionally, do you think the examples support the purpose of the essay, or should the author have chosen different examples? Be prepared to explain your opinion.

Don't Judge a Person . . .

Knowing what is on a person's play list has become so popular, Web sites and forums are dedicated to answering just that question. On YouTube, people have posted videos creatively sharing what is on their play lists. In magazines, celebrities are often asked what is on their play list, and the article that follows then dissects the celebrity's

1

continued

personality based upon his or her music choices. Unfortunately, people are often judged by the type of music they listen to, but stereotyping people according to their music often creates an incorrect picture.

One example of music listeners who are frequently mislabeled is rap music fans. Rap music is often stereotyped as angry, sexual, and violent. Because of this, people who listen to rap are often labeled as gang members or trouble-makers. There are listeners who like it because it symbolizes gangs and trouble, but many people have much simpler reasons for listening. Some people like to listen to rap because the songs usually have very strong rhythms, which can be hypnotic and fun. Others like to listen to rap because they find it therapeutic; the rappers sing about topics that many of the listeners are experiencing, but don't know how to deal with. When Common, a rapper and poet, was invited to a poetry event at the White House, many people were astonished and upset. Picturing a president listening to rap and inviting that artist to the White House was too much. The president shouldn't be inviting rappers to the White House. Common's performance, however, was not angry, sexual, or violent, and those who heard him praised his performance.

Christian music listeners are another group that is often mislabeled. Because of the nature of Christian music, listeners are often labeled as "goody-two-shoes" or naive. Most listeners of Christian music like that it incorporates many genres, including rap, but doesn't usually contain vulgar language or sexually explicit lyrics.

A final group of music listeners that is often wrongly stereotyped is country music listeners. These listeners are often labeled as "pickup-driving hunters" and "hicks." However, many country music fans are urbanites who have spent very little time in the country. Other fans of country music like it because, like Christian music, the songs are often less vulgar and racy than other popular forms of music. Despite his sexy, superstar "nonhick" image, actor Taylor Lautner listens to several types of music, including country.

Countless numbers of people are judged or stereotyped by what music they listen to. However, wrapping someone in a label according to the music he or she listens to is often more wrong than right. As the saying goes, "Don't judge a book by its cover," or in this case don't judge a person by his or her play list.

2 TEACHING TIP
Read this essay aloud. In tandem with having students follow the "Directions for Reading the Essay" above, ask them to underline the thesis statement, specific examples, and transitions before answering the questions.

3

4

5

About the Main Idea and Author's Purpose

1. In your own words, write the main idea of the essay.

The author is persuading the reader not to judge people by the music they listen to. She then gives examples that support this idea using three types of music.

2. What is the author's purpose, and how can you determine this?

To persuade the reader. The author uses examples to show how different people

listen to different music and not everyone fits into the stereotype.

ESL NOTE
To achieve greater coherence, nonnative speakers should review the transitions for exemplification and comparison-contrast essays. These include: additive transitions (to introduce categories), transitions to show similarities and differences, transitions to introduce examples, and transitions to indicate the importance of a category.

About Unity

3. Which sentence in paragraph 2 of "Don't Judge a Person . . ." should be omitted in the interest of paragraph unity? (Write the opening words.)

The president shouldn't be . . .

About Support

4. After which sentence in paragraph 3 is more support needed? (Write the opening words.)

Most listeners of Christian music like the fact . . .

About Coherence

5. List the transitional words used at the beginning of paragraphs 2, 3, and 4.

One example

Another group

A final group

Mixed Modes

6. What are the different types of modes the author employs in her paragraphs to create such a fluid essay?

Exemplification and classification

About the Introduction and/or Conclusion

7. What method of introduction is used in the opening paragraph? (Circle the letter of the answer.)

   a. Anecdote

   b. Idea that is the opposite of the one to be developed

   c. Broad, general statement narrowing to a thesis

   d. Quotation

Writing an Essay with Emphasis on Division and Classification

EXAMINING CATEGORIES

Choose one of the following subjects as the basis for an essay that emphasizes division and classification. Once you have chosen a topic, you will want to decide what other modes of writing will help support your purpose and review the relevant chapters. If your essay requires description, review Chapter 8; if it requires comparison or contrast, review Chapter 11. Remember, all essays are a mix of writing modes.

Music	Pet owners	Vacations
DVDs	Junk food	Bosses
Catalogs	College courses	Voicemail messages
Fiction	Dating couples	Breakfast foods
Web sites	Shoppers	Parties

GETTING TO KNOW YOUR COLLEGE LIBRARY

The library on your campus is a central part of the learning process. At some point, most classes will require students to use the library for projects that need research. In this assignment, you will be asked to visit your campus library and interview a librarian to find out all the resources available. Once you have gathered your information, you will want to classify the types of services offered at your library, supporting the classifications with detailed information. This assignment will require you to review Chapter 6, "Exemplification"; Chapter 8, "Description"; Chapter 13, "Division-Classification"; Chapter 17, "Information Literacy"; and Chapter 21, "Writing a Research Paper."

In this essay that emphasizes division or classification, you will write with a specific purpose and for a specific audience.

DESCRIBING THE IDEAL JOB Unsure about your career direction, you have gone to a job counseling center. To help select the work best suited for you, a counselor has asked you to write a detailed description of your "ideal job," which will be used to match you to different types of employment.

To describe your "ideal job," choose three categories from the following list:

Activities done on the job

Skills used on the job

People you work with

Physical environment

Salary and fringe benefits

Opportunities for advancement

WRITING ASSIGNMENT 1

Personal

TEACHING TIP
Encourage students to use the four steps to complete these assignments, including prewriting and revision.

WRITING ASSIGNMENT 2

Academic

BEYOND THE CLASSROOM

Division-Classification

Work

continued

In your essay, explain your ideals for each category (Chapter 13, "Division-Classification"). You will also need to use specific examples to illustrate your points like anecdotes (Chapter 7, "Narration") and possibly researched support (the three Part 5 chapters).

Developing an Essay with Emphasis on Argument

Considering Purpose and Audience

When you write an essay that has an emphasis on argument, your main purpose is to convince readers that your particular view or opinion on an issue or topic is correct. In addition, at times, you may have a second purpose for your essay: to persuade your audience to take some sort of action.

in a writer's words

" *Words are, of course, the most powerful drug used by mankind.*"

—Rudyard Kipling

While consideration of your audience is important for all essay forms, it is absolutely critical to the success of an essay that is persuasive in tone. Depending on the main point you choose, your audience may be firmly opposed to your view or somewhat supportive of it. As you begin planning, consider what your audience already knows and how it feels about the main point of your essay. Say, for example, you want to argue that public schools should require students to wear uniforms. Using this example, ask yourself what opinion your audience holds about school uniforms. What are likely to be their objections to your argument? Why would people not support your main point? What, if anything, are the merits of the opposing point of view? In order to "get inside the head" of your opposition, you might even want to interview a few people you're sure will disagree with you: say, for instance, a student with a very funky personal style who you know would dislike wearing a uniform. By becoming aware of the points of view your audience might have, you will know how to proceed in researching your rebuttal to their arguments. By directly addressing your opposition, you add credibility to your argument and increase the chances that others will be convinced that your main point is valid.

The purpose of your essay will determine what research should be included (Part 5), what tone should be taken, and what modes of writing should be used for support. As you have seen in the paragraph development sections, different modes require different forms of writing, so it is important to look at the specific modes and writing techniques where and when needed.

Student Essay to Consider

Directions for Reading the Essay: As you read the following essay, circle areas that strike you as interesting or especially descriptive, underline areas that seem to be out of place or need work, place stars by any areas where you think additional information could be added, and mark the different modes of writing within this essay. Additionally, determine if the examples the author provided are persuasive enough, and if not, what would have offered better support. Be prepared to discuss your opinion.

AAA Gets an A for Service

1   When many people pack for road trips, they include things like clothes, food, games, more food, and, for some, GPS units. What many people forget to pack is a membership in the American Automobile Association (AAA). AAA offers travel planning, roadside service, and peace of mind. Although many people use GPS units, nothing should replace a service like AAA.

2   Trip planning is one of the services that AAA offers that a GPS unit cannot truly do. Although many people like to plan trips on their own, having a service like AAA can add a whole new dimension to the planning. They offer a service that organizes all the travel, whether road, air, train, or boat. A wonderful product is the TripTik—road trip ideas that include roadside interests, fun sites, restaurants, navigational directions that can be downloaded and printed, and gas station locations. Although GPS units can offer similar things, AAA's TripTik information is regularly updated and verified. Another positive thing about the TripTik is that it can be printed, so the passenger can follow along, making suggestions and providing backup just in case travelers lose cell service or the GPS unit fails. When my husband and I were on a trip, our GPS unit started misreading our location. We were in the mountains, so our cell phones weren't helpful either. Because we had printed our driving directions, we were able to make it to our hotel with no delays.

3   Another great service that AAA offers is a free selection of guidebooks that are available in both online and print format. Travelers can get guidebooks for states, regions, and cities. The guidebooks contain everything from information about hotels and restaurants to activities to do in that area. The guidebooks also provide detailed background information, so travelers can become their own tour guides. To purchase similar guidebooks at a bookstore would be an annoyance. Although they also contain lists of restaurants, hotels, and activities, GPS units don't have teams of people visiting these venues and rating them on cleanliness, service, quality of food and value for money. And while many people would use their cell phones to find these services, cell service can often be weak or nonexistent in certain areas of the country. During one trip, on an unplanned overnight stay in Montana, our cell phones wouldn't access any data and our car's GPS unit listed only two questionable-sounding motels. Luckily, we had ordered a print copy of the Montana guidebook, so we consulted it and found a great place that had been approved by AAA and offered a discounted price for AAA members.

4   One of the best benefits of AAA is the emergency roadside service. If a car breaks down, the driver can call AAA to get help.

TEACHING TIP
Read this essay aloud. Ask students to underline the thesis statement, specific examples, and transitions before answering the questions.

continued

AAA will send someone out to change a flat tire, jumpstart the car, or even deliver gas. If the person dispatched to help cannot provide assistance, he or she will call for a tow truck to take the car and its passengers to a nearby garage. Again, like the restaurant and hotel guides, the tow truck will be AAA-approved and should be free to the AAA customer. Additionally, the tow truck will take the car to an approved garage that has proven itself to be honest and reliable. No task is too small for AAA, even retrieving keys locked in the car.

Technology is great and having a GPS unit in a car is a comfort to many drivers. However, one comfort that all drivers should have is the knowledge that they packed their card containing their AAA membership number and the toll-free number that reaches live operators. GPS units may offer navigational security, but they cannot replace the security that AAA provides its members.

5

QUESTIONS

About the Main Idea and Author's Purpose

1. In your own words, write the main idea of the essay.

   The author offers reasons why everyone should include an AAA membership in his or her packing list.

2. What is the author's purpose, and how can you determine this?

   Persuasion. The author's examples point out the benefits of AAA but ignore any drawbacks to having a membership.

About Unity

3. Which sentence in paragraph 3 should be omitted in the interest of paragraph unity? (Write the opening words.)

   To purchase similar guidebooks . . .

About Support

4. After which sentence in paragraph 4 is more support needed? (Write the opening words.)

   No task is too small . . .

About Coherence

5. What transition words does the author use at the beginning of each paragraph?

   . . . one of the services . . .

   Another great service . . .

   One of the best . . .

ESL NOTE
To achieve coherence and grammatical accuracy in their writing, nonnative students would benefit from instruction in the context of an argumentative paragraph. Among Spanish-speaking students, a typical error is: "I *am* agree," which is a direct translation. A review of connectors that show adding information would be helpful too.

Mixed Modes

6. What are the different types of modes the author employs in her paragraphs to create such a persuasive essay?

Exemplification, narration, comparison and/or contrast

About the Introduction and/or Conclusion

7. What method is used in the conclusion?
   a. Summary and final thoughts
   b. Recommendation
   c. Thought-provoking question

Writing an Essay with Emphasis on Argument

SUPPORTING AN ARGUMENT

Write an essay in which you argue *for* or *against* the statement: "An employer should be able to use information from social networking sites such as *MySpace* and *Facebook* before hiring a job applicant."

Support and defend your essay by drawing on your reasoning ability and general experience. Use the modes of writing that will best help you support your essay. If you use any research, refer to Part 5 to help you locate, document, and cite your information properly.

WRITING ASSIGNMENT 1

Work

TEACHING TIP
Encourage students to use the four steps, to complete these assignments, including prewriting and revision.

WRITING A LETTER TO THE COLLEGE PRESIDENT

Write a letter to the president of your college about something that needs to be changed on campus; it could be parking issues, tuition, schedules, fees, and so on. In your letter, explain what the problem is, why it needs to be fixed, and offer a solution. Keeping your audience in mind, you will want to maintain a formal tone and provide solid evidence. Your evidence might include the effects of the problem (Chapter 10), anecdotes of fellow students' experiences (Chapter 7), and/or examples from other colleges that have had the same problem (Chapter 11 and Part 5).

WRITING ASSIGNMENT 2

Academic

In this essay that emphasizes argument, you will write with a specific purpose and for a specific audience.

RAISING AWARENESS You care deeply about the issues in your community. As a concerned citizen, you would like to make others aware of a growing problem—for example, a rise in auto thefts, speeding in a school zone, graffiti on the roadways, or illegal dumping. Write a letter to the editor of your local newspaper in which you argue why more should be done to address this problem. Provide convincing reasons to support your position and address any skepticism that readers may have. Good research (Part 5) and anecdotes (Chapter 7) will help provide valid reasons to support your position.

BEYOND THE CLASSROOM

Argument

Personal

As you are reading the following essay written by Serena for a health and wellness class, think about what advice you would offer her as she prepares to write her final draft. Does her essay cover all four bases of effective writing? To be sure, use the checklist that follows.

TEACHING TIP
Ask students to discuss with a partner what advice they would give this writer.

The Common Cold

[1]According to the US Department of Health and Human Services, "each year in the United States, there are millions of cases of the common cold. Adults have an average of 2–3 colds per year, and children have even more." [2]That's a lot of stuffy noses, sore throats, and coughs. [3]Since the cold is so common, it would make sense that scientists should have found a cure by now. [4]However, common does not mean simple, and the common cold is very complex.

[5]First of all, a cold is caused by a virus, and it's not just one type of virus. [6]More than two hundred viruses cause colds by attacking healthy cells of the nose, throat, or lungs. [7]The virus then gets into the cells and takes control. [8]A single virus makes hundreds or thousands of cold viruses inside each cell. [9]Eventually, the cell bursts open and dies. [10]The viruses, though, escape and attack healthy cells (United States, Dept. of Health and Human Services, Centers for Disease Control and Prevention). [11]By now the victim is sneezing and coughing. [12]His or her throat is sore. [13]The virus keeps infecting healthy cells.

[14]Second, only the body can fight cold viruses. [15]Billions of white blood cells travel in the blood. [16]White blood cells make antibodies. [17]These proteins attach themselves to viruses and destroy them.

[18]In addition, there isn't much the victim can do to fight a cold. [19]The US Department of Health and Human Services stresses that antibiotic drugs don't work against viruses. [20]Nose drops and cough medicines only relieve symptoms. [21]Chicken soup seems to help. [22]Vitamin C may help too. [23]My doctor has told me that a dose of 1,000 milligrams of vitamin C on the first day of a cold may quicken recovery.

[24]Most importantly, people need to be healthy so they don't catch a cold at all. [25]They should eat a well-balanced diet and get eight hours of sleep each day. [26]They should exercise regularly. [27]They should stay away from coughing, sneezing people, because the cold virus spreads through the air. [28]The cold virus can live up to three hours outside the body. [29]That means it can be picked up from touching money, doorknobs, and other people. [30]So people should wash their hands often. [31]Prevention are the best action.

Works Cited

United States, Department of Health and Human Services, Centers for Disease Control and Prevention. "Common Colds: Protect Yourself and Others." *Diseases and Conditions,* 12 February 2018. www.cdc.gov/features/rhinoviruses/index.html.

A WRITER'S CHECKLIST

Unity

✓ The thesis statement can be found in sentence number _____4_____.

✓ Why do you think the writer chose to place the thesis statement where she did?
Answers may vary.

Support

✓ Fill in the supporting points for the thesis statement in the following brief outline:

The common cold is complex and has no cure.

    a. *A cold is caused by a virus.*

    b. *Only your body can fight a cold virus.*

    c. *Little can be done to fight a cold.*

    d. *Prevention is important.*

✓ Does Serena provide specific evidence for each point? *No. More details are needed in the second supporting paragraph.*

Coherence

✓ Has Serena effectively used transitional words? If so, what are those words? If not, where should she include them? *Yes, Serena has effectively used the transitional words first of all, second, in addition, and most importantly.*

✓ Which method of organization did Serena use? *Emphatic* How do you know?
The words most importantly are used in the last supporting paragraph.

Sentence Skills

✓ Has Serena avoided wordiness and used concise wording? *Yes*

✓ Were the sentences varied? *No. There are many short simple sentences that could have been combined to create more variety.*

✓ Can you find any other sentence skills mistakes, as listed on the inside back cover of the book?
Sentence 31 has a subject-verb agreement mistake.

Collaborative Activity

In your group or class, make an outline of Serena's essay. Looking at the outline, can you think of any additional supporting details that could be added to make this essay more effective?

TEACHING TIP
Encourage everyone in the class to participate in this collaborative activity.

©Jacob Lund/
Shutterstock

PART 5

Research-Based Writing

PART FIVE SHOWS YOU HOW TO

- locate and evaluate online sources
- use the library in the context of the digital world
- cite and incorporate sources to write research-based papers

PART FIVE ALSO GIVES YOU PRACTICE

- writing a paraphrase
- writing a summary
- taking effective notes
- writing a literary analysis
- writing a research paper

EXPLORING WRITING PROMPT:

Navigating all the information that is now available can sometimes be overwhelming for students. Think about a time you had to find information for a project. What were your first steps? Were you able to easily locate what you needed or was it difficult to find the right information? How did you determine what information was credible and what wasn't? Brainstorm about your experiences and be ready to share them with a classmate.

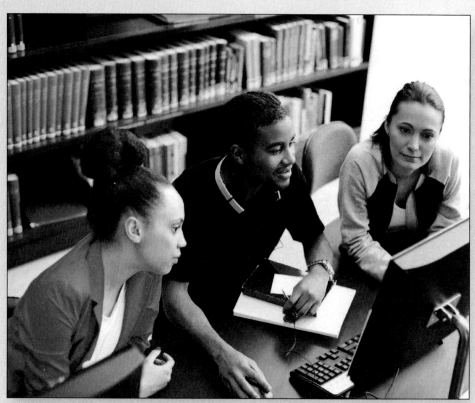

©Jacob Lund/Shutterstock

RESPONDING TO IMAGES

*Think about your experiences using the Internet and school library while locating
reliable resources for an assignment. Take a few moments to write out your
thoughts. In this chapter, you will learn strategies to help you navigate all the
information you can access online and in your college library.*

Engaging in research means dealing with a lot of information from different sources. One of the keys to good research is understanding how to navigate all the information that is available to you. Students have the option of using college libraries and public libraries, the Internet, and other media sources like television and radio. Finding and choosing the right information to use in an essay can be overwhelming for many students.

Often, students begin their research by going online, which usually nets more results than are possible to evaluate. This can cause frustration and wasted time as students try to figure out where to start and what to read. Especially when operating under a time crunch, students don't always select the best resources for their papers. Knowing how to properly approach online research by using the right search engines and search terms and the right databases, as well as knowing how to find credible information, will save both time and effort.

While you will most likely do a majority of your research online, you should always start with your college library, as it will provide you with the best sources. Because, like most libraries, it has a variety of print, online, and media sources available, it can be challenging to navigate the resources in a college library. However, the librarians are there to help students find the right sources.

Knowing how to identify the best and most appropriate sources for your work and how to use each source accurately will help you in your research. It will also significantly reduce the amount of time you'll need to spend locating usable sources. This chapter will introduce you to managing and evaluating resources to help you efficiently research information that supports the purpose of each essay that you write.

Using Online Sources Effectively

Locating Sources Efficiently

Most students think that going to Google, typing in some terms, and beginning to read links that look interesting is the best way to begin researching. This type of research can lead to an overwhelming number of results, as well as links to sites like Wikipedia that are not reliable resources for academic research. This can all take more time than necessary, or more time than students have, to determine which results are valid and will provide the best information for their research essays.

Because search engines like Google go through a vast amount of information to find articles containing any of the words you have put into your search, knowing what search engine to use for information gathering, how to best search, and how to sift through the results is important for all researchers.

Search Engines

While most people think of Google when they look up information, it is not the only option. Students often use other engines like Bing, Yahoo!, and Baidu. There are also meta search engines, which retrieve information from specific sites like Twitter or Instagram. Specialized search engines like Google Scholar, which only searches scholarly articles, and Wolfram Alpha, which creates data comparisons, can be helpful for students doing specific types of research projects. Being familiar with specialized search engines can save you time, as these engines focus their searches in specific areas.

Searching with Keywords and Boolean Operators

Familiarity with strong search terms (keywords) is also important when "Googling." If you want to write a paper on recent Supreme Court decisions about education and you type in *supreme court decisions*, using Google will get you over 197 million results. However, if you narrow your search to *supreme court decisions education 21st century*, the results narrow to just over two million.

Knowing how to best use keywords will help you save time. Keywords, like *supreme court decisions* above, are the general terms that are entered into search engines. When keywords are typed into a search, documents with all those words will be included in the list of results. However, because all the words are included, no matter how insignificantly they have been used within the document, thousands, if not millions of results will be returned. This is why you need to be as specific as possible. Narrowing a search to *supreme court decisions education 21st century* will net fewer results because you have expanded all the specific words that must be contained in the document.

Understanding Boolean operators can also help you narrow your searches. By adding quotation marks around words, and by using AND, OR, or NOT, you can quickly change your results. In the earlier Google search, changing the phrase to *supreme court decisions AND education AND 21st century* causes the results to reduce to seven million, but by changing the phrase to "supreme court decisions AND education," the results drop to just nine. Boolean operators can be used with any of the search engines.

Databases

Databases, like JSTOR and Academic Search Elite, are services that offer you the ability to search and access periodicals and journals online. Most databases have to be accessed through a subscription service, so your library will be your best source. However, if your library doesn't subscribe to a certain database that you need to use, many offer individual subscriptions for reasonable fees. In this way, you can, for example, read editions of *The Harvard Review* from the past thirty years. Common library databases will be discussed in more detail later in the chapter.

Evaluating Online Sources

The quality and reliability of information you find on the Internet will vary widely, and it is your responsibility to learn how to differentiate between valuable information and propaganda. Most reputable journals, news sources, and published books have editors and other staff members to verify information, thus giving you some assurance that care has been taken with the information. Online, however, no such quality control exists. Anyone with a bit of computer know-how can create a Web site, and it is very common for the information on sites to change overnight. The designer of a Web site may be a Nobel Prize winner, a leading authority in a specialized field, a high school student, or an off-balance zealot. While the following information focuses on Web sites and other online sources, you should evaluate all your research (including print and media) in this manner to be sure you are using sources that are credible and support the purpose of your paper.

Determining the Reliability of an Online Source

Be careful, then, to look closely at any source in the following ways:

1. **Internet address:** In a Web address (the uniform resource locator or URL), the three letters following the "dot" are the domain. The most common domains are .com (usually a commercial organization); .edu (educational institution); .gov (government organization); or .org (nonprofit or sometimes for-profit organization). A common misconception is that a Web site's reliability can be determined by its domain. This is not the case, as almost anyone can get a Web address ending in .com, .edu, .org, or any of the other domains. Therefore, it is important that you examine every Web site carefully, considering the four points that follow.

2. **Publisher or sponsor:** Who maintains the site? Is the organization/ group/individual reputable? What is the domain? Remember, these don't determine reliability, but they can help you find out who is responsible for the Web site.

3. **Author:** What credentials does the author have (if any)? Has the author published other material on the topic? Is the author known to have a particular stance (bias) on this topic? You may need to do some additional research through a Web search or library database search to find this information.

4. **Date:** Is the information up to date? Check at the top or bottom of the document for copyright, publication, or revision dates. Knowing such dates will help you decide whether the material is current enough for your purposes.

5. **Internal evidence:** Does the author seem to proceed objectively— presenting all sides of a topic fairly before arguing his or her own views? Does the author produce solid, adequate support for his or her views?

TEACHING TIP
Have your students evaluate a news source like CNN, ABC, or Fox, for credibility and bias. Have them describe the bias and explain why they think this bias exists.

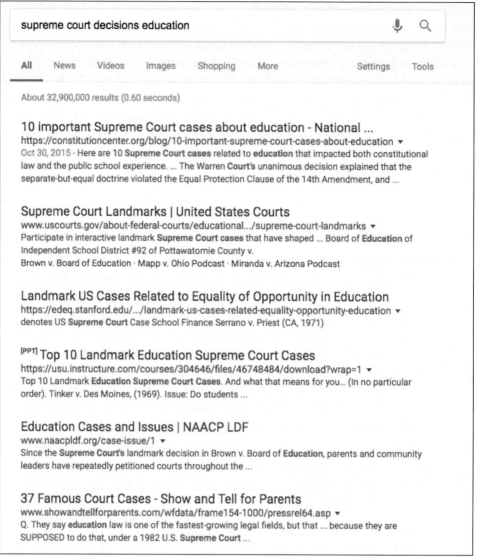

Results from a keyword search on Google using: supreme court decisions education
Source: Google, Inc.

Compare the image above with the image on the facing page. These two images show the different results a student could expect when using Google versus Google Scholar. Although the same search terms were used, the results on Google Scholar were not only fewer, but they were more focused and research based.

Examine the number of results and types of results in the first image:

- The first result is from the Constitution Center, an institution that was established by Congress to publish constitutional information. While it is a reputable source, you will still need to verify any information you use from this site.

- The second result is from a government Web site, so it too should be reputable. However, you will still need to look at the summaries with an objective eye and check the original sources to make sure the summaries are accurate.

- The third result is from an educational source. Since this source is Stanford, students may automatically assume that it is more reputable than a state university; however, the article has the title "Landmark US Cases . . .", which means the author of the article has determined that these are important cases, so there may be some bias.

- The fourth result directly takes students to a PowerPoint that has no author listed. While the actual PowerPoint *seems* to have good information, and its URL shows it is from USU (Utah State University), without being able to verify the original source of the PowerPoint, students should avoid using such a source.

- The final result is a Web site geared toward parents. The author's bio provides information that seems to show she is credible (a graduate of the University of Missouri School of Journalism) but may have biases that affect how she presents material.

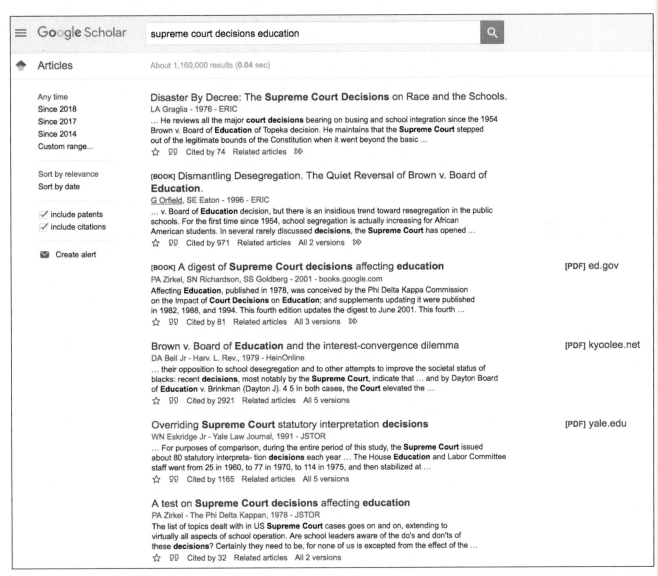

Results from a keyword search on Google Scholar using: supreme court decisions education

Source: Google, Inc.

Now, examine the results from Google Scholar in the second image:

- You can see all the results are from articles cited in other studies, based on research and published in specialized journals. These sources, while as potentially biased as organizations, do go through more steps in order to be published, so their credibility is already potentially stronger than the organizations and newspapers. You will still need to spend time analyzing the sources to determine how valuable they will be for your research, but you won't need to spend as much time determining whether or not the sources are credible.

Using Critical Thinking to Examine Online Sources

Once you have determined whether or not a source is reliable, you then need to work through the material to determine how well it will support the purpose of your essay. You will first want to analyze the author's argument, think about whether or not you have seen a similar opinion expressed elsewhere, and ask yourself if it endorses or counters the argument you are presenting (just because it counters your argument doesn't mean you cannot use it). As you look at the author's argument, you want to think about whether or not the author's support is valid and verifiable. Just because someone repeats something multiple times doesn't make it true. Another good way to verify your source is to look at the sources he or she has cited. If the author is citing obviously biased sites or fake news sites, no matter how good his or her argument sounds, it is most likely based on poor information. When you decide that the resource will work in your research, you will want to familiarize yourself with it by reading it several times and determining how you see it fitting into your paper.

| **ACTIVITY 1** | Follow each set of directions to complete Parts A, B, and C of this activity. |

TEACHING TIP
You may want to ask your students to work in teams for this activity.

NOTE
Answers will vary.

Part A

Go to www.google.com and search for *Bill of Rights*. Then complete the items below.

1. How many items did your search yield? 126 million

2. What are the first three listings? billofrightsinstitute.org, a Wikipedia entry, and the National Center for Constitutional Studies

3. Look through the first four pages of entries to find an example of each of the following domains: .edu, .gov, .org, and .com. Pick one site with each domain and write its full address.

   a. Address of one .com site: http://www.history.com/topics/bill-of-rights

   b. Address of one .gov site: https://www.archives.gov/founding-docs/bill-of-rights-transcript

   c. Address of one .org site: https://www.billofrightsinstitute.org

   d. Address of one .edu site: https://www.law.cornell.edu/constitution/billofrights

Part B

Circle one of the sites you identified and use it to complete the following evaluation.

NOTE
Answers will vary.

4. Name of site's author or authoring institution: <u>US National Archives and</u>

<u>Records Administration</u>

5. Why did you choose this site? <u>It is a government site, so it is generally accepted</u>

<u>as reputable, though students should still remain cautious.</u>

6. Is the site's information current (within two years)? <u>No, but it contains all</u>

<u>the archives of the actual Bill of Rights, plus explanations and educational infor-</u>

<u>mation. Since the Bill of Rights has not changed, this information is still reliable.</u>

7. Does the site serve an obvious business purpose (with advertising or

attempts to sell products)? <u>No.</u>

8. Does the site have an obvious connection to a governmental, commercial,

business, or religious organization? If so, which one? <u>Yes—the federal</u>

<u>government.</u>

9. Does the site's information seem fair and objective? <u>Yes.</u>

10. Based on the information above, would you say the site appears reliable?

<u>Yes.</u>

Part C

Try the following four search terms and compare the results on Google and Google Scholar. On a separate sheet of paper, write down the number of returned results and the type of result that is listed in first place. Once you have compared each, choose one site and evaluate it for reliability. Explain what you have observed.

NOTE
At the end of this chapter are sample results from this activity, along with an explanation of what students should understand about different search engines and search terms.

Bill of Rights

"Bill of Rights"

"Bill of Rights" AND challenges

"Bill of Rights AND challenges"

Using the Library in the Context of the Digital World

College libraries occupy both physical and virtual space. Getting familiar with both will benefit you well as you embark on your college journey.

Most students know that libraries' physical buildings provide study space, computer workstations, and copying machines. Libraries also contain reading areas, which contain recent copies of magazines and newspapers. Other

TEACHING TIP
If your library offers instructional sessions, consider setting up a session early in the semester to help students feel comfortable with the resources available.

features that you will find in the library are the rows of books, known as stacks, that can be perused and checked out; DVDs and CDs that can be borrowed; general reference materials that can be used in the library; and the special materials that instructors put on reserve for specific class use.

The online resources can usually be accessed via your college library's home page, which typically contains information including location, hours, catalog of holdings, and selected databases. Some library home pages offer features like instant chat with a librarian, access to other college catalogs, research tools, subject guides, and lists of Web sites that librarians have found to be useful and credible. Students can usually access their library's online resources from their personal computers and from the computers in the library.

You should become familiar with your library and expect to use most, if not all, of its features at some point in your college experience. The more familiar you are with everything your library has to offer, the less time you will spend locating the information you need. Getting to know your librarians is an excellent way to start developing this familiarity and to help you navigate all the library has to offer. After a brief discussion of the role of librarians, we will examine the various resources—both print and online—a library offers.

Librarians

The number-one resource available to use through your college library is the college librarian. Librarians are knowledgeable about the resources available to you and can quickly point you to the materials you need. Most academic librarians collaborate with the departments on campus to make sure students' needs are being met, and often set up subject guides or reserve materials that might be helpful for projects they know faculty are assigning. Librarians are also experts at finding information, and they can often help you locate online and print sources in minutes rather than the days it might take you. They are also very skilled at helping you evaluate your sources.

Reference Materials

Defining Primary and Secondary Sources

There are two types of sources students can use in their research. Primary sources are original sources; they include conference presentations, dissertations, memoirs, photographs and paintings, speeches, works of literature, and government documents. Secondary sources, on the other hand, analyze, interpret, or comment on primary sources. Secondary sources include biographies, literature reviews, or articles written about primary sources.

General and Reserved References

General references include encyclopedias, world fact books, dictionaries, atlases, manuals, and so on. Most of these can be found online, but if you do want a print source, be aware that these are often for library use only, so you will want to be prepared to spend an hour or two in the library.

Many libraries will have certain books, periodicals, reports, videos, and journals that cannot be taken out of the library. Instead, you will have to check out the material for a certain period of time, often two hours, and remain in the library while you read or view the material. It is common that professors will put such materials on reserve for students to use, but will restrict the use to ensure all students have a chance to work with the material.

Library Catalog

The library catalog, accessible both online and on site, is your entry point to the holdings in your library. These holdings can include print books, e-books, downloadable audio books, CDs, and DVDs. Most libraries have agreements with each other, so if a book or item isn't available at your library, you may have the option of requesting it from another library. Your college library Web site and librarians should have this information readily available.

Finding a Book

There are numerous ways to find books using your library's catalog. You can search by author, title, keyword(s), or subject.

Author, Title, Keyword(s), or Subject If you are looking for a specific book or specific author, the easiest search would be an author or title search. For example, suppose you want to see if the library has the book *Origin* by Dan Brown. You could check for the book through:

1. An *author* search, in which you would look under *Brown, Dan.*

2. A *title* search, in which you would look under *Origin.*

However, if you are looking for books on specific topics, a keyword or subject search is your better choice. For example, if you are looking for a book about symbology, you could check for a book through:

3. A *keyword* search. In this case, since the subject of the book is symbology and cryptology, you could look under words like these or you could look under words like *thriller* and *action.* Keyword searches are the most common way to begin research because the system will look for that term anywhere in the record. Just as is true of the use of search engines, keyword searches are the easiest searches to employ when using online catalogs.

4. A *subject* search. Subject searches use very limited and defined vocabulary. While a good subject search can yield the best results, unless you know for sure what the subject search terms should be (in this case, "Robert Langdon—code and cipher stories" or "Robert Langdon—fictional hero"), subject searches should be done with the aid of a librarian.

Summary Points: Using Keywords and Subject Searches

- Searching by keyword allows for considerable flexibility of vocabulary and search parameters. Keyword searches for books in a library catalog work much the same way as keyword searches in search engines.

- Searching by subject requires knowledge of very controlled vocabulary and search parameters. It is best used with the aid of a librarian.

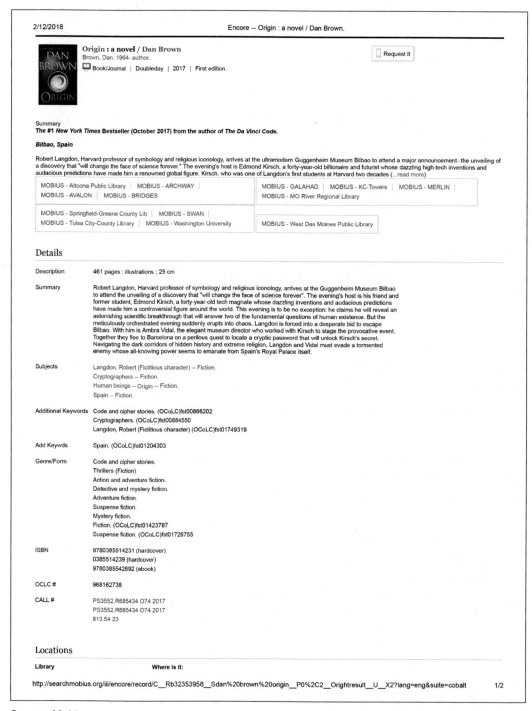

Source: Mobius

These facing pages show an example of an online catalog entry for Brown's book, *Origin*. Note that in addition to giving you the publisher (Doubleday) and year of publication (2017), the entry also tells you the book's physical location and its call number—each of which will help you find it in the library. If you need to request the book from another library, your library will have a specific spot (front desk, reference desk, etc.) where the book will be waiting upon delivery.

2/12/2018   Encore -- Origin : a novel / Dan Brown.

MOBIUS - Altoona Public Library	Altoona Public Library	Mys Brown	DUE 02-19-18
MOBIUS - ARCHWAY	STLCC-FP Best Sellers	F B87756o	Not Requestable
MOBIUS - ARCHWAY	STLCC-FV Best Sellers	F B87756o	Not Requestable
MOBIUS - ARCHWAY	STLCC-M Currently Popular	F B87756o	DUE 02-20-18
MOBIUS - AVALON	TRUMAN Popular Reading	PS3552.R685434 O74 2017	DUE 03-02-18
MOBIUS - AVALON	UCM Best Sellers	PS3552 .R685434 O74 2017	DUE 02-23-18
MOBIUS - BRIDGES	Maryville Univ Hot Reads	Fiction	DUE 03-07-18
MOBIUS - BRIDGES	Lindenwood Univ Popular Reading Collection	PS3552.R685434 O74 2017	DUE 03-07-18
MOBIUS - GALAHAD	MAC General Collection	PS 3552 .R685434 O74 2017	DUE 02-26-18
MOBIUS - KC-Towers	NW Owens PopularC	MYS 813 B8776or	DUE 02-16-18
MOBIUS - MERLIN	UMSL TJ/MERC BESTSELLERS LEVEL 3	PS3552.R685434 O74 2017	DUE 05-17-18
MOBIUS - MO River Regional Library	Main Walk-in Bestseller	BRO	DUE 02-20-18
MOBIUS - MO River Regional Library	Main Fiction	BRO	DUE 03-01-18
MOBIUS - MO River Regional Library	Osage Fiction	BRO	DUE 02-20-18
MOBIUS - MO River Regional Library	Mobile Fiction	BRO	DUE 12-11-17
MOBIUS - Springfield-Greene County Lib	No local holdings		
MOBIUS - SWAN	WorldCat Link		
MOBIUS - SWAN	Cottey New Books	813.54 B812or 2017	DUE 03-05-18
MOBIUS - Tulsa City-County Library	BIXBY Adult	Mystery	DUE 02-13-18
MOBIUS - Tulsa City-County Library	BROKEN ARROW Adult	Mystery	DUE 02-16-18
MOBIUS - Tulsa City-County Library	BROOKSIDE Adult	Mystery	DUE 02-14-18
MOBIUS - Tulsa City-County Library	CENTRAL 2 Adult Circulating	Mystery	AVAILABLE
MOBIUS - Tulsa City-County Library	COLLINSVILLE Adult	Mystery	1 HOLD
MOBIUS - Tulsa City-County Library	GLENPOOL Adult	Mystery	AVAILABLE
MOBIUS - Tulsa City-County Library	H&K KAISER Adult	Mystery	DUE 02-22-18
MOBIUS - Tulsa City-County Library	HARDESTY 2nd flr Adult	Mystery	DUE 02-20-18
MOBIUS - Tulsa City-County Library	HELMERICH Adult	Mystery	DUE 02-22-18
MOBIUS - Tulsa City-County Library	JENKS Adult	Mystery	DUE 02-24-18
MOBIUS - Tulsa City-County Library	KENDALL-WHITTIER Adult	Mystery	AVAILABLE
MOBIUS - Tulsa City-County Library	KISHNER Adult	Mystery	AVAILABLE
MOBIUS - Tulsa City-County Library	MARTIN Adult	Mystery	DUE 02-21-18
MOBIUS - Tulsa City-County Library	MAXWELL PARK Adult	Mystery	DUE 02-20-18
MOBIUS - Tulsa City-County Library	NATHAN HALE Adult	Mystery	DUE 02-20-18
MOBIUS - Tulsa City-County Library	OWASSO Adult	Mystery	DUE 12-22-17 +1 HOLD
MOBIUS - Tulsa City-County Library	PRATT Adult	Mystery	DUE 02-24-18
MOBIUS - Tulsa City-County Library	RUDISILL Adult	Mystery	DUE 02-21-18
MOBIUS - Tulsa City-County Library	SCHUSTERMAN Adult	Mystery	DUE 02-16-18
MOBIUS - Tulsa City-County Library	SOUTH B.A. Adult	Mystery	DUE 02-22-18
MOBIUS - Tulsa City-County Library	SUBURBAN ACRES Adult	Mystery	DUE 12-30-17 +1 HOLD
MOBIUS - Tulsa City-County Library	ZARROW Adult	Mystery	DUE 02-16-18
MOBIUS - Tulsa City-County Library	SKIATOOK Adult	Mystery	DUE 02-16-18
MOBIUS - Tulsa City-County Library	CHARLES PAGE Adult	Mystery	DUE 02-14-18
MOBIUS - Washington University	Olin Library Level 1 PopLit Thriller	PS3552.R685434 O74 2017	DUE 02-07-18 +1 HOLD
MOBIUS - West Des Moines Public Library	Adult Collection		1 copy in process
MOBIUS - West Des Moines Public Library	Adult Collection		2 copies in process
MOBIUS - West Des Moines Public Library	Adult Collection		1 copy in process
MOBIUS - West Des Moines Public Library	Adult Collection		1 copy in process
MOBIUS - West Des Moines Public Library	Adult Collection		2 copies in process

Permanent Link

http://encore.searchmobius.org/iii/encore/record/C__Rb32353958

http://searchmobius.org/iii/encore/record/C__Rb32353958__Sdan%20brown%20origin__P0%2C2__Orightresult__U__X2?lang=eng&suite=cobalt   2/2

Source: Mobius

Answer the questions and/or follow the directions for each item.	**ACTIVITY 2**

NOTE
Answers will vary.

1. What is the title of one book by JoJo Moyes? Example: *Still Me.*

2. Who is the author of *The Great Alone*? (Remember to look up the title under *Great*, not *The*.) Kristin Hannah

3. List one book and its author dealing with the subject of "American presidents."

Answers will vary. Example: *Humor in the White House: The Wit of Five American*

Presidents by Arthur A. Sloane

4. Look up a book that is titled *Horse Soldiers* and obtain the following information:

   a. Author: Doug Stanton

   b. Publisher: Scribner

   c. Date of Publication: 2009

   d. Call number: DS371.412.S73 2009

   e. One subject heading: Afghan War

5. Look up a book written by Melinda Leigh and obtain the following information:

   a. Title: Midnight Obsession

   b. Publisher: Montlake Romance

   c. Date of Publication: 2017

   d. Call number: 951949176

   e. One subject heading: kidnapping

Book Stacks

The book stacks are the library shelves where books are arranged according to their call numbers. The call number, as distinctive as a Social Security number, always appears on the catalog entry for any book. It is also pasted onto the spine of every book in the library. If your library has open stacks (ones that you are permitted to enter), there is a basic procedure to finding a book. Suppose you are looking for *Origin*, which has the call number PS3552. R685434 074 2017 in the Library of Congress system. (Libraries using the Dewey decimal system have call letters made up entirely of numbers rather than letters and numbers. However, you use the same basic method to locate a book.) The first place you would look is the section that holds the P's. You would then want to look for the PS's, which will be listed alphabetically. Once you've located the section housing the PS's, you would then look for PS3552 and finally R685434 074 2017. If your library has closed stacks (ones you are not permitted to enter), you will have to write down the title, author, and call number and ask a reference librarian get the book for you.

Periodicals

Periodicals—magazines, journals, and newspapers—are available in both print and electronic form. They contain recent or very specialized information about a subject, which may not be available in a book. Most libraries will have print copies of many of the magazines and journals students enjoy reading like *Rolling Stone* and *People*, and more scholarly sources like the *Econometrica*, *Science*, and *the Journal of the American Medical Association*. If the source isn't available in print, check with your librarian to see if the resource is available online through one of the databases your college subscribes to. If not, the librarian may be able to secure it through an interlibrary loan or may be able to direct you to a nearby library that has that source, either in print or electronic form.

Using Databases

As mentioned earlier in this chapter, most college and public libraries provide online computer-search services known as online databases or library subscription services. Using any of these services, you will be able to type in keywords and quickly search many periodicals for articles on your subject. Some databases, such as General Science Index, are discipline-specific, but others, such as Academic Search Premier, are more general.

The search process can vary depending on the database you are using. As in searching the library catalog, your best choices are using an author or title search if you know the specific piece you are trying locate or a keyword search if you are trying to gather information on a topic. Just as in a regular online research, using Boolean operators can help you narrow your results. Use a subject search only if you know exactly what vocabulary to use.

Often articles you find will be shown as "full text." That means that you can print out the entire article from your computer. In other cases, only an abstract (summary) of the article will be available. However, abstracts are valuable too, for they allow you to determine whether the article is relevant to your research and whether you should continue searching for the full text.

Finally, database articles appear in *html* (hypertext markup language) or *pdf* (portable document format) format or in both. Articles in .html have been reformatted for publication on the Internet. Those in .pdf are exact reproductions of a print document. Note that some databases are among many compiled by the same provider. EBSCOhost, Infotrac, and ProQuest are such providers.

Following are a few online databases that have proven useful for new student researchers and are often available through college libraries. (You should become familiar with your college's offerings, as not all databases are offered at all colleges.) If you are unsure which databases will be most useful for your research, reference librarians are skilled and knowledgeable in exactly this area and can help you locate the best source of information.

Academic Search Elite (EBSCO) covers a variety of disciplines and includes full-text articles and abstracts of articles from thousands of journals.

American History Online (Facts on File Reference Suite) contains hundreds of primary-source documents.

ERIC (Education Resources Information Center) makes available articles from professional journals, reports, and speeches having to do with education.

JSTOR (Journal Storage) provides full-text articles found in back issues of journals in the humanities, social sciences, and natural sciences.

Lexis-Nexis Academic Universe has full-text access to over 10,000 journals, covering local and world news, legal cases, and business.

ProQuest Research Library provides articles covering a variety of topics including education, law, psychology, arts, and business.

Science Online (Facts on File Reference Suite) contains thousands of diagrams, experiments, videos, biographies, and essays.

ACTIVITY 3	Look up a recent article on *influenza* using one of your library's online databases and fill in the following information:

NOTE
Answers will vary.

a. Name of the index you used _____

b. Article title _____

c. Author (if given) _____

d. Name of magazine _____

e. Pages _____

f. Date _____

Sample results for Activity 1, Part C:

The following result numbers will change, but provide good snapshot numbers from one particular point in time. The key thing to note is that the proportions and relationships among the results will remain constant.

Bill of Rights Google: 126 million results. The first result is a definition.

Google Scholar: 2.14 million results. The first result is an academic article about digital rights.

"Bill of Rights" Google: 42.9 million results. The first result is a definition.

Google Scholar: 441,000 results. The first result is an academic article about digital rights.

"Bill of Rights" AND challenges Google: 13.9 million results. The first result is ushistory.org.

Google Scholar: 116,000 results. The first result is an academic article about corporations and the Bill of Rights.

"Bill of Rights AND challenges" Google: 5 results. The first result is The James Madison Legacy Project online course about the constitution.

Google Scholar: 2 results. The first result is an academic article discussing a court case in Fifth Circuit Court.

Working with Sources

©Spotmatik Ltd/Shutterstock

RESPONDING TO IMAGES

Think about the experiences you have had writing a source-based essay. What types of struggles and successes did you experience? If you haven't written a source-based essay before, what concerns might you have? Using a prewriting technique of your choice, answer these questions as thoughtfully and thoroughly as you can.

TEACHING TIP
Ask students to complete this writing prompt in class.

Most writing in college will require students to use information from outside sources. In order to properly incorporate original source material and avoid plagiarism, you will need to first understand what you are reading, which may require you to do a second or third reading, take careful notes, and choose how to incorporate the information. As a writer, you will need to decide whether or not to summarize or paraphrase the material or use a direct quotation. The general rule is, if the author says it brilliantly, use the author's words (quotation); if the author's ideas are great, but you can rewrite it to better fit your essay, use paraphrase or summary.

In this chapter, you will learn how to write summaries and paraphrases, be given a brief introduction to using direct quotations, and view how these characteristics work within a literary analysis and a source-based essay.

TEACHING TIP
Let your students know about "paper mills" and plagiarism prevention Web sites. Point out that students can readily cheat, but instructors can easily catch them.

Identifying and Avoiding Plagiarism

If you fail to properly document information that you have incorporated into your essay and is not your own, you will be stealing. The formal term is *plagiarizing*—using someone else's work as your own. This is true whether you borrow a single image, idea, sentence, or entire essay.

One example of plagiarism is turning in a friend's paper (or a paper you purchased) as if it were your own. Another example is copying an article found in a magazine, newspaper, journal, or on the Internet and turning it in as your own. By copying someone else's work, you risk being failed or even expelled. Equally, plagiarism deprives you of what can be a most helpful learning and organization experience—researching and writing about a selected topic in detail.

Plagiarism presents a specific risk for the different writing activities treated in this chapter. For that reason, within each major section, you will find a brief discussion that focuses on that activity and on what writers need to watch for specifically in order to avoid plagiarizing.

Writing a Summary

At some point in a course, your instructor may ask you to write a summary of a book, an article, a TV show, or the like. In a *summary* (also referred to as a *précis* or an *abstract*), you reduce material in an original work to its main points and key supporting details. Unlike an outline, however, a summary does not use symbols such as I, A, 1, 2, etc., to indicate the relationships among parts of the original material.

A summary may consist of a single word, a phrase, several sentences, or one or more paragraphs. The length of any summary you prepare will depend on your instructor's expectations and the length of the original work. Most often, you will be asked to write a summary consisting of one paragraph. Summaries can be written as stand-alone pieces or incorporated into paragraphs and essays as detailed support.

TEACHING TIP
Stress to students that their personal opinions should not appear in a summary.

Writing a summary brings together a number of important reading, study, and writing skills. To condense the original assigned material, you must preview, read, evaluate, organize, and perhaps outline it. Summarizing, then, can be a real aid to understanding; you must "get inside" the material and realize fully what is being said before you can reduce its meaning to a few words.

You need to be extra careful to avoid accidental plagiarism when writing a summary. A helpful method is to make sure you fully understand the material first, and then to avoid consulting the original piece while writing your summary. You can then inspect for plagiarism by checking your words and phrases against the original, making sure that the words used are your own and not the author's. You should also examine your sentence structure to confirm that you are not mimicking the author's sentence structure and merely inserting a new word here and there. Finally, you need to make sure you have credited the original source in your summary, either by in-text citation or by crediting the author within the summary.

How to Summarize an Article

To write a summary of an article, follow the steps described below. If the assigned material is a TV show or film, adapt the suggestions accordingly.

1. Take a few minutes to preview the work. You can preview an article in a magazine by taking a quick look at the following:

   a. *Title.* A title often summarizes what an article is about. Think about the title for a minute, and about how it may condense the meaning of the article.

   b. *Subtitle.* A subtitle, if given, is a short summary appearing under or next to the title. For example, in a *Newsweek* article titled "Growing Old, Feeling Young," the following sentence appeared: "Not only are Americans living longer, they are staying active longer—and their worst enemy is not nature, but the myths and prejudices about growing old." In short, the subtitle often provides a quick insight into the meaning of an article.

   c. *First and last several paragraphs.* In the first several paragraphs, the author may introduce you to the subject and state the purpose of the article. In the last several paragraphs, the writer may present conclusions or a summary. The previews or summaries can give you a quick overview of what the entire article is about.

   d. *Other items.* Note any heads or subheads that appear in the article. They often provide clues to the article's main points and give an immediate sense of what each section is about. Look carefully at any pictures, charts, or diagrams that accompany the article. Page space in a magazine or journal is limited, and such visual aids are generally used only to illustrate important points in the article. Note any words or phrases set off in *italic type* or **boldface type**; such words have probably been emphasized because they deal with important points in the article.

2. Read the article for all you can understand the first time through. Do not slow down or turn back. Check or otherwise mark main points and key supporting details. Pay special attention to all the items noted in the preview. Also, look for definitions, examples,

and enumerations (lists of items), which often indicate key ideas. You can also identify important points by turning any heads into questions and reading to find the answers to the questions.

3. Go back and reread more carefully the areas you have identified as most important. Also, focus on other key points you may have missed in your first reading.

4. Take notes on the material. Concentrate on getting down the main ideas and the key supporting points.

5. Prepare the final draft of your summary, keeping these points in mind:

ESL NOTE
Remind nonnative speakers to use paraphrasing in their summaries. A review of strategies for effective paraphrasing might be helpful.

TEACHING TIP
Review plagiarism with your students.

   a.   In your first sentence, identify the title and author of the work. If your summary is not part of an essay, with in-text citations and a "Works Cited" page, then you should also include the date of publication and publication name. The two examples that follow show the different formats.

   b.   The first sentence of your summary should also be written as a topic sentence and should contain the main idea or thesis of the original work in your own words.

   c.   Do not write an overly detailed summary. Remember that the purpose of a summary is to reduce the original work to its main points and essential supporting details.

   d.   Express the main points and key supporting details in your own words. Do not imitate the style of the original work.

   e.   Never insert your own ideas or opinions into the summary. Be careful not to use loaded language. For instance, saying "the author tries to support her claims with studies" or "the author supports her claims with weak information" implies an opinion of how well argued the original piece is. A good summary, instead, would simply state, "the author supports her claims with studies."

   f.   Periodically refer to the author (by last name) or article to emphasize that this is a summary. In addition, use signal words (*argues, illustrates, asserts, observes, writes, reports*) to remind readers that the ideas being presented are directly from the article.

   g.   Quote from the material only to illustrate key points. Limit your quotations. A one-paragraph summary should not contain more than one quoted sentence or phrase.

   h.   Preserve the balance and proportion of the original work. If the original devoted 70 percent of its space to one idea and only 30 percent to another, your summary should reflect that emphasis.

   i.   Revise your final draft, paying attention to the four bases of effective writing (*unity, support, coherence,* and *sentence skills*) explained in Part 2.

   j.   Write the final draft of the summary.

A Model Summary of an Article

Here is a model summary of a magazine article that would stand on its own:

> In the article "Mayor of Rust," originally printed in the February 11, 2011, edition of *The New York Times Magazine*, author Sue Halpern profiles an unlikely politician who is trying to turn around his city. She first introduces her readers to John Fetterman, a tattoo-covered, bald, six-foot-eight man whom she met at the Aspen Ideas Festival. She hints that she is fascinated by him because he doesn't fit the typical picture of a politician, but she is also aware that he has also been working hard to improve his town of Braddock, Pennsylvania. What is significant, according to the author, is that Braddock is a town that has lost most of its business and population, so Fetterman has employed unusual tactics to rebuild the town. The author goes into great detail explaining the different programs Fetterman has instigated. She also interviews numerous current residents who have differing opinions of Fetterman's tactics. Halpern's article presents an in-depth look at what one person can do with heart and grit.

TEACHING TIP
You might have students read "Mayor of Rust," which is in the anthology at the back of the book.

Here is a model summary of a magazine article that is used in an essay containing a "Works Cited" page. Note that the publication information is not needed within the text, but it is available in the "Works Cited" entry. As shown here, the first time you cite an article, you need to reference the article's title. However, the second or subsequent time you cite this article, you would refer only to the author's last name, as in "[Author last name] also points out . . ."

> In the article "Mayor of Rust," author Sue Halpern profiles an unlikely politician who is trying to turn around his city. She first introduces her readers to John Fetterman, a tattoo-covered, bald, six-foot-eight, man whom she met at the Aspen Ideas Festival. She hints that she is fascinated by him because he doesn't fit the typical picture of a politician, but he has also been working hard to improve his town of Braddock, Pennsylvania. What is significant, according to the author, is that Braddock is a town that has lost most of its business and population, so Fetterman has employed unusual tactics to rebuild the town. The author goes into great detail explaining the different programs Fetterman has instigated. She also interviews numerous current residents who have differing opinions of Fetterman's tactics. Halpern's article presents an in-depth look at what one person can do with heart and grit.

continued

Work Cited

Halpern, Sue. "Mayor of Rust." *The New York Times Magazine*, 11 Feb. 2011, www.nytimes.com/2011/02/13/ magazine/13Fetterman-t.html. Accessed 19 Sept. 2018.

ACTIVITY 1

Answers will vary.

Write a summary of the following article. Your topic sentence should introduce the name of the article, the main purpose/thesis of the article, and the publication information. The rest of your summary should include only factual information that expresses the main points of the article. Your concluding sentence should express the closing idea presented in the article.

TEACHING TIP
Encourage students to annotate this article, underlining the thesis statement and main points.

TEACHING TIP
You might want to point out that since there is no author name provided for this sample article, students won't need to include this information in their topic sentence.

Power Learning

Jill had not done as well in high school as she had hoped. Since college involved even more work, it was no surprise that she didn't do better there.

The reason for her so-so performance was not a lack of effort. She attended most of her classes and read her textbooks. And she never missed handing in any assignment, even though it often meant staying up late the night before homework was due. Still, she just got by in her classes. Before long, she came to the conclusion that she simply couldn't do any better.

Then one day, one of her instructors said something to make her think otherwise. "You can probably build some sort of house by banging a few boards together," he said. "But if you want a sturdy home, you'll have to use the right techniques and tools. Building carefully takes work, but it gets better results. The same can be said of your education. There are no shortcuts, but there are some proven study skills that can really help. If you don't use them, you may end up with a pretty flimsy education."

Jill signed up for a study-skills course and found out a crucial fact—that learning how to learn is the key to success in school. There are certain dependable skills that have made the difference between disappointment and success for generations of students. These techniques won't free you from work, but they will make your work far more productive. They include three important areas: time control, classroom note-taking, and textbook study.

Time Control

Success in college depends on time control. *Time control* means that you deliberately organize and plan your time, instead of letting it

1

2

3

4

5

continued

drift by. Planning means that you should never be faced with an overdue term paper or a cram session the night before a test.

There are three steps involved in time control. *First,* you should prepare a large monthly calendar. Buy a calendar with a large white block around each date, or make one yourself. At the beginning of the college semester, circle important dates on this calendar. Circle the days on which tests are scheduled; circle the days when papers are due. This calendar can also be used to schedule study plans. At the beginning of the week, you can jot down your plans for each day. An alternative method would be to make plans for each day the night before. On Tuesday night, for example, you might write down "Read Chapter 5 in psychology" in the Wednesday block. Hang this calendar where you will see it every day—your kitchen, bedroom, even your bathroom!

6

The *second step* in time control is to have a weekly study schedule for the semester—a chart that covers all the days of the week and all the waking hours in each day. Below is part of one student's schedule:

7

Time	Mon.	Tue.	Wed.	Thurs.	Fri.	Sat.	
6:00 A.M.							
7:00	Breakfast	Breakfast	Breakfast	Breakfast	Breakfast		
8:00	Math	STUDY	Math	STUDY	Math	Breakfast	
9:00	STUDY	Biology	STUDY	Biology	STUDY	Job	
10:00	Psychology	↓	Psychology	↓	Psychology		
11:00		English		English			
12:00	Lunch		Lunch		Lunch	↓	

On your own schedule, fill in all the fixed hours in each day—hours for meals, classes, job (if any), and travel time. Next, mark time blocks that you can *realistically* use for study each day. Depending on the number of courses you are taking and the demands of these courses, you may want to block off five, ten, or even twenty or more hours of study time a week. Keep in mind that you should not block off time that you do not truly intend to use for study. Otherwise, your schedule will be a meaningless gimmick. Also, remember that you should allow time for "rest and relaxation." You will be happiest, and able to accomplish the most, when you have time for both work and play.

The *third step* in time control is to make a daily or weekly "to do" list. This may be the most valuable time-control method you ever use. On this list, write down the things you need to do for the following day or the following week. If you choose to write a weekly

8

continued

list, do it on Sunday night. If you choose to write a daily list, do it the night before. Here is part of one student's daily list:

```
To Do                        Tuesday
*1.  Review biology notes before class
*2.  Proofread English paper due today
*3.  See Dick about game on Friday
*4.  Get gas for car
*5.  Read next chapter of psychology text
```

You may use a three- by five-inch notepad or a small spiral-bound notebook for this list. Carry the list around with you during the day. Always concentrate on doing the most important items first. To make the best use of your time, mark high-priority items with an asterisk and give them precedence over low-priority items. For instance, you may find yourself wondering what to do after dinner on Thursday evening. Among the items on your list are "Clean inside of car" and "Review chapter for math quiz." It is obviously more important for you to review your notes at this point; you can clean out the car some other time. As you complete items on your "to do" list, cross them out. Do not worry about unfinished items. They can be rescheduled. You will still be accomplishing a great deal and making more effective use of your time.

Classroom Note-Taking

One of the most important single things you can do to perform well in a college course is to take effective class notes. The following hints should help you become a better note-taker.   9

First, attend class faithfully. Your alternatives—reading the text, reading someone else's notes, or both—cannot substitute for the class experience of hearing ideas in person as someone presents them to you. Also, in class lectures and discussions, your instructor typically presents and develops the main ideas and facts of the course—the ones you will be expected to know on exams.   10

Another valuable hint is to make use of abbreviations while taking notes. Using abbreviations saves time when you are trying to get down a great deal of information. Abbreviate terms that recur frequently in a lecture and put a key to your abbreviations at the top of your notes. For example, in sociology class, *eth* could stand for *ethnocentrism;* in a psychology class, *STM* could stand for *short-term memory.* (When a lecture is over, you may want to go back and write out the terms you have abbreviated.) Also, use *e* for *example; def* for *definition; info* for *information;* + for *and;* and so on. If you use the same abbreviations all   11

continued

the time, you will soon develop a kind of personal shorthand that makes taking notes much easier.

A third hint for taking notes is to be on the lookout for signals of importance. Write down whatever your instructor puts on the board. If he or she takes the time to put material on the board, it is probably important, and the chances are good that it will come up later on exams. Always write down definitions and enumerations. Enumerations are lists of items. They are signaled in such ways as "The four steps in the process are . . ."; "There were three reasons for . . ."; "The two effects were . . ."; "Five characteristics of . . ."; and so on. In your notes, always number such enumerations (1, 2, 3, etc.). They will help you understand relationships among ideas and organize the material of the lecture. Watch for emphasis words—words your instructor may use to indicate that something is important. Examples of such words are "This is an important reason . . ."; "A point that will keep coming up later . . ."; "The chief cause was . . ."; "The basic idea here is . . ."; and so on. Always write down the important statements announced by these and other emphasis words. Finally, if your instructor repeats a point, you can assume that it is important. You might put an *R* for *repeated* in the margin so that later you will know that your instructor stressed it.   12

Next, be sure to write down the instructor's examples and mark them with an *e*. The examples help you understand abstract points. If you do not write them down, you are likely to forget them later, when they are needed to help make sense of an idea.   13

Also, be sure to write down the connections between ideas. Too many students merely copy terms the instructor puts on the board. They forget that, as time passes, the details that serve as connecting bridges between ideas quickly fade. You should, then, write down the relationships and connections in class. That way you'll have them to help tie together your notes later on.   14

Review your notes as soon as possible after class. You must make them as clear as possible while they are fresh in your mind. A day later may be too late, because forgetting sets in very quickly. Make sure that punctuation is clear, that all words are readable and correctly spelled, and that unfinished sentences are completed (or at least marked off so that you can check your notes with another student's). Add clarifying or connecting comments wherever necessary. Make sure that important ideas are clearly marked. Improve the organization if necessary so that you can see at a glance main points and relationships among them.   15

Finally, try in general to get down a written record of each class. You must do this because forgetting begins almost immediately. Studies have shown that within two weeks you are likely to have forgotten 80 percent or more of what you have heard. And in four   16

continued

weeks you are lucky if 5 percent remains! This is so crucial that it bears repeating: To guard against the relentlessness of forgetting, it is absolutely essential that you write down what you hear in class. Later you can concentrate on working to understand fully and to remember the ideas that have been presented in class. And then, the more complete your notes are, the more you are likely to learn.

Textbook Study

In many college courses, success means being able to read and study a textbook skillfully. For many students, unfortunately, textbooks are heavy going. After an hour or two of study, the textbook material is as formless and as hard to understand as ever. But there is a way to attack even the most difficult textbook and make sense of it. Use a sequence in which you preview a chapter, mark it, take notes on it, and then study the notes.   17

Previewing

Previewing a selection is an important first step to understanding. Taking the time to preview a section or chapter can give you a bird's-eye view of the way the material is organized. You will have a sense of where you are beginning, what you will cover, and where you will end.   18

There are several steps in previewing a selection. First, study the title. The title is the shortest possible summary of a selection and will often tell you the limits of the material you will cover. For example, the title "FDR and the Supreme Court" tells you to expect a discussion of President Roosevelt's dealings with the Court. You know that you will probably not encounter any material dealing with FDR's foreign policies or personal life. Next, quickly read over the first and last paragraphs of the selection; these may contain important introductions to, and summaries of, the main ideas. Then briefly examine the headings and subheadings in the selection. Together, the headings and subheadings are a mini-outline of what you are reading. Headings are often main ideas or important concepts in capsule form; subheadings are breakdowns of ideas within main areas. Finally, read the first sentence of some paragraphs, look for words set off in **boldface** or *italics*, and look at pictures or diagrams. After you have previewed a selection in this way, you should have a good general sense of the material to be read.   19

Marking

You should mark a textbook selection at the same time that you read it through carefully. Use a felt-tip highlighter to shade   20

continued

material that seems important, or use a ballpoint pen and put symbols in the margin next to the material: stars, checks, or NB (*nota bene,* Latin for "note well"). What to mark is not as mysterious as some students believe. You should try to find main ideas by looking for clues: definitions and examples, enumerations, and emphasis words.

1. *Definitions and examples:* Definitions are often among the most important ideas in a selection. They are particularly significant in introductory courses in almost any subject area, where much of your learning involves mastering the specialized vocabulary of that subject. In a sense, you are learning the "language" of psychology or business or whatever the subject might be.

   Most definitions are abstract, and so they usually are followed by one or more examples to help clarify their meaning. Always mark off definitions and at least one example that makes a definition clear to you. In a psychology text, for example, we are told that "rationalization is an attempt to reduce anxiety by deciding that you have not really been frustrated." Several examples follow, among them: "A young man, frustrated because he was rejected when he asked for a date, convinces himself that the girl is not very attractive or interesting."

2. *Enumerations:* Enumerations are lists of items (causes, reasons, types, and so on) that are numbered 1, 2, 3, ... or that could easily be numbered. They are often signaled by addition words. Many of the paragraphs in this book, for instance, use words like *First of all, Another, In addition,* and *Finally* to signal items in a series. Other textbooks also use this very common and effective organizational method.

3. *Emphasis words:* Emphasis words tell you that an idea is important. Common emphasis words include phrases such as *a major event, a key feature, the chief factor, important to note, above all,* and *most of all.* Here is an example: "The most significant contemporary use of marketing is its application to nonbusiness areas, such as political parties."

Note-Taking

Next, you should take notes. Go through the chapter a second time, rereading the most important parts. Try to write down the main ideas in a simple outline form. For example, in taking notes on a psychology selection, you might write down the heading "Defense Mechanisms." Below the heading you would define them, number and describe each kind, and give an example of each.

21

22

23

24

25

continued

Defense Mechanisms

a. Definition: unconscious attempts to reduce anxiety

b. Kinds:

(1) Rationalization: An attempt to reduce anxiety by deciding that you have not really been frustrated.

Example: A man turned down for a date decides that the woman was not worth going out with anyway.

(2) Projection: Projecting onto other people motives or thoughts of one's own.

Example: A wife who wants to have an affair accuses her husband of having one.

Studying Notes

To study your notes, use repeated self-testing. For example, look at the heading "Defense Mechanisms" and say to yourself, "What are the kinds of defense mechanisms?" When you can recite them, then say to yourself, "What is rationalization?" "What is an example of rationalization?" Then ask yourself, "What is projection?" "What is an example of projection?" After you learn each section, review it, and then go on to the next section.   26

Do not simply read your notes; keep looking away and seeing if you can recite them to yourself. This self-testing is the key to effective learning.   27

Summary: Textbook Study

In summary, remember this sequence for dealing with a textbook: preview, mark, take notes, study the notes. Approaching a textbook in this methodical way will give you very positive results. You will no longer feel bogged down in a swamp of words, unable to figure out what you are supposed to know. Instead, you will understand exactly what you have to do, and how to go about doing it.   28

Take a minute now to evaluate your own study habits. Do you practice many of the above skills in order to take effective classroom notes, control your time, and learn from your textbooks? If not, perhaps you should. The skills are not magic, but they are too valuable to ignore. Use them carefully and consistently, and they will make academic success possible for you. Try them, and you won't need convincing.   29

Write a summary of one of the readings in the anthology. In your first sentence, include the name of the reading, the author's full name, and a statement that explains the author's purpose. For example, you might write: In "The Professor Is a Dropout," by Beth Johnson, the author profiles a woman who initially dropped out of school in first grade, but eventually earned a graduate degree and became a professor at a university.

Write a paragraph-length summary of a cover story of interest to you in a recent issue of *Time*, *GQ*, or *The New Yorker*.

EXPLORING WRITING ONLINE

Visit one of these TV network Web sites and select one of your favorite TV shows. Watch a video of an entire episode or find an episode that you have already seen, and then read the synopsis or recap of that episode. Next, write a summary of your own.

CBS.com: http://www.cbs.com

ABC.com: http://abc.go.com

NBC.com: http://www.nbc.com

Fox Broadcasting: http://www.fox.com

©Tetra Images/ Shutterstock

Writing a Paraphrase

In a paraphrase, you report the information in your own words and your own writing style, without condensing it. You should paraphrase when the original information is important, but you can write it more clearly in your own words. Since you are not condensing it, a paraphrase usually compares in length to the original work. Unlike a summary, which can be created as a stand-alone paper, paraphrases are only used within a larger essay.

Students must be careful when paraphrasing in order to avoid plagiarism. Simply changing one or two words from the original is not a paraphrase. In order to successfully paraphrase something, you should read the information, set it aside, and then try to explain what you just read in your own words and writing style. Remember, as with summaries, if you don't fully understand the information you have just read, you won't be able to write a successful paraphrase. You should preview, read, and evaluate the information before attempting to write about it using your own words and writing style.

How to Paraphrase Information from an Article

To paraphrase information from an article, follow steps 1 and 2 for "How to Summarize an Article," then follow the steps below. If the assigned material is a TV show or film, adapt the suggestions accordingly.

1. Find and reread a paragraph or two that you have identified as important.

2. Set the article aside. Without looking at the original source and using your own words, write down what you have just read.

3. Compare your version with the original source. Using quotation marks, mark any words or phrases that are directly from the original source.

4. Revise any sentences that are structured closely to the original source.

5. At the bottom of your version, write down the source information, including page number, so you can properly credit the information when you use it.

Here is a sample passage followed by two model paraphrases. The first one is unacceptable. Note the sections that are too closely related to the original source. The second one properly conveys the meaning of the passage without following the original sentence structure or using the original words.

Original Passage

> A *scratch outline* is an excellent sequel to the first four prewriting techniques. A scratch outline often follows freewriting, questioning, list-making, or diagramming, or it may gradually emerge in the midst of these strategies. In fact, trying to make a scratch outline is a good way to see if you need to do more prewriting. If you cannot come up with a solid outline, then you know you need to do more prewriting to clarify your main point or its several kinds of support.

Paraphrase A

> A *scratch outline* is a good follow-up to the first prewriting techniques. A scratch outline often follows diagramming, questioning, list-making, or freewriting, or it may emerge in the middle of these strategies. In reality, making a scratch outline is the best way to see if you need to prewrite more. If you cannot come up with a firm outline, then you know you need to do more prewriting to explain your claim and support.

Paraphrase B

A *scratch outline* is a good technique to use after you have spent time prewriting with your chosen method. By creating a scratch outline, you can see the holes in your argument and support, so you can figure out where you may need to do additional prewriting. The weaker your outline, the more obvious it is you need to spend more time prewriting.

ACTIVITY 4

Here are two sets of passages from the anthology of readings at the end of this book. Each set begins with an original passage and an MLA-formatted bibliographic entry demonstrating how a student would cite the use of such a passage in the "Works Cited" page. Each set is followed by two possible paraphrases of the passage. One is an acceptable paraphrase, but the other is unacceptable because the sentences and ideas too closely follow the original structure and/or use the original words. Identify the acceptable paraphrase with an A and the unacceptable paraphrase with a U.

SET 1: ORIGINAL PASSAGE

Propaganda is a systematic effort to influence people's opinions, to win them over to a certain view or side. Propaganda is not necessarily concerned with what is true or false, good or bad. Propagandists simply want people to believe the messages being sent. Often, propagandists will use outright lies or more subtle deceptions to sway people's opinions. In a propaganda war, any tactic is considered fair.

McClintock, Ann. "Propaganda Techniques in Today's Advertising." *Exploring Writing: Paragraphs and Essays,* authored by Zoé L. Albright and John Langan, 4th ed., McGraw-Hill Education, 2020, pp. 605–610.

___A___   a. Propaganda is information that is created to get people to believe certain things and think certain ways. Propagandists are people who create and promote propaganda, and they are not concerned with whether or not their messages are true, partially true, or outright lies. Their only concern is selling their message and getting people to believe it. They believe that all is fair in the propaganda war.

___U___   b. *Propaganda* is an organized effort to impact other people's views, to get them to agree with a certain view or side. Propaganda is not concerned with true or false. Propagandists only want people to trust the messages being sent. Often, people who make propaganda will use blatant lies or deceptions to get people to change their opinions. Any tactic is considered fair in a propaganda war.

TEACHING TIP
Have students discuss why these passages are acceptable or unacceptable. Encourage them to carefully examine the original passage.

TEACHING TIP
Point out to students that the citations following each passage are MLA formatted to demonstrate how students would cite the use of passages from an anthology (like the one at the end of this textbook). Students should also be made aware of the text permission citations at the end of the chapter, which illustrate how a permissioned source is legally required to be noted in another publication.

SET 2: ORIGINAL PASSAGE

What does "a positive attitude" mean? Well, for one thing, it means avoiding the zombie syndrome. It means not only showing up for your classes, but also doing something while you're there. Really listen. Take notes. Ask a question if you want to. Don't just walk into a class, put your mind in neutral, and drift away to never-never land.

O'Keeney, Brian. "How to Make It in College, Now That You're Here." *Exploring Writing: Paragraphs and Essays,* authored by Zoé L. Albright and John Langan, 4th ed., McGraw-Hill Education, 2020, pp. 655–660.

____U____ a. What does it mean to have a positive attitude? First, it means shunning the zombie syndrome. It means showing up for your classes and also doing something while you're there. Listen. Take notes. Ask a question. Don't put your mind in neutral after you walk into a class and drift away.

____A____ b. The question is about what it means to have a positive attitude. Instead of being a passive, lifeless student, a student with a positive attitude is an active learner. This student shows up to class in both body and mind, ready to learn and engage. Also, this student participates in class by listening, taking notes, and asking questions.

ACTIVITY 5

Choose two nonconsecutive paragraphs from one of the readings in the anthology that has either been assigned by your instructor or chosen by you, and write a paraphrase of each paragraph. Make sure you include the original paragraphs with your work, so you and your instructor can compare them.

Using Direct Quotations

Unlike a summary or paraphrase, a direct quotation must be written exactly as it appears in the original work. There are three ways that direct quotations are generally presented. For shorter passages, quotation marks are used. For longer complete passages, the material is indented as a block of text and no quotation marks are used. The same formatting applies to longer passages with omitted material, but for these passages, ellipses are included to indicate the omitted text. (Each "Original Passage" in the preceding paraphrasing activity is an example of a direct quotation.)

Each of these categories is explained further and illustrated in the following sections. These examples have been taken from the "Power Learning" essay you worked with in Activity 1. The paragraph location of each quotation is explained, so you can refer to the original essay and see the quotation in its original context. When you incorporate quotes into your essays, you will need to follow proper MLA format. For complete MLA format for using in-text citations, refer to Chapter 21.

Unlike summaries and paraphrases—where accidental plagiarism can occur as students try to use their own words to report others' words and ideas—there is less risk of plagiarism in the use of direct quotations. However, if you forget to use quotation marks or block indents and/or forget to credit the author, plagiarism can occur. Thus, it is critical to pay careful attention to your use of another author's words throughout all your writing.

Short Quotations

In order to include a brief sentence or two of direct text from an original source, use a short quotation. As you insert the quoted material into your own writing, a transition is usually needed. Examine the two examples below. Notice that in the second example, the writer builds the direct quote into a larger sentence and in so doing, places the letter "t" in brackets. This shows that the word was lowercased by the student and not by the author of the quotation.

> The author states, "Success in college depends on time control." (paragraph 5)

> The author emphasizes there are three steps to good time control. She explains that "[t]he second step in time control is to have a weekly study schedule for the semester—a chart that covers all the days of the week and all the waking hours in each day." (paragraph 7)

Long Complete Quotations

If you want to use a complete section that is longer than four lines, you should block the quotation, which means you'll need to indent it by an extra margin to set it off from the rest of the essay. (This will result in an indent of ½ inch from the left margin.) Block quotations do not use quotation marks. In the example below, the first paragraph was written by a student as a lead-in to the direct quotation from "Power Learning." Notice how the quotation is set off by the extra indent.

> In the essay "Power Learning" several strategies for successful studying are presented. In the section about note-taking, good attendance is stressed as the most important key to success:

> > First, attend class faithfully. Your alternatives—reading the text, reading someone else's notes, or both—cannot substitute for the class experience of hearing ideas in person as someone presents them to you. Also, in class lectures and discussions, your instructor typically presents and develops the main ideas and facts of the course—the ones you will be expected to know on exams. (paragraph 10)

Quotations with Omitted Information

If you are using a longer quotation that includes information unrelated to your topic, you may omit the irrelevant words as long as you don't change the overall meaning. To show such an omission, use three spaced periods (known as *ellipsis points*) in place of the deleted words:

> The author offers three clear steps to good time control, "First, you should prepare a large monthly calendar … circle important dates on this calendar. Circle the days on which tests are scheduled; circle the days when papers are due." (paragraph 6)

Note that in the following example there are four periods in the first line of the quotation—the first dot is the period at the end of the sentence.

> The author's final step in time control focuses on lists. "The third step in time control is to make a daily or weekly to-do list…. On this list, write down the things you need to do for the following day of the following week." (paragraph 8)

in a writer's words

" *Write what you really think and mean, not what you think you should write and not what you thought you would think and not what you hope it will mean, but what is really authentic and true.*"

—Susan Orlean

TEACHING TIP
Direct students to the diagram of the four bases in Chapter 5.

Writing a Literary Analysis or Source-Based Essay

Each semester, you will probably be asked by at least one instructor to write an assignment that will require you to use outside sources to support your argument. In English classes, this type of essay is often a literary analysis, an assignment that requires students to read a book, short story, or poem and analyze different aspects of the work. While these assignments don't necessarily demand research on the part of the student, they will require the student to use information from the original source as essay support. Regardless of whether students use only the original source or bring in additional outside sources for their analysis, this information will need to be incorporated and cited properly.

Writing a literary analysis, a source-based essay, or a research essay will require careful note-taking, proper integration of information, in-text citation, and a "Works Cited" page regardless of whether you are using one, two, or ten sources. The following pages will explain how to properly incorporate and document your sources.

Planning Ahead and Taking Notes

The purpose of a literary analysis or source-based essay is to thoroughly develop a main point about the literary work or topic that is neither too narrow nor too broad. You want your support to focus on the development of that topic, not stray in multiple directions. When you are writing a literary analysis or source-based essay, you will need to read thoroughly and take notes on the material you plan to use to support your ideas.

Preparing a Scratch Outline

As you carefully read through the material you have gathered, think about the content and organization of your paper. Begin deciding what information you will present and how you will arrange it. Prepare a scratch outline that shows both the paper's working thesis and the areas that support the thesis. Try to include at least three areas, if not more, of support.

Working Thesis: _____

Support:

- _____

- _____

- _____

- _____

See Chapter 2 for further discussion about and additional models of scratch outlines.

Keeping Careful Notes

With this tentative outline in mind, you can begin taking notes on the information that you expect to include in your paper. For each source, you will want to create a document or use note cards. Don't use loose-leaf or notebook paper; doing so makes it harder to organize your notes as you prepare to draft your paper. Notes should be in the form of direct quotations and summaries in your own words. At times, you may also paraphrase, but you will probably summarize much more often than you will paraphrase.

When you create your notes, you want to make sure you include all relevant bibliographic information—title of source, author, page number, publication information. If you are using only your original work in your essay, keeping track of sources is much simpler; however, if you choose to use additional sources, it is important that you keep clear notes as to where your quotes originate. As you choose information that you think you are going to use, you should copy it word-for-word and enclose it within quotation marks. If you want to paraphrase or summarize the information, you should write your paraphrase or summary with the page number and a notation stating what you have created.

Taking Notes Using a Direct Quotation

As stated earlier, a *direct quotation* must be written exactly as it appears in the original work. Several examples of note cards with direct quotations follow.

Lewis, C. S. *The Magician's Nephew*. The MacMillan Company, 1955.

"A voice had begun to sing. It was very far away and Digory found it hard to decide from what direction it was coming. Sometimes it seemed to come from all directions at once. Sometimes he almost thought it was coming out of the earth beneath them. Its lower notes were deep enough to be the voice of the earth herself. There were no words. It was hardly a tune. But it was beyond comparison, the most beautiful sound he had ever heard." (This is a direct quotation found on page 87.)

Note with
Direct Quotation

Note with Direct Quotation
and Ellipsis

> **Lewis, C. S. *The Magician's Nephew*. The MacMillan Company, 1955.**
>
> "A voice had begun to sing. It was very far away and Digory found it hard to decide from what direction it was coming. Sometimes it seemed to come from all directions at once. Sometimes he almost thought it was coming out of the earth beneath them. Its lower notes were deep enough to be the voice of the earth ... [and was] the most beautiful sound he had ever heard." (This is a direct quotation found on page 87.)

(The words *and was* in brackets show that the words were added by the student and not by the author of the quotation.)

Taking Notes Using a Summary

Remember that in a *summary*, you condense the original material and use your own words.

Note with Summary

> **Lewis, C. S. *The Magician's Nephew*. The MacMillan Company, 1955.**
>
> Digory heard a song that seemed to come from everywhere and surrounded him. After listening for a while, he believed it to be the most amazing thing he had ever heard. (This is a summary of the quote on page 87 that is part of paragraph 6.)

Taking Notes Using a Paraphrase

Remember that in a *paraphrase*, you report the information in your own words and writing style without condensing it.

Note with Paraphrase

> **Lewis, C. S. *The Magician's Nephew*. The MacMillan Company, 1955.**
>
> Digory heard a sound he had never heard before that was the most amazing thing he had ever heard. It seemed like a song, but no one was singing any words. He couldn't place where it was originating because it sounded like it came from the Earth. (This is a paraphrase of the quote on page 87 that is part of paragraph 6.)

Helpful Tips on Taking Notes

Keep the following in mind as you take notes.
    If you are using note cards:

- Write on only one side of each card.

- Write only one kind of information, from one source, on any one card.

- Identify the source and page number on every card.

- Identify whether you have written a quotation, summary, or paraphrase on every card.

If you are keeping notes in a document:

- Create a new document for each source.

- Identify the author, title, and publication information at the top of the document. Write it in proper MLA format.

- Identify the page number at the end of each note.

- Identify whether you have written a quotation, summary, or paraphrase at the end of each note.

Always record the exact source and page from which you take each piece of information. In a literary analysis, source-based essay, or research essay, you must document all information that is not common knowledge or not a matter of historical record. For example, the birth and death dates of J. D. Salinger are established facts and do not need documenting. On the other hand, who first published *Lolita* is a specialized fact and should be documented. In addition, as you read several sources on a subject, you will develop a sense of what authors regard as generally shared, or common, information and what is more specialized information that requires documentation.

ACTIVITY 6

Answers will vary.

Read the following paragraphs from sources that a student might use to gather material for a literary analysis, source-based essay, or research essay. Then, on a separate sheet of paper, create three separate notes for each:

1. In the first note, use a direct quotation in which you indicate the omission of certain words or phrases by using ellipses.

2. In the second note, write a paraphrase of the paragraph.

3. In the third note, write a summary of the paragraph.

   Be sure to provide the source information at the beginning of the notes.

PARAGRAPH A

Cooper, Susan Fenimore. "August." 1887. *Quotidiana,* edited by Patrick Madden. 3 June 2008, essays.quotidiana.org/cooper_s/august/. Accessed 24 Sept. 2018.

"There is not a single town of any size within a distance of forty miles, yet already the rural population of this county is quite large. The whole country, within a wide circuit north, south, east and west, partakes of the same general character; mountain ridges, half tilled, half wood, screening cultivated valleys, sprinkled with farms and hamlets, among which some pretty stream generally winds its way. The waters in our immediate neighborhood all flow to the southward, though only a few miles to the north of our village, the brooks are found running in an opposite course, this valley lying just within the borders of the dividing ridge. The river itself, though farther south it becomes one of the great streams of the country, cannot boast of much breadth so near its source, and running quietly among the meadows, half screened by the groves and thickets, scarcely shows in the general view."

PARAGRAPH B

Verne, Jules. *Around the World in 80 Days*. Routledge, 1873. *Lit2Go*, etc.usf
.edu/lit2go/55/around-the-world-in-80-days/. Accessed 24 Sept. 2018.

"During his brief interview with Mr. Fogg, Passepartout had been
carefully observing him. He appeared to be a man about forty years of
age, with fine, handsome features, and a tall, well-shaped figure; his hair
and whiskers were light, his forehead compact and unwrinkled, his face
rather pale, his teeth magnificent. His countenance possessed in the highest degree what physiognomists call "repose in action," a quality of those
who act rather than talk. Calm and phlegmatic, with a clear eye, Mr. Fogg
seemed a perfect type of that English composure which Angelica Kauff-
mann has so skilfully *[sic]* represented on canvas. Seen in the various
phases of his daily life, he gave the idea of being perfectly well-balanced,
as exactly regulated as a Leroy chronometer. Phileas Fogg was, indeed,
exactitude personified, and this was betrayed even in the expression of his
very hands and feet; for in men, as well as in animals, the limbs themselves
are expressive of the passions."

Citing Sources

Format

TEACHING TIP
Point out that
documentation helps
readers locate information,
so accuracy is important.

The model papers in this chapter show acceptable formats for a source-based
or research paper, including the style recommended by the Modern Language
Association (MLA). Be sure to note carefully the comments and directions
that are set in small print in the margins of each page.

Documentation of Sources

You must reveal the sources (books, articles, and so on) of borrowed information in your paper. Whether you quote directly or paraphrase or summarize
ideas in your own words, you must acknowledge your sources. Here you will
learn a simplified and widely accepted documentation style used by the MLA.

Citations within a Paper

When citing a source, you must mention the author's name and the relevant
page number. The author's name may be given either in the sentence itself or
in parentheses following the sentence. Here are two examples:

In *The Way We Really Are*, Stephanie Coontz writes, "Right up
through the 1940s, ties of work, friendship, neighborhood, ethnicity,
extended kin, and voluntary organizations were as important a source
of identity for most Americans, and sometimes a more important
source of obligation, than marriage and the nuclear family" (37).

"Some . . . are looking for a way to reclaim family closeness in
an increasingly fast-paced society.... Still others worry about unsavory
influences in school—drugs, alcohol, sex, violence" (Kantrowitz and
Wingert 66).

There are several points to note about citations within a paper:

- When referring to an author within the parenthetical citation, use only the last name.

- There is no punctuation between the author's name and the page number.

- The parenthetical citation is placed after the borrowed material but before the period at the end of the sentence.

- If you are using more than one work by the same author, include a shortened version of the title within the parenthetical citation. For example, suppose you were using two books by Stephanie Coontz, and you included a second quotation from her book *The Way We Really Are.* Your citation within the text would be

  (Coontz, *Really Are* 39).

  Note that a comma separates the author's last name from the abbreviated title and page number.

- Use the abbreviation *qtd. in* when citing a quotation from another source. For example, a quotation from Edward Wolff on page 2 of the model paper (in the next chapter) is from a book not by Wolff but by Sylvia Ann Hewlett and Cornel West. The citation is therefore handled as follows:

The economist Edward Wolff explains the loss of time:
> Over a thirty-year time span, parental time has declined 13 percent. The time parents have available for their children has been squeezed by the rapid shift of mothers into the paid labor force, by escalating divorce rates and the subsequent abandonment of children by their fathers, and by an increase in the number of hours required on the job. (qtd. in Hewlett and West 48)

Citations at the End of a Paper

Your paper should end with a list of "Works Cited" that includes all the sources actually used in the paper. (Don't list any other sources, no matter how many you have read.) Look at the "Works Cited" page in the model source-based essay in this chapter and the model research paper in the next chapter and note the following points:

- The list is organized alphabetically according to the authors' last names. Entries are not numbered.

- Entries are double-spaced, with no extra space between entries.

- After the first line of each entry, there is a half-inch indentation for each additional line in the entry.

TEACHING TIP
Students often use the outdated term "bibliography" rather than "works cited." Point out that the word "bibliography" means a "list of books."

Model Entries for a List of "Works Cited"

Model "Works Cited" entries are given below. Use these entries as a guide when you prepare your own list.

Book by One Author

Bryson, Bill. *A Short History of Nearly Everything.* Broadway
    Books, 2003.

Note that the author's last name is written first. This is followed by the title of the book with the first word and all major words capitalized. Next comes the name of the publisher and the date of publication.

Two or More Entries by the Same Author

- - -. *I'm a Stranger Here Myself.* Broadway Books, 2005.

If you cite two or more sources by the same author (in the example above, a second book by Bill Bryson is cited) do not repeat the author's name. Instead, begin the entry with three hyphens followed by a period. Arrange works by the same author alphabetically by title. The words *A, An,* and *The* are ignored when alphabetizing by title.

Book by Two Authors

Simon, David, and Edward Burns. *The Corner.* Broadway Books, 2000.

For a source with two authors, give both authors' names but reverse only the first author's name.

Magazine Article

Kalb, Claudia. "Brave New Babies." *Newsweek,* 26 Jan. 2009, pp. 45–52.

Newspaper Article

Farrell, Greg. "Online Time Soars at Office." *USA Today,* 18 Feb.
    2009, pp. A1–2.

For articles where the date of the publication includes a month, abbreviate all months in your entries, except May, June, and July. For newspapers, include both a section and page number if available (*pp. A1-2* in the example above). If the article is not printed on consecutive pages, list the first page followed by a plus sign (*+*). In that case, the above example would read *pp. A1+.*

Editorial

"Fouling the Air." Editorial. *The New York Times,* 23 Aug. 2009, p. A12.

List an editorial as you would any signed or unsigned article, but indicate the nature of the piece by adding *Editorial* after the article's title.

Article in a Professional Journal

Andrews, Elmer. "The Gift and the Craft: An Approach to the Poetry
    of Seamus Heaney." *Twentieth Century Literature,* vol. 31, no. 4,
    Winter 1985, pp. 368–79.

Selection in an Edited Collection

Paige, Satchel. "Rules for Staying Young." *Baseball: A Literary Anthology,*
    edited by Nicholas Dawidoff, Library of America, 2002, p. 318.

Revised or Later Edition

Henslin, James M. *Essentials of Sociology.* 5th ed., Allyn & Bacon, 2004.

Edition information (*revised ed., 2nd ed., 3rd ed.,* and so on) is placed right after the title.

Krugman, Paul. "The Angry People." *The Great Unraveling.* Norton, 2003, pp. 272–74.

Chapter or Section in a Book by One Author

Funding Your Education. United States Department of Education, Office of Federal Student Aid, 2014.

Pamphlet

"Musically Speaking." *60 Minutes,* reported by Lesley Stahl, season 36, episode 1, CBS, 28 Sept. 2003.

Television Program

Nolan, Christopher, director. *The Dark Knight.* Warner Bros., 2008.

Film

Springsteen, Bruce. "The Wrestler." *Working on a Dream,* Columbia Records, 2009.

Sound Recording

McClintock, Ann. Personal interview. 23 June 2004.

Personal Interview

Procopiou, Christina. "The Wind Turbines Saving the Galápagos Islands." *Newsweek,* 29 May 2016, www.newsweek.com/wind-turbines-saving-galapagos-islands-464423.

Article in an Online Magazine

TEACHING TIP
Because students often rely on Web sites, spend time teaching them how to document electronic sources.

Include URLs for online source entries. Do not include http:// or https:// as part of any URLs in your entries.

"Being Chased in Dreams." *Dreams and Nightmares,* Elemental Expressions, www.dreamsnightmares.com/chasedindreams.html. Accessed 17 May 2016.

Article from a Web Site

When no author is given, list the title of the article first. For online sources, include the date the Web site or page was published or last updated, whichever is most recent. If an online source has no publication date (as in the example above), then include a date of access at the end of the entry. Although this is no longer required, it is strongly advised, especially if the page does not have a copyright date.

Carta, Stefano. "Music in Dreams and the Emergence of the Self." *Journal of Analytical Psychology,* vol. 54, no. 1, 2009, pp. 85–102. *Academic Search Premier,* doi:10.1111/j.1468-5922.2008.01759.x.

Article in Reference Database

Include complete print publication information for the article, and then list the name of the database and a URL or DOI for the article. A DOI (digital object identifier) is a number assigned by publishers to some professional journal articles; if you see a DOI listed for an article, include that in your citation instead of a URL.

Graham, Vanessa. "Teenager Problems." Received by Sonya Philips, 12 Apr. 2009.

E-mail

Saujnai, Reshma. "Teach Girls Bravery, Not Perfection." *TED,* Feb. 2016, www.ted.com/talks/reshma_saujani_teach_girls_bravery_not_perfection.

Online Video

When the name of a Web site and the name of the publisher or sponsor for the Web site are the same (as with *TED* in the example above), do not include a publisher or sponsor in your citation.

| ACTIVITY 7 | On a separate sheet of paper, convert the information in each of the following references into the correct form for a list of "Works Cited." Use the appropriate model above as a guide. |

1. A book by David Anderegg called *Worried All the Time* and published by Free Press in 2003.
    1. Anderegg, David. *Worried All the Time*. Free Press, 2003.
2. An article by Susan Page titled "No Experience Necessary" on pages 1A–2A of the September 29, 2007, issue of *USA Today*.
    2. Page, Susan. "No Experience Necessary." *USA Today*, 29 Sept. 2007, pp. 1A–2A.
3. A book by Michael W. Passer and Ronald E. Smith titled *Psychology: The Science of Mind and Behavior* and published in a fourth edition by McGraw-Hill Education in 2008. 3. Passer, Michael W., and Ronald E. Smith.
    Psychology: The Science of Mind and Behavior. 4th ed., McGraw-Hill Education, 2008.
4. An article by Mark Miller titled "Parting with a Pet" dated October 7, 2003, found on the *Newsweek* Web site, at this URL: www.newsweek.com/parting-pet-138971.
    4. Miller, Mark. "Parting with a Pet." *Newsweek*, 7 Oct. 2003, www.newsweek.com/parting-pet-138971.
5. An article titled "The World's Loudest Animal Might Surprise You" written by Ella Davies and posted on April 1, 2016, on the Web site titled *BBC*, which is also sponsored by BBC, at this URL: www.bbc.com/earth/story/20160331-the-worlds-loudest-animal-might-surprise-you.
    5. Davies, Ella. "The World's Loudest Animal Might Surprise You." *BBC*, 1 Apr. 2016, www.bbc.com/earth/story/20160331-the-worlds-loudest-animal-might-surprise-you.

A Model Literary Analysis

Here is a literary analysis written by a student for her class. Notice how the essay makes a claim about the literature and uses information from the novel to support the claim.

Introductory paragraph
including thesis.

Notice the first
body paragraph
gives a summary
of the novel.

I Know Why the Caged Bird Sings: Depth and Emotion through Words

In *I Know Why the Caged Bird Sings* Maya Angelou tells the story of her earliest years. Angelou, a dancer, poet, and television producer as well as a writer, has continued her life story in three more volumes of autobiography. *I Know Why the Caged Bird Sings* is the start of Maya Angelou's story; in this book, she writes with extraordinary clarity about the pains and joys of being black in America.   1

I Know Why the Caged Bird Sings covers Maya Angelou's life from age three to age sixteen. When the book opens, she is a gawky little girl in a white woman's cut-down lavender silk   2 dress. She has forgotten the poem she had memorized for the Easter service, and all she can do is rush out of the church. At this point, Angelou is living in Stamps, Arkansas, with her grandmother and uncle. The town is rigidly segregated: "People in Stamps used to say that the whites in our town were so prejudiced that a Negro couldn't buy vanilla ice cream" (40). Yet Angelou has some good things in her life: her adored older brother Bailey, her success in school, and her pride in her grandmother's quiet strength and importance in the black community. There is laughter, too, as when a preacher is interrupted in midsermon by an overly enthusiastic woman shouting, "Preach it, I say preach it!" The woman, in a frenzied rush of excitement, hits the preacher with her purse; his false teeth fly out of his mouth and land at Angelou's feet. Shortly after this incident, Angelou and her brother are taken by her father to live in California with their mother. Here, at age eight, she is raped by her mother's boyfriend, who is mysteriously murdered after receiving only a suspended sentence for his crime. She returns, silent and withdrawn, to Stamps, where the gloom is broken when a friend of her mother introduces her to the magic of great books. Later, at age thirteen, Angelou returns to California. She learns how to dance. She runs away after a violent family fight and lives for a month in a junkyard. She becomes the first black female to get a job on the San Francisco streetcars. She graduates from high school eight months pregnant. And she survives.

Maya Angelou's writing style is impressive and vivid. For example, she describes the lazy dullness of her life in Stamps: "Weekdays revolved in a sameness wheel. They turned into themselves so steadily and inevitably that each seemed to be the original of yesterday's rough draft" (93). She also knows how to bring a scene to life, as when she describes her eighth-grade graduation. For months, she has been looking forward to this event, knowing she will be honored for her academic successes. She is even happy with her appearance: her hair has become pretty, and her yellow dress is a miracle of hand-sewing. But the ceremony is spoiled when the speaker—a white man—implies that the only success available to blacks is in athletics. Angelou remembers: "The man's dead words fell like bricks around the auditorium and too many settled in my belly. . . . The proud graduating class of 1940 had dropped their heads" (152). Later, Angelou uses a crystal-clear image to describe her father's mistress sewing: "She worked the thread through the flowered cloth as if she were sewing the torn ends of her life together" (208). With such vivid details and figures of speech, Maya Angelou re-creates her life for her readers.

3

TEACHING TIP
Explain to students that this literary analysis does not include full MLA formatting, such as headings and headers, as this model is focused on students reading and understanding the structure and content of this type of essay.

Connection: Notice the topic sentence reconnects with the thesis statement.

Quotation: In this quote, the student uses ellipses to signal where original material has been omitted.

The strong images of the injustices suffered by blacks two generations ago are well done and incredibly powerful. The description of seven-year-old Maya—when some "powhitetrash" girls torment her dignified grandmother, calling her "Annie" and mimicking her mannerisms—is emotional and raw. In another incident, Mrs. Cullinan, Angelou's white employer, decides that Marguerite (Angelou's real name) is too difficult to pronounce and so renames her Mary. This loss of her name—a "hellish horror" (91)—is another humiliation suffered at white hands, and Angelou leaves Mrs. Cullinan's employ soon afterward. Later, Angelou encounters overt discrimination when a white dentist tells her grandmother, "Annie, my policy is I'd rather stick my hand in a dog's mouth than in a nigger's" (160)—and only slightly less obvious prejudice when the streetcar company refuses to accept her application for a conductor's job. Over and over again, Angelou is the victim of a white society. 4

Although these injustices are disheartening, Angelou's triumphs are inspiring. Angelou is thrilled when she hears the radio broadcast of Joe Louis's victory over Primo Camera: "A Black boy. Some Black mother's son. He was the strongest man in the world" (114). She weeps with pride when the class valedictorian leads her and her fellow eighth-graders in singing the Negro National Anthem. And there are personal victories, too. One of these comes after her father has gotten drunk in a small Mexican town. Though she has never driven before, she manages to get her father into the car and drives fifty miles through the night as he lies intoxicated in the backseat. Finally, she rejoices in the birth of her son: "He was beautiful and mine. Totally mine. No one had bought him for me" (245). Angelou shows us, through these examples, that she is proud of her race—and of herself. 5

I Know Why the Caged Bird Sings is a remarkable book. Angelou could have been just another casualty of race prejudice. Yet by using her intelligence, sensitivity, and determination, she succeeds in spite of the odds against her. And by writing with such power, she lets the readers share her defeats and joys. She also teaches a vital lesson: with strength and persistence, all people can escape their cages—and sing their songs. 6

Work Cited

Angelou, Maya. I *Know Why the Caged Bird Sings*. Random House, 1969.

Student Paper: A Model Source-Based Essay

Here is a source-based essay written by a student for his English composition course. In this assignment, the student was asked to react to *The Essay on Self-Reliance* by Ralph Waldo Emerson. Notice how the essay incorporates quotations to support the student's claim. This essay is MLA formatted and shows a proper heading, headers, in-text citations, and "Works Cited" page.

Gafford 1

Harry Gafford

Professor Sharif

English Composition 1

5 Dec. 2019

Self-Reliance or How I Learned to Stop Worrying and

Achieve the American Dream by Being a Nonconformist

Over the years, many people have decided to pack up what they own and travel far and wide to the United States to become US citizens. In search of one thing, they leave behind the world they've known to move to the United States. That one thing they seek is a chance to achieve the American Dream. People of all kinds travel many miles from all around the world and endure many hardships, just for the chance of becoming one of the multitude of success stories. Many people who try to achieve the American Dream don't succeed; those who find success are paragons of the ideals put forth by Ralph Waldo Emerson's *The Essay on Self-Reliance*. By using Emerson's personal philosophy of devoted hard work, perseverance under adversity, and a willingness to become a nonconformist as a guide, anyone can work toward his or her version of the American Dream.

Hard work is something that doesn't come easily to anyone. One of Emerson's first principles is that the universe won't just hand out good; people must strive for it, as "no kernel of nourishing corn can come to him but through his toil

Book titles are written in italics.

Thesis statement that asserts a claim.

Gafford 2

bestowed on that plot of ground which is given to him to till" (10). Most people don't wake up with success or have it handed down from above. It comes through effort over time. One example of someone who has achieved great success through hard work is Ursula Burns, the former CEO of Xerox. She grew up in a housing project in New York City and was a good student, eventually attending Polytechnic Institute of New York and Columbia University. She began at Xerox as an intern in 1980 and after decades of pushing herself, became the CEO in 2009 (Mont). Nothing was just handed to Burns. She worked her way up through the chain of command, and her efforts continually got her noticed and promoted.

Connection: Notice the topic sentence reconnects with the thesis statement.

This leads to the second principle: hard work alone doesn't always bear fruit immediately; patience and perseverance are needed while people wait for their efforts to pay off. Stephen King is an example of someone who needed strong perseverance to get where he is. Before he became a famous author, King was a high school teacher and wrote in the evenings and on weekends. His first book, *Carrie*, was rejected thirty times (Jacques). Had King not persevered, Americans wouldn't know the wonderful, creepy characters of Pennywise, Cujo, Jack Torrance, and the very scary car, Christine. Despite reportedly wanting to give up, King kept trying and finally realized the success he deserved.

This information is written in the student's own words, but it originated from Renee Jacques's article. Because it is a paraphrase, the student doesn't need to use quotations, but he still needs to credit the original author.

Most important is Emerson's idea of nonconformity. A person who seeks the accomplishment embodied by the American Dream must be ready to tear down barriers and stand proudly above the masses. Most of the time, when someone attempts to carve out a path in society, he or she will find critics and skeptics rising to deter him or her from moving

Gafford 3

forward. Steve Jobs, cofounder of Apple Computer, Inc., and creator of the Macintosh line of personal computers, is a recent example. In the early 1980s, Jobs had a revolutionary idea to make computers easier to use by incorporating a simple visual interface with a mouse. Many dismissed the idea as a sales gimmick. After a few years, that idea changed the computing industry. That change established Steve Jobs as a leader of the computing world. He was "a nonconformist by nature" (Mishra) and not afraid to challenge the status quo and ignore disbelievers. Those who dare to achieve the American Dream must be ready to sail through a sea of critics. They must remain headstrong, dismiss the naysayers, and stray from the pack. The people who follow this philosophy will find the American Dream, while those who stay with the herd won't find success nearly as easily.

Becoming the embodiment of the American Dream is by no means easy. Those who want the dream must not be afraid to put their faith in Emerson and follow his personal philosophy, which is encapsulated in *The Essay on Self-Reliance*. A common thread among Ursula Burns, Stephen King, and Steve Jobs is that they are followers of the ideas penned by Emerson. They had a hearty devotion to hard work. They lived a life of perseverance, bouncing back after their failures. Lastly, they were willing to accept a path of nonconformity. People who are ready to achieve the American Dream must live the ideals of self-reliance and can thus themselves rise above the crowd.

Quotation: In this quotation, the student has cited the author's last name. As it is an online source (see "Works Cited"), no page number is necessary.

Thesis reasserted in conclusion.

Gafford 4

Works Cited

Emerson, Ralph Waldo. *The Essay on Self-Reliance.* The Roycrofters, 1908.

Jacques, Renee. "16 Wildly Successful People Who Overcame Huge Obstacles to Get There." *Huffpost*, 6 Dec. 2017, www .huffingtonpost.com/2013/09/25/successful-people-obstacles_ n_3964459.html. Accessed 28 Apr. 2018.

Mishra, Akansha. "Steve Jobs Embraced Life's Hardships." *The Independent Florida Alligator*, 14 Oct. 2011, www.alligator. org/opinion/columns/article_c0090004-f61d-11e0-8389- 001cc4c03286.html. Accessed 28 Apr. 2018.

Mont, Joe. "10 People Living the American Dream." *The Street*, 4 July 2011, www.thestreet.com/story/11173382/1/10-people-living-the- american-dream.html. Accessed 30 Apr. 2018.

EXPLORING WRITING ONLINE

©Tetra Images/Shutterstock

Visit the *Quotidiana* Web site at http://essays.quotidiana.org/ and select a short story to read. Read the story and write an essay that analyzes the story, like the model literary analysis, or uses the lessons in the story to connect to your life, like the model source-based essay.

TEXT CREDITS

Writing a Research Paper

©Images & Stories/Alamy Stock Photo

RESPONDING TO IMAGES

If you were to write a research paper on war, what would you focus on? War itself is too broad a topic to cover in one paper. You would need to select a more limited topic to write about—for example, the effect of war on the economy. Looking at the above photograph of American soldiers interacting with local people, can you think of some other limited topics you might cover in a research paper?

CHAPTER PREVIEW:

Step 1: Get Started by Creating a Schedule

Step 2: Select a Topic That You Can Readily Research

Step 3: Limit Your Topic and Make the Purpose of Your Paper Clear

Step 4: Brainstorm and Gather Information on Your Limited Topic

Step 5: Keep Track of Your Sources and Take Notes

Step 6: Write the Paper

Step 7: Create a "Works Cited" Page

A Model Research Paper

TEACHING TIP
Ask students to complete this writing prompt in class.

Writing a research essay will require many of the same skills as writing a source-based essay; however, it will also require good organization and time management. Many students who are assigned research papers find themselves running out of time because they spend too many hours trying to gather research, reading the research, or changing the focus of their papers at the last minute. This chapter will explain how to create a realistic schedule, organize your notes, and break down the writing of the essay into smaller, more manageable steps.

Step 1: Get Started by Creating a Schedule

Writing a research paper will require you to be very organized in order to complete all the steps necessary in a timely fashion. Getting started is often the hardest part. The inclination is that your paper isn't due for several weeks, so there is no rush to begin. This type of attitude can get you in trouble. Instead, you should figure out your schedule and get started as soon as you have been assigned the paper.

Creating an effective and realistic schedule is an important first step. It is best to work backward from the date your paper is due. You should always build in more time than you think it will take and have a contingency plan that will allow you to handle unexpected interruptions and changes. For instance, if your instructor gives you three weeks to produce a rough draft, with a final due date of May 3, 2019, you will want to map out a schedule to stay on track. First, fill in the due dates for the rough and final drafts. You will then want to work backward to make sure you allot enough time for research and drafting. A sample working schedule is shown here.

<u>Final Draft Due</u>	May 3, 2019
Edit	
Revise	
<u>Rough Draft Due</u>	April 26, 2019
Works Cited Created and Checked	
Rough Draft	
Outline	April 19, 2019
Bibliography Created and Checked	
Research Read and Annotated	April 15, 2019
Research Collected	
Create a Working Thesis	April 9, 2019
Limit the Topic	
Choose Topic	
Preliminary Research	April 7, 2019

Step 2: Select a Topic That You Can Readily Research

Many professors will assign a topic, but if you need to select your own topic, you will want to add time in your research schedule to find one that interests you enough to work with for an extended period of time. Remember, if your professor has given you a list of topics to avoid, don't waste your time trying to figure out a way to write about one of those topics.

To quickly find a topic that interests you and has enough material to work with, you should first consult your library resources. For example, if you initially choose the broad topic "parenting," try to find at least three academic resources on parenting. These sources could be current parenting books or journal articles on parenting.

If you decide you need more information and are planning to use the Internet or library, you may want to review Chapter 19, as it covers how to narrow search results, how to use better search engines like Google Scholar, and how to get help from librarians.

Step 3: Limit Your Topic and Make the Purpose of Your Paper Clear

Like any paper that is source-based, a research essay should *thoroughly* develop a *limited* topic. Your paper's length will determine how broad or narrow your topic will need to be. Therefore, as you read through books and articles, look for ways to limit your general topic.

For instance, the broad subject "death" could be reduced to euthanasia or the unfair pricing practices in some funeral homes. "Divorce" might be limited to its most damaging effects on the children of divorced parents; "stress in everyday life" could be narrowed to methods of reducing stress in the workplace.

Do not expect to limit your topic and make your purpose clear all at once. You may have to do quite a bit of reading as you work out a narrowed focus for your paper. Note that many research essays have one of two general purposes: (1) to defend a point—for example, to provide evidence that elected officials should serve no more than a single term; or (2) to present information—for example, to discuss the effects of diet on heart disease.

Step 4: Brainstorm and Gather Information on Your Limited Topic

Once you have narrowed your topic, you should brainstorm what you already know about the topic. This will help you focus your research and save you time. For instance, if you have chosen to write about problems students encounter in high school, you could reflect on your own experiences as well as the experiences of your friends. You might focus on problems in the classroom or social problems both inside and outside of school. You might even think about some of the problems you or your friends experienced on social media.

After you have a good sense of your limited topic, you can begin gathering relevant information. A helpful way to proceed is to sign out the books that you need from your library. In addition, make copies of all relevant articles from magazines, newspapers, or journals. If your library has an online periodicals database, you may be able to print out those articles.

In other words, take the steps needed to get all your key source materials together in one place. You can then sit and work on these materials in a quiet, unhurried way in your home or some other place of study.

Step 5: Keep Track of Your Sources and Take Notes

As you are researching, you need to keep careful and thorough track of your sources. As you learned in Chapter 20, "Working with Sources," doing this is important because you have to know where your information originates so that you can cite it properly. To keep track of your sources, you should create a bibliography—a list of everything you have read and consulted. This should be formatted just as a "Works Cited" page is formatted. To keep your print sources organized, you should staple your documents, so the individual pages don't get lost or mixed up. All print sources should be kept in a single folder that is dedicated to that writing assignment. To keep electronic sources organized, save each source as a separate document, and store all sources in one electronic folder that is dedicated to that writing assignment.

You will make use of your sources by creating a scratch outline and taking good notes in preparation for writing your essay. Chapter 2 and Chapter 20 provide detailed coverage of how to create a scratch outline and of the kinds of notes you should take.

Step 6: Write the Paper

After you have finished your reading and note-taking, you should have a fairly clear idea of the plan of your paper. Regardless of whether or not your instructor requires it, you should create an outline and use it as a guide to writing your first full draft. Your outline should build from your informal scratch outline, giving you a thorough, detailed roadmap and helping you to figure out where your research will best fit into your essay before you even begin writing.

You can prepare either a topic outline (thesis plus supporting words and phrases) or a sentence outline (complete sentences). As an example, a topic outline appears in the model essay at the end of this chapter. Note that roman numerals are used for first-level headings, capital letters for second-level headings, and Arabic numbers for third-level headings.

In an *introduction,* include a thesis statement expressing the purpose of your paper and indicate the plan of development that you will follow. The section on writing introductions for an essay (Chapter 17) is also appropriate for the introductory section of the research paper. Notice that the model research paper at the end of this chapter uses a two-paragraph introduction.

As you move from *introduction* to *main body* to *conclusion,* strive for unity, support, and coherence so that your paper will be clear and effective. Repeatedly ask, "Does each of my supporting paragraphs develop the thesis of my paper?" Use the checklist on the inside back cover of this book to make sure that your paper follows all four bases of effective writing.

Step 7: Create a "Works Cited" Page

To create a "Works Cited" page, go back to your working bibliography and read through your essay to note the sources that you used. As you encounter a source, check it off on your bibliography. Once you have checked off each source used, you can then refer to your notes to transfer those sources into a "Works Cited" page. This page will always be located at the end of your essay. Chapter 20 provides additional information about creating a "Works Cited" page.

A Model Research Paper

Successful Families:

Fighting for Their Kids

by

Sonya Philips

English 101

Professor Lessing

6 May 2019

Model Title Page

While the *MLA Handbook* does not require a title page or an outline for a paper, your instructor may ask you to include one or both. Here is a model title page.

The title should begin about one-third of the way down the page. Center the title. Double-space between lines of the title and your name. Also center and double-space the instructor's name and the date.

1 inch

1/2 inch

Philips 1

Sonya Philips

Professor Lessing

English 101

6 May 2019

Successful Families: Fighting for Their Kids

It's a terrible time to be a teenager, or even a teenager's parent. That message is everywhere. Television, magazines, and newspapers are all full of frightening stories about teenagers and families. They say that America's families are falling apart, that kids don't care about anything, and that parents have trouble doing anything. . . .

Model First Page of MLA-Style Paper

Papers written in MLA style use the simple format shown here. There is no title page or outline.

Double-space all 4 lines

Double-space between lines. Leave a one-inch margin on all sides.

Model Outline Page

Use this format if your instructor asks you to submit an outline of your paper.

After the title page, number all pages in the upper-right corner, a half-inch from the top. Place your name before the page number. Use small roman numerals on outline pages. Use arabic numerals on pages following the outline.

The word *Outline* (without underlining or quotation marks) is centered one inch from the top. Double-space between lines. Leave a one-inch margin on all sides.

TEACHING TIP
Consider using this model paper for a scavenger hunt. For example, ask students to find an in-text citation, a direct quote, and a "Works Cited" entry for a Web site.

Philips i

Outline

Thesis: Although these are difficult times to be raising teenagers, successful families are finding ways to cope with the challenges.

I.   Meeting the challenge of spending quality time together

    A.   Barriers to spending quality time

        1.   Increased working hours

        2.   Rising divorce rates

        3.   Women in workforce

    B.   Danger of lack of quality time

    C.   Ways found to spend time together

        1.   Working less and scaling back lifestyle

        2.   Home schooling

II. Meeting the challenge of creating sense of community

    A.   Lack of traditional community ties

    B.   Ways found to create sense of community

        1.   Intentional communities

        2.   Religious ties

III. Meeting the challenge of limiting the negative impact of media and technology

    A.   Negative impact of media and technology

        1.   Creation of environment without protection

        2.   Flood of uncontrolled, inappropriate information

    B.   Ways of controlling media and technology

        1.   Banning TV

        2.   Using technology in beneficial ways

Philips 1

Successful Families: Fighting for Their Kids

It's a terrible time to be a teenager or even a teenager's parent. That message is everywhere. Television, magazines, and newspapers are all full of frightening stories about teenagers and families. They say that America's families are falling apart, that kids don't care about anything, and that parents have trouble doing anything about it. Bookstores are full of disturbing titles like these: *Parenting Your Out-of-Control Teenager, Teenage Wasteland, Unhappy Teenagers,* and *Teen Torment.* These books describe teenage problems that include apathy, violence, suicide, sexual abuse, depression, loss of values, poor mental health, crime, gang involvement, and drug and alcohol addiction.

Naturally, caring parents are worried by all this. Their worry showed in a 2002 national poll in which 76% of parents said that raising children was "a lot harder" than it was when they were growing up (Farkas). But just as most popular TV shows don't give a realistic view of American teens, these frightening books and statistics do not provide a complete picture of what's going on in families today. The fact is that not all teens and families are lost and without values. While they struggle with problems in our culture like everyone else, successful families are doing what they've always done: finding ways to protect and nurture their children. They are fighting the battle for their families in three ways: by fighting against the loss of

Here is a full model paper. It assumes the writer has included a title page.

Double-space between lines of the text. Leave a one-inch margin all the way around the page. Your name and page number should be one-half inch from the top of the page.

Common knowledge is not documented.

This typical citation shows the source by giving the author's last name or (if no author is provided) the title of the article (and if relevant, a page number). "Works Cited" then provides full information about the source.

Thesis, followed by plan of development.

Philips 2

Source is identified by name and area of expertise.

quality family time, by fighting against the loss of community,

and by fighting against the influence of the media.

It's true that these days, parents face more challenges than

ever before when it comes to finding quality time to spend with

their children. The economist Edward Wolff explains the loss of

time:

Direct quotations of four typed lines or more are indented five spaces (or one-half inch) from the left margin. Quotation marks are not used.

> Over a thirty-year time span, parental time has declined
>
> 13%. The time parents have available for their children has
>
> been squeezed by the rapid shift of mothers into the paid
>
> labor force, by escalating divorce rates and the subsequent
>
> abandonment of children by their fathers, and by an
>
> increase in the number of hours required on the job. The
>
> average worker is now at work 163 hours a year more than
>
> in 1969, which adds up to an extra month of work annually.
>
> (qtd. in Hewlett and West 48)

The abbreviation *qtd.* means *quoted*. No comma is used between the author's names and the page number.

As a result, more children are at home alone than ever before.

And this situation does leave children vulnerable to getting into

trouble. Richardson and others, in their study of five thousand

eighth-graders in California, found that children who were

home alone after school were twice as likely to experiment

with drugs and alcohol as children who had a parent (or

another adult) home in the after-school hours.

When citing a work in general, not part of a work, it is best to include the author's name in the text instead of using a parenthetical citation. No page number is needed, as the citation refers to the findings of the study overall.

But creative parents still come up with ways to be there for

their kids. For some, it's been a matter of cutting back on

working hours and living more simply. For example, in her

book *The Shelter of Each Other*, Mary Pipher tells the story of

a couple with three-year-old twin boys. Eduardo worked sixty-

hour weeks at a factory. Sabrina supervised checkers at a

K-Mart, cared for the boys, and tried to watch over her mother,

who had cancer. Money was tight, especially since day care

Philips 3

was expensive and the parents felt they had to keep the twins stylishly dressed and supplied with new toys. The parents were stressed over money problems, their lack of time together, and especially having so little time with their boys. It bothered them that the twins had begun to cry when their parents picked them up at day care, as if they'd rather stay with the day-care workers. Finally, Sabrina and Eduardo made a difficult decision. Sabrina quit her job, and the couple invited her mother (whose illness was in remission) to live with them. With three adults pooling their resources, Sabrina and Eduardo found that they could manage without Sabrina's salary. The family no longer ate out, and they gave up their cable TV. Their sons loved having their grandmother in the house. Sabrina was able to begin doing relaxed, fun projects with the boys. They planted a garden and built a sandbox together. Sabrina observed, "I learned I could get off the merry-go-round" (195). Other parents have "gotten off the merry-go-round" by working at home, even if it means less money than they had previously.

> Only the page number is needed, as the author has already been named in the text.

Some parents even home-school their children as a way to be sure they have plenty of time together. Home schooling used to be thought of as a choice made only by very religious people or back-to-nature radicals. Now, teaching children at home is much less unusual. It's estimated that as many as 2 million American children are being home-schooled. Harvard even has an admissions officer whose job it is to review applications from home-schooled kids. Parents who home-school have different reasons, but according to a cover story in *Newsweek*, "Some . . . are looking for a way to reclaim family closeness in an increasingly fast-paced society. . . . Still others worry about unsavory influences in school—drugs, alcohol, sex, violence"

> When omitting a word or words from a quotation, indicate the deleted word or words by using ellipsis marks, which are three periods (. . .). In this instance, the fourth period represents the end of the sentence.

Philips 4

(Kantrowitz and Wingert 66). Home schooling is no guarantee that a child will resist those temptations, but some families do believe it's a great way to promote family closeness. One fifteen-year-old, home-schooled since kindergarten, explained why he liked the way he'd been raised and educated. He ended by saying, "Another way I'm different is that I love my family. One guy asked me if I'd been brainwashed. I think it's spooky that liking my family is considered crazy" (Pipher 103).

Many parents can't quit their jobs or teach their children at home. But some parents find a second way to nurture their children, through building community ties. They help their children develop a healthy sense of belonging by creating links with positive, constructive people and activities. In the past, community wasn't so hard to find. In *The Way We Really Are*, Stephanie Coontz writes, "Right up through the 1940s, ties of work, friendship, neighborhood, ethnicity, extended kin, and voluntary organizations were as important a source of identity for most Americans, and sometimes a *more* important source of obligation, than marriage and the nuclear family" (37). Even when today's parents were teenagers, neighborhoods were places where kids felt a sense of belonging and responsibility. But today "parents . . . mourn the disappearance of neighborhoods where a web of relatives and friends kept a close eye on everyone's kids. And they worry their own children grow up isolated, knowing more about the cast of *Friends* than the people in surrounding homes" (Donahue D1).

One way that some families are trying to build old-fashioned community is through "intentional community" or "cohousing." Begun in Denmark in 1972, the cohousing movement is modeled after the traditional village. It brings together a number of families

Ellipses show where the student has omitted material from the original source. The quoted material is not capitalized because the student has blended it into a sentence with an introductory phrase.

Philips 5

who live in separate houses but share some common space. For instance, families might share central meeting rooms, dining areas, gardens, day care, workshops, or office space. They might own tools and lawn mowers together, rather than each household having its own. The point is that they treat their neighbors as extended family, not as strangers. As described on the site *The Cohousing Association of the United States*, cohousing is "a type of collaborative housing that attempts to overcome the alienation of modern subdivisions in which no one knows their neighbors, and there is no sense of community." In its 2010 directory, the Fellowship for Intentional Communities organization estimates that "several thousand" such communities exist in North America.

Other families turn to religion as a source of community. Michael Medved and Diane Medved, authors of *Saving Childhood*, are raising their family in a religious Jewish home. Their children attend Jewish schools, go to synagogue, and follow religious customs. They frequently visit, eat, play with, and are cared for by neighboring Jewish families. The Medveds believe their family is stronger because of their belief "in planting roots—in your home, in your family, in your community. That involves making a commitment, making an investment both physically and emotionally, in your surroundings" (200). Other religious traditions offer families a similar sense of community, purpose, and belonging. Marcus and Tracy Glover are members of the Nation of Islam. They credit the Nation with making their marriage and family strong and breaking a three-generation cycle of single motherhood (Hewlett and West 201–02).

A third way that families are fighting to protect their children is by controlling the impact of the media and

Cited material extends from one page to another, so both page numbers are given.

technology. Hewlett and West and Pipher use similar words to describe this impact. As they describe growing up today, Hewlett and West write about children living "without a skin" (xiii), and Pipher writes about "houses without walls" (12). These authors mean that today—unlike in the old days when children were protected from the outside world while they were in their homes—the home offers little protection. Even in their own living rooms, all children have to do is to turn on a TV, radio, or computer to be hit with a flood of violence, sick humor, and often weird sexuality. Children are growing up watching shows like *The Osbournes,* a program that celebrated two spoiled, foul-mouthed children and their father—a burnt-out rock star slowed by years of carefree drug abuse. A recent article in *Science* magazine offered the most damning link yet between TV watching and antisocial behavior. Reporting on the results of its seventeen-year study that followed viewers from youth to adulthood, *Science* found that the more television a teen watched, the higher the chances he or she would commit violent acts later in life. Of kids who watched an hour or less TV a day, fewer than 6% of teens went on to commit assaults, robberies, or other violent acts as adults. But nearly 28% of teens who watched TV three or more hours a day did commit crimes of violence (Anderson and Bushman 2377–79). Sadly many parents seem to have given up even trying to protect their growing kids against the flood of televised garbage. They are like the mother quoted in *USA Today* as saying, "How can I fight five hundred channels on TV?" (Donahue D1).

Fortunately, some parents are still insisting on control over the information and entertainment that comes into their homes.

Some ban TV entirely from their homes. More try to find a way to use TV and other electronics as helpful tools, but not allow them to dominate their homes. One family in Nebraska, the Millers, who home-school their children, described to Mary Pipher their attitude toward TV. They hadn't owned a TV for years, but they bought one so that they could watch the Olympics. The set is now stored in a closet unless a program is on that the family agrees is worthwhile. Some programs the Millers have enjoyed together include the World Cup soccer games, the TV drama *Sarah Plain and Tall*, and an educational TV course in sign language. Pipher was impressed by the Miller children, and she thought their limited exposure to TV was one reason why. In Pipher's words:

> Calm, happy children and relaxed, confident parents are so rare today. Probably most notable were the long attention spans of the children and their willingness to sit and listen to the grown-ups talk. The family had a manageable amount of information to deal with. They weren't stressed by more information than they could assimilate. The kids weren't overstimulated and edgy. Nor were they sexualized in the way most kids now are. (107)

Pipher's words describe children raised by parents who won't give in to the idea that their children are lost. Such parents structure ways to be present in the home, build family ties to a community, and control the impact of the media in their homes. Through their efforts, they succeed in raising nurtured, grounded, successful children. Such parents acknowledge the challenges of raising kids in today's America, but they are up to the job.

The conclusion provides a summary and restates the thesis.

"Works Cited" entries should be double-spaced and should always appear on a separate, titled page.

Titles of books, magazines, and the like should be italicized.

Include a complete URL for all online sources.

Include the date you accessed a Web source if no publication or posting date is available for that source.

Philips 8

Works Cited

Anderson, Craig A., and Brad J. Bushman. "The Effects of Media Violence on Society." *Science,* 29 Mar. 2002, pp. 2377–79.

"Communities Directory." *Fellowship for Intentional Community,* www.ic.org/directory. Accessed 25 Apr. 2012.

Coontz, Stephanie. *The Way We Really Are.* Basic Books, 1997.

Donahue, Deirdre. "Struggling to Raise Good Kids in Toxic Times." *USA Today,* 1 Oct. 1998, pp. D1+.

Farkas, Steve, et al. "A Lot Easier Said Than Done: Parents Talk about Raising Children in Today's America." *Public Agenda,* State Farm Companies Foundation / Public Agenda, 2002, www.publicagenda.org/files/easier_said_than_done.pdf.

Hewlett, Sylvia Ann, and Cornel West. *The War against Parents: What We Can Do for America's Beleaguered Moms and Dads.* Houghton Mifflin, 1998.

Kantrowitz, Barbara, and Pat Wingert. "Learning at Home: Does It Pass the Test?" *Newsweek,* 5 Oct. 1998, pp. 64–70.

Medved, Michael, and Diane Medved. *Saving Childhood: Protecting Our Children from the National Assault on Innocence.* HarperCollins, 1998.

Pipher, Mary. *The Shelter of Each Other.* Ballantine Books, 1997.

"What Is Cohousing?" *The Cohousing Association of the United States,* 4 Oct. 2011, www.cohousing.org/what_is_cohousing.

RESPONDING TO IMAGES

Although the student writer of the research paper emphasized the impact of TV on children, she referred to the computer as another source of "violence, sick humor, and often weird sexuality." In your opinion, which do you feel is more dangerous for children when unsupervised, the computer or the TV? Why?

©Onoky Photography/Glow Images

EXPLORING WRITING ONLINE

Visit the *Plagiarism.org* Web site at http://www.plagiarism.org to learn more about what plagiarism is and how to avoid it. Read the section "Understanding Plagiarism," and then write a paragraph about this issue using a pattern of development, such as cause and/or effect, comparison and/or contrast, or argumentation. If you reference the Web site, be sure to avoid plagiarism yourself.

©Tetra Images/ Shutterstock

TEACHING TIP
Demonstrate one or more online citation generators to your students, expressing that relying on an online source does not take the place of using a reputable textbook or handbook.

A WRITER'S TEMPLATE: Across Disciplines

As you are reading the following essay written by Sanaa for her developmental writing class, think about what advice you would offer her as she writes her final draft. Does her essay cover all four bases of effective writing and reflect accurate incorporation of research and citations? To be sure, use the checklist that follows.

Junk Food's Adverse Effects

[1]Many students don't understand the harmful effects that junk food can have on the body. [2]In 2012, when the federal mandate changed the kinds of foods offered in school cafeterias, many students became upset. [3]They didn't like the fact that the foods they had enjoyed were no longer available in their schools. [4]This is because they didn't understand that the food they were eating was harming their bodies. [5]Eating unhealthy foods and junk food can lead to depression, obesity, and diabetes.

[6]One symptom of eating too many unhealthy foods is depression. [7]Children need healthy foods because their bodies require the nutrients to grow stronger, and without proper nutrition, the body doesn't function properly. [8]A study by the University of Las Palmas de Gran Canaria and the University of Granada found that people who eat junk food and "fast food . . . are 51% more likely to develop depression" (Plataforma). [9]Depression can lead to other problems like addiction, isolation, and suicide.

[10]Another harmful effect of eating too much junk food is obesity. [11]Once a rare condition, it has become common. [12]In fact, "over two-thirds of adults are overweight or obese, and one in three Americans is obese" (Balentine). [13]The Centers for Disease Control and Prevention states "childhood obesity is a serious problem in the United States" and findings show that obesity among teenagers was 20.5% between 2011 and 2014 ("Childhood Obesity Facts"). [14]There are a lot of kids in my school who are obese. [15]Obesity is at the top of the list of the many problems in the United States and being obese can lead to other health problems like heart disease, breathing problems, and high blood pressure.

[16]A third health issue that can result from eating unhealthy food is diabetes. [17]Obesity can lead to insulin resistance. [18]It is a main cause of diabetes. [19]Because people who are obese have more fatty tissue, their cells can become resistant to insulin. [20]Getting in the way of insulin's role in lowering blood sugar. (Mayo Clinic) [21]The problems that can stem from diabetes range from nerve damage to vision problems to death.

[22]While the mandate in 2012 was not popular, and was eventually overturned, it did increase awareness of what children are eating each day in their school cafeterias. [23]It also raised awareness of how these food choices can lead to depression, epidemic obesity, and the rise in diabetes.

Works Cited

Plataforma SINC. "Link between fast food and depression confirmed." *ScienceDaily*, 30 March 2012, www.sciencedaily.com/releases/2012/03/120330081352.htm.

Balentine, Jerry R. "Obesity Symptoms, Causes, Treatment: How Common Is Obesity?" *MedicineNet*, www.medicinenet.com/obesity_weight_loss/article.htm#what_causes_obesity. Accessed 8 March 2019.

"Childhood Obesity Facts." *Centers for Disease Control and Prevention*, 10 April, 2017, www.cdc.gov/obesity/data/childhood.html.

"Type 2 Diabetes." *Mayo Clinic*, 2018, www.webmd.com/depression/guide/untreated-depression-effects#1. Accessed 8 March 2019.

A WRITER'S CHECKLIST

Unity

✔ The thesis statement can be found in sentence number __5__ .

✔ Does all the information in the essay help support the thesis? No. Sentence 14 should be deleted in the interest of unity.

Support

✔ Does Sanaa provide specific evidence for each point? Yes

✔ What two methods of incorporating sources does Sanaa use in sentence 13? a direct quotation and a paraphrase

✔ Does Sanaa properly document her information? No, her citation in sentence 20 is incorrect and should say ("Type 2 Diabetes") and the period should come after the citation.

✔ Is Sanaa's "Works Cited" page properly formatted? No. She has listed her sources in the order she used them rather than alphabetical order. Also, entries should be double-spaced, with no extra space between entries.

Coherence

✔ Does Sanaa use transitions and other connective devices between paragraphs? Yes

If so, list them here: One symptom, Another, A third

Sentence Skills

✔ Can you find any sentence skills mistakes, as listed on the inside back cover of the book? Sentence 15 is a run-on, and sentence 20 is a fragment.

Introduction and/or Conclusion

✔ Does Sanaa have a satisfactory conclusion? No. If not, what would you suggest Sanaa does to improve her conclusion? The conclusion has only two sentences and should be developed a bit more.

Collaborative Activity
In your group or class, work together to fix the documentation errors. Then, look up her sources to decide if she used credible sources to support her claims.

©Jacob Lund/
Shutterstock

PART **6** Handbook of Sentence Skills

SECTION I
Grammar

SECTION II
Mechanics

SECTION III
Punctuation

SECTION IV
Word Use

SECTION V
Tests

PART SIX WILL

- explain the basic skills needed to write clear, error-free sentences

- provide numerous activities so that you can practice these skills enough to make them habits

- contain editing tests at the end of each section to offer additional practice activities

- provide editing tests at the end of the Part to offer an opportunity to review overall sentence-skills knowledge

EXPLORING WRITING PROMPT:
College writing requires accuracy and correctness in grammar, mechanics, punctuation, and word use—all of which are covered in Part Six. However, we are seeing more and more examples of incorrect writing in shop windows, on bulletin boards, in posters that advertise concerts or movies, in restaurant menus, or in product advertisements. We also experience inaccurate use of English in music, on television, and in the movies.

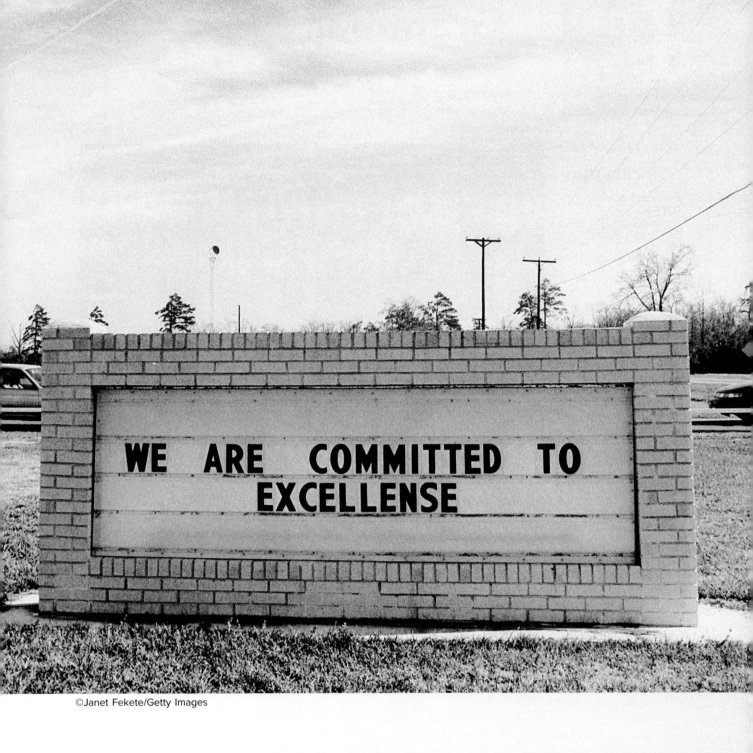

©Janet Fekete/Getty Images

Keep a list of such examples in a notebook or in your journal over a seven-day period. You can start with the sign pictured above. What sentence-skills mistake do you notice? Then, find an article online on any popular subject or activity that interests you. Rewrite it, correcting errors in grammar, mechanics, punctuation, and especially word use. If possible, condense the article by using fewer words than the original.

Grammar

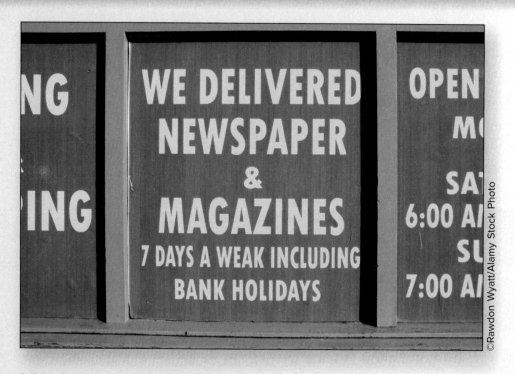

©Rawdon Wyatt/Alamy Stock Photo

RESPONDING TO IMAGES

Can you find the grammar errors in the sign above? What could be done to make the sign grammatically correct?

Subjects and Verbs

The basic building blocks of English sentences are subjects and verbs. Understanding them is an important first step toward mastering a number of sentence skills.

Every sentence has a subject and a verb. Who or what the sentence speaks about is called the *subject;* what the sentence says about the subject is called the *verb.* In the following sentences, the subject is underlined once and the verb twice.

The <u>boy</u> <u><u>cried</u></u>.

That <u>fish</u> <u><u>smells</u></u>.

Many <u>people</u> <u><u>applied</u></u> for the job.

The <u>show</u> <u><u>is</u></u> a documentary.

A Simple Way to Find a Subject

To find a subject, ask *who* or *what* the sentence is about. As shown below, your answer is the subject.

Who is the first sentence about? The <u>boy</u>

What is the second sentence about? That <u>fish</u>

Who is the third sentence about? Many <u>people</u>

What is the fourth sentence about? The <u>show</u>

A Simple Way to Find a Verb

To find a verb, ask what the sentence *says about* the subject. As shown below, your answer is the verb.

What does the first sentence *say about* the boy? He <u><u>cried</u></u>.

What does the second sentence *say about* the fish? It <u><u>smells</u></u>.

What does the third sentence *say about* the people? They <u><u>applied</u></u>.

What does the fourth sentence *say about* that show? It <u><u>is</u></u> a documentary.

CHAPTER PREVIEW

A Simple Way to Find a Subject

A Simple Way to Find a Verb

More about Subjects and Verbs

TEACHING TIP
Bring a photo of a DNA molecule to class. Tell your students that just as amino acids are the building blocks of DNA, subjects and verbs are the building blocks of sentences.

TEACHING TIP
In groups, have students brainstorm a list of nouns. Then have them brainstorm a list of verbs. Now ask them to create several sentences using these nouns, which will function as subjects and verbs. Encourage everyone to be creative.

ESL NOTE
Discuss the differences between English and other languages in terms of word order, usage of subject pronouns, and verb forms. In some languages, a verb does not require a subject pronoun. In other languages, the verb precedes the subject. In still other languages, there are no inflections on verbs.

A second way to find the verb is to put *I, you, we, he, she, it,* or *they* in front of the word you think is a verb. If the result makes sense, you have a verb. For example, you could put *he* in front of *cried* in the first sentence, with the result, *he cried,* making sense. Therefore, you know that *cried* is a verb. You could use the same test with the other three verbs as well.

Finally, it helps to remember that most verbs show action. In the sentences already considered, the three action verbs are *cried, smells,* and *applied.* Certain other verbs, known as *linking verbs,* do not show action. They do, however, give information about the subject. In "The show is a documentary," the linking verb *is* joins the subject (*show*) with a word that identifies or describes it (*documentary*). Other common linking verbs include *am, are, was, were, feel, appear, look, become,* and *seem.*

| ACTIVITY 1 | In each of the following sentences, draw one line under the subject and two lines under the verb. |

1. The children's abandoned toys collected dust in the attic.
2. Long-distance running requires mental and physical discipline.
3. Maddy sprained her ankle while playing beach volleyball.
4. My roommate owes me money for this month's rent.
5. A cockroach scampered across the kitchen floor.
6. The patient's lab results arrived in the mail.
7. My ex-husband called me yesterday.
8. On New Year's Day, my grandmother prepared traditional Japanese *ozoni* soup.
9. Sarah's mother visits her grandchildren every summer.
10. During the winter season, everyone needs a flu shot.

More about Subjects and Verbs

1. A sentence may have more than one verb, more than one subject, or several subjects and verbs.

   The engine coughed and sputtered.

   Broken glass and empty cans littered the parking lot.

   Marta, Nilsa, and Robert met after class and headed downtown.

2. The subject and verb of the sentence never appear within a prepositional phrase. A *prepositional phrase* is simply a group of words that begins with a preposition. Following is a list of the more commonly used prepositions.

Prepositions				
about	before	despite	into	throughout
above	behind	down	like	to
across	below	during	near	toward
after	beneath	except	of	under
against	beside	far	off	underneath
along	between	for	on, onto	until
among	beyond	from	out	up
around	by	in	over	upon
as	concerning	including	since	with
at	considering	inside	through	without

Crossing out prepositional phrases will help you find the subject or subjects of a sentence.

A stream of cold air seeps in through the space below the door.

Specks of dust dance gently in a ray of sunlight.

The people in the apartment above ours fight loudly.

The murky waters of the polluted lake spilled over the dam.

The amber lights on its sides outlined the tractor-trailer in the hazy dusk.

3. Many verbs consist of more than one word. (The extra verbs are called *auxiliary,* or *helping,* verbs.) Here, for example, are some of the many forms of the verb *work.*

Forms of *work*		
work	worked	should work
works	were working	will be working
does work	have worked	can work
is working	had worked	could be working
are working	had been working	must have worked

4. Words like *not, just, never, only,* and *always* are not part of the verb, although they may appear within the verb.

Ruby has never liked cold weather.

Our boss will not be singing with the choir this year.

The intersection has not always been this dangerous.

TEACHING TIP
You may want to explain to students that a prepositional phrase provides specific details about position or movement. Ask students to identify prepositions that describe position (for example, "behind") and ones that describe movement (for example, "during").

TEACHING TIP
For added practice, have students identify the many forms of the verb "talk."

ESL NOTE
Using correct verb tenses and forms is very confusing for nonnative speakers. Have students identify the verb tenses for each of the forms in the box.

TEACHING TIP
Introduce students to infinitives, which are verbs preceded by the preposition to. Remind students that an infinitive is not the main verb of a sentence.

5. A verb preceded by *to* is never the verb of a sentence.

   At night, my son likes to read under the covers.

   Eve decided to separate from her husband.

6. An *-ing* word by itself is never the verb of a sentence. (It may be part of the verb, but it must have a helping verb in front of it.)

   They going on a trip this weekend.

   (not a sentence, because the verb is not complete)

   They are going on a trip this weekend. (a sentence)

ACTIVITY 2	Draw a single line under subjects and a double line under verbs. Cross out prepositional phrases as necessary to find the subjects.

TEACHING TIP
For added practice, ask students to circle the infinitives in this activity.

1. A thick layer of dust covers the top of our refrigerator.

2. In June, sagging Christmas decorations were still hanging in the windows of the abandoned house.

3. The people in the all night coffee shop seemed weary and lost.

4. Every plant in the dim room bent toward the small window.

5. A glaring headline about the conviction of a local congressman attracted my attention.

6. Two of the biggest stores in the mall are going out of business.

7. The battery tester's tiny red lights suddenly started to flicker.

8. A neighbor of mine does all her work at home and e-mails it to her office.

9. The jar of peppercorns tumbled from the spice shelf and shattered on the floor.

10. The scar in the hollow of Jon's throat is the result of an emergency operation to clear his windpipe.

REVIEW TEST

TEACHING TIP
You may want to use this review test to assess what your students have learned.

(Academic)

Draw a single line under the subjects and a double line under the verbs. Note that many sentences have multiple subjects and multiple verbs. Cross out prepositional phrases as necessary to find the subjects.

1. John Muir is known as the "Father of the National Park Service."

2. Muir was born in Scotland, but his family moved to the United States in 1849.

3. As a freshman at the University of Wisconsin, he studied chemistry, but was soon introduced to botany.

4. In 1866, Muir moved to Indianapolis for a job in a factory, and his life was changed forever.

5. As Muir was working on a machine, a tool slipped and struck Muir in the eye.

6. After his remarkable recovery, Muir realized that he should follow his dreams of study and exploration.

7. In 1867, Muir embarked on a 1,000-mile journey from Indianapolis to Florida, where he studied the flora and fauna, met people, and learned about America.

8. After his long walk, Muir sailed to San Francisco and immediately traveled to Yosemite.

9. His experience in Yosemite and Ralph Waldo Emerson's essays on nature inspired Muir.

10. He published articles about his experiences.

11. After Yosemite, Muir traveled to Utah, Alaska, and Mt.Rainier.

12. With the importance of the natural world in mind, Muir convinced President Roosevelt that Yosemite, Mt. Rainier, and the Grand Canyon must be protected.

13. In 1890, 1500 acres of Yosemite were established as preserved land.

14. This paved the way for the creation of over fifty protected parks now within the United States National Park System.

Sentence Sense

TEACHING TIP
Have your students define what the word *instinct* means. Encourage them to find examples, such as the "fight or flight" instinct.

TEACHING TIP
Get students to talk about past school experiences that were "unrewarding or unpleasant" and how those experiences affect their sentence sense.

ESL NOTE
Nonnative students' "sentence sense" will be derived from their first language. Ask students to compare their native language to English. Not only will ESL students benefit from this discussion, but native students will develop an understanding of cultural diversity in languages.

What Is Sentence Sense?

As a speaker of English, you already possess the most important of all sentence skills. You have *sentence sense*—an instinctive feel for where a sentence begins, where it ends, and how it can be developed. You learned sentence sense automatically and naturally, as part of learning the English language, and you have practiced it through all the years that you have been speaking English. It is as much a part of you as your ability to speak and understand English is a part of you.

Sentence sense can help you recognize and avoid fragments and run-ons, two of the most common and most serious sentence-skills mistakes in written English. Sentence sense will also help you to properly place commas and spot awkward and unclear phrasing. Many of the following chapters will give you detailed practice using commas correctly, avoiding fragments and run-ons, and creating clarity.

Sentence sense can also assist you in adding variety to your sentences, by helping you determine how many simple sentences, compound sentences, and complex sentences you should use to create a well-developed, coherent paragraph. Too many simple sentences—sentences that contain one independent clause—can create a choppy-sounding paragraph. Adding compound sentences—sentences that contain two or more independent clauses—can take some of the choppiness out of your paragraph. Additionally, complex sentences—sentences that contain one independent clause and one or more dependent clauses—can make your paragraph flow better while adding needed variety. Chapter 4, "The Third and Fourth Steps in Writing," offers additional background information as well as suggestions for creating good compound and complex sentences.

You may ask, "If I already have this 'sentence sense,' why do I still make mistakes in punctuating sentences?" One answer could be that your past school experiences in writing were unrewarding or unpleasant. English courses may have been a series of dry writing topics and heavy doses of "correct" grammar and usage, or they may have given no attention at all to sentence skills. For any of these reasons, or perhaps for other reasons, the instinctive sentence skills you practice while speaking may turn off when you start writing. The very act of picking up a pen may shut down your natural system of language abilities and skills.

Turning On Your Sentence Sense

Chances are that you don't *read a paper aloud* after you write it, or you don't do the next best thing: read it "aloud" in your head. But reading aloud is essential to turn on the natural language system within you. By reading aloud, you will be able to hear the points where your sentences begin and end. In addition, you will be able to pick up any trouble spots where your thoughts are not communicated clearly and well.

The activities that follow will help you turn on and rediscover the enormous language power within you. You will be able to see how your built-in sentence sense can guide your writing just as it guides your speaking.

Each item that follows lacks basic punctuation. There is no period to mark the end of one sentence and no capital letter to mark the start of the next. Read each item aloud (or in your head) so that you "hear" where each sentence begins and ends. Your voice will tend to drop and pause at the point of each sentence break. Draw a light slash mark (/) at every point where you hear a break. Then go back and read the item a second time. If you are now sure of each place where a split occurs, insert a period and change the first small letter after it to a capital. Minor pauses are often marked in English by commas; these are already inserted. Part of item 1 is done for you as an example.

1. I take my dog for a walk on Saturdays in the big park by the lake. I do this very early in the morning before children come to the park. That way I can let my dog run freely. He jumps out the minute I open the car door and soon sees the first innocent squirrel. Then he is off like a shot and doesn't stop running for at least half an hour.

2. When Nico first started college, he did not know what major to pursue. At first, he wanted to become a computer software engineer, but he struggled in his math classes. A counselor suggested that he might think about entering a technical program since he is skilled with his hands. For instance, last summer he helped his neighbors renovate their kitchen and bathroom. He also assisted in the building of a house through Habitat for Humanity. Now Nico is considering the carpentry technology program.

3. When I sit down to write, my mind is blank. All I can think of is my name, which seems to me the most boring name in the world. Often I get sleepy and tell myself I should take a short nap. Other times I start daydreaming about things I want to buy. Sometimes I decide I should make a telephone call to someone I know. The piece of paper in front of me is usually still blank when I leave to watch my favorite television show.

4. One of the biggest regrets of my life is that I never told my father I loved him. I resented the fact that he had never been able to say the words "I love you" to his children. Even during the long period of my father's

illness, I remained silent and unforgiving. $\overset{T}{\cancel{t}}$hen one morning he was dead, with my words left unspoken. $\overset{A}{\cancel{a}}$ guilt I shall never forget tore a hole in my heart. I determined not to hold in my feelings with my daughters. $\overset{T}{\cancel{t}}$hey know they are loved, because I both show and tell them this. $\overset{A}{\cancel{a}}$ll people, no matter who they are, want to be told that they are loved.

5. A month ago, Christina decided to become a vegetarian. $\overset{S}{\cancel{s}}$he never really liked meat all that much, except for an occasional hamburger or grilled steak. $\overset{S}{\cancel{s}}$he decided to give up meat because she read about the health benefits that a vegetarian lifestyle could provide. $\overset{A}{\cancel{a}}$lso, she knew that eating more fruits, vegetables, and grains would be beneficial. $\overset{S}{\cancel{s}}$ome of her friends asked if she opposed the killing of animals, which she had not considered. $\overset{E}{\cancel{e}}$verything was going well for Christina and her new lifestyle. $\overset{S}{\cancel{s}}$he began to try new recipes, shop at the local farmers' market, and even feel more energetic. $\overset{T}{\cancel{t}}$hen last Saturday she went out to dinner at an Italian restaurant with her friends. $\overset{W}{\cancel{w}}$ithout thinking, Christina ordered her favorite item on the menu, Shrimp Scampi. $\overset{A}{\cancel{a}}$fter she was halfway through her meal, one of her friends said, "Christina, you're eating meat!" $\overset{S}{\cancel{s}}$he was stunned for she had completely forgotten about being a vegetarian. $\overset{S}{\cancel{s}}$he felt disappointed in herself, especially since there were several vegetarian pasta dishes on the menu. $\overset{O}{\cancel{o}}$ne of her friends smiled nonchalantly and said, "Don't worry, Christina, you're a pescatarian—someone who's mostly a vegetarian but occasionally eats fish and seafood." Christina smiled and happily finished her meal.

Summary: Using Sentence Sense

You probably did well in locating the end stops in these selections—proving to yourself that you *do* have sentence sense. This instinctive sense will help you deal with fragments and run-ons, perhaps the two most common sentence-skills mistakes.

Remember the importance of *reading your paper aloud.* By reading aloud, you turn on the natural language skills that come from all your experience of speaking English. The same sentence sense that helps you communicate effectively in speaking will help you communicate effectively in writing.

Fragments

Every sentence must have a subject and a verb and must express a complete thought. A word group that lacks a subject or a verb and does not express a complete thought is a *fragment*. Following are the most common types of fragments that people write:

1. Dependent-word fragments
2. *-ing* and *to* fragments
3. Added-detail fragments
4. Missing-subject fragments

Once you understand what specific kinds of fragments you might write, you should be able to eliminate them from your writing. The following pages explain all four types.

Dependent-Word Fragments

Some word groups that begin with a dependent word are fragments. Following is a list of common dependent words. Whenever you start a sentence with one of these words, you must be careful that a fragment does not result.

Dependent Words		
after	if, even if	when, whenever
although, though	in order that	where, wherever
as	since	whether
because	that, so that	which, whichever
before	unless	while
even though	until	who
how	what, whatever	whose

In the example below, the word group beginning with the dependent word *After* is a fragment.

> After I cashed my paycheck. I treated myself to dinner.

TEACHING TIP
You may want to teach
your students about
dependent and
independent clauses.

A *dependent statement*—one starting with a dependent word like *after*—cannot stand alone. It depends on another statement to complete the thought. *After I cashed my paycheck* is a dependent statement. It leaves us hanging. We expect to find out, in the same sentence, *what happened after* the writer cashed the check. When a writer does not follow through and complete a thought, a fragment results.

To correct the fragment, simply follow through and complete the thought:

> After I cashed my paycheck, I treated myself to dinner.

Remember, then, that *dependent statements by themselves are fragments*. They must be attached to a statement that makes sense standing alone.

Here are two other examples of dependent-word fragments:

> I won't leave the house. Until I hear from you.

> Rory finally picked up the socks. That he had thrown on the floor days ago.

Until I hear from you is a fragment; it does not make sense standing by itself. We want to know in the same statement *what cannot happen* until I hear from you. The writer must complete the thought. Likewise, *That he had thrown on the floor days ago* is not in itself a complete thought. We want to know in the same statement what *that* refers to.

Additional information about dependent words and phrases can be found in Chapter 4. In this section, dependent words are also referred to as subordinating words.

How to Correct a Dependent-Word Fragment

In most cases you can correct a dependent-word fragment by attaching it to the sentence that comes after it or the sentence that comes before it. Look at how the fragments above have been corrected:

> After I cashed my paycheck, I treated myself to dinner.

> (The fragment has been attached to the sentence that comes after it.)

> I won't leave the house until I hear from you.

> (The fragment has been attached to the sentence that comes before it.)

> Rory finally picked up the socks that he had thrown on the floor days ago.

> (The fragment has been attached to the sentence that comes before it.)

TEACHING TIP
Reiterate to your students
that there are two ways to
correct a dependent-word
fragment: join the fragment
to a complete sentence or
get rid of the dependent
word. Use the clingy
girlfriend or boyfriend as
an analogy. Some people
say that there are only two
ways to deal with them:
marry them ("join" them) or
break up (get rid of the
dependency).

Another way of connecting a dependent-word fragment is simply to eliminate the dependent word by rewriting the sentence:

> I cashed my paycheck and then treated myself to dinner.

> I will wait to hear from you.

> He had thrown them on the floor days ago.

TIPS

   a. Use a comma if a dependent-word group comes at the *beginning* of a sentence (see also Chapter 37).

      After I cashed my paycheck, I treated myself to dinner.

     However, do not generally use a comma if the dependent-word group comes at the *end* of a sentence.

      I won't leave the house until I hear from you.

      Rory finally picked up the socks that he had thrown on the floor days ago.

   b. Sometimes the dependent words *who, that, which,* or *where* appear not at the very start, but *near* the start, of a word group. A fragment often results:

      I drove slowly past the old brick house. The place where I grew up.

     The place where I grew up is not in itself a complete thought. We want to know in the same statement *where was the place* the writer grew up. The fragment can be corrected by attaching it to the sentence that comes before it:

      I drove slowly past the old brick house, the place where I grew up.

Turn each of the following dependent-word groups into a sentence by adding a complete thought. Use a comma after the dependent-word group if a dependent word starts the sentence. Note the examples.

ACTIVITY 1

TEACHING TIP
Point out that a dependent-word group can start or end a sentence. For example, "Until I die" could appear in a sentence two ways: "I plan to eat chocolate until I die" or "Until I die, I plan to eat chocolate."

EXAMPLES

   Although I felt miserable

   Although I felt miserable, I tried to smile for the photographer.

   The man who found my wallet

   The man who found my wallet returned it the next day.

1. After I received my tax return

   After I received my tax return, I deposited the money into my savings account.

Answers will vary. Examples are shown.

2. Before I had a job

   Before I had a job, I never had any money.

3. Because I studied so hard for my exams

   Because I studied so hard for my exams, I passed all my classes.

4. Since getting my college degree is so important

Since getting my college degree is so important, I make sure to study every day.

_____

5. Unless I eat breakfast

Unless I eat breakfast, I am hungry all morning.

_____

ACTIVITY 2

Underline the dependent-word fragment in each item. Then rewrite the items, correcting each fragment by attaching it to the sentence that comes before or the sentence that comes after it—whichever sounds more natural. Use a comma after the dependent word group if it starts the sentence.

1. <u>Whenever I spray deodorant.</u> My cat arches her back. She thinks she is hearing a hissing enemy.

   . . . deodorant, my cat . . .

   _____

2. My father, a pharmaceutical representative, was on the road all week. We had a great time playing football in the house. <u>Until he came home for the weekend.</u>

   . . . house until he . . .

   _____

3. <u>If Kim takes too long saying good-bye to her boyfriend.</u> Her father will start flicking the porch light. Then he will come out with a flashlight.

   . . . boyfriend, her father . . .

   _____

4. Scientists are studying mummified remains. <u>That are thousands of years old.</u> Most of the people were killed by parasites.

   . . . remains that are thousands . . .

   _____

5. <u>After I got to class.</u> I realized my report was still on the kitchen table. I had been working there the night before.

   . . . class, I realized . . .

   _____

-ing and to Fragments

When an -ing word appears at or near the start of a word group, a fragment may result. Such fragments often lack a subject and part of the verb. In the items below, underline the word groups that contain -ing words. Each is a fragment.

1. Ellen walked all over the neighborhood yesterday. <u>Trying to find her dog Bo.</u> Several people claimed they had seen him only hours before.

2. We sat back to watch the movie. <u>Not expecting anything special.</u> To our surprise, we clapped, cheered, and cried for the next two hours.

3. I telephoned the balloon store. <u>It being the day before our wedding anniversary.</u> I knew my wife would be surprised to receive a dozen heart-shaped balloons.

People sometimes write *-ing* fragments because they think that the subject of one sentence will work for the next word group as well. Thus, in item 1 the writer thinks that the subject *Ellen* in the opening sentence will also serve as the subject for *Trying to find her dog Bo.* But the subject must actually be in the same sentence.

TEACHING TIP
Stress to your students that the subject must be in the same sentence as the *-ing* word group.

How to Correct *-ing* Fragments

1. Attach the fragment to the sentence that comes before it or the sentence that comes after it, whichever makes sense. Item 1 could read: "Ellen walked all over the neighborhood yesterday, trying to find her dog Bo."

2. Add a subject and change the *-ing* verb part to the correct form of the verb. Item 2 could read: "We didn't expect anything special."

3. Change *being* to the correct form of the verb be (*am, are, is, was, were*). Item 3 could read: "It was the day before our wedding anniversary."

How to Correct *to* Fragments

When *to* appears at or near the start of a word group, a fragment sometimes results:

> At the Chinese restaurant, Tim used chopsticks. To impress his date. He spent one hour eating a small bowl of rice.

The second word group is a fragment and can be corrected by adding it to the preceding sentence:

> At the Chinese restaurant, Tim used chopsticks to impress his date.

Underline the *-ing* fragment in each of the following items. Then correct the item by using the method described in parentheses.	**ACTIVITY 3**

EXAMPLE

<u>Stepping hard on the accelerator.</u> Armon tried to beat the truck to the intersection. He lost by a hood.
(Add the fragment to the sentence that comes after it.)

Stepping hard on the accelerator, Armon tried to beat the truck to the intersection.

1. Marble-sized hailstones fell from the sky. <u>Flattening the young plants in the cornfield.</u> A year's work was lost in an hour.
(Add the fragment to the preceding sentence.)

. . . sky, flattening . . .

_____

_____

TEACHING TIP
For these activities, you may want to go over the answers in class. Ask students to discuss the choices they made to correct these fragments.

2. A noisy fire truck suddenly raced down the street. <u>Coming to a stop at my house.</u> My home security system had sent a false alarm.
(Correct the fragment by adding the subject *it* and changing *coming* to the proper form of the verb, *came*.)

... street. It came to a stop at my house ...

3. My phone doesn't ring. Instead, a light on it blinks. <u>The reason for this being that I am partially deaf.</u>
(Correct the fragment by changing *being* to the proper form of the verb, *is*.)

The reason for this is that I am ...

Underline the *-ing* or *to* fragment in each item. Then rewrite each item, correcting the fragment by using one of the three methods described above.

1. <u>Looking at the worm on the table.</u> Shelby groaned. She knew she wouldn't like what the biology teacher said next.

... table, Shelby groaned ...

2. I put a box of baking soda in the freezer. <u>To get rid of the musty smell.</u> However, my ice cubes still taste like old socks.

... freezer to get rid of the musty smell ...

3. <u>Staring at the clock on the far wall.</u> I nervously began my speech. I was afraid to look at any of the people in the room.

... wall, I nervously began my speech ...

4. Jerome sat quietly at his desk. <u>Fantasizing about the upcoming weekend.</u> He might meet the girl of his dreams at Saturday night's party.

... desk, fantasizing about ...

5. <u>To get to the bus station from here.</u> I have to walk two blocks out of my way. The sidewalk is torn up because of construction work.

... from here, I have to ...

Added-Detail Fragments

Added-detail fragments lack a subject and a verb. They often begin with one of the following words:

also	especially	except	for example
like	including	such as	

Underline the one added-detail fragment in each of the following items:

1. Before a race, I eat starchy foods. <u>Such as bread and spaghetti.</u> The carbohydrates provide quick energy.

2. Dante is taking a night course in auto mechanics. <u>Also, one in plumbing.</u> He wants to save money on household repairs.

3. My son keeps several pets in his room. <u>Including hamsters and mice.</u>

People often write added-detail fragments for much the same reason they write *-ing* fragments. They think the subject and verb in one sentence will serve for the next word group. But the subject and verb must be in *each* word group.

TEACHING TIP
Draw attention to this point.

How to Correct Added-Detail Fragments

1. Attach the fragment to the complete thought that precedes it. Item 1 could read: "Before a race, I eat starchy foods, such as bread and spaghetti."

2. Add a subject and a verb to the fragment to make it a complete sentence. Item 2 could read: "Dante is taking a night course in auto mechanics. Also, he is taking one in plumbing."

3. Insert the fragment within the preceding sentence. Item 3 could read: "My son keeps several pets, including hamsters and mice, in his room."

Underline the fragment in each of the following items. Then make it a sentence by rewriting it, using the method described in parentheses.

ACTIVITY 5

EXAMPLE

My mother likes watching daytime television shows. <u>Especially old movies and soap operas.</u> She says that daytime television is less violent. (Add the fragment to the preceding sentence.)

My mother likes watching daytime television shows, especially old movies and

soap operas.

1. Mateo works evenings in a movie theater. He enjoys the fringe benefits. <u>For example, seeing the new movies first.</u>
(Correct the fragment by adding the subject and verb *he sees*.)

. . . For example, he sees the new movies first.

2. Ethan's fingernails are ragged from years of working as a mechanic. And his fingertips are always black. <u>Like ink pads.</u>
    (Attach the fragment to the preceding sentence.)

    . . . black, like ink pads.

3. Electronic devices keep getting smarter. <u>Such as Amazon Echo and Google Home.</u> Now families can hook up all their devices to one system that can be controlled by a smartphone.
    (Correct the fragment by inserting it in the preceding sentence.)

    Electronic devices, such as Amazon Echo and Google Home, keep getting

    smarter. Now families. . .

ACTIVITY 6	Underline the added-detail fragment in each item. Then rewrite to correct the fragment. Use one of the three methods described on the previous page.

Methods of correction may vary.

1. Left-handed students face problems. <u>For example, right-handed desks.</u> Spiral notebooks can also be uncomfortable to use.

    . . . problems. For example, they must sit at right-handed desks . . .

2. Mrs. Fields always wears her lucky clothes to bingo. <u>Such as a sweater printed with four-leaf clovers.</u> She also carries a rhinestone horseshoe.

    . . . clothes, such as a sweater printed with four-leaf clovers, to bingo . . .

3. Hundreds of moths were swarming around the stadium lights. <u>Like large flecks of snow.</u> However, I knew they couldn't be snow—it was eighty degrees outside.

    . . . lights like large flecks of snow . . .

4. Trevor buys and sells collectors' items. <u>For instance, comic books and movie posters.</u> He sets up a display at local flea markets and carnivals.

    . . . items. For instance, he buys and sells comic books and movie posters . . .

5. I wonder now why I had to learn certain subjects. <u>Such as geometry.</u> No one has ever asked me about the hypotenuse of a triangle.

    . . . subjects, such as geometry. No one . . .

Missing-Subject Fragments

In each item below, underline the word group in which the subject is missing:

1. Alicia loved getting wedding presents. <u>But hated writing thank-you notes.</u>

2. Noah has orange soda and potato chips for breakfast. <u>Then eats more junk food, like root beer and cookies, for lunch.</u>

ESL NOTE
Some nonnative speakers will omit subject pronouns because it is acceptable in their native language.

How to Correct Missing-Subject Fragments

1. Attach the fragment to the preceding sentence. Item 1 could read: "Alicia loved getting wedding presents but hated writing thank-you notes."

2. Add a subject (which can often be a pronoun standing for the subject in the preceding sentence). Item 2 could read: "Then he eats more junk food, like root beer and cookies, for lunch."

Underline the missing-subject fragment in each item. Then rewrite that part of the item needed to correct the fragment. Use one of the two methods of correction described above.

ACTIVITY 7

1. Every other day, Kara runs two miles. <u>Then does fifty crunches.</u> She hasn't lost weight, but she looks trimmer and more muscular.

   . . . miles. Then she does . . .

   _____

Methods of correction may vary.

2. I like all kinds of fresh pizza. <u>But refuse to eat frozen pizza.</u> The sauce is always dried out, and the crust tastes like leather.

   . . . pizza. But I refuse. . .

   _____

TEACHING TIP
You may want to complete this activity as an entire class.

3. Many people are allergic to seafood. They break out in hives when they eat it. <u>And can even have trouble breathing.</u>

   . . . they eat it, and they can even . . .

   _____

4. To distract the upset toddler, the mother started singing Sandra Boynton's "Pajama Time." <u>Then started dancing.</u> The young child stopped crying and started clapping.

   . . . "Pajama Time." Then she started dancing.

   _____

5. Last semester, I took six courses. <u>And worked part-time in a discount drugstore.</u> Now that the term is all over, I don't know how I did it.

   . . . courses and worked . . .

   _____

> **A Review: How to Check for Sentence Fragments**
>
> 1. Read your paper aloud from the *last* sentence to the *first*. You will be better able to see and hear whether each group you read is a complete thought.
>
> 2. If you think a word group may be a fragment, ask yourself: Does this contain a subject and a verb and express a complete thought?
>
> 3. More specifically, be on the lookout for the most common fragments:
>   - Dependent-word fragments (starting with words like *after, because, since, when,* and *before*)
>   - *-ing* and *to* fragments (*-ing* and *to* at or near the start of a word group)
>   - Added-detail fragments (starting with words like *for example, such as, also,* and *especially*)
>   - Missing-subject fragments (a verb is present but not the subject)

REVIEW TEST 1

Personal

Each word group in the following student paragraph is numbered. In the space provided, write C if a word group is a complete sentence; write F if it is a fragment. You will find eight fragments in the paragraph.

_____C_____ 1. ¹I'm starting to think that there is no safe place left. ²To ride

_____F_____ 2. a bicycle. ³When I try to ride on the highway, in order to

_____F_____ 3. go to school. ⁴I feel like a rabbit being pursued by predators.

_____C_____ 4. ⁵Drivers whip past me at high speeds. ⁶And try to see how

_____C_____ 5. close they can get to my bike without actually killing me.

_____F_____ 6. ⁷When they pull onto the shoulder of the road or make a

_____F_____ 7. right turn. ⁸Drivers completely ignore my vehicle. ⁹On city

_____C_____ 8. streets, I feel more like a cockroach than a rabbit. ¹⁰Drivers

_____C_____ 9. in the city despise bicycles. ¹¹Regardless of an approaching

_____C_____ 10. bike rider. ¹²Street-side car doors will unexpectedly open.

_____F_____ 11. ¹³Frustrated drivers who are stuck in traffic will make nasty

_____C_____ 12. comments. ¹⁴Or shout out obscene propositions. ¹⁵Even

_____C_____ 13. pedestrians in the city show their disregard for me. ¹⁶While

_____F_____ 14. jaywalking across the street. ¹⁷The pedestrian will treat

_____C_____ 15. me, a law-abiding bicyclist, to a withering look of disdain.

_____F_____ 16. ¹⁸Pedestrians may even cross my path deliberately. ¹⁹As if to

_____C_____   17. prove their higher position in the pecking order of the city

_____C_____   18. streets. [20]Today, bicycling can be hazardous to the rider's

_____F_____   19. health.

_____C_____   20.

Now (on separate paper) correct the fragments you have found. Attach the fragments to sentences that come before or after them or make whatever other change is needed to turn each fragment into a sentence.

Answers will vary for this part of the test.

REVIEW TEST 2

Each of the following items includes a fragment. Make whatever changes are needed to turn the fragments into sentences.

EXAMPLE

One of the most popular series of books in the twenty-first century has been the Millennium trilogy/ ᵇ̶Ȿy Stieg Larsson.

1. Larsson was an outspoken Swedish writer and journalist/ ʷW̶ho died in 2004 from a heart attack. He was fifty.

2. His books became an instant sensation/ ⁱI̶n Sweden and by 2010 had sold more than 20 million copies in 41 countries.

3. The first book of the series, *The Girl with the Dragon Tattoo*, is a suspenseful novel about a computer hacker/ Lisbeth Salander, and a journalist, Mikael Blomqvist, who work to solve a financial fraud mystery.

4. The second book, *The Girl Who Played with Fire*, finds Mikael trying to save Lisbeth/ ᶠF̶rom being arrested for a triple murder.

5. The third book, *The Girl Who Kicked the Hornet's Nest*, focuses on Lisbeth's planned revenge against those who tried to kill her/ ᵃA̶nd on Mikael's help in implementing her plan.

6. Unlike many trilogies, the Millennium trilogy does not have a conclusive ending/ ᵇB̶ecause Larsson didn't plan for it to be only a trilogy.

7. He died before he could finish the series/ ʷW̶hich he planned to be ten books.

8. It's surprising that it wasn't until 2011 that the first book was made into a movie in America/ ˢȘince all three books were made into movies in Sweden in 2009.

REVIEW TEST 3

Academic

Read the paragraph below and correct each fragment. You should find a total of six fragments.

  Many college students find that having social lives can be very expensive, Which means they need to find ways to save money. Most colleges have numerous activities, That are free or cost little. For instance, colleges may have art galleries that are free to visit or free movie nights. Some colleges even bring bands to campus and charge students a nominal fee. Students can also use their local library, To provide free or inexpensive entertainment. Many libraries, both on campus and off, have free programs that include classes, speakers, and activities. Libraries are also filled with books and movies, That can be checked out at no cost to the student. Although eating out is another expense that students often have, There are creative ways to cut dining costs as well. The easiest way to cut costs is not to eat out and instead to invite friends to each bring a dish for an old fashioned pot-luck dinner. If eating out is a must, Many students can take advantage of "all-you-can-eat" buffets and "before 4:00" specials. Part of college life is the social life, but activities, movies, concerts, and dining out can quickly deplete a person's wallet, so saving and planning is essential.

Run-Ons

What Are Run-Ons?

A *run-on* is two complete thoughts that are run together with no adequate sign given to mark the break between them.*

Some run-ons have no punctuation at all to mark the break between the thoughts. Such run-ons are known as *fused sentences:* they are fused, or joined together, as if they were only one thought.

Fused Sentences

The bus stopped suddenly I spilled coffee all over my shirt.

Mario told everyone in the room to be quiet his favorite show was on.

In other run-ons, known as *comma splices*, a comma is used to connect, or "splice" together, the two complete thoughts. However, a comma alone is *not enough* to connect two complete thoughts. Some stronger connection than a comma alone is needed.

Comma Splices

The bus stopped suddenly, I spilled coffee all over my shirt.

Mario told everyone in the room to be quiet, his favorite show was on.

Comma splices are the most common kind of run-on. Students sense that some kind of connection is needed between two thoughts, and so they often put a comma at the dividing point. But the comma alone is *not sufficient*. A stronger, clearer mark is needed between the two complete thoughts.

*Notes:
1. Some instructors regard all run-ons as fused sentences. But for many other instructors, and for our purposes in this book, the term *run-on* applies equally to fused sentences and comma splices. The bottom line is that you do not want either fused sentences or comma splices in your writing.
2. Some instructors refer to each complete thought in a run-on as an *independent clause*. A clause is simply a group of words having a subject and a verb. A clause may be *independent* (expressing a complete thought and able to stand alone) or *dependent* (not expressing a complete thought and not able to stand alone). Using this terminology, we'd say that a run-on is two independent clauses run together with no adequate sign given to mark the break between them.
3. Chapter 4, "The Third and Fourth Steps in Writing," demonstrate how to take simple sentences and make them compound or complex sentences without creating run-ons.

ESL NOTE
Nonnative speakers do not always know about sentence boundaries in English. In an attempt to combine simple sentences, they may write run-ons. They need to learn to use appropriate connectors and correct punctuation in English.

TEACHING TIP
Bring a Band-Aid to class. Ask two volunteers to come to the front of the room. Explain to your students that each person represents a complete thought (sentence). Ask your volunteers to hold up one of their hands, and then "splice" them together with the Band-Aid, which represents a comma. Tell your students that the two people are now a comma splice and that the "comma" is not strong enough to hold the two "thoughts" together.

ESL NOTE
Nonnative speakers may use *now* or *then* as a conjunction to connect simple sentences.

A Warning: Words That Can Lead to Run-Ons

People often write run-ons when the second complete thought begins with one of the following words:

I	we	there	now
you	they	this	then
he, she, it	that	next	

Whenever you use one of these words in writing a paper, remember to be on the alert for run-ons.

How to Correct Run-Ons

Here are three common methods of correcting a run-on:

1. Use a period and a capital letter to break the two complete thoughts into separate sentences:

    The bus stopped suddenly. I spilled coffee all over my shirt.

    Mario told everyone in the room to be quiet. His favorite show was on.

2. Use a comma plus a joining word (*and, but, for, or, nor, so, yet*) to connect the two complete thoughts:

    The bus stopped suddenly, and I spilled coffee all over my shirt.

    Mario told everyone in the room to be quiet, for his favorite show was on.

TEACHING TIP
You may want to review semicolons with your students.

3. Use a semicolon to connect the two complete thoughts:

    The bus stopped suddenly; I spilled coffee all over my shirt.

    Mario told everyone in the room to be quiet; his favorite show was on.

A fourth method of correcting a run-on is to use *subordination*. The following activities will give you practice in the first three methods. Subordination is described fully in Chapter 4, in the section of the book that deals with sentence variety.

Method 1: Period and a Capital Letter

One way of correcting a run-on is to use a period and a capital letter between the two complete thoughts. Use this method especially if the thoughts are not closely related or if another method would make the sentence too long.

ACTIVITY 1

In each of the following run-ons, locate the point at which one complete thought ends and another begins. Each is a *fused sentence*—that is, each consists of two sentences fused, or joined together, with no punctuation at all between them. Reading each sentence aloud will help you "hear" where a major break or split between the thoughts occurs. At such a point, your voice will probably drop and pause.

Correct the run-on by putting a period at the end of the first thought and a capital letter at the start of the next thought.

EXAMPLE

    Jessica's tablet doesn't work anymore. $\overset{S}{\cancel{s}}$he spilled a glass of soda on it.

1. The men at the door claimed to have paving material left over from another job. $\overset{T}{\cancel{t}}$hey wanted to pave our driveway for a "bargain price."

2. Linh, a paralegal who speaks Vietnamese, helps other people from her country write wills. $\overset{S}{\cancel{s}}$he assists others by going with them when they have to appear in court.

3. Vicky has her own unique style of dressing. $\overset{S}{\cancel{s}}$he wore a tuxedo with a red bow tie to her cousin's wedding.

4. In the summer, ants are attracted to water. $\overset{T}{\cancel{t}}$hey will often enter a house through the dishwasher.

5. Humans have managed to adapt to any environment. $\overset{T}{\cancel{t}}$hey can survive in Arctic wastes, tropical jungles, and barren deserts.

6. A six-year-old child uses over two thousand words. $\overset{H}{\cancel{h}}$e or she also understands over 20,000 words.

7. I rummaged around the crowded drawer looking for a pair of scissors. $\overset{T}{\cancel{t}}$hen it suddenly stabbed me in the finger.

8. Squirrels like to jump from trees onto our roof. $\overset{T}{\cancel{t}}$heir footsteps sound like ghosts running around our attic.

9. Today I didn't make good time driving to work. $\overset{E}{\cancel{e}}$very traffic light along the way was red.

10. Since I got my own laptop, I've saved so much time studying. I never have to wait for the library computers anymore.

Method 2: Comma and a Joining Word

Another way of correcting a run-on is to use a comma plus a joining word to connect the two complete thoughts. Joining words (also called *conjunctions*) include *and, but, for, or, nor, so*, and *yet*. Here is what the four most common joining words mean:

   and   in addition

   Cassie works full-time for an accounting firm, and she takes evening classes.

(*And* means *in addition:* Cassie works full-time for an accounting firm; *in addition*, she takes evening classes.)

   but   however, on the other hand

   I checked out the job boards, but I knew my dream job wouldn't be listed.

TEACHING TIP
For this activity, read each sentence aloud as your students make corrections.

TEACHING TIP
Caution students against using the word "and" too often to join complete thoughts.

ESL NOTE
Nonnative speakers need to learn the usage of coordinating conjunctions and the required punctuation. Some will put a comma after the conjunction because they may be confusing it with a conjunctive adverb ("But, I knew my dream job wouldn't be listed" vs. "However, I knew my dream job wouldn't be listed").

(*But* means *however:* I checked out the job boards; *however*, I knew my dream job wouldn't be listed.)

for   because

Lizards become sluggish at night, for they need the sun's warmth to maintain an active body temperature.

(*For* means *because:* Lizards become sluggish at night *because* they need the sun's warmth to maintain an active body temperature.)

so   as a result, therefore

The canoe touched bottom, so Dave pushed it toward deeper water.

(*So* means *as a result:* The canoe touched bottom; *as a result*, Dave pushed it toward deeper water.)

ACTIVITY 2

Insert the joining word (*and, but, for, so*) that logically connects the two thoughts in each sentence.

TEACHING TIP
Consider making a game out of this activity. See how quickly your students can complete the activity correctly. You may want to ask them to create a set of game rules first.

1. Sarah is a great mountain climber, _____but_____ she is afraid of heights.

2. The large dog was growling at me, _____and_____ there were white bubbles of foam around its mouth.

3. The library had just closed, _____so_____ I couldn't get any of the reserved books.

4. He checked on the new baby every five minutes, _____for_____ he was afraid that something would happen to her.

5. Kate thought the milk was fresh, _____but_____ it broke up into little sour flakes in her coffee.

6. My neighbor has a dog who loves to run, _____so_____ she takes him to the dog park every day.

7. Napoleon is famous for being a French general, _____but_____ he was also the author of a romance novel, *Clisson and Eugénie.*

8. Although I like most creatures, I am not fond of snakes, _____and_____ I like spiders even less.

9. My sister wants to exercise more and use her car less, _____so_____ she walks to the grocery store.

10. Max spends hours every day on his computer, _____and_____ he often has the television on at the same time.

ACTIVITY 3

Add a complete and closely related thought to go with each of the following statements. Use a comma plus the indicated joining word when you write the second thought.

EXAMPLE

for The journalist interviewed the children at my son's school _____
    , for she was writing a story about bullying on campus.

1. Most reality TV shows are unoriginal _____
   , but I find the underhanded behavior amusing.

2. Ryan enrolled in an online class _____
   , for he works full time all the way across town.

3. My mom taught me to respect others _____
   , and she also taught me to respect myself.

4. The warehouse fire occurred late last night _____
   , so the morning newspaper didn't cover the story.

5. Sharla called in sick to work today _____
   , but she still managed to attend class.

but   Answers will vary; examples are given.

for

and

so

but

ACTIVITY 4

Correct each run-on with either (1) a period and a capital letter or (2) a comma and a logical joining word. Do not use the same method of correction for every sentence.

Some of the run-ons are fused sentences (there is no punctuation between the two complete thoughts), and some are comma splices (there is only a comma between the two complete thoughts). One sentence is correct.

TEACHING TIP
For this activity, read each sentence aloud as your students make corrections.

EXAMPLE
                                    so
There was a strange odor in the house, ̧Elias called the gas company immediately.

Answers may vary; examples are shown.

                                   , and
1. I suffer from seasonal allergies ̧ the worst season is spring when all the trees are in bloom.

                                   P
2. Christmas is a great holiday. ̧people decorate their houses so nicely.

                              so
3. The children on the bus were very loud, ̧the bus driver often had a headache.

4. The cake baking in the oven smelled wonderful, and my mouth watered at the thought of eating it. Correct

                                          , but
5. The new book by Anita Diamante is extremely interesting ̧one of her best books is *The Red Tent*.

                                   T
6. Meteorologists have very interesting jobs, ̧they use science to predict the weather.

                                       A
7. Interviewing for a new job is very stressful. ̧anticipating what questions will be asked is difficult.

                                          so
8. Many people have problems getting rid of junk, ̧their homes quickly become filled and cluttered.

                              , but
9. The car stalled on the railroad tracks ̧the train engineer quickly applied the brakes and avoided an accident.

                                                 W
10. John bought a new car from the dealership down the road, ̧we have purchased two cars from that same dealership.

Method 3: Semicolon

TEACHING TIP
Write "Complete thought; complete thought" on the board, and then circle the semicolon. Stress that both thoughts in the sentence must be complete.

A third method of correcting a run-on is to use a semicolon to mark the break between two thoughts. A *semicolon* (;) looks like a period above a comma and is sometimes called a *strong comma*. A semicolon signals more of a pause than a comma alone but not quite the full pause of a period. When it is used to correct run-ons, the semicolon can be used alone or with a transitional word.

Semicolon Alone

ESL NOTE
The semicolon is often used differently in other languages. Nonnative speakers would benefit from comparing its usage in their native language.

Here are some earlier sentences that were connected with a comma plus a joining word. Now they are connected by a semicolon alone. Notice that the semicolon alone—unlike the comma alone—can be used to connect the two complete thoughts in each sentence:

My neighbor has a dog who loves to run; she takes him to the dog park every day.

The children on the bus were very loud; the bus driver often had a headache.

Napoleon is famous for being a French general; he was also the author of a romance novel, *Clisson and Eugénie.*

The large dog was growling at me; there were white bubbles of foam around its mouth.

Meteorologists have very interesting jobs; they use science to predict the weather.

Using semicolons can add to sentence variety. For some people, however, the semicolon is a confusing punctuation mark. Keep in mind that if you are not comfortable using it, you can and should use one of the first two methods of correcting run-ons.

| ACTIVITY 5 | Insert a semicolon where the break occurs between the two complete thoughts in each of the following sentences. |

TEACHING TIP
For this activity, read each sentence aloud as students make corrections.

EXAMPLE

Neither my dad nor my mom attended college; I plan to be the first person in my family to earn a bachelor's degree.

1. Everyone at the fundraising event brought canned goods; the organizers hoped to donate several thousand pounds of food to the local food pantry.

2. The council member was censured for his comments; he quickly apologized when he realized that others found his remarks offensive.

3. Kaitlyn spends a lot of time studying for classes; she usually listens to music at the same time.

4. Someone from the credit card company called this afternoon; I am a month behind in my payments.

5. The attorney called her witness to the stand; the witness, however, was too nervous to answer questions.

6. Thomas suffers from cherophobia; he has an aversion to being happy.

7. Ben & Jerry's first ice cream store opened in 1978; the owners took a correspondence course through Penn State to learn how to make ice cream.

8. Adrian thinks that he owns the remote control; he doesn't realize that I removed the batteries from it.

9. Insulin medication was made from beef- and pork-based products until 1982; people with diabetes now use insulin made from genetically altered bacteria.

10. Mari is lactose intolerant; she never eats ice cream or drinks milk.

Semicolon with a Transitional Word

A semicolon can be used with a transitional word and a comma to join two complete thoughts. Here are some examples:

Larry believes in being prepared for emergencies; therefore, he stockpiles canned goods in his basement.

I tried to cash my paycheck; however, I had forgotten to bring identification.

Athletic shoes must fit perfectly; otherwise, wearers may injure their feet or ankles.

A short nap at the end of the day relaxes me; in addition, it gives me the energy to spend the evening on my homework.

Some zoo animals have not learned how to be good parents; as a result, baby animals are sometimes brought up in zoo nurseries and even in private homes.

People use seventeen muscles when they smile; on the other hand, they use forty-three muscles when they frown.

Following is a list of common transitional words (also known as *adverbial conjunctions*), with brief meanings.

Transitional Word	Meaning
however	but
nevertheless	however
on the other hand	however
instead	as a substitute
meanwhile	in the intervening time
otherwise	under other conditions
indeed	in fact
in addition	also, and
also	in addition
moreover	in addition
furthermore	in addition
as a result	thus, therefore

continued

TEACHING TIP
Caution students against using transitional words too often.

ESL NOTE
Nonnative speakers need to learn the meanings of these transitional words. Group them according to meaning or usage (e.g., contrast, time, explanation or emphasis, addition of information, and result). Tell students that *but* often connects simple sentences. *Also* is used in other positions in a sentence (e.g., "He is also late"). *Also* and *but* are used more often in spoken English. Substitute other transitional words from the same category (*also*—addition; *but*—contrast) in written expression.

Transitional Word	Meaning
thus	as a result
consequently	as a result
therefore	as a result

<table>
</table>

ACTIVITY 6

For each sentence, choose a logical transitional word from the box above, and write it in the space provided. Use a semicolon *before* the connector and a comma *after* it.

EXAMPLE

I dread going to parties ____; however,____ my husband loves meeting new people.

Some answers may vary.

1. Jackie suffers from migraine headaches ____; therefore,____ her doctor has advised her to avoid caffeine and alcohol.

2. Hunter's apartment is always neat and clean ____; on the other hand,____ the interior of his car looks like the aftermath of a tornado.

3. I try to attend all my math classes ____; otherwise,____ I'll get too far behind to pass the weekly quizzes.

4. Jabril was singing Mary J. Blige tunes in the shower ____; meanwhile,____ his toast was burning in the kitchen.

5. The reporter was tough and experienced ____; however,____ even he was stunned by the tragic events.

A Note on Subordination

ESL NOTE
Nonnative speakers may write dependent clauses as complete sentences because they hear them used in spoken English. Some languages consider dependent clauses acceptable in written form.

TEACHING TIP
You may want to provide several more examples of subordination for your students.

A fourth method of joining related thoughts is to use subordination. *Subordination* is a way of showing that one thought in a sentence is not as important as another thought. (Subordination is explained in full in Chapter 4.) Below are three earlier sentences, recast so that one idea is subordinated to (made less important than) the other idea. In each case, the subordinate (or less important) thought is underlined. Note that each subordinate clause begins with a dependent word.

<u>Because the library had just closed</u>, I couldn't get any of the reserved books.

<u>When he saw a car stalled on the railroad tracks</u>, the train engineer quickly applied the brakes and avoided an accident.

I didn't make good time driving to work today <u>because every traffic light along the way was red</u>.

A Review: How to Check for Run-Ons

1. To see if a sentence is a run-on, read it aloud and listen for a break marking two complete thoughts. Your voice will probably drop and pause at the break.

continued

2. To check an entire paper, read it aloud from the *last* sentence to the *first*. Doing so will help you hear and see each complete thought.

3. Be on the lookout for words that can lead to run-on sentences:

I	he, she, it	they	this	then	now
you	we	there	that	next	

4. Correct run-ons by using one of the following methods:

Period and a capital letter

Comma and a joining word (*and, but, for, or, nor, so, yet*)

Semicolon, alone or with a transitional word

Subordination

TEACHING TIP
Introduce students to the correction symbol "r-o" for a run-on and "cs" for comma splice.

REFLECTIVE ACTIVITY

Reread any essay you wrote for Chapter 18. Are there any run-ons in your paper? Correct them using what you learned in Chapter 25.

©mavo/Shutterstock

REVIEW TEST 1

Correct each run-on with either (1) a period and a capital letter or (2) a comma (if needed) and the joining word *and, but, for*, or *so*. Do not use the same method of correction for every sentence.

Some of the run-ons are fused sentences (there is no punctuation between the two complete thoughts), and some are comma splices (there is only a comma between the two complete thoughts). One sentence is correct.

1. Our boss expects us to work four hours without a break, *but* he wanders off to a vending machine at least once an hour.

   Some answers may vary.

2. The children in the next car were making faces at other drivers. *W*when I made a face back, they giggled and sank out of sight.

3. Chuck bent over and lifted the heavy tray. *T*then he heard an ominous crack in his back.

   TEACHING TIP
You may want to use these review tests to assess what your students have learned.

4. The branches of the tree were bare*, and* they made a dark feathery pattern against the orange-pink sunset.

5. In the dark alley, the air smelled like rotten garbage*, and* a large rat lurked in the shadows.

6. Our class wanted to do something for the hurricane victims, ^so we sent a donation to the Red Cross.

7. My ex-husband hit me just once in our marriage. ~F~five minutes later I was packed and walking out the door.

8. Aunt Jeanne thought a warm dry climate would improve her health, ^so she moved to Arizona.

9. ~Even though o~One of Johnny Cash's most famous songs is "A Boy Named Sue," Shel Silverstein is the author of the song.

10. We stocked our backpacks with energy bars, and we also brought bags of dried apricots and peaches.   *Correct*

REVIEW TEST 2

Answers may vary.

Correct each run-on by using (1) a period and a capital letter, (2) a comma and a joining word, or (3) a semicolon. Do not use one method exclusively.

1. Every April, millions of people celebrate Earth Day, ^but few probably know the history of how and why Earth Day came to be.

2. In 1970, Wisconsin senator Gaylord Nelson helped pass a resolution that declared April 22 as a national celebration of Earth Day; ^Americans at that time were not as aware of environmental concerns as they have become.

3. In the 1960s, many cities were suffering from smog-filled air, ^and pollution was so bad some rivers even caught fire!

4. To raise awareness of the problem, Senator Nelson decided to "shake up the political establishment." ^H~he~ forced the issue onto the national agenda.

5. During the 1970s and 1980s, Earth Day was a relatively small celebration; ^in 1990, Dennis Hayes organized a worldwide celebration, resulting in over 200 million people in 141 countries celebrating.

6. Earth Day support continued to grow. ^I~in~ 2000, on the 30th anniversary of Earth Day, 184 countries celebrated.

7. Some people gather at rallies or march in parades in world capitals; ^other people hold smaller celebrations that include picking up litter, planting trees, and making energy-efficient choices in their homes.

Locate and correct the five run-ons in the passage that follows. Do not use the same method of correction for every sentence.

Note:
Corrections will vary; here are some possibilities.

Employers are always looking for great employees who are conscientious, focused, and analytical. First, conscientious employees take pride in their work and want to do their best; they make sure they contribute the best work possible and meet deadlines. If they run into a problem, they first try to solve it on their own. If they cannot solve the problem, they seek the help necessary to complete the task. Second, focused employees don't waste time. They arrive punctually and use the time at work to do work; they don't talk frivolously to their friends or family on the phone. They don't surf the Internet for amusing YouTube videos, and they don't stand around idly chatting with coworkers. Finally, analytical employees see a problem and work to solve the issue because they are striving to make things better. If they see a better way that something could be done, they try to implement it. Employees who have these three qualities will always be in demand.

Regular and Irregular Verbs

ESL NOTE
In some languages, the
verb changes with every
pronoun. Therefore, some
nonnative students will
overgeneralize and omit
endings, especially third-
person singular present
and -ed (simple past).

ESL NOTE
In some languages, the
time marker indicates the
time of the action.
Consequently, some
nonnative speakers will not
add any endings to verbs
the way we do in English.

Regular Verbs

A Brief Review of Regular Verbs

Every verb has four principal parts: *present, past, past participle,* and *present participle.* These parts can be used to build all the verb *tenses*—the times shown by verbs.

Most verbs in English are regular. The past and past participle of a regular verb are formed by adding *-d* or *-ed* to the present. The *past participle* is the form of the verb used with the helping verbs *have, has,* or *had* (or some form of *be* with passive verbs). The *present participle* is formed by adding *-ing* to the present.

For a more in-depth look at verb tense and helping verbs, see Chapter 28. Here are the principal parts of some regular verbs:

Present	Past	Past Participle	Present Participle
shout	shouted	shouted	shouting
prepare	prepared	prepared	preparing
surprise	surprised	surprised	surprising
tease	teased	teased	teasing
frighten	frightened	frightened	frightening

Present Tense Endings

The verb ending *-s* or *-es* is needed with a regular verb in the present tense when the subject is *he, she, it,* or any one person or thing.

He reads every night.

She watches television every night.

It appears they have little in common.

Some verbs in the sentences that follow need -*s* or -*es* endings. Cross out each incorrect verb form and write the correct form in the space provided.

__forgets__   1. Keri-Ann usually ~~forget~~ to turn off her cell phone during class.

__makes__   2. My mom ~~make~~ the best lasagna in the world.

__takes__   3. Kurt ~~take~~ his son to the babysitter every morning.

__plans__   4. Marcela ~~plan~~ to major in criminology once she completes her prerequisites.

__feels__   5. If I don't stretch when I wake up, my body ~~feel~~ stiff throughout the day.

Past Tense Endings

The verb ending -*d* or -*ed* is needed with a regular verb in the past tense.

This morning I completed my research paper.

The recovering hospital patient walked slowly down the corridor.

Some students hissed when the new assignment was given out.

Some verbs in the sentences that follow need -*d* or -*ed* endings. Cross out each incorrect verb form and write the correct form in the space provided.

__managed__   1. Last year one of my classmates ~~manage~~ to earn a full scholarship to a four-year university.

__interviewed__   2. The police officer ~~interview~~ several witnesses at the scene of the accident yesterday.

__realized__   3. This morning Alexis ~~realize~~ that she had left her backpack in a carrel at the library.

__planted__   4. I ~~plant~~ rosemary and basil in the garden last spring.

__asked__   5. The manager greeted each customer and ~~ask~~ them for their feedback on the new menu items.

Irregular Verbs

Irregular verbs have irregular forms in past tense and past participle. For example, the past tense of the irregular verb *choose* is *chose*; its past participle is *chosen*.

Almost everyone has some degree of trouble with irregular verbs. When you are unsure about the form of a verb, you can check the following list of irregular verbs. (The present participle is not shown on this list because it is formed simply by adding -*ing* to the base form of the verb.) Or you can check a dictionary, which gives the principal parts of irregular verbs.

A List of Irregular Verbs

Present	Past	Past Participle
arise	arose	arisen
awake	awoke *or* awaked	awoken *or* awaked
be (am, are, is)	was (were)	been
become	became	become
begin	began	begun
bend	bent	bent
bite	bit	bitten
blow	blew	blown
break	broke	broken
bring	brought	brought
build	built	built
burst	burst	burst
buy	bought	bought
catch	caught	caught
choose	chose	chosen
come	came	come
cost	cost	cost
cut	cut	cut
do (does)	did	done
draw	drew	drawn
drink	drank	drunk
drive	drove	driven
eat	ate	eaten
fall	fell	fallen
feed	fed	fed
feel	felt	felt
fight	fought	fought
find	found	found
fly	flew	flown
freeze	froze	frozen
get	got	got *or* gotten
give	gave	given
go (goes)	went	gone
grow	grew	grown
have (has)	had	had
hear	heard	heard
hide	hid	hidden
hold	held	held
hurt	hurt	hurt
keep	kept	kept

continued

Present	Past	Past Participle
know	knew	known
lay	laid	laid
lead	led	led
leave	left	left
lend	lent	lent
let	let	let
lie	lay	lain
light	lit	lit
lose	lost	lost
make	made	made
meet	met	met
pay	paid	paid
ride	rode	ridden
ring	rang	rung
run	ran	run
say	said	said
see	saw	seen
sell	sold	sold
send	sent	sent
shake	shook	shaken
shrink	shrank	shrunk
shut	shut	shut
sing	sang	sung
sit	sat	sat
sleep	slept	slept
speak	spoke	spoken
spend	spent	spent
stand	stood	stood
steal	stole	stolen
stick	stuck	stuck
sting	sting	stung
swear	swore	sworn
swim	swam	swum
take	took	taken
teach	taught	taught
tear	tore	torn
tell	told	told
think	thought	thought
wake	woke *or* waked	woke *or* waked
wear	wore	worn
win	won	won
write	wrote	written

Cross out the incorrect verb form in each of the following sentences. Then write the correct form of the verb in the space provided.

EXAMPLE

__flown__   After it had ~~flew~~ into the picture window, the dazed bird huddled on the ground.

__worn__   1. She had ~~wore~~ her best dress for the party, but it still wasn't fancy enough.

__stood__   2. As Jane ~~stands~~ in the aisle at the grocery store and stared at the different types of bread, she couldn't choose which one to purchase.

__swum__   3. Even though my son is eight years old, he has never ~~swam~~.

__grown__   4. The children had ~~grew~~ much taller over the course of the summer, so their mother took them shopping for new clothes.

__known__   5. If I had ~~knew~~ how much I would like Indian food, I would have started eating it much earlier in my life.

__rode__   6. Jacob was afraid of horses, so it was quite a triumph when he finally ~~rides~~ one.

__shook__   7. After the earthquake ~~shaked~~ the building, the people were relieved that no one was hurt.

__brought__   8. He was asked to bring chips and salsa to the party, but he ~~brang~~ a vegetable platter instead.

__lay__   9. The young child was very tired so he ~~lied~~ down to take a nap.

__fed__   10. Last night, before he went to bed, Grayson ~~feeds~~ his pets.

Three Problematic, Common Irregular Verbs

The verbs *be*, *have*, and *do* are often problematic because they are irregular even in the present tense. The following charts have the proper conjugations of *be*, *have*, and *do*.

Be

Present Tense		Present Tense Examples	
I am	we are		
you are	you are		
he/she/it is	they are	the cat is	the cats are
Past Tense		**Past Tense Examples**	
I was	we were		
you were	you were		
he/she/it was	they were	the cat was	the cats were

Have

Present Tense		Present Tense Examples	
I have	we have		
you have	you have		
he/she/it has	they have	Allan has	Allan and Dave have
Past Tense		**Past Tense Examples**	
I had	we had		
you had	you had		
he/she/it had	they had	Allan had	Allan and Dave had

Do

Present Tense		Present Tense Examples	
I do	we do		
you do	you do		
he/she/it does	they do	the professor does	the professors do
Past Tense		**Past Tense Examples**	
I did	we did		
you did	you did		
he/she/it did	they did	the professor did	the professors did

> **TIP**   Many people have trouble with one negative form of *do*. They will say, for example, "He don't agree" instead of "He doesn't agree," or they will say "The door *don't* work" instead of "The door doesn't work." Be careful to avoid the common mistake of using *don't* instead of *doesn't*.

Fill in the blanks with the correct forms of *be, have,* or *do*.

ACTIVITY 4

My cat, Tugger, __is__ the toughest animal I know. He __has__ survived many close calls. Three years ago, he __was__ caught inside a car's engine. He __had__ one ear torn off and lost his sight in one eye. We __were__ surprised that he lived through the accident. Within weeks, though, he __was__ back to normal. Then, last year, we __were__ worried that we would lose Tugger. Lumps that __were__ growing on his back turned out to be cancer. However, the vet __did__ an operation that saved Tugger's life. We really believe that Tugger __does__ have nine lives.

REVIEW TEST 1

Cross out the incorrect verb form or tense in each sentence. Then write the correct form or tense in the space provided.

established   1. The Declaration of Independence was signed in 1776 and ~~establishes~~ the United States as an independent country.

was   2. George Washington ~~is~~ elected the first president of the United States in 1789.

was   3. The philosophical idea of Manifest Destiny, the belief that the United States should expand across the continent, ~~were~~ popular throughout the 1840s and 1850s.

claimed   4. Between 1861 and 1865, the Civil War ~~claim~~ over 600,000 American lives.

prohibited   5. The Eighteenth Amendment, which was signed in 1919 and ~~prohibits~~ the sale of alcohol, was repealed by the Twenty-First Amendment in 1933.

avoided   6. The United States ~~avoids~~ fighting in World War II until Japan attacked Pearl Harbor on December 7, 1941.

admitted   7. In 1959, President Eisenhower ~~admit~~ Alaska and Hawaii as the 49th and 50th states.

took   8. As the first man on the moon, Neil A. Armstrong ~~takes~~ "one small step for man, one giant leap for mankind" on July 20, 1969 and established NASA and the United States as leaders in space exploration.

became   9. In 1974, President Richard Milhous Nixon ~~becomes~~ the first American president to resign from office.

celebrated   10. The United States ~~celebrate~~ its 200th anniversary in the year 1976.

was   11. Geraldine Ferraro ~~were~~ the first female vice-presidential candidate in 1984; she was followed twenty-four years later, in 2008, by vice-presidential candidate Sarah Palin.

REVIEW TEST 2

Write short sentences that use the form requested for the following verbs.

EXAMPLE

Past of *grow* I grew my own tomatoes last year.

1. Past of *know* I knew I could pass the course, and I did.

2. Present of *take* To get to work, Liz takes two buses and a subway.

3. Past participle of *give* Mom has always given me good advice.

4. Past participle of *write* _Have you ever written a narrative essay?_

5. Past of *do* _As a schoolchild, I never did my homework until the last minute._

6. Past of *talk* _They talked for an hour before finally hanging up._

7. Present of *begin* _An opera usually begins with an overture._

8. Past of *go* _After work, Todd went shopping._

9. Past participle of *see* _I have not seen my cousin for years._

10. Present of *drive* _My kids drive me crazy sometimes._

Subject-Verb Agreement

ESL NOTE
Some common agreement areas to watch for with ESL students:

- third-person singular in the present
- subject and verb do not agree when words come in between them
- verb in a relative clause does not agree with the noun that the clause modifies
- verb does not agree when the subject is a gerund or infinitive
- verb does not agree when *there* or *here* is used to announce the subject ("Here are the textbook.")
- verb does not agree when *one* is used ("One of the boys go.")

A verb must agree with its subject in number. A *singular subject* (one person or thing) takes a singular verb. A *plural subject* (more than one person or thing) takes a plural verb. Mistakes in subject–verb agreement are sometimes made in the following situations:

1. When words come between the subject and the verb
2. When a verb comes before the subject
3. With compound subjects
4. With indefinite pronouns

Each of these situations is explained in this chapter. Additional information about subjects and verbs can be found in Chapter 22.

Words between Subject and Verb

Words that come between the subject and the verb do not change subject–verb agreement. In the sentence

The sharp <u>fangs</u> in the dog's mouth <u>look</u> scary.

the subject (*fangs*) is plural, and so the verb (*look*) is plural. The words that come between the subject and the verb are a prepositional phrase: *in the dog's mouth*. They do not affect subject–verb agreement. (A list of prepositions can be found in Chapter 22.)

To help find the subject of certain sentences, you should cross out prepositional phrases.

The lumpy <u>salt</u> ~~in the shakers~~ <u>needs</u> to be changed.

An old <u>chair</u> ~~with broken legs~~ <u>has sat</u> in our basement for years.

ACTIVITY 1

©Jacob Lund/
Shutterstock

Working in groups of two, underline the subject and lightly cross out any words that come between the subject and the verb. Then double-underline the verb in parentheses that you believe is correct.

1. Some <u>members</u> ~~of the parents' association~~ (<u><u>want</u></u>, wants) to ban certain books from the school library.

2. Chung's trench <u>coat</u>, ~~with its big lapels and shoulder flaps~~, (make, <u><u>makes</u></u>) him feel like a tough private eye.

3. Misconceptions ~~about apes like the gorilla~~ (has, <u>have</u>) turned a relatively peaceful animal into a terrifying monster.

4. The rising <u>cost</u> ~~of necessities like food and shelter~~ (force, <u>forces</u>) many elderly people to live in poverty.

5. In my opinion, a few <u>slices</u> ~~of pepperoni pizza~~ (<u>make</u>, makes) a great evening.

TEACHING TIP
Remind students that the object in a prepositional phrase is not the subject in the sentence.

Verb before Subject

A verb agrees with its subject even when the verb comes *before* the subject. Words that may precede the subject include *there, here*, and, in questions, *who, which, what*, and *where*.

Here are some examples of sentences in which the verb appears before the subject:

There <u>are</u> wild <u>dogs</u> in our neighborhood.

In the distance <u>was</u> a <u>billow</u> of black smoke.

Here <u>is</u> the <u>newspaper</u>.

Where <u>are</u> the children's <u>coats</u>?

If you are unsure about the subject, ask *who* or *what* of the verb. With the first example above, you might ask, "*What* are in our neighborhood?" The answer, *wild dogs*, is the subject.

ESL NOTE
This is a common problem for nonnative speakers. Tell them that *there* and *here* announce the subject, so they can look ahead in the sentence for correct subject–verb agreement.

Write the correct form of each verb in the space provided.	**ACTIVITY 2**

1. There <u>are</u> dozens of frenzied shoppers waiting for the store to open. (is, are)

2. Here <u>are</u> the notes from yesterday's anthropology lecture. (is, are)

3. When <u>do</u> we take our break? (do, does)

4. There <u>were</u> scraps of yellowing paper stuck between the pages of the cookbook. (was, were)

5. At the very bottom of the grocery list <u>was</u> an item that meant a trip all the way back to aisle one. (was, were)

Compound Subjects

A *compound subject* is two subjects separated by a joining word, such as *and*. Subjects joined by *and* generally take a plural verb.

A patchwork <u>quilt</u> and a sleeping <u>bag</u> <u>cover</u> my bed in the winter.

<u>Brandon</u> and <u>Carrie</u> <u>are</u> a contented couple.

TEACHING TIP
You may want to provide additional examples of compound subjects joined by "either . . . or," "neither . . . nor," and "not only . . . but also."

When subjects are joined by *either . . . or, neither . . . nor, not only . . . but also,* the verb agrees with the subject closer to the verb.

Neither the <u>negotiator</u> nor the union <u>leaders</u> <u>want</u> the strike to continue.

The nearer subject, *leaders,* is plural, and so the verb is plural.

Neither the union <u>leaders</u> nor the <u>negotiator</u> <u>wants</u> the strike to continue.

In this version, the nearer subject, *negotiator,* is singular, so the verb is singular.

ACTIVITY 3	Write the correct form of the verb in the space provided.

(know, knows)

1. The driver and her passenger _____know_____ that they are at fault for the auto accident.

(are, is)

2. The coffee and dessert _____are_____ ready to be served.

(encourage, encourages)

3. Not only my teachers but also my wife ___encourages___ me to work hard in college.

(was, were)

4. Before the birth of my son, video games and television _____were_____ important to me.

(interest, interests)

5. Neither accounting nor marketing _____interests_____ Dustin, but he still plans to major in business.

ESL NOTE
Nonnative speakers also have problems with indefinite pronouns, especially when *either* and *neither* are used as correlative conjunctions.

Indefinite Pronouns

The following words, known as *indefinite pronouns,* always take singular verbs:

TEACHING TIP
The pronouns "everyone" and "everybody" are often mistaken as plural. Point out to students that the word "-one" is always singular.

(*-one* words)	(*-body* words)	(*-thing* words)	
one	nobody	nothing	each
anyone	anybody	anything	either
everyone	everybody	everything	neither
someone	somebody	something	

TIP   *Both* always takes a plural verb.

Write the correct form of the verb in the space provided.

ACTIVITY 4

1. Neither of those Web sites _____is_____ credible.   (are, is)

2. Somebody in the classroom __knows__ who stole my wallet.   (know, knows)

3. Both of the professors you mentioned _____are_____ hard, but you will learn   (are, is)
   a lot in their classes.

4. One of these downloaded movie rentals __needs__ to be watched within   (need, needs)
   twenty-four hours.

REVIEW TEST 1

In the space provided, write the correct form of the verb shown in the margin.

1. Tornadoes _____are_____ massive storms characterized by rotating columns   (is, are)
   of air that create funnels.

2. Almost a third of all the tornadoes in the United States _____occur_____ in   (occurs, occur)
   Tornado Alley, an area that covers Nebraska, Kansas, Oklahoma, and
   Texas.

3. The majority of tornadoes _____develop_____ between April and June.   (develops, develop)

4. Tornado watches _____are_____ often issued to alert people that weather   (is, are)
   conditions could produce tornadoes.

5. If either a storm chaser or radar _____spots_____ a tornado, a warning is   (spots, spot)
   issued.

6. Storm chasers _____are_____ people who attempt to get close to the torna-   (is, are)
   does to film, study, or just experience the storm.

7. When the National Weather Service _____issues_____ tornado warnings, peo-   (issues, issue)
   ple prepare by seeking safety in basements or shelters.

8. Hail, heavy rain, and a greenish black sky _____are_____ signs that a tor-   (is, are)
   nado may occur.

9. Tornadoes are measured on the Fujita Scale, which _____rates_____ the   (rates, rate)
   storms based on an estimate of the strength of the winds.

10. Although the Fujita Scale rates tornadoes from F0 to F6, most meteorol-   (feels, feel)
    ogists _____feel_____ an F6 tornado is inconceivable.

REVIEW TEST 2

Cross out the incorrect verb form in each sentence. In addition, underline the
subject or subjects that go with the verb. Then write the correct form of the
verb in the space provided.

TEACHING TIP
You may want to use these
review tests to assess
what your students have
learned.

___are___   1. Why ~~is~~ Jonathan and his friends cutting their hair so short?

___is___   2. Neither of my essays for history or economics ~~are~~ well written.

were   3. A 3-D <u>printer</u>, a pair of Bose <u>headphones</u>, and a <u>Google Daydream</u> ~~was~~ on my daughter's wish list.

look   4. The <u>mangoes</u> on the tree ~~looks~~ ripe.

are   5. There ~~is~~ the <u>mayor</u> and the school board <u>candidates</u>.

prevents   6. The annoying <u>barking</u> from the neighbor's dogs ~~prevent~~ me from studying.

_is_   7. <u>One</u> of my sports heroes ~~are~~ snowboarder Chloe Kim, who won a gold medal in the snowboard halfpipe in 2018.

make   8. Three <u>eggs</u>, grated <u>cheese</u>, and chopped <u>ham</u> ~~makes~~ for a hearty omelet.

thinks   9. A <u>person</u> in his or her twenties often ~~think~~ that retirement planning isn't necessary.

has   10. <u>Each</u> of the contestants on the new game show ~~have~~ a chance of winning the million-dollar grand prize.

More about Verbs

The purpose of this chapter is to provide additional information about verbs. Some people will find the grammatical terms here a helpful reminder of what they've learned earlier, in school, about verbs. For them, the terms will increase their understanding of how verbs function in English. Other people may welcome more detailed information about terms used elsewhere in the text. In either case, remember that the most common mistakes people make with verbs have been treated in previous chapters of the book.

Verb Tense

Verbs tell us the time of an action. The time that a verb shows is usually called *tense*. The most common tenses are the simple present, past, and future. In addition, there are nine tenses that enable us to express more specific ideas about time than we could with the simple tenses alone. Following are the twelve verb tenses and examples of each tense. Read them over to increase your sense of the many different ways of expressing time in English.

Tenses	Examples
Present	I *work*.
	Alejandro *works*.
Past	Abigail *worked* on her car.
Future	You *will work* on a new project next week.
Present perfect	He *has worked* on his term paper for a month.
	They *have worked* out a compromise.
Past perfect	The nurse *had worked* two straight shifts.
Future perfect	Next Monday, I *will have worked* here exactly two years.
Present progressive	I *am working* on my speech for the debate. You *are working* too hard.
	The tape recorder *is* not *working* properly.
Past progressive	He *was working* in the basement. The contestants *were working* on their talent routines.
Future progressive	My son *will be working* in our store this summer.
Present perfect progressive	Sarah *has been working* late this week.

continued

CHAPTER PREVIEW

Verb Tense

Helping Verbs

Verbals

- **Infinitive**

- **Participle**

- **Gerund**

TEACHING TIP
Write "tense = time" on the board. You may also want to write "agreement = number" on the board.

TEACHING TIP
Ask students to provide another example for each of the other verb tenses.

ESL NOTE
Nonnative speakers need to learn the usage and forms of verb tenses so that the reader can understand when events and actions take place. This chart can be expanded to the function and form of all verb tenses in English.

ESL NOTE
To assist nonnative speakers in understanding the usages in verb tenses in English, compare: present versus present perfect, present versus present progressive, simple past versus past perfect.

Tenses	Examples
Past perfect progressive	Until recently, I *had been working* nights.
Future perfect progressive	My mother *will have been working* as a nurse for forty-five years by the time she retires.

ACTIVITY 1   On a separate paper, write twelve sentences using the twelve verb tenses.

Answers will vary.

Helping Verbs

There are three common verbs that can either stand alone or combine with (and "help") other verbs. Here are the verbs and their forms:

TEACHING TIP
Point out which helping verbs are in the present tense and which ones are in the past tense.

be (am, are, is, was, were, being, been)
have (has, having, had)
do (does, did)

Here are examples of the helping verbs:

Used Alone	Used as Helping Verbs
I *was* confident.	I *was becoming* confident.
Lance *has* the answer.	Lance *has remembered* the answer.
My mom *did* a good job raising me.	My mom *did raise* me well.

There are nine helping verbs (traditionally known as *modals*, or *modal auxiliaries*) that are always used in combination with other verbs. Here are the nine verbs and a sentence example of each:

ESL NOTE
ESL writers have many problems with modals, such as using the wrong modal to express intended meaning, or using the wrong form of the verb after the modal. Another common mistake is that the time reference of the modal is wrong ("I should not exercise so much yesterday"). Nonnative speakers might benefit from a chart that contains the modal, function, form in the present, future, and past.

can	I *can study* for my sociology exam this weekend.
could	I *could* not *find* my professor after class.
may	The quiz *may cover* last week's assigned readings.
might	Steve *might attend* the group study session tonight.
shall	I *shall ask* my classmate Arnel to help me with my math homework.
should	She *should know* the answers because she attended the lecture.

continued

will	Tara *will want* to attend the biology field trip to the tidal pools.
would	The person at the counter *would* not *tell* me when the financial aid forms were due.
must	You *must ask* questions when you don't understand.

ESL NOTE
In English, verbs can be followed by other verbs, some by an infinitive, some by a gerund, and some by a base form of the verb. Nonnative speakers need to study commonly used forms.

Note from the examples that these verbs have only one form. They do not, for instance, add an *-s* when used with *he, she, it,* or any one person or thing.

On separate paper, write nine sentences using the nine helping verbs.

ACTIVITY 2

Answers will vary.

Verbals

Verbals are words formed from verbs. Verbals, like verbs, often express action. They can add variety to your sentences and vigor to your writing style. The three kinds of verbals are *infinitives, participles,* and *gerunds.*

Additional information about infinitives can be found in Chapter 24. Additional information about participles and gerunds can be found in Chapters 24 and 32.

Infinitive

An infinitive is *to* plus the base form of the verb.

I love *to dance.*

Lina hopes *to write* for a newspaper.

I asked the children *to clean* the kitchen.

Participle

A participle is a verb form used as an adjective (a descriptive word). The present participle ends in *-ing.* The past participle ends in *-ed* or has an irregular ending.

Peering into the cracked mirror, the *crying* woman wiped her eyes.

The *astounded* man stared at his *winning* lottery ticket.

Swinging a sharp ax, Omar split the *rotted* beam.

Gerund

A gerund is the *-ing* form of a verb used as a noun.

Swimming is the perfect exercise.

Eating junk food is my diet downfall.

Through *doodling,* people express their inner feelings.

ACTIVITY 3

Answers will vary.

TEACHING TIP
For this activity, suggest that students write sentences that are specific to their own lives.

On separate paper, write three sentences using infinitives, three sentences using participles, and three sentences using gerunds. At least three of your sentences must be written about the photograph below.

©Valerie Martin

REFLECTIVE ACTIVITY

©mavo/Shutterstock

Reread any paragraph you wrote for an assignment in Chapter 7, "Narration," or any essay you wrote for Chapter 18, "Patterns of Essay Development." Do you see any verb problems or subject-verb agreement problems in your paper? If so, correct them using what you learned in Chapters 26-28.

Pronoun Agreement and Reference

Nouns name persons, places, or things. *Pronouns* are words that take the place of nouns. In fact, the word *pronoun* means "for a noun." Pronouns are short-cuts that keep you from unnecessarily repeating words in writing. Here are some examples of pronouns:

Parker left *his* camera on the bus.
(*His* is a pronoun that takes the place of *Parker's.*)

Elena drank the coffee even though *it* was cold.
(*It* replaces *coffee.*)

As I turned the newspaper's damp pages, *they* disintegrated in my hands.
(*They* is a pronoun that takes the place of *pages.*)

This chapter presents rules that will help you avoid two common mistakes people make with pronouns. The rules are:

1. A pronoun must agree in number with the word or words it replaces.

2. A pronoun must refer clearly to the word it replaces.

Pronoun Agreement

A pronoun must agree in number with the word or words it replaces. If the word a pronoun refers to is singular, the pronoun must be singular; if that word is plural, the pronoun must be plural. (Note that the word a pronoun refers to is known as the *antecedent.*)

Delaney showed me her antique wedding band.

Students enrolled in the art class must provide their own supplies.

In the first example, the pronoun *her* refers to the singular word *Delaney*; in the second example, the pronoun *their* refers to the plural word *Students*.

CHAPTER PREVIEW
Pronoun Agreement
• **Indefinite Pronouns**
Pronoun Reference

ESL NOTE
Nonnative speakers may have difficulty with pronoun agreement because in their native language the pronoun may agree with the noun it modifies. For example, a Spanish speaker might say, "Delaney showed me *their* rings" instead of "*Delaney* showed me *her* rings."

TEACHING TIP
Introduce students to the term "antecedent."

Write the appropriate pronoun (*their, they, them, it*) in the blank space in each of the following sentences.

EXAMPLE

I bought a used bicycle and gave ___it___ a new coat of paint.

1. Melinda and Jo bought tickets for the concert, and __they__ also made reservations for dinner at the new Italian restaurant on Sanchez Avenue.

2. The leftover pizza was cold, but I decided to eat ___it___ for breakfast.

3. The teachers at my college are very committed, for __they__ often stay after class to help students.

4. Leon's children are coming over on Friday, and then ___their___ mother will pick them up on Sunday night.

5. This morning, Jada forgot to bring the quarterly sales report, so she caught a cab home before the meeting to get ___it___.

Indefinite Pronouns

The following words, known as *indefinite pronouns,* are always singular.

(-*one* words)	(-*body* words)	
one	nobody	each
anyone	anybody	either
everyone	everybody	neither
someone	somebody	

If a pronoun in a sentence refers to one of these singular words, the pronoun should be singular.

Somebody left her shawl in the women's restroom.

One of the busboys just called and said he would be an hour late.

Everyone in the club must pay his dues next week.

Each circled pronoun is singular because it refers to an indefinite pronoun. There are two important points to remember about indefinite pronouns:

1. In the last example, if everyone in the club was a woman, the pronoun would be *her.* If the club had women and men, the pronoun would be *his or her:*

   Everyone in the club must pay his or her dues next week.

Traditionally, writers used the masculine pronoun (*he, him, his*) to refer to both women and men; however, most writers now use *he or she, him or her,* and *his or hers* to avert an implied gender bias. To avoid using the masculine pronoun or the somewhat awkward *or* constructions, a sentence can often be rewritten in the plural:

> Club members must pay their dues next week.

2. In informal spoken English, *plural* pronouns are often used with the indefinite pronouns. Many people would probably not say:

> Everybody has his or her own opinion about the election.

Instead, they would be likely to say:

> Everybody has their own opinion about the election.

Here are other examples:

> Everyone in the choir must buy their robes.

> Everybody in the line has their ticket ready.

> No one in the class remembered to bring their books.

TEACHING TIP
Take an opinion poll in class to see if students use the plural pronouns with indefinite pronouns.

In such cases, the indefinite pronouns are clearly plural in meaning, and using plural pronouns with them helps people avoid the awkward *his or her.* In time, the plural pronoun may be accepted in formal speech or writing. Until then, however, you should use the grammatically correct singular form in your writing.

Underline the correct pronoun.	**ACTIVITY 2**

1. Neither of the potential buyers had really made up (<u>her</u>, their) mind.

2. Not one of the new cashiers knows what (<u>he</u>, they) should be doing.

3. Each of these computers has (<u>its</u>, their) drawbacks.

4. Anyone trying to reduce (<u>his or her</u>, their) salt intake should avoid canned and processed foods.

5. If anybody calls when I'm out, tell (<u>him</u>, them) I'll return in an hour.

Pronoun Reference

A sentence may be confusing and unclear if a pronoun appears to refer to more than one word or does not refer to any specific word. Look at this sentence:

> Malia was annoyed when they failed her car for a faulty turn signal.

Who failed her car? There is no specific word that *they* refers to. Be clear:

> Malia was annoyed when the inspectors failed her car for a faulty turn signal.

Here are sentences with other faulty pronoun references. Read the explanations of why they are faulty and look carefully at how they are corrected.

TEACHING TIP
Ask students to underline the pronouns in these sentences and circle their antecedents.

Faulty

Peter told Alan that his wife was unhappy.
(Whose wife is unhappy: Peter's or Alan's? Be clear.)

Kia is really a shy person, but she keeps it hidden.
(There is no specific word that *it* refers to. It would not make sense to say, "Kia keeps shy hidden.")

Jodie attributed her success to her husband's support, which was generous.
(Does *which* mean that Jodie's action was generous or that her husband's support was generous?)

Clear

Peter told Alan, "My wife is unhappy."

Kia is really a shy person, but she keeps her shyness hidden.

Generously, Jodie attributed her success to her husband's support. *Or:* Jodie attributed her success to her husband's generous support.

ACTIVITY 3

Answers may vary.

Rewrite each of the following sentences to make clear the vague pronoun reference. Add, change, or omit words as necessary.

EXAMPLE

Amanda's sister picked up her daughter from the babysitter after work.

Amanda's sister picked up Amanda's daughter from the babysitter after work.

1. Andrew went down to the shoe store but didn't find one that fit him.

   Andrew went down to the shoe store but didn't find a pair of shoes that fit him.

2. To check out books at the library, they will ask students if they have a valid student identification card.

   To check out books at the library, the librarians will ask students if they have
   a valid student identification card.

3. Roberto told Hudson that his computer-animated art project was well designed.

   Roberto told Hudson that Hudson's computer-animated art project was well
   designed.

4. Jiggling her key into the rusty padlock, Susan knew that she had found the right one.

   Jiggling her key into the rusty padlock, Susan knew that she had found the
   right key.

5. Yumiko visited the counseling center because they could help her decide on a major.

   Yumiko visited the counseling center because the counselors could help her
   decide on a major.

Cross out the pronoun error in each sentence, and write the correct word(s) on the line following the sentence. Then, in the space provided, write whether the rule being followed is about pronoun agreement or about pronoun reference.

TEACHING TIP
You may want to use this review test to assess what your students have learned.

EXAMPLES

___Pronoun Agreement___ Many students begin college without any idea what ~~he or she~~ are going to study. ___they___

___Pronoun Reference___ The years pass quickly, and ~~they~~ will soon need to focus on a main interest. ___students___

___Pronoun Agreement___ 1. If a person wants to become a high school history teacher, ~~they~~ should major in secondary education. ___he or she___

___Pronoun Reference___ 2. Astronomers are scientists who study the stars; ~~they~~ are often out late at night. ___these scientists___

___Pronoun Agreement___ 3. College students wanting to be cryptologists need to study math, and ~~he or she~~ also must be good at solving puzzles and creating and breaking codes. ___they___

___Pronoun Agreement___ 4. Anybody who wants to be a firefighter will need to be in top physical condition to pass ~~their~~ physical examination. ___his or her___

___Pronoun Reference___ 5. Not all food service workers need college degrees, but ~~they~~ can help with advancement. ___the degrees___

___Pronoun Agreement___ 6. A student who wants to study the field of biomedical engineering should be prepared to spend ~~his~~ college years taking chemistry, biology, anatomy, and engineering classes. ___his or her___

___Pronoun Reference___ 7. Zoologists work at zoos and aquariums with animals, and ~~they~~ sometimes live in natural habitats to learn more. ___the zoologists___

___Pronoun Agreement___ 8. A student who wants to work outdoors could choose to be a fish and game warden, but ~~they~~ should be prepared to major in wildlife management. ___he or she___

Pronoun Types

This chapter describes some common types of pronouns: subject and object pronouns, possessive pronouns, and demonstrative pronouns.

Subject and Object Pronouns

Most pronouns change their form depending on what place they occupy in a sentence. In the box that follows is a list of subject and object pronouns.

Subject Pronouns	Object Pronouns
I	me
you	you (no change)
he	him
she	her
it	it (no change)
we	us
they	them

Subject Pronouns

Subject pronouns are subjects of verbs.

> He served as a soldier in Iraq. (*He* is the subject of the verb *served.*)
>
> *They* are moving into Kari's old apartment. (*They* is the subject of the verb *are moving.*)
>
> We students should have a say in the decision. (*We* is the subject of the verb *should have.*)

Following are several rules for using subject pronouns—and several kinds of mistakes people sometimes make with subject pronouns.

Rule 1

Use a subject pronoun when you have a compound subject (more than one subject).

Incorrect	**Correct**
My brother and *me* are Bruno Mars fanatics.	My brother and *I* are Bruno Mars fanatics.
Him and *me* know the lyrics to all of Bruno's songs.	*He* and *I* know the lyrics to all of Bruno's songs.

ESL NOTE
Nonnative speakers may repeat the subject as they do in their native language ("When the *airplane it's* arriving, I will call my friend to pick me up.").

> **T I P** **for Rule 1**
> If you are not sure what pronoun to use, try each pronoun by itself in the sentence. The correct pronoun will be the one that sounds right. For example, "Him knows the lyrics to all of Bruno's songs" does not sound right; "He knows the lyrics to all of Bruno's songs" does.

Rule 2

Use a subject pronoun after forms of the verb *be*. Forms of *be* include *am, are, is, was, were, has been, have been,* and others.

It was *I* who left the light on.

It may be *they* in that car.

It is *he.*

The sentences above may sound strange and stilted to you because they are seldom used in conversation. When we speak with one another, forms such as "It was me," "It may be them," and "It is him" are widely accepted. In formal writing, however, the grammatically correct forms are still preferred.

TEACHING TIP
Point out that "it" is often a vague pronoun.

> **T I P** **for Rule 2**
> You can avoid having to use a subject pronoun after *be* by simply rewording a sentence. Here is how the preceding examples could be reworded:
>
> I was the one who left the light on.
> They may be in that car.
> He is here.

Rule 3

Use subject pronouns after *than* or *as*. The subject pronoun is used because a verb is understood after the pronoun.

You play better than I (play). (The verb *play* is understood after *I.*)

Jenna is as bored as I (am). (The verb *am* is understood after *I.*)

We don't need the money as much as they (do). (The verb *do* is understood after *they.*)

> **TIP**
>
> **for Rule 3**
> Avoid mistakes by mentally adding the "missing" verb at the end of the sentence.

Object Pronouns

Object pronouns (me, him, her, us, them) are the objects of verbs or prepositions. (*Prepositions* are connecting words like *for, at, about, to, before, by, with,* and *of.* See also Chapter 22.)

> Kelsea helped me. (*Me* is the object of the verb *helped.*)
>
> We took *them* to the college. (*Them* is the object of the verb *took.*)
>
> Leave the children with *us.* (*Us* is the object of the preposition *with.*)
>
> I got in line behind *him.* (*Him* is the object of the preposition *behind.*)

People are sometimes uncertain about what pronoun to use when two objects follow a verb.

Incorrect	**Correct**
I gave a gift to Morgan and *she.*	I gave a gift to Morgan and *her.*
She came to the movie with Adrianna and *I.*	She came to the movie with Adrianna and *me.*

> **TIP**
>
> If you are not sure what pronoun to use, try each pronoun by itself in the sentence. The correct pronoun will be the one that sounds right. For example, "I gave a gift to she" does not sound right; "I gave a gift to her" does.

ACTIVITY 1	Underline the correct subject or object pronoun in each of the following sentences. Then show whether your answer is a subject or object pronoun by circling the S or O in the margin. The first one is done for you as an example.

TEACHING TIP
After students complete this activity, go over the answers in class.

S　(O)　1. The sweaters Mom knitted for Vince and (I, <u>me</u>) are too small.

(S)　O　2. The umpire and (<u>he</u>, him) started to argue.

(S)　O　3. No one has a quicker temper than (<u>she</u>, her).

(S)　O　4. Your grades prove that you worked harder than (<u>they</u>, them).

(S)　O　5. (<u>We</u>, Us) runners train indoors when the weather turns cold.

(S)　O　6. (<u>She</u>, Her) and Sienna never put the cap back on the toothpaste.

Ⓢ   O   7. Chris and (<u>he</u>, him) are the most energetic kids in the first
              grade.

S   Ⓞ   8. Arguing over clothes is a favorite pastime for my sister and
              (I, <u>me</u>).

S   Ⓞ   9. The rest of (they, <u>them</u>) will be arriving in about ten minutes.

S   Ⓞ   10. The head of the ticket committee asked Maggie and (I, <u>me</u>)
              to help with sales.

Possessive Pronouns

Here is a list of possessive pronouns:

my, mine	our, ours
your, yours	your, yours
his	their, theirs
her, hers	
its	

Possessive pronouns show ownership or possession.

Adam revved up *his* motorcycle and took off.

The keys are *mine*.

 TIP   A possessive pronoun *never* uses an apostrophe. (See also
Chapter 36.)

Incorrect

That coat is *hers'*.

The card table is *theirs'*.

Correct

That coat is *hers*.

The card table is *theirs*.

Cross out the incorrect pronoun form in each of the sentences below. Write the
correct form in the space at the left.

ACTIVITY 2

EXAMPLE

___hers___   Those Nintendo games are ~~hers'~~.

___its___   1. I didn't know that the blender I bought at the garage sale had
              lost ~~its'~~ blade.

___theirs___   2. Several strangers at the park asked the couple if the unleashed
              dog was ~~theirs'~~.

ESL NOTE
Remind nonnative
speakers that in English,
the possessive pronoun
agrees with the possessor,
not the object it modifies.
A Spanish speaker might
say, "I have their books"
instead of "I have my
books." This can be an
error that causes confusion
for the reader.

hers	3. Kimi's chemistry professor wondered if the correct answers were indeed ~~hers'~~.
ours	4. The boxes of donated items for the annual food drive are ~~ours'~~.
yours	5. You should tell everyone that the idea was entirely ~~yours'~~.

Demonstrative Pronouns

Demonstrative pronouns point to or single out a person or thing. There are four demonstrative pronouns:

this	these
that	those

Generally speaking, *this* and *these* refer to things close at hand; *that* and *those* refer to things farther away. The four demonstrative pronouns are also commonly used as demonstrative adjectives.

Is anyone using *this* spoon?

I am going to throw away *these* magazines.

I just bought *that* black pickup truck at the curb.

Pick up *those* toys in the corner.

 TIP Do not use *them, this here, that there, these here,* or *those there* to point out. Use only *this, that, these,* or *those.*

| ACTIVITY 3 | Cross out the incorrect pronoun form of the demonstrative pronoun, and write the correct form in the space provided. |

EXAMPLE

Those	~~Them~~ pizza boxes are empty.
This	1. ~~This here~~ iPod is outdated.
those	2. Bring ~~them~~ files to the meeting on Monday.
those	3. The salesperson politely asked ~~them~~ customers if they needed help.
that	4. I baked ~~that there~~ apple pie with Splenda.
those	5. What do ~~them~~ Japanese *kanji* characters on your tattoo mean?

Re-read any paragraph you wrote for an assignment in Chapter 8, "Description," or any essay you wrote while studying Chapter 18, "Patterns of Essay Development." Ask yourself if you see any pronoun-agreement problems in your writing. Are there any problems with pronoun types as explained in Chapters 29 and 30? If so, correct them using what you learned in those chapters.

©mavo/Shutterstock

REVIEW TEST

Read the paragraph and underline the correct word in the parentheses.

Many people have heard of the Bill & Melinda Gates Foundation, but few know (its, it's) history or (its, their) purposes. In 1975, Bill Gates and Paul Allen founded Microsoft, which was nothing more than two very smart men and (his, their) ideas. By 1986, Microsoft had gone public and Gates was a billionaire. In 1994, (he, him) created the William H. Gates Foundation that focused on health issues around the world. In 1997, (he, him) and (his, his') wife, Melinda, created the Gates Library Foundation to help fund libraries and help provide free Internet access to Americans through library access. In 1999, (they, them) renamed the Gates Library Foundation; it became known as the Gates Learning Foundation. (This, These) broadened (its, it's) focus to include initiatives for helping low-income students prepare and pay for college. In 2000, the William H. Gates Foundation and the Gates Learning Foundation merged to become the Bill & Melinda Gates Foundation. Since 1994, the foundation has provided funds of more than three billion dollars through (its, their) Global Development Program to help create sustainable solutions in poorer countries. Some of (these, them) programs are agricultural development, financial services for the poor, and initiatives for educating about and establishing clean water, good sanitation, and healthful hygiene. The foundation has also funded over fourteen billion dollars in its Global Health Program. (This, This here) program finances initiatives that focus on saving lives in poor countries through vaccinations, neonatal and infant health care, and treatment of illnesses such as HIV/AIDS, malaria, and tuberculosis. A third program, the United States Program, has received almost six billion dollars to continue to fund the programs started by the Gates Learning Foundation. All of (these, those) programs have had an impact on millions of lives through the founders' belief that "every life has equal value."

TEACHING TIP
You may want to use this review test to assess what your students have learned.

Academic

Adjectives and Adverbs

TEACHING TIP
For each sentence, ask students to underline the word that the adjective describes.

ESL NOTE
Many nonnative speakers experience difficulty with adjectives:

1. Word order: In some languages, the adjective follows the noun it modifies.
2. Word form: In some languages, the adjective agrees with the word it modifies in number and gender.
3. Nonnative students also have difficulty distinguishing between *-ing* and *-ed* adjectives.

Adjectives

What Are Adjectives?

Adjectives describe nouns (names of persons, places, or things) or pronouns.

Keiko is a *wise* woman. (The adjective *wise* describes the noun *woman.*)

She is also *funny.* (The adjective *funny* describes the pronoun *she.*)

I'll carry the *heavy* bag of groceries. (The adjective *heavy* describes the noun *bag.*)

It is *torn.* (The adjective *torn* describes the pronoun *it.*)

Adjectives usually come before the word they describe (as in *wise* woman and *heavy* bag). But they also come after forms of the verb *be* (*is, are, was, were,* and so on). They also follow verbs such as *look, appear, seem, become, sound, taste,* and *smell.*

That road is *slippery.* (The adjective *slippery* describes the road.)

The dogs are *noisy.* (The adjective *noisy* describes the dogs.)

Those customers were *impatient.* (The adjective *impatient* describes the customers.)

Your room looks *neat.* (The adjective *neat* describes the room.)

RESPONDING TO IMAGES

Describe this artwork using as many specific details as possible. How many adjectives did you use? Circle them.

©Edwin Verin/Shutterstock

Using Adjectives to Compare

Adjectives are often used to compare things or people. Use the comparative form of the adjective if two or more people or things are being compared. Use the superlative form of the adjective if three or more people or things are being compared.

For all one-syllable adjectives and some two-syllable adjectives, add *-er* when comparing two things and *-est* when comparing three or more things.

> Josh's beard is *longer* than mine, but Lee's is the *longest.*

> Meg may be the *quieter* of the two sisters; but that's not saying much, since they're the *loudest* girls in school.

For some two-syllable adjectives and all longer adjectives, use *more* when comparing two things and *most* when comparing three or more things.

> Liza Minnelli is *more famous* than her sister; but their mother, Judy Garland, is still the *most famous* member of the family.

> The red letters on the sign are *more noticeable* than the black ones, but the fluorescent letters are the *most noticeable.*

You can usually tell when to use *more* and *most* by the sound of a word. For example, you can probably tell by its sound that "carefuller" would be too awkward to say and that *more careful* is thus correct. But there are many words for which both *-er* or *-est* and *more* or *most* are equally correct. For instance, either "a more fair rule" or "a fairer rule" is correct.

To form negative comparisons, use *less* and *least.*

> During my first dance class, I felt *less graceful* than an injured elephant.

> When the teacher came to our house to complain to my parents, I offered her the *least* comfortable chair in the room.

Points to Remember about Comparing

Point 1

Use only one form of comparison at a time. That is, do not use both an *-er* ending and *more* or both an *-est* ending and *most:*

Incorrect	Correct
My mother's fruitcake is always *more heavier* than my grandmother's.	My mother's fruitcake is always *heavier* than my grandmother's.
Get Out is the *most frighteningest* movie I've ever seen.	*Get Out* is the *most frightening* movie I've ever seen.

Point 2

Learn the irregular forms of the words shown below.

	Comparative (for comparing two things)	Superlative (for comparing three or more things)
bad	worse	worst
good, well	better	best
little (in amount)	less	least
much, many	more	most

Do not use both *more* and an irregular comparative or *most* and an irregular superlative.

Incorrect	Correct
It is *more better* to give than to receive.	It is *better* to give than to receive.
Last night I got the *most worst* headache I ever had.	Last night I got the *worst* headache I ever had.

ACTIVITY 1

Add to each sentence the correct form of the word in the margin.

EXAMPLES

bad

wonderful

good

young

bad

unusual

little

The ___worst___ job I ever had was baby-sitting for spoiled four-year-old twins.

The ___most wonderful___ day of my life was when my daughter was born.

1. The ___best___ chocolate cake I ever ate had bananas in it.

2. Aunt Sonja is the ___youngest___ of the three sisters.

3. A rain that freezes is ___worse___ than a snowstorm.

4. That's the ___most unusual___ home I've ever seen—it's shaped like a teapot.

5. Being painfully shy has made Erin the ___least___ friendly person I know.

Adverbs

What Are Adverbs?

Adverbs describe verbs, adjectives, or other adverbs. They usually end in *-ly*.

The father *gently* hugged the sick child. (The adverb *gently* describes the verb *hugged*.)

Newborns are *totally* innocent. (The adverb *totally* describes the adjective *innocent*.)

The lecturer spoke so *terribly* fast that I had trouble taking notes. (The adverb *terribly* describes the adverb *fast*.)

A Common Mistake with Adverbs and Adjectives

People often mistakenly use an adjective instead of an adverb after a verb.

Incorrect	Correct
Sam needs a haircut *bad*.	Sam needs a haircut *badly*.
She gets along *easy* with others.	She gets along *easily* with others.
You might have lost the race if you hadn't run so *quick* at the beginning.	You might have lost the race if you hadn't run so *quickly* at the beginning.

Underline the adjective or adverb needed. (Remember that adjectives describe nouns, and adverbs describe verbs and other adverbs.)

TEACHING TIP
You may want to do this activity with the entire class.

1. As Beyoncé spoke, the audience listened (attentive, <u>attentively</u>).

2. I added a teaspoon of (<u>dark</u>, darkly) sugar to the teriyaki steak marinade.

3. The couple talked (continuous, <u>continuously</u>) during the movie.

4. The moon shone (bright, <u>brightly</u>) the night that Ava and I went fishing.

5. Our teacher assured us that the pop quiz contained (<u>easy</u>, easily) questions.

Well and *Good*

Two words that are often confused are *well* and *good*. *Good* is an adjective; it describes nouns. *Well* is usually an adverb; it describes verbs. But *well* (rather than *good*) is used as an adjective when referring to health.

Write *well* or *good* in each of the sentences that follow.

1. If you kids do a ____good____ job cleaning your bedrooms, I'll take you out for some ice cream.

2. If I organize the office records too ____well____, my bosses may not need me anymore.

3. After eating a pound of chocolate, I didn't feel too ____well____.

4. When Jon came out, he discovered who his ____good____ friends really were.

5. Just because brothers and sisters fight when they're young doesn't mean they won't get along ____well____ as adults.

Review a paragraph you wrote for an assignment in Chapter 8, "Description," or an essay you wrote for Chapter 18, "Patterns of Essay Development." Underline all of the adjectives and adverbs in the paper. Are there any problems with these words? If so, correct them using what you learned in Chapter 31.

©mavo/Shutterstock

REVIEW TEST 1

TEACHING TIP
You may want to use these review tests to assess what your students have learned.

ESL NOTE
Some nonnative students have difficulty with the placement of frequency adverbs (*always, sometimes, never*). They also make errors in the placement of a series of adverbials of time and place ("I went at 10 p.m. to the movies" instead of "I went to the movies at 10 p.m."). Tell students that time adverbials can often begin or end a sentence and that's why you place them at the end of the sentence. It can also add sentence variety ("At 10 p.m., I went to the movies").

Underline the correct word in parentheses.

1. The waitress poured (littler, <u>less</u>) coffee into my cup than yours.

2. Humid air seems to make Gabriel's asthma (more worse, <u>worse</u>).

3. The movie is so interesting that the three hours pass (quick, <u>quickly</u>).

4. The talented boy sang as (confident, <u>confidently</u>) as a seasoned performer.

5. Our band played so (good, <u>well</u>) that a local firm hired us for its annual dinner.

6. Norah is always (<u>truthful</u>, truthfully), even when it might be better to tell a white lie.

7. The driver stopped the bus (sudden, <u>suddenly</u>) and yelled, "Everybody out!"

8. Shirts and pants in the same color make a person look (more thin, <u>thinner</u>) than ones in contrasting colors.

9. Your intentions may have been (<u>good</u>, well), but I'd prefer that you ask before arranging a blind date for me.

10. Our cat likes to sit in the (<u>warmest</u>, most warm) spot in any room—by a fireplace, on a windowsill in the sunshine, or on my lap.

REVIEW TEST 2

There are eight adjective and adverb errors in the following paragraph. Draw a line through each error and above that word, write the correct word(s).

Every year, sightseers to Washington, D.C., visit parts of the Smithsonian Institution, which is the world's ~~larger~~ *largest* museum complex. It consists of nineteen different museums and galleries, which are ~~real~~ *very/really* big, along with nine of the ~~most best~~ *best* research facilities in the world. Three ~~extreme~~ *extremely* popular museums are the National Air and Space Museum, the National Museum of Natural History, and the National Museum of American History. The National Zoo is also under the jurisdiction of the Smithsonian Institution and is home to over 2,000 animals. Like the museums, the zoo is very big and cannot be toured ~~quick~~ *quickly*, so visitors should plan to spend the entire day. When tourists visit the Smithsonian, they often choose the ~~popularest~~ *most popular* museums, but this can mean dealing with ~~hugely~~ *huge* crowds. Those who wish to avoid crowds might want to visit ~~least~~ *lesser* known museums like the Postal Museum.

Misplaced and Dangling Modifiers

Misplaced Modifiers

Misplaced modifiers are words that, because of awkward placement, do not describe what the writer intended them to describe. A misplaced modifier can make a sentence confusing or unintentionally funny. To avoid this, place words as close as possible to what they describe.

Misplaced Words	Correctly Placed Words
Declan couldn't drive to work in his small sports car *with a broken leg*. (The sports car had a broken leg?)	With a broken leg, Declan couldn't drive to work in his small sports car. (The words describing Declan are now placed next to *Declan*.)
The sound system was sold to us by a charming salesman *with a money-back guarantee*. (The salesman had a money-back guarantee?)	The sound system with a money-back guarantee was sold to us by a charming salesman. (The words describing the sound system are now placed next to it.)
He *nearly* brushed his teeth for twenty minutes every night. (He came close to brushing his teeth but in fact did not brush them at all?)	He brushed his teeth for nearly twenty minutes every night. (The meaning—that he brushed his teeth for a long time—is now clear.)

Underline the misplaced word or words in each sentence. Then rewrite the sentence, placing related words together and thereby making the meaning clear.

ACTIVITY 1

EXAMPLES

Sliced cucumbers were placed on my weary eyes that were chilled in the refrigerator.

Sliced cucumbers that were chilled in the refrigerator were placed on my weary eyes.

Professor Ng spoke about the national housing crisis during her lecture.

During her lecture, Professor Ng spoke about the national housing crisis.

1. The tortilla soup was prepared by my mother-in-law on the stove.

The tortilla soup on the stove was . . .

2. The customer spoke to the branch manager <u>with a service complaint.</u>

   The customer with a service complaint spoke . . .

3. Nico added a mango to his fruit smoothie, <u>which was grown in his own yard.</u>

   Nico added a mango, which was grown in his own yard, to . . .

4. Emily deposited the money that she would use to pay for her college tuition <u>in the bank.</u>

   Emily deposited in the bank the money that . . .

5. Mari watched the movie on her portable DVD player <u>that her friends recommended.</u>

   Mari watched the movie that her friends recommended on . . .

6. I <u>nearly</u> sent out two dozen job applications this week alone.

   I sent out nearly two dozen job applications . . .

7. The motivational speaker talked about his former drug addiction <u>speaking from experience.</u>

   Speaking from experience, the motivational speaker talked . . .

8. I knew that I should avoid the traffic accident on the highway <u>listening to the radio.</u>

   Listening to the radio, I knew that . . .

9. The man asked the pharmacist for cough syrup <u>with a sore throat.</u>

   The man with a sore throat asked the pharmacist . . .

10. I gave a sizable donation to the candidate <u>at the end of the political fundraiser event.</u>

    At the end of the political fundraiser event, I gave . . .

Dangling Modifiers

A modifier that opens a sentence must be followed immediately by the word it is meant to describe. Otherwise, the modifier is said to be dangling, and the sentence takes on an unintended meaning. For example, in the sentence

TEACHING TIP
Get students to think about what the word "dangling" means.

While reading the newspaper, my dog sat with me on the front steps.

the unintended meaning is that the *dog* was reading the paper. What the writer meant, of course, was that *he* (or *she*), the writer, was reading the paper. The writer should have said,

While reading the newspaper, *I* sat with my dog on the front steps.

The dangling modifier could also be corrected by placing the subject within the opening word group:

While *I* was reading the newspaper, my dog sat with me on the front steps.

Here are other sentences with dangling modifiers. Read the explanations of why they are dangling, and look carefully at how they are corrected.

Dangling	Correct
Shaving in front of the steamy mirror, the razor nicked Eli's chin. (*Who* was shaving in front of the mirror? The answer is not *razor* but *Eli*. The subject *Eli* must be added.)	Shaving in front of the steamy mirror, *Eli* nicked his chin with the razor. *Or:* While *Eli* was shaving in front of the steamy mirror, he nicked his chin with the razor.
While turning over the bacon, hot grease splashed my arm. (*Who* is turning over the bacon? The answer is not *hot grease*, as it unintentionally seems to be, but *I*. The subject *I* must be added.)	While *I* was turning over the bacon, hot grease splashed my arm. *Or:* While turning over the bacon, *I* was splashed by hot grease.
Taking the exam, the room was so stuffy that Keisha almost fainted. (*Who* took the exam? The answer is not the *room* but *Keisha*. The subject Keisha must follow the modifier.)	Taking the exam, *Keisha* found the room so stuffy that she almost fainted. *Or:* When *Keisha* took the exam, the room was so stuffy that she almost fainted.
To impress the interviewer, punctuality is essential. (*Who* is to impress the interviewer? The answer is not *punctuality* but *you*. The subject *you* must be added.)	To impress the interviewer, *you* must be punctual. *Or:* For *you* to impress the interviewer, punctuality is essential.

The examples above show two ways of correcting a dangling modifier. Decide on a logical subject and do one of the following:

1. Place the subject *within* the opening word group:

   While *Eli* was shaving in front of the steamy mirror, he nicked his chin.

 TIP In some cases, an appropriate subordinating word such as *when* must be added and the verb may have to be changed slightly as well.

2. Place the subject right *after* the opening word group:

   Shaving in front of the steamy mirror, *Eli* nicked his chin.

Note: Some instructors might consider the third example on this page a misplaced modifier since the subject of the phrase *taking the exam*—Keisha—does appear later in the sentence. However, since correcting the error would involve omitting one word (*was*) and changing additional words (*Keisha found the room so stuffy that she*), this type of error is classified as a dangling modifier in *Exploring Writing: Paragraphs and Essays*. In general, if a word group is a participial phrase, and if the phrase occurs at the beginning of the sentence but modifies a subject that does not appear until later in the sentence, it is called a dangling rather than a misplaced modifier.

| ACTIVITY 2 | Look at the opening words in each sentence and ask, *Who?* The subject that answers the question should be nearby in the sentence. If it is not, provide the logical subject by using either method of correction just described. |

EXAMPLE

While pitching his tent, a snake bit Parker on the ankle.

While Parker was pitching his tent, a snake bit him on the ankle.

Or: While pitching his tent, Parker was bitten on the ankle by a snake.

Answers may vary.

1. Dancing on their hind legs, the audience cheered wildly as the elephants paraded by.

   The audience cheered wildly as the elephants, dancing on their hind legs,

   paraded by.

2. Last seen wearing dark glasses and a blond wig, the police spokesperson said the suspect was still being sought.

   The police spokesperson said the suspect, last seen wearing dark glasses

   and a blond wig, was . . .

3. Pouring out the cereal, a coupon fell into my bowl of milk.

   As I poured out the cereal, a coupon fell . . .

4. Escorted by dozens of police motorcycles, I knew the limousine carried someone important.

   Because it was escorted by dozens of police motorcycles, I knew the limousine . . .

5. Tired and exasperated, the fight we had was inevitable.

   We were tired and exasperated, so the fight we had . . .

6. Packed tightly in a tiny can, Joe had difficulty removing the anchovies.

   Joe had difficulty removing the anchovies, which were packed tightly . . .

7. Kicked carelessly under the bed, Raquel finally found her sneakers.

   Raquel finally found her sneakers, which were kicked carelessly under the bed.

8. Working at the copy machine, the morning dragged on.

   As I worked at the copy machine, the morning . . .

Reread any paragraph you wrote for an assignment in Chapter 9, "Process," or any essay you wrote while studying Chapter 18, "Patterns of Essay Development." Ask yourself if any of your sentences contain misplaced or dangling modifiers. If so, correct them using what you learned in Chapter 32. In each case, make sure you understand why the correction is much better than the original.

REVIEW TEST 1

Write MM for *misplaced modifier* or C for *correct* in the space provided for each sentence.

TEACHING TIP
You may want to use these review tests to assess what your students have learned.

MM   1. While in Vegas, I almost spent five hundred dollars at one slot machine.

C   2. While in Vegas, I spent almost five hundred dollars at one slot machine.

C   3. Roberto patiently waited as the meal he ordered was being prepared in the kitchen.

MM   4. Roberto patiently waited as the meal was being prepared in the kitchen he ordered.

MM   5. Chloe registered for her two summer classes on Monday.

C   6. On Monday, Chloe registered for her two summer classes.

C   7. Behind the sofa, the dog hid the biscuit that was given to him by his owner.

MM   8. The dog hid the biscuit that was given to him by his owner behind the sofa.

MM   9. I ordered a new hard drive that was refurbished from the Web site.

C   10. I ordered from the Web site a new hard drive that was refurbished.

REVIEW TEST 2

Write DM for *dangling modifier* or C for *correct* in the space provided for each sentence.

DM   1. While riding the bicycle, a vicious-looking German shepherd snapped at Jayden's ankles.

C   2. While Jayden was riding the bicycle, a vicious-looking German shepherd snapped at his ankles.

_____C_____   3. Afraid to look his father in the eye, Charley kept his head bowed.

_____DM_____   4. Afraid to look his father in the eye, Charley's head remained bowed.

_____DM_____   5. Boring and silly, I turned the YouTube video off.

_____C_____   6. I turned off the boring and silly YouTube video.

_____C_____   7. Munching leaves from a tall tree, the giraffe fascinated the children.

_____DM_____   8. Munching leaves from a tall tree, the children were fascinated by the giraffe.

_____DM_____   9. At the age of twelve, several colleges had already accepted the child genius.

_____C_____   10. At the age of twelve, the child genius had already been accepted by several colleges.

REVIEW TEST 3

Answers may vary; examples are shown.

Make the changes needed to correct the misplaced and dangling modifiers in the following sentences.

1. Willa Cather, author of *O Pioneers*, often wrote about women doing unusual things in her books.

   Willa Cather, author of O Pioneers, often wrote in her books about women

   doing unusual things.

2. Edgar Allan Poe's "The Fall of the House of Usher" is a deeply disturbing story that contains the standard features of mysterious death, haunted houses, and a barren landscape of a Gothic story.

   Edgar Allan Poe's "The Fall of the House of Usher" is a deeply disturbing story

   that contains the standard features of a Gothic story of mysterious death, haunted

   houses, and a barren landscape.

3. Kate Chopin wrote about the oppression of women in traditional society in many stories.

   Kate Chopin wrote many stories about the oppression of women in traditional

   society.

4. In "And of Clay Are We Created," Isabel Allende writes about how the death of a young girl affects a young man with deep feeling.

   In "And of Clay Are We Created," Isabel Allende writes about how the death of

   a young girl deeply affects a young man.

5. Often reflecting very real situations and violent deaths, Ambrose Bierce wrote many short stories.

   Ambrose Bierce wrote many short stories that often reflect very real situations and violent deaths.

6. Reading "The Metamorphosis" by Franz Kafka, an unexplained fear of apples and large bugs is caused.

   Many people find that reading "The Metamorphosis" by Franz Kafka causes an unexplained fear of apples and large bugs.

7. F. Scott Fitzgerald is best known for his novel, which takes place in the 1920s, *The Great Gatsby*.

   F. Scott Fitzgerald is best known for his novel, The Great Gatsby, which takes place in the 1920s.

8. Credited as the father of the American short story, "Rip Van Winkle" was written by Washington Irving.

   Credited as the father of the American short story, Washington Irving wrote "Rip Van Winkle."

9. Although "The Lottery" by Shirley Jackson was written in 1948, it is influencing other stories still in the twenty-first century.

   Although "The Lottery" by Shirley Jackson was written in 1948, it is still influencing other stories in the twenty-first century.

10. Overlooking the connection and courage her family offers in "Everyday Use," Alice Walker writes about a young woman, Dee, who strives to find her identity.

    In "Everyday Use," Alice Walker writes about a young woman, Dee, who overlooks the connection and courage her family offers and strives to find her identity.

REVIEW TEST 4

Complete the following sentences. In each case, a logical subject should follow the opening words.

EXAMPLE

Looking through the door's peephole, *I couldn't see who rang the doorbell.*

1. Noticing the light turn yellow, *Zach slowed the car down.*

2. Being fragile, *the vase broke when I set it down too hard.*

3. While washing the car, *the kids got soaking wet.*

4. Although very expensive, *the coat did not wear well.*

5. Driving past the cemetery, *Terry had gloomy thoughts of death.*

Answers will vary; examples are shown.

SECTION I: GRAMMAR EDITING TEST I

Decide which of the following items are fragments or run-ons and which are correct. Place your answers in the spaces at the bottom by writing F for fragment, RO for run-on, and C for correct. Then correct the incorrect items by rewriting them in the margins or between the lines.

1. The heart is a ~~muscle. 2. That~~ *muscle that* pumps blood throughout the body. 3. The human heart is about the size of one's closed fist ~~it is~~ *and* shaped like a pear. 4. Located in the ~~chest, 5. It~~ *chest, it* can be found slightly to the left of the breastbone. 6. The human heart has two ~~compartments. 7. Which~~ *compartments, which* are divided into two other chambers. 8. The upper sections are called the ~~atria, the~~ *atria, and the* lower ones are called the ventricles. 9. The heart also contains ~~valves. 10. Which~~ *valves, which* control the flow of blood.

1. __C__   2. __F__   3. __RO__   4. __F__   5. __C__

6. __C__   7. __F__   8. __RO__   9. __C__   10. __F__

SECTION I: GRAMMAR EDITING TEST II

In the margins or between the lines, rewrite the following paragraph to correct problems in subject–verb agreement, verb forms, and pronoun agreement and pronoun reference.

Starbucks may ~~has~~ *have* gotten its start in 1971, but coffee and coffee-houses ~~has~~ *have* been around much longer. There are many legends surrounding the beginnings of coffee, including one about an Ethiopian goatherd who found ~~them~~ *his* goats munching on the berries (raw beans) of the local coffee plants, but most believe ~~it~~ *coffee* was first roasted and brewed in the fifteenth century. Sufi monasteries in Yemen ~~is~~ *are* credited for this discovery. In the 1500s, coffee was very popular in Egypt, Turkey, and Persia. Travelers to these countries ~~discover~~ *discovered* coffee and ~~bring~~ *brought* it to Europe. People ~~are drinking~~ *drank* coffee at

continued

home, but the most popular way to drink it was at a coffeehouse.

Coffee *gains* popularity throughout Europe, as it was seen as a safe
~~gains~~ *gained*

drink that enhanced ~~their~~ *people's* abilities to think and reason. In fact, people

believe the French Revolution was started at the Café de Foy in

1789. By the nineteenth century, coffeehouses ~~are~~ *were* the place to see

and be seen. Many famous writers, musicians, and politicians ~~meets~~ *met*

in coffeehouses to exchange ideas and implement new policies. In

the twenty-first century, people who purchase coffee and relax in the

atmosphere of Starbucks cafés should know that ~~he or she was~~ *they are* part

of hundreds of years of tradition.

SECTION I: GRAMMAR EDITING TEST III

On the lines that follow, rewrite this e-mail to correct problems with adjectives
and adverbs, with misplaced or dangling modifiers, and with pronoun agreement and reference.

From: rose889@gmail.com
Sent: Saturday, August 24, 2019 12:03 PM
To: dodgers69@comcast.net
Subject: your recovery

Dad,

　　Mom called me on my cell late last night to tell me that you
have not been feeling good over the past few days because your
medications are making you dizzy and weak. However, the doctor
said that by taking your medicines regularly, your condition should
improve within weeks. I know that you'll feel a lot better then.
Remember that following the doctor's orders close is the only way to
recovery. Sticking with the plan, your health sure will return and you
can face the future more confident than ever.

　　You are lucky that your lungs suffered only minor damage.
Smoking cigarettes for that long, serious illnesses could have been
contracted. Of course we all hope that you never smoke again.
Going back to cigarettes, your current struggle to get healthy will
have been for nothing. Remember that a full recovery never comes
quick. However, each day your condition will improve, slow but sure.

continued

You will actually feel yourself getting more and more stronger as the months without cigarettes pass. Your sense of smell will return, and foods will taste more better than ever. Your clothes will stop stinking so bad, too. Finally, your urge to have a smoke will become less stronger, and you will wonder what made you start smoking in the first place.

Love,
Rose

Dad,

Mom called me on my cell late last night to tell me that you have not been feeling well over the past few days because your medications are making you dizzy and weak. However, the doctor said that if you take your medicines regularly, your condition should improve within weeks. I know that you'll feel a lot better then. Remember that following the doctor's orders closely is the only way to recovery. Sticking with the plan, your health surely will return and you can face the future more confidently than ever.

You are lucky that your lungs suffered only minor damage. Smoking cigarettes for that long, you could have contracted serious illnesses. Of course we all hope that you never smoke again. If you go back to cigarettes, your current struggle to get healthy will have been for nothing. Remember that a full recovery never comes quickly. However, each day your condition will improve, slowly but surely. You will actually feel yourself getting stronger and stronger as the months without cigarettes pass. Your sense of smell will return, and foods will taste better than ever. Your clothes will stop stinking so badly too. Finally, your urge to have a smoke will become weaker, and you will wonder what made you start smoking in the first place.

Love,
Rose

Mechanics

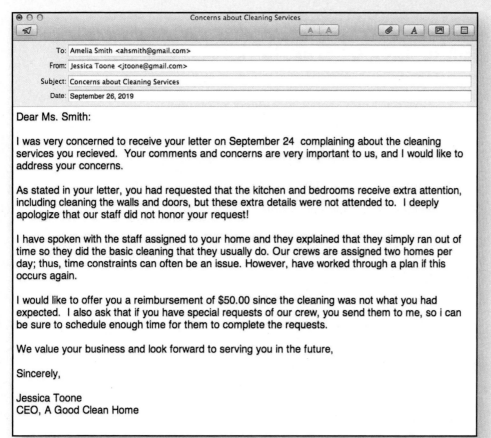

To: Amelia Smith <ahsmith@gmail.com>
From: Jessica Toone <jtoone@gmail.com>
Subject: Concerns about Cleaning Services
Date: September 26, 2019

Dear Ms. Smith:

I was very concerned to receive your letter on September 24 complaining about the cleaning services you recieved. Your comments and concerns are very important to us, and I would like to address your concerns.

As stated in your letter, you had requested that the kitchen and bedrooms receive extra attention, including cleaning the walls and doors, but these extra details were not attended to. I deeply apologize that our staff did not honor your request!

I have spoken with the staff assigned to your home and they explained that they simply ran out of time so they did the basic cleaning that they usually do. Our crews are assigned two homes per day; thus, time constraints can often be an issue. However, have worked through a plan if this occurs again.

I would like to offer you a reimbursement of $50.00 since the cleaning was not what you had expected. I also ask that if you have special requests of our crew, you send them to me, so i can be sure to schedule enough time for them to complete the requests.

We value your business and look forward to serving you in the future,

Sincerely,

Jessica Toone
CEO, A Good Clean Home

To: Sami Jones <srjones@gmail.com>
From: Jessica Toone <jtoone@gmail.com>
Subject: [No Subject]
Date: September 26, 2019

Hey Sami -- FWIW, i had another complaint about my cleaning crew. I thot i had trained them well enough, but this is the 3rd complaint this week about the crew doing a rotton job. I just don't know what to do, i feel like I should just fire them, but then maybe it's just the houses we are working with. I'm losing $ because I have to keep giving refunds to these jerky customers. Geez – there getting there houses cleaned for next to nothing, but they still complain! B4N jess

RESPONDING TO IMAGES

People often forget to apply sentence skills to their writing when composing e-mails. The two e-mails pictured here are geared toward different audiences, but both contain sentence-skills mistakes. As discussed in Chapter 1, such mistakes are not acceptable in a formal e-mail. Do you think sentence-skills mistakes should be excusable in informal e-mails? Compare the different audiences, form, and style of each e-mail; then find and correct the three errors in the first e-mail.

Capital Letters

Main Uses of Capital Letters

Capital letters are used with

1. First word in a sentence or direct quotation
2. Names of persons and the word *I*
3. Names of particular places and institutions
4. Names of days of the week, months, and holidays
5. Names of commercial products
6. Titles of books, magazines, newspapers, articles, stories, poems, films, television shows, songs, papers that you write, and the like
7. Names of companies, associations, unions, clubs, religious and political groups, and other organizations

Each use is illustrated in this chapter.

First Word in a Sentence or Direct Quotation

The new car dealership opened last week.

The teacher said, "There will be a quiz tomorrow."

"If you need help," said Teri, "call me. I'll be over in no time."

In the third example above, *If* and *I'll* are capitalized because they start new sentences. But *call* is not capitalized, because it is part of the first sentence.

Names and Titles

Names of Persons and the Word I

Last night, I saw a hilarious movie starring Kathryn Hahn and Mila Kunis.

Names of Particular Places and Institutions

Although Justin dropped out of Port Charles High School, he eventually earned his diploma and enrolled in Northern Essex Community College.

But   Use small letters if the specific name is not given.

Although Justin dropped out of high school, he eventually earned his diploma and enrolled in college.

Names of Days of the Week, Months, and Holidays

On the last Friday afternoon in May, the day before Memorial Day, my boss is having a barbecue for all the employees.

But   Use small letters for the seasons—summer, fall, winter, spring.

Most people feel more energetic in the spring and fall.

ESL NOTE
In some languages, days, months, and holidays are not capitalized.

Names of Commercial Products

Marta installed a new Pioneer AVH-X5800BHS receiver in her Subaru Legacy.

But   Use small letters for the *type* of product (receiver, car, and so on).

Titles of Books, Magazines, Newspapers, Articles, Stories, Poems, Films, Television Shows, Songs, Papers That You Write, and the Like

We read the book *The Grapes of Wrath*, by John Steinbeck, for our history class.

In the doctor's waiting room, I watched *Property Brothers*, read an article in *Shape*, and leafed through the *The News-Herald*.

Names of Companies, Associations, Unions, Clubs, Religious and Political Groups, and Other Organizations

Aisha Dhanial is a Muslim, and her best friend is a Southern Baptist.

The Hyde Park Hip Hop Group has won many competitions.

Brian, a member of Bricklayers Local 431 and the Knights of Columbus, works for Ace Construction.

Underline the words that need capitals in the following sentences. Then write the capitalized form of each word in the space provided. The number of spaces tells you how many corrections to make in each case.

ACTIVITY 1

EXAMPLE

In our biology class, each student must do a report on an article in the magazine *scientific american*.   __Scientific__   __American__

1. Meghan's collection of <u>beatles</u> souvenirs includes a pair of tickets from their last concert in <u>candlestick park</u> in San Francisco.

   __Beatles__   __Candlestick__   __Park__

2. Yumi read in *natural health* magazine that <u>abraham lincoln</u> suffered from severe depression.

   __Natural__   __Health__   __Abraham__   __Lincoln__

3. When <u>i</u> have a cold, I use <u>vicks</u> ointment and chew <u>halls</u> lozenges.

   __I__   __Vicks__   __Halls__

TEACHING TIP
Consider making a game out of this activity. See how quickly your students can complete the activity correctly. You may want to ask them to create a set of game rules first.

4. Since no parents volunteered for the job, the <u>boy scouts</u> in <u>springfield, illinois</u>, have a college student as troop leader.

   <u>Boy</u>   <u>Scouts</u>   <u>Springfield</u>   <u>Illinois</u>

5. A nature trail for the blind in <u>cape cod, massachusetts</u>, has signs written in Braille that encourage visitors to smell and touch the plants.

   <u>Cape</u>   <u>Cod</u>   <u>Massachusetts</u>

6. Some of the most popular items at a restaurant called <u>big river</u> are <u>chilean</u> sea bass and <u>atlantic</u> clam chowder.

   <u>Big</u>   <u>River</u>   <u>Chilean</u>   <u>Atlantic</u>

7. My father is a confirmed Dallas <u>cowboys</u> fan, though he lives in <u>boston</u>.

   <u>Cowboys</u>   <u>Boston</u>

8. Isabella bought a <u>diet pepsi</u> to wash down her <u>hostess twinkie</u>.

   <u>Diet</u>   <u>Pepsi</u>   <u>Hostess</u>   <u>Twinkie</u>

9. Dominic listened to songs by Thelonious Monk and John Coltrane on his iPhone while Grace read an article in *glamour* titled "What Do <u>men</u> Really <u>want?</u>"

   <u>Glamour</u>   <u>Men</u>   <u>Want</u>

10. After having her baby, <u>dana</u> received a card from one of her friends that read, "<u>congratulations</u>, we all knew you had it in you."

   <u>Dana</u>   <u>Congratulations</u>

Other Uses of Capital Letters

Capital letters are also used with

1. Names that show family relationships
2. Titles of persons when used with their names
3. Specific school courses
4. Languages
5. Geographic locations
6. Historical periods and events
7. Races, nations, and nationalities
8. Opening and closing of a letter

Each use is illustrated on the following pages.

TEACHING TIP
Ask students to create a sentence for each use of capital letters.

Names and Titles

Names That Show Family Relationships

All his life, Father has been addicted to gadgets.

I browsed through Grandmother's collection of old photographs.

Aunt Florence and Uncle Bill bought a mobile home.

But   Do not capitalize words like *mother, father, grandmother, grandfather, uncle, aunt,* and so on when they are preceded by a possessive word (such as *my, your, his, her, our, their*).

All his life, my father has been addicted to gadgets.

I browsed through my grandmother's collection of old photographs.

My aunt and uncle bought a mobile home.

Titles of Persons When Used with Their Names

I contributed to Senator McClure's campaign fund.

Is Dr. Cuezze on vacation?

Professor Sharif announced that there would be no tests in the course.

But   Use lowercase letters when titles appear by themselves, without specific names.

I contributed to my senator's campaign fund.

Is the doctor on vacation?

The professor announced that there would be no tests in the course.

Specific School Courses

The college offers evening sections of Education 200, Introduction to Teaching, Educational Psychology, and Children's Literature for Elementary Teachers.

But   Use lowercase letters for general subject areas.

The college offers evening sections of many education courses.

Miscellaneous Categories

Languages

My grandfather's Polish accent makes his English difficult to understand.

ESL NOTE
In some languages, names of languages are not capitalized.

Geographic Locations

He grew up in the Midwest but moved to the South to look for a better job.

But   Use lowercase letters in directions.

Head west for five blocks and then turn south on State Street.

Historical Periods and Events

During the Middle Ages, the Black Death killed over one-quarter of Europe's population.

Races, Nations, and Nationalities

The questionnaire asked if the head of our household was Caucasian, African American, Asian, Latino, or American Indian.

Tanya has lived on army bases in Guam, Germany, and Alabama.

Denise's beautiful features reflect her Chinese and Mexican parentage.

Opening and Closing of a Letter

Dear Sir: Sincerely yours,

Dear Ms. Henderson: Truly yours,

Capitalize only the first word in a closing.

ACTIVITY 2

Underline the words that need capitals in the following sentences. Then write the capitalized forms of the words in the spaces provided. The number of spaces tells you how many corrections to make in each case.

TEACHING TIP
Consider making a game out of these activities. See how quickly your students can complete the activity correctly. You may want to ask them to create a set of game rules first.

1. The students at the <u>university</u> of <u>hawaii</u> enjoyed visiting the beach, <u>mauna loa</u>, and Honolulu.

   University   Hawaii   Mauna   Loa

2. <u>Secretary</u> of <u>state</u> <u>henry</u> <u>kissinger</u> played a major role during <u>president</u> Nixon's years in office.

   Secretary   State   Henry   Kissinger   President

3. The students in <u>american</u> <u>indian</u> <u>literature</u> 267 decided that *tracks* by <u>louise erdrich</u> was their favorite book.

   American   Indian   Literature   *Tracks*

   Louise   Erdrich

4. John and <u>sue</u> are taking a cruise through the <u>panama canal</u>.

   Sue   Panama   Canal

5. Three countries I would like to visit one day are <u>greece</u>, <u>morocco</u>, and <u>india</u>.

   Greece   Morocco   India

Unnecessary Use of Capitals

ACTIVITY 3

Many errors occur when capitalization is used when it is not needed. Underline the incorrectly capitalized words in the following sentences, and write the correct forms in the spaces provided. The number of spaces tells you how many corrections to make in each sentence.

CHAPTER 33   Capital Letters   517

1. George Washington's <u>Forces</u> starved at Valley Forge because Pennsylvania <u>Farmers</u> preferred to sell food to the British for cash.

   ____forces____   ____farmers____

2. The virus damaged the files on my <u>Brother's</u> Dell <u>Computer</u>.

   ____brother's____   ____computer____

3. The <u>Country</u> cheered during the 2008 Summer Olympics when Michael Phelps won a record-breaking eight <u>Gold</u> <u>Medals</u> in Beijing.

   ____country____   ____gold____   ____medals____

4. In his <u>Book</u> titled *Offbeat Museums*, Saul Rubin tells about various <u>Unusual</u> <u>Museums</u>, such as the Kansas Barbed Wire <u>museum</u>.

   ____book____   ____unusual____   ____museums____   ____Museum____

5. The theory of relativity, which Einstein developed when he was only twenty-six, led to the invention of the <u>Electron</u> <u>Microscope</u>, <u>Television</u>, and <u>Atomic</u> bomb.

   ____electron____   ____microscope____   ____television____   ____atomic____

Add or delete capitals where needed in the following sentences. You should make forty-one corrections in all.

EXAMPLE

My favorite quote about ~~T~~hinking is from the ~~f~~rench philosopher, Descartes, who stated, "~~i~~ think, therefore ~~i~~ am."

1. In 1841, Ralph Waldo ~~e~~merson wrote, "~~w~~hat is the hardest task in the world? ~~t~~o think."

2. George ~~b~~ernard ~~s~~haw, the ~~i~~rish playwright, once wrote, "~~f~~ew people think more than two or three times a year; I have made an ~~I~~nternational reputation for myself by thinking once a week."

3. The saying, "A man is but the product of his thoughts; what he thinks, he becomes," was written by Mohandas ~~k~~. Gandhi in *ethical religion*.

4. ~~w~~illiam ~~j~~ames, a nineteenth-century ~~a~~merican ~~P~~hilosopher, stated, "~~a~~ great many people think they are thinking when they are merely rearranging their prejudices."

5. Don Marquis, a ~~N~~ewspaper columnist, challenged people by stating, "~~i~~f you make people think they're thinking, ~~T~~hey'll love you; but if you really make them think, they'll hate you."

You may want to use these review tests to assess what your students have learned.

Academic

6. In "faculties of the mind," the marquis of halifax wrote, "A man may dwell
so long upon a thought that it may take him prisoner."

7. In 1854, Henry David Thoreau wrote *walden; or life in the woods,* a book
that reflected on life and meaning. In it, he stated, "if i were confined to a
corner of a garret all my days, like a spider, the world would be just as large
to me while i had my thoughts about me."

8. "great thoughts spring from the heart," was written in the Eighteenth century
by Vauvenargues, a french essayist.

9. Samuel Butler, best known for his novel, *the way of all flesh*, once wrote,
"all Thinking is … a state of unrest tending towards equilibrium."

10. albert schweitzer wrote, "Renunciation of thinking is a Declaration of
spiritual bankruptcy."

REVIEW TEST 2

On separate paper, write

Answers will vary.

1. Seven sentences demonstrating the seven main uses of capital letters.

2. Eight sentences demonstrating the eight other uses of capital letters.

Numbers and Abbreviations

Numbers

Here are three helpful rules for using numbers.

Rule 1

Spell out numbers that take no more than two words. Otherwise, use the numbers themselves.

> In Jody's kitchen is her collection of seventy-two cookbooks.
>
> Jody has a file of 350 recipes.
>
> It will take about two weeks to fix the computer database.
>
> Since a number of people use the database, the company will lose over 150 workdays.
>
> Only twelve students have signed up for the field trip.
>
> Nearly 250 students came to the lecture.

Rule 2

Be consistent when you use a series of numbers. If some numbers in a sentence or paragraph require more than two words, then use numbers for the others, too.

> After the storm, maintenance workers unclogged 46 drains, removed 123 broken tree limbs, and rescued 3 kittens who were stuck in a drainpipe.

Rule 3

Use numbers to show dates, times, addresses, percentages, and chapters of a book.

> The burglary was committed on October 30, 2018, but not discovered until January 2, 2019.
>
> Before I went to bed, I set my alarm for 6:45 a.m. (*But*: Spell out numbers before *o'clock*. For example: I didn't get out of bed until seven o'clock.)
>
> The library is located at 45 West 52nd Street.
>
> When you take the skin off a piece of chicken, you remove about 40 percent of the fat.
>
> The name of the murderer is revealed in Chapter 8 on page 236.

CHAPTER PREVIEW
Numbers
Abbreviations

TEACHING TIP
Write several sentences on the board in which you intentionally break these rules. Ask students to identify the mistakes.

| **ACTIVITY 1** | Cross out the mistakes in numbers and write the corrections in the spaces provided. |

1. The Pan-Pacific Festival will begin at ~~four-thirty~~ in front of the park band-stand at ~~ninety-four~~ North ~~Fifty-Third~~ Street.

   _____4:30_____　　　　_____94_____　　　　_____53rd_____

2. Christine spent ~~8~~ hours writing all ~~15~~ pages of her English paper.

   _____eight_____　　　　_____fifteen_____

3. My supervisor wants me to finish at least ~~sixty~~ percent of the projects by July ~~fifteen~~.

   _____60_____　　　　_____15_____

Abbreviations

Using abbreviations can save you time when you take notes. In formal writing, however, you should avoid most abbreviations. Listed below are some of the few abbreviations that are considered acceptable in compositions. Note that a period is used after most abbreviations.

1. Mr., Mrs., Ms., Jr., Sr., Dr. when used with names:

   Mrs. Johnson　　　　Dr. Garcia　　　　Howard Kelley, Jr.

2. Time references:

   a.m. or A.M.　　　　p.m. or P.M.　　　　B.C., A.D.

3. Initials in a person's name:

   J. Edgar Hoover　　　　John F. Kennedy　　　　Samuel L. Jackson

4. Organizations, technical words, and company names known primarily by their initials:

   IBM　　　UNICEF　　　ABC　　　IRS　　　NBA　　　FAA

| **ACTIVITY 2** | Cross out the words that should not be abbreviated, and correct them in the spaces provided. |

1. I hope to graduate with my ~~deg.~~ by mid ~~Aug.~~, if not sooner.

   _____degree_____　　　　_____August_____

2. Galen needs to make an ~~appt.~~ with Dr. Wong, who is an endocrinologist, in ~~Feb.~~ to monitor his diabetes.

   _____appointment_____　　　　_____February_____

3. I want to find an inexpensive ~~apart.~~ near campus with one ~~bdrm.~~ and a separate kitchen.

   _____apartment_____　　　　_____bedroom_____

REFLECTIVE ACTIVITY

Review a paragraph you wrote for an assignment in Chapter 10, "Cause and/or Effect," or an essay you wrote while studying Chapter 18, "Patterns of Essay Development." Do you find any errors in mechanics, capitalization, or the use of numbers and abbreviations? If so, correct them according to what you learned in Chapters 33–34.

©mavo/Shutterstock

REVIEW TEST

The following e-mail contains errors in capitalization and the use of numbers and abbreviations. Rewrite the e-mail to correct these errors in the margins or in spaces between the lines. You should make twenty-five corrections in all.

TEACHING TIP
You may want to use this review test to assess what your students have learned.

From: Sarah L. *Leet*

Sent: Saturday, August 24, 2019

To: ~~Prof.~~ *Professor* Jane Smith

Subject: Spanish 2 Schedule, Weeks 1- ~~three~~ *3*

Hi ~~Prof.~~ *Professor* Smith:

~~i~~ *I* wanted to make sure I had our assignments clear for the next ~~3~~ *three* weeks in ~~Span.~~ *Spanish* class. By ~~Sept. eight~~ *September 8*, I am supposed to learn to count from ~~1~~ *one* to twenty-one and study Chapter ~~One~~ *1* in the

textbook. For the next week of class, I will need to read Chapters 2 and 3 and complete the ~~5~~ *five* exercises on ~~pg. sixty-three~~ *page 63*. In the third week of class, I will need to visit ~~Wash. h.s.~~ *Washington High School* from 9:30 ~~am~~ *a.m.* until ~~one-thirty pm~~ *1:30 p.m.* each day. During the visit, each of us in class will work with the ~~h.s. Span. Class.~~ *high school Spanish class* Is this right?

Thank you.

Sarah ~~leet~~ *Leet*

SECTION II: MECHANICS EDITING TEST I

The following sentences contain errors in capitalization and in the use of numbers and abbreviations. Rewrite these sentences to correct these errors in the margins or in spaces between lines. You should make twenty-five corrections in all.

> Aaron Copland was an important ~~american~~ ***American*** ¢omposer. Born in
> *New York City* *November*   *19*
> ~~new york city~~ on ~~november nineteenth~~, 1900, he studied music in
> *Paris France*
> ~~paris, france~~, during the early years of the twentieth century.
>   *Great*
> Copland's early works were inspired by jazz. During the ~~great~~
> *Depression*
> ~~depression~~ of the 1930s and 1940s, however, he turned to folk
>   *Lincoln Portrait*
> songs, using themes from this music in works entitled ~~lincoln portrait~~,
> *Billy   kid*   *Spring*
> ~~billy~~ the ~~kid~~, and his masterpiece *Appalachian* ~~*spring*~~. During this
>
> period, he also wrote scores for films like *Of Mice and Men*, which
>   *John Steinbeck's*
> is based on ~~john steinbeck's~~ novel of the same name. One of
>   *Fanfare*   *Common Man*
> Copland's most famous works is "~~fanfare~~ for the ~~common man~~,"
>   *1940s*
> which appears in a symphony he wrote in the ~~nineteen forties~~.
>   *December   2*   *New*
> Copland died on ~~dec. the second~~, 1990, in Tarrytown, ~~N.~~ York, at the
>
> age of ninety.

SECTION II: MECHANICS EDITING TEST II

The following paragraphs contain errors in capitalization and the use of numbers and abbreviations. Rewrite each paragraph to correct these errors in the margins or in spaces between lines. You should make twenty-six corrections in all.

> The metric system, a standard system of measurement, was
>   *France*   *1791*
> officially adopted in ~~france~~ in ~~seventeen ninety-one~~. Today it is used
>   *Europe*   *world*
> in continental ~~europe~~ and in other parts of the ~~World~~, except for
> *English*   *countries*   *scientific*
> ~~english~~-speaking ~~Countries~~. It is also used by the ~~Scientific~~
>
> community around the globe. It is based on the meter, which
>   *thirty-six inches*
> measures a little more than ~~36 ins.~~, or about one yard. Another
>
> metric unit is the gram. One hundred grams are known as

continued

a centigram; one thousand grams are called a kilogram. These units

measure an object's ~~Mass~~ mass. A gram is very small. In fact, an ounce,

a measurement in the ~~english~~ English system, equals ~~28~~ twenty-eight grams. The liter,

another metric unit, measures volume. A liter equals about ~~1 Eng.~~ one English

quart.

    The English system, still in use in Great Britain and the United

~~Sts.,~~ States, has different units. For example, measurements of length

include the inch, the foot, and the ~~yd.~~ yard. The inch is equivalent to about

~~two-and-one-half~~ 2.5 centimeters in the metric system. The English

system also includes a furlong, which is ~~two hundred and twenty~~ 220

yards or about ~~two hundred and one~~ 201 meters; it also includes the

mile, which is ~~five thousand two hundred and eighty-nine~~ 5,289 feet—

slightly more than ~~one-and-one-half~~ 1.5 kilometers. ~~finally~~ Finally, the ~~Engl.~~ English

~~S~~system measures volume in pints, quarts, and gallons. One ~~gln.~~ gallon is

approximately ~~four-and-one-half~~ 4.5 liters.

SECTION

III

Punctuation

RESTRICTED TELEPHONE
POLICE & SENATOR'S <u>ONLY</u>

<u>NOT</u> FOR STAFF
OR PUBLIC USE

©Douglas Graham/Getty Images

RESPONDING TO IMAGES

Can you find the punctuation error in the sign pictured here? What should be done to correct it?

Apostrophe

The two main uses of the apostrophe are

   1. To show the omission of one or more letters in a contraction

   2. To show ownership or possession

Each use is explained in this chapter.

Apostrophe in Contractions

A *contraction* is formed when two words are combined to make one word. An apostrophe is used to show where letters are omitted in forming the contractions. Here are two contractions:

   have + not = haven't (the *o* in *not* has been omitted)

   I + will = I'll (the *wi* in *will* has been omitted)

Following are some other common contractions:

I + am = I'm	it + is = it's
I + have = I've	it + has = it's
I + had = I'd	is + not = isn't
who + is = who's	could + not = couldn't
do + not = don't	I + would = I'd
did + not = didn't	they + are = they're

Will + not has an unusual contraction: won't.

TEACHING TIP
Ask students if they have ever confused a contraction with a possessive pronoun. Most students will say yes.

Write the contractions for the words in parentheses. One is done for you.

1. (Is not) __Isn't__ the trigonometry exam scheduled for the last week of December?

2. I (do not) __don't__ know (who is) __who's__ invited to Dillon's birthday party.

3. (It is) __It's__ unfortunate that the classes I need to take (are not) __aren't__ offered this semester.

TEACHING TIP
You may want to complete this activity with the entire class.

4. Our teacher (can not) ___can't___ expect us to know all the answers because (we are) ___we're___ still learning the material.

5. (I have) ___I've___ a reservation at the Italian restaurant for Saturday night, but I (could not) ___couldn't___ get tickets to the concert.

> **TIP** Even though contractions are common in everyday speech and in written dialogue, it is often best to avoid them in formal writing.

Apostrophe to Show Ownership or Possession

To show ownership or possession, we can use such words as *belongs to, possessed by, owned by*, or (most commonly) *of*.

the skateboard *that belongs to* Audrey

the toys *possessed by* children

the 3-D printer *owned by* the school

the gentleness *of* my father

But the apostrophe plus *s* (if the word does not end in *s*) is often the quickest and easiest way to show possession. Thus we can say

Audrey's skateboard

children's toys

the school's 3-D printer

my father's gentleness

Points to Remember

1. The *'s* goes with the owner or possessor (in the examples given, *Audrey, children, the school, my father*). What follows is the person or thing possessed (in the examples given, *the skateboard, the toys, the 3-D printer, gentleness*).

2. There should not be a break between the word and *'s*.

Audrey's   not   Audrey 's

Yes   No

3. An apostrophe and *s* are used to show possession with a singular word even if the word already ends in *s*: for example, Iris's purse (the purse belonging to Iris).

Working in pairs with a fellow classmate, rewrite the *italicized* part of each of the sentences below, using '*s* to show possession. Remember that the '*s* goes with the owner or possessor.

©Jacob Lund/
Shutterstock

EXAMPLE

The wing of the bluejay was broken.

The bluejay's wing was broken.

1. *The annoying voice of the comedian* irritated me, so I changed the TV channel.

   The comedian's annoying voice

2. *The performance of the quarterback* is inconsistent.

   The quarterback's performance

3. *The thin hand belonging to the old woman* felt as dry as parchment.

   The old woman's thin hand

4. *In the window of the jewelry store* is a sign reading "Ears Pierced While You Wait."

   In the jewelry store's window

5. A fly flew into *the mouth of the TV weatherperson.*

   the TV weatherperson's mouth

6. *The new denim shirt belonging to Lamont* was as scratchy as sandpaper.

   Lamont's new denim shirt

7. *The hair belonging to Rachel* is usually not green–she colored it for Halloween.

   Rachel's hair

8. *The bowl of cereal belonging to Dennis* refused to snap, crackle, or pop.

   Dennis's bowl of cereal

9. *The Honda owned by Poppy* was crammed with boxes and furniture.

   Poppy's Honda

10. *The previous tenant of the apartment* had painted all the walls bright green.

    The apartment's previous tenant

Add '*s* to each of the following words to make it the possessor or owner of something. Then write sentences using the words. The first one is done for you.

1. rock star   rock star's

   The rock star's limousine pulled up to the curb.

Sentences will vary;
examples are given.

2. Felipe <u>Felipe's</u>

   Felipe's name is the Spanish version of Philip.

3. pilot <u>pilot's</u>

   The pilot's last message was "We're losing altitude!"

4. neighbor <u>neighbor's</u>

   Our neighbor's yard is filled with flowers.

5. school <u>school's</u>

   The school's enrollment is about five hundred students.

6. soldier <u>soldier's</u>

   The soldier's family sent him a weekly letter.

TEACHING TIP
Encourage your students to talk about whether they make this mistake, which many of them may do.

Apostrophe versus Possessive Pronouns

Do not use an apostrophe with possessive pronouns. They already show ownership. Possessive pronouns include *his, hers, its, yours, ours,* and *theirs.*

Incorrect	**Correct**
The files are on his' laptop.	The files are on his laptop.
The restored Model T is theirs'.	The restored Model T is theirs.
The decision is yours'.	The decision is yours.
The plaid suitcase is ours'.	The plaid suitcase is ours.
The lion charged its' prey.	The lion charged its prey.

TEACHING TIP
Emphasize that this rule only applies to plurals ending in -s.

Apostrophe versus Simple Plurals

When you want to make a word plural, just add an *s* at the end of the word. Do not add an apostrophe. For example, the plural of the word *movie* is *movies,* not *movie's* or *movies'.*

Look at this sentence:

Connor coveted his roommate's collection of music downloads and Xbox games.

The words *downloads* and *games* are simple plurals, meaning more than one download, more than one game. The plural is shown by adding *s* only. On the other hand, the *'s* after *roommate* shows possession—that the roommate owns the downloads and games.

ACTIVITY 4   Insert an apostrophe where needed to show possession in the following sentences. Write *plural* above words where the *s* ending simply means more than one thing.

EXAMPLE
                                  plural
    Ryan's computer has two viruses.
                     plural
1. Old historic houses are Sam's main interest, but he also likes modern
   plural
   houses.

2. Reurbanization districts are popping up all over the country. John's house
   is in such a district.
   plural
3. Old mansions are often refurbished and used as wedding venues.
   plural   *plural*
4. Dimitri's porch has a large swing that the neighbors' kids like to use.
   plural
5. Andrea's husband collects cars and currently has three classic convertibles
   plural   *plural*
   and two racecars.
   plural
6. Eric's home has a private pool, but Michele's family uses the neighborhood
   pool.
7. Jason's car has been hit twice this week, so he is parking in his brother's
   garage.
8. My best friend's cupcakes come in flavors like chocolate raspberry and
   plural   *plural*
   pink lemonade.
9. Tim's shoe collection includes forty pairs of Birkenstocks.
   plural   *plural*
10. The administrative assistant's office was broken into and his computers
    plural
    were stolen.

Apostrophe with Plurals Ending in -s

Plurals that end in -s show possession simply by adding the apostrophe, rather
than an apostrophe plus s.

the Thompsons' porch

the players' victory

her parents' motor home

the Killers' latest CD

the soldiers' hats

TEACHING TIP
Stress the difference
between possession for
singular words ending in
"s" and plural words
ending in "s."

Add an apostrophe where needed.

ACTIVITY 5

1. Several campers' tents collapsed during the storm.

2. The Murrays' phone bills are often over $400 a month.

3. Many buildings' steep steps make it difficult for wheelchair users to gain
   access.

4. The twins' habit of dressing alike was started by their mother when they
   were children.

5. At the crowded intersection, several young men rushed out to wash the
   cars' windshields.

REVIEW TEST

In the paragraph below, underline the words that either need apostrophes or have misused apostrophes. Then, in the spaces between the lines, correct the mistakes. You should make eleven corrections in all.

Spiders'
Spiders silk is an amazing substance! Paul Hillyard says in *The Book of the Spider* (1994), "For an equal [diameter], spider silk is stronger than steel and about as strong as nylon. It is, however much more resilient and can stretch

times
several time's before breaking—it is twice as elastic as nylon and more difficult

its
to break than rubber." Because of it's strength and durability, many scientists

spiders'
are studying spider's dragline silk, a silk that can be extended 30 to 50 percent

its
of it's length before it breaks. The U.S. Army is interested in spider silk to

products
use in product's like bulletproof vests, and medical scientists are interested in

studies
creating artificial ligaments and tendons from spider silk. All these study's

qualities
show that spider silk has the qualities' to be useful, but creating enough has proven difficult. One researcher, however, has been genetically modifying goats

goats'
to produce the spider silk protein in the goats milk. Once the milk is specially

Researchers
processed, threads of spider silk are created. Researchers' are also studying

plants'
alfalfa plants ability to produce the silk protein. It's highly likely that one day in the near future, spider silk may be mass produced by nonspider methods.

Quotation Marks

The two main uses of quotation marks are

1. To set off the exact words of a speaker or writer

2. To set off the titles of short works

Each use is explained here.

 TIP Quotation marks are also used in research papers to signify direct quotes. See Chapter 20.

Quotation Marks to Set Off the Words of a Speaker or Writer

Use quotation marks to show the exact words of a speaker or writer.

"I feel as though I've been here before," Angie murmured to her husband.
(Quotation marks set off the exact words that Angie spoke to her husband.)

Ben Franklin once wrote, "To lengthen thy life, lessen thy meals."
(Quotation marks set off the exact words that Ben Franklin wrote.)

"Did you know," said the nutrition expert, "that it's healthier to be ten pounds overweight?"
(Two pairs of quotation marks are used to enclose the nutrition expert's exact words.)

The biology professor said, "Ants are a lot like human beings. They farm their own food and raise smaller insects as livestock. And, like humans, ants send armies to war."
(Note that the end quotation marks do not come until the end of the biology professor's speech. Place quotation marks before the first quoted word and after the last quoted word. As long as no interruption occurs in the speech, do not use quotation marks for each new sentence.)

TIP In the four examples above, notice that a comma sets the quoted part off from the rest of the sentence. Also, observe that commas and periods at the end of a quotation always go *inside* quotation marks.

TEACHING TIP
You may want to provide an example so that students can see you put the period inside the quotation marks.

| **ACTIVITY 1** | Complete the following statements, which explain how capital letters, commas, and periods are used in quotations. Refer to the four previous examples as guides. |

1. Every quotation begins with a _____capital_____ letter.

2. When a quotation is split (as in the sentence about the nutrition expert), the second part does not begin with a capital letter unless it is a _____new_____ sentence.

3. _____Commas_____ are used to separate the quoted part of a sentence from the rest of the sentence.

4. Commas and periods that come at the end of a quotation go _____inside_____ the quotation marks.

The answers are *capital, new, Commas,* and *inside.*

| **ACTIVITY 2** | Place quotation marks around the exact words of a speaker or writer in the sentences that follow. |

1. Several people have been credited with saying, "The more I see of people, the more I like dogs."

2. Merryl asked, "Do you give a discount to senior citizens?"

3. "This hamburger is raw!" cried Liam.

4. The bumper sticker on the rear of the battered old car read, "Don't laugh—it's paid for."

5. "I know why Robin Hood robbed only the rich," said the comedian. "The poor don't have any money."

6. "These knives," proclaimed the television announcer, "are not sold in any store."

7. "When chefs go to great lengths," the woman at the diet center said, "I go to great widths."

8. "If I go with you to the dinner party," my friend said, "you must promise not to discuss politics."

9. On a tombstone in a Maryland cemetery are the words "Here lies an atheist, all dressed up and no place to go."

10. The columnist advised, "Be nice to people on your way up because you'll meet them on your way down."

| **ACTIVITY 3** | |

1. Write a sentence in which you quote a favorite expression of someone you know. In the same sentence, identify the person's relationship to you.

EXAMPLE   <u>My grandfather loves to say, "It can't be as bad as all that."</u>

_____

_____

2. Write a quotation that contains the words *Jacques asked Rhianna*. Write a second quotation that includes the words *Rhianna replied*.

"What time is it?" Jacques asked Rhianna.

"How should I know?" Rhianna replied.

_____

_____

_____

3. Quote an interesting sentence or two from a book, magazine, or other published work. In the same sentence, identify the title and author of the work.

EXAMPLE   <u>In *The Dilbert Desk Calendar* by Scott Adams, the cartoon</u>

<u>character Dilbert says, "I can please only one person per day. Today isn't your</u>

<u>day, and tomorrow isn't looking good either."</u>

_____

_____

_____

_____

Indirect Quotations

An indirect quotation is a rewording of someone else's comments rather than a word-for-word direct quotation. The word *that* often signals an indirect quotation.

Direct Quotation

The nurse said, "Some babies cannot tolerate cows' milk." (The nurse's exact spoken words are given, so quotation marks are used.)

Tristan's note to Hailee read, "I'll be home by 7:30." (The exact words that Tristan wrote in the note are given, so quotation marks are used.)

Indirect Quotation

The nurse said that some babies cannot tolerate cows' milk. (We learn the nurse's words indirectly, so no quotation marks are used.)

Tristan left a note for Hailee saying that he would be home by 7:30. (We learn Tristan's words indirectly, so no quotation marks are used.)

ACTIVITY 4   Rewrite the following sentences, changing words as necessary to convert the sentences into direct quotations. The first one has been done for you as an example.

1. Leona asked me if I wanted to study at the library after class.

   Leona asked me, "Do you want to study at the library after class?"

2. My supervisor said that I should apply for the opening in Seattle.

   My supervisor said, "You should apply for the opening in Seattle."

3. Heidi asked if she could order the Catch of the Day without the béarnaise sauce.

   Heidi asked, "Could I order the Catch of the Day without the béarnaise

   sauce?"

4. The witness testified in court that she saw the suspect flee the convenience store with a gun.

   The witness testified in court, "I saw the suspect flee the convenience store

   with a gun."

5. Professor Quigley said that he grades on a curve.

   Professor Quigley said, "I grade on a curve."

Quotation Marks to Set Off Titles of Short Works

TEACHING TIP
Bring newspapers, magazines, poetry books, and music CDs to class. Ask students to write out several long and short titles, using quotation marks and italics as needed.

Titles of short works are usually set off by quotation marks, while titles of long works are italicized. Use quotation marks to set off titles of such short works as articles in books, newspapers, or magazines; chapters in a book; short stories; poems; and songs. But you should italicize titles of books, newspapers, magazines, plays, movies, CDs, albums, and television shows. Following are some examples.

Quotation Marks	Italics
the essay "On Self-Respect"	in the book *Slouching Towards Bethlehem*
the article "The Problem of Acid Rain"	in the newspaper the *New York Times*
the article "Living with Inflation"	in the magazine *Newsweek*
the chapter "Chinese Religion"	in the book *Paths of Faith*
the story "Hands"	in the book *Winesburg, Ohio*

the poem "When I Have Fears"   in the book *Complete Poems of John Keats*

the song "Ziggy Stardust"   in the album *Changes*

the television show *CSI:NY*

the movie *Dunkirk*

> **TIP** When you are typing a paper, you should always italicize longer works; however, if you are handwriting a paper, you should underline longer works. For example, *The Hunger Games* by Suzanne Collins would be handwritten <u>The Hunger Games</u> by Suzanne Collins.

Use quotation marks as needed. Underline titles that should be italicized. Once you have completed the activity, go over your answers with a partner.

ACTIVITY 5

©Jacob Lund/ Shutterstock

1. My personal trainer told me to read the article "Five Ways to Trick Yourself into Eating Less," which appeared in <u>Newsweek</u>.

2. The title of Maya Angelou's autobiography <u>I Know Why the Caged Bird Sings</u> comes from Paul Laurence Dunbar's poem "Sympathy."

3. I was so inspired to read the chapter "It's About How to Live Your Life" in Randy Pausch's book <u>The Last Lecture</u>.

4. Everyone in the class was inspired after reading Beth Johnson's article "The Professor Is a Dropout" about Guadalupe Quintanilla.

5. The movie <u>The Fellowship of the Ring</u>, which starred Viggo Mortensen as Aragon, was originally cast with Stuart Townsend in that role.

6. The movie <u>Alien</u> has many spin-offs, including an entire film series, novels, comic books, and video games.

7. The history test will cover the chapters "The First World War" and "The Second World War."

8. The American Broadcasting Company's <u>ABC's Wide World of Sports</u> was the longest running sports show on television.

9. Michael Jackson holds the record for the highest selling album, entitled <u>Thriller</u>, with such songs as "Beat It" and "Billie Jean."

10. I am reading the essay "Of Our Spiritual Strivings," which was first published in W.E.B. DuBois's <u>The Souls of Black Folk</u>.

Other Uses of Quotation Marks

Quotation marks are also used as follows:

1. To set off special words or phrases from the rest of a sentence:

In grade school, we were taught a little jingle about the spelling rule "*i* before *e*."

What is the difference between "it's" and "its"?

(In this book, *italics* are often used instead of quotation marks to set off words.)

2. To mark off a quotation within a quotation:

The physics professor said, "For class on Friday, do the problems at the end of the chapter titled 'Work and Energy.'"

Brendan remarked, "Did you know that Humphrey Bogart never actually said, 'Play it again, Sam' in the movie *Casablanca*?"

> **TIP**   A quotation within a quotation is indicated by *single* quotation marks, as shown above.

REVIEW TEST 1

Insert quotation marks where needed in the sentences that follow. One sentence is correct; mark that sentence with a *C*.

1. The May 2011 issue of *Diabetes Forecast* included articles such as "Kids, I Have Diabetes: How to Talk to Children about Your Disease" and "Dreaming of a Healthy Tomorrow."

2. An article titled "Nat Strand's Amazing Ways" highlighted Nat Strand, who was part of a two-woman team to win a million-dollar race around the world.

3. Carolyn Butler wrote about how the winner of CBS's reality show *The Amazing Race* had the added challenge of controlling her diabetes while racing. C

4. "The race," said Strand, "is probably the hardest situation you can imagine for a diabetic."

5. In the article, Butler asked Strand, "How do you pack light when you have diabetes—and absolutely no idea where you are going?"

6. Strand replied, "I had so much [diabetes-related] stuff that I didn't even pack a hairbrush."

7. When asked about the boiled sheep's head she had to eat during one challenge, Strand replied, "I just gritted my teeth and hoped that since it was protein, it was low-carb."

8. Later in the article, Strand's teammate Kat Chang remarked, "I definitely have a new respect and understanding for diabetes—that it is just so, so so difficult to manage, and it is absolutely 24/7."

9. After describing what the race was like for Strand and discussing the outpouring of support for the diabetic competitor, Butler wrote, "In June she [Strand] will lobby members of Congress with the Juvenile Diabetes Research Foundation."

10. Strand ended her interview saying, "I'm never going to say diabetes is easy—
I'm never going to say it's something I would choose if I had a choice—but
it's not a limitation."

Source: Butler, C., "Race of a lifetime. Nat Strand's amazing ways," *Diabetes Forecast*, 64(5) May 2011, 39–45.

REVIEW TEST 2

Go through the comics section of a newspaper to find a comic strip that amuses you. Be sure to choose a strip in which two or more characters are speaking to each other. Write a full description that will enable people who have not read the comic strip to visualize it clearly and appreciate its humor. Describe the setting and action in each panel, and enclose the words of the speakers in quotation marks.

Answers will vary.

Comma

TEACHING TIP
As you begin this section, briefly provide at least one example of each comma use so that your students will have reference points.

ESL NOTE
Sometimes nonnative speakers will use a comma instead of a period. Compare the use of commas and periods in English.

TEACHING TIP
Ask volunteers to read these sentences aloud. Encourage students to listen for pauses and breaks.

TEACHING TIP
Stress this rule: "If in doubt, leave it out."

Six Main Uses of the Comma

Commas are used mainly as follows:

1. To separate items in a series

2. To set off introductory material

3. On both sides of words that interrupt the flow of thought in a sentence

4. Between two complete thoughts connected by *and, but, for, or, nor, so, yet*

5. To set off a direct quotation from the rest of a sentence

6. For certain everyday material

You may find it helpful to remember that the comma often marks a slight pause or break in a sentence. Read aloud the sentence examples given for each rule and listen for the minor pauses or breaks that are signaled by commas.

Comma between Items in a Series

Use commas to separate items in a series.

My favorite kinds of books are spy thrillers, historical fiction, and science fiction.

The golfer retightened his glove, adjusted his stance, and took a practice swing.

The yoga instructor told us to inhale, exhale, and relax.

Joe peered into the hot, still-smoking engine.

A. The final comma in a series, also called the Oxford comma, is optional, but it is often used. Students should plan to use it in academic writing.

B. A comma is used between two descriptive words in a series only if *and* inserted between the words sounds natural. You could say:

Joe peered into the hot *and* still-smoking engine.

But notice in the following sentence that the descriptive words do not sound natural when *and* is inserted between them. In such cases, no comma is used.

Owen wore a pale green tuxedo. (A pale *and* green tuxedo does not sound right, so no comma is used.)

Place commas between items in a series.

1. The nursery was furnished with a convertible crib, a changing table, and a glider chair.

2. Upon coming home, Alyssa threw her keys on the table, turned on her computer, and checked her e-mail messages.

3. The tourists snapped photos of the forceful, awe-inspiring lava cascades that erupted from the mountain.

4. The serene, solitary forest is an ideal place to go for a relaxing meditation.

5. The interviewer's friendly, open smile made the nervous job applicant suddenly feel at ease.

TEACHING TIP
For this activity, read each sentence aloud as students add commas.

Comma after Introductory Material

Use a comma to set off introductory material.

Just in time, Laney applied the brakes and avoided a car accident.

Muttering under his breath, Hassan reviewed the terms he had memorized.

In a wolf pack, the dominant male holds his tail higher than the other pack members.

Although he had been first in the checkout line, Damien let an elderly woman go ahead of him.

After the fire, we slogged through the ashes of the burned-out house.

TEACHING TIP
Ask volunteers to read these sentences aloud. Encourage students to listen for pauses and breaks.

 TIP If the introductory material is brief, the comma is sometimes omitted. In the activities here, however, you should include the comma.

Place commas after introductory material.

1. Entering school this fall, Ezra will begin studying to be a lawyer.

2. As the weather was sunny and warm, the family decided to go to the beach.

3. Before she went to the store, Jane wrote out a list of items she needed to buy.

4. If I had studied better, I don't think I would have failed the exam.

5. Although flying is a quicker way to travel, some people prefer to drive.

Comma around Words That Interrupt the Flow of Thought

TEACHING TIP
Ask volunteers to read these sentences aloud. Encourage students to listen for pauses and breaks.

Use a comma on both sides of words or phrases that interrupt the flow of thought in a sentence.

The leather car seat, sticky from the heat, clung to my skin.

Aniya's Galaxy S9, which her parents gave her as a birthday gift, occupies all her spare time.

The alpine tundra, cool and breezy, was a welcome respite from the heat of the valley floor.

Usually, by reading a sentence aloud, you can "hear" words that interrupt the flow of thought. In cases where you are not sure if certain words are interrupters, remove them from the sentence. If it still makes sense without the words, you know that the words are interrupters and that the information they give is nonessential. *Such nonessential or extra information is set off with commas.*

In the sentence

Sue Dodd, who goes to yoga class with me, was in a serious car accident.

the words *who goes to yoga class with me* are extra information not needed to identify the subject of the sentence, *Sue Dodd.* Commas go around such nonessential information. On the other hand, in the sentence

The woman who goes to yoga class with me was in a serious accident.

the words *who goes to yoga class with me* supply essential information— information needed for us to identify the woman being spoken of. If the words were removed from the sentence, we would no longer know exactly who was in the accident: "The woman was in a serious accident." Here is another example:

The Sea Runners, a novel by Ivan Doig, is the most thrilling adventure story I've ever read.

Here the words *a novel by Ivan Doig* could be left out, and we would still know the basic meaning of the sentence. Commas are placed around such nonessential material. But in the sentence

Ivan Doig's novel *The Sea Runners* is the most thrilling adventure story I've ever read.

the title of the novel is essential. Without it the sentence would read, "Ivan Doig's novel is the most thrilling adventure story I've ever read." We would not know which of Ivan Doig's novels was so thrilling. Commas are not used around the title because it provides essential information.

Most of the time you will be able to "hear" words that interrupt the flow of thought in a sentence and will not have to think about whether the words are essential or nonessential.

Use commas to set off interrupting words.

1. A slight breeze, hot and damp, ruffled the bedroom curtains.

2. The defrosting chickens, loosely wrapped in plastic, left a pool on the counter.

3. Caleb's wallet, which he kept in his front pants pocket, was linked to his belt with a metal chain.

4. Mr. Delgado, who is an avid Yankees fan, remembers the grand days of Mickey Mantle and Yogi Berra.

5. The fleet of tall ships, a majestic sight, made its way into the harbor.

TEACHING TIP
For this activity, read each sentence aloud as students add commas.

Comma between Complete Thoughts

Use a comma between two complete thoughts connected by *and, but, for, or, nor, so, yet.*

Caden moved his car inside the garage, but the predicted ice storm never arrived.

I like wearing comfortable clothing, so I buy yoga pants and sweatshirts.

Layla loves to travel to different countries, for she enjoys experiencing unfamiliar cultures.

A. The comma is optional when the complete thoughts are short.

The movie started and Ethan put on his 3-D glasses.

Many people left but the band played on.

I made a wrong turn so I doubled back.

B. Be careful not to use a comma to separate two verbs that belong to one subject. The comma is used in sentences made up of two complete thoughts (two subjects and two verbs). In the sentence

The doctor stared over his bifocals and lectured the teen about vaping.

there is only one subject (*doctor*) and a double verb (*stared* and *lectured*). No comma is needed. Likewise, the sentence

Dean switched the lamp on and off and then tapped it with his fingers.

has only one subject (*Dean*) and a double verb (*switched* and *tapped*); therefore, no comma is needed.

TEACHING TIP
Ask volunteers to read these sentences aloud. Encourage students to listen for pauses and breaks.

ESL NOTE
Nonnative speakers may put a comma after the joining word. Remind them that commas precede coordinating conjunctions.

Place a comma before a joining word that connects two complete thoughts (two subjects and two verbs). Remember, do *not* place a comma within a sentence that has only one subject and a double verb. (Some items may be correct as given.)

TEACHING TIP
For this activity, read each sentence aloud as students add commas.

1. Armand left work early to pick up his daughter from school and take her to basketball practice.   Correct

2. He can spend hours circling the parking lot looking for a spot near the store, or he can easily park a few yards away and get some exercise.

3. Our professor told us that the quiz would cover material we learned since the last exam, but the quiz also covered material that we learned before the exam.

4. Kristine was worried that she would lose her sales job, so she began taking accounting classes at the local community college.

5. Only a few people attended the game, but that did not discourage the players from playing to their utmost and winning the division title.

6. I used last night's leftovers to make a delicious chicken salad sandwich for lunch and prepare a chicken casserole for the freezer.   Correct

7. I made an appointment with a personal financial advisor, for I need to start planning for retirement.

8. Austin promised that he would teach me how to play Texas Hold'em, and I promised that I would help him with his math homework.

9. Claire was worried about her father's health, so she made an appointment for him with a doctor at the community clinic.

10. The customer tried on dozens of outfits but walked out of the store without purchasing a single item.   Correct

Comma with Direct Quotations

Use a comma to set off a direct quotation from the rest of a sentence.

The protester yelled, "It is wrong to treat people as second-class citizens!"

"Now is the time to yield to temptation," my horoscope read.

"I'm sorry," said the restaurant host. "You'll have to wait."

"For my first writing assignment," said Scott, "I have to turn in a five-hundred-word description of a stone."

 TIP Commas and periods at the end of a quotation go inside quotation marks. See also Chapter 36.

ACTIVITY 5 Use commas to set off direct quotations from the rest of the sentence.

1. The coach announced, "In order to measure your lung capacity, you're going to attempt to blow up a plastic bag with one breath."

2. "A grapefruit," said the comedian, "is a lemon that had a chance and took advantage of it."

3. My father asked, "Did you know that the family moving next door has thirteen children?"

4. "Speak louder," a man in the back row said to the guest speaker. "I paid fifty dollars to hear you talk, not whisper."

5. The zookeeper explained to the visitors, "We can't tell the sex of a giant tortoise for almost ten years after its birth."

Comma with Everyday Material

Use a comma with certain everyday material.

If you're the last to leave, Paul, please switch off the lights.	Persons
Nathaniel, I think we're on the wrong road.	Spoken to
Did you see the playoff game, Lisa?	
June 30, 2020, is the day I make the last payment on my car.	Dates
I buy discount children's clothing from Isaac's Baby Wear Factory, Box 900, Chicago, Illinois 60614.	Addresses

TIP No comma is used before a zip code.

Dear Santa,	Sincerely yours,	Openings and Closings of Letters
Dear Roberto,	Truly yours,	

TIP In formal letters, a colon is used after the opening:
Dear Sir: *or* Dear Madam: *or* Dear Allan: *or* Dear Ms. Mohr:

The insurance agent sold me a $10,000 term life insurance policy.	Numbers

---

ACTIVITY 6

Place commas where needed.

1. Would you mind, Perlita, if I used your name as a reference on this job application?

2. The pad thai served at Mekong's Restaurant, 5001 South Prince Street, is authentic.

3. Approximately 1,500 protesters flooded City Hall on September 12, 2019, to voice their concern about the proposed educational cuts.

4. The report indicates, Chelsey, that 5,012 customers purchased extended warranties during the first quarter.

5. The community center's address is 94-1201 Mojave Drive, San Jose, California 95102.

TEACHING TIP
For this activity, read each sentence aloud as students add commas.

REVIEW TEST 1

Insert commas where needed. In the space provided below each sentence, summarize briefly the rule that explains the comma or commas used

1. "First impressions," the job recruiter said, "are crucial during a job interview."

   commas with direct quotation

Wording of rules may vary.

TEACHING TIP
You may want to use these
review tests to assess
what your students have
learned.

2. I had wanted to buy roses for Jo on Valentine's Day, but the florist said that I should have placed an order at least a month ago.

   comma between two complete thoughts

3. The motivational speaker ended her presentation by saying, "Remember that you can make a difference."

   comma to set off a direct quotation

4. At the age of forty-three, John F. Kennedy was the youngest person to be elected to the office of United States President.

   comma after introductory material

5. The driver, who was clearly at fault, took his eyes off the road while texting his girlfriend.

   commas with words interrupting the flow of thought

6. More than two weeks into the semester, I still need to buy textbooks for my chemistry, astronomy, and history classes.

   commas with items in a series

REVIEW TEST 2

Insert commas where needed. Mark the one sentence that is correct with a *C*.

1. A person studying art history will have to learn about the many different movements like French Impressionism, Art Nouveau, Cubism, Surrealism, and Pop Art.

2. From 1869 to 1890, French Impressionism was very popular.

3. Artists like Claude Monet, Camille Pissarro, and Paul Gauguin challenged the art world with their painting styles.

4. Edgar Degas, a French Impressionist, was most famous for his paintings of ballet dancers.

5. The era of Art Nouveau, which lasted from 1890 to 1910, was not limited to paintings.

6. Many artists during this period also worked with furniture, buildings, and jewelry.

7. René Lalique, a French architect, became famous for his Art Nouveau glass.

8. Another movement, Cubism, occurred from 1908 to 1914.   C

9. Pablo Picasso used to be credited with creating Cubism, but now he shares that honor with Georges Braque.

10. From 1920 to 1930, Surrealism was the popular way to paint, and this movement was led by André Breton.

11. The most famous Surrealist painter, Salvador Dali, painted *The Persistence of Memory.*

12. Dali, like other Surrealist painters, painted illogical pictures that were meant to represent images from the subconscious mind.

13. Pop Art, a movement characterized by popular culture, occurred between 1955 and 1970.

14. Andy Warhol was most famous for his screen prints of Marilyn Monroe, his soup cans, and his Coca-Cola bottles.

REVIEW TEST 3

In the following passage, there are ten missing commas. Add the commas where needed. The types of mistakes to look for are shown in the box preceding the passage.

> 2 commas missing between items in a series
> 1 comma missing after introductory material
> 4 commas missing around interrupting words
> 2 commas missing between complete thoughts
> 1 comma missing with a direct quotation

When I was about ten years old, I developed several schemes to avoid eating liver, a food I despise. My first scheme involved my little brother. Timmy, too young to realize what a horrible food liver is, always ate every bit of his portion. On liver nights, I used to sit next to Tim and slide my slab of meat onto his plate when my parents weren't paying attention. This strategy worked until, older and wiser, Tim decided to reject his liver along with the rest of us. Another liver-disposal method I used was hiding the meat right on the plate. I'd cut the liver into tiny squares half the size of postage stamps, and then I would carefully hide the pieces. I'd put them inside the skin of my baked potato, beneath some mashed peas, or under a crumpled paper napkin. This strategy worked perfectly only if my mother didn't look too closely as she scraped the dishes. Once she said to me, "Do you know you left a lot of liver on your plate?" My best liver trick was to hide the disgusting stuff on a three-inch-wide wooden ledge that ran under our dining-room table. I'd put little pieces of liver on the ledge when Mom wasn't looking; I would sneak the dried-up scraps into the garbage early the next day. Our dog would sometimes smell the liver, try to get at it, and bang his head noisily against the bottom of the table. These strategies seemed like a lot of work, but I never hesitated to take whatever steps I could. Anything was better than eating a piece of meat that tasted like old socks soaked in mud.

REVIEW TEST 4

On separate paper, write six sentences, one illustrating each of the six main comma rules.

Answers will vary.

Other Punctuation Marks

TEACHING TIP
Ask students to help you
create several more
examples using colons.

Colon (:)

Use the colon at the end of a complete statement to introduce a list, a long quotation, or an explanation.

1. List:

> The store will close at noon on the following dates: November 26, December 24, and December 31.

2. Quotation:

> In his book *Life Lines,* Forrest Church maintains that people should cry more: "Life is difficult. Some people pretend that it is not, that we should be able to breeze through. Yet hardly a week passes in which most of us don't have something worth crying about."

3. Explanation:

> Here's a temporary solution to stop the noise made by a dripping faucet: tie a string to it and let the drops slide down the string to the sink.

ACTIVITY 1

Place colons where needed in the sentences below:

1. Bring these items to registration: a ballpoint pen, your student ID card, and a check made out to the college.

2. Willa Cather, the American author, had an insightful comment about plots: "There are only two or three human stories, and they go on repeating themselves as fiercely as if they had never happened before."

3. The road was closed because of an emergency: an enormous tree had fallen and blocked both lanes.

Semicolon (;)

The main use of the semicolon is to mark a break between two complete thoughts, as explained in Chapter 25. Another use is to mark off items in a series when the items themselves contain commas. Here are some examples:

> Maya's children are named Melantha, which means "black flower"; Yonina, which means "dove"; and Cynthia, which means "moon goddess."

> My parents' favorite albums are *Rubber Soul,* by the Beatles; *Songs in the Key of Life,* by Stevie Wonder; and *Bridge over Troubled Water,* by Simon and Garfunkel.

Working in pairs with a classmate, place semicolons where needed in the sentences below.

1. Teens who are under sixteen have to be creative to earn money; my sister is very entrepreneurial.

2. She had a profitable summer: by mowing lawns, she earned $1,200; by walking the neighbors' dogs, $1,440; and by babysitting on the weekends, $1000.

3. Her favorite dogs to walk were Pip, a German shepherd; Klaus, a tiny schnauzer; and Bruce, a three-legged Chihuahua.

©Jacob Lund/ Shutterstock

Dash (—)

A dash signals a pause longer than a comma but not as complete as a period. Use a dash to set off words for dramatic effect:

I was so exhausted that I fell asleep within seconds—standing up.

He had many good qualities—sincerity, honesty, and thoughtfulness—yet he had few friends.

The pardon from the governor finally arrived—too late.

 TIPS
a. A dash can be formed on a keyboard by striking the hyphen twice (--). Computer software also has a symbol for the dash. In handwriting, a dash is as long as two letters would be.
b. Be careful not to overuse dashes.

Place dashes where needed in the following sentences.

1. The women's 5K race held each May in honor of Mother's Day attracts participants of all ages.

2. The stolen car was found abandoned on the freeway minus the car's sound system and the owner's personal belongings.

3. After months of working on my research paper, I could hope for only one thing an A to reward me for all my hard work.

TEACHING TIP
You may want to ask students to complete this activity in pairs.

Parentheses ( )

Parentheses are used to set off extra or incidental information from the rest of a sentence:

In 1913, the tax on an annual income of $4,000 (a comfortable wage at that time) was one penny.

Arthur C. Clarke, author of science fiction books (including *2001: A Space Odyssey*), was inspired as a young man by the magazine *Astounding Stories*.

TEACHING TIP
Ask students to help you create several more examples using parentheses.

> **TIP**   Do not use parentheses too often in your writing.

| ACTIVITY 4 | Working with a partner, add parentheses where needed. |

©Jacob Lund/
Shutterstock

1. President Taft (1909–1913) established many things during his term in office, including a postal savings system.

2. Zachary Taylor was in office for one short year (1849–1850).

3. Franklin D. Roosevelt (FDR) and John F. Kennedy (JFK) are often referred to by their initials.

Hyphen (-)

1. Use a hyphen with two or more words that act as a single unit describing a noun.

   The light-footed burglar silently slipped open the sliding glass door.

   While being interviewed on the late-night talk show, the quarterback announced his intention to retire.

   With a steady hand, Bryce wiped the paint-splattered glass window pane.

2. Use a hyphen to divide a word at the end of a line of writing or typing. When you need to divide a word at the end of a line, divide it between syllables. Use your dictionary to be sure of correct syllable divisions.

   Selena's first year at college was filled with numerous new pressures and responsibilities.

> **TIPS**   a. Do not divide words of one syllable.
> b. Do not divide a word if you can avoid dividing it.

| ACTIVITY 5 | Place hyphens where needed. |

TEACHING TIP
You may want to ask students to complete this activity in pairs.

1. The apartment complex was no longer a laughter-filled place once the neighborhood children had grown and moved out.

2. Samantha, who is usually a high-strung person, decided to start yoga and meditation.

3. My last-minute efforts produced a poorly written paper, which I was embarrassed to submit to my professor.

REFLECTIVE ACTIVITY

Look over a paragraph you wrote for an assignment in Chapter 11, "Comparison and/or Contrast," or an essay you wrote while studying Chapter 18, "Patterns of Essay Development." Do you notice any errors with apostrophes, quotation marks, commas, or other punctuation marks? If so, correct them using what you learned in Chapters 35–38.

REVIEW TEST

At the appropriate spot, place the punctuation mark shown in the margin.

— 1. A bad case of flu, a burglary, the death of an uncle—it was not what you would call a pleasant week.

( ) 2. My grandfather (who will be ninety in May) says that hard work and a glass of wine every day are the secrets of a long life.

: 3. Mark Twain offered this advice to writers: "The difference between the right word and the nearly right word is the difference between lightning and the lightning bug."

- 4. The passengers in the glass-bottomed boat stared at the colorful fish in the water below.

( ) 5. Ellen's birthday (December 27) falls so close to Christmas that she gets only one set of presents.

; 6. The dog-show winners included Freckles, a springer spaniel; King Leo, a German shepherd; and Big Guy, a miniature schnauzer.

— 7. I feel I have two chances of winning the lottery—slim and none.

- 8. Cold-hearted stepmothers are a fixture in many famous fairy tales.

; 9. Some people need absolute quiet in order to study; they can't concentrate with the soft sounds of a radio, air conditioner, or television in the background.

: 10. A critic reviewing a bad play wrote, "I saw the play under the worst possible circumstances: the curtain was up."

TEACHING TIP
You may want to use this review test to assess what your students have learned.

SECTION III: PUNCTUATION EDITING TEST I

Correct the following paragraphs by adding and/or removing marks of punctuation as needed. You should make twenty-seven corrections.

      headaches
Migraine headache's affect millions of people in the United States. This illness attacks all segments of the population, both adults and children. However, it is more common in females than in males.
Migraines
Migraine's are so serious a problem that they cause millions of lost work and study hours in factories, warehouses, offices, stores, schools, and colleges. An essay entitled"What Are Migraine Headaches?" describes the problem in the following words:"an intense throbbing or pounding pain."The pain from migraines is most often unilateral; in other words, it is on one side of the head.

      Nausea, vomiting, dizziness, sensitivity to light, and even diarrhea are other symptoms that migraines can cause. The most effective
                                               drugs
remedy is a good night's sleep; however, there are several drug's that can also help. A migraine patient should also avoid certain foods: sharp cheeses, red wines, and some types of nuts. Smoking also
                                                cigarettes and
makes things worse, so doctors advise staying away from cigarettes, and other tobacco products.

SECTION III: PUNCTUATION EDITING TEST II

Correct the following paragraph by adding and/or removing marks of punctuation as needed. You should make twenty corrections.

      Bossypants was published in 2011; it contains many funny short stories and essays about the author, Tina Fey. Some of the short
stories
storie's, like"Peeing in Jars with Boys";"Sarah, Oprah, and Captain Hook, or How to Succeed by Sort of Looking Like Someone Else"; and"A Childhood Dream, Realized"focus on her life during her years on *Saturday Night Live.* Another short story,"Young Men's Christian

continued

Association," tells about one of her first jobs as a front desk clerk at the Evanston, Illinois, YMCA. Her shortest chapter, "What Turning Forty Means to Me," is only three sentences long! She even offers advice to her readers: "Do your thing and don't care if they like it." Although it won't ever be considered a classic piece of literature like Shakespeare's *Romeo and Juliet,* it is a book that will create laughter in thousand's of homes.

thousands

SECTION

IV

Word Use

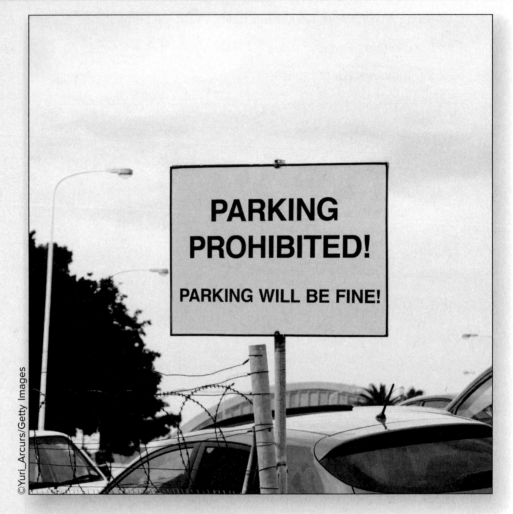

©Yuri_Arcurs/Getty Images

RESPONDING TO IMAGES

Sometimes making a spelling error or confusing similar words can give your writing a completely different and unintended meaning! What error was made in the sign above, and how does it change the sign's meaning?

Commonly Confused Words

Homonyms

Some words are commonly confused because they have the same sounds but different meanings and spellings; such words are known as *homonyms*. Following are a number of homonyms. Complete the activity for each set of words, and check off and study the words that give you trouble.

TEACHING TIP
You may want to ask students to complete this activity in pairs, and then go over some of the answers in class. Encourage students to identify words that still confuse them.

all ready   completely prepared

already   previously; before

> I was *all ready* for the test when I learned that my teacher had cancelled class.

> It was *already* May by the time I thought about applying for college.

Fill in the blanks: Sasha was ___all ready___ for bed by nine o'clock, and she had ___already___ laid out her clothes for the next day.

brake   stop

break   come apart

> The mechanic advised me to add *brake* fluid to my car.

> During a commercial *break*, Marie lay on the floor and did fifty crunches.

Fill in the blanks: Tim, a poor driver, would always ___brake___ at the last minute and would usually ___break___ the speed limit as well.

complement   a thing that completes, enhances, or perfects

compliment   a polite expression of praise

> A glass of fresh squeezed orange juice is the perfect *complement* to a breakfast of eggs, bacon, and hash browns.

> The teacher was so impressed with the group's hard work that she gave each student an individual *compliment*.

Fill in the blanks: Libby is wearing a royal blue shirt and bright floral headband that ___complement___ her blue eyes, so I made sure to ___compliment___ her.

course   part of a meal; a school subject; direction; progression of time

coarse   rough

During the *course* of the evening, I had to endure my date's *coarse* behavior.

Fill in the blanks: When the waitress brought the main ___course___, I was surprised that the cornmeal used for the hush puppies was so ___coarse___.

| hear | perceive with the ear |
| here | in this place |

I can *hear* the performers so well from *here* that I don't want to change my seat.

Fill in the blanks: The chairperson explained that the meeting was being held ___here___ in the auditorium to enable everyone to ___hear___ the debate.

| hole | an empty spot |
| whole | entire |

A *hole* in the crumbling brick mortar made a convenient home for a small bird and its *whole* family.

Fill in the blanks: The ___hole___ in Matt's argument wouldn't exist if he put his ___whole___ concentration into his thinking.

| its | belonging to it |
| it's | shortened form of "it is" or "it has" |

ESL NOTE
Nonnative speakers also confuse *its* and *it's*. Help them distinguish these two words by generating some additional examples.

It's unfortunate that your college is unable to finance all *its* students' tuition.

Fill in the blanks: I withdrew my application because ___it's___ too difficult to start a new job at the end of the semester, even though the job and ___its___ fringe benefits were tempting.

| knew | past form of *know* |
| new | not old |

No one *knew* our *new* phone number, but the obscene calls continued.

Fill in the blanks: Even people who ___knew___ Charlie well didn't recognize him with his ___new___ beard.

| know | to understand |
| no | a negative |

By the time students complete that course, they *know* two computer languages and have *no* trouble writing their own programs.

Fill in the blanks: Dogs and cats usually ___know___ by the tone of the speaker's voice when they are being told "___no___."

passed	went by; succeeded in; handed to
past	a time before the present; by, as in "I drove past the house"

Travis *passed* up the offer to play basketball with his friends because he remembered his *past* mistakes, which included neglecting his homework.

Fill in the blanks: This __past__ year, LeMarcus was determined to move up in the company, and thus he was not __passed__ over for the promotion.

peace	calm
piece	a part

The best *piece* of advice she ever received was to maintain her own inner *peace*.

Fill in the blanks: Upon hearing that __piece__ of music, my angry mood was gradually replaced by one of __peace__.

plain	simple
plane	aircraft

The *plain* box contained a very expensive model *plane* kit.

Fill in the blanks: After unsuccessfully trying to overcome her fear, Selena finally admitted the __plain__ truth: she was terrified of flying in a __plane__.

principal	main; a person in charge of a school
principle	a law or standard

If the *principal* ingredient in this stew is octopus, I'll abandon my *principle* of trying everything at least once.

Fill in the blanks: Our __principal__ insists that all students adhere to every school __principle__ regarding dress, tardiness, and smoking.

right	correct; opposite of "left"
write	to put words on paper

Our professor was *right* when she said that it's difficult to *write* a research paper without plagiarizing, even unintentionally.

Fill in the blanks: I tried to __write__ down the directions correctly, but I obviously didn't record the __right__ street address because I am lost now.

sight	the ability to see, a place or thing worth seeing
site	a location, place, Web site

The *site* where my home stood before the fire was a sad *sight* to see.

Fill in the blanks: After looking at different ___sites___ on the computer, I decided that the ___site___ of the Battle of Gettysburg would be a memorable ___sight___ I'd never forget.

their	belonging to them
there	at that place; a neutral word used with verbs like *is, are, was, were, have,* and *had*
they're	shortened form of "they are"

The tenants *there* are complaining because *they're* being cheated by *their* landlord.

Fill in the blanks: The tomatoes I planted ___there___ in the back of the garden are finally ripening, but ___their___ bright red color will attract hungry raccoons, and I fear ___they're___ going to be eaten.

| threw | past form of *throw* |
| through | from one side to the other; finished |

When my daughter was a toddler, she often *threw* a tantrum when she was *through* eating.

Fill in the blanks: As the children moved ___through___ the museum, one of them ___threw___ a candy wrapper into the display area.

to	verb part, as in *to smile;* toward, as in "I'm going *to* heaven"
too	overly, as in "The pizza was *too* hot"; also, as in "The coffee was hot, *too.*"
two	the number 2

I ran *to* the car *to* roll up the windows. (The first *to* means "toward"; the second *to* is a verb part that goes with *roll.*)

That amusement park is *too* far away; I hear that it's expensive, *too.* (The first *too* means "overly"; the second *too* means "also.")

The *two* players (2 players) jumped up to tap the basketball away.

Fill in the blanks: The ___two___ of them have been dating for a year, but lately they seem ___to___ be arguing ___too___ often to pretend nothing is wrong.

| wear | to have on |
| where | in what place |

Where I will *wear* a purple feather boa is not the point; I just want to buy it.

Fill in the blanks: ___Where___ were we going the night I refused to ___wear___ a tie?

weather	atmospheric conditions
whether	if it happens that; in case; if

Although meteorologists are *weather* specialists, even they can't predict *whether* a hurricane will change course.

Fill in the blanks: The gloomy __weather__ report in the paper this morning ended all discussion of __whether__ to pack a picnic lunch for later.

whose	belonging to whom
who's	shortened form of "who is" and "who has"

Tell me *who's* the person *whose* dirty dishes are left in the workroom sink?

Fill in the blanks: The emcee asked the guests, " __Who's__ the person __whose__ birthday is closest to the guest of honor's?"

your	belonging to you
you're	shortened form of "you are"

You're confident that *your* grades are high enough to earn you a scholarship next year.

Fill in the blanks: If __you're__ sure that you can pay the rent, you and __your__ family should move into a larger apartment.

Other Words Frequently Confused

Not all frequently confused words are homonyms. Here is a list of other words that people often confuse. Complete the activities for each set of words, and check off and study the words that give you trouble.

a, an	Both *a* and *an* are used before other words to mean, approximately, "one."

Generally you should use *an* before words starting with a vowel (*a, e, i, o, u*):

ESL NOTE
Nonnative speakers need additional practice with *a/an* and *a/an* versus the omission of articles.

an orange   an umbrella   an indication   an ape   an effort

Generally you should use *a* before words starting with a consonant (all other letters):

a genius   a movie   a speech   a study   a laptop

Fill in the blanks: The morning after the party, I had __a__ pounding headache and __an__ upset stomach.

accept	(ăk sĕpt′)	to receive; agree to
except	(ăk sĕpt′)	excluding; but

I wanted to *accept* the job offer, *except* that I already committed to staying at my current job for another year.

Fill in the blanks: Do you __accept__ your spouse for who he or she is, or do you say, "I love you, __except__ for your faults"?

advice   (ăd vīs′)   noun meaning "an opinion"

advise   (ăd vīs′)   verb meaning "to counsel, to give advice"

I have learned not to take my sister's *advice* on straightening out my life.

A counselor can *advise* you about the courses you'll need next year.

Fill in the blanks: Sabine is so troubled about losing her job that I will __advise__ her to seek the __advice__ of a professional counselor.

affect   (uh fĕkt′)   verb meaning "to influence"

effect   (ĭ fĕkt′)   verb meaning "to cause something"; noun meaning "result"

The bad weather will definitely *affect* the outcome of the election.

If we can *effect* a change in Michael's attitude, he may do better in his courses.

One *effect* of the strike will be dwindling supplies in the supermarkets.

Fill in the blanks: Scientists have studied the __effect__ of large quantities of saccharine on lab animals but have yet to learn how similar amounts __affect__ human beings.

allude   to refer to something indirectly

elude   to avoid or escape someone or something

His stories always *allude* to Shakespearean themes and plots.

The young boy tried to *elude* his mom because he knew he was going to be in trouble.

Fill in the blanks: The thieves were arrested after attempting to __elude__ the police. None of the thieves would tell where the jewels were hidden, but one did __allude__ to where they might be found.

among   implies three or more

between   implies only two

The committee had to choose one person *among* five applicants, not *between* two applicants as previously thought.

Fill in the blanks: __Between__ you and me, I would rather live by myself than __among__ friends.

awhile   adverb meaning for a moment or a brief time

a while   noun meaning an indefinite period of time

> The mother told the child to go play *awhile*, but after *a while*, she noticed it was very quiet, so she went looking for him.

Fill in the blanks: Sampson watched his friends play __awhile__, but then decided he hadn't read any of his favorite books in __a while__, so he headed inside.

beside   along the side of

besides   in addition to

> *Besides* doing daily inventories, I have to stand *beside* the cashier whenever the store gets crowded.

Fill in the blanks: __Besides__ those books on the table, I plan to use these magazines stacked __beside__ me while doing my research paper.

compose   to write or create; to make up of or constitute; to calm or settle

comprise   to be made up of; to include or contain

> I am going to *compose* a new short story this weekend.
>
> Many ingredients *compose* a good gooey butter cake.
>
> After crying for some time, she began to *compose* herself, so she could talk.
>
> Guacamole *comprises* many ingredients, including avocados, onions, tomatoes, and jalapeños.

Fill in the blanks: The test __comprises__ twenty multiple-choice questions, as well as a question that requires students to __compose__ an essay.

definitely   without a doubt

defiantly   in a manner that shows resistance or disobedience

> The child knew he was *definitely* in trouble after he *defiantly* refused to clean up his room.

Fill in the blanks: I knew that I __definitely__ wanted to be a teacher, but my parents wanted me to be a doctor, so I __defiantly__ refused to apply to medical school.

farther   by a greater literal distance; over a great expanse

further   go beyond a certain point; refers to figurative distance

> The better culinary school is *farther* away from my home, but I want to go *further* in my career, so I am willing to make the longer commute.

Fill in the blanks: The bus ride from my hotel to my friend's house was <u>farther</u> than I'd expected, but the longer trip allowed me to read <u>further</u> in my book.

| fewer | used with things that can be counted |
| less | refers to amount, value, or degree |

ESL NOTE
Nonnative speakers need to learn to distinguish between what can be counted and what cannot.

I've taken *fewer* classes this semester, so I hope to have *less* trouble finding time to study.

Fill in the blanks: This beer advertises that it has <u>fewer</u> calories and is <u>less</u> filling.

| former | refers to the first of two items named |
| latter | refers to the second of two items named |

ESL NOTE
Nonnative speakers might also confuse *for* and *during* because in their native language these words are not distinguished.

Camila enjoys cooking and gardening: the *former* allows her to try new recipes, and the *latter* provides her with fresh vegetables to use in her dishes.

Fill in the blanks: When Nikki learned that she had the flu, she immediately called her shift manager and her history professor. She told the <u>former</u> that she would miss work, and she told the <u>latter</u> that she would miss class.

| learn | to gain knowledge |
| teach | to give knowledge |

I can't *learn* a new skill unless someone with lots of patience *teaches* me.

Fill in the blanks: Because she is quick to <u>learn</u> new things, Mandy has offered to <u>teach</u> me how to play the latest video games.

| loose | (lo͞os) | not fastened; not tight-fitting |
| lose | (lo͞oz) | to misplace; fail to win |

In this strong wind, the house may *lose* some of its *loose* roof shingles.

Fill in the blanks: A <u>loose</u> wire in the television set was causing us to <u>lose</u> the picture.

| quiet | (kwī′ĭt) | peaceful |
| quite | (kwīt) | entirely; really; rather |

ESL NOTE
Nonnative speakers will also confuse *quiet* and *quite*. They might also confuse *quit*. All three words are similar except for the vowel sounds. These are called minimal pairs.

Julia seems *quiet* and demure, but she has *quite* a temper at times.

Fill in the blanks: Most people think the library is <u>quite</u> a good place to study, but I find the extreme <u>quiet</u> distracting.

than   (thăn)   used in comparisons

then   (thĕn)   at that time

I made more money *then*, but I've never been happier *than* I am now.

Fill in the blanks: I wanted to purchase a Subaru Crosstrek more ___than___ a Honda CR-V, but ___then___ I was offered a better price at Honda, so now I drive a CR-V.

ESL NOTE
In addition to confusing *than* and *then*, nonnative speakers confuse *than* and *that*. In Spanish, "que" means both.

These sentences check your understanding of *its, it's; there, their, they're; to, too, two;* and *your, you're*. Underline the two incorrect spellings in each sentence. Then spell the words correctly in the spaces provided.

ACTIVITY 1

They're _it's_	1. There still complaining about the weather even though its sunny and warm.
its _two_	2. The dog chewed it's bone while too other dogs watched.
their _there_	3. Although I told them not to park by the tree, there car is parked their.
You're _to_	4. "Your going to be late," said his mother. "The carpool is not going too wait for you."
You're _to_	5. Since your the fastest runner on the team, you're going two run the anchor leg.
too _they're_	6. Your clothes are to wild for me, but I think their perfect for you.
There _two_	7. Their were to things I needed to buy at the store, but I forgot both.
Your _too_	8. You're aunt has a very nice house, but she has two many pillows on her furniture, and I couldn't even sit down!
too _their_	9. John and Sarah spent to much money on there wedding, but their honeymoon was very inexpensive.
too _it's_	10. It's to late to return their car since I wrecked it this afternoon and its totaled!

REVIEW TEST 1

Underline the correct word in the parentheses. Rather than guessing, look back at the explanations of the words when necessary.

1. I (know, no) that several of the tenants have decided (to, too, two) take (their, there, they're) case to court.

2. (Whose, Who's) the author of that book about the (affects, effects) of eating (to, too, two) much protein?

TEACHING TIP
You may want to use these review tests to assess what your students have learned.

3. In our supermarket is a counter (<u>where</u>, wear) (your, <u>you're</u>) welcome to sit down and have free coffee and doughnuts.

4. (Its, <u>It's</u>) possible to (loose, <u>lose</u>) friends by constantly giving out unwanted (<u>advice</u>, advise).

5. For a long time, I couldn't (<u>accept</u>, except) the fact that my husband wanted a divorce; (<u>then</u>, than) I decided to stop being angry and get on with life.

6. I spent the (hole, <u>whole</u>) day browsing (threw, <u>through</u>) the chapters in my business textbook, but I didn't really study them.

7. The newly appointed (<u>principal</u>, principle) is (<u>quite</u>, quiet) familiar with the problems (hear, <u>here</u>) at our school.

8. I found that our cat had (all ready, <u>already</u>) had her kittens (<u>among</u>, between) the weeds (<u>beside</u>, besides) the porch.

9. I (advice, <u>advise</u>) you not to take children to that movie; the special (affects, <u>effects</u>) are (to, <u>too</u>, two) frightening.

10. It seems that nobody will ever be able to (learn, <u>teach</u>) Mario to take (<u>fewer</u>, less) chances with his car.

REVIEW TEST 2

Answers will vary.

On separate paper, write short sentences using the ten words shown below.

1. except

2. it's

3. your

4. among

5. there

6. through

7. whose

8. here

9. whether

10. than

Effective Word Choice

Choose your words carefully when you write. Always take the time to think about your word choices rather than simply use the first word that comes to mind. You want to develop the habit of selecting words that are precise and appropriate for your purpose. One way you can show sensitivity to language is by avoiding slang, clichés, and inflated words.

Slang

We often use slang expressions when we talk because they are so vivid and colorful. However, slang is usually out of place in formal writing. Here are some examples of slang:

Mario exercises daily to keep his *six-pack abs*.

Laura needs a *triple* from Starbucks if she plans to *pull an all-nighter*.

My sister knows how to *dish it out*, but I can *throw* some *'tude*, too.

The new restaurant's food really *grossed me out*.

Slang expressions have a number of drawbacks. They go out of date quickly, they become tiresome if used excessively in writing, and they may communicate clearly to some readers but not to others. Also, the use of slang can be an evasion of the specific details that are often needed to make one's meaning clear in writing. For example, in "The new restaurant's food really grossed me out," the writer has not provided specific details about the food necessary for us to clearly understand the statement. Was the food poorly cooked, undercooked, rotten, or too exotic? What was it that caused the writer to dislike the food? In general, then, you should avoid slang in your writing. If you are in doubt about whether an expression is slang, it may help to check a recently published hardbound dictionary.

Rewrite the following sentences, replacing the italicized slang words with more formal ones.

EXAMPLE

My neighbor keeps his TV on 24-7, which *drives me up the wall*.

My neighbor keeps his TV on constantly, which irritates me.

1. I *crammed* for my test all night, but I *bombed* it anyway.

. . . studied . . . failed

CHAPTER PREVIEW
Slang
Clichés
Inflated Words

TEACHING TIP
Get students to use slang in class. They will probably hesitate, which underscores why they should avoid using slang in their writing.

ESL NOTE
Many nonnative speakers have learned English from their American peers. Help them distinguish between what is acceptable in spoken language but not acceptable in written expression (e.g., "I don't want to *lay a guilt trip on you*" versus "I don't want you to *feel guilty*").

ACTIVITY 1

TEACHING TIP
You may want to do this activity as an entire class.

Answers may vary.

2. My sister has such *FOMO* that she is involved in everything.

My sister has such a fear of missing out on things . . .

_____

_____

3. When I first met Nick, I thought he was *choice,* but he turned out to be *a hater* and didn't want me to have other friends.

. . . cool [or fun] . . . jealous

_____

_____

4. Keira couldn't understand why Luke was *ghosting* her since their last date had been *clutch*.

. . . . no longer communicating with . . . really wonderful.

_____

_____

5. My friend likes *chillaxin'* after school before she does her *h/w*.

. . . relaxing and unwinding . . . homework

_____

_____

Clichés

A *cliché* is an expression that has been worn out through constant use. Here are some typical clichés:

short but sweet	last but not least
drop in the bucket	work like a dog
had a hard time of it	all work and no play
word to the wise	it goes without saying
it dawned on me	at a loss for words
sigh of relief	taking a big chance
too little, too late	took a turn for the worse
singing the blues	easier said than done
in the nick of time	on top of the world
too close for comfort	time and time again
saw the light	make ends meet

TEACHING TIP
Ask students to offer other clichés.

Clichés are common in speech but make your writing seem tired and stale. Also, they are often an evasion of the specific details that you must work to provide in your writing. You should, then, avoid clichés and try to express your meaning in fresh, original ways.

Underline the cliché in each of the following sentences. Then substitute specific, fresh words for the trite expression.

EXAMPLE

My boyfriend has stuck with me through thick and thin.

through good times and bad

Rewritten statements may vary.

1. As the only girl in an otherwise all-boy family, I got away with murder.

   . . . was spoiled. (or: . . . could do anything I wanted.)

2. When I realized I'd lost my textbook, I knew I was up the creek without a paddle.

   . . . in serious trouble.

3. My suggestion is just a shot in the dark, but it's better than nothing.

   . . . just a guess . . .

4. Abigail got more than she bargained for when she offered to help Miles with his math homework.

   . . . more work than she expected . . .

5. Alex is pushing his luck by driving a car with bald tires.

   . . . taking a risk . . .

6. On a hot, sticky midsummer day, iced tea or any frosty drink really hits the spot.

   . . . is really refreshing. (or: is really satisfying.)

7. Nadia thanks her lucky stars that she was born with brains, beauty, and humility.

   . . . is grateful . . .

8. Anything that involves mathematical ability has always been right up my alley.

   . . . easy for me. (or: I've always done well at anything that . . .)

9. Your chance of buying a good used car from that dealer is one in a million.

   . . . slim.

10. Even when we are up to our eyeballs in work, our boss wonders if we have enough to do.

    . . . overloaded with work . . . (or: . . . very busy . . .; or: . . . overworked . . .)

ACTIVITY 3

©Jacob Lund/
Shutterstock

> Write a short paragraph describing the kind of day you had. Try to put as many clichés as possible into it. For example, "I got up at the crack of dawn, ready to take on the world. I grabbed a bite to eat. . . ." Once you are finished, exchange paragraphs with a partner. Each of you should read the other's paragraph aloud. By making yourself aware of clichés in this way, you should lessen the chance that they will appear in your writing.

Inflated Words

Some people feel that they can improve their writing by using fancy, elevated words rather than simple, natural words. They use artificial, stilted language that more often obscures their meaning than communicates it clearly. This frequently occurs when students attempt to use a dictionary or thesaurus, but just pick words at random to replace the simpler words. Using college-level vocabulary is a way to improve your writing, but you must be careful in choosing words. Not only can certain choices sound artificial, but another problem may arise when words are chosen without enough thought. Since many words can act as nouns, verbs, adjectives, and adverbs, using the wrong part of speech often leads to obscured meaning.

Here are some unnatural-sounding sentences:

It was a marvelous gamble to procure some slumber.

We relished the delectable noon-hour repast.

The officer apprehended the imbibed operator of the vehicle.

The female had an affectionate spot in her heart for domesticated canines.

The same thoughts can be expressed more clearly and effectively by using plain, natural language, as below:

It was an excellent chance to get some sleep.

We enjoyed the delicious lunch.

The officer arrested the drunk driver.

The woman had a warm spot in her heart for dogs.

Here are some other inflated words and simpler words that could replace them:

Inflated Words	Simpler Words
amplitude	fullness or abundance
terminate	finish
subsequent to	after
delineate	describe or explain
facilitate	assist or help
moribund	dying or wasting away
manifested	established or shown
to endeavor	to attempt or to try
habituated	accustomed or familiar

Cross out the inflated words in each sentence. Then substitute clear, simple language for the inflated words.

Rewritten versions may vary.

EXAMPLE

A man dressed in odd ~~attire accosted~~ me on the street.

... clothing stopped ...

1. Tyler ~~utilized~~ Natalie's ~~conceptualization~~ to create a video on YouTube.

   ... used ... idea ...

2. My six-year-old daughter plans to ~~facilitate a termination~~ of world hunger.

   ... help end ...

3. Leanne ~~aspires~~ to legally change her ~~identification~~ to "Li Ahn."

   ... wants ... name ...

4. I ~~enlightened~~ the cashier about the ~~calculation discrepancy~~ on our bill.

   ... told ... mistake ...

5. Only Jonah ~~comprehended~~ what ~~transpired~~ at the ~~finalization~~ of the movie.

   ... understood ... happened ... end ...

Certain words are italicized in the following paragraph. These words are either clichés, slang, or inflated. In the space between the lines, replace the italicized words with more effective diction. One italicized phrase is not needed at all; simply cross that one out.

Performance evaluations can be *the worst of times* [stressful] for both employee and employer. Employers *check out* [review] how the employee has performed over a certain period of time and then *facilitate an interview with* [interview] the employee. One of the things employers focus on is improvement. Under areas of improvement, employers write things like: *needs to initiate proper arrival time at work* [needs to show up to work on time], *needs to facilitate excellent group collaboration* [needs to work with groups], and needs to increase production. Another area that employers focus on is goal setting because this gives an employee something to work toward. Sometimes goal setting might identify skill areas that need improvement, but often it involves something simple like increasing production ~~*by a big percent*~~ or setting up a fifteen-minute break every afternoon. After focusing on the things that employees need to improve, and *fleecing it out* [solving problems], employers will

Rewritten versions may differ.

TEACHING TIP
You may want to use this review test to assess what your students have learned.

often chat about the employee's accomplishments. This is when both the employee

and employer have a chance to *revel in* [enjoy] the positive part of the review. Accom-

plishments that employers like to highlight are things like *working like a dog,* [hard work]

landing large accounts, or overall positive behavior. Although performance eval-

uations can *generate heart palpitations* [be stressful], they often help employers and employees

implement changes that attain positive personnel performance. [create plans for better job performance.]

SECTION IV: WORD USE EDITING TEST I

There are fifteen incorrect words or phrases in the following paragraph. Rewrite the paragraph to correct word-use problems. Use the margins and the space between the lines.

Young people today have ~~quiet~~ [quite] a few advantages beyond what
~~they're~~ [their] parents and grandparents had. Beside computers and cell
phones, they have a ~~hole~~ [whole] shelf full of gadgets that make ~~there~~ [their]
~~life's~~ [lives] easier. For example, to ~~brake~~ [break] up the monotony of waiting in a
doctor's office, at a bus stop, or in a long line at the grocery store,
they put on their earbuds and listen to ~~the latest tunes~~ [their favorite music], for ~~ours~~ [hours] if
they have to. In addition, they have an easier time communicating
with friends ~~then there~~ [than their] parents did. When they are not able to
~~hang out with the guys~~ [be with friends], they simply ~~transmit~~ [send] them an e-mail or a text.
~~Last but not least~~ [Finally], technology has made it possible for them to
download hundreds of ~~hot~~ [new] songs and videos, so finding an endless
supply of entertainment is ~~a breeze~~ [easy].

SECTION IV: WORD USE EDITING TEST II

Rewrite the following paragraph to correct word-use and other sentence-skills problems. Use the margins and the space between the lines.

Wording of corrections may vary.

Alan Paton (1903–1988), ~~who's~~ *whose* novels ~~zeroed in~~ *focused* on the struggle for human and civil rights in South Africa, was that country's finest author ~~and writer~~. Paton opposed the political system known as apartheid, the principle purpose of which was to keep the races ~~apart and~~ separate. More importantly, it also denied basic liberties to blacks and other nonwhites ~~in the country of South Africa~~. ~~Time and time again~~, *Frequently* Paton was ~~hassled~~ *harassed* by the ~~cops~~ *police*. ~~The reason for this was~~ because he ~~wanted to ditch the whole~~ *opposed* apartheid ~~system~~. The ~~guys in charge of the country~~ *authorities* even ~~busted~~ *outlawed* the Liberal Party, which ~~Paton~~ *he* had established in 1953 to oppose the Nationalist Party. The Nationalists ~~favored and~~ supported apartheid. The government also confiscated Paton's passport and tried to ~~shut~~ *silence* him ~~up~~. But ~~that was easier said then done~~ *they were not successful*. Paton's message about the evils of apartheid got out through his novels, the most famous of which is *Cry, the Beloved Country* (1948). Paton's ~~believe~~ *belief* in racial equality ~~among people of different races~~ contributed to the eventual abolishment of apartheid in 1995.

Tests

©Education Images/Universal Images Group/Getty Images

RESPONDING TO IMAGES

Sometimes making a spelling error can create an embarrassing situation. What error was made in the sign above, and how might it reflect on the school or college located on that avenue?

Editing Tests

The twelve editing tests in this chapter will give you practice in revising to correct sentence-skills mistakes. Remember that if you don't edit carefully, you run the risk of undermining much of the work you have put into a paper. If readers see too many surface flaws, they may assume that you don't place much value on what you have to say, and they may not give your ideas a fair hearing. Revising to eliminate sentence-skills errors is a basic part of clear, effective writing.

In nine of the tests, the spots where errors occur have been underlined; your job is to identify and correct each error. In the rest of the tests, you must locate, as well as identify and correct, the errors.

EDITING TIPS

Here are tips that can help you edit the next-to-final draft of a paper for sentence-skills mistakes:

1. Have at hand two essential tools: a good dictionary and a sentence-skills handbook (you can use Chapter 4 and Part 6 of this book).

2. Use a sheet of paper to cover your essay so that you will expose only one sentence at a time. Look for errors in grammar, spelling, and typing. It may help to read each sentence out loud. If a sentence does not read clearly and smoothly, chances are something is wrong.

3. Pay special attention to the kinds of errors you yourself tend to make. For example, if you tend to write run-ons or fragments, be especially on the lookout for those errors.

4. Proofreading symbols that may be of particular help are the following:

    ⟋ℯ delete   draw two ~~two~~ conclusions ⟋ℯ

    ^ insert missing letter or word   achi̭eve

    cap, lc add a capital   My english Class
               (or a lowercase) letter

EDITING TEST 1

TEACHING TIP
You may want to use these editing tests to assess what your students have learned.

In the spaces at the bottom, write the numbers of the ten word groups that contain fragments or run-ons. Then, in the spaces between the lines and in the margin, edit by making the necessary corrections.

¹I remember my childhood as being generally happy and can recall experiencing some of the most carefree times of my life. ²But I can also remember, even more vividly, other moments/ ³When I was deeply frightened. ⁴As a child, I was truly terrified of the dark and of getting lost. ⁵These fears were very real/ they caused me some extremely uncomfortable moments.

⁶Maybe it was the strange way things looked and sounded in my familiar room at night/ ⁷That scared me so much. ⁸The streetlight outside or passing car lights would create shadows in my room. ⁹As a result, clothes hung over a chair ~~taking~~ on the shape of an unknown beast.

¹⁰Out of the corner of my eye, I saw curtains move when there was no breeze. ¹¹A tiny creak in the floor would sound a hundred times louder than in daylight, my imagination would take over/ ¹²Creating burglars and monsters on the prowl. ¹³Because darkness always made me feel so helpless/ ¹⁴I would lie there motionless so that the "enemy" would not discover me.

¹⁵Another of my childhood fears was that I would get lost/ ¹⁶Especially on the way home from school. ¹⁷After school, all the buses lined up along the curb, I was terrified that I'd get on the wrong one. ¹⁸Scanning the bus windows for the faces of my friends/ ¹⁹I'd also look to make sure that the bus driver was the same one I had had in the morning.

1. ___3___   3. ___7___   5. ___11___   7. ___13___   9. ___17___
2. ___5___   4. ___9___   6. ___12___   8. ___16___   10. ___18___

Margin annotations: ℓ; ℓc; :; ℓ / ℓc; took; and / ,; ℓc; ,; ,; ℓc / when,; ,

EDITING TEST 2

Identify the ten mistakes at the underlined spots in the student paper that follows. From the box below, choose the letter that describes each mistake and write that letter in the space provided. (The same kind of mistake may appear more than once.) Then, in the spaces between the lines, edit and correct each mistake.

a. fragment	e. homonym error
b. run-on	f. subject-verb agreement error
c. missing comma	g. inconsistent verb tense
d. apostrophe error	h. wordiness

Personal

doesn't
Eating in fast-food restaurants <u>don't</u> need to be completely
  1
King, I
unhealthy. Although I often stop at Wendy's or Burger <u>King. I</u>
  2
there
find ways to make healthful choices <u>their</u>. For one thing, I order
  3
sandwiches that are as plain as possible. A broiled hamburger or fish
isn't
sandwich isn't so bad, as long as it <u>isnt</u> covered with melted cheese,
  4
fatty sauces, bacon
<u>fatty sauces bacon</u>, or other extras that pile on the fat and calories.
  5
is   *potatoes*
Another health-conscious choice <u>are</u> to skip deep-fat-fried <u>potatoe's</u>
                                  6   7
cholesterol; instead
loaded with salt and heavy with <u>cholesterol, instead</u>, I can order a
                                  8
plain baked potato from Wendy's and add just a bit of butter and salt
take
for taste. In addition, I <u>took</u> advantage of healthful items on menus.
  9
For example, most fast-food places now offer green salads and low-
order
fat chicken choices. Finally, I <u>entreat upon the personnel to get me</u> a
                                  10
sensible beverage—ice water or coffee—instead of soda or a milk

shake.

1. __f__   3. __e__   5. __c__   7. __d__   9. __g__

2. __a__   4. __d__   6. __f__   8. __b__   10. __h__

EDITING TEST 3

Identify the ten sentence-skills mistakes at the underlined spots in the student paper that follows. From the box below, choose the letter that describes each mistake and write that letter in the space provided. (The same kind of mistake may appear more than once.) Then, in the spaces between the lines, edit and correct each mistake.

a. fragment	d. dangling modifier
b. run-on	e. missing comma
c. inconsistent verb tense	f. homonym error

Some corrections may vary.

winter. I
I had a strange experience last winter, I was shopping for Christmas
<u>1</u>

presents when I came to a small clothing shop. I was going to pass it
by, until
by, Until I saw a beautiful purple robe on a mannequin in the window.
<u>2</u>
When I stopped to look at it,
Stopping to look at it, the mannequin seemed to wink at me. I was
<u>3</u> *;*

really startled, I looked around to see if anyone else was watching.
<u>4</u> *head,*
Shaking my head I stepped closer to the window. Then I really began
<u>5</u> *sanity. It*   *its*
to question my sanity, it looked as if the mannequin moved it's legs.
<u>6</u>   <u>7</u> *smiled*
My face must have shown alarm because the mannequin then smiles.
and   *relief. It*   <u>8</u>
And even waved her arm. I sighed with relief, it was a human model
<u>9</u>   <u>10</u>

after all.

1. __b__   3. __d__   5. __e__   7. __f__   9. __a__

2. __a__   4. __b__   6. __b__   8. __c__   10. __b__

EDITING TEST 4

Identify the ten sentence-skills mistakes at the underlined spots in the student paper that follows. From the box below, choose the letter that describes each mistake and write that letter in the space provided. (The same kind of mistake may appear more than once.) Then, in the spaces between the lines, edit and correct each mistake.

a. run-on	e. wordiness
b. mistake in subject–verb agreement	f. slang
c. faulty parallelism	g. missing comma
d. missing quotation marks	

I think

It is this writer's opinion that smokers should quit smoking for
‾‾‾‾‾‾‾‾‾‾‾‾‾‾‾‾‾‾‾‾
        1

the sake of those who are around them. Perhaps the most helpless

                                        are   *babies.*
creatures that suffer from being near a smoker is unborn babies,
                                       ‾‾   ‾‾‾‾‾‾
                                        2   3
According.
according to Dr. Sears, a leading pediatric expert, one study suggests
‾‾‾‾‾‾‾
   3

that the risk of having an undersized baby is doubled if pregnant

women are exposed to cigarette smoke for about two hours a day.
                                            should avoid
Pregnant women should refrain from smoking and to avoid smoke-
                                           ‾‾‾‾‾‾‾
                                              4

filled rooms. The American Heart Association has stated that passive

smoking is very dangerous, so spouses of smokers are also
at risk
in bigtrouble. They are more likely than spouses of nonsmokers to die
‾‾‾‾‾‾‾
   5   *to develop*
of heart disease and the development of fatal cancers. Office workers
                     ‾‾‾‾‾‾‾‾‾‾‾‾‾‾‾
                             6

are a final group that can be harmed by a smoke-filled environment.
                        said,
The US Surgeon General has said "Workers who smoke are a health
                         ‾‾‾‾
                          7
       coworkers."
risk to their coworkers. While ~~it is undoubtedly true that~~ one can argue
              ‾‾‾‾‾‾‾‾   ‾‾‾‾‾‾‾‾‾‾‾‾‾‾‾‾‾‾‾‾‾‾‾
                 8   9
                                  themselves, they
that smokers have the right to hurt themselves they do not have the
                                    ‾‾‾‾‾‾‾‾‾‾‾‾‾‾‾
                                         10

right to hurt others. Smokers should abandon their deadly habit for the

health of others at home and at work.

Some corrections may vary.

1. _e_   3. _a_   5. _f_   7. _g_   9. _e_

2. _b_   4. _c_   6. _c_   8. _d_   10. _g_

EDITING TEST 5

Identify the ten sentence-skills mistakes at the underlined spots in the student paper that follows. From the box below, choose the letter that describes each mistake and write that letter in the space provided. (The same kind of mistake may appear more than once.) Then, in the spaces between the lines, edit and correct each mistake.

a. fragment	e. dangling modifier
b. run-on	f. missing comma
c. mistake in subject–verb agreement	g. wordiness
d. misplaced modifier	h. slang

Some corrections may vary.

The United States will never be a drug-free society but we [society, but] [1]

could eliminate many of our drug-related problems by legalizing

drugs. ~~Drugs~~ would be sold by companies and not criminals ~~if they~~ [If drugs were legal, they] [∧]

~~were legal.~~ The drug trade would then take place like any business [business,] [2] [3]

freeing the police and courts to devote their time to other problems. [freeing]

Lawful drugs would be sold at a fair price, no one would need to steal [price, so]

in order to buy them. By legalizing drugs, organized crime ~~would lose~~ [we would deprive] [of one of] [4] [5] [∧]

~~one of~~ its major sources of revenue. ~~It goes without saying that~~ we [We] [6]

would, instead, create important tax revenues for the government.

Finally, if drugs was sold through legal outlets, we could reduce drug [were] [7]

problems among our young people. It would be illegal to sell drugs to

people under a certain age. Just as is the case now with alcohol. And [age, just] [8]

because the profits on drugs would no longer be out of sight, there [be so high,] [9]

would be little incentive for drug pushers to sell to young people.

Decriminalizing drugs, in short, could be a solution. ~~To~~ many of the [solution to] [10]

problems that result from the illegal drug trade.

1. __f__   3. __f__   5. __e__   7. __c__   9. __h__

2. __d__   4. __b__   6. __g__   8. __a__   10. __a__

EDITING TEST 6

Identify the ten sentence-skills mistakes at the underlined spots in the student paper that follows. From the box below, choose the letter that describes each mistake and write that letter in the space provided. (The same kind of mistake may appear more than once.) Then, in the spaces between the lines, edit and correct each mistake.

a. fragment	e. mistake with quotation marks
b. run-on	f. mistake in pronoun point of view
c. mistake in subject–verb agreement	g. cliché
d. mistake in verb tense	h. missing comma

One reason that I enjoy the commute to school is that the drive
uninterrupted
gives me <u>uninterupted</u> time to myself. The classes and socializing
are 1
at college <u>is</u> great, and so is the time I spend with my family, but
2
me
sometimes all this togetherness keeps <u>you</u> from being able to think.
3 *alone, for*
In fact, I look forward to the time I have <u>alone, it</u> gives me a chance
4
to plan what I'll accomplish in the day ahead. For example, one Tuesday
announced
afternoon my history professor <u>announces</u> that a rough outline for
5 *Fortunately*
our semester report was due that Friday. <u>By happy chance</u>, I had already
6
reading, and
done some <u>reading and</u> I had checked my proposed topic with her
7 *evening,*
the week before. <u>Therefore, on the way home in the car that evening</u>
8
I planned the entire history report in my mind. Then all I had to do
when I got home was quickly jot it down before I forgot it. <u>When I
morning, she
handed the professor the outline at 8:30 Wednesday morning.</u> She
9
asked me <u>"if I had stayed up all night working on it."</u> She was amazed
10
when I told her that I owed it all to commuting.

Personal

Some corrections may vary.

1. _g_   3. _f_   5. _d_   7. _h_   9. _a_
2. _c_   4. _b_   6. _g_   8. _a_   10. _e_

EDITING TEST 7

Identify the ten sentence-skills mistakes at the underlined spots in the student paper that follows. From the box below, choose the letter that describes each mistake and write that letter in the space provided. (The same kind of mistake may appear more than once.) Then, in the spaces between the lines, edit and correct each mistake.

a. fragment	f. misplaced modifier
b. run-on	g. homonym error
c. mistake in subject–verb agreement	h. apostrophe error
d. missing comma	i. cliché
e. missing capital letters	

Some corrections may vary.

The Appalachian Trail, also known as the A.T. runs along the *[A.T., runs]*
1
Appalachian mountain range from Maine to Georgia. The trail is over
2,100 miles long and passes threw fourteen states there are four *[through]* *[states. There]*
2   3
main types of hikers on the trail. "Thru-hikers" hike the entire trail in
one continuous journey that often takes six months. "Flip-floppers"
complete the entire trail in one journey to avoid crowds and weather, *[in discontinuous sections, to]*
4   *[avoid crowds and weather.]*
in discontinuous sections. "Section-hikers" hike different sections and
complete the entire trail over several year's. "Day-hikers" hike short *[years]*
5
parts of the trail with know attempt to complete the entire trail. The *[no]*
6
majority of the two to three million visitors to the A.T. each year
are day-hikers; however, about 2,000 people a year attempt to
"thru-hike." Averaging only 250 successful hikers who feel like they *["thru-hike," averaging]*
7   8
are on top of the world. To keep the trail clean and healthy for all the
visitors, thousands of volunteers, along with the national park service *[National Park Service]*
9
and USDA Forest Service, spends over 200,000 hours a year *[spend]*
10
maintaining the trail.

1. __d__   3. __b__   5. __h__   7. __a__   9. __e__

2. __g__   4. __f__   6. __g__   8. __i__   10. __c__

EDITING TEST 8

Each numbered box in the application below contains a sentence-skills mistake. Identify each of the ten mistakes. As you find each, write the type of mistake you found in the space provided. Then correct it next to your answer. The first one has been done for you.

1. missing comma: August 15, 2019

2. missing capital letters: Carson City

3. unnecessary quotation marks: Food Server

4. slang: as soon as possible

5. missing capital: Kennedy High School

6. homonym error: Course

7. missing capital: Outlet

8. missing comma: Carson City, NV 89706

9. apostrophe error: Sales Clerk

10. fragment: I also stock shelves.

Some corrections may vary.

Work

DT Food Services Ltd. • Employment Application			1. Date of Application *August 15 2019*	
Social Security # *123-45-6789*	Last Name *Lee-Thomas*		First Name *Leona*	Middle Initial *F.*
Address (Street number and name) *550 Tenth Avenue*		2. City, State, and Zip Code *carson city, NV 89706*		
3. Desired Position *"Food Server"*	4. Date Available to Start *Asap!*	Home Phone		Business Phone

EDUCATION

Schools	Name and Location	Dates Attended (mo/yr) From: To:	Grad?	Major/Minor Course Work	Type of Degree
High School	5. *Kennedy High school*	*9/01 to 6/05*	YES *X* NO		
College or University	*Washoe Community College*	*9/05 to 6/06*	YES NO *X*		
Other Training or Education	6. *Coarse in typing*		YES *X* NO		

WORK HISTORY (include volunteer experience. Use additional sheets if necessary.)			
7. Current or Last Employer: *Grocery outlet*		8. Address: *120 South Carson Street* *Carson City NV 89706*	
9. Job Title: *Sales' Clerk*		Supervisor's Name and Title *Julie Leroy, Manager*	Phone Number *775-333-3333*
Dates Employed (mo/yr-mo/yr) *10/15 to present*	Starting Salary *$8.50/hour*	Ending or Current Salary *$9.50/hour*	Reason for Leaving *Currently employed but seeking new opportunities*

10. List major duties in order of their importance in the job: *I operate the cash register. Also stock shelves.*

EDITING TEST 9

Each underlined area in the cover letter below contains a sentence-skills mistake. Identify the mistake and write its item number in the appropriate space in the box below. Then correct the mistake in the space above each error.

missing colon: __1__	homonym error: __5__ , __9__
missing apostrophe: __2__	dangling modifier: __3__
dropped verb ending: __4__	fragment: __6__
missing word: __7__	run-on: __8__
missing comma: __10__	

Some corrections may vary.

Karen Sanchez

Personnel Officer

Bay Adventures

Tampa, FL 33619

^{1}Dear Ms. Sanchez — *Sanchez:*

^{2}I am replying to your ad in last Sundays newspaper that — *Sunday's*

indicated an opening in Bay Adventures for a recreational activities

coordinator. ^{3}Athletic and outgoing, the position seems ideal for me. — *Since I am athletic and outgoing,*

^{4,5}I spend the past two years working at an after-school program — *spent*

wear I developed fun activities for children in grades K-6. My job — *where*

required me to think of creative yet safe ways to promote physical

fitness. ^{6}And encourage teamwork and cooperation among the kids. — *fitness, and*

^{7}Also, I took several physical education classes at University of — *at the University*

Tampa. ^{8}I learned about sports psychology, I even took a class on — *psychology. I even*

exercise techniques. Right now, I hope to apply what I have learned,

which is why I am very interested in your job.

Please feel free to call me for an interview. ^{9}Thank you for you're — *your*

consideration.

^{10}Sincerely — *Sincerely,*

Mark Rankins

EDITING TEST 10

Each underlined area in the cover letter below contains a sentence-skills mistake. Identify the mistake and write its item number in the appropriate space in the box below. Then correct the mistake in the space above each error.

missing period: __1__	missing colon: __2__
homonym error: __3__	slang: __4__
faulty parallelism: __6__	fragment: __5__ , __7__
run-on: __8__	apostrophe error: __9__ , __10__

August, 28, 2019

¹[Mr] Gordon Hebling   *Mr.*

Western Savings Bank

122 Mijo Way

Tucson, AZ 85706

²Dear Mr. [Hebling]   *Hebling:*

³I attended a career fair last week at the Tucson Convention Center and discovered that [you're] company is hiring part-time and   *your*
relief tellers. ⁴A [guy] I spoke to told me that I would be ideal for the   *representative*
position because of my experience working as a cashier.

I currently work as a cashier at an electronics [store. ⁵But would]   *store, but I*
like to start a career in banking. My job requires me to be
responsible and accurate. ⁶I understand the importance of customer
service and [how good communicating is important.]   *good communication.*
⁷[In addition to my work experience.] ⁸I am proficient with   *experience, I am*
[Excel, I have used several computer systems.] ⁹,¹⁰If I am hired, I can   *Excel, and I*
work at various [bank's] because I have a valid [drivers'] license and   *banks* ... *driver's*
my own car.

Please feel free to call me at (520) 222-2222. I hope that I will
have an opportunity to talk with you in person.

Sincerely,

Monique Williamson

 Work

Some corrections may vary.

EDITING TEST 11

Each underlined area in the résumé excerpt below contains a sentence-skills mistake. Identify the mistake and write its item number in the appropriate space in the box below. Then correct the mistake in the space above each error.

missing capital letter: __1__ , __10__	inconsistent verb tense: __7__
dangling modifier: __4__	run-on: __9__
faulty parallelism: __3__	apostrophe error: __8__
fragment: __5__ , __6__	missing comma: __2__

Work

Some corrections may vary.

Alyssa Leong

Bagley
[1]597 bagley Street
Torrance, CA
[2]Torrance CA 90501

Phone: (310) 555-5555 aleong@xyz.net

Objective

I hope to find a position as a certified nurse assistant at a nursing

full-time hours
facility that will offer me rewarding work, [3]hours that are full time, and

medical benefits.

Summary of Qualifications

working, I have experience taking care of people.
[4]Caring, competent, and hard working, my experience caring for

people is present. [5]Having volunteered at an adult residential care
two years, I
home for two years. I am aware of the responsibilities for providing
home, I
basic care. [6]At the care home. [7]I helped staff members and sometimes
dressed   supervisors
fed, bathed, and dress clients. [8]My supervisors' encouraged me to

enroll in a certified nursing assistant program. [9]In 2015, I completed a
training, and I
six-month training, I also received my CNA certification.

Education

2017	Certified Nursing Assistant Program	Los Angeles Adult Community School
2015	Diploma	Roosevelt High School

Work History

Central Adult Residential
9/2015–6/2017   Volunteer[10]South central adult residential Care Home

- Assisted clients with personal hygiene and recreational activities

- Provided companionship

EDITING TEST 12

Each numbered line in the résumé below contains a sentence-skills mistake. Identify the mistake and write its item number in the appropriate space in the box below. Then correct the mistake in the space above each error.

Work

missing capital letter: __1__, __10__   homonym error: __8__

faulty parallelism: __3__   missing -s ending: __4__, __6__

missing comma: __2__   apostrophe error: __5__, __9__

inconsistent verb tense: __7__

Kalani Bowers

Avenue   St. Louis, MO
[1]203 Mahogany avenue • [2]St. Louis MO 63103 • (314) 777-7777

• kalanib@xxx.mail

OBJECTIVE

[3]I wish to find a full-time sales position with an opportunity for
personal growth
advancement and growing personally.

WORK HISTORY

Dave's Electronics, St. Louis, MO

2011 to present

Inventory Clerk

- [4]Used a computer system to catalog and monitor inventory
appliances
(electronics and appliance)
inventories
- [5]Conducted quarterly physical inventories'

CPK Trading Company, St. Louis, MO

2008 to 2011

Data Entry Clerk
invoices
- [6]Processed payments and invoice
Maintained
- [7]Maintain and audited numerous databases
two
- [8]Entered daily sales receipts for too branch locations
reports
- [9]Generated reports' and memoranda

EDUCATION

Diploma, St. Anthony's High School, Columbia, MO (2008)

SPECIAL SKILLS

- Experienced with Windows, Word, and Excel
C.P.R
- [10]c.p.r. certified

Some corrections may vary.

As you are reading the following essay written by Reynaldo for a nutrition class, think about what advice you would offer him as he prepares to write his final draft. Does his essay cover all four bases of effective writing? To be sure, use the checklist that follows.

A Balanced Diet

[1]The human body works twenty-four hours a day. [2]It's always
                   repairing. It's   *Its*
building and repairing, it's always feeding and cleansing itself. [3]It's
                                        thought
goal is to be ready for any movement, breath, or how you think.

[4]A person's quality of life depends on how well his or her body

works. [5]How well the body works depends on how much energy it

gets. [6]Energy comes from the food that is eaten. [7]Food contains

nutrients that a body needs for growth and energy.
                               balanced
       [8]People who eat a balenced diet give their body the six

essential nutrients it needs: minerals, water, carbohydrates, fats,

proteins, and vitamins. [9]Minerals are nutrients that build bones and

teeth. [10]Minerals also form red blood cells and other substances.
Water   *are*
[11]water aids digestion and waste removal. [12]Carbohydrates is the

body's main source of energy. [13]Two carbohydrates are sugars from

foods such as fruits and vegetables and starches found in rice,

potatoes, and bread. [14]Fats help build cell membranes. [15]Proteins

repair and grow body tissues. [16]Finally, vitamins help the body use
carbohydrate, fats
carbohydrates fats, and proteins.

       [17]Everyone should follow the nutritional food pyramid created by
                            Department
the United States department of Agriculture (USDA). [18]This pyramid
shows
showing the daily number of servings a person should eat from five

food groups plus fats and oils. [19]The food pyramid has six levels.
                                 contains
[20]The first and largest part of the pyramid contained the bread,

cereal, rice, and pasta group from which the body needs six ounces

every day. [21]The next two levels are vegetables and then fruits.

continued

²²The USDA recommends two and a half cups of vegetables and two cups of fruits. ²³The next part of the pyramid is the smallest level. ²⁴It contains fats, oils, and sweets. ²⁵These foods have few nutrients, so people should eat them sparingly. ²⁶The final two levels are the milk, yogurt, and cheese group and the meat, poultry, fish, dry beans, eggs, and nuts group. ²⁷~~They~~ *People* need three cups of the milk group and five and a half ounces of meat or beans. ²⁸These recommended daily amounts are based on a 2,000-calorie diet.

Unity

✔ Is there a clear thesis statement? _____Yes_____ If so, write it below:

Food contains nutrients that your body needs for growth and energy.

✔ Is all the material on target in support of the thesis statement? _Yes_

✔ Can you find any problems with unity in any of the supporting paragraphs? _No_ .

Support

✔ Is additional specific evidence needed anywhere in the essay? _No_

Coherence

✔ Does Reynaldo use transitions and other connective devices in the second supporting paragraph?

_____Yes_____ If yes, list them here:

___First___   ___The next level___   ___The third level___   ___Finally___

Sentence Skills

✔ Can you identify the ten sentence-skills mistakes in the essay? Write the sentence number of each mistake in the space provided:

run-on ___2___   mistake in subject–verb agreement ___12___

faulty parallelism ___3___   incorrect apostrophe ___3___

missing comma ___16___   pronoun mistake ___27___

spelling mistake ___8___   inconsistent verb tense ___20___

sentence fragment ___18___   capitalization mistake ___17___

Introduction and/or Conclusion

✔ Does Reynaldo provide a satisfying conclusion, one that brings his essay to a natural and graceful end? _No_ If not, what advice would you offer Reynaldo regarding his conclusion? _Reynaldo could provide his readers with information on how to find out the recommended daily amounts that are right for them, possibly by going to the USDA Web site. (Answers will vary.)_

Collaborative Activity

Together with your group or class, edit and correct each sentence-skills mistake in Reynaldo's essay.

©Jacob Lund/
Shutterstock

CORRECTION SYMBOLS

Here is a list of symbols the instructor may use when marking papers.

Agr	Correct the mistake in agreement of subject and verb or pronoun and the word the pronoun refers to
Apos	Correct the apostrophe mistake
Bal	Balance the parts of the sentence so they have the same (parallel) form
Cap	Correct the mistake in capital letters
Coh	Revise to improve coherence
Comma	Add a comma
CS	Correct the comma splice
DM	Correct the dangling modifier
Det	Support or develop the topic more fully by adding details
Frag	Attach the fragment to a sentence or make it a sentence
lc	Use a lowercase (small) letter rather than a capital
MM	Correct the misplaced modifier
¶	Indent for a new paragraph
No ¶	Do not indent for a new paragraph
Pro	Correct the pronoun mistake
Quot	Correct the mistake in quotation marks
R-O	Correct the run-on
Sp	Correct the spelling error
Trans	Supply or improve a transition
Und Ital	Underline italics
Verb	Correct the verb or verb form
Wordy	Omit needless words
WC	Replace the word marked with a more accurate one (word choice)
?	Write the illegible word clearly
/	Eliminate the word, letter, or punctuation mark so slashed
^	Add the omitted word or words
; / : / - / —	Add semicolon, colon, hyphen, or dash
()	Add parentheses
✓	You have something fine or good here: an expression, a detail, an idea

Readings for Writers

Introduction to the Readings

Nineteen Reading Selections

PART SEVEN WILL

- provide you with nineteen essays on a variety of thought-provoking topics

- develop your literal and inferential reading skills through guided reading comprehension questions

- develop your critical thinking skills through discussion questions

- develop your writing skills through structure and technique questions and writing assignments

EXPLORING WRITING PROMPT:

Ta-Nehisi Coates has received praise during the last few years for his direct, opinionated political writing, but he has also gained a lot of critics. In fact, Coates closed his Twitter account in 2017 because of contentious exchanges with some who criticized his ideas. Standing up for your beliefs can often be difficult, especially when social media makes it easy for people to insult and harass others. How do you feel about people shutting down their accounts because of negativity? Have you had negative interactions on social media? If so, what actions, if any, did you take to address the negativity?

Author/writer Ta-Nehisi Coates speaks onstage during the March 2018 SXSW Convergence Keynote at the Austin Convention Center in Austin, Texas.

Introduction to the Readings

TEACHING TIP
Ask students to discuss
how they feel about
reading. Many students do
not enjoy it. Explore why.

ESL NOTE
Nonnative students might
require some strategies
for understanding
vocabulary in context
(e.g., punctuation clues,
synonyms, antonyms,
definition clues,
experience, understanding
the logic). Otherwise, they
will rely upon a dictionary,
which can make the
reading assignments
difficult and tedious.

The nineteen reading selections in Part 7 will help you find topics for writing. These selections deal in various ways with interesting, often thought-provoking concerns or experiences of contemporary life. Subjects of the essays include growth mindset; free college tuition; how the minimum wage affects society; why social media can be beneficial for people's careers; practical advice on surviving the first year of college; ways the media influence our attitudes; and how students should approach the job market. The varied subjects should inspire lively class discussions as well as serious individual thought. The selections should also provide a continuing source of high-interest material for a wide range of writing assignments.

The selections serve another purpose as well. They will help develop reading skills, with direct benefits to you as a writer. One benefit is that, through close reading, you will learn how to recognize the thesis in a selection and to identify and evaluate the supporting material that develops the thesis. In your own writing, you will aim to achieve the same essential structure: an overall thesis followed by detailed, valid support for that thesis. A second benefit is that close reading will also help you explore a selection and its possibilities thoroughly. The more you understand about what is said in a piece, the more ideas and feelings you may have about writing on an assigned topic or a related topic of your own. A third benefit of close reading is that you will become more aware of authors' stylistic devices—for example, their introductions and conclusions, their ways of presenting and developing a point, their use of transitions, their choice of language to achieve a particular tone. Recognizing these devices in other people's writing will help you enlarge your own range of ideas and writing techniques.

The Format of Each Selection

Each selection begins with a short overview that gives helpful background information as well as a brief idea of the topic of the reading. The selection is followed by three sets of questions:

- First, there are ten "Reading Comprehension" questions to help you measure your understanding of the material. These questions involve several important reading skills: understanding vocabulary in context, recognizing a subject or topic, determining a thesis or main idea, identifying key supporting points, and making inferences. Answering the questions will enable you and your instructor to check your basic understanding of a selection quickly. More significantly, as you move from one selection to the next, you will sharpen your reading skills as well as strengthen your thinking skills—two key factors in making you a better writer.

- Following the comprehension questions are questions on "Structure and Technique" that focus on aspects of a writer's craft, and questions on "Critical Reading and Discussion" that involve you in reading carefully and thinking actively about a writer's ideas.

- Finally, several writing assignments accompany each selection (one for a paragraph and two for essays). The assignments range from personal narratives to expository and persuasive paragraphs and essays about issues in the world at large. Many assignments provide detailed guidelines on how to proceed, including suggestions for prewriting and appropriate methods of development. When writing your paragraph and essay responses to the readings, you will have opportunities to apply all the methods of development presented in Parts 3 and 4 of this book.

How to Read Well: Four General Steps

Skillful reading is an important part of becoming a skillful writer. Following is a series of four steps that will make you a better reader—both of the selections here and in your reading at large.

1. Concentrate As You Read

To improve your concentration, follow these tips:

- First, read in a place where you can be quiet and alone. Don't choose a spot where there is a TV or music on or where friends or family are talking nearby.

- Next, sit upright when you read. If your body is in a completely relaxed position, sprawled across a bed or nestled in an easy chair, your mind is also going to be completely relaxed. The light muscular tension that comes from sitting in a straight chair promotes concentration and keeps your mind ready to work.

- Third, consider using your index finger (or a pen) as a pacer while you read. Lightly underline each line of print with your index finger as you read down a page. Hold your hand slightly above the page and move your finger at a speed that is a little too fast for comfort. This pacing with your index finger, like sitting upright in a chair, creates a slight physical tension that will keep your body and mind focused and alert.

2. Skim Material Before You Read It

In skimming, you spend about two minutes rapidly surveying a selection, looking for important points and skipping secondary material. Follow this sequence when skimming:

- Begin by reading the overview that precedes the selection.

- Then study the title of the selection for a few moments. A good title is the shortest possible summary of a selection; it often tells you in several words—or even a single word—just what a selection is about. For example, the title "The Professor Is a Dropout" suggests that you're going to read about someone who dropped out but returned to school.

- Next, form a question (or questions) based on the title. For instance, for the selection titled "The Professor Is a Dropout," you might ask,

TEACHING TIP
Keep in mind that a student with a learning disability may have a difficult time skimming.

"How can someone be both a professor and a dropout?" "What happened?" "How did the person make the change?" Using a title to form questions is often a key to locating a writer's thesis, your next concern in skimming.

- Read the first and last couple of paragraphs in the selection. Very often a writer's thesis, *if* it is directly stated, will appear in one of these places and will relate to the title.

- Finally, look quickly at the rest of the selection for other clues to important points. Are there any subheads you can relate in some way to the title? Are there any words the author has decided to emphasize by setting them off in *italic* or **boldface** type? Are there any major lists of items signaled by words such as *first, second, also, another,* and so on?

3. Read the Selection Straight Through with a Pen in Hand

Read the selection without slowing down or turning back; just aim to understand as much as you can the first time through. This is the time to read for the overall content. During your second reading of the selection, write a check or star beside answers to basic questions you formed from the title, and beside other ideas that seem important. Number lists of important points: 1, 2, 3, ... Circle words you don't understand. Write question marks in the margins next to passages that are unclear and that you will want to reread.

4. Work with the Material

Go back and reread passages that were not clear the first time through. Look up words that block your understanding of ideas and write their meanings in the margin. Also, reread carefully the areas you identified as most important; doing so will enlarge your understanding of the material. Now that you have a sense of the whole, prepare a short written outline of the selection by answering these questions:

- What is the thesis?
- What key points support the thesis?
- What seem to be other important ideas in the selection?

By working with the material in this way, you will significantly increase your understanding of a selection. Effective reading, just like effective writing, does not happen all at once. Rather, it must be worked on. Often you begin with a general impression of what something means, and then, by working at it, you move to a deeper level of understanding.

How to Answer the Comprehension Questions: Specific Hints

The ten reading comprehension questions that follow each selection involve several important reading skills:

- Understanding vocabulary in context
- Summarizing the selection in a title

- Determining the main idea

- Recognizing key supporting details

- Making inferences

TEACHING TIP
Stress to your students the importance of answering these questions.

The following hints will help you apply each of these reading skills:

- *Vocabulary in context.* To decide on the meaning of an unfamiliar word, consider its context. Ask yourself, "Are there any clues in the sentence that suggest what this word means?"

- *Subject or title.* Remember that the title should accurately describe the *entire* selection. It should be neither too broad nor too narrow for the material in the selection. It should answer the question "What is this about?" as specifically as possible. Note that you may at times find it easier to answer the title question *after* the main-idea question.

- *Main idea.* Choose the statement that you think best expresses the main idea—also known as the *central point* or *thesis*—of the entire selection. Remember that the title will often help you focus on the main idea. Then ask yourself, "Does most of the material in the selection support this statement?" If you can answer "yes," you have found the thesis.

TEACHING TIP
In pairs, ask students to apply these hints to a specific reading section.

- *Key details.* If you were asked to give a two-minute summary of a selection, the key, or major, details are the ones you would include in that summary. To determine the key details, ask yourself, "What are the major supporting points for the thesis?"

- *Inferences.* Answer these questions by drawing upon the evidence presented in the selection and your own common sense. Ask yourself, "What reasonable judgments can I make on the basis of the information in the selection?"

The readings in Part 7 are categorized according to three main themes: Goals and Values; Education and Learning; and Challenging Society. Additionally, these readings represent how authors use a variety of rhetorical modes within their essays to support their points. A complete list of these readings, grouped by rhetorical mode, is provided at the front of this book. It is titled "Readings Listed by Rhetorical Mode" and directly follows the Table of Contents.

Goals and Values

◼️ READINGS

What Students Need to Know about Today's Job Crisis

Don Bertram

PREVIEW

Finding a job in America may be more difficult than it has ever been before. What are the factors that make the job hunt so much more challenging today—and what must students do to increase their chances for employment? Above all, how can students avoid an all-too-common trap in today's economy: post-high-school study and significant debt, but no job to show for it?

Many Jobs Have Disappeared Forever

To begin with, students must recognize a hard truth: Many jobs in America 1 **have disappeared forever.** There is a well-known story about a meeting that President Barack Obama had with the late Steve Jobs of Apple Computer, America's most profitable corporation. Apple at one time boasted that its products were made in the United States. But now almost all of its millions of iPods, iPhones, iPads, and other products are manufactured overseas—benefiting hundreds of thousands of workers there. Why can't all that work making Apple products come home, Obama was said to have asked. Jobs's reply was unambiguous: "Those jobs aren't coming back," he said.

The globalization of jobs is simply a reality of today. Many American 2 companies, like Apple, have shipped their jobs overseas to places like China, India, and Latin America, where workers are willing to work for a fraction of the pay they would receive in the United States. Companies go overseas because they are increasingly owned by institutional investors who focus on the bottom line, rather than on what might be better, in the long run, for American workers. "American business is about maximizing shareholder value," says Allen Sinai, chief global economist at the research firm Decision Economics.

Once companies decided to set up manufacturing sites in other countries, 3 with cheaper costs and higher profits, American manufacturing could not compete, and many blue-collar manufacturing jobs for the middle class disappeared. Thirty or forty years ago, the country had an abundance of low-skill, decent-paying manufacturing jobs in the automobile, steel, textile, furniture, apparel and electronics assembly industries, among others. Instead of going to college, a person could work in a factory and still enjoy a middle-class life with a house, a yearly vacation, and the chance to eat steak in a restaurant on a Saturday night. But those days are gone.

Relatedly, the manufacturing jobs that *do* remain in America have been 4 reduced by automation, which has helped companies cut over 6 million jobs

TEACHING TIP
Ask students to discuss jobs they have seen become automated in the past few years.

since 2000. As one executive said, "You basically don't want workers. You try to find capital equipment to replace them." Today there are all kinds of factory robots that perform tasks that once gave people a living wage.

The rapid growth of computer-based technology has also eliminated many 5 traditional jobs. Picture the 1960s advertising agency in the cable TV show *Mad Men*, and think about the abundance of people there who were hired to do jobs now handled electronically by small machines. Secretaries have been replaced by word processing, voice mail, e-mail and scheduling software; accounting staff by Excel; people in the art department by desktop design programs. And today the need for workers of all kinds has been reduced by, for example, online banking, self-service checkouts at the supermarket, and the use of home computers or smartphones to do one-click ordering of food, clothing, shoes, health and beauty aids, books, music, movies, games, tools, and an endless range of sports, electronics, and automotive products.

Also cutting deeply into American jobs has been "outsourcing"—the transfer 6 of many white-collar jobs to the much cheaper labor market overseas. Enabled by global computer networks, questions and problems that were once dealt with by workers in the U.S. are now answered by someone at a computer and phone station in India. The back-office operations of banks, investment houses, and insurance companies are increasingly handled by bright, talented people, hired at low wages, in countries halfway around the world. And many companies have or plan to set up white-collar operations in other countries. A case in point: Pharmaceutical giant Merck & Co. Inc., which operates a plant near Philadelphia, announced plans to invest $1.5 billion in research development in China—enough to build a facility large enough to house 600 employees, who will work on discovering new drugs, testing them, and getting regulatory approval. Global competition for jobs with people in other parts of the world is a reality that is likely to increase over time.

The Reduced Value of a College Degree

A second key factor in today's economy is that not only have many jobs disap- 7 **peared, but a college degree no longer means what it once did.** In the past, a student with a college diploma could walk out the college door, and companies would almost be waiting on the doorstep, ready to offer him or her an interesting white-collar job. Today, chances are that unless students have prepared themselves for jobs in marketable areas, there will be no one waiting at their doorstep except the lenders who have provided them with the loans needed to earn their degree.

Here are a few all-too-typical stories; there are countless others just like 8 them.

1.　Kelsey, 23, graduated from a university in Ohio with a degree in marketing 9 and $120,000 in student debt. Unable to get a job in her major, she is now working two restaurant jobs and has given up her apartment to live with her parents. Her mother, who co-signed on the loans, took out a life insurance policy on her daughter. "If anything ever happened, God forbid, that is my debt also," said her mother.

Kelsey didn't seem like a perfect financial fit for a school that costs nearly 10 $50,000 a year. Her father and mother have modest incomes, and she has four sisters. But when she visited the school, she was won over by faculty and admissions staff members who urge students to pursue their dreams rather than obsess on the sticker price. "I was an 18-year-old and they really sold me," Kelsey says. "But no one told me that when I would graduate, I'd owe like $900 a month.

2. Michael, 22, graduated in 2010 with a creative writing degree. Today he 11 is making just above the minimum wage in his job as a barista, serving customers at a Seattle coffeehouse. In the beginning he sent three or four résumés a day, but employers questioned his lack of experience or the practical worth of his major, and he has lost his job-hunting momentum. He is fortunate in getting financial help from his parents to help pay off student loans.

3. Laura, 29, unemployed and with $100,000 in student debt, graduated with 12 honors and two B.A.s, served in the Peace Corps, then graduated with a master's degree in public administration. Despite her accomplishments, she searches fruitlessly for work and lives on food stamps in South Philadelphia. At last count, she had applied for more than 250 jobs, from government service to boutique clerk to waitress. She talked about the blue-collar parents that have supported her along the way: "My parents' hopes are in me, and I feel I'm letting them down. My generation wants to succeed, and given the chance, we could shine. But so many things are holding us back."

4. Wanda makes $8.50 an hour working for an employment training center 13 in Florida. She dropped out of a for-profit college after she ran out of money, even with the loans. She has stopped opening her student loan bills but thinks they now total over $90,000. She's a single mother who knows she cannot pay it. "She's worse off than when she started," an adviser says. "Debt with no degree."

5. "I always used to say that I couldn't wait to get out of here when I graduate 14 and have a career instead of just a job," Reid, 24, says as he sweeps the grocery store aisles where he still works as what he calls a "glorified janitor." Reid graduated 18 months ago with a degree in corporate finance. He hasn't been able to find a job in investment banking or wealth management as he had hoped, and his student loans are over $50,000 and growing. After a year of fruitless job searching, Reid lowered his expectations. No one was hiring investment specialists, because far fewer people had money to invest. "So I changed my approach and expectations," Reid explains. Although he was overqualified, he began applying for low-paying positions at call centers. "But even with those," he says, "they were looking for older, more experienced, and even better qualified workers. That's how bad the job situation is."

6. Eric got a degree in history from the University of Pennsylvania, and he 15 still owes $20,000 for his degree. He's applied for a least 100 jobs—"any job that looked like something I can do"—but nothing has developed. Now he's a chess tutor for elementary school kids. He believes he was misled: "The good schools project this image that if you have our degree, it's a ticket to any job you want—which is obviously total B.S.," he says. "I don't think I was properly informed of the negative side to all this. And he adds: "If this is what it's like for people who go to the best colleges, how is it for everyone else?"

Five Important "Don'ts"

Given the loss of so many jobs in America, and the fact that a college degree no 16
longer means what it once did, here are five guidelines that students should keep
in mind:

1. **Don't choose a college because you've fallen in love with it.** Parents 17
and students often fall in love with pretty campuses. To compete for
the parent dollar, education experts say, college officials have long
believed that they must manufacture nothing short of Shangri-La University: heaven on earth, with cable and Internet. Health facilities,
major athletic complexes, libraries, speedy Internet service—an entire
society is replicated. "On the college tour," says one student advisor,
"they don't take you to the philosophy department. They show you
the gym." The appealing extras cost money, and all too often schools
pass along those costs to incoming students in the form of ever-
increasing tuition.

   Listen to the advice of Barmak Nassirian, associate executive direc- 18
tor of the American Association of Collegiate Registrars and Admissions Officers in Washington. Too many students, he says, don't
understand that when they go to college, they're entering places of
business, not cathedrals on a hill: "A lot of schools have stopped being
anything but self-sustaining bureaucracies." His advice: "Pick a more
Spartan school near home, and commute."

2. **Don't assume a college will give you important advice about either career** 19
prospects or student debt. Some schools are responsible in educating
students about today's job challenges. But as one expert has said, "Many
colleges are just trying to fill seats. Warm bodies in classrooms help
pay for the comfortable salaries of tenured faculty and administrative
personnel. They present school as an opportunity, but it reaches a point
where they're just taking people's money. As a result, students leave
school with serious debt and without a marketable degree."

   Carl Van Horn, direction of the John J. Heldrich Center for Work- 20
force Development at Rutgers University, is one of an increasing number of voices saying that colleges need to do better to prepare their
students for today's changed labor market. Van Horn says, "Colleges
have a moral responsibility to educate students about job prospects, but
few offer anything other than advice to start a job search six weeks
before graduation."

   Today's reality is that a college degree itself is no ticket to success. 21
About 50 percent of college graduates are working in jobs that don't
require a bachelor's degree, according to economist Paul Harrington
of Drexel University. Students in four-year colleges, he says, don't give
sufficient thought to how their majors connect to jobs in the real
world.

   As for student debt, the Obama administration has tried to make 22
college pricing easier to understand. Colleges and universities are now
required to post calculators on their websites that explain the net tuition
price after grants and loans, but critics say the calculators can be confusing, misleading or hard to find. And the administration has proposed

that colleges be required to offer a "shopping sheet" to make it easier for families to measure the true costs and benefits. "We just have to get them much more information," said Education Secretary Arne Duncan. "If you're going to college, you need to know not what the first year costs. You need to know what it's going to cost for the long haul." One student advisor has said, "When a college suggests that students take out $5,000 in loans, I wish they'd put 5,000 one-dollar bills on a table in front of them and explain that debt will follow them for life. Then maybe they could see just what they're getting into." Nassarian adds that lenders have been only too happy to work with schools. "What's better than owning a piece of a student for life?"

In light of the above, an important rule of thumb is to not get into 23 **major debt.** Regard any student loan for more than $2,500 a year as a danger to your future. Like mortgages lugged around for life, student loans can follow you to the grave and can't be discharged in bankruptcy. Lenders can legally collect on those loans by attaching money from your wages and even from your social security.

3. **Don't start college unless you're reasonably sure you can finish.** The one 24 thing worse than student debt is student debt without a diploma. Only about 40 percent of all four-year college students who start school ever complete it, and among community college students, just one in five earns an associate's degree within three years. Students drop out due to family demands and the need to find some kind of work. As a result, the United States has the highest college dropout rate in the industrialized world. The danger of dropping out is especially high for children of low-income families.

4. **Don't go to a for-profit school.** (To see a list of such schools, Google 25 "for-profit schools" or go to specific online sites dedicated to these types of schools.) Students at for-profit schools often complain that they were misled about educational costs and that their job prospects were exaggerated. Many for-profit institutions have a track record of very high tuitions—sometimes twice that of nonprofit schools—and low graduation rates. Government reports and lawsuits have accused some for-profit colleges of outright fraud, including doctoring attendance records or peddling near-worthless degrees. Never go to a for-profit school without checking first to see if there is a comparable program offered at a nearby community college.

5. **Don't assume that you will need a college degree. Instead, you may want to** 26 **get a certification or some other postsecondary training in a growing career field.** Former Labor Secretary Robert Reich says, "Too many families cling to the mythology that their child can be a success only if he or she has a college degree." Such an assumption poorly serves candidates who might be better off taking career-related courses, attending a vocational-training school, or learning about other ways to enter the work force.

A report called *Pathways to Prosperity* recently released by Harvard 27 University states, in some of the strongest terms yet, that a "college for all" emphasis may actually harm many American students—keeping them from having a smooth transition from adolescence to adulthood and a viable career. The Harvard report concludes: "The American system for preparing young people to lead productive and prosperous lives as adults is clearly badly broken." It is a system that doesn't do a good job showing students the link between their learning and the jobs to which they aspire. The college-for-all rhetoric should be broadened to become "post-high-school credential for all."

And writing recently in *The Atlantic*, Jordan Weissmann adds: "When 28 there were fewer graduates, a generic college degree used to be a valuable credential. Now that the market is flooded, diplomas count less, and specific skills count more. This means that, in many instances, associate's and technical degrees may be more financially valuable than a liberal-arts degree. After all, some of the fastest growing job categories are expected to be in so-called 'middle-skill' positions such as nursing, which do not require a full, four-year education. It's one more sign that, for people seeking to fix America's employment picture, 'college for all' is the wrong mantra. We need to be talking about 'skills for all' instead."

Other voices express a similar conclusion: One unemployed college 29 graduate observed, "I was raised to think that what you needed was a college degree," he said. "That's not the game anymore. It's what you major in." And an employment adviser comments: "Our current college system doesn't work. You get a degree but wind up in a high school labor market job you could have had before college. But now you're worse off because you have all the debt you incurred getting that college degree." And an education researcher concludes: "The mainstream American approach to education is obsolete. The solution to today's problems starts with education—specifically, work-linked education, the teaching of particular skills to do a particular job. We should not be emphasizing college but career training."

Two Important "Do's"

1. **Do pursue some kind of post-high-school skills development.** In today's 30 economy, job applicants with only high school degrees are among the worst off; just three out of 10 can expect to make $35,000 a year or more in their lifetimes, predicts Georgetown University economist Jeff Strohl. One education reporter has said that in today's world facing the future even with a postsecondary degree "is like being a lifeboat in a roiling sea," but "facing the future with a high school degree is like being in the water."

And writes Adam Davidson in the *New York Times*: "Though it's no 31 guarantee, a B.A. or some kind of technical training is at least a prerequisite for a decent salary. It's hard to see any great future for high-school dropouts or high-school graduates with no technical skills. They most often get jobs that require little judgment and minimal training, like stocking shelves, cooking burgers, and cleaning offices. Employers generally see these unskilled workers as commodities—one is as good as any other—and thus each worker has very little bargaining power, especially now that unions are weaker. There are about 40 million of these low-skilled people in our work force. They're vying for jobs that are likely to earn near the minimum wage with few or no benefits, and they have a high chance of being laid off many times in a career. . . . The rest of us, meanwhile, should go to school, learn some skills and prepare for a rocky road."

It's worth noting that most community colleges remain a bargain— 32 a way to make postsecondary education affordable. Average tuition is often about $3,000 a year, compared to a four-year school costing tens of thousands more. And a student can save thousands more by commuting to a community college close to home.

2. **Do sail your own ship in looking for a job.** The Harvard report *Pathways* 33 *to Prosperity* notes that much so-called career counseling is inadequate and nonexistent, with counselors lacking the expertise needed for quality career guidance in today's world. For that reason, you need to take charge of the fact *that it's up to you* to research career and job possibilities. Some students lack street smarts, and they just drift passively and blindly with the tide, not looking or planning ahead for the challenges and dangers that await. Don't be a patsy; your life is in your hands—no one else's.

Here's what you should start to do: Educate yourself about what all 34 the adults in your life do to make a living. Educate yourself about the kinds of jobs that are available in the region of the country where you live. Educate yourself about the strongest jobs possibilities by visiting the *Occupational Outlook Handbook* (www.bis.gov/ooh/)—the government website that lists the strongest job possibilities for today. (Right now the fastest growing occupations up to 2020 are projected to be personal care aides, home health aides, masonry, carpenter and plumber helpers, veterinary technicians, physical and occupational therapy assistants, meeting and event planners, interpreters and translators, medical secretaries, and family therapists.) Use the Internet to educate yourself as well about how to prepare a good résumé and a good cover letter when applying for jobs, as well as how to handle a job interview.

And, in general, keep in mind that the U.S. economy is one that 35 has shifted from the production of vital goods to a service-based collection of jobs. Ask yourself, "What kind of service-providing job can I prepare for?" For example, one of the largest growth fields in the country today is health care. If your funds are severely limited, consider earning a certificate as a personal care aide or home health aide; chances are that certificate will quickly get you a job with a regular paycheck you can use to gradually take courses in a promising career direction.

Final Thoughts

Knowledge is power. To secure a meaningful job, you must first understand 36 the challenges in today's economy. The first challenge is that many jobs have disappeared, and the second is that a college degree no longer leads to a job in the way it once did. With these facts in mind, apply the "Don't's" and "Do's" presented here. Then proceed one careful step at a time in exploring directions you feel will have the best chance of opening job doors. Remember, it's up to you to make the search for a good job a primary and ongoing goal in your life. I wish you success.

READING COMPREHENSION

1. The word *unambiguous* in "Why can't all that work making Apple products come home, Obama was said to have asked. Jobs's reply was unambiguous: 'Those jobs aren't coming back,' he said" (paragraph 1) means
   a. promising.
   b. clever.
   c. straightforward.
   d. indirect.

2. The word *generic* in "When there were fewer graduates, a generic college degree used to be a valuable credential. Now that the market is flooded, diplomas count less, and specific skills count more" (paragraph 28) means
   a. general.
   b. specific.
   c. competitive.
   d. technical.

3. The word *mantra* in "It's one more sign that, for people seeking to fix America's employment picture, 'college for all' is the wrong mantra. We need to be talking about 'skills for all' instead" (paragraph 29) means
   a. image.
   b. message.
   c. explanation.
   d. definition.

4. Which of the following would be the best alternative title for this selection?
   a. College: The Gateway to Guaranteed Employment
   b. Avoid College, Avoid Debt
   c. College and Employment: A Losing Combination
   d. Employment Realities in the Twenty-First Century

5. Which sentence best expresses the central point of the entire selection?
   a. Globalization, automation, and outsourcing are the reasons why it is now difficult for many Americans to get good-paying jobs.
   b. Because many American jobs have disappeared, students need to pursue some kind of post–high school education that will provide them with marketable skills.
   c. There are ways that today's students can avoid falling into the trap of becoming unemployed or under-employed.
   d. Because they have failed to prepare themselves for the current job market, about 50 percent of college graduates are working in jobs that don't require a college degree.

6. The implied main idea of paragraphs 8–16 is that
   a. today it's common for young, college graduates to be deeply in debt and unemployed or underemployed.

b. many young American college graduates are deeply in debt due to the high cost of their college education.

c. today a college degree is worthless.

d. many of today's recent college graduates are surprised that they have to work so hard to obtain even low-paying jobs.

7. Which sentence best expresses the main idea of paragraph 35?

a. There are many reasons why it is important to become well educated.

b. The *Occupational Outlook Handbook* lists the strongest job possibilities for today.

c. There are lots of job openings in the field of health care and in certain trades such as masonry, carpentry, and plumbing.

d. It's important to educate yourself about the strongest job possibilities for today and the near future.

8. According to the selection, students who are shopping for a college should enroll at

a. the one with the best overall academic reputation.

b. the one with the newest health facilities, athletic complexes, and libraries.

c. the one that functions more like a business, not a cathedral on a hill.

d. the Spartan one close to home.

9. According to Education Secretary Arne Duncan,

a. not all students need to acquire a post–high school education.

b. students need to know what college will cost for the long haul.

c. it is only important for students to know what the first year of college will cost.

d. students should avoid taking out any loans to pay for their college education.

10. According to Bertram, students should NOT

a. expect that their college will prepare them for today's job market.

b. automatically think that they need a four-year college degree.

c. enroll at a for-profit school when a community college offers a comparable program.

d. all of the above.

STRUCTURE AND TECHNIQUE

1. In the section "The Reduced Value of a College Degree," Bertram highlights six different students' experiences. What is the purpose in presenting these stories? Why do you believe he presents them numerically?

2. Bertram employs the use of bold text and headlines throughout the essay. Why do you think the author chose this strategy?

3. Bertram often uses testimony by authorities to support his points. Where in his essay does he use such support? What do you think it adds to his piece?

4. Is the author's purpose to educate readers about the job crisis or to persuade readers to do something? What specific points in the article lead you to that opinion?

CRITICAL READING AND DISCUSSION

1. According to the author, why have so many American jobs been outsourced to countries like China, India, and Latin America?

2. On the basis of paragraphs 19–21, we can infer that like other businesses, colleges need to make money to survive. Do you agree with this statement? Do you think, as the author implies, that this need to make money sometimes overshadows quality of education?

3. Were you surprised by any of the information presented in this article? Did you expect that your degree would guarantee you a high-paying job? Explain.

WRITING ASSIGNMENTS

Assignment 1: Writing a Paragraph

Imagine that you have completed your post-secondary education and that you now have skills for which there is a steady demand. Write a cover letter for a job that you would like to have. In your cover letter, describe the personal qualities and educational background that would make you an ideal candidate for the job. Look at some sample cover letters on the Internet to get an idea of the proper format for such a letter.

Assignment 2: Writing an Essay

In the selection, Bertram recommends educating yourself about what the adults in your life do to make a living. Take his advice and speak with three people you know regarding what they do for a living. Be sure to ask them how and why they got into this particular field, and whether or not they are satisfied with what they are currently doing. After you are done, write an essay summing up what you've learned by talking with them. Your thesis sentence might be similar to the following:

"Talking with _____, _____, and _____ about what they do for a living was an eye-opening experience."

or

"I learned several things about the working world after speaking with _____, _____, and _____."

Assignment 3: Writing an Essay

Don Bertram states that because so much career counseling is inadequate and nonexistent, it's up to you to research career and job possibilities. Take a few minutes and brainstorm a list of careers and/or jobs that you are interested in. Then pick three items from your list and research these three, using such resources as the Occupational Outlook Handbook (www.bis.gov/ooh/); United States Jobs, Careers, and Education Resources (http://usa.careers.org); and others. Afterward, write an essay that, in your own words, presents the results of your research. Your thesis statement might be similar to one of the following:

> According to my research, three strong job possibilities in my region of the country are
>
> _____, _____, and _____.
>
> or
>
> According to my research, there is a strong demand for _____ and _____, but not for _____.

The body of your essay should describe in detail what the occupational outlook is for each career, what the salary is for each career, and what a person would need to do to prepare for each career. You might conclude your essay by explaining which career most appeals to you, and why. You may want to review Part 5 to help you find credible results and properly incorporate your sources.

Propaganda Techniques in Today's Advertising

Ann McClintock

PREVIEW

Advertisers want your business, and they will use a variety of clever ad slogans to get it. If you've ever responded to ads, you have been swayed by the effective use of propaganda. You may associate the word *propaganda* with the tactics used by strong-arm governments. But Ann McClintock provides evidence that we are the targets of propaganda every day and that it shapes many of our opinions and decisions.

Americans, adults and children alike, are being seduced. They are being brainwashed. And few of us protest. Why? Because the seducers and the brainwashers are the advertisers we willingly invite into our homes. We are victims, content—even eager—to be victimized. We read advertisers' propaganda messages in newspapers and magazines; we watch their alluring images on television. We absorb their messages and images into our subconscious. We all do it—even those of us who claim to see through advertisers' tricks and therefore feel immune to advertising's charm. Advertisers lean heavily on propaganda to sell products, whether the "products" are a brand of toothpaste, a candidate for office, or a particular political viewpoint.

Propaganda is a systematic effort to influence people's opinions, to win them over to a certain view or side. Propaganda is not necessarily concerned with what is true or false, good or bad. Propagandists simply want people to believe

1

2

TEACHING TIP
You might ask your students to write for ten minutes about what the word "propaganda" means to them.

the messages being sent. Often, propagandists will use outright lies or more subtle deceptions to sway people's opinions. In a propaganda war, any tactic is considered fair.

When we hear the word "propaganda," we usually think of a foreign menace: 3 anti-American radio programs broadcast by a totalitarian regime or brainwashing tactics practiced on hostages. Although propaganda may seem relevant only in the political arena, the concept can be applied fruitfully to the way products and ideas are sold in advertising. Indeed, the vast majority of us are targets in advertisers' propaganda war. Every day, we are bombarded with slogans, print and Internet pop-up ads, commercials, packaging claims, billboards, trademarks, logos, and designer brands—all forms of propaganda. One study reports that each of us, during an average day, is exposed to over *five hundred* advertising claims of various types. This saturation may even increase in the future, since current trends include ads on movie screens, shopping carts, videocassettes, and even public television.

What kind of propaganda techniques do advertisers use? There are seven 4 basic types:

1. **Name Calling.** Name calling is a propaganda tactic in which negatively 5 charged names are hurled against the opposing side or competitor. By using such names, propagandists try to arouse feelings of mistrust, fear, and hate in their audiences. For example, a political advertisement may label an opposing candidate a "loser," "fence-sitter," or "warmonger." Depending on the advertiser's target market, labels such as "a friend of big business" or "a dues-paying member of the party in power" can be the epithets that damage an opponent. Ads for products may also use name calling. An American manufacturer may refer, for instance, to a "foreign car" in its commercial—not an "imported" one. The label of foreignness will have unpleasant connotations in many people's minds. A childhood rhyme claims that "names can never hurt me," but name calling is an effective way to damage the opposition, whether it is another car maker or a congressional candidate.

2. **Glittering Generalities.** Using glittering generalities is the opposite of 6 name calling. In this case, advertisers surround their products with attractive—and slippery—words and phrases. They use vague terms that are difficult to define and that may have different meanings to different people: *freedom, democratic, all-American, progressive, Christian,* and *justice.* Many such words have strong affirmative overtones. This kind of language stirs positive feelings in people, feelings that may spill over to the product or idea being pitched. As with name calling, the emotional response may overwhelm logic. Target audiences accept the product without thinking very much about what the glittering generalities mean—or whether they even apply to the product. After all, how can anyone oppose "truth, justice, and the American way"?

    The ads for politicians and political causes often use glittering gen- 7 eralities because such "buzzwords" can influence votes. Election slogans include high-sounding but basically empty phrases like the following:

    "He cares about people." (That's nice, but is he a better candidate than his opponent?)

"Vote for progress." (Progress by whose standards?)
"They'll make this country great again." (What does "great" mean?
Does "great" mean the same thing to others as it does to me?)
"Vote for the future." (What kind of future?)
"If you love America, vote for Phyllis Smith." (If I don't vote for
Smith, does that mean I don't love America?)

Ads for consumer goods are also sprinkled with glittering general- 8
ities. Product names, for instance, are supposed to evoke good feelings:
Luvs diapers, *Stayfree* feminine hygiene products, *Joy* liquid detergent,
Loving Care hair color, *Almost Home* cookies, *Yankee Doodle* pastries.
Product slogans lean heavily on vague but comforting phrases: . . .
General Electric "brings good things to life," and Dow Chemical "lets
you do great things." Chevrolet, we are told, is the "heartbeat of
America," and Chrysler boasts cars that are "built by Americans for
Americans."

3. Transfer. In transfer, advertisers try to improve the image of a product 9
by associating it with a symbol most people respect, like the American
flag or Uncle Sam. The advertisers hope that the prestige attached to
the symbol will carry over to the product. Many companies use transfer
devices to identify their products: Lincoln Insurance shows a profile of
the president; Continental Insurance portrays a Revolutionary War min-
uteman; Amtrak's logo is red, white, and blue; Liberty Mutual's corporate symbol is the Statue of Liberty; Allstate's name is cradled by a pair
of protective, fatherly hands.

Corporations also use the transfer technique when they sponsor 10
prestigious shows on radio and television. These shows function as symbols of dignity and class. Kraft Corporation, for instance, sponsored
a "Leonard Bernstein Conducts Beethoven" concert, while Gulf Oil is
the sponsor of *National Geographic* specials and Mobil supports public
television's *Masterpiece Theater.* In this way, corporations can reach an
educated, influential audience and, perhaps, improve their public image
by associating themselves with quality programming.

Political ads, of course, practically wrap themselves in the flag. Ads 11
for a political candidate often show either the Washington Monument,
a Fourth of July parade, the Stars and Stripes, a bald eagle soaring over
the mountains, or a white-steepled church on the village green. The
national anthem or "America the Beautiful" may play in the background.
Such appeals to Americans' love of country can surround the candidate
with an aura of patriotism and integrity.

4. Testimonial. The testimonial is one of advertisers' most-loved and most- 12
used propaganda techniques. Similar to the transfer device, the testimonial capitalizes on the admiration people have for a celebrity to make
the product shine more brightly—even though the celebrity is not an
expert on the product being sold.

Print and television ads offer a nonstop parade of testimonials: 13
here's William Shatner for Priceline.com; here's basketball star Michael
Jordan eating Wheaties; a slew of well-known people (including pop star
Madonna) advertise clothing from Gap; and Jerry Seinfeld assures us

he never goes anywhere without his American Express card. Testimonials can sell movies, too; newspaper ads for films often feature favorable comments by well-known reviewers. And, in recent years, testimonials have played an important role in pitching books; the backs of paperbacks frequently list complimentary blurbs by celebrities.

Political candidates, as well as their ad agencies, know the value of 14 testimonials. Barbra Streisand lent her star appeal to the presidential campaign of Bill Clinton, while Arnold Schwarzenegger endorsed George Bush. Even controversial social issues are debated by celebrities. The nuclear freeze, for instance, starred Paul Newman for the pro side and Charlton Heston for the con.

As illogical as testimonials sometimes are (Pepsi's Michael Jackson, 15 for instance, was a health-food adherent who did not drink soft drinks), they are effective propaganda. We like the *person* so much that we like the *product* too.

5. **Plain Folks.** The plain folks approach says, in effect, "Buy me or vote 16 for me. I'm just like you." Regular folks will surely like Bob Evans's Down on the Farm Country Sausage or good old-fashioned Country-time Lemonade. Some ads emphasize the idea that "we're all in the same boat." We see people making long-distance calls for just the reasons we do—to put the baby on the phone to Grandma or to tell Mom we love her. And how do these folksy, warmhearted (usually saccharine) scenes affect us? They're supposed to make us feel that AT&T—the multinational corporate giant—has the same values we do. Similarly, we are introduced to the little people at Ford, the ordinary folks who work on the assembly line, not to bigwigs in their executive offices. What's the purpose of such an approach? To encourage us to buy a car built by these honest, hardworking "everyday Joes" who care about quality as much as we do.

Political advertisements make almost as much use of the "plain 17 folks" appeal as they do of transfer devices. Candidates wear hard hats, farmers' caps, and assembly-line coveralls. They jog around the block and carry their own luggage through the airport. The idea is to convince voters that the candidates are average people, not the elite—not wealthy lawyers or executives but common citizens.

6. **Card Stacking.** When people say that "the cards were stacked against 18 me," they mean that they were never given a fair chance. Applied to propaganda, card stacking means that one side may suppress or distort evidence, tell half-truths, oversimplify the facts, or set up a "straw man"—a false target—to divert attention from the issue at hand. Card stacking is a difficult form of propaganda both to detect and to combat. When a candidate claims that an opponent has "changed his mind five times on this important issue," we tend to accept the claim without investigating whether the candidate had good reasons for changing his mind. Many people are simply swayed by the distorted claim that the candidate is "waffling" on the issue.

Advertisers often stack the cards in favor of the products they are 19 pushing. They may, for instance, use what are called "weasel words." These are small words that usually slip right past us, but that make the difference between reality and illusion. The weasel words are underlined in the following claims:

> "Helps control dandruff symptoms." (The audience usually interprets this as stops dandruff.)
> "Most dentists surveyed recommend sugarless gum for their patients who chew gum." (We hear the "most dentists" and "for their patients," but we don't think about how many were surveyed or whether or not the dentists first recommended that the patients not chew gum at all.)
> "Sticker price $1,000 lower than most comparable cars." (How many is "most"? What car does the advertiser consider "comparable"?)

Advertisers also use a card stacking trick when they make an unfinished claim. For example, they will say that their product has "twice as much pain reliever." We are left with a favorable impression. We don't usually ask, "Twice as much pain reliever as what?" Or advertisers may make extremely vague claims that sound alluring but have no substance: Toyota's "Oh, what a feeling!"; Vantage cigarettes' "the taste of success"; "The spirit of Marlboro"; Coke's "the real thing." Another way to stack the cards in favor of a certain product is to use scientific-sounding claims that are not supported by sound research. When Ford claimed that its LTD model was "400% quieter," many people assumed that its LTD must be quieter than all other cars. When taken to court, however, Ford admitted that the phrase referred to the difference between the noise level inside and outside the LTD. Other scientific-sounding claims use mysterious ingredients that are never explained as selling points: Retsyn, "special whitening agents," "the ingredient doctors recommend."

7. Bandwagon. In the bandwagon technique, advertisers pressure, "Everyone's doing it. Why don't you?" This kind of propaganda often succeeds because many people have a deep desire not to be different. Political ads tell us to vote for the "winning candidate." The advertisers know we tend to feel comfortable doing what others do; we want to be on the winning team. Or ads show a series of people proclaiming, "I'm voting for the senator. I don't know why anyone wouldn't." Again, the audience feels under pressure to conform.

In the marketplace, the bandwagon approach lures buyers. Ads tell us that "nobody doesn't like Sara Lee" (the message is that you must be weird if you don't). They tell us that "most people prefer Brand X two to one over other leading brands" (to be like the majority, we should buy Brand X). If we don't drink Pepsi, we're left out of "the Pepsi generation." To take part in "America's favorite health kick," the National Dairy Council asks us, "Got Milk?" And Honda motorcycle ads, praising the virtues of being a follower, tell us, "Follow the leader. He's on a Honda."

Why do these propaganda techniques work? Why do so many of us buy the products, viewpoints, and candidates urged on us by propaganda messages? They work because they appeal to our emotions, not to our minds. Often, in fact, they capitalize on our prejudices and biases. For example, if we are convinced that environmentalists are

TEACHING TIP
Ask students to provide other examples of worthwhile advertising, such as Mothers Against Drunk Driving and anti-smoking campaigns.

radicals who want to destroy America's record of industrial growth and progress, then we will applaud the candidate who refers to them as "treehuggers." Clear thinking requires hard work: analyzing a claim, researching the facts, examining both sides of an issue, using logic to see the flaws in an argument. Many of us would rather let the propagandists do our thinking for us.

Because propaganda is so effective, it is important to detect it and 24 understand how it is used. We may conclude, after close examination, that some propaganda sends a truthful, worthwhile message. Some advertising, for instance, urges us not to drive drunk, to become volunteers, to contribute to charity. Even so, we must be aware that propaganda is being used. Otherwise, we have consented to handing over to others our independence of thought and action.

READING COMPREHENSION

1. The word *epithets* in "labels such as 'a friend of big business' or 'a dues-paying member of the party in power' can be the epithets that damage an opponent" (paragraph 5) means
   a. courtesies.
   b. descriptive labels.
   c. assurances.
   d. delays.

2. The words *capitalizes on* in "the testimonial capitalizes on the admiration people have for a celebrity" (paragraph 12) mean
   a. reports about.
   b. ignores.
   c. cuts back on.
   d. takes advantage of.

3. Which of the following would be a good alternative title for this selection?
   a. The World of Advertising
   b. Common Persuasion Techniques in Advertising
   c. Propaganda in Politics
   d. Common Advertising Techniques on Television

4. Which sentence best expresses the main idea of the selection?
   a. Americans may be exposed daily to over five hundred advertising claims of some sort.
   b. The testimonial takes advantage of the admiration people have for celebrities, even though they have no expertise on the product being sold.
   c. People should detect and understand common propaganda techniques, which appeal to the emotions rather than to logic.
   d. Americans need to understand that advertising, a huge industry, affects their lives in numerous ways.

5. The propaganda technique in which a product is associated with a symbol or image most people admire and respect is
   a. glittering generalities.
   b. transfer. *(circled)*
   c. testimonials.
   d. bandwagon.

6. The technique in which evidence is withheld or distorted is called
   a. glittering generalities.
   b. bandwagon.
   c. plain folks.
   d. card stacking. *(circled)*

7. The technique that makes a political candidate seem to be just like the people an ad is aimed at is
   a. glittering generalities.
   b. bandwagon.
   c. plain folks. *(circled)*
   d. card stacking.

8. A way to avoid being taken in by propaganda is to use
   a. our emotions.
   b. name calling.
   c. clear thinking. *(circled)*
   d. our subconscious.

9. The author implies in paragraph 16 that
   a. most Americans do not frequently call their grandmothers.
   b. multinational corporations do not have the same values as average citizens. *(circled)*
   c. Bob Evans is an American celebrity.
   d. executives at AT&T and Ford are hardworking and honest.

10. From paragraphs 23 and 24, we can conclude that the author feels
    a. we are unlikely to analyze advertising logically unless we recognize it as propaganda. *(circled)*
    b. propaganda should not be allowed.
    c. if we don't want to hand over to others our independence, we should ignore all propaganda.
    d. we should not support the "products, viewpoints, and candidates urged on us by propaganda messages."

STRUCTURE AND TECHNIQUE

1. In paragraph 1, McClintock's choice of words reveals her attitudes toward both propagandists and the public. What specific words reveal her attitudes, and what attitudes do they represent?

2. What key term does McClintock define in paragraph 2? Why does she define it here? Where else in the essay does she use the technique of definition?

3. McClintock uses parentheses in two lists, the ones in paragraphs 7 and 19. What purpose do these parentheses serve?

4. McClintock provides abundant examples throughout her essay. Why does she provide so many examples? What does she accomplish with this technique?

CRITICAL READING AND DISCUSSION

1. Some of the propaganda techniques listed in the selection have contrasting appeals. How do name-calling and glittering generalities contrast with each other? Testimonials and plain folks?

2. Why are ads that use the bandwagon approach so effective? What ads have you seen recently that use that approach?

3. The author states, "Americans, adults and children alike, are being seduced." What might be the differences between the ways adults and children react to the seductions of advertising?

4. McClintock states, "We are victims, content—even eager—to be victimized" (paragraph 1). Do you agree? Is this article likely to change how you view ads in the future? Why or why not?

RESPONDING TO IMAGES

What propaganda technique (or techniques) does this advertisement use? Is it effective? Why or why not?

©Lars A. Niki

WRITING ASSIGNMENTS

Assignment 1: Writing a Paragraph

Imagine that you work for an ad agency and have been asked to come up with a campaign for a new product (for example, a car, a perfume, a detergent, jeans, beer, a toothpaste, a deodorant, or an appliance). Write a paragraph in which you describe the propaganda technique(s) that might be used to sell the product and how these claims could persuade the public to buy. Be specific about the general look, the character, and the wording of your ad and about how it fits in with the technique(s) you suggest.

Assignment 2: Writing an Essay

Analyze three ads currently appearing on television or in print. Show that each ad uses one or more of the propaganda techniques McClintock discusses. Be specific about product names, what the ad looks like, kinds of characters in the ad, and so on. Don't forget that all your specific details should back up your point that each ad uses a certain propaganda technique (or techniques) to sell a product. Your thesis will make some overall statement about the three ads, such as either of these:

Beer advertisements use a variety of propaganda techniques.

Glittering generalities are used to sell very different types of products.

Assignment 3: Writing an Essay

Do some informal "market research" on why people buy the products they do. Begin by asking at least ten people why they bought a particular brand-name item. You might question them about something they're wearing (designer jeans, for example). Or you might ask them what toothpaste they use, what car they drive, what pain reliever they take, or what chicken they eat—or ask about any other product people use. Take notes on the reasons people give for their purchases.

Then write an essay with the thesis "My research suggests that people often buy products for three reasons." Include in your introductory paragraph your plan of development—a list of the three reasons that were mentioned most often by the people you interviewed. Develop your supporting paragraphs with examples drawn from the interviews. As part of your support, use quotations from the people you spoke with.

The Great Spirit

Zitkala-Ša

PREVIEW

Zitkala-Ša (1876–1938) is a Lakota Sioux whose birth name is Gertrude Simmons. In her late teens, she adopted the name Zitkala-Ša, which means "Red Bird." She attended White's Manual Labor Institute and Earlham College, both Quaker schools. In addition to publishing short stories, books, and essays, Zitkala-Ša was secretary of the Society of the American Indian and founded the National Council of American Indians. In this essay, which is part of her book *American Indian Stories*, she discusses her connection to her native beliefs.

Source: The National Museum of American History

When the spirit swells my breast I love to roam leisurely among the green 1
hills; or sometimes, sitting on the brink of the murmuring Missouri, I marvel
at the great blue overhead. With half-closed eyes I watch the huge cloud shadows in their noiseless play upon the high bluffs opposite me, while into my
ear ripple the sweet, soft cadences of the river's song. Folded hands lie in my
lap, for the time forgot. My heart and I lie small upon the earth like a grain
of throbbing sand. Drifting clouds and tinkling waters, together with the
warmth of a genial summer day, bespeak with eloquence the loving Mystery
round about us. During the idle while I sat upon the sunny river brink, I grew
somewhat, though my response be not so clearly manifest as in the green grass
fringing the edge of the high bluff back of me.

At length retracing the uncertain footpath scaling the precipitous embank- 2
ment, I seek the level lands where grow the wild prairie flowers. And they, the
lovely little folk, soothe my soul with their perfumed breath.

Their quaint round faces of varied hue convince the heart which leaps with 3
glad surprise that they, too, are living symbols of omnipotent thought. With
a child's eager eye I drink in the myriad star shapes wrought in luxuriant color
upon the green. Beautiful is the spiritual essence they embody.

I leave them nodding in the breeze, but take along with me their impress 4
upon my heart. I pause to rest me upon a rock embedded on the side of a foot-
hill facing the low river bottom. Here the Stone-Boy, of whom the American
aborigine tells, frolics about, shooting his baby arrows and shouting aloud with
glee at the tiny shafts of lightning that flash from the flying arrow-beaks. What
an ideal warrior he became, baffling the siege of the pests of all the land till he
triumphed over their united attack. And here he lay—Inyan our great-great-
grandfather, older than the hill he rested on, older than the race of men who
love to tell of his wonderful career.

Interwoven with the thread of this Indian legend of the rock, I fain would 5
trace a subtle knowledge of the native folk which enabled them to recognize
a kinship to any and all parts of this vast universe. By the leading of an ancient
trail I move toward the Indian village.

With the strong, happy sense that both great and small are so surely enfolded 6
in His magnitude that, without a miss, each has his allotted individual ground
of opportunities, I am buoyant with good nature.

Yellow Breast, swaying upon the slender stem of a wild sunflower, warbles 7
a sweet assurance of this as I pass near by. Breaking off the clear crystal song,
he turns his wee head from side to side eyeing me wisely as slowly I plod with
moccasined feet. Then again he yields himself to his song of joy. Flit, flit
hither and yon, he fills the summer sky with his swift, sweet melody. And
truly does it seem his vigorous freedom lies more in his little spirit than in
his wing.

With these thoughts I reach the log cabin whither I am strongly drawn by 8
the tie of a child to an aged mother. Out bounds my four-footed friend to meet
me, frisking about my path with unmistakable delight. Chän is a black shaggy
dog, "a thoroughbred little mongrel" of whom I am very fond. Chän seems to
understand any words in Sioux, and will go to her mat even when I whisper the
word, though generally I think she is guided by the tone of the voice. Often she
tries to imitate the sliding inflection and long-drawn-out voice to the amusement
of our guests, but her articulation is quite beyond my ear. In both my hands I
hold her shaggy head and gaze into her large brown eyes. At once the dilated

pupils contract into tiny black dots, as if the roguish spirit within would evade my questioning.

Finally resuming the chair at my desk I feel in keen sympathy with my [9] fellow-creatures, for I seem to see clearly again that all are akin. The racial lines, which once were bitterly real, now serve nothing more than marking out a living mosaic of human beings. And even here men of the same color are like the ivory keys of one instrument where each resembles all the rest, yet varies from them in pitch and quality of voice. And those creatures who are for a time mere echoes of another's note are not unlike the fable of the thin sick man whose distorted shadow, dressed like a real creature, came to the old master to make him follow as a shadow. Thus with a compassion for all echoes in human guise, I greet the solemn-faced "native preacher" whom I find awaiting me. I listen with respect for God's creature, though he mouths most strangely the jangling phrases of a bigoted creed.

As our tribe is one large family, where every person is related to all the [10] others, he addressed me—

"Cousin, I came from the morning church service to talk with you." [11]

"Yes?" I said interrogatively, as he paused for some word from me. [12]

Shifting uneasily about in the straight-backed chair he sat upon, he began: [13] "Every holy day (Sunday) I look about our little God's house, and not seeing you there, I am disappointed. This is why I come today. Cousin, as I watch you from afar, I see no unbecoming behavior and hear only good reports of you, which all the more burns me with the wish that you were a church member. Cousin, I was taught long years ago by kind missionaries to read the holy book. These godly men taught me also the folly of our old beliefs.

"There is one God who gives reward or punishment to the race of dead [14] men. In the upper region the Christian dead are gathered in unceasing song and prayer. In the deep pit below, the sinful ones dance in torturing flames.

"Think upon these things, my cousin, and choose now to avoid the after- [15] doom of hell fire!" Then followed a long silence in which he clasped tighter and unclasped again his interlocked fingers.

Like instantaneous lightning flashes came pictures of my own mother's mak- [16] ing, for she, too, is now a follower of the new superstition.

"Knocking out the chinking of our log cabin, some evil hand thrust in [17] a burning taper of braided dry grass, but failed of his intent, for the fire died out and the half-burned brand fell inward to the floor. Directly above it, on a shelf, lay the holy book. This is what we found after our return from a several days' visit. Surely some great power is hid in the sacred book!"

Brushing away from my eyes many like pictures, I offered midday meal to [18] the converted Indian sitting wordless and with downcast face. No sooner had he risen from the table with "Cousin, I have relished it," than the church bell rang.

Thither he hurried forth with his afternoon sermon. I watched him as he [19] hastened along, his eyes bent fast upon the dusty road till he disappeared at the end of a quarter of a mile.

The little incident recalled to mind the copy of a missionary paper brought [20] to my notice a few days ago, in which a "Christian" pugilist commented upon a recent article of mine, grossly perverting the spirit of my pen. Still I would not forget that the pale-faced missionary and the hoodooed aborigine are both God's creatures, though small indeed their own conceptions of Infinite Love.

A wee child toddling in a wonder world, I prefer to their dogma my excursions into the natural gardens where the voice of the Great Spirit is heard in the twittering of birds, the rippling of mighty waters, and the sweet breathing of flowers.

Here, in a fleeting quiet, I am awakened by the fluttering robe of the Great 21 Spirit. To my innermost consciousness the phenomenal universe is a royal mantle, vibrating with His divine breath. Caught in its flowing fringes are the spangles and oscillating brilliants of sun, moon, and stars.

READING COMPREHENSION

1. The word *cadences* in "while into my ear ripple the sweet, soft cadences of the river's song" (paragraph 1) means
   a. general modulation of the voice.
   b. general rhythm of sounds.
   c. rhythmic flow of words.
   d. rhythmic flow of events.

2. The word *manifest* in "though my response be not so clearly manifest as in the green grass fringing the edge of the high bluff back of me" (paragraph 1) means
   a. to make clear or evident; show plainly.
   b. a list or invoice of goods transported by truck or train.
   c. relating to conscious feelings, ideas, and impulses.
   d. to record a list of passengers or cargo.

3. The word *precipitous* in "at length retracing the uncertain footpath scaling the precipitous embankment" (paragraph 2) means
   a. violently hurled or flung down.
   b. done suddenly and without careful consideration.
   c. dangerously slippery and narrow.
   d. dangerously high or steep.

4. The word *buoyant* in "I am buoyant with good nature" (paragraph 6) means
   a. unsinkable.
   b. optimistic.
   c. weightless.
   d. bouncy.

5. Which of the following would be a good alternative title for this selection?
   a. My Connection to the Universe
   b. My Cousin's Road to Priesthood
   c. The Sioux Way
   d. My Cousin's Disappointment

6. Which sentence best expresses the main idea of the selection?

   a. Zitkála-Šá explains why she has decided to convert from her native beliefs to Christianity.

   (b.) Zitkála-Šá explains why she will continue to follow her native beliefs even though her family has converted to Christianity.

   c. Zitkála-Šá explains why nature is so important to her.

   d. Zitkála-Šá explains why her cousin has converted to Christianity and has become a priest.

7. From the description "a thoroughbred little mongrel" (paragraph 8), we can conclude that

   (a.) her dog is well-behaved and noble.

   b. her dog is large and mangy.

   c. her dog is small and ornery.

   d. her dog is aggressive and protective.

8. What does the author mean when she says "men of the same color are like the ivory keys of one instrument" (paragraph 9)?

   a. The racial lines between American Indians and Caucasians is musical, like a piano.

   (b.) Even men of the same race have their own individual characteristics and are different from one another.

   c. The lines between races are bitter and defined, and nothing will change the racial tensions.

   d. She feels connected to all men and women regardless of their racial background.

9. Why is the "native preacher" disappointed?

   a. He has been unable to convert most of the people in the tribe.

   (b.) He has been unable to convert Zitkála-Šá to his new faith.

   c. His Sunday services are not as full as he would like them to be.

   d. Zitkála-Šá has demonstrated unbecoming behavior for a woman.

10. How does the preacher explain his belief in the power of the Bible to Zitkála-Šá?

   a. He tells the story of how he saw the power of the Bible in the missionaries who spoke with him.

   (b.) He tells the story of how his cabin had been set afire, but the fire quickly died out when it got near the Bible.

   c. He tells the story of when he was being attacked by a mongrel, but the dog stopped the minute he held the Bible in front of him.

   d. He tells the story of when he was sitting out in nature, listening to the birds, and when he began reading from the Bible, the birds stopped singing to listen.

STRUCTURE AND TECHNIQUE

1. Does the author clearly state her thesis? If so, where is it stated? If not, write her thesis in your own words.

2. The majority of the selection is written as the narrator's internal thoughts. How does this affect the opinion of the audience?

3. What rhetorical modes does Zitkala-Ša use to create a well-written essay?

CRITICAL READING AND DISCUSSION

1. Why do you think the author uses so much imagery in her writing?

2. Why do you think Zitkala-Ša uses the simile of the piano when discussing race? How does the use of the simile help convey and explain the author's message?

3. Who or what do you believe the narrator is in conflict with?

4. Reflect upon your own faith and values. Do you believe the same things as your parents and extended family? Have you ever questioned your parents' or your beliefs? Has anyone else ever questioned you? Do you think you could be as steadfast as Zitkala-Ša if you were confronted as she was?

WRITING ASSIGNMENTS

TEACHING TIP
Guide students to use specific details and avoid vague language.

Assignment 1: Writing a Paragraph

Write a paragraph that explains how you felt about this reading. Did you like it? Why or why not? What did you agree or disagree with? Why?

Assignment 2: Writing an Essay

In this essay Zitkala-Ša discusses her beliefs, which are different from her family's beliefs. Have you experienced a situation in which your beliefs have differed from your parents'?

If so, write an essay that explains what you believe versus what your parents believe and how this has affected your family. For instance, if you strongly believe in Buddhism, but your parents are Catholic, how have you navigated these differences? Do you talk about your religious views? Do your parents try to convert you or make you go to church with them? Do they accept your different views?

If not, write an essay that explores some of your parents' beliefs that you haven't really questioned. Decide why you haven't questioned them and whether you should always go along with your parents' beliefs or start to critically examine them and formulate your own ideas. For instance, if your parents are Catholic, and you have just accepted the Catholic doctrine up to this point, are there any other religious doctrines that you find yourself drawn to, but might challenge Catholic tradition? What would happen if you were to find a different doctrine more in line with your own ideas?

Assignment 3: Writing an Essay

In this essay, Zitkala-Ša focuses on how connected she feels to nature. She provides many details to paint a picture of what her surroundings are like. She talks about the "murmuring Missouri," "wild prairie flowers," and a bird who "warbles a sweet assurance."

For this essay, write about a place where you feel absolutely peaceful and connected. It could be a favorite place on your college campus, a peaceful park in your home town, or a remote wilderness area. You should create a thesis that asserts why this location is special to you, and then create an essay that profiles that location's importance. Two thesis statements have been provided to give you ideas:

> A quiet corner of my college library is the place I go to when I need to center myself, focus on my studies, and find meaning.

> James A. Reed Wildlife Center is my favorite place to spend a day when I need to be alone.

Advice to Youth

Mark Twain

PREVIEW

Mark Twain, born Samuel Langhorne Clemens, is one of America's most famous authors. Best known for the controversial book *The Adventures of Huckleberry Finn* Twain wrote dozens of novels, nonfiction pieces, short stories, and essays. Twain did not plan on becoming a writer, but through his many adventures and failures, he found an outlet for his voice and humor. In this essay, Twain uses satire to advise and lecture about morality.

Source: Library of Congress Prints and Photographs Division [LC-USZ62-5513]

Being told I would be expected to talk here, I inquired what sort of talk I ought to make. They said it should be something suitable to youth—something didactic, instructive, or something in the nature of good advice. Very well. I have a few things in my mind which I have often longed to say for the instruction of the young; for it is in one's tender early years that such things will best take root and be most enduring and most valuable. First, then. I will say to you my young friends—and I say it beseechingly, urgingly— 1

Always obey your parents, when they are present. This is the best policy in the long run, because if you don't, they will make you. Most parents think they know better than you do, and you can generally make more by humoring that superstition than you can by acting on your own better judgment. 2

Be respectful to your superiors, if you have any, also to strangers, and sometimes to others. If a person offend you, and you are in doubt as to whether it was intentional or not, do not resort to extreme measures; simply watch your chance and hit him with a brick. That will be sufficient. If you shall find that he had not intended any offense, come out frankly and confess yourself in the wrong when you struck him; acknowledge it like a man and say you didn't mean 3 to. Yes, always avoid violence; in this age of charity and kindliness, the time has gone by for such things. Leave dynamite to the low and unrefined.

Go to bed early, get up early—this is wise. Some authorities say get up with   4
the sun; some say get up with one thing, others with another. But a lark is really
the best thing to get up with. It gives you a splendid reputation with everybody
to know that you get up with the lark; and if you get the right kind of lark, and
work at him right, you can easily train him to get up at half past nine, every
time—it's no trick at all.

Now as to the matter of lying. You want to be very careful about lying; oth-   5
erwise you are nearly sure to get caught. Once caught, you can never again be in
the eyes to the good and the pure, what you were before. Many a young person
has injured himself permanently through a single clumsy and ill finished lie, the
result of carelessness born of incomplete training. Some authorities hold that the
young ought not to lie at all. That of course, is putting it rather stronger than
necessary; still while I cannot go quite so far as that, I do maintain, and I believe
I am right, that the young ought to be temperate in the use of this great art until
practice and experience shall give them that confidence, elegance, and precision
which alone can make the accomplishment graceful and profitable. Patience, dil-
igence, painstaking attention to detail—these are requirements; these in time, will
make the student perfect; upon these only, may he rely as the sure foundation for
future eminence. Think what tedious years of study, thought, practice, experience,
went to the equipment of that peerless old master who was able to impose upon
the whole world the lofty and sounding maxim that "Truth is mighty and will
prevail"—the most majestic compound fracture of fact which any of woman born
has yet achieved. For the history of our race, and each individual's experience, are
sewn thick with evidences that a truth is not hard to kill, and that a lie well told
is immortal. There is in Boston a monument of the man who discovered anesthe-
sia; many people are aware, in these latter days, that that man didn't discover it
at all, but stole the discovery from another man. Is this truth mighty, and will it
prevail? Ah no, my hearers, the monument is made of hardy material, but the lie
it tells will outlast it a million years. An awkward, feeble, leaky lie is a thing which
you ought to make it your unceasing study to avoid; such a lie as that has no more
real permanence than an average truth. Why, you might as well tell the truth at
once and be done with it. A feeble, stupid, preposterous lie will not live two years—
except it be a slander upon somebody. It is indestructible, then of course, but that
is no merit of yours. A final word: begin your practice of this gracious and beautiful art early—begin now. If I had begun earlier, I could have learned how.

Never handle firearms carelessly. The sorrow and suffering that have been   6
caused through the innocent but heedless handling of firearms by the young!
Only four days ago, right in the next farm house to the one where I am spending
the summer, a grandmother, old and gray and sweet, one of the loveliest spirits
in the land, was sitting at her work, when her young grandson crept in and got
down an old, battered, rusty gun which had not been touched for many years
and was supposed not to be loaded, and pointed it at her, laughing and threat-
ening to shoot. In her fright she ran screaming and pleading toward the door
on the other side of the room; but as she passed him he placed the gun almost
against her very breast and pulled the trigger! He had supposed it was not
loaded. And he was right—it wasn't. So there wasn't any harm done. It is the
only case of that kind I ever heard of. Therefore, just the same, don't you meddle
with old unloaded firearms; they are the most deadly and unerring things that

have ever been created by man. You don't have to take any pains at all with them; you don't have to have a rest, you don't have to have any sights on the gun, you don't have to take aim, even. No, you just pick out a relative and bang away, and you are sure to get him. A youth who can't hit a cathedral at thirty yards with a Gatling gun in three quarters of an hour, can take up an old empty musket and bag his grandmother every time, at a hundred. Think what Waterloo would have been if one of the armies had been boys armed with old muskets supposed not to be loaded, and the other army had been composed of their female relations. The very thought of it make one shudder.

There are many sorts of books; but good ones are the sort for the young to 7 read. Remember that. They are a great, an inestimable, and unspeakable means of improvement. Therefore be careful in your selection, my young friends; be very careful; confine yourselves exclusively to Robertson's *Sermons*, Baxter's *Saint's Rest*, *The Innocents Abroad*, and works of that kind.

But I have said enough. I hope you will treasure up the instructions which 8 I have given you, and make them a guide to your feet and a light to your understanding. Build your character thoughtfully and painstakingly upon these precepts, and by and by, when you have got it built, you will be surprised and gratified to see how nicely and sharply it resembles everybody else's.

READING COMPREHENSION

1. The word *didactic* in ". . . something suitable to youth—something didactic" (paragraph 1) means
   a. intended to teach a moral lesson.
   b. intended to help with pronunciation.
   c. youthful and fun.
   d. intended to entertain.

2. The word *superstition* in ". . . by humoring that superstition" (paragraph 2) most closely refers to
   a. custom.
   b. belief not based on reason or knowledge.
   c. act or ritual derived from custom.
   d. fact.

3. The word *inestimable* in ". . . a great, an inestimable, and unspeakable means of improvement" (paragraph 7) most closely means
   a. too large to be counted.
   b. valuable beyond measure.
   c. very limited.
   d. very predictable.

4. What would be the best alternative title for this selection?
   a. Do as I Say, Not as I Do
   b. Lying Is the Best Way to Get What You Want
   c. What Not to Do
   d. Adventures of Twain

5. Which statement below represents the main idea of the selection?
    a. Think for yourself. *(circled)*
    b. Don't question advice; follow it!
    c. Morality requires obedience.
    d. Parents are always correct.

6. Why, according to Twain, should people be careful of lying?
    a. It is morally wrong.
    b. It can be very difficult.
    c. It is an art that needs to be practiced.
    d. It can hurt a person's reputation. *(circled)*

7. True or False? ___True___ Twain believes that firearms are OK, as long as they are handled correctly.

8. True or False? ___False___ Twain is a great liar and believes that everyone should learn how to properly tell lies.

9. If Twain's style could be described with one word, which one would it be?
    a. funny
    b. serious
    c. depressing
    d. sarcastic *(circled)*

10. Which of the following subjects is not covered in "Advice to Youth"?
    a. respect
    b. reading
    c. study habits *(circled)*
    d. guns

STRUCTURE AND TECHNIQUE

TEACHING TIP
Satire is a difficult technique for many students to understand. You might want to present several other satirical pieces to help students understand how satire is written and used.

1. Twain employs the technique of satire, using ridicule to expose or denounce something, in this essay. Although it seems he is giving bad advice, he is actually giving good advice. Why do you think he uses satire instead of writing plainly and in a straightforward manner?

2. Twain breaks up his essay into six very specific rules; do you think he left out any rules? Explain.

3. Do you think Twain's speech would have been more effective if he had not used satire? Explain.

CRITICAL READING AND DISCUSSION

1. In paragraph 3, Twain discusses the idea of being respectful to superiors and strangers and ends the paragraph with the idea that violence is "unrefined." Do you agree or disagree? Explain.

2. In paragraph 4, Twain is actually addressing the old saying, "The early bird gets the worm." Do you think that people who get up earlier are more productive and morally upright? Why do you think this saying became so popular?

3. According to this essay, lying is an art, to be practiced from an early age. What does modern society say about lying?

4. Twain is an author and essayist, yet one of his shortest paragraphs gives advice about reading, and he suggests staying confined to a very short list of books. Without knowing any details about these books, what do you think Twain is actually warning his listeners about?

WRITING ASSIGNMENTS

Assignment 1: Writing a Paragraph

Write a paragraph that discusses what audience you believe Twain was addressing in this speech, what event was being held, and why he had been asked to speak. Use evidence from the text–vocabulary and advice–to support your claim.

Assignment 2: Writing an Essay

Write an essay that instructs a group of people about how to do something. Imagine you are giving a commencement address or speaking at an elementary school. Topics for your essay could be teaching a group of younger children how to behave; a group of high school freshmen how to succeed in high school; or a group of college students how to make and keep friends. Incorporating humor into your essay can help you make your point, but don't focus so much on the humor that the message is lost. If you choose to mimic Twain's style, you may want to include statements like "always talk behind people's backs" or "never read the directions on a test," but remember to use support for the opposite idea. (For example, describe what happens if someone doesn't read the directions.)

Assignment 3: Writing an Essay

Write an essay about advice you have been given while growing up. You should create a thesis statement that tells whether the advice you have been given is either good or bad. Use the rest of your essay to support your thesis by offering examples of the advice and how it did or did not help you.

Inaugural Address

John F. Kennedy

PREVIEW

This is the speech delivered by John Fitzgerald Kennedy to his fellow Americans after taking the oath of office as the thirty-fifth president of the United States on January 20, 1961. In his first speech as president, he attempts to summarize the enormous task confronting not just him, but everyone striving for freedom and world peace. President Kennedy evokes an urgency when addressing the various problems confronting the United States, and yet he also engages the rest of the world through his speech. In particular, he calls on the world's leaders to aim for a higher purpose of their own lands and people, while at the same time asking the American people to join him in participating in the transformation of the United States.

Source: Library of Congress Prints and Photographs Division [LC-USZ62-117124]

Vice President Johnson, Mr. Speaker, Mr. Chief Justice, President Eisenhower, 1
Vice President Nixon, President Truman, reverend clergy, fellow citizens, we
observe today not a victory of party, but a celebration of freedom—symbolizing
an end, as well as a beginning—signifying renewal, as well as change. For I have
sworn before you and Almighty God the same solemn oath our forebears pre-
scribed nearly a century and three quarters ago.

The world is very different now. For man holds in his mortal hands the 2
power to abolish all forms of human poverty and all forms of human life. And
yet the same revolutionary beliefs for which our forebears fought are still at issue
around the globe—the belief that the rights of man come not from the generosity
of the state, but from the hand of God.

We dare not forget today that we are the heirs of that first revolution. Let 3
the word go forth from this time and place, to friend and foe alike, that the
torch has been passed to a new generation of Americans, born in this century,
tempered[1] by war, disciplined by a hard and bitter peace, proud of our ancient
heritage and unwilling to witness or permit the slow undoing of those human
rights to which this Nation has always been committed, and to which we are
committed today at home and around the world.

Let every nation know, whether it wishes us well or ill, that we shall pay 4
any price, bear any burden, meet any hardship, support any friend, oppose any
foe, to assure the survival and the success of liberty.

This much we pledge and more.   5

To those old allies whose cultural and spiritual origins we share, we pledge 6
the loyalty of faithful friends. United, there is little we cannot do in a host of
cooperative ventures.[2] Divided, there is little we can do—for we dare not meet
a powerful challenge at odds and split asunder.

To those new States whom we welcome to the ranks of the free, we pledge 7
our word that one form of colonial control shall not have passed away merely
to be replaced by a far more iron tyranny. We shall not always expect to find
them supporting our view. But we shall always hope to find them strongly supporting their own freedom—and to remember that, in the past, those who fool-
ishly sought power by riding the back of the tiger ended up inside.

To those peoples in the huts and villages across the globe struggling to break 8
the bonds of mass misery, we pledge our best efforts to help them help themselves, for whatever period is required, not because the Communists may be
doing it, not because we seek their votes, but because it is right. If a free society
cannot help the many who are poor, it cannot save the few who are rich.

To our sister republics south of our border, we offer a special pledge—to 9
convert our good words into good deeds in a new alliance for progress—to assist
free men and free governments in casting off the chains of poverty. But this
peaceful revolution of hope cannot become the prey of hostile powers. Let all
our neighbors know that we shall join with them to oppose aggression or subversion[3] anywhere in the Americas. And let every other power know that this
Hemisphere intends to remain the master of its own house.

To that world assembly of sovereign states, the United Nations, our last best 10
hope in an age where the instruments of war have far outpaced the instruments
of peace, we renew our pledge of support—to prevent it from becoming merely

[1]*tempered:* strengthened.
[2]*ventures:* undertaking that is of uncertain outcome.
[3]*subversion:* attempt to overthrow or undermine the government.

a forum for invective—to strengthen its shield of the new and the weak and to enlarge the area in which its writ may run.

Finally, to those nations who would make themselves our adversary, we offer [11] not a pledge but a request—that both sides begin anew the quest for peace, before the dark powers of destruction unleashed by science engulf all humanity in planned or accidental self-destruction.

We dare not tempt them with weakness. For only when our arms are sufficient beyond doubt can we be certain beyond doubt that they will never be employed. [12]

But neither can two great and powerful groups of nations take comfort from [13] our present course—both sides overburdened by the cost of modern weapons, both rightly alarmed by the steady spread of the deadly atom, yet both racing to alter that uncertain balance of terror that stays the hand of mankind's final war.

So let us begin anew, remembering on both sides that civility is not a sign [14] of weakness, and sincerity is always subject to proof. Let us never negotiate out of fear. But let us never fear to negotiate.

Let both sides explore what problems unite us instead of belaboring those [15] problems which divide us.

Let both sides, for the first time, formulate serious and precise proposals [16] for the inspection and control of arms and bring the absolute power to destroy other nations under the absolute control of all nations.

Let both sides seek to invoke the wonders of science instead of its terrors. [17] Together let us explore the stars, conquer the deserts, eradicate[4] disease, tap the ocean depths, and encourage the arts and commerce.

Let both sides unite to heed in all corners of the earth the command of [18] Isaiah—to "undo the heavy burdens . . . and let the oppressed go free."

And if a beachhead[5] of cooperation may push back the jungle of suspicion, [19] let both sides join in creating a new endeavor, not a new balance of power, but a new world of law, where the strong are just and the weak secure and the peace preserved.

All this will not be finished in the first 100 days. Nor will it be finished in [20] the first 1,000 days, nor in the life of this administration, nor even perhaps in our lifetime on this planet. But let us begin.

In your hands, my fellow citizens, more than mine, will rest the final success [21] or failure of our course. Since this country was founded, each generation of Americans has been summoned to give testimony to its national loyalty. The graves of young Americans who answered the call to service surround the globe.

Now the trumpet summons us again—not as a call to bear arms, though [22] arms we need—not as a call to battle, though embattled we are—but a call to bear the burden of a long twilight struggle, year in and year out, "rejoicing in hope, patient in tribulation"—a struggle against the common enemies of man: tyranny, poverty, disease, and war itself.

Can we forge against these enemies a grand and global alliance, North and [23] South, East and West, that can assure a more fruitful life for all mankind? Will you join in that historic effort?

In the long history of the world, only a few generations have been granted [24] the role of defending freedom in its hour of maximum danger. I do not shrink

[4]*eradicate:* get rid of.
[5]*beachhead:* an initial accomplishment that opens the way for further developments.

from this responsibility—I welcome it. I do not believe that any of us would exchange places with any other people or any other generation. The energy, the faith, the devotion which we bring to this endeavor will light our country and all who serve it—and the glow from that fire can truly light the world.

And so, my fellow Americans: ask not what your country can do for you— 25 ask what you can do for your country.

My fellow citizens of the world: ask not what America will do for you, but 26 what together we can do for the freedom of man.

Finally, whether you are citizens of America or citizens of the world, ask of 27 us here the same high standards of strength and sacrifice which we ask of you. With a good conscience our only sure reward, with history the final judge of our deeds, let us go forth to lead the land we love, asking His blessing and His help, but knowing that here on earth God's work must truly be our own.

READING COMPREHENSION

1. In paragraph 10, President Kennedy uses the word *invective*. This most closely means
   a. abuse or insult.
   b. barrier.
   c. inclusion.
   d. communication.

2. In paragraph 15, he uses the term *belaboring*. This most closely means
   a. not using.
   b. designing.
   c. discriminating.
   d. overemphasizing.

3. What would be a good alternate title for this selection?
   a. Let Freedom Ring
   b. JFK: Our Youngest President
   c. JFK Addresses the Nation for the First Time as President
   d. America's First Catholic President

4. What is the main idea of this selection?
   a. President Kennedy addresses the nation with a call to service.
   b. President Kennedy wants to help the world become one.
   c. The world reaches out to America for help and support.
   d. President Kennedy addresses world leaders to come together.

5. In paragraph 4, President Kennedy states to nations that wish us well or ill, that we (the United States) would pay any price for the following
   a. our standing in the world.
   b. our monetary value.
   c. our survival and success of liberty.
   d. our land.

6. How does President Kennedy suggest we explore the wonders of science?

   a. tap the ocean depths

   b. eradicate disease

   c. explore the stars

   (d.) all of the above

7. In his speech, President Kennedy refers to all of the following except this common enemy of man.

   (a.) money

   b. disease

   c. war

   d. tyranny

8. President Kennedy states that world peace lies not in his hands but in those of

   a. United Nations representatives.

   b. his Cabinet members.

   c. smaller nations.

   (d.) his fellow citizens.

9. Who is President Kennedy speaking to when he says "ask not what your country can do for you–ask what you can do for your country"?

   a. fellow citizens of the world

   (b.) fellow Americans

   c. Communists

   d. the United Nations

10. Which of the following adjectives describes President Kennedy's speech?

   a. dull

   b. long

   (c.) inspiring

   d. terrifying

STRUCTURE AND TECHNIQUE

1. President Kennedy's address is brief in nature yet contains his principal message as the thesis statement. Where is this thesis statement located? How does he support the thesis in his address? What examples or rationales does he provide?

2. The president uses the word "Let" many times during the address. How does the use of this word affect his message? What does he wish to accomplish with its use?

3. In paragraph 23, President Kennedy asks two questions: "Can we forge against . . . for all mankind? Will you join in that historic effort?" What roles do these questions play at the end of the address? Why do you believe he left these questions for last? Would their placement at the beginning of the address have been as successful? If so, why? If not, why not?

4. In paragraph 25 he makes his famous "ask not" quote. Why does he include this statement at the end of his speech? Would the statement have worked elsewhere in the speech? What does the statement mean to you?

CRITICAL READING AND DISCUSSION

1. The presidential inaugural address begins with an acknowledgement that the world has changed and that change is required to move forward. In addition, President Kennedy refers to America's forefathers and their contributions to the American cause. How does invoking the forefathers' efforts apply to the subsequent efforts Kennedy will ask of the American people? Where in the passage is this call to action made? Is this effective?

2. President Kennedy begins some of his paragraphs with "To_____." He is asking specific groups to work cooperatively with him. What does invoking each group do to the address? How would the different groups react if they had not been mentioned? Why do you believe the president felt it was necessary to call special attention to these individual groups?

3. Once President Kennedy completes his request of support from the various groups mentioned, he begins to suggest the path America as a nation should take. He lists four requests. What are they and what do they represent to him, the nation, and the world?

WRITING ASSIGNMENTS

Assignment 1: Writing a Paragraph

Write a paragraph about the current president of the United States. Describe his or her personality and what you like or dislike about him or her. How does he or she rate compared to other presidents? Do you relate to his or her view of the world? What do you admire about him or her? What decisions has he or she made that you agree or disagree with?

Assignment 2: Writing an Essay

Historically, President Kennedy was considered a good leader. Even though he died young, many feel admiration and respect for his vision. What do you believe makes for a good leader of the United States? What are some of the qualities an American president should possess?

Write an essay about your ideal American president. This is a descriptive essay where you may use vivid details to support your points.

Assignment 3: Writing an Essay

Write an essay in which you contrast a good president and a bad president. Make a list of the qualities that make one excellent and the other ineffective or worse. Focus on three pairs of contrasting qualities, using either a one-side-at-a-time or a point-by-point method of development (see Chapter 11).

Neat People vs. Sloppy People

Suzanne Britt

©Suzanne Britt

PREVIEW

This amusing article written by Suzanne Britt depicts the virtues of sloppy people, while expressing that neat people are not kind people at all. She uses various methods and circumstances to give us the reasons she believes neat people are uncaring and ruthless with very few feelings. On the other hand, she claims sloppy people are kind-hearted perfectionists who are misunderstood. They are visionaries within a world that does not understand their creative minds and higher purpose.

I've finally figured out the difference between neat people and sloppy people. The distinction is, as always, moral. Neat people are lazier and meaner than sloppy people. 1

Sloppy people, you see, are not really sloppy. Their sloppiness is merely the unfortunate consequence of their extreme moral rectitude.[1] Sloppy people carry in their mind's eye a heavenly vision, a precise plan, that is so stupendous, so perfect, it can't be achieved in this world or the next. 2

Sloppy people live in Never-Never Land. Someday is their métier.[2] Someday they are planning to alphabetize all their books and set up home catalogs. Someday they will go through their wardrobes and mark certain items for tentative mending, and certain items for passing on to relatives of similar shape and size. Someday sloppy people will make family scrapbooks into which they will put newspaper clippings, postcards, locks of hair, and the dried corsage from their senior prom. Someday they will file everything on the surface of their desks, including the cash receipts from coffee purchases at the snack shop. Someday they will sit down and read all the back issues of *The New Yorker*. 3

For all these noble reasons and more, sloppy people never get neat. They aim too high and wide. They save everything, planning someday to file, order, and straighten out the world. But while these ambitious plans take clearer and clearer shape in their heads, the books spill from the shelves onto the floor, the clothes pile up in the hamper and closet, the family mementos accumulate in every drawer, the surface of the desk is buried under mounds of paper, and the unread magazines threaten to reach the ceiling. 4

Sloppy people can't bear to part with anything. They give loving attention to every detail. When sloppy people say they're going to tackle the surface of the desk, they really mean it. Not a paper will go unturned; not a rubber band will go unboxed. Four hours or two weeks into the excavation, the desk looks exactly the same, primarily because the sloppy person is meticulously[3] creating new piles of papers with new headings and scrupulously stopping to read all the old book catalogs before he throws them away. A neat person would just bulldoze the desk. 5

Neat people are bums and clods at heart. They have cavalier[4] attitudes toward possessions, including family heirlooms. Everything is just another 6

[1] *rectitude:* honesty and correct moral behavior.
[2] *métier:* specialty.
[3] *meticulously:* carefully, precisely.
[4] *cavalier:* careless.

dustcatcher to them. If anything collects dust, it's got to go and that's that. Neat people will toy with the idea of throwing the children out of the house just to cut down on the clutter.

Neat people don't care about process. They like results. What they want to do is get the whole thing over with so they can sit down and watch the rasslin'[5] on TV. Neat people operate on two unvarying principles: Never handle any item twice, and throw everything away. 7

The only thing messy in the neat person's house is the trash can. The minute something comes to a neat person's hand, he will look at it, try to decide if it has immediate use and, finding none, throw it in the trash. 8

Neat people are especially vicious with mail. They never go through their mail unless they are standing directly over a trash can. If the trash can is beside the mailbox, even better. All ads, catalogs, pleas for charitable contributions, church bulletins and money-saving coupons go straight into the trash can without being opened. All letters from home, postcards from Europe, bills and paychecks are opened, immediately responded to, then dropped in the trash can. Neat people keep their receipts only for tax purposes. That's it. No sentimental salvaging of birthday cards or the last letter a dying relative ever wrote. Into the trash it goes. 9

Neat people place neatness above everything, even economics. They are incredibly wasteful. Neat people throw away several toys every time they walk through the den. I knew a neat person once who threw away a perfectly good dish drainer because it had mold on it. The drainer was too much trouble to wash. And neat people sell their furniture when they move. They will sell a La-Z-Boy recliner while you are reclining in it. 10

Neat people are no good to borrow from. Neat people buy everything in expensive little single portions. They get their flour and sugar in two-pound bags. They wouldn't consider clipping a coupon, saving a leftover, reusing plastic nondairy whipped cream containers or rinsing off tin foil and draping it over the unmoldy dish drainer. You can never borrow a neat person's newspaper to see what's playing at the movies. Neat people have the paper all wadded up and in the trash by 7:05 A.M. 11

TEACHING TIP
Ask students to write down their own examples to define neat and sloppy people.

Neat people cut a clean swath through the organic as well as the inorganic world. People, animals, and things are all one to them. They are so insensitive. After they've finished with the pantry, the medicine cabinet, and the attic, they will throw out the red geranium (too many leaves), sell the dog (too many fleas), and send the children off to boarding school (too many scuffmarks on the hardwood floors). 12

READING COMPREHENSION

1. The word *heirlooms* in paragraph 6 refers to
   a. family vacations.
   b. pictures of the family.
   c. objects reflecting the family history.
   d. another name for neat people.

2. In paragraph 3, the word *tentative* can be defined as
   a. clearly stated.
   b. thoroughly investigated.

[5]*rasslin'*: Southern style of professional wrestling.

c.   intensely disliked.

(d.) possible.

3. Which of the following would be a good alternate title for the selection?

a.   A Sloppy Person's Manifesto

b.   The Virtues of Being Neat

c.   Household Duties and Internal Conflicts

(d.) Sloppy vs. Mean People: A Personal Analysis

4. Which of the following sentences best expresses the main idea of the selection?

a.   Sloppy and neat people vary in many ways.

b.   There are three major differences between neat and sloppy people.

(c.) There are many reasons why neat people are mean.

d.   Sloppy people have a lot of emotional baggage.

5. The author suggests that there are many reasons sloppy people never get neat; they include all of these except

a.   they aim too high and wide.

b.   they save everything.

c.   they are attached to sentimental mementos.

(d.) they go through their closets and give away clothing.

6. According to the author, neat people do all of these except

a.   spend lots of money on expensive things.

b.   go through their mail next to the trash can.

(c.) keep all receipts for three years.

d.   throw away toys and clothes easily.

7. Neat people do not care about their family, pets, or friends because they

(a.) are insensitive.

b.   are thrifty with their purchases.

c.   love to invite people over to their homes.

d.   do not take organization seriously.

8. In the selection, author Suzanne Britt makes a distinction between neat and sloppy people and concludes that

a.   sloppy people are meaner than neat people.

b.   neat people have a lot of things stocked up in their spaces.

c.   neat people prefer their children to messes.

(d.) sloppy people are nicer than neat people.

9. According to Britt, neat people

a.   are very conservative about their money and expenses.

(b.) value order over sentimentality.

c.   hate all who are not like them.

d.   don't understand what sloppy people are thinking.

10. We can conclude that Suzanne Britt is

   a.   a neat person.

   b.   a sloppy person.

   c.   a little of both.

   d.   neither neat nor sloppy.

STRUCTURE AND TECHNIQUE

1. "Neat People vs. Sloppy People" is written in a form that most closely resembles which pattern of development (narration, exemplification, comparison/contrast, description, or process)? Explain.

2. The effectiveness of the article can be attributed to the format the author used to explain her point of view. In your opinion, how does Suzanne Britt support her thesis statement that neat people are meaner and uncaring and that sloppy people are better individuals? Explain.

3. The article is almost written as if it were a list of attributes. Few examples are given about sloppy people while most examples are about the negative aspects of neat people. Do you think this made for an effective article? Do you think it was too one-sided and not enough examples were given about sloppy people?

4. Throughout the article, Britt alternates between neat and sloppy people, but at no point does she point out the positive attributes that neat people could possibly have. Does this style weaken her argument in any way? If yes, why? If not, why not?

CRITICAL READING AND DISCUSSION

TEACHING TIP
Use item 1 as a prompt for a short in-class writing assignment.

1. According to Britt, who is a more decent person, a neat or sloppy person? What examples does she give that make you believe this is so?

2. In paragraph 7, Britt mentions that neat people don't care about process. Do you believe this is true? Are there any aspects of neat people that you believe are process-oriented? What are some examples that you can think of where being neat is more desirable than being sloppy?

3. What does Britt mean in paragraph 12 when she writes that "neat people cut a clean swath through the organic as well as the inorganic world"? Explain what she meant by inorganic.

4. In paragraph 6 Britt uses the term *cavalier* to express the attitudes of neat people towards family and possessions. How do you interpret the word *cavalier* in this passage? How does the use of this word to describe their attitudes affect the tone of the article? Does it reinforce the author's main idea, or does it take away from it?

WRITING ASSIGNMENTS

Assignment 1: Writing a Paragraph

Suzanne Britt talks about the differences between neat and sloppy people.

Write a paragraph about the differences between two siblings or friends. For example, one can be outgoing and the other introverted. What types of problems can occur in a family with different views on cleanliness and appropriation of chores? You can also write about a time you had to compromise to get along with someone who had different habits than you, a roommate, for example.

Assignment 2: Writing an Essay

According to Britt, neat people are inherently mean people as well. In her opinion, they may even give priority to order and simplicity over a creative environment. She claims that sloppy people are nicer and have more creativity.

Write an essay about a person you believe to be either a "neat freak" or a "sloppy couch potato." You can divide the essay into sections, dedicating body paragraphs to physical attributes and then behavioral differences. Mention if this individual is a part of your family, yourself, or a friend. Does Britt's analysis apply to the person you describe?

Assignment 3: Writing an Essay

In the article, Suzanne Britt talks mostly about the negative qualities of neat people. When she describes sloppy people she uses details and examples that praise the sloppy person's behavior. The article is written so that the reader comes away with a skewed view of neat people. What are some of the negative qualities of sloppy people? What are some of the obstacles and conflicts that sloppy people could encounter?

Consider including aspects such as what might happen to people who are chronically unprepared or disorganized—for instance, losing job opportunities or missing appointments.

A Few Good Monuments Men: Saving Art from Looting and Destruction—Especially in the Middle East—Is a Military Matter

The British Army is recruiting experts who fancy themselves George Clooney 2.0 to preserve global cultural treasure.

Noah Charney

©Noah Charney

PREVIEW

Noah Charney is an author and art historian who is best known for his book *The Art Thief*. He has also written numerous essays that explore topics in the art world, including this article that first appeared in *Salon* in 2016. In it, Charney examines different efforts—including partnerships between military and university personnel—to preserve historical artifacts in war zones.

The British Army recently announced that it would be recruiting 15 to 20 new 1
officers with specializations in art, archaeology and antiquities who will be
deployed in the field, just behind the front lines, to help identify, protect and
track art and antiquities that are in danger of being damaged, looted or
destroyed.

This is, of course, particularly relevant to Middle Eastern conflicts, where 2
groups like ISIS have shown a giddy eagerness to destroy ancient monuments,
on the scale of whole cities like Palmyra and Nimrud, as well as individual pre-
Islamic statuary that are deemed heretical. Of course, the flip side to this is that
these groups are also happy to profit off the very objects they condemn, and
they are funding their activities through illicit trade in antiquities.

These works of great artistry and historical importance—which cannot 3
exactly be blamed for not being Islamic artworks, if they were created a millennium before the Prophet Muhammad was born—can be saved from the mallet
if they are destined for the auctioneer's hammer.

Not long ago, scholars like me (I'm a specialist in the history of art 4
crime) had to work hard to convince not just the general public but also
authorities, police and politicians that art crime, particularly illicit trade in
antiquities, funded organized crime and terrorism. No longer. This stance
has been vindicated, unfortunately, in scores of destructive ways, most obviously through ISIS videos of iconoclasm. The only remaining questions concern the scale of the earnings from looted antiquities and what to do to stem
the flow.

The most direct way to curb the looting is to discourage First World buyers 5
from purchasing anything that is not 100 percent clearly *not* from recent exca-
vations in Middle Eastern conflict zones. But while those in the art trade talk
a good game, there's profit to be had, from major galleries and online auction
sites (where it is easy for a seller to hide his or her identity, difficult to be sure
of an object's provenance, and where some objects have been advertised as being
still covered in desert sand, as if this were a selling point). The documentary
"Blood Antiques" chillingly shows how certain Brussels art dealers, for instance,
collude with actors posing as people with looted antiquities to sell, even as some
still have desert sand on them.

So the need is clear to help protect surviving monuments from iconoclasts 6
and do what we can to limit the funds for fundamentalist groups. Curbing art
crime is one way to do that. The U.K. and France are among the governments
that have recently dedicated tens of millions to protecting cultural heritage. The
National Endowment for the Humanities in the United States recently launched
a new grant for projects with that same goal. So it stands to reason that the
military would reinstate officers who might be described as modern-day Monuments Men.

***

It is fitting that the Monuments Men 2.0 should be spearheaded by the 7
British because they were the masterminds behind the original incarnation. The
highest-profile among the officers were Americans, promoted by recent books
like "Monuments Men," which focused on George Stout (whose fictional avatar
was played by Clooney in his film of the same name) and my own "Stealing the
Mystic Lamb," which focused on Monuments Men Robert Posey and Lincoln

Kirstein. (Fictionalized versions of the latter were played by Bill Murray and Bob Balaban in the "Monuments Men" film.)

8   But the core of the program was British, led by Sir Leonard Woolley, a rumpled, opinionated archaeologist, a buddy of Agatha Christie and someone in desperate need of a rollicking biography, preferably penned by the master of World War II intrigue romps, Ben MacIntyre. Woolley's project has its origins in January 1943, when archaeologists Mortimer Wheeler and John Ward-Perkins visited archaeological sites like Leptis Magna in North Africa.

9   A team of Italian archaeologists had recently excavated the site, but the excavated objects were just left there unprotected. British soldiers were inadvertently damaging ruins without realizing that the stones were of cultural or historical importance. The two prepared homemade "out of bounds" signs to show people where to avoid treading.

TEACHING TIP
Have students talk about their experiences visiting museums and viewing exhibits, including antiquities, from other countries. Have them speculate about how the museum acquired the artwork and how the artwork became available to the museum.

10   Thus began a movement to educate soldiers in the field, for with knowledge of the treasures they might encounter came consideration to protect them. What Wheeler conceived was later enacted by Woolley, as part of the British War Office. But Woolley envisioned this as an advisory role not one that would actually send officers into war zones. That would be the American contribution.

11   Meanwhile, in the United States at the outset of World War II, a group of American museum leaders, including Paul Sachs of Harvard's Fogg Museum and Alfred Barr of the Museum of Modern Art, drew up a list of cultural heritage objects that might be in danger in the course of the fighting on continental Europe. This list was linked to maps that were distributed to officers, along with General Dwight Eisenhower's important directive to avoid damaging cultural sites whenever possible. There is no record of a previous general making such a statement.

12   While it was up to field commanders to apply it (and if the lives of humans were at stake, they took precedence over objects) and there were some major-league "oopses," like the art-rich monastery of Monte Cassino being horribly bombed despite the fact that no Nazis were hiding in it, the principle was important.

13   An estimated 5 million cultural heritage objects were stolen, looted, damaged or destroyed during World War II, but the greatest treasures stolen by the Nazis and their dedicated art and archive-theft unit, the Einsatzstab Reichsleiter Rosenberg, were saved, thanks to the heroic efforts of the underfunded, underappreciated Monuments Men.

14   "The just-announced creation of the UK's Cultural Heritage Protection Unit, (a.k.a. the Monuments Men and Women Returned) is very significant," Judge Arthur Tompkins told *Salon*. "This represents another tangible and practical initiative to safeguard art and culture where they are often most at risk, by way of a specialist unit which will in turn act as a strategically beneficial force-multiplier on the ground," said Tompkins, who is the author of "Art Crime and Its Prevention" and the forthcoming "Plundering Beauty: A Concise Illustrated History of Art Crime in War." "It is another piece of the mosaic which is gradually, but with increasing momentum, rebuilding and enhancing the core national and international structures of cultural protection during armed conflict."

***

There have been officers who have functioned as the Monuments Men did 15 during World War II in the decades since. Italy's Carabinieri military police have had dozens of officers from their Division for the Protection of Cultural Heritage in conflict zones for years. Colonel Matthew Bogdanos, a former U.S. Marine, was in charge of recovering objects looted from the National Museum in Baghdad during the Iraq War. Lt. Col. Timothy Purbrick, an art dealer in his civilian life, has led a cultural property protection working group in the British Army for the last two years, and the new unit will be an extension of the fine work he has done.

The U.S. Army employs archaeologists like Laurie Rush, whose role has 16 been to train soldiers in how to respect and protect cultural heritage sites in the field. "The British initiative is good news for all of us who work with the military on issues of cultural property protection," Rush said. "I have had the added good fortune to be able to work directly with key members of the British military, like [Lt. Col.] Purbrick and my counterpart Richard Osgood, so I know that the British effort is in extremely good hands."

Rush was also behind a most coveted, not-for-sale trinket: cultural heritage 17 protection playing cards, distributed to soldiers in the field. Each features a picture of an at-risk object or monument, so that troops can learn as they play poker.

The Association for Research into Crimes against Art (full disclosure: I'm 18 its founder) has for years been teaching post-graduate students and professionals about protecting art. Dozens of graduates of its summer-long Postgraduate Program in Art Crime and Culture Heritage Protection have expressed interest in joining some sort of new incarnation of the Monuments Men, but opportunities have been lacking. No longer.

"While art historians, provenance experts, and criminologists might seem 19 like unlikely war heroes, the fact that the military recognizes the need for these types of experts, to advise commanders and to work with civilian authorities after battles, is hugely important," said Lynda Albertson, CEO of the association. "As the military are planning before and during a conflict, it is important for officers in charge to think 'what are the historically significant places we need to protect in a conflict, and how do we preserve what is damaged as a result of military necessity.'"

To that end, the Association for Research into Crimes against Art has 20 a scholarship set aside as part of its postgraduate training program to advance the knowledge of cultural heritage experts in uniform, providing training to cultural-property-protection personnel who are working with the military at the national or multinational level. Recent scholars have come from conflict-zone countries: Iraq, Yemen and Syria.

Over the past two years, governments have finally recognized the severity 21 of art crime, above all illicit looting and trade of antiquities and openly condemned it, dedicating impressive funding to curbing it. Now the British Army is going a step further and recruiting officers to enter the fray and help save art. It is an important step, recognizing not only that art is of great importance as the tangible relic of past and present civilizations but also because it is something to safeguard against those who would destroy or illicitly profit from it, using it a weapon in the war against terror.

Noah Charney, "A Few Good Monuments Men," *Salon*, December 11, 2016. This article first appeared in Salon.com, at http://www.Salon.com. An online version remains in the Salon archives. Reprinted with permission.

READING COMPREHENSION

1. The word *heretical* in "individual pre-Islamic statuary that are deemed heretical" (paragraph 2) means
   a. freethinking.
   b. idolatrous.
   c. dissenting.
   d. nonconforming.

2. The word *illicit* in "funding their activities through illicit trade" (paragraph 2) means
   a. illegal; illegitimate.
   b. extracted; extorted.
   c. brought out; evoked.
   d. dirty; improper.

3. The word *vindicated* in "this stance has been vindicated, unfortunately, in scores of destructive ways" (paragraph 4) means
   a. absolved.
   b. disproven.
   c. supported.
   d. established.

4. Which of the following would be a good alternative title for this selection?
   a. Protecting Cultures
   b. Military Roles
   c. Black-Market Sales
   d. Art Imitating Life

5. Which sentence best expresses the main idea of the selection?
   a. Art historians make the best soldiers because they can preserve art as well as fight the enemy.
   b. Safeguarding art from war zones has become an important part of militaries' missions.
   c. The military has a long history of trying to preserve artwork in war zones.
   d. Keeping art out of the hands of fundamentalists has become a main priority for the British army.

6. According to the author, what are groups like ISIS doing?
   a. They are destroying art and historical artifacts in every city they conquer.
   b. They are selling art and historical artifacts to support their war efforts.
   c. They are both selling and destroying pieces of art and historical artifacts.
   d. They are selling some pieces of art and artifacts to build up the cities they conquer.

7. What does the author mean by "discourage First World buyers from purchasing" (paragraph 5)?

   a. If people in developed countries, First World countries, stopped buying illegal artifacts, there would be no market, and could help stop the business.

   b. If people in developed countries, First World countries, stopped buying illegal artifacts, more items would be destroyed.

   c. If First World buyers went to the countries where the artifacts originate, they could buy these items much more cheaply.

   d. If First World buyers wouldn't purchase all the artifacts, the art historians would be able to buy and preserve them.

8. According to the essay, how many new officers are going to be hired?

   a. 10–15

   b. 15–20

   c. 20–25

   d. 25–30

9. According to the essay, about how many objects were stolen or destroyed during World War II?

   a. 2 million

   b. 3 million

   c. 4 million

   d. 5 million

10. The Association for Research into Crimes against Art does all of the following EXCEPT:

    a. train post-graduates about protecting art.

    b. train professionals about protecting art.

    c. train governments about protecting art.

    d. train military personnel about protecting art.

STRUCTURE AND TECHNIQUE

1. What type of introduction does Charney use? How does it enhance the essay?

2. What point of view does the author employ? Why do you think he uses this approach? Do you think this approach is effective?

3. How does Charney establish his credibility as an authority on this topic? Give specific examples.

4. Charney breaks his essay into three distinct parts. Explain the purpose of each part. Do you think this is an effective way to write this essay? Explain your answers.

TEACHING TIP
Ask students to meet in small groups, each one to discuss a different question in the "Critical Reading and Discussion" section.

CRITICAL READING AND DISCUSSION

1. Why does the author think that the recruitment efforts of the military are a good thing?

2. Explain how the military practice of preserving art and artifacts in war zones emerged. Describe the efforts of both the British and the Americans in developing this practice.

3. Reread paragraph 17. What do you think about this method of helping soldiers learn what to look for? Explain your answer.

WRITING ASSIGNMENTS

Assignment 1: Writing a Paragraph

In his essay, Charney explains that he started the Association for Research into Crimes against Art to teach people how to protect art. Write a paragraph in which you describe an organization that you believe should be started to help educate people to protect something valuable to your community.

Assignment 2: Writing an Essay

Over the years, educators have experimented with different ways to help students learn. Gamification (motivating students by using video game design and gaming elements) became a popular movement in the early 2000s. Teachers were told to "flip their classrooms" (switch the kinds of activities traditionally done in-class with those typically done out of the classroom) in the 2010s. Like the soldiers' playing cards, trying to find new and creative ways to educate people has often been at the forefront of educational movements.

For this essay, you are to reflect upon your own educational background and come up with three creative ways that teachers could have helped you learn. For instance, if you struggled with comma use, maybe your teacher could have created games like "pin the comma on the sentence" to help you better understand punctuating sentences with commas. Another example might be having your history teacher include watching short documentaries as part of your homework, so you could "see" the history you were learning about.

Assignment 3: Writing an Essay

Charney writes about ongoing efforts to preserve artifacts in war zones. For this essay, you will either focus on one of these specific programs or a specific person who is involved in one of the programs, and you will then write a profile of the program or the person.

If you choose to research a program, you will want to learn the origin and history of the program, how effective the program has been, and how it chooses and trains its preservationists. A thesis statement for this type of essay could look like this:

The US Immigrations and Customs Enforcement agency takes great pride in the work it has done through its Cultural Property, Art and Antiquities Investigations unit.

OR

The members of the Art Loss Register have worked tirelessly to return stolen art to its original owners.

If you choose to research a person, you will want to learn how the person got involved in the preservation of art, what types of antiquities that person specializes in, and how effective that person has been. A thesis statement for this type of essay could look like this:

> Captain Edith A. Standen was instrumental in the preservation of many works of art during World War II.

RESPONDING TO IMAGES

©Print Collector/Getty Images

Look at the photo of the men trying to salvage a statue of John Milton that was damaged during a London bombing in 1940. What impact does this photo have on you? How might a photo like this affect people's thinking about war?

On Homecomings

Everyone wants some place to retreat, to collapse, to be at home—but you can't always go home again.

Ta-Nehisi Coates

©Shahar Azran/Getty Images

PREVIEW

Ta-Nehisi Coates is an American journalist, author, and comic book writer who is a national correspondent for *The Atlantic*. He has contributed to the *Washington Post* and the *New York Times Magazine* among other publications. He is well known for his social and political writings. In this essay, he explains how his first book, *Between the World and Me*, made his dreams both possible and impossible.

In the summer of 2001, my family and I moved into the Prospect-Lefferts Garden neighborhood in Brooklyn, New York. I was 25. My partner was 24. Our son was 11 months. Prospect-Lefferts Garden is a lovely neighborhood marked by quiet streets and some of the most beautiful architecture in the city. There are several blocks lined with perfectly preserved limestones and brownstones. There is a strong sense of community. Block parties are a tradition. And for those of us who fear the suburbs, Flatbush Avenue hums at the neighborhood's border. When we moved into the neighborhood, it was predominantly black. A haircut was a two-minute walk away. Great jerk chicken was everywhere. My best friend from college lived on the same block. On Friday evenings you could find us out on his stoop with Jack and Coke in hand (which we drank back then), watching the world go by.

I didn't make much money back then. I spent much of my creative energies, in that first year, freelancing for *The Washington Monthly* at 10 cents a word. If I earned $5,000 that year, I would be surprised. Whatever steadiness there was in the house came from my partner, who seemed to not share my uncanny talent for getting fired. In all things, she was a rock and if I have prospered since then, if I have become anything more as a writer and as a man, it is mostly to her credit. Back then, I was certain that it was time to get a real job. No, she would say. You need to write. The upshot of her support is neither vague nor symbolic. One of those articles I freelanced was an attempt to understand the killing of my friend, Prince Jones. Fourteen years later, that article blossomed into *Between the World and Me*.

2 TEACHING TIP
Have students share some examples of what their neighborhoods are like.

My partner—now my wife—loved our old Brooklyn neighborhood. We eventually had to leave after a dispute with our landlord, but we dreamed of moving back. We'd return to visit friends, and gentrification would always be Topic A. Prospect-Lefferts Garden was still black. But most of the young couples moving in were not. We didn't have the money to move in back then, but that didn't stop us from fantasizing. We imagined ourselves as aiding in the preservation of a black presence. But there were more personal reasons, too. We wanted to be closer to our friends in the neighborhood. And I wanted, in some tangible way, to reward my partner's investment in me. I think that had a lot more to do with my insecurities than with her stated desires. We all carry our stories.

Between the World And Me was originally conceived under a different, far worse, title. It was supposed to be a compilation of Civil War essays. It was not supposed to be a big book. Writers don't prepare for people to read them, so much as they prepare for no one to read them. Anonymity, not celebrity, is the usual result of slogging through a book, no matter how great it is. When celebrity came to me—and I must now admit that it has—a world was thrust upon me, one that I had, in so many ways, spent my life angled against.

Everything—good and bad—about *Between the World And Me* shocked the hell out of me. I was shocked that Toni Morrison agreed to blurb the book. I was shocked that Cornel West objected to this. I was shocked at how much my old homes—West Baltimore and Howard University—embraced the book. I was shocked to see bell hooks and Kevin Powell attacking it. I was shocked at how many white people read the book. I was shocked at how the fact of white people reading the book came to exert a kind of gravity. I was shocked that I lost some friends. I was shocked at how the book resonated with black and Arab people in France. One of the great moments of life was being in Paris, sitting in the 108 Café in the 19th, building with the people of the diaspora, and understanding that the old pan-African spirit had not yet died.

I was shocked at the royalties. But as soon as I saw them, I knew what I would do with them. I called my old buddy and asked him if anything was available in that neighborhood, in the Prospect-Lefferts Garden which we loved so much. I was thinking of finally being able to take all of our books out of storage. I was thinking of my mother, who would have a space of her own, and could come and stay for as long as she liked. I was thinking of my partner, who was by then my wife, and how much she had given me and made possible.

My friend found a house on Lincoln Road. He dubbed it "The Dream." He told me my wife would love it. She did. I did. There was, by then, a storm around the book, people asking for crazy things, and offering crazier things, still. We thought we'd found a port in that storm. Unlike Park Slope, Fort Green, or Williamsburg, Prospect-Lefferts Garden had always been low-key. In our early years in New York, we felt like we were in on a secret. 7

But no one keeps secrets in Brooklyn. A few weeks after we bought, another friend sent an item from a local blog gossiping about our possible purchase. We didn't expect to live anonymously. We thought there might be some interest and we took some steps to dissuade that interest. Those steps failed. Last week, the *New York Post*, and several other publications, reported on the purchase. They ran pictures of the house. They named my wife. They photoshopped me in the kitchen. They talked to the seller's broker. The seller's broker told them when we'd be moving in. The seller's broker speculated on our plans for renovation. They rummaged through my kid's Instagram account. They published my home address. 8

Some of my acquaintances went on Facebook and shared these articles. Other people called up my actual friends and joked about the purchase. Very little of this conversation was negative. Much of it was of the congratulatory "Nigga, we made it" variety. But all of it was premised on a kind of obliviousness, an inability to imagine how horrifying it would be to see all the details of your new life out there for the world to see. It is true what they say about celebrity—people suddenly don't quite see you. You walk into a room and you are not a person, so much as symbol of whatever someone needs you to be. 9

But the world is real. And you can't really be a black writer in this country, take certain positions, and not think about your personal safety. That's just the history. And you can't really be a human being and not want some place to retreat into yourself, some place to collapse, some place to be at peace. That's just neurology. One shouldn't get in the habit of crying about having a best-selling book. But you can't really sell enough books to become superhuman, to salve that longing for home. 10

I want you to know that I have been struggling, these past few months, to write about politics. I feel people, all around me, uninterested in questions and enthralled with prophecy. The best part of writing is the constant searching, the twisting, the turning, the back-and-forth, the things you think you understand, the things you understand more than you know. Prophecy has no real use for writing as discovery. And when people want prophets, they will make you into one, no matter your strenuous objections. If the world wants a "Writer Moves to Brooklyn Brownstone" story, it's going to have one, no matter your thoughts. You are their symbol. This is all a very poor excuse for not writing. I find myself stuck in the past, pining for another time, blinded by nostalgia, longing for my old horde, longing for my old home. 11

Within a day of seeing these articles, my wife and I knew that we could never live in Prospect-Lefferts Garden, that we could never go back home. If anything happened to either of us, if anything happened to our son, we'd never forgive ourselves. Even the more likely, more benign, examples were disconcerting— fans showing up at your door (this happened once) or waiting for you on your stoop. Our old neighborhood was not as quiet as we thought. Nothing is quiet anymore—least of all us. 12

READING COMPREHENSION

1. The word *gentrification* in "We'd return to visit friends, and gentrification would always be Topic A" (paragraph 3) means
   a. neighborhood renovations that make a neighborhood much hipper and cooler.
   b. neighborhood renovations that bring in artists and creative business owners.
   c. neighborhood renovations that bring in middle class people and drive out the local, often poorer people.
   d. neighborhood renovations that bring in new businesses and families, and in turn help local families.

2. The word *royalties* in "I was shocked at the royalties" (paragraph 6) means
   a. the wealthy people who lived in the neighborhood.
   b. the famous and successful people who live in the neighborhood.
   c. the rights granted to an individual or corporation.
   d. fees paid to a writer for use of his or her material.

3. The word *prophecy* in "uninterested in questions and enthralled with prophecy" (paragraph 11) means
   a. divinely inspired prediction.
   b. action, function, or faculty of a prophet.
   c. to foretell or predict as if by divine inspiration.
   d. to speak as a mediator between God and humankind.

4. Which of the following would be a good alternative title for this selection?
   a. My First Success
   b. Moving to Brooklyn
   c. Facing New Realities
   d. An Author's Dilemma

5. Which sentence best expresses the main idea of the selection?
   a. Coates's celebrity status was something he had been working for his whole life, so he was thrilled when he finally achieved it.
   b. Coates's unexpected celebrity status changed his life in ways he couldn't have predicted, which had an impact on his family's dreams.
   c. Living in Prospect-Lefferts Garden was a dream for Coates and his family, and they were thrilled when they finally found the perfect home.
   d. Coates and his family decided to move to Prospect-Lefferts Garden because it was an up-and-coming neighborhood.

6. What does the author mean by "blocks lined with perfectly preserved limestones and brownstones"?
   a. older row houses that have been renovated and cared for
   b. different types of old growth trees that provide dappled shade

    c. a type of landscaping in which stones are used for edging

    d. a type of decoration that uses stone columns along the sidewalks

7. What event became the basis of Coates's book *Between the World and Me*?

    a. an incident in Prospect-Lefferts Garden

    (b.) the murder of Prince Jones

    c. a compilation of Civil War essays

    d. his confrontation with Cornel West

8. According to the essay, which of the following people did like his book?

    a. Kevin Powell

    b. bell hooks

    (c.) Arab people in France

    d. black people in Canada

9. According to the essay, which of the following did NOT happen to Coates as he was planning to move to Prospect-Lefferts Garden?

    a. Pictures of his new house were printed in newspapers.

    b. Coates was photoshopped into pictures of the new kitchen.

    c. The address of the new house was published.

    (d.) People combed through his child's Facebook account.

10. We can infer from the essay that Coates

    (a.) was unprepared for the celebrity he acquired.

    b. wishes he had never written a book.

    c. is thankful for his public voice to affect change.

    d. is excited about writing his next book.

STRUCTURE AND TECHNIQUE

1. In his first two paragraphs, Coates presents a lot of numbers. Explain what you believe is his purpose in doing this.

2. Reread paragraph 10. Coates breaks several grammar and essay rules in this paragraph. Discuss why you think he chose to do this. Do you think it is effective, or do you think he should have followed conventions? Explain your reasons.

3. Reread Coates's conclusion. Does it reassert the thesis? Does it follow any of the model conclusions in the text?

CRITICAL READING AND DISCUSSION

1. In paragraph 3, Coates writes "We imagined ourselves as aiding in the preservation of a black presence." What do you think he means by this?

2. In paragraph 4, Coates writes, "Writers don't prepare for people to read them, so much as they prepare for no one to read them." Explain what you believe he means.

TEACHING TIP
Have students work in groups to answer the questions in the "Critical Reading and Discussion" section. Then have the groups present their answers to the class.

3. In paragraph 11, Coates states, "The best part of writing is the constant searching, the twisting, the turning, the back-and-forth, the things you think you understand, the things you understand more than you know." What do you think of his explanation about why he likes to write? Do you feel the same way? Explain your answer.

4. What do you think about what happened to Coates and his family? Do you think the *New York Post* was wrong? How about the seller's broker? What about looking through the social media accounts? What do you think Coates should have done? What would you have done in this situation?

WRITING ASSIGNMENTS

Assignment 1: Writing a Paragraph

Coates ends paragraph 3 by saying, "We all carry our stories." For this assignment, you are to write a paragraph that tells a story you carry, a story that defines you. You might choose to tell a story about a specific scar you have or how you fell in love with your partner or why you quit high school. Remember to use vivid details to help your reader understand the importance of the story.

Assignment 2: Writing an Essay

Ta-Nehisi Coates mentions several famous people, including Toni Morrison, Cornel West, bell hooks, and Kevin Powell. For this essay, you are to choose one of these four people and learn about their lives, their writings and activism, their beliefs, and their impact on society. You will then write a profile of your chosen person.

Because you will need to incorporate quotations, paraphrases, and/or summaries, you will want to read Chapter 20, "Working with Sources," in order to properly incorporate and cite your information.

Assignment 3: Writing an Essay

Invasion of privacy is often in the news, whether it concerns a celebrity whose private life has been made public or personal data that has been stolen or sold. For this essay, you have two choices:

OPTION 1: If you have had experience with your personal information being made public, write an essay about the experience. For instance, if you had a private diary stolen and it was shared either through social media or by students gossiping, explain how the diary was stolen, what happened when the information was shared, and how you handled the invasion of privacy.

OPTION 2: Research the privacy laws in your state and learn about what types of penalties are given for different types of violations. Then write an essay in which you explain to students at your school what the laws are, what the penalties are, and how people can avoid having their private information made public.

Education and Learning

The Professor Is a Dropout

Beth Johnson

©Beth Johnson

PREVIEW

After being mistakenly labeled "retarded" and humiliated into dropping out of first grade, Lupe Quintanilla knew she wanted nothing more to do with formal education. Life as a wife and mother would satisfy her . . . and it did, until she saw her own children being pushed aside as "slow learners." Driven to help them succeed, Lupe took steps that dramatically changed her life.

1   Guadalupe Quintanilla is an assistant professor at the University of Houston. She is president of her own communications company. She trains law enforcement officers all over the country. She was nominated to serve as the U.S. Attorney General. She's been a representative to the United Nations.

2   That's a pretty impressive string of accomplishments. It's all the more impressive when you consider this: "Lupe" Quintanilla is a first-grade dropout. Her school records state that she is retarded, that her IQ is so low she can't learn much of anything.

3   How did Lupe Quintanilla, "retarded" nonlearner, become Dr. Quintanilla, respected educator? Her remarkable journey began in the town of Nogales, Mexico, just below the Arizona border. That's where Lupe first lived with her grandparents. (Her parents had divorced.) Then an uncle who had just finished medical school made her grandparents a generous offer. If they wanted to live with him, he would support the family as he began his medical practice.

4   Lupe, her grandparents, and her uncle all moved hundreds of miles to a town in southern Mexico that didn't even have paved roads, let alone any schools. There, Lupe grew up helping her grandfather run his little pharmacy and her grandmother keep house. She remembers the time happily. "My grandparents were wonderful," she said. "Oh, my grandfather was stern, authoritarian, as Mexican culture demanded, but they were also very kind to me." When the chores were done, her grandfather taught Lupe to read and write Spanish and do basic arithmetic.

5   When Lupe was 12, her grandfather became blind. The family left Mexico and went to Brownsville, Texas, with the hope that doctors there could restore his sight. Once they arrived in Brownsville, Lupe was enrolled in school. Although she understood no English, she was given an IQ test in that language. Not surprisingly, she didn't do very well.

6   Lupe even remembers her score. "I scored a sixty-four, which classified me as seriously retarded, not even teachable," she said. "I was put into first grade with a class of six-year-olds. My duties were to take the little kids to the bathroom and to cut out pictures." The classroom activities were a total mystery to Lupe—they were all conducted in English. And she was humiliated by the other children, who teased her for being "so much older and so much dumber" than they were.

TEACHING TIP
Ask students to speculate how Lupe Quintanilla was able to earn her doctorate and become a respected educator.

After four months in first grade, an incident occurred that Lupe still does 7
not fully understand. As she stood in the doorway of the classroom waiting to
escort a little girl to the bathroom, a man approached her. He asked her, in
Spanish, how to find the principal's office. Lupe was delighted. "Finally someone in this school had spoken to me with words I could understand, in the
language of my soul, the language of my grandmother," she said. Eagerly, she
answered his question in Spanish. Instantly her teacher swooped down on her,
grabbing her arm and scolding her. She pulled Lupe along to the principal's
office. There, the teacher and the principal both shouted at her, obviously very
angry. Lupe was frightened and embarrassed, but also bewildered. She didn't
understand a word they were saying.

"Why were they so angry? I don't know," said Lupe. "Was it because I spoke 8
Spanish at school? Or that I spoke to the man at all? I really don't know. All I
know is how humiliated I was."

When she got home that day, she cried miserably, begging her grandfather 9
not to make her return to school. Finally he agreed.

From that time on, Lupe stayed at home, serving as her blind grand-father's 10
"eyes." She was a fluent reader in Spanish, and the older man loved to have her
read newspapers, poetry, and novels aloud to him for hours.

Lupe's own love of reading flourished during these years. Her vocabulary was 11
enriched and her imagination fired by the novels she read—novels which she
learned later were classics of Spanish literature. She read *Don Quixote*, the famous
story of the noble, impractical knight who fought against windmills. She read
thrilling accounts of the Mexican revolution. She read *La Prensa*, the local Spanish-
language paper, and *Selecciones*, the Spanish-language version of *Reader's Digest*.

When she was just 16, Lupe married a young Mexican-American dental 12
technician. Within five years, she had given birth to her three children, Victor,
Mario, and Martha. Lupe's grandparents lived with the young family. Lupe was
quite happy with her life. "I cooked, sewed, cleaned, and cared for everybody,"
she said. "I listened to my grandmother when she told me what made a good
wife. In the morning I would actually put on my husband's shoes and tie the
laces—anything to make his life easier. Living with my grandparents for so long,
I was one generation behind in my ideas of what a woman could do and be."

Lupe's contentment ended when her children started school. When they 13
brought home their report cards, she struggled to understand them. She could
read enough English to know that what they said was not good. Her children
had been put into a group called "Yellow Birds." It was a group for slow learners.

At night in bed, Lupe cried and blamed herself. It was obvious—not only 14
was she retarded, but her children had taken after her. Now they, too, would
never be able to learn like other children.

But in time, a thought began to break through Lupe's despair: Her children 15
didn't seem like slow learners to her. At home, they learned everything she taught
them, quickly and easily. She read to them constantly, from the books that she
herself had loved as a child. *Aesop's Fables* and stories from *1,001 Arabian Nights*
were family favorites. The children filled the house with the sounds of the songs,
prayers, games, and rhymes they had learned from their parents and grandparents. They were smart children, eager to learn. They learned quickly—in Spanish.

A radical idea began to form in Lupe's mind. Maybe the school was wrong 16
about her children. And if the school system could be wrong about her children—
maybe it had been wrong about her, too.

Lupe visited her children's school, a daring action for her. "Many Hispanic 17 parents would not dream of going to the classroom," she said. "In Hispanic culture, the teacher is regarded as a third parent, as an ultimate authority. To question her would seem most disrespectful, as though you were saying that she didn't know her job." That was one reason Lupe's grandparents had not interfered when Lupe was classified as retarded. "Anglo teachers often misunderstand Hispanic parents, believing that they aren't concerned about their children's education because they don't come visit the schools," Lupe said. "It's not a lack of concern at all. It's a mark of respect for the teacher's authority."

At her children's school. Lupe spoke to three different teachers. Two of them 18 told her the same thing: "Your children are just slow. Sorry, but they can't learn." A third offered a glimmer of hope. He said, "They don't know how to function in English. It's possible that if you spoke English at home they would be able to do better."

Lupe pounced on that idea. "Where can I learn English?" she asked. The 19 teacher shrugged. At that time there were no local English-language programs for adults. Finally he suggested that Lupe visit the local high school. Maybe she would be permitted to sit in the back of a classroom and pick up some English that way.

Lupe made an appointment with a counselor at the high school. But when 20 the two women met, the counselor shook her head. "Your test scores show that you are retarded," she told Lupe. "You'd just be taking space in the classroom away from someone who could learn."

Lupe's next stop was the hospital where she had served for years as a vol- 21 unteer. Could she sit in on some of the nursing classes held there? No, she was told, not without a diploma. Still undeterred, she went on to Texas Southmost College in Brownsville. Could she sit in on a class? No; no high-school diploma. Finally she went to the telephone company, where she knew operators were being trained. Could she listen in on the classes? No, only high-school graduates were permitted.

That day, leaving the telephone company. Lupe felt she had hit bottom. She 22 had been terrified in the first place to try to find an English class. Meeting with rejection after rejection nearly destroyed what little self-confidence she had. She walked home in the rain, crying. "I felt like a big barrier had fallen across my path," she said. "I couldn't go over it; I couldn't go under it; I couldn't go around it."

But the next day Lupe woke with fresh determination. "I was motivated by 23 love of my kids," she said. "I was not going to quit." She got up; made breakfast for her kids, husband, and grandparents; saw her children and husband off for the day; and started out again. "I remember walking to the bus stop, past a dog that always scared me to death, and heading back to the college. The lady I spoke to said, 'I told you, we can't do anything for you without a high-school degree.' But as I left the building, I went up to the first Spanish-speaking student I saw. His name was Gabito. I said, 'Who really makes the decisions around here?' He said, 'The registrar.'" Since she hadn't had any luck in the office building, Lupe decided to take a more direct approach. She asked Gabito to point out the registrar's car in the parking lot. For the next two hours she waited beside it until its owner showed up.

Impressed by Lupe's persistence, the registrar listened to her story. But 24 instead of giving her permission to sit in on a class and learn more English, he insisted that she sign up for a full college load. Before she knew it, she was enrolled in four classes: basic math, basic English, psychology, and typing. The registrar's parting words to her were, "Don't come back if you don't make it through."

With that "encouragement," Lupe began a semester that was part nightmare, part dream come true. Every day she got her husband and children off to school, took the bus to campus, came home to make lunch for her husband and grandparents, went back to campus, and was home in time to greet Victor, Mario, and Martha when they got home from school. In the evenings she cooked, cleaned, did laundry, and got the children to bed. Then she would study, often until three in the morning.   25

"Sometimes in class I would feel sick with the stress of it," she said. "I'd go to the bathroom and talk to myself in the mirror. Sometimes I'd say, 'What are you doing here? Why don't you go home and watch *I Love Lucy?*"   26

But she didn't go home. Instead, she studied furiously, using her Spanish-English dictionary, constantly making lists of new words she wanted to understand. "I still do that today," she said. "When I come across a word I don't know, I write it down, look it up, and write sentences using it until I own that word."   27

Although so much of the language and subject matter was new to Lupe, one part of the college experience was not. That was the key skill of reading, a skill Lupe possessed. As she struggled with English, she found the reading speed, comprehension, and vocabulary that she had developed in Spanish carrying over into her new language. "Reading," she said, "reading was the vehicle. Although I didn't know it at the time, when I was a girl learning to love to read, I was laying the foundation for academic success."   28

She gives credit, too, to her Hispanic fellow students. "At first, they didn't know what to make of me. They were eighteen years old, and at that time it was very unfashionable for an older person to be in college. But once they decided I wasn't a 'plant' from the administration, they were my greatest help." The younger students spent hours helping Lupe, explaining unfamiliar words and terms, coaching her, and answering her questions.   29

That first semester passed in a fog of exhaustion. Many mornings, Lupe doubted she could get out of bed, much less care for her family and tackle her classes. But when she thought of her children and what was at stake for them, she forced herself on. She remembers well what those days were like. "Just a day at a time. That was all I could think about. I could make myself get up one more day, study one more day, cook and clean one more day. And those days eventually turned into a semester."   30

To her own amazement perhaps as much as anyone's, Lupe discovered that she was far from retarded. Although she sweated blood over many assignments, she completed them. She turned them in on time. And, remarkably, she made the dean's list her very first semester.   31

After that, there was no stopping Lupe Quintanilla. She soon realized that the associate's degree offered by Texas Southmost College would not satisfy her. Continuing her Monday, Wednesday, and Friday schedule at Southmost, she enrolled for Tuesday and Thursday courses at Pan American University, a school 140 miles from Brownsville. Within three years, she had earned both her junior college degree and a bachelor's degree in biology. She then won a fellowship that took her to graduate school at the University of Houston, where she earned   32 a master's degree in Spanish literature. When she graduated, the university offered her a job as director of the Mexican-American studies program. While in that position, she earned a doctoral degree in education.

How did she do it all? Lupe herself isn't sure. "I hardly know. When I think 33 back to those years, it seems like a life that someone else lived." It was a rich and exciting but also very challenging period for Lupe and her family. On the one hand, Lupe was motivated by the desire to set an example for her children, to prove to them that they could succeed in the English-speaking academic world. On the other hand, she worried about neglecting her family. She tried hard to attend important activities, such as parents' meetings at school and her children's sporting events. But things didn't always work out. Lupe still remembers attending a baseball game that her older son, Victor, was playing in. When Victor came to bat, he hit a home run. But as the crowd cheered and Victor glanced proudly over at his mother in the stands, he saw she was studying a textbook. "I hadn't seen the home run," Lupe admitted. "That sort of thing was hard for everyone to take."

Although Lupe worried that her children would resent her busy schedule, 34 she also saw her success reflected in them as they blossomed in school. She forced herself to speak English at home, and their language skills improved quickly. She read to them in English instead of Spanish—gulping down her pride as their pronunciation became better than hers and they began correcting her. (Once the children were in high school and fluent in English, Lupe switched back to Spanish at home, so that the children would be fully comfortable in both languages.) "I saw the change in them almost immediately," she said. "After I helped them with their homework, they would see me pulling out my own books and going to work. In the morning, I would show them the papers I had written. As I gained confidence, so did they." By the next year, the children had been promoted out of the Yellow Birds.

Even though Victor, Mario, and Martha all did well academically, Lupe 35 realized she could not assume that they would face no more obstacles in school. When Mario was in high school, for instance, he wanted to sign up for a debate class. Instead, he was assigned to woodworking. She visited the school to ask why. Mario's teacher told her, "He's good with his hands. He'll be a great carpenter, and that's a good thing for a Mexican to be." Controlling her temper, Lupe responded, "I'm glad you think he's good with his hands. He'll be a great physician someday, and he is going to be in the debate class."

Today, Lupe Quintanilla teaches at the University of Houston, where she 36 has developed several dozen courses concerning Hispanic literature and culture. Her cross-cultural training for law enforcement officers, which helps bring police and firefighters and local Hispanic communities closer together, is renowned throughout the country. Former President Ronald Reagan named her to a national board that keeps the White House informed of new programs in law enforcement. She has received numerous awards for teaching excellence, and there is even a scholarship named in her honor. Her name appears in the Hispanic Hall of Fame, and she has been co-chair of the White House Commission on Hispanic Education.

The love of reading that her grandfather instilled in Lupe is still alive. She 37 thinks of him every year when she introduces to her students one of his favorite poets, Amado Nervo. She requires them to memorize these lines from one of Nervo's poems: "When I got to the end of my long journey in life, I realized that I was the architect of my own destiny." Of these lines, Lupe says, "That is something that I deeply believe, and I want my students to learn it before the end of their long journey. We create our own destiny."

Her love of reading and learning has helped Lupe create a distinguished 38 destiny. But none of the honors she has received means more to her than the success of her own children, the reason she made that frightening journey to seek classes in English years ago. Today Mario is a physician. Victor and Martha are lawyers, both having earned doctor of law degrees. And so today, Lupe likes to say, "When someone calls the house and asks for 'Dr. Quintanilla,' I have to ask, 'Which one?' There are four of us—one retarded and three slow learners."

READING COMPREHENSION

1. The word *flourished* in "Lupe's own love of reading flourished during these years. Her vocabulary was enriched and her imagination fired by the novels she read" (paragraph 11) means
   a. grew. *(circled)*
   b. stood still.
   c. was lost.
   d. remained.

2. The word *instilled* in "The love of reading that her grandfather instilled in Lupe is still alive" (paragraph 37) means
   a. frightened.
   b. established. *(circled)*
   c. forced.
   d. forgot.

3. Which of the following would be a good alternative title for this selection?
   a. Difficulties Facing Spanish-Speaking Students
   b. Unfair Labeling
   c. Balancing School and Family
   d. A Courageous Mother's Triumph *(circled)*

4. Which sentence best expresses the main idea of the selection?
   a. Lupe, a first-grade dropout, eventually earned a doctoral degree and created a professional career.
   b. Lupe Quintanilla's experience proves that the educational system must be set up to accommodate non-English-speaking children.
   c. Through hard work and persistence combined with a love of reading and learning, Lupe has created a distinguished career and helped her children become professionals. *(circled)*
   d. In school, Spanish-speaking students may experience obstacles as they aim for professional careers.

5. Lupe realized that her children were not retarded when
   a. they got good grades at school.
   b. she saw how quickly they learned at home. *(circled)*

c. they were put in the group called "Yellow Birds."

d. they read newspapers, poetry, and novels to her.

6. Lupe's training for law enforcement officers

   a. teaches them to speak Spanish.

   b. teaches Hispanic literature and culture.

   c. offers a scholarship named in her honor.

   (d.) brings police, firefighters, and local Hispanic communities together.

7. According to Lupe, Hispanic parents rarely visit their children's schools because they

   a. do not consider schoolwork important.

   (b.) think doing so would be disrespectful to the teacher.

   c. are ashamed of their English language skills.

   d. are usually working during school visitation hours.

8. "Once they arrived in Brownsville, Lupe was enrolled in school. Although she understood no English, she was given an IQ test in that language. Not surprisingly, she didn't do very well" (paragraph 5). From these sentences, we might conclude that

   (a.) an IQ test in a language that the person tested doesn't know is useless.

   b. although Lupe was not very intelligent at first, she became more intelligent once she learned English.

   c. Lupe really did know English.

   d. there are no IQ tests in Spanish.

9. We might conclude from the reading that

   a. a school system's judgment about an individual is always accurate.

   b. it is often better for a child to stay home rather than attend school.

   (c.) by paying attention and speaking up, parents may remove obstacles to their children's education.

   d. working parents should accept the fact that they cannot attend important events in their children's lives.

10. The last line of the reading suggests that

   a. retarded people can become successful professionals.

   (b.) people should not blindly accept other people's opinions of them.

   c. Lupe's children are smarter than she is.

   d. all of the above.

STRUCTURE AND TECHNIQUE

1. Johnson begins the essay by listing Lupe Quintanilla's accomplishments, then revealing that Quintanilla was once classified as retarded. What introductory technique is Johnson employing? Why is it effective here?

2. Paragraphs 3–11 are devoted to the first fifteen years of Lupe's life. But the next decade or so is covered in only two paragraphs (12–13). Why

might Johnson have presented Lupe's earlier life in so much more detail? Do you agree with her decision?

3. In paragraph 2, Johnson writes that "[Lupe's] school records state that she is retarded. . . ." But in the next sentence, she writes, "How did Lupe Quintanilla, 'retarded' nonlearner, become Dr. Quintanilla, respected educator?" Why does Johnson put the word "retarded" in quotation marks in the second sentence, but not in the first? What is she implying? Can you find another place where Johnson makes similar use of quotation marks?

4. At one point, Johnson switches from the topic of Lupe's success in college to the topic of the challenges that continued to face her children in school. In what paragraph does she make that switch? What transitional words does she use to alert the reader to her new direction?

CRITICAL READING AND DISCUSSION

1. In the course of the essay, what characteristics and attitudes does Lupe suggest are typical of Hispanic culture? Does she seem sympathetic, critical, or neutral about those qualities or attitudes? How has she dealt with cultural expectations in her own life?

2. How has Lupe handled the question of what language to use with her children? If you grew up in a two-language household, how did your family deal with the issue? How would you approach the issue with children of your own?

3. Do you think Lupe's grandfather was right in allowing her to quit school? What factors do you imagine might have gone into his decision?

4. Lupe credits her fellow Hispanic students with giving her valuable support in college. Is there anyone in your life—a teacher, family member, or friend—who has helped you through challenging times in your education? Explain what obstacles you faced and how this person helped you overcome them.

WRITING ASSIGNMENTS

Assignment 1: Writing a Paragraph

Write a paragraph that takes as its topic sentence one of the following statements:

Schools need to be prepared to help non-English-speaking students catch up with other students at their grade level.

The responsibility for catching non-English-speaking students up to their grade level rests solely with the students and their families.

Support your topic sentence with several points.

Assignment 2: Writing an Essay

Lupe Quintanilla is an outstanding example of someone who has taken charge of her life. She has been, to echo the poet whose work she teaches, the architect of her own destiny. Choose a person you know who, in your opinion, has done a fine job of taking charge of his or her own destiny. Write an essay about this person. You might describe three areas of life in which the person has taken control. Alternatively, you might narrate three incidents from the person's life that illustrate his or her admirable self-determination.

Assignment 3: Writing an Essay

Lupe had to struggle in order to balance her school responsibilities with her roles as a wife and mother. Write an essay in which you identify aspects of your life that you need to juggle along with your responsibilities as a student. They may include a job, a spouse or significant other, children, household chores, pets, extracurricular activities, a difficult living situation, or anything else that poses a challenge to your academics. Provide vivid, real-life illustrations of how each of those responsibilities sometimes conflicts with your studies.

How to Make It in College, Now That You're Here

Brian O'Keeney

PREVIEW

The author of this selection presents a compact guide to being a successful student. He will show you how to pass tests, how to avoid becoming a student zombie, how to find time to fit in everything you want to do, and how to deal with personal problems while keeping up with your studies. These and other helpful tips have been culled from the author's own experience and his candid interviews with fellow students.

Today is your first day on campus. You were a high school senior three months 1 ago. Or maybe you've been at home with your children for the last ten years. Or maybe you work full time and you're coming to school to start the process that leads to a better job. Whatever your background is, you're probably not too concerned today with staying in college. After all, you just got over the hurdle (and the paperwork) of applying to this place and organizing your life so that you could attend. And today, you're confused and tired. Everything is a hassle, from finding the classrooms to standing in line at the bookstore. But read my advice anyway. And if you don't read it today, clip and save this article. You might want to look at it a little further down the road.

By the way, if this isn't your very first day, don't skip this article. Maybe 2 you haven't been doing as well in your studies as you'd hoped. Or perhaps you've had problems juggling your work schedule, your class schedule, and your social life. If so, read on. You're about to get the inside story on making it in college. On the basis of my own experience as a final-year student, and after dozens of interviews with successful students, I've worked out a no-fail system for coping with college. These are the inside tips every student needs to do well in school. I've put myself in your place, and I'm going to answer the questions that will cross (or have already crossed) your mind during your stay here.

What's the Secret to Getting Good Grades?

It all comes down to getting those grades, doesn't it? After all, you came here 3
for some reason, and you're going to need passing grades to get the credits or
degree you want. Many of us never did much studying in high school; most
of the learning we did took place in the classroom. College, however, is a lot
different. You're really on your own when it comes to passing courses. In fact,
sometimes you'll feel as if nobody cares if you make it or not. Therefore, you've
got to figure out a study system that gets results. Sooner or later, you'll be
alone with those books. After that, you'll be sitting in a classroom with an
exam sheet on your desk. Whether you stare at that exam with a queasy stomach or whip through it fairly confidently depends on your study techniques.
Most of the successful students I talked to agreed that the following eight
study tips deliver solid results.

1. Set Up a Study Place. Those students you see "studying" in the cafeteria 4
or game room aren't learning much. You just can't learn when you're dis-
tracted by people and noise. Even the library can be a bad place to study if
you constantly find yourself watching the clouds outside or the students walking through the stacks. It takes guts to sit, alone, in a quiet place in order to
study. But you have to do it. Find a room at home or a spot in the library
that's relatively quiet—and boring. When you sit there, you won't have much
to do except study.

2. Get into a Study Frame of Mind. When you sit down, do it with the attitude 5
that you're going to get this studying done. You're not going to doodle in your
notebook or make a list for the supermarket. Decide that you are going to
study and learn *now*, so that you can move on to more interesting things as
soon as possible.

3. Give Yourself Rewards. If you sweat out a block of study time, and do 6
a good job on it, treat yourself. You deserve it. You can "psych" yourself up
for studying by promising to reward yourself afterward. A present for yourself
can be any thing from a favorite TV show to a relaxing bath to a dish of
double chocolate ice cream.

4. Skim the Textbook First. Lots of students sit down with an assignment 7
like "Read chapter five, pages 125–150" and do just that. They turn to page
125 and start to read. After a while, they find that they have no idea what
they just read. For the last ten minutes, they've been thinking about their five-
year-old or what they're going to eat for dinner. Eventually, they plod through
all the pages but don't remember much afterward.

In order to prevent this problem, skim the textbook chapter first. This 8
means: look at the title, the subtitles, the headings, the pictures, the first and
last paragraphs. Try to find out what the person who wrote the book had in
mind when he or she organized the chapter. What was important enough to
set off as a title or in bold type? After skimming, you should be able to explain
to yourself what the main points of the chapter are. Unless you're the kind of
person who would step into an empty elevator shaft without looking first,
you'll soon discover the value of skimming.

5.   Take Notes on What You're Studying. This sounds like a hassle, but it 9
works. Go back over the material after you've read it, and jot down keywords
and phrases in the margins. When you review the chapter for a test, you'll
have handy little things like "definition of rationalization" or "example of
assimilation" in the margins. If the material is especially tough, organize a separate sheet of notes. Write down definitions, examples, lists, and main ideas.
The idea is to have a single sheet that boils the entire chapter down to a
digestible lump.

6.   Review After You've Read and Taken Notes. Some people swear that talking 10
to yourself works. Tell yourself about the most important points in the chapter.
Once you've said them out loud, they seem to stick better in your mind. If
you can't talk to yourself about the material after reading it, that's a sure sign
you don't really know it.

7.   Give Up. This may sound contradictory, but give up when you've had 11
enough. You should try to make it through at least an hour, though. Ten
minutes here and there are useless. When your head starts to pound and your
eyes develop spidery red lines, quit. You won't do much learning when you're
exhausted.

8.   Take a College Skills Course if You Need It. Don't hesitate or feel embar- 12
rassed about enrolling in a study skills course. Many students say they wouldn't
have made it without one.

How Can I Keep Up with All My Responsibilities Without Going Crazy?

You've got a class schedule. You're supposed to study. You've got a family. 13
You've got a husband, wife, boyfriend, girlfriend, child. You've got a job. How
are you possibly going to cover all the bases in your life and maintain your
sanity? This is one of the toughest problems students face. Even if they start
the semester with the best of intentions, they eventually find themselves tearing their hair out trying to do everything they're supposed to do. Believe it or
not, though, it is possible to meet all your responsibilities. And you don't have
to turn into a hermit or give up your loved ones to do it.

The secret here is to organize your time. But don't just sit around half the 14
semester planning to get everything together soon. Before you know it, you'll be
confronted with midterms, papers, family, and work all at once. Don't let yourself reach that breaking point. Instead, try these three tactics:

1.   Monthly Calendar. Get one of those calendars with big blocks around the 15
dates. Give yourself an overview of the whole term by marking down the due
dates for papers and projects. Circle test and exam days. This way those days
don't sneak up on you unexpectedly.

2.   Study Schedule. Sit down during the first few days of this semester and 16
make up a sheet listing the days and hours of the week. Fill in your work and
class hours first. Then try to block out some study hours. It's better to study
a little every day than to create a huge once-or-twice-a-week marathon session.
Schedule study hours for your hardest classes for the times when you feel most
energetic. For example, I battled my tax law textbook in the mornings; when

I looked at it after 7:00 p.m., I might as well have been reading Chinese. The usual proportion, by the way, is one hour of study time for every class hour.

In case you're one of those people who get carried away, remember to leave blocks of free time, too. You won't be any good to yourself or anyone else if you don't relax and pack in the studying once in a while. 17

3. "To Do" List. This is the secret that, more than any other, got me through college. Once a week (or every day if you want to), write a list of what you have to do. Write down everything from "write English paper" to "buy cold cuts for lunch." The best thing about a "to do" list is that it seems to tame all those stray "I have to" thoughts that nag at your mind. Just making the list seems to make the tasks "doable." After you finish something on the list, cross it off. Don't be compulsive about finishing everything; you're not Superman or Wonder Woman. Get the important things done first. The secondary things you don't finish can simply be moved to your next "to do" list. 18

What Can I Do If Personal Problems Get in the Way of My Studies?

One student, Roger, told me this story:

> Everything was going OK for me until the middle of the spring semester. I went through a terrible time when I broke up with my girlfriend and started seeing her best friend. I was trying to deal with my ex-girlfriend's hurt and anger, my new girlfriend's guilt, and my own worries and anxieties at the same time. In addition to this, my mother was sick and on a medication that made her really irritable. I hated to go home because the atmosphere was so uncomfortable. Soon, I started missing classes because I couldn't deal with the academic pressures as well as my own personal problems. It seemed easier to hang around my girlfriend's apartment than to face all my problems at home and at school. 19

Another student, Marian, told me;

> I'd been married for eight years and the relationship wasn't going too well. I saw the handwriting on the wall, and I decided to prepare for the future. I enrolled in college, because I knew I'd need a decent job to support myself. Well, my husband had a fit because I was going to school. We were arguing a lot anyway, and he made it almost impossible for me to study at home. I think he was angry and almost jealous because I was drawing away from him. It got so bad that I thought about quitting college for a while. I wasn't getting any support at home, and it was just too hard to go on. 20

Personal troubles like these are overwhelming when you're going through them. School seems like the least important thing in your life. The two students above are perfect examples of this. But if you think about it, quitting or failing school would be the worst thing for these two students. Roger's problems, at least with his girlfriends, would simmer down eventually, and then he'd regret having left school. Marian had to finish college if she wanted to be able to live independently. Sometimes, you've just got to hang tough. 21

But what do you do while you're trying to live through a lousy time? First 22 of all, do something difficult. Ask yourself, honestly, if you're exaggerating small problems as an excuse to avoid classes and studying. It takes strength to admit this, but there's no sense in kidding yourself. If your problems are serious, and real, try to make some human contacts at school. Lots of students hide inside a miserable shell made of their own troubles and feel isolated and lonely. Believe me, there are plenty of students with problems. Not everyone is getting A's and having a fabulous social and home life at the same time. As you go through the term, you'll pick up some vibrations about the students in your classes. Perhaps someone strikes you as a compatible person. Why not speak to that person after class? Share a cup of coffee in the cafeteria or walk to the parking lot together. You're not looking for a best friend or the love of your life. You just want to build a little network of support for yourself. Sharing your difficulties, questions, and complaints with a friendly person on campus can make a world of difference in how you feel.

Finally, if your problems are overwhelming, get some professional help. Why 23 do you think colleges spend countless dollars on counseling departments and campus psychiatric services? More than ever, students all over the country are taking advantage of the help offered by support groups and therapy sessions. There's no shame attached to asking for help, either; in fact, almost 40 percent of college students (according to one survey) will use counseling services during their time in school. Just walk into a student center or counseling office and ask for an appointment. You wouldn't think twice about asking a dentist to help you get rid of your toothache. Counselors are paid—and want—to help you with your problems.

Why Do Some People Make It and Some Drop Out?

Anyone who spends at least one semester in college notices that some students 24 give up on their classes. The person who sits behind you in accounting, for example, begins to miss a lot of class meetings and eventually vanishes. Or another student comes to class without the assignment, doodles in a notebook during the lecture, and leaves during the break. What's the difference between students like this and the ones who succeed in school? My survey may be nonscientific, but everyone I asked said the same thing: attitude. A positive attitude is the key to everything else—good study habits, smart time scheduling, and coping with personal difficulties.

What does "a positive attitude" mean? Well, for one thing, it means avoiding 25 the zombie syndrome. It means not only showing up for your classes, but also doing something while you're there. Really listen. Take notes. Ask a question if you want to. Don't just walk into a class, put your mind in neutral, and drift away to never-never land.

Having a positive attitude goes deeper than this, though. It means being 26 mature about college as an institution. Too many students approach college classes like six-year-olds who expect first grade to be as much fun as *Sesame Street*. First grade, as we all know, isn't as much fun as *Sesame Street*. And college classes can sometimes be downright dull. If you let a boring class discourage you so much that you want to leave school, you'll lose in the long run. Look at your priorities. You want a degree, or a certificate, or a career. If you have to, you can make it through a less-than-interesting class in order to achieve

TEACHING TIP
Encourage students to do
a scratch outline of
O'Keeney's essay.

what you want. Get whatever you can out of every class. But if you simply can't stand a certain class, be determined to fulfill its requirements and be done with it once and for all.

After the initial high of starting school, you have to settle in for the long 27 haul. If you follow the advice here, you'll be prepared to face the academic crunch. You'll also live through the semester without giving up your family, your job, or *Monday Night Football*. Finally, going to college can be an exciting time. You do learn. And when you learn things, the world becomes a more interesting place.

READING COMPREHENSION

1. The word *queasy* in "with a queasy stomach" (paragraph 3) means
    a. strong.
    b. healthy.
    c. full.
    d. nervous.

2. The word *tactics* in "try these three tactics" (paragraph 14) means
    a. proofs.
    b. problems.
    c. methods.
    d. questions.

3. Which of the following would be a good alternative title for this selection?
    a. Your First Day on Campus
    b. Coping with College
    c. How to Budget Your Time
    d. The Benefits of College Skills Courses

4. Which sentence expresses the main idea of the selection?
    a. In high school, most of us did little homework.
    b. You should give yourself rewards for studying well.
    c. Sometimes personal problems interfere with studying.
    d. You can succeed in college by following certain guidelines.

5. According to the author, "making it" in college means
    a. studying whenever you have any free time.
    b. getting a degree by barely passing your courses.
    c. quitting school until you solve your personal problems.
    d. getting good grades without making your life miserable.

6. If your personal problems seem overwhelming, you should
    a. drop out for a while.
    b. exaggerate them to teachers.
    c. avoid talking about them.
    d. get help from a professional.

7. Which of the following is NOT described by the author as a means of time control?

    a. monthly calendar

    b. to-do list

    c. study schedule

    (d.) flexible job hours

8. We can infer that the writer of this essay

    (a.) cares about college students and their success.

    b. dropped out of college.

    c. is very disorganized.

    d. is an A student.

9. From the selection we can conclude that

    a. college textbooks are very expensive.

    (b.) it is a good practice to write notes in your textbook.

    c. taking notes on your reading takes too much time.

    d. a student should never mark up an expensive book.

10. The author implies that

    a. fewer people than before are attending college.

    b. most college students experience no problems during their first year.

    c. all college students experience overwhelming problems.

    (d.) coping with college is difficult.

STRUCTURE AND TECHNIQUE

1. O'Keeney uses a highly structured format in his essay. What are some of the features of this format? Why do you think O'Keeney structured his essay in this way?

2. Does the author clearly state his thesis? If so, where is it stated, and how?

3. What method of introduction does the author use in the section on personal problems (starting with paragraph 19)? What is the value of using this method?

4. Throughout his essay, O'Keeney addresses his audience in the second person—using the word *you*. How does such a technique advance his main point?

TEACHING TIP
As students discuss this question, remind them that second-person point of view should be used in very limited situations, and ask them to focus on why this particular situation is appropriate.

CRITICAL READING AND DISCUSSION

1. What, according to O'Keeney, is the secret of getting good grades? Have you used any of O'Keeney's study methods? If so, how useful do you think they have been for you? Are there any that you haven't used, but might try? Explain your answer.

2. What does O'Keeney recommend students do in order to manage their time and responsibilities more effectively? Which of these suggestions are you most likely to use? Which are you least likely to use? Why?

3. What is the secret the author says got him through college? What do you think is the most helpful or important suggestion the author makes in the selection? Give reasons for your choice.

4. Do you agree with the author that Roger and Marian should stay in school? Are there any situations in which it would be better for students to quit school or leave, at least temporarily? Explain, giving examples to support your answer.

RESPONDING TO IMAGES

What tips from O'Keeney's essay might the student in this photograph find beneficial?

©John Lund/Getty Images

WRITING ASSIGNMENTS

Assignment 1: Writing a Paragraph

Write a paragraph contrasting college *as you thought it would be* with college *as it is.* You can organize the paragraph by focusing on three specific things that are different from what you expected, or you can cover three general areas of difference. For instance, you may decide to contrast your expectations about (1) a college dorm room, (2) your roommate, and (3) dining-hall food with reality. Or you could contrast your expectations about (1) fellow students, (2) college professors, and (3) college courses with reality.

Refer to the section in Chapter 11 on methods of developing comparison and contrast paragraphs to review point-by-point and one-side-at-a-time development. Be sure to make an outline of your paragraph before you begin to write.

Assignment 2: Writing an Essay

Write a letter to Roger or Marian, giving advice on how to deal with the personal problem mentioned in the article. You could recommend any or all of the following:

Face the problem realistically. (By doing what?)

Make other contacts at school. (How? Where?)

See a counselor. (Where? What should this person be told?)

Realize that the problem is not so serious. (Why not?)

Ignore the problem. (How? By doing what instead?)

In your introductory paragraph, explain why you are writing the letter. Include a thesis statement that says what plan of action you are recommending. Then, in the rest of the letter, explain the plan of action in detail.

Assignment 3: Writing an Essay

Write an essay similar to the one you've just read that explains how to succeed in some other area of life—for example, a job, a sport, marriage, child rearing. First, brainstorm three or four problem areas a newcomer to this experience might encounter. Then, under each area you have listed, jot down some helpful hints and techniques for overcoming these problems. For example, a process paper on "How to Succeed As a Restaurant Server" might describe the following problem areas in this kind of job:

Developing a good memory

Learning to do tasks quickly

Coping with troublesome customers

Each supporting paragraph in this paper would discuss specific techniques for dealing with these problems. Be sure that the advice you give is detailed and specific enough to really help a person in such a situation.

You may find it helpful to look over the essay that emphasizes process in Chapter 18.

L.A. Targets Full-Time Community College Students for Free Tuition

Anna M. Phillips

PREVIEW

Anna M. Phillips is a journalist who has worked for the *Tampa Bay Times*, the *New York Times*, and the *Los Angeles Times*. A graduate of Columbia University, Phillips focuses much of her writing on educational topics. This article examines a program that Los Angeles implemented to help college students.

TEACHING TIP
Ask students to discuss
the financial responsibilities
they have while in college
and what type of program
would really help them get
through college.

At 19, Maria Medrano of Echo Park is already halfway to earning her associate's degree at Los Angeles City College. 1

Her sister, who is three years older, works during the day to support their family and takes classes at night. So even though she started community college earlier than her little sister, she'll end up graduating later. 2

"If I had to work, I wouldn't be as focused as I am right now," Medrano said as she sat hunched over an unfinished essay in LACC's student union. "I'd be struggling, as I'm seeing my sister struggle." 3

At Los Angeles' nine community colleges, Medrano's sister's experience is the norm. Many students are burdened by rent payments, textbook costs, and average tuition fees of $1,300 a year, and 73% go to school part time. Research shows that they are less likely than their fulltime peers to complete a degree or transfer to a four-year college. 4

That's one reason for a new plan promoted by Mayor Eric Garcetti to offer graduating high school students one year of free community college. 5

L.A. College Promise, first proposed during Garcetti's State of the City address last spring, applies only to graduates of L.A. Unified high schools. And only fulltime students who maintain a 2.0 grade point average can receive the aid. 6

The hope is to persuade students to quit their day jobs and focus on college. 7

"A lot of our students work and go to school and so we're hoping that some of them will decide to go full time because of the extra help," said Scott Svonkin, president of the board of the Los Angeles Community College District. "We're taking one barrier, one burden, away. And we know if they go full time, students succeed in astronomically higher numbers." 8

A financial aid program run by the California Community Colleges Board of Governors already allows most graduates of L.A. public schools to attend local community colleges for free. About 69% of these students have all of their tuition fees waived, according to a district official. Other qualifying students receive assistance for tuition and textbooks from the Cal Grant program, the largest source of state-funded college aid. 9

The mayor's plan—which is expected to cost $3 million the first year—targets an estimated 2,100 students who will graduate from L.A. high schools in 2017 and whose families' earnings probably will be too high to qualify them for a Board of Governors tuition waiver. Though families in this situation may make too much money to be eligible, they often still make too little to support their children through college. 10

L.A. College Promise resembles President Obama's proposal in his 2015 State of the Union address to offer two free years of community college to all U.S. students. It also includes proposals to help students fill out financial aid applications, which can be dauntingly complex, and to give them priority when registering for classes to ensure they aren't locked out of the courses they need to graduate. Extending the tuition benefits to two years is the ultimate goal, Svonkin said. 11

"When I look at the underlying thinking, I'm fairly encouraged," said Thomas Bailey, a professor of economics and education at Teachers College at Columbia University and director of its Community College Research Center. "The kind of reforms that surround L.A.'s plan, reforms that deal with the problems students face, those are as important or probably more important than the tuition assistance itself." 12

The Promise proposal could lead to an increase in enrollment at community 13 colleges, Bailey said. In states that have offered similar assistance, students who previously did not think they could afford college applied. Some discovered only then that they would have qualified for financial aid anyway.

To pay for the program, the Mayor's Fund for Los Angeles has raised 14 $1.8 million, said Garcetti spokeswoman Connie Llanos, including an $800,000 donation from the Karsh Family Foundation, $400,000 from the Broad Foundation and a $200,000 contribution from the L.A. Dodgers. The rest of the money is expected to come from the community college district, which so far has raised $30,000.

"We're going to solicit from every company in Los Angeles that has their 15 name on a building downtown," Svonkin said. "If they can afford to put their name on a building, they can afford to donate to this."

Convincing students to attend community college full time, however, may 16 take more than offering one free year.

Even with a tuition waiver, Medrano said she relies on her parents to help 17 her pay for textbooks, which can cost her as much as $500 a semester.

Full-time student Katherine Castillo, 18, can rattle off a list of her expenses 18 that aren't entirely covered by her Cal Grant, which pays for most of her tuition. There's the $200 a month toward an apartment in Koreatown that she shares with her mother, not to mention the textbooks, school supplies, and daily transportation to and from the City College campus.

Castillo has a discounted Metro TAP card offered to college and voca- 19 tional students, and several campus programs distribute vouchers for books— but so far no one has volunteered to buy her groceries or write a check to her landlord.

"I need to help my mom out and I need to pay for my own personal needs 20 like clothing, food, etc.," she said. "So the initiative is going to be useful, but it's not going to be useful for the students who actually do need the extra cash."

Castillo said she is pretty sure she will have to look for a job next semester. 21 Once she's working, she plans to go to school part time.

READING COMPREHENSION

1. The word *barrier* in "We're taking one barrier, one burden, away" (paragraph 8) means

    a. anything built or serving to bar passage.

    b. any natural bar or obstacle.

    c. anything that retrains or obstructs progress.

    d. a limit or a boundary of any kind.

2. The word *reforms* in "The kind of reforms that surround L.A.'s plan, reforms that deal with the problems students face" (paragraph 12) means

    a. improvements to something that is wrong.

    b. amendments of conduct or beliefs.

    c. to abandon evil conduct or error.

    d. to improve by altering or substituting.

3. The word *solicit* in "We're going to solicit from every company in Los Angeles" (paragraph 15) means
   a. to make petition to; entreat.
   b. to urge something strongly.
   (c.) to approach with a request.
   d. to proposition a person.

4. Which of the following would be a good alternative title for this selection?
   a. Helping Students Graduate College
   (b.) Financial Help from Unusual Sources
   c. Wasteful Federal and State Spending
   d. Why Students Fail College

5. Which sentence best expresses the main idea of the selection?
   a. College students who have parents who help them attend college have a much easier time graduating than students whose parents are unable to help financially.
   b. College students are unable to afford going to college full time, so most attend part time.
   c. The mayor of Los Angeles and the L.A. Community College District are implementing a new program to help more students afford attending California universities.
   (d.) The mayor of Los Angeles and the L.A. Community College District are implementing a new program to help more students afford college as full-time students in order to help their chances at graduation.

6. According to the essay, how many community colleges are in Los Angeles?
   a. 5
   (b.) 9
   c. 18
   d. 19

7. According to the essay, how many students have all their tuition waived in Los Angeles community colleges?
   (a.) 69% of college students
   b. 73% of college students
   c. 2,100 students
   d. all of the L.A. public school students

8. *True or False?* ____False____ The L.A. College Promise is based on the plan laid out by President Barack Obama in his 2015 State of the Union Address.

9. The author writes about Maria Medrano because she is benefitting from the new program; however, the author also points out that the cost of textbooks is not covered and can cost as much as
   a. $900 a year.
   b. $1,300 a year.

(c.) $500 a semester.

d. $200 a semester.

10. According to the essay, students in Los Angeles can also get help with

a. grocery bills.

b. rent.

(c.) transportation.

d. school supplies.

STRUCTURE AND TECHNIQUE

1. How would you describe the author's tone in this essay? Is it formal or informal? What are the basic feelings that pervade the essay?

2. What rhetorical modes does Phillips use to create this well-written essay?

3. The author quotes a number of different people in her essay. What is the purpose of all these quotations?

4. Reread the concluding sentence. What is the author's purpose in ending the essay this way?

CRITICAL READING AND DISCUSSION

1. The author provides a percentage for how many students attend community colleges part time. Find that percentage, and then discuss whether you think this number is similar to community colleges in your area. Are the reasons for attending part time as laid out in the essay the same as those that pertain to part-time students in your home area? If not, what are the differences?

2. If California already has the Cal Grant, why, according to the author, is the mayor of Los Angeles implementing the L.A. College Promise?

3. In paragraph 11, the author explains some additional features of the L.A. College Promise. Reread this paragraph, identify the additional features, and discuss your opinion of them.

4. In paragraph 14, the author explains how the mayor plans to fund the new program. How much is the program expected to cost? How much has the mayor raised? How much have the community colleges raised? How much remains to be raised and what are the community colleges planning to do to raise this amount? Discuss your reaction to these numbers and the plans.

WRITING ASSIGNMENTS

Assignment 1: Writing a Paragraph

This essay highlights many of the costs that college students juggle in order to attend college. Write a paragraph in which you discuss your college experience: whether you attend full time or part time; the costs you are responsible for; any help that you receive; and whether you juggle your class load with work.

Assignment 2: Writing an Essay

The rising costs of higher education are commonly discussed in the news, social media, and education forums. Many states, like California, have come up with programs to help students lower their costs, especially if they attend community colleges for the first two years. If your state has such a program, write an essay in which you discuss what the program is, what the requirements are for students to qualify for and participate in the program, and what the success rates are for the program. If your state doesn't have such a program, research a program in another state, and then write an essay that argues why your state should implement such a program.

Assignment 3: Writing an Essay

Write a critical analysis of the Phillips essay. Are the arguments in Phillips's essay clear? Do you feel that Phillips has successfully supported her arguments? If not, in what areas should she have gone deeper? What types of support would have helped her argument? Have any ideas been overemphasized or underemphasized? Has the author made any assumptions about her readers that could have an impact on how well the essay is received? Does the author have an evident bias that affects how her information is presented?

Once you have read through the essay and answered as many questions as possible, you will need to create a thesis that emphasizes your overall impression of the essay. You will then need to organize your ideas around your thesis, so you can create a strong argument. You may need to look at Chapter 14, "Argument" and Chapter 20, "Working with Sources" to help you integrate quotes, paraphrases, and summaries from the article into your essay.

Carol Dweck Revisits the "Growth Mindset"

Carol Dweck

©Carol Dweck

PREVIEW

Carol S. Dweck earned her PhD in Social and Developmental Psychology from Yale University and is the Lewis and Virginia Eaton Professor of Psychology at Stanford University. In this article, Dweck looks at how her research has been interpreted and applied.

For many years, I secretly worked on my research. I say "secretly" because, once upon a time, researchers simply published their research in professional journals—and there it stayed. 1

However, my colleagues and I learned things we thought people needed to know. We found that students' mindsets—how they perceive their abilities—played a key role in their motivation and achievement, and we found that if we changed students' mindsets, we could boost their achievement. More precisely, students who believed their intelligence could be developed (a growth mindset) 2 outperformed those who believed their intelligence was fixed (a fixed mindset). And when students learned through a structured program that they could "grow their brains" and increase their intellectual abilities, they did better. Finally, we found that having children focus on the process that leads to learning (like hard work or trying new strategies) could foster a growth mindset and its benefits.

So a few years back, I published my book *Mindset: The New Psychology of Success* to share these discoveries with educators. And many educators have applied the mindset principles in spectacular ways with tremendously gratifying results.   3

This is wonderful, and the good word continues to spread. But as we've watched the growth mindset become more popular, we've become much wiser about how to implement it. This learning—the common pitfalls, the misunderstandings, and what to do about them—is what I'd like to share with you, so that we can maximize the benefits for our students.   4

A growth mindset isn't just about effort. Perhaps the most common misconception is simply equating the growth mindset with effort. Certainly, effort is key for students' achievement, but it's not the only thing. Students need to try new strategies and seek input from others when they're stuck. They need this repertoire of approaches—not just sheer effort—to learn and improve.   5

TEACHING TIP
Ask students if they have heard the terms "growth mindset" and/or "fixed mindset." Have them share their experiences with these terms.

We also need to remember that effort is a means to an end to the goal of learning and improving. Too often nowadays, praise is given to students who are putting forth effort, but *not learning*, in order to make them feel good in the moment: "Great effort! You tried your best!" It's good that the students tried, but it's not good that they're not learning. The growth-mindset approach helps children feel good in the short *and* long terms, by helping them thrive on challenges and setbacks on their way to learning. When they're stuck, teachers can appreciate their work so far, but add: "Let's talk about what you've tried, and what you can try next."   6

Recently, someone asked what keeps me up at night. It's the fear that the mindset concepts, which grew up to *counter* the failed self-esteem movement, will be used to *perpetuate* that movement. In other words, if you want to make students feel good, even if they're not learning, just praise their effort! Want to hide learning gaps from them? Just tell them, "Everyone is smart!" The growth mindset was intended to help close achievement gaps, not hide them. It is about telling the truth about a student's current achievement and then, together, doing something about it, helping him or her become smarter.   7

I also fear that the mindset work is sometimes used to justify why some students aren't learning: "Oh, he has a *fixed* mindset." We used to blame the child's environment or ability.   8

Must it always come back to finding a reason why some children just can't learn, as opposed to finding a way to help them learn? Teachers who understand the growth mindset do everything in their power to unlock that learning.   9

A few years ago, my colleague in Australia, Susan Mackie, detected an outbreak of what she called "false growth mindset." She was seeing educators who claimed to have a growth mindset, but whose words and actions didn't reflect it. At first, I was skeptical. But before long, I saw it, too, and I understood why.   10

In many quarters, a growth mindset had become the right thing to have, the right way to think. It was as though educators were faced with a choice: Are you an enlightened person who fosters students' well-being? Or are you an   11 unenlightened person, with a fixed mindset, who undermines them? So, of course, many claimed the growth-mindset identity. But the path to a growth mindset is a journey, not a proclamation.

Let's look at what happens when teachers, or parents, claim a growth mind- 12 set, but don't follow through. In recent research, Kathy Liu Sun found that there were many math teachers who endorsed a growth mindset and even said the words "growth mindset" in their middle school math classes, but did not follow through in their classroom practices. In these cases, their students tended to endorse more of a fixed mindset about their math ability. My advisee and research collaborator Kyla Haimovitz and I are finding many parents who endorse a growth mindset, but react to their children's mistakes as though they are problematic or harmful, rather than helpful. In these cases, their children develop more of a fixed mindset about their intelligence.

How can we help educators adopt a deeper, true growth mindset, one that will 13 *show in their classroom practices?* You may be surprised by my answer: Let's legitimize the fixed mindset. Let's acknowledge that (1) we're all a mixture of fixed and growth mindsets, (2) we will probably always be, and (3) if we want to move closer to a growth mindset in our thoughts and practices, we need to stay in touch with our fixed mindset thoughts and deeds.

If we "ban" the fixed mindset, we will surely create false growth-mindsets. 14 (By the way, I also fear that if we use mindset measures for accountability, we will create false growth mindsets on an unprecedented scale.) But if we watch carefully for our fixed mindset triggers, we can begin the true journey to a growth mindset.

What are your triggers? Watch for a fixed mindset reaction when you face 15 challenges. Do you feel overly anxious, or does a voice in your head warn you away? Watch for it when you face a setback in your teaching, or when students aren't listening or learning. Do you feel incompetent or defeated? Do you look for an excuse? Watch to see whether criticism brings out your fixed mindset. Do you become defensive, angry, or crushed instead of interested in learning from the feedback? Watch what happens when you see an educator who's better than you at something you value. Do you feel envious and threatened, or do you feel eager to learn? Accept those thoughts and feelings and work with and through them. And keep working with and through them.

My colleagues and I are taking a growth-mindset stance toward our message 16 to educators. Maybe we originally put too much emphasis on sheer effort. Maybe we made the development of a growth mindset sound too easy. Maybe we talked too much about people having one mindset or the other, rather than portraying people as mixtures. We are on a growth-mindset journey, too.

TEACHING TIP
Ask students to brainstorm some of their triggers and then compare their list with a partner.

READING COMPREHENSION

1. The word *foster* in "the process that leads to learning (like hard work or trying new strategies) could foster a growth mindset" (paragraph 2) means
   a. to promote further; encourage.
   b. to care for; cherish; nurture.
   c. to feed or nourish.
   d. to bring up a child.

2. The word *implement* in "we've become much wiser about how to implement it" (paragraph 4) means

    a. an instrument; tool.

    b. a means.

    c. to fulfill; perform.

    (d.) to put into effect.

3. The word *counter* in "which grew up to counter the failed self-esteem movement" (paragraph 7) means

    a. a surface for food preparation.

    b. a long narrow table with stools.

    (c.) to oppose; contradict.

    d. to compute or add up.

4. Which of the following would be a good alternative title for this selection?

    (a.) Continuing to Grow

    b. The New Psychology of Success

    c. It's All About Effort

    d. Banning the Fixed Mindset

5. Which sentence best expresses the main idea of the selection?

    a. Carol Dweck feels that her theory of growth mindset is going to be the answer to education's problems.

    (b.) Carol Dweck believes the message to educators about growth mindset has not been interpreted properly.

    c. Carol Dweck realizes that her theory of growth mindset needs to be studied again because it has basic flaws.

    d. Carol Dweck believes that too many educators have fixed mindsets, so they are unable to teach growth mindset.

6. *True or False?* ___False___ According to the author, growth mindset is just about effort.

7. According to the essay, what keeps the author up at night?

    a. a fear that her research is faulty and the theory is flawed

    b. a fear that other researchers will undermine her current theories

    c. a fear that growth mindset will be taken over by the self-esteem movement

    (d.) a fear that growth mindset will lead to a failed self-esteem movement

8. According to the author, what is wrong with the comment, "Oh, he has a fixed mindset"?

    a. It is used to explain that a child's ability is a result of his environment.

    b. There is nothing wrong with a fixed mindset, so it shouldn't be used to explain a problem.

    (c.) This phrase is used to justify why a child might not be learning.

    d. This phrase is used to explain why teachers struggle to teach.

9. What did Kathy Liu Sun find about the math teachers she researched?

   a. They promoted the growth mindset and were experiencing success in their classrooms.

   (b.) They said they were teaching growth mindset, but in actuality, were not.

   c. They endorsed growth mindset, but their students endorsed a fixed mindset.

   d. They endorsed a fixed mindset, but their students tried to adopt a growth mindset.

10. Which of the following things does Dweck feel students should NOT do in order to adopt a growth mindset?

    a. seek input from others

    b. put in effort

    (c.) feel good based on praise

    d. try new strategies

STRUCTURE AND TECHNIQUE

1. Dweck's essay doesn't follow traditional format in that her thesis is not in the first paragraph. Find her thesis, explain what type of thesis it is (persuasive, narrative, etc.), and discuss why you think she placed it in that location.

2. Throughout the essay, Dweck uses italics frequently. What is her purpose in italicizing the words and phrases she does?

3. Why do you think Dweck chooses to use dialogue instead of merely describing what teachers and parents often say?

4. Dweck ends with the statement "We are on a growth-mindset journey, too." Why do you think she chooses to end her essay in this manner?

CRITICAL READING AND DISCUSSION

1. Dweck offers a lot of information about how students can adopt a growth mindset but, at the same time, explains that often parents and teachers undermine students' mindsets. Describe what Dweck sees as parents' and teachers' problematic behavior.

2. Why does the author want to legitimize a fixed mindset? What reasons does she provide?

3. According to the author, what is a false growth mindset?

4. Why does the author encourage people to watch out for their triggers? What is the ultimate goal in monitoring these trigger situations?

WRITING ASSIGNMENTS

Assignment 1: Writing a Paragraph

React to the essay. According to Carol Dweck, what is a "growth mindset," and why is it important? Think about your past learning experiences. Do you feel you have had a growth mindset, a fixed mindset, or a combination of both? What do you think has influenced these reactions? Support your answer with examples from your own experiences.

Assignment 2: Writing an Essay

Dweck asks her readers to look at their triggers to learn when they are reacting with a fixed mindset. Reread paragraph 15, and as a prewriting activity, answer the questions she poses. Then, using this prewriting, write an essay that discusses when you have triggers, what your responses have been in the past, and how you can adjust those responses in the future.

Assignment 3: Writing an Essay

Dweck's essay looks back at her growth mindset theory. She reflects on and reviews how this mindset has been practiced and implemented over the years. For this assignment, research growth mindset and learn as much about the theory as possible. Then write an essay in which you discuss what you have learned. Explain to your readers what you understand about growth mindset, why growth mindset has been shown to be beneficial to students, and how you think it should be implemented in the classroom.

You should plan to use direct quotations, paraphrases, and/or summaries in your essay, so you should be familiar with Chapter 20, "Working with Sources" to help you properly incorporate and cite your sources.

In Praise of the F Word

Mary Sherry

©Mary Sherry

PREVIEW

What does it take to get by in high school? Too little, according to the author, a teacher in an "educational-repair shop." In this article, which originally appeared in *Newsweek*, Mary Sherry describes the ways she sees students being cheated by their schools and proposes a remedy you may find surprising.

Tens of thousands of eighteen-year-olds will graduate this year and be handed 1
meaningless diplomas. These diplomas won't look any different from those awarded to their luckier classmates. Their validity will be questioned only when their employers discover that these graduates are semiliterate.

Eventually a fortunate few will find their way into educational-repair shops— 2   TEACHING TIP
adult-literacy programs, such as the one where I teach basic grammar and writ-   Ask students to speculate
ing. There, high school graduates and high school dropouts pursuing   what the "F word" means
graduate-equivalency certificates will learn the skills they should have learned   in Mary Sherry's essay.
in school. They will also discover that they have been cheated by our educational
system.

As I teach, I learn a lot about our schools. Early in each session I ask my 3
students to write about an unpleasant experience they had in school. No writer's
block here! "I wish someone had made me stop doing drugs and made me

study." "I liked to party, and no one seemed to care." "I was a good kid and didn't cause any trouble, so they just passed me along even though I didn't read well and couldn't write." And so on.

I am your basic do-gooder, and prior to teaching this class I blamed the poor 4 academic skills our kids have today on drugs, divorce, and other impediments to the concentration necessary for doing well in school. But, as I rediscover each time I walk into the classroom, before a teacher can expect students to concentrate, he has to get their attention, no matter what distractions may be at hand. There are many ways to do this, and they have much to do with teaching style. However, if style alone won't do it, there is another way to show who holds the winning hand in the classroom. That is to reveal the trump card[1] of failure.

I will never forget a teacher who played that card to get the attention of one 5 of my children. Our youngest, a world-class charmer, did little to develop his intellectual talents but always got by—until Mrs. Stifter.

Our son was a high school senior when he had her for English. "He sits in 6 the back of the room talking to his friends," she told me. "Why don't you move him to the front row?" I urged, believing the embarrassment would get him to settle down. Mrs. Stifter looked at me steely-eyed over her glasses. "I don't move seniors," she said. "I flunk them." I was flustered. Our son's academic life flashed before my eyes. No teacher had ever threatened him with that before. I regained my composure and managed to say that I thought she was right. By the time I got home I was feeling pretty good about this. It was a radical approach for these times, but, well, why not? "She's going to flunk you," I told my son. I did not discuss it any further. Suddenly English became a priority in his life. He finished out the semester with an A.

I know one example doesn't make a case, but at night I see a parade of 7 students who are angry and resentful for having been passed along until they could no longer even pretend to keep up. Of average intelligence or better, they eventually quit school, concluding that they were too dumb to finish. "I should have been held back," is a comment I hear frequently. Even sadder are those students who are high school graduates who say to me after a few weeks of class, "I don't know how I ever got a high school diploma."

Passing students who have not mastered the work cheats them and the 8 employers who expect graduates to have basic skills. We excuse this dishonest behavior by saying kids can't learn if they come from terrible environments. No one seems to stop to think that—no matter what environments they come from— most kids don't put school first on their list unless they perceive that something is at stake. They'd rather be sailing.

Many students I see at night could give expert testimony on unemployment, 9 chemical dependency, and abusive relationships. In spite of these difficulties, they have decided to make education a priority. They are motivated by the desire for a better job or the need to hang on to the one they've got. They have a healthy fear of failure.

People of all ages can rise above their problems, but they need to have 10 a reason to do so. Young people generally don't have the maturity to value education in the same way my adult students value it. But fear of failure, whether economic or academic, can motivate both.

---

[1]*trump card:* in bridge, a card of the suit that ranks highest; thus, something powerful, often held in reserve to be used at the right moment.

Flunking as a regular policy has just as much merit today as it did two 11 generations ago. We must review the threat of flunking and see it as it really is—a positive teaching tool. It is an expression of confidence by both teachers and parents that the students have the ability to learn the material presented to them. However, making it work again would take a dedicated, caring conspiracy between teachers and parents. It would mean facing the tough reality that passing kids who haven't learned the material—while it might save them grief for the short term—dooms them to long-term illiteracy. It would mean that teachers would have to follow through on their threats, and parents would have to stand behind them, knowing their children's best interests are indeed at stake. This means no more doing Scott's assignments for him because he might fail. No more passing Jodi because she's such a nice kid.

This is a policy that worked in the past and can work today. A wise teacher, 12 with the support of his parents, gave our son the opportunity to succeed—or fail. It's time we returned this choice to all students.

READING COMPREHENSION

1. The word *validity* in "[The diplomas'] validity will be questioned only when . . . employers discover that these graduates are semiliterate" (paragraph 1) means

    a. soundness.

    b. dates.

    c. age.

    d. supply.

2. The word *impediments* in "I blamed the poor academic skills our kids have today on drugs, divorce, and other impediments to concentration" (paragraph 4) means

    a. questions.

    b. paths.

    c. skills.

    d. obstacles.

3. Which of the following would be a good alternative title for this selection?

    a. Learning to Concentrate in School

    b. Teaching English Skills

    c. A Useful Tool for Motivating Students

    d. Adult-Literacy Programs

4. Which sentence best expresses the main idea of the selection?

    a. Many adults cannot read or write well.

    b. English skills can be learned through adult-literacy programs.

    c. Schools should include flunking students as part of their regular policy.

    d. Before students will concentrate, the teacher must get their attention.

5. Sherry's night students are

    a. usually unemployed.

    b. poor students.

    (c.) motivated to learn.

    d. involved with drugs.

6. According to the author, many students who get "passed along"

    a. are lucky.

    b. never find a job.

    c. don't get into trouble.

    (d.) eventually feel angry and resentful.

7. Sherry feels that to succeed, flunking students as a regular policy requires

    a. adult-literacy programs.

    b. graduate-equivalency certificates.

    (c.) the total cooperation of teachers and parents.

    d. a strong teaching style.

8. The author implies that our present educational system is

    a. the best in the world.

    b. doing the best that it can.

    c. very short of teachers.

    (d.) not demanding enough of students.

9. *True or False?* ___*True*___ Sherry implies that high school students often don't realize the value of academic skills.

10. From the selection, we may conclude that the author based her opinion on

    a. recent statistics.

    b. educational research.

    (c.) her personal and professional experiences.

    d. expert professional testimony.

STRUCTURE AND TECHNIQUE

1. In current vocabulary, "the F word" usually refers to something other than "fail." Why do you think Mary Sherry used the term in her title, rather than simply using "fail" or "failure"? What effect does her title have on the reader?

2. In which paragraph does the author first mention her thesis? What is her main method of development, and how is it related to that thesis? Where does she use narration to support her thesis?

3. What contrast transition is used in the first sentence of paragraph 10? What ideas are being contrasted within that sentence?

4. In paragraph 11, how many times does Sherry use "mean" or "means"? What might her purpose be for repeating this word so frequently?

CRITICAL READING AND DISCUSSION

1. Sherry writes that "before a teacher can expect students to concentrate, he has to get their attention, no matter what distractions may be at hand" (paragraph 4). What examples of distractions does Sherry mention? Find several in her essay. Can you think of others—perhaps ones that existed in your own high school?

2. What does Sherry mean by calling the program she teaches in an "educational-repair shop"? What does the term tell us about Sherry's attitude toward high schools?

3. Sherry writes, "Young people generally don't have the maturity to value education in the same way my adult students value it." Do you agree or disagree? Support your view with details and observations from your own experience.

4. Do you feel your high school teachers made an honest effort to give you the skills you need—and to make you aware of the importance of those skills? If not, what should your school have done that it did not do?

WRITING ASSIGNMENTS

Assignment 1: Writing a Paragraph

Write a paragraph that has as its topic sentence one of the following statements:

> Students have no one to blame but themselves if they leave school without having learned basic skills.

> When students graduate or quit school lacking basic skills, they are the victims of an inadequate educational system.

> Flunking students has more disadvantages than advantages.

Support your topic sentence with several points.

Assignment 2: Writing an Essay

Sherry proposes using "flunking as a regular policy" as a way to encourage students to work harder. What else might school systems do to help students? Write an essay in which you suggest a few policies for our public schools and give the reasons you think those changes will be beneficial. Following are some policies you may wish to consider:

More writing in all classes

Shorter summer vacations

Less emphasis on memorization and more on thinking skills

A language requirement

A daily quiet reading session in elementary grades

Assignment 3: Writing an Essay

Here are two letters to the editor, written by teachers in response to Sherry's article:

Letter 1

Mary Sherry's essay that supports flunking students as a tool to teach is very ill-informed. My school district discourages teachers giving out failing grades because they are then held accountable. District officials see it as a reflection of teaching practices, not student ability. Even more significant is the fact that students today have so much more to deal with that a failing grade often means nothing. For students who have abusive parents, are suffering bullying in school, or are dealing with addiction, the last thing they are concerned with is whether or not they are passing eleventh-grade English. The fears they are facing are much stronger than the fear of a failing grade.

Sean Herrington
Gillette, Wyoming

Letter 2

Ms. Sherry is absolutely correct that flunking students is what schools should do. However, if it isn't a partnership, or conspiracy as Sherry calls it, between parents and teachers, it won't work. During my second year of teaching high school, I had a student refuse to submit any parts of her research paper. Despite sending numerous notes home, I heard nothing until the day grades came out. All of a sudden, the student's mother was angry at me and demanded that I allow the student to work with me for an hour after school each day to make up the work. She was so angry at my refusal that she took it to my principal, and it escalated. Had we been partners rather than adversaries, her daughter would have probably learned much more from her failing grade than she did.

Mila D. Honnaker
Salem, Oregon

These letters suggest that if schools want to try flunking as a regular policy, they will have to plan carefully. Write an essay in which you discuss ways to make failing poor students work as a regular policy. Your thesis statement can be something like this: "In order for a policy of flunking to work, certain policies and attitudes would need to be changed in many schools." As support in your essay, use the ideas in these letters, Sherry's ideas, and any other ideas you have heard or thought of. Describe your supporting ideas in detail and explain why each is necessary or useful.

Challenging Society

Is Sex All That Matters?

Joyce Garity

PREVIEW

From the skimpy clothing in ads to the suggestive themes in many of today's TV comedies, our young people are bombarded with sexuality. How does the constant stream of sexual images influence their behavior and dreams? In considering that question, social worker Joyce Garity focuses on one young woman named Elaine, alone and pregnant with her second child.

A few years ago, a young girl lived with me, my husband, and our children 1 for several months. The circumstances of Elaine's coming to us don't matter here; suffice it to say that she was troubled and nearly alone in the world. She was also pregnant—hugely, clumsily pregnant with her second child. Elaine was seventeen. Her pregnancy, she said, was an accident; she also said she wasn't sure who had fathered her child. There had been several sex partners and no contraception. Yet, she repeated blandly, gazing at me with clear blue eyes, the pregnancy was an accident, and one she would certainly never repeat.

Eventually I asked Elaine, after we had grown to know each other well 2 enough for such conversations, why neither she nor her lovers had used birth control. She blushed—porcelain-skinned girl with one child in foster care and another swelling the bib of her fashionably faded overalls—stammered, and blushed some more. Birth control, she finally got out, was "embarrassing." It wasn't "romantic." You couldn't be really passionate, she explained, and worry about birth control at the same time.

I haven't seen Elaine for quite a long time. I think about her often, though. 3 I think of her as I page through teen fashion magazines in the salon where I have my hair cut. Although mainstream and relatively wholesome, these magazines trumpet sexuality page after leering page. On the inside front cover, an advertisement for Guess jeans features junior fashion models in snug denim dresses, their legs bared to just below the crotch. An advertisement for Liz Claiborne fragrances shows a barely clad young couple sprawled on a bed, him painting her toenails. An advertisement for Obsession cologne displays a waif-thin girl draped stomach-down across a couch, naked, her startled expression suggesting helplessness in the face of an unseen yet approaching threat.

I think of Elaine because I know she would love these ads. "They're so 4 beautiful," she would croon, and of course they are. The faces and bodies they show are lovely. The lighting is superb. The hair and makeup are faultless. In the Claiborne ad, the laughing girl whose toenails are being painted by her handsome lover is obviously having the time of her life. She stretches luxuriously on a bed heaped with clean white linen and fluffy pillows. Beyond the sheer blowing curtains of her room, we can glimpse a graceful wrought-iron balcony.

Looking at the ad, Elaine could only want to be her. Any girl would want to be her. Heck, I want to be her.

But my momentary desire to move into the Claiborne picture, to trade lives with the exquisite young creature pictured there, is just that—momentary. I've lived long enough to know that what I see is a marketing invention. A moment after the photo session was over, the beautiful room was dismantled, and the models moved on to their next job. Later, the technicians took over the task of doctoring the photograph until it reached full-blown fantasy proportions.

Not so Elaine. After months of living together and countless hours of watching her yearn after magazine images, soap-opera heroines, and rock goddesses, I have a pretty good idea of why she looks at ads like Claiborne's. She sees the way life—her life—is supposed to be. She sees a world characterized by sexual spontaneity, playfulness, and abandon. She sees people who don't worry about such unsexy details as birth control. Nor, apparently, do they spend much time thinking about such pedestrian topics as commitment or whether they should act on their sexual impulses. Their clean sunlit rooms are never invaded by the fear of AIDS, of unwanted pregnancy, of shattered lives. For all her apparent lack of defense, the girl on the couch in the Obsession ad will surely never experience the brutality of rape.

Years of exposure to this media-invented, sex-saturated universe have done their work on Elaine. She is, I'm sure, completely unaware of the irony in her situation: She melts over images from a sexual Shangri-la,[1] never realizing that her attempts to mirror those images left her pregnant, abandoned, living in the spare bedroom of a stranger's house, relying on charity for rides to the welfare office and supervised visits with her toddler daughter.

Of course, Elaine is not the first to be suckered by the cynical practice of using sex to sell underwear, rock groups, or sneakers. Using sex as a sales tool is hardly new. At the beginning of this century, British actress Lily Langtry shocked her contemporaries by posing, clothed somewhat scantily, with a bar of Pear's soap. The advertisers have always known that the masses are susceptible to the notion that a particular product will make them more sexually attractive. In the past, however, ads used euphemisms, claiming that certain products would make people "more lovable" or "more popular." What is a recent development is the abandonment of any such polite double-talk. Advertising today leaves no question about what is being sold along with the roasted peanuts or artificial sweetener. "Tell us about your first time," coyly invites the innuendo[2] filled magazine advertisement for Campari liquor. A billboard for Levi's shows two jeans-clad young men on the beach, hoisting a girl in the air. The boys' perfect, tan bodies are matched by hers, although we see a lot more of hers: bare midriff, short shorts, cleavage. She caresses their hair; they stroke her legs. A jolly fantasy where sex exists without consequences.

But this fantasy is a lie—one which preys on young people. Studies show that by the age of twenty, 75 percent of Americans have lost their virginity. In many high schools—and an increasing number of junior highs—virginity is regarded as an embarrassing vestige of childhood, to be disposed of as quickly as possible. Young people are immersed from their earliest days in a culture that parades sexuality at every turn and makes heroes of the advocates of sexual excess. Girls, from toddlerhood on up, shop in stores packed with clothing once

---

[1]*Shangri-la:* an imaginary paradise on earth (the name of a beautiful faraway place in the novel *Lost Horizon*).
[2]*innuendo:* subtle suggestion.

thought suitable only for streetwalkers—lace leggings, crop tops, and wedge-heeled boots. Parents drop their children off at concerts featuring simulated on-stage masturbation or pretended acts of copulation. Young boys idolize sports stars like the late Wilt Chamberlain, who claimed to have bedded 20,000 women. And when the "Spur Posse," eight California high school athletes, were charged with systematically raping girls as young as ten as part of a "scoring" ritual, the beefy young jocks were rewarded with a publicity tour of talk shows, while one father boasted to reporters about his son's "manhood."

In a late, lame attempt to counterbalance this sexual overload, most schools 10 offer sex education as part of their curriculums. (In 1993, forty-seven states recommended or required such courses.) But sex ed classes are heavy on the mechanics of fertilization and birth control—sperm, eggs, and condoms—and light on any discussion of sexuality as only one part of a well-balanced life. There is passing reference to abstinence as a method of contraception, but little discussion of abstinence as an emotionally or spiritually satisfying option. Promiscuity is discussed for its role in spreading sexually transmitted diseases. But the concept of rejecting casual sex in favor of reserving sex for an emotionally intimate, exclusive, trusting relationship—much less any mention of waiting until marriage—is foreign to most public school settings. "Love and stuff like that really wasn't discussed" is the way one Spur Posse member remembers his high school sex education class.

TEACHING TIP
Ask your students to
discuss these questions
with a partner.

Surely teenagers need the factual information provided by sex education 11 courses. But where is "love and stuff like that" talked about? Where can they turn for a more balanced view of sexuality? Who is telling young people like Elaine, my former houseguest, that sex is not an adequate basis for a healthy, respectful relationship? Along with warnings to keep condoms on hand, is anyone teaching kids that they have a right to be valued for something other than their sexuality? Madison Avenue, Hollywood, and the TV, music, and fashion industries won't tell them that. Who will?

No one has told Elaine—at least, not in a way she comprehends. I haven't 12 seen her for a long time, but I hear of her occasionally. The baby boy she bore while living in my house is in a foster home, a few miles from his older half-sister, who is also in foster care. Elaine herself is working in a local convenience store—and she is pregnant again. This time, I understand, she is carrying twins.

READING COMPREHENSION

1. The word *dismantled* in "A moment after the photo session was over, the beautiful room was dismantled, and the models moved on to their next job" (paragraph 5) means

    a. used.

    b. photographed.

    c. taken apart.

    d. perfected.

2. The word *vestige* in "In many high schools—and an increasing number of junior highs—virginity is regarded as an embarrassing vestige of childhood" (paragraph 9) means

    a. reversal.

    b. activity.

   (c.) remainder.

   d. error.

3. Which of the following would be a good alternative title for this selection?

   a. Teens and Birth Control

   b. The Use of Sex to Sell Products

   (c.) An Unbalanced View of Sexuality

   d. The Advantages of Casual Sex

4. Which sentence best expresses the main idea of the selection?

   a. Sexual images have helped our society become more open and understanding about a natural part of life.

   b. We live in a society ruled by Madison Avenue, Hollywood, and the TV, music, and fashion industries.

   c. Sex education courses, required in most states, have not done enough to teach our children about sexuality and responsible behavior.

   (d.) Nothing, not even sex education, is counteracting the numerous sexual images in our society that encourage irresponsible, casual sex.

5. According to the author, Elaine probably likes to look at sexy magazine ads because

   a. she doesn't have high moral standards.

   b. she wishes she could afford the products being advertised.

   (c.) they portray the kind of life she'd like to lead.

   d. they remind her of her life before she had children.

6. In contrast to Elaine, the author

   (a.) understands that most ads portray an unreal world.

   b. finds ads like the Claiborne ad distasteful.

   c. never looks at fashion magazines.

   d. does not have children.

7. Elaine

   a. wanted to become pregnant.

   (b.) thinks birth control isn't romantic.

   c. never finished high school.

   d. has a healthy fear of AIDS.

8. We can conclude the author believes that

   a. sex is a private matter that should not be discussed.

   (b.) many young people view sex as an adequate basis for a relationship.

   c. Madison Avenue; Hollywood; and the TV, music, and fashion industries have completely destroyed all morality in America.

   d. virginity is an embarrassing vestige of childhood.

9. The author implies that

   a. sexy ads should be illegal.

   b. schools should teach contraception at an earlier age.

(c.) sex should be reserved for an exclusive, loving relationship.

d. casual sex is sometimes, though not always, a good idea.

10. The author suggests that sex education classes

a. are a major cause of casual, unprotected sex.

(b.) should include the role of sex in a meaningful relationship.

c. should not include the mechanics of fertilization and birth control.

d. have taken over a role that rightfully belongs to parents.

STRUCTURE AND TECHNIQUE

1. To support her views about sexuality in popular culture, Garity presents the case of Elaine. Why has the author chosen to focus so much of her essay on Elaine? What would have been lost if Garity had omitted Elaine?

2. List the details that Garity provides as she describes the Claiborne ad. Why does she go to such lengths to describe it? Why might she think it important for the reader to see it so clearly?

3. Garity uses a number of examples to support her claim about the prevalence of sex in popular culture. Cite some of these examples and explain how they support her argument.

4. Throughout paragraph 11, Garity poses a series of questions. What does she gain by using this technique?

CRITICAL READING AND DISCUSSION

1. How do you think Garity felt about Elaine? Affectionate? Scornful? Resentful? Disapproving? Pitying? Explain your answer, pointing out evidence from Garity's text.

2. In paragraph 7, the author says that Elaine is "completely unaware of the irony in her situation." In an ironic situation, there is an inconsistency between what might be expected and what actually happens. What about Elaine's situation is ironic?

3. The author lists numerous examples to illustrate and support her claim that "young people are immersed from their earliest days in a culture that parades sexuality at every turn and makes heroes of advocates of sexual excess." What examples can you think of to add to her list? Describe and explain them.

4. In arguing against the emphasis on sexuality in our culture, Garity focuses on potential dangers to young women. How do you think this highly sexualized culture affects young men? Are they also at risk? Explain.

WRITING ASSIGNMENTS

Assignment 1: Writing a Paragraph

Garity accuses the advertising, film, TV, music, and fashion industries of contributing to our sex-saturated society by parading "sexuality at every turn."

Choose one industry from that list, and write your own paragraph about how it portrays sexuality.

There is more than one way you can approach this assignment. In a paragraph on the fashion industry, for instance, you could focus on types of clothing being promoted, ads in print, and ads on TV. In a paragraph on the music industry, you might discuss three musicians and how their lyrics and their performances promote a particular view of sex. Whatever your choice, include specific, colorful descriptions, as Garity does when discussing ads and fashions. (See, for example, paragraphs 3 and 8.)

Assignment 2: Writing an Essay

Garity suggests that sex education courses should include more than the "mechanics of fertilization and birth control" (paragraph 10). Write an essay describing several ways you feel sex education classes could incorporate "love and stuff like that." Begin by selecting three general approaches that could be used in a sex education class to get students to think about what a rich, balanced romantic relationship is made of. For example, you might focus on three of the following:

Discussion of what students seek in a relationship

Discussion of a fictional relationship, such as that of Romeo and Juliet or two characters on a TV show

Discussion of the lyrics of a popular song

Bringing into class a psychologist who deals with problems in relationships

Bringing into class one or more couples who have been together for many years

Discuss each method you choose in a separate paragraph. Describe in detail how the method would work, using hypothetical examples to illustrate your points.

Assignment 3: Writing an Essay

Advertisements represent many elements of our society. Choose an element other than sexuality, and analyze the way ads of any kind (in magazines and newspapers, on billboards and buses, on TV and radio and the Internet) portray that subject. Following are some areas of our lives that are commonly represented in ads:

Family life

Women's roles

Men's roles

Possessions

Looks

Health

In analyzing an ad, consider what images and words are used, how they are intended to appeal to the audience, and what values they promote. Use the conclusion you come to as the thesis of your essay. For example, an essay on men's roles might make this point: "Many of today's TV ads promote participation of fathers in domestic activities."

Support your conclusion with colorful descriptions of several ads. Make your descriptions detailed enough so that your readers can "see" the elements of ads you refer to. Be sure to focus on the parts of the ads that support the point you are trying to make. You could organize your essay by devoting a paragraph each to three significant ads. Or you could devote each support paragraph to one of several important points about the subject you've chosen. For instance, an essay about fathers' roles at home might discuss child care, cleaning, and cooking. A paragraph on each of those topics might refer to two or more ads.

Mayor of Rust

Sue Halpern

©Sophie McKibben

PREVIEW

Sue Halpern, a former Rhodes Scholar and Guggenheim Fellow, has a Ph.D. from Oxford University, has taught at Columbia University's College of Physicians and Surgeons, and is currently a scholar-in-residence at Middlebury College. She is also the director of Face of Democracy, a nonprofit project that teaches documentary journalism to high school students. In this article, which appeared in the *New York Times Magazine,* she profiles a young man who is trying to make a difference in his town.

At the Aspen Ideas Festival in Colorado last July, John Fetterman, the mayor 1 of Braddock, a small Pennsylvania town ten miles upriver from Pittsburgh, was introduced by Dana Gioia, former chairman of the National Endowment for the Arts, as a man who demonstrates "how ideas can change the world." It was four days into the weeklong festival, and Fetterman, a forty-one-year-old, 6-foot-8 white man with a shaved head, a fibrous black beard, and tattoos up one arm and down the other, was presenting a slideshow about how art could bring social change to a town where one-third of its 2,671 residents, a majority of whom are African-American and female, live in poverty. Fetterman projected pictures of old, bustling Braddock, which steel made until the middle of the twentieth century and unmade throughout the rest. Its main street was packed with shoppers, its storefronts filled with wares. Then he turned to Braddock as it is today.

"We've lost 90 percent of our population and 90 percent of our buildings," 2 he said. "Ninety percent of our town is in a landfill. So we took a two-pronged approach. We created the first art gallery in the four-town region, with artists' studios. We did public art installations. And, I don't know if you consider it arts, exactly, but I consider growing organic vegetables in the shadow of a steel mill an art, and that has attracted homesteading."

Fetterman displayed a picture of a furniture store, which the nonprofit he 3 founded bought in 2009 for $15,000, and an abandoned church, which is being turned into a community center, and former building lots that are now green spaces, and an outdoor pizza oven, made with bricks from a demolished building, and a house belonging to two of the homesteaders who have moved to Braddock from "all over the country."

"They bought this house for $4,300," Fetterman told the crowd, "and put 4 in a lot of sweat equity, and now it looks like something you'd see in a magazine." The audience was enchanted. Here was a guy in biker boots bringing the Park Slope (Aspen, Marin, Portland, Santa Fe) ethos—organic produce, art installations, an outdoor bread oven—to the disenfranchised. "What was Braddock like before we took office? Braddock was a notorious community that was steeped in violence. But as of—knock on wood—today, we are now twenty-seven months without a homicide." The audience began to clap and didn't stop for a long time.

As the event wound down, Gioia asked Fetterman to explain the numbers 5 tattooed on his arms. "This one," the mayor said, holding out his right forearm, "is the Braddock ZIP code, 15104. And this one," he said, switching arms, "are the dates of the five people we lost to senseless violence in Braddock since I took office." The audience clapped again. When the applause died out, people swarmed the mayor. A woman from a foundation in Dallas wanted to make a grant. "Whatever you're interested in, we have projects up the wazoo," he said. A sculptor offered one of her pieces. "We use art to combat the dark side of capitalism," Fetterman replied. A man asked how many people had made the move to Braddock. "It's the same as 4,000 people moving into Pittsburgh," Fetterman said, not offering a real number. Then Lynn Goldsmith, a photographer known for her portraits of rock stars, asked if she could take his picture, and in the shade of the building, the mayor struck a pose, unsmiling, arms out.

With appearances this past year or so on "The Colbert Report," CBS News 6 Sunday Morning, PBS, and CNN, John Fetterman has become the face of Rust Belt renewal. He was dubbed America's "coolest mayor" by *The Guardian* and the Mayor of Hell by *Rolling Stone*. *The Atlantic* included him in its "Brave New Thinkers" issue of 2009. In contrast to urban planners caught up in political wrangling, budget constraints, and bureaucratic shambling, Fetterman embraces a do-it-yourself aesthetic and a tendency to put up his own money to move things along. He has turned a thirteen-block town into a sampling of urban renewal trends: land-banking (replacing vacant buildings with green space, as in Cleveland); urban agriculture (Detroit); championing the creative class to bring new energy to old places (an approach popularized by Richard Florida); "greening" the economy as a path out of poverty (as Majora Carter has worked to do in the South Bronx); embracing depopulation (like nearby Pittsburgh). Thrust into the national spotlight, Fetterman has become something of a folk hero, a Paul Bunyan of hipster urban revival, with his own Shepard Fairey block print—the Fetterman mien with the word "mayor" underneath. *This,* the poster suggests, is what a mayor should be.

I met Mayor John, as he likes to be called, for the first time on a warm 7 summer day. We sat on the porch of a former convent, across the street from Andrew Carnegie's first American steel mill, the Edgar Thomson Steel Works, which now employs fewer than one-tenth of the workers it used to and was sending a steady cloud of steam and particulates into a perfect blue sky. Next door, at a school-turned-gallery, two New York artists were taking down a show. Nearby, on a parcel of land called Braddock Farms run by the Pittsburgh non-profit Grow Pittsburgh, a lone young man pulled weeds. Behind the convent, students from a charter school a couple of towns over were tending a bee colony. Mayor John, who wore low-hanging jeans and a black T-shirt, said the bees were found in one of the town's many abandoned buildings and "repurposed."

Had I sat there all day, as the beekeepers and artists and farmers wandered 8 in and out of view, listening to Fetterman explain how the population of Braddock had gone from 20,000 people crammed into houses built fast and cheap in 1920, to less than 2,700 now, and how, as the population dwindled, the stores all closed, too, and how he paid a guy out of his own pocket to drive around town giving out ice cream to poor kids because their town was "a food desert," and taken in his explanation that Braddock was gentrification-proof because "even if housing prices tripled, which they'd never do, a house would still only cost $15,000," I might have been so convinced of the answer that I would have forgotten to ask the question: Is Braddock a model for bringing a Rust Belt town back to life?

Urban decline has been around just about as long as there have been cities, 9 but the degeneration of America's industrial heartland, because it cuts across a wide swath of the country and is as much about jobs as it is about habitation, has seemed both intractable and inevitable. Earlier efforts to address it involved razing whole neighborhoods and erecting Robert Moses-inspired projects. But in places like Youngstown, Detroit, and Pittsburgh, as well as satellites like Braddock, where urban blight was not just a matter of run-down neighborhoods but of manufacturing plants packing up and moving away, even such radical solutions offered little hope. It's one thing to replace substandard housing stock, quite another to reinvent an economy.

Typically, when John Fetterman talks about his town, he starts with the long 10 list of businesses that once lined its main street. "In 2010," Fetterman then invariably says, "those numbers have dropped to zero." It is a stunning, almost unfathomable decline, and it suggests why Braddock has become a favorite media stand-in for Rust Belt devastation, even if what Fetterman says is not precisely true. A medical clinic, auto garages, a florist, an optometrist, three markets, a preschool, a parochial school, a dollar store, and Carnegie's first public library continue to do business alongside empty buildings wrapped in barbed wire.

John Fetterman showed up in Braddock in 2001. He had tried the family 11 business, insurance, but it didn't take, and he ended up joining AmeriCorps and moving to Pittsburgh in the late '90s. After a two-year interlude at Harvard's Kennedy School studying education and social policy, Fetterman was hired to start a program for at-risk youth in Braddock, a town beset by violence. Two years later, Fetterman bought the church that he planned to turn into a community center; it was part of his Aspen slideshow, which he planned to turn into a community center. He squatted in the church for a while, then, entranced by the town's "malignant beauty," bought the warehouse next door and turned it into a Dwell-worthy loft, topped by two remodeled shipping containers for additional living space. Four years after arriving in town, he ran for mayor.

In Braddock, executive decisions are made by an elected six-person borough 12 council, and day-to-day municipal affairs are run by a nonelected borough manager. The mayor, who works for a salary of $150 a month, has two main functions: to break a tie and to oversee the police (he has veto power but can be overruled by a majority council vote). Fetterman knew this, of course, but he thought being mayor would give him a "bully pulpit." Fetterman made no attempt to hide his belief that most of the borough council members had little interest in furthering the fortunes of the town and were using their positions mainly to benefit themselves. The borough manager, Ella B. Jones (who was later charged with forgery and theft of $178,000 of the town's money, a charge to which she pleaded not guilty), considered Fetterman to be a wealthy interloper, the "great white hope" of Braddock, as Jones put it. "Council makes the laws," Jones said in 2006. "They do it all. They have the vote. They make the rules. And he doesn't."

So Fetterman built a back door—he started a nonprofit organization called 13 Braddock Redux, financed until recently primarily by family money. (His father is its largest individual donor.) Because Fetterman is the head of a nonprofit that uses Fetterman money, and because for the longest time it had only two other members, Jeb Feldman, a friend, and Helen Wachter, the head of the countywide KEYS-AmeriCorps program (which supplied volunteers to the nonprofit, including an assistant for Fetterman), Braddock Redux is known around town as John's Nonprofit. Before it became part of Braddock Redux, the Fettermans put up the money for the church next to the mayor's house, which is popularly called John's Church. Braddock Redux owns the convent across the street from the steel mill, which is known as John's Convent. Feldman has the title to the convent school, which is known as Jeb's School. The church houses the county's summer program, the Braddock Youth Project, among other things. The convent sometimes serves as a hostel for potential "urban pioneers," and the middle school as a gallery and studio space. By heading a nonprofit that is a major property owner, the mayor was able to advance what he calls his "social-justice agenda" without having much political power, or the burden of it, either.

In 2009, when the Levi's jeans company wanted to use Braddock to promote 14 a line of work clothes, it approached Fetterman, not the borough council. The million and a half dollars Levi's offered in exchange went to John's Nonprofit, for John's Church and community center, rather than the town's coffers. It was a closed loop that didn't sit well with some of the mayor's constituents, even those who voted for him in the last election, in 2009, which he won, 294 to 103.

"I came back to Braddock because I was interested in what John was doing," 15 Pat Morgan, a church musician told me one evening after a borough council meeting. "But he doesn't play well with others. He decides we need a youth center, and he's going to put it here, but I never hear him come to one of these council meetings and say, 'You know what, I've got some money, what should we do with it?' If you're casting yourself as the mayor who speaks for Braddock, we want him to at least pretend that we have a say in any of this."

It was a sentiment I would hear numerous times, from longtime residents 16 like the filmmaker Tony Buba ("John's idea of grass roots is Astroturf") as well as from transplants. Because he ran a nonprofit, Fetterman operated with limited public accountability. It was efficient—Braddock Redux could buy a building and get the H. J. Heinz Company Foundation to donate $100,000 to put a green roof on it and bypass the pesky part where people debate the pros and cons. But as a consequence, no matter how sincere Fetterman's "social justice agenda," it is, in the end, often perceived as his.

"The key to urban reclamation is citizen participation," David Lewis told 17 me when I visited him in Homestead, another struggling Mon Valley borough across the river from Braddock. An architect and urban planner known for his emphasis on community participation, Lewis was instrumental in a massive redevelopment project there called the Waterfront. "You start with the people," Lewis said.

Fetterman, who did convene a group of residents to plan the community center, likes to say that he won the last election 2 to 1. "The election was a referendum on the things I've done," he said. 18

Levi's Braddock ad campaign had its debut in movie theaters across the country on July 4th weekend. "We were taught how the pioneers went into the West. They opened their eyes and made up what things could be," a girl intoned. "A long time ago, things got broken here. People got sad and left. Maybe the world breaks on purpose so we can have work to do. People think there aren't frontiers anymore. They can't see how frontiers are all around us." 19

That same weekend, billboards with Braddock, PA, along the bottom appeared in Times Square and across the country. They featured portraits of some of the finer-looking denizens of the town, like Dave Rosenstraus, whose company, Fossil Free Fuel, was the one new business in town (which recently spawned another, still with the same partners); Jack Samuel, a member of a straight-edge-vegan-punk-rock collective; and Deanne Dupree, whose boyfriend was the last homicide in town. They carried the affirming slogan "Everybody's Work Is Equally Important," which had a touch of irony in a place where so many people cannot find jobs. 20

The urban-pioneer motif in the Levi's ads was part of the Braddock revival story from the beginning. One of the first things Fetterman did when he took office was offer free studio space to artists. "It's hard to appreciate how big a leap of faith it was," the mayor told me. "No way artists are going to come out to Braddock" from Pittsburgh "at nine at night for studio space. The perception was that it was too dangerous." It was easy to segue from there to offering—or at least pointing to the availability of—cheap housing to anyone willing to make up what could be. Still, according to Fetterman, "we have never tried to bring people in. It's just like media interest. They've just found us." 21

That media interest was itself an invitation, and it began with a colorful spread in 2007 in the magazine *ReadyMade.* In the accompanying article, the mayor declared: "We need to get people excited about living in Braddock again. For D.I.Y.-ers, this town is a dream." The article, which highlighted Fetterman's own rugged homesteading experience, flew around the Internet and was picked up by the mainstream media. The *Daily Beast* did a "live chat." *The New York Times* published three separate articles. Japanese and Swiss television crews showed up. So did the curious, the adventurous, the idealistic. "Braddock would not be possible if it were not for the Internet," Fetterman said. "To be able to type in 'Braddock' and pull up this wealth of information and you can draw your own beliefs on it—it's impossible to overstate that." 22

In Aspen, when Fetterman was asked how many "modern pioneers" had moved to Braddock, he framed his answer as an equivalence: it was like 4,000 people moving to Pittsburgh, he said, which sounded like a lot. The actual number is currently twenty-three, in ten households. Modern pioneering turns out to be harder than just fixing a wrecked house, which turns out to be hard enough. Gutting and renovating a structure that wasn't built well the first time can easily compete with having a regular job. In Braddock, a successful modern pioneer typically requires family money, savings, or another outside means of support, and even then it's often a stretch. 23

And, for "urban pioneers" and longtime residents, it can be challenging to 24
live in a place that is getting so much attention. They resent their town being
cast as a wasteland. They resent hearing that it "broke on purpose." They resent
that some of the good things done by groups not affiliated with the mayor, like
a new, state-of-the-art senior housing complex, or the thirty-six new homes and
rental units built by the Mon Valley Initiative, which house eighty-nine people
and have brought an influx of working families to Braddock (most headed by
women employed in a range of jobs in the area), rarely find their way into the
prevailing narrative. And they resent that one man's vision is represented as
their collective vision, even while acknowledging that some of his actions, like
planting fruit trees in abandoned lots, using Levi's money to finance a children's
librarian and helping to get a new playground donated to the town make Braddock a more appealing, and most likely safer, place.

"I get jealous reading those stories because I want to live in that place," Jodi 25
Morrison said. Morrison grew up a few towns over and moved to Braddock
from Brooklyn in 2008 after learning about its progressive mayor. Morrison,
who is thirty-three, was showing me the colossal bank building she bought
almost three years ago for $125,000. At the time, Morrison wasn't sure what
she was going to do with it but figured it didn't matter. She'd come to Braddock,
and the spirit of the place would move her. Not long after that, the roof sprang
a massive leak. "My life here has become reactionary," Morrison said. "It's
whatever crisis has come up that week that I have to fix. I'm way overwhelmed.
I don't know how I am going to do this alone."

A few blocks away, Morrison's friends Jenny and Kevin Fremlin are not 26
just overwhelmed; they're angry. The couple, who are in their thirties,
moved here from Juneau, Alaska, after an exploratory visit. They liked what
they saw: arts groups working with kids, a potluck at a neighbor's house
and the 17,000-square-foot former Chevy dealership that Fetterman's sister,
Kristin, and her partner, Joel Rice, were converting (for about $250,000)
into a magnificent furniture workshop, loft, greenhouse and textile studio.
The Fremlins were eager to buy a $5,000 house but agreed to manage John's
Convent in exchange for free housing on its third floor. By the time they
arrived from Alaska, dog and possessions in tow, it had been declared
uninhabitable.

Paradoxically, it can be difficult to find a home in Braddock. Many buildings 27
are slated for demolition, and there is a relatively profitable Section 8 rental
market for those that aren't. Eventually, with the mayor's help, the Fremlins
found a house on one of the more crime-ridden streets.

That was more than two years ago. Their $5,000 house has now cost them 28
nearly $60,000, and they are broke. There was drive-by shooting out front. They
own a shotgun because it is more intimidating than a handgun. "Most people
come here because of the hype that you can get houses cheap and fulfill your
dreams," said Jenny, who runs an online communications design business. "We
came here so we could work less and do the projects we wanted, and we're
working more than we ever did."

Kevin, her husband, agreed. "We've spent every dime we had and then 29
some," he said. "It's a hard pill to swallow when you realize you have squandered
your nest egg. Squandered. It's gone."

Scale is a tricky variable when it pertains to turning around a city, especially 30
one as small as Braddock. From 2000 to 2009, the population has declined by

241; about 600 jobs were lost last year alone when the University of Pittsburgh Medical Center closed the local hospital. Those are big numbers in a small place, and they represent a tide that even a personality as large as Fetterman's is unable to hold back. Nonetheless, tearing down a single abandoned building and returning the lot to green space, or renovating a dilapidated house, has its own significance: it suggests something else is possible.

"We have made our lives here, started a family and support local events and fundraisers, even if we aren't always happy about living here and hope to move out," Jenny Fremlin wrote in a recent e-mail. On their own, she and Jodi Morrison are starting a "friends of the library group" and hope someday to open a used bookstore in an unused part of the library. 31

For the mayor, though, fostering civic engagement is not a necessary corollary to urban homesteading. "If someone wants to buy a house and live their life and pay their taxes, that's fine," Fetterman said. "Ninety percent of old Braddock walked away. That left a lot of chaos in town." 32

Which raises the question: Is urban renewal just a matter of showing up? 33

On Wood Street, Jack Samuel, the twenty-five-year-old straight-edge vegan punk rocker and Levi's model, was hanging out in one of the two houses he and the six other members of the Some Ideas Collective bought last year. The group wanted an inexpensive "live-work" space where they could play music, write, and work on bikes. They bought a house for $6,000 from a filmmaker who was moving on. It was run-down, but for kids whose goal was to "make life cheap enough" so they could "binge work and then be free," it was just fine. 34

"My goal is to build for myself a life that meets my needs most effectively," Samuel explained last summer. "So that means the lowest possible overhead costs day to day. If you qualify for food stamps, that's that much less money you have to make. I've been on food stamps for the last few months." 35

Samuel and his collective did not move to Braddock with the intent of "fixing it." That idea, he said, "is potentially very colonial or paternalistic." "I got a little blinded by the image of Braddock that has been portrayed by the media, that all this place is is an artist's compound. And then getting here, it's like, 'Oh, there are just people who live here.' This is home for a lot of people, a lot of low-income people in particular." 36

James Smith, a thirty-two-year-old Braddock native, often hangs out in the dollar-store parking lot with a group of friends. A graduate of the local high school, Smith can find only temp work, like cleaning Heinz Stadium after Steelers' games. The weekly farmers' market in Braddock is OK, Smith says, but even if he wanted to shop there, he couldn't afford it. Jobs and public transportation to get to them remain in short supply. Nothing that was happening in Braddock—not the green roof on the old furniture store, not the screen printing studio run by members of a socially conscious arts collective, not beehives, not the Shepard Fairey art installation on a nearby wall, not the Levi's ad campaign—has changed the most essential facts of his life: he is poor and without prospects. "The mayor is doing good things for the kids, and that does matter most, the future," he told me. "But what about the future that was neglected? Our generation, the generation before us. There is nothing for us." 37

One afternoon at the mayor's house, the former warehouse he shares with his wife and young son, I asked him how having seven underemployed twenty-somethings move to town was a strategy for change. "What's better, having 38 a group of kids like Jack buy a house, or waiting another six years till the buildings fall in on themselves?" the mayor asked.

A few weeks later I got an e-mail from Fetterman. "I know I am not Braddock's savior, never felt that way, and never will," he wrote. "There's no 'Rudystyle ending' waiting for me where I get carried off the field and everything turns out OK for me or for Braddock," he continued, referring to the Notre Dame football legend.   39

I'd heard the mayor use that analogy a number of times before; it had   40
seemed like a throwaway line. Reading it now, though, I realized that it went some way toward explaining why the mayor of such a small town had got so much attention. The Braddock story has the appeal of an inspirational sports movie: we want this guy to win the game against all odds. We want to believe that all it takes to fix a town is—to borrow a phrase from Samuel and his friends—"some ideas."

READING COMPREHENSION

1. The word *disenfranchised* in "Here was a guy in biker boots bringing the Park Slope ethos . . . to the disenfranchised" (paragraph 5) means
   a. not interested, disengaged.
   b. independent.
   c. deprived of power, marginalized.
   d. forbidden to vote.

2. The word *reclamation* in "The key to urban reclamation is citizen participation" (paragraph 17) means
   a. change.
   b. restoration.
   c. decline.
   d. revision.

3. Which of the following would be a good alternative title for this selection?
   a. Grow Pittsburgh
   b. Biker Boy Buys Votes
   c. A Disastrous Mayor
   d. Finding a Future

4. Which sentence best expresses the main idea of the selection?
   a. Everyone in Braddock is excited about the mayor's vision.
   b. The mayor is trying to revitalize his town, despite the obstacles.
   c. More and more towns in America are dying because of the lack of jobs.
   d. People who don't want to work should move to towns like Braddock.

5. What do the tattoos on Fetterman's arm stand for?
   a. the birthdates of his children
   b. the important fraternity dates from his college days

c. the number of people killed in Braddock since he took office and the address of City Hall

(d.) the dates of the people killed in Braddock since he took office and the zip code of Braddock

6. What qualifications does Fetterman have to be mayor?

a. past experience working in insurance

b. attendance at Harvard's Kennedy School studying social policy

c. running a program for at-risk youth

(d.) all of the above

7. Halpern uses the term "Rust Belt town" to describe Braddock. Based on contextual clues, what does this term mean?

a. A dirty, dingy town with lots of rusty buildings.

b. A town that no longer produces any type of industrial product and now focuses on green products.

(c.) A town that used to thrive by manufacturing industrial products, but now has multiple factories that are shut down.

d. A town that used to create a lot of products, but has now focused on producing only one type of product.

8. Why does Fetterman believe his position offers him a "bully pulpit"?

(a.) He doesn't feel the city council has revitalization of Braddock at the forefront of its agenda, so he believes his position is to "bully" the council into making revitalization its top priority.

b. He wants to run and dominate the town, so he feels that becoming mayor will allow him to do whatever he wants.

c. Bullying has been a problem in Braddock, so the mayor feels that his position will now allow him to eradicate all forms of bullying.

d. The city council has had a history of bullying the residents into participating in projects they don't like, so Fetterman sees his position as the one to put a stop to this bullying.

9. What does Halpern mean by "Fetterman built a back door" (paragraph 13)?

a. He figured out how to fix most of the run-down buildings.

b. He figured out a way to work with the city council.

c. He started a non-profit organization.

(d.) He figured out a way around all the red tape of the city council.

10. The author implies that

(a.) many of the current residents of Braddock have been surprised by what real life is like in the town.

b. the mayor of Braddock is a con artist.

c. only someone with a degree from an elite college could take on such a project.

d. the film about Braddock was a joke.

STRUCTURE AND TECHNIQUE

1. What method of introduction—brief story, stating importance of topic, or broad-to-narrow—does Halpern use? Why do you think she chose this way to begin her article?

2. Halpern employs the use of dialogue throughout her article. Why do you think she does this, and do you find it effective?

3. What pattern(s) of development does Halpern use in her article?

4. Analyze how the tone changes throughout the article.

CRITICAL READING AND DISCUSSION

1. What is Halpern's purpose in using these details—shaved head, tattoos, 6-foot-8—in her description of Fetterman ?

2. The slogan, "Everybody's Work Is Equally Important," was featured on billboards across the country. The author stated that this slogan was ironic when applied to Braddock because so many were out of work. Why do you think this slogan was featured? Do you agree that it is ironic, or might it have a different purpose? Explain your reasoning.

3. Not all the people interviewed are happy with Fetterman and the way he is running things, yet he has been reelected. Why do you think Fetterman is handling the revitalization of Braddock in the manner he is?

4. The article ends on a realistic, rather than a happy, note. Instead of touting Fetterman as the savior of Braddock, Halpern portrays the reality of trying to save a dying town. Why wouldn't Halpern want to end her article on a more positive note? Do you think she supports Fetterman? Do you think she condones his actions?

WRITING ASSIGNMENTS

Assignment 1: Writing a Paragraph

Fetterman has spent personal money to help revitalize Braddock. You are to write a paragraph explaining what you would do if you were given a million dollars, with the stipulation that it had to be used to benefit others in your community. You will want to explain in detail what you would do with the money, how it would benefit your community, and your reasons for selecting certain causes and not others.

Assignment 2: Writing an Essay

In paragraph 14, Halpern refers to the Levi's ad campaign: "A long time ago, things got broken here. People got sad and left. Maybe the world breaks on purpose so we can have work to do. People think there aren't frontiers any-more. They can't see how frontiers are all around us." Write an essay in which you respond to the quote and discuss whether or not you agree with the ideas being presented by the advertisement.

Assignment 3: Writing an Essay

Fetterman sometimes bypassed the city council to get things done—much to the annoyance of many of the members. Most people, however, have to work through proper channels. Write a letter to your city council discussing something that needs to be done to improve your community or discussing the need to streamline a process, such as applying for a permit to demolish a blighted building, improving a playground, or getting speed bumps installed to slow traffic.

RESPONDING TO IMAGES

When you think of the word "mayor," is this the picture that comes to mind? How do you think our perceptions of jobs affect who we believe should be doing these jobs? And, conversely, how do our images of different people affect our thinking about how well they might fit a particular job?

©ANDREW RUSH/AP Images

Why You May Need Social Media for Your Career

John Warner

©Robert Grant

PREVIEW

John Warner is an author and professor. He has written several books and contributed articles to the *Chicago Tribune* and *Inside Higher Ed*. He has taught creative writing at Clemson University and College of Charleston, both in South Carolina. This article examines social media as a career catalyst rather than a pastime or hobby.

Writing recently in the *New York Times*, Georgetown associate professor of computer science Cal Newport recommended that people should "quit social media because it can hurt your career." 1

Unlike those who believe that a social media presence is *necessary* to improve their job prospects (not sure who these people are, but never mind), Prof. Newport 2 sees social media use as the enemy of "deep thinking," which in turn hinders professional development.

TEACHING TIP
Ask students to discuss what they think the author means by "deep thinking."

Prof. Newport's theory in his own words: "In a capitalist economy, the market rewards things that are rare and valuable. Social media use is decidedly not rare or valuable. Any 16-year-old with a smartphone can invent a hashtag or repost a viral article. The idea that if you engage in enough of this low-value activity, it will somehow add up to something of high value in your career is the same dubious alchemy that forms the core of most snake oil and flimflam in business." 3

We can begin to see the edges of the argument fray already, for example conflating all social media use with the reposting of memes or other trivial things. For those interested, social media can be an outlet for important alternative perspectives, as illustrated just yesterday by a thread of tweets authored by Nicole Hemmer, a professor who studies extremist right wing ideologies, in response to a particularly poorly argued *New York Times* op-ed. 4

But the core shortcoming of Prof. Newport's argument is here: "Professional success is hard, but it's not complicated. The foundation to achievement and fulfillment, almost without exception, requires that you hone a useful craft and then apply it to things that people care about. This is a philosophy perhaps best summarized by the advice Steve Martin used to give aspiring entertainers: 'Be so good they can't ignore you.' If you do that, the rest will work itself out, regardless of the size of your Instagram following." 5

Here we have a pretty unremarkable description of the so-called "meritocracy," but one that those who live in the real world recognize as a fantasy. Among those who recognize this as fantasy are the vast majority of professional comedians who will eagerly tell you about the funniest comedians they know, hands down, but you've never heard of them because. . . 6

. . . because professional success is actually pretty damn complicated. If I was being uncharitable, I might even call what Prof. Newport's peddling snake oil.[1] 7

Well meaning snake oil, no doubt, but oversimplified flimflam nonetheless. Yes, we should all strive to be good, but Prof. Newport's vision presumes a level playing field where the same moves (or "hacks" as he calls them) by different people will garner the same results, but we know this is not true. 8

For example, academia, which seems to have been kind to Prof. Newport, is not equally hospitable for all who choose to participate. 9

Take two of my favorite writers/scholars, Tressie McMillan Cottom and Roxane Gay. As women of color, history shows us they likely need to be better than "good" in order to receive the recognition that Prof. Newport believes will come if you do what the meritocracy asks. These women had every reason to believe that their being good would indeed be ignored. 10

TEACHING TIP
Encourage students to look up Cottom and Gay's social media sites.

And so each in their own way used social media not to tweet memes or fart around, but to advocate for recognition of their (and others') "goodness." In addition to their distinguished scholarly and professional work they utilized the tool of social media to become public voices. They made space for themselves that otherwise might not have been available. 11

It worked. Not only do Professors Cottom and Gay now frequently publish in prestige outlets like *The Atlantic* or the *New York Times*, but they also have 12

[1]There's an additional disconnect in Prof. Newport's work in that all of his advice to students is to "do less," i.e., find the "hacks" and shortcuts to "success." *Born Standing Up*, Steve Martin's memoir of becoming a comedian that Newport references is all about the opposite, that there are no shortcuts.

established platforms independent of those outlets where they may be heard. Prof. Cottom's essay "Finding Hope in a Loveless Place," for my money the most profound work of commentary in the wake of the recent election, became a viral read after being posted on her own blog.

But for Profs Cottom and Gay, entering into a conversation to which many 13 think they do not belong comes with a price, as the racist and sexist invective they are subject to on social media is grotesque.[2] Even as they have made themselves indispensable to the cultural conversation, there are people who seek to drive them out. I am going to go on a limb and say that Prof. Newport has never experienced this, and not only because he chooses not to be on social media, but because he is unlikely to be treated as an interloper.

There is no "hack" to undo racism or sexism. You cannot "nudge" a white 14 supremacist towards a more enlightened world view.

Neither is there a "hack" to undo a generation of privatizing the public 15 space, which has left a lot of young scholars in the humanities who are "so good they can't be ignored" nonetheless work without the security of tenurable employment. This work is supposed to have "value," isn't it? Prof. Newport's ethos asks us to ignore this sort of injustice.

The source of Prof. Newport's narrow gaze is the same flaw we see in all 16 self-help books, a singular focus on the success stories. His oeuvre: *How to Win at College, How to Become a Straight A Student, How to Be a High School Superstar* are all targeted to the relatively privileged, those who are competing from the already rarefied air, for example, those for whom the advice not to take so many A.P. courses may apply because their high schools actually offer A.P. courses.

Prof. Newport peddles a fantasy, a lie, one that resonates with a narrow slice 17 of the professional class and all but erases the experiences of those who have been traditionally marginalized. I don't want to lie to my students, which is why I tell them hard, focused work is necessary, but there's no guarantee it's enough because what is "valuable" has not all that much to do with our values.

I tell my students success is complicated, failure too for that matter. If we 18 want a world where hard work counts, we have to work towards making a world that truly rewards those values.

READING COMPREHENSION

1. The word *engage* in "if you engage in enough of this low-value activity" (paragraph 3) means
   a. to begin and carry on an occupation or interest.
   b. to pledge oneself; to make a guarantee.
   c. to hold the attention of and cause to participate.
   d. to bind someone to do something, especially a pledge to marry.

2. The word *conflating* in "conflating all social media use with the reposting of memes or other trivial things" (paragraph 4) means
   a. separating.
   b. amalgamating.

[2]I've debated with myself as to whether or not to illustrate this with specific examples, but have ultimately chosen not to because, A. The worst perpetrators of the hateful responses seem to desire and feed off the specific attention, and B. The evidence is readily available if you go look for yourself.

   c.   combining.

   (d.) confusing.

3. The word *interloper* in "he is likely to be treated as an interloper" (paragraph 13) means

   a.   alien.

   b.   refugee.

   (c.) intruder.

   d.   stranger.

4. Which of the following would be a good alternative title for this selection?

   (a.) Using Public Space to Get Noticed

   b.   Privatizing the Public Space

   c.   Social Media Wastes Time

   d.   Prestigious Publishing

5. Which sentence best expresses the main idea of the selection?

   a.   People must have a strong social media presence in order to get ahead in life.

   b.   People must avoid wasting time on social media as it has no positive bearing on careers.

   (c.) Strategically using social media to create a presence can be helpful for many who are trying to advance their careers.

   d.   Strategically using social media to push ideas and causes is a sure way for people to become known in their fields.

6. What does the author mean by pointing out that academia might have been hospitable to Professor Newport, but this isn't the case for all who choose to participate?

   a.   Students were probably friendly to Professor Newport but might treat other professors more hostilely.

   (b.) Other academics probably welcomed and included Professor Newport, but not all academics are treated this way by other professors.

   c.   Professor Newport probably found college easy to navigate, but not all students have this experience.

   d.   Professor Newport is probably very helpful and welcoming to his students, but this isn't the case with every professor.

7. What does the author mean by "they made space for themselves that otherwise would not have been made available"?

   a.   Academia is now embracing social media use, and academics who use it are going to be welcomed.

   b.   Academia has always been a men's club that has done everything in its power to keep out women academics.

   (c.) Academia has not been open to women and people of color, so in order to break into academia, they have had to do things differently.

   d.   Academia has always required people to be creative in order to become a part of its culture.

8. According to the essay, where was Professor Cottom's most profound work published?

   a. *The Atlantic*

   b. the *New York Times*

   c. the college newspaper

   d. her own blog

9. According to the essay, who comprises the audience for Professor Newport's books and writings?

   a. minority students

   b. privileged students

   c. college students

   d. journalism students

10. We can conclude that the author's beliefs about social media have been influenced by

    a. other professors' research.

    b. other professors' experiences.

    c. other writers' articles.

    d. other students' experiences.

STRUCTURE AND TECHNIQUE

1. What type of introduction does Warner use?

2. What points of view (first person, second person, and/or third person) does the author employ? Why do you think he uses this approach? Do you think the approach is effective?

3. What rhetorical modes does Warner use to create his well-written essay?

4. Warner doesn't include a traditional concluding paragraph that looks back at the thesis. Why do you think he does this, and do you think his conclusion is effective?

CRITICAL READING AND DISCUSSION

1. Do you agree with Professor Newport's opinion that social media usage is a "low-value activity" that can hurt your career prospects or with John Warner's opinion that social media usage can help people create space for themselves, leading to career prospects?

2. Why do you think the author highlighted Tressie McMillan Cottom and Roxane Gay as examples instead of other, better known people who have used social media to further their careers?

3. Think about your planned career field. Do you believe it is easier for some people to get into that field? Whom do you think it caters to? Do you believe social media use, or some other medium, will help or hurt your career options? What other activities could you engage in to increase your chances at a career in your chosen field?

WRITING ASSIGNMENTS

Assignment 1: Writing a Paragraph

Think about your social media use. What types do you use? Do you interact with social media every day, multiple times a day, or just a few times a week? Write a paragraph in which you discuss whether or not you think your social media use is a benefit or a drawback in your daily life.

Assignment 2: Writing an Essay

Critique the essay. Are the arguments in Warner's essay clear? Do you feel that Warner successfully supports his arguments? If not, in what areas should he have gone deeper? What types of support would have helped his argument? Have any ideas been overemphasized or underemphasized? Are there any statements that you find to be unclear? Has the author made any assumptions about his readers that could have an impact on how well the essay is received? Does the author have an evident bias that affects how his information is presented?

Once you have read through the essay and answered as many questions as possible, you will need to create a thesis that emphasizes your overall impression of the essay. You will then need to organize your ideas around your thesis, so you can create a strong argument. You may need to look at Chapter 14, "Argument" and Chapter 20, "Working with Sources" to help you integrate quotes, paraphrases, and summaries from the article into your essay.

Assignment 3: Writing an Essay

Professor Newport believes that social media can hurt an individual's career. Many professors also argue that social media can hurt a student's education and hinder his or her chances of graduating.

Write an essay in which you argue whether or not social media use has a positive or negative impact on students' classwork, grades, and graduation rates. You may need to do some research to find statistics or other articles that support your argument. If you do research, you will want to review Part 5, "Research-Based Writing," in order to find good sources and properly incorporate your outside sources and their ideas into your essay.

Lincoln's Second Inaugural Address (1865)

Abraham Lincoln

PREVIEW

Abraham Lincoln was the sixteenth president of the United States and is most revered for the Emancipation Proclamation and his leadership through the Civil War in preserving the Union. On March 4, 1865, he delivered this Inaugural Address for his second term, forty-three days before he was assassinated and about two months before the Civil War officially ended.

At this second appearing to take the oath of the Presidential office there is 1
less occasion for an extended address than there was at the first. Then a statement somewhat in detail of a course to be pursued seemed fitting and proper.
Now, at the expiration of four years, during which public declarations have
been constantly called forth on every point and phase of the great contest
which still absorbs the attention and engrosses the energies of the nation, little
that is new could be presented. The progress of our arms, upon which all else
chiefly depends, is as well known to the public as to myself, and it is, I trust,
reasonably satisfactory and encouraging to all. With high hope for the future,
no prediction in regard to it is ventured.

On the occasion corresponding to this four years ago all thoughts were 2
anxiously directed to an impending civil war. All dreaded it, all sought to avert
it. While the inaugural address was being delivered from this place, devoted
altogether to *saving* the Union without war, insurgent agents were in the city
seeking to *destroy* it without war-seeking to dissolve the Union and divide effects
by negotiation. Both parties deprecated war, but one of them would *make* war
rather than let the nation survive, and the other would *accept* war rather than
let it perish, and the war came.

One-eighth of the whole population were colored slaves, not distributed gen- 3
erally over the Union, but localized in the southern part of it. These slaves
constituted a peculiar and powerful interest. All knew that this interest was somehow the cause of the war. To strengthen, perpetuate, and extend this interest was
the object for which the insurgents would rend the Union even by war, while the
Government claimed no right to do more than to restrict the territorial enlarge-
ment of it. Neither party expected for the war the magnitude or the duration
which it has already attained. Neither anticipated that the *cause* of the conflict
might cease with or even before the conflict itself should cease. Each looked for
an easier triumph, and a result less fundamental and astounding. Both read the
same Bible and pray to the same God, and each invokes His aid against the other.
It may seem strange that any men should dare to ask a just God's assistance in
wringing their bread from the sweat of other men's faces, but let us judge not,
that we be not judged. The prayers of both could not be answered. That of neither
has been answered fully. The Almighty has His own purposes. "Woe unto the
world because of offenses; for it must needs be that offenses come, but woe to
that man by whom the offense cometh." If we shall suppose that American slavery is one of those offenses which, in the providence of God, must needs come,
but which, having continued through His appointed time, He now wills to remove,
and that He gives to both North and South this terrible war as the woe due to
those by whom the offense came, shall we discern therein any departure from
those divine attributes which the believers in a living God always ascribe to Him?
Fondly do we hope, fervently do we pray, that this mighty scourge of war may
speedily pass away. Yet, if God wills that it continue until all the wealth piled by
the bondsman's two hundred and fifty years of unrequited toil shall be sunk, and
until every drop of blood drawn with the lash shall be paid by another drawn
with the sword, as was said three thousand years ago, so still it must be said "the
judgments of the Lord are true and righteous altogether."

With malice toward none, with charity for all, with firmness in the right as 4
God gives us to see the right, let us strive on to finish the work we are in, to
bind up the nation's wounds, to care for him who shall have borne the battle
and for his widow and his orphan, to do all which may achieve and cherish
a just and lasting peace among ourselves and with all nations.

READING COMPREHENSION

1. The word *ventured* in "With high hope for the future, no prediction in regard to it is ventured" (paragraph 1) means
   a. undertaken.
   b. hazardous.
   c. risky.
   d. guaranteed.

2. The word *deprecated* in "Both parties deprecated war" (paragraph 2) means
   a. did not appreciate.
   b. hoped for.
   c. disapproved of.
   d. protested against.

3. The word *fundamental* in "Each looked for an easier triumph, and a result less fundamental and astounding" (paragraph 3) means
   a. original.
   b. indispensable.
   c. primitive.
   d. significant.

4. Which of the following would be a good title for Lincoln's speech?
   a. Let Us Look Toward Healing
   b. Let Us Search for Causes
   c. Who Will Win This War?
   d. Slavery, the South, and War

5. Which sentence best expresses the main idea of the selection?
   a. Lincoln wanted to expose the real reasons behind the Civil War, so he would be seen as a strong president.
   b. Lincoln wanted to be sure Americans understood why the Civil War had happened, the toll it had taken, and that the country could move forward.
   c. Lincoln wanted to place blame on those who fought in the Civil War, so he could shame them into putting an end to it.
   d. Lincoln wanted to present himself as an authoritative, judgmental president who would not tolerate any more civil unrest.

6. What does Lincoln claim was happening while he delivered his first Inaugural Address in 1861?
   a. Soldiers were fighting each other in several Civil War battles.
   b. Insurgents were undermining the American government and trying to dissolve the Union (the United States).
   c. Confederate and Union troops were recruiting young men in preparation for the impending civil war.
   d. Both Union and Confederate lawmakers were working tirelessly to find a way to avoid the impending war.

7. According to the essay, what percentage of the population was made up of slaves?

   (a.) one-eighth
   b.   one-quarter
   c.   three-fifths
   d.   three-quarters

8. To whom is Lincoln referring when he says, "Both read the same Bible and pray to the same God"?

   a.   Protestants and Catholics
   (b.) Northerners and Southerners
   c.   generals and privates
   d.   slaves and slave owners

9. According to Lincoln, what is divine punishment for the sin of slavery?

   a.   war-seeking insurgents
   b.   malice and judgment
   (c.) scourge of war
   d.   progress of our arms

10. *True or False?* _____*True*_____ Lincoln believed that all Americans, both Northerners and Southerners, were complicit in allowing slavery.

STRUCTURE AND TECHNIQUE

1. Lincoln uses a good deal of alliteration and repetition. Find some examples and be ready to discuss their effectiveness and purpose.

2. What point of view (first person, second person, or third person) does Lincoln employ? Do you think this approach is effective?

3. What do you believe Lincoln's purpose is when he says, "let us judge not, that we be not judged"? Have you heard a similar thought expressed elsewhere? Explain your answer.

4. Lincoln's address is very short and contains only four paragraphs. Discuss why you think he thought this was appropriate. Use the essay for support.

CRITICAL READING AND DISCUSSION

1. React to this statement: ". . . one of them would *make* war rather than let the nation survive, and the other would *accept* war rather than let it perish." Identify the two parties Lincoln is referring to and explain the differences in each party's position.

2. In paragraph 3, Lincoln claims "neither party expected for the war the magnitude or the duration which it has already attained." Look up statistics about the Civil War and be prepared to discuss them in class.

3. What do you think Lincoln means when he states, "With malice toward none, with charity for all. . ."? What is his purpose in using these words?

4. Lincoln makes several attempts to unify Northerners and Southerners, even as the war continues. Find several statements that he uses to create unity among the people.

WRITING ASSIGNMENTS

Assignment 1: Writing a Paragraph

Most people consider Abraham Lincoln to be one of the greatest presidents in America, although in his lifetime he was unpopular with many. Write a paragraph about someone you admire because of his or her values and convictions, even if his or her beliefs are not popular with mainstream ideas.

TEACHING TIP
Guide students to use specific details and avoid vague language.

Assignment 2: Writing an Essay

Many people do not believe that slavery was a main causative factor of the Civil War; however, Lincoln states, "These slaves constituted a peculiar and powerful interest. All knew that this interest was somehow the cause of the war." Write an essay in which you react to this statement. You will need to provide evidence as to why you believe his claim to be true or false. Because you will be advancing an argument, you will want to review Chapter 14, "Argument." And because the defense of your argument will require additional research, you will want to be familiar with Chapter 20, "Working with Sources" and Chapter 21, "Writing a Research Paper" in order to properly incorporate and cite your outside information.

Assignment 3: Writing an Essay

John F. Kennedy's Inaugural Address is included in Part 7, Section I. Read Kennedy's address, and then write an essay in which you compare and/or contrast his speech with Lincoln's address. You might want to focus on themes, tones, structure, and promises.

You will need to use evidence from both addresses to support your essay, so you will want to be familiar with Chapter 20, "Working with Sources" in order to properly incorporate and cite the information.

Serena Williams Is the Greatest

The player's record-tying championship at Wimbledon means as much for the world outside of tennis as it does for the sport itself.

Vann R. Newkirk II

PREVIEW

Vann Newkirk is a staff writer for *The Atlantic*. He graduated from Morehouse College with a B.S. in biology and the University of North Carolina at Chapel Hill with a M.S.P.H. in health policy and management. As a journalist, he focuses on politics, policy, and health policy and has contributed to *Daily Kos*, *GQ*, and *Ebony*.

©John Sciulli/Getty Images

Last week, for me, was about Alton Sterling, Philando Castile, and the list of 1
names of hundreds more black bodies that they joined. It was about protests
and it was about anger. It was about 11 police officers wounded and five killed
in a tragic slaughter in Dallas. It was about grief, and it was about my personal
despair that the curtain of racism, inequality, rage, and violence that has covered the country since time immemorial may never be lifted.

Saturday, though, was also about Serena Williams and the magic of her easy 2
7–5 6–3 victory over Angelique Kerber at Wimbledon. For over an hour I had
a respite from digesting and covering a week of pain as I watched Serena blast
serve after serve and raise a single fist in joy after the final point was won. On
Saturday Williams claimed her 22nd women's tennis Grand Slam title, tying
Steffi Graf for the most in the Open Era. On Saturday, she swatted away any—
already dubious—claims that she might not be the greatest.

The importance of Serena's victory and her sixth Wimbledon doubles cham- 3
pionship win with her sister Venus is intimately connected with the week of
trauma and the fact that cries of "black lives matter" currently ring out in the
streets. Those cries are a demand for justice, yes, and that demand is inspirational to anyone who believes in said justice. But they're also rooted in a fear
that a better tomorrow may never come, and in terror and grief over the present
cavalcade of images of dead black bodies. Saturday was a rare instance in which
a sporting event was transfigured into something more, a symbolic victory that
both helped assuage trauma and provided real hope. No living athlete—perhaps
of any gender or in any sport—has represented the spirit of that hope more than
Serena.

The very facts of her life make her an almost too-perfect representative of 4
the basic struggle against racism and prejudice that people of color in the country still face. She and Venus spent their early childhood in Compton, California,
learning the game of tennis on public courts secured by gang members in jeans,
and hydrating with water from a taco stand. Although the sisters later received
the insulated homeschooling and private tennis lessons that define prodigies,
the Williams sisters were often reminded of their race and the fact that it made
them outsiders, no matter how much they dominated.

There was the Indian Wells incident, in which the sisters declined to partic- 5
ipate in the tournament for 14 years after Venus withdrew from a match with
Serena and the crowd subjected the family to boos and alleged verbal abuse.
There are the banal attacks on Serena's body image and femininity. There are
the issues of her marketability in contrast to Maria Sharapova, a far inferior
tennis player who, prior to being banned on doping charges, outpaced Serena
in earnings everywhere but on the court. And then there are the daily racial
slurs and innuendo that every black person of renown has to deal with. Her
success is both an exemplar of the necessary and exhausting business of
blackness—twice as good, twice as humble, twice as nice, twice as amazing—that
black people have to deal in just in order to survive and a glimmer of hope that
on their Sisyphean struggle they might finally see the top of the slope.

That Serena is a black woman is not tangential or merely related to her 6
importance as a symbol of hope, but central to it. Black activism today has been
a conscious redress of its most glaring weaknesses through most of history: the
marginalization of women and queer people. Athletes have often served as symbols of hope for black activism, but rarely have women been accepted as those
symbols. Serena is the perfect hero for today's time and the simple fact is that

no straight man could serve as a symbol that so perfectly encapsulates what Serena does. She is what we want our daughters to be. She is what I'd want my sons to be.

I wrote about Muhammad Ali after his death and how his skills in the ring 7 and his message of blackness, boldness, and beauty became a voice for black America and a balm for its ills in the critical time of rage and sorrow after Martin Luther King Jr.'s death. He was larger than life because he had to be—an incredibly unfair burden that he bore all the same. If the stakes today are less than then, the burden for Serena seems just as heavy. She has carried that burden with the same real, raw humanity and brashness of Ali—perfect in its imperfection—and has managed to cope with the twin perils of racism and misogyny while carrying it. While nobody asks for that burden, and carrying the weight of expectations of thousands (maybe millions) of people is entirely unfair, Serena has accepted it.

TEACHING TIP
Ask students to discuss other incidents of racism and misogyny that Williams has experienced and would support the author's thesis.

The most remarkable part of Serena's victory at Wimbledon Saturday wasn't 8 the flawless and somewhat easy victory over an opponent who just couldn't match her serve, but what happened after. The questions from reporters came almost immediately, not about her victory itself, but the violence of the week before.

"I feel anyone in my color in particular is of concern. I do have nephews 9 that I'm thinking, 'Do I have to call them and tell them, don't go outside. If you get in your car, it might be the last time I see you?'" Serena said. "I don't think that the answer is to continue to shoot our young black men in the United States." Even in the wake of the tragic killings in Dallas, Serena was instrumental in urging that people not yield to the agenda of one man with a gun.

And so she walked off, her place in tennis and sports lore as one of the 10 greatest athletes to ever suit up solidified. But that greatness doesn't only come from what she accomplished inside the lines; it's also from what she means outside of them. The most enduring image from Wimbledon won't be of one of her 13 aces or 39 winners, but of her walking off the court, her hair streaming in the wind, as the crowd cheered on. A single fist, raised.

READING COMPREHENSION

1. The word *digesting* in "I had a respite from digesting and covering a week of pain" (paragraph 2) means
   a. to bear with patience; endure.
   b. to convert food into energy for the body.
   c. to absorb and use.
   d. to arrange in convenient order.

2. The word *tangential* in ". . . that Serena Williams is a black woman is not tangential or merely related to her importance" (paragraph 6) means
   a. pertaining to the nature of a tangent or line; being or moving in the direction of a tangent or line.
   b. digressive, as from a subject under consideration.
   c. merely touching; slightly connected; diverging.
   d. tending to digress or to reply to questions obliquely.

3. The word *misogyny* in "... managed to cope with the twin perils of racism and misogyny" (paragraph 7) means
   a. envy of other women.
   b. contempt for women.
   c. radicalism.
   d. discrimination.

4. Which of the following would be a good alternative title for this selection?
   a. Black Lives Matter
   b. The Grand Slam Queen
   c. Compton, Indian Wells, and Beyond
   d. An Athlete to Revere

5. Which sentence best expresses the main idea of the selection?
   a. Serena Williams's status as one of the greatest athletes of all time has also forced her to carry the weight of expectations of thousands of minorities.
   b. Serena Williams is one of the greatest athletes of all time and should be recognized alongside Mohammad Ali.
   c. Too many people expect Serena Williams to be ladylike and quiet and are disappointed when she doesn't live up to those expectations.
   d. The Williams sisters have become symbols to thousands of African American girls, and because of them, tennis has become more racially diverse.

6. According to this essay, how many Grand Slam titles has Williams earned?
   a. 6
   b. 11
   c. 14
   d. 22

7. According to the author, why is Williams an "almost too-perfect representative of the basic struggle against racism"?
   a. She grew up privileged.
   b. She was homeschooled and took private tennis lessons.
   c. She was from Compton and started out on public courts.
   d. She is an outspoken member of Black Lives Matter.

8. Why did fourteen years pass before Williams competed at Indian Hills?
   a. She and her sister had been treated poorly when Venus had to withdraw.
   b. She was subjected to numerous comments about her body.
   c. Indian Hills tournament organizers refused to invite her.
   d. She was unable to qualify for the tournament for almost fourteen years.

9. To whom does the author compare Serena Williams in importance?
   a. Muhammad Ali
   b. Martin Luther King Jr.
   c. Philando Castile
   d. Alton Sterling

10. *True or False?* _____False_____ After Williams's win at Wimbledon, the reporters asked poignant questions about her tennis skills and performance on the court.

STRUCTURE AND TECHNIQUE

1. Writers are often told to use only one point of view in a piece of writing, but the author breaks this rule. What points of view are used? Why does he switch points of view? Do you find it effective?

2. Newkirk uses a good deal of figurative language in paragraph 5. Locate an example that you find effective and explain why.

3. What type of conclusion does Newkirk use? Discuss why you think he ends his essay in this manner.

CRITICAL READING AND DISCUSSION

1. The author suggests that many in the Black Lives Matter movement fear that a "better tomorrow may never come." React to this statement. What is the author trying to help the reader understand?

2. The author states that "the Williams sisters were often reminded of their race and the fact that it made them outsiders." What do you think the author means by this statement? What evidence does the author offer to support this view?

3. The author says, "Athletes have often served as symbols of hope for black activism, but rarely have women been accepted as those symbols." Do you agree or disagree with this statement? Explain your answer.

4. While this essay focuses on an incredible athlete, much of the underlying message is that racism is still very prevalent. Discuss incidents of racism you have witnessed or experienced firsthand. What do you think can be done to help eliminate racism?

WRITING ASSIGNMENTS

Assignment 1: Writing a Paragraph

If you were given an opportunity to have dinner with the author, Vann Newkirk, or with any of the people mentioned in the article, whom would you choose and why? Use the essay to support your answer.

Assignment 2: Writing an Essay

Newkirk's essay is a profile of the athlete, Serena Williams. Like Williams, there are many athletes whom people look up to and admire. Write an essay in which you profile an athlete who, in your opinion, exemplifies a good role model. Your essay should identify specific traits that demonstrate why this person is a good role model. You will want to include details that support your claim that this person does in fact have the traits that make him or her a good role model.

Assignment 3: Writing an Essay

Newkirk references the Black Lives Matter movement, which was started in 2013. Like many movements, much misinformation has been disseminated about Black Lives Matter. In Chapter 19, "Information Literacy" you were introduced to methods for examining online information; checking the credibility and validity of sites and authors; and locating reliable sources. For this essay, you should implement this knowledge to research Black Lives Matter or another important social movement. You will then write an exemplification essay to explain how the movement was started and to describe its mission, as well as to refute some of the misinformation that has been disseminated.

Raise the Minimum Wage, Reduce Crime?

A new White House report links higher hourly incomes to lower rates of lawbreaking.

Juleyka Lantigua-Williams

©Jason Honyotski/Juleyka Lantigua-Williams

PREVIEW

Juleyka Lantigua-Williams is a writer, editor, and journalist whose articles have appeared in the *Chicago Tribune*, the *Los Angeles Times*, *Jet,* and *The Atlantic*. She received her B.A. from Skidmore College and her M.S. in Journalism from Boston University.

American labor activists have mounted a national campaign to increase the   1
minimum wage. They have made many arguments about the rising cost of living, the long-term effects of poverty, and the obstacles even faced by families who have two incomes. But in a new study, the White House has made a novel argument: Raising the minimum wage reduces crime by 3 to 5 percent.

The Council of Economic Advisers, which advises the president on national   2
economic policy, recently unveiled key findings that cast doubt on the criminal justice system's ability to reduce and prevent crime. "Research has established that rising incarceration is not principally responsible for the reduction in crime, and that higher levels of imprisonment have occurred despite—not because of—changes in underlying criminal activity," states the report. This is

a significant finding: For decades, incarceration advocates promoted the opposite idea. So, if putting people in jails and prisons does not reduce crime, what does?

More education, more job opportunities, school enrichment activities, and a basic living wage are among the factors listed in the study. "Higher wages for low-skilled workers reduce both property and violent crime, as well as crime among adolescents," the authors write. "The impact of wages on crime is substantial . . . a 10 percent increase in wages for non-college educated men results in approximately a 10 to 20 percent reduction in crime rates." More concretely, the Council calculates that raising the minimum wage to $12 by 2020 "would result in a 3 to 5 percent crime decrease (250,000 to 510,000 crimes) and a societal benefit of $8 to $17 billion dollars."

3

TEACHING TIP
Ask students to talk about the starting wages at their first jobs and how easy/difficult it was to pay their bills on those wages.

"The research on this is really clear and really consistent; it cuts across party lines," said Jason Furman, the Council's chairman and President Obama's chief economist, at a White House forum. For example, the Council estimates that "a 10 percent increase in wages for non-college educated men leads to a 10 to 20 percent reduction in crime rates."

4

The Council outlined several specific policy recommendations for state governments and private businesses in dealing with the formerly incarcerated. The Obama administration has already instructed the Office of Personnel Management—the government's HR department, effectively—to delay criminal-background checks beyond initial job applications, for example. And the Departments of Justice and Labor will establish a National Clean Slate Clearinghouse to help legal-aid programs, public-defenders offices, and reentry-services providers with "record cleaning and expungement."

5

But there are some practical obstacles involved with these seemingly straightforward recommendations. Over 46,000 state and federal laws restrict "employment, occupational licenses, and business licenses for people with criminal records," according to the report. Around 70 percent of employers conduct criminal background checks. Additionally, there are more than 1,000 mandatory license exclusions for people with records of misdemeanors and nearly 3,000 exclusions for felony records, per the American Bar Association. The Council also determined that "applicants with criminal records were 50 percent less likely to receive an interview request or job offer." The combined results of these practices are multiple, leaving people to struggle with chronic underemployment, a purgatory of low-wage jobs, stagnant skill sets, and a lack of professional mobility. Most drastically, it means that formerly incarcerated people earn considerably less than other workers—between 10 and 40 percent less, according to Council's report.

6

The irony is that many among the currently incarcerated might not have ever committed crimes if more employment and higher wages were available. Even summer jobs for disadvantaged young people have a meaningful impact on the crime rate; in one case, the probability of incarceration dropped by 10 percent for those who participated in such programs in New York City, according to the Council. In some instances, the Council writes, "states with more flexible labor market conditions for individuals with criminal records may have lower recidivism rates." Offering a higher minimum wage and improved standard of living to those who most need it isn't just about reducing poverty—it would have a quantifiable impact on the country's overall crime rate.

7

READING COMPREHENSION

1. The word *novel* in "the White House has made a novel argument" (paragraph 1) means
   a. a fictitious prose narrative of considerable length.
   b. something that is different from anything seen before.
   c. an imperial enactment in standard law.
   d. a new decree or amendment.

2. The word *recidivism* in "individuals with criminal records may have lower recidivism rates" (paragraph 7) means
   a. employment.
   b. imprisonment.
   c. parole.
   d. relapse.

3. The word *quantifiable* in "it would have a quantifiable impact on the country's overall crime rate" (paragraph 7) means
   a. significant.
   b. desirable.
   c. lasting.
   d. imperceptible.

4. Which of the following would be a good alternative title for this selection?
   a. $15 Minimum Wage Is Fair
   b. The Criminal Justice System Is Flawed
   c. Incarceration Doesn't Work
   d. What Really Has an Impact on Crime

5. Which sentence best expresses the main idea of the selection?
   a. The White House regularly studies and gives recommendations about how to lower crime rates.
   b. Research shows that a $12 minimum wage should be mandatory in every state.
   c. Research shows that increasing the minimum wage has a direct impact on crime rates.
   d. People who are currently in jail could have avoided a life of crime had they had better job opportunities.

6. According to the article, raising the minimum wage reduces crime by how much?
   a. 3 to 5 percent
   b. 5 to 10 percent
   c. 10 percent
   d. 10 to 20 percent

7. According to the essay, what does the Council of Economic Advisers do?

    a. outlines policy related to employment opportunities for people on parole

    (b.) advises the president on national budgetary and fiscal policy

    c. researches information related to monetary policy in the United States

    d. advises the Secretary of Labor about when interest rates should be raised

8. According to the article, what would NOT result if the minimum wage were raised to $12 per hour?

    a. 250,000 to 510,000 fewer crimes would be committed.

    b. $8 to $17 billion dollars would be added to the economy.

    c. Fewer people would be incarcerated for committing crimes.

    (d.) More people would have access to better education.

9. According to the author, how many companies conduct criminal background checks?

    a. 10 to 25 percent

    (b.) 70 percent

    c. about 1,000

    d. about 3,000

10. What did the summer program in New York City demonstrate?

    a. Students who participated in the program returned the following summer.

    b. Students with summer jobs have higher grade point averages in school.

    c. Disadvantaged youth who participated enrolled in college at a higher rate.

    (d.) Disadvantaged youth who participated had a lower probability of incarceration.

STRUCTURE AND TECHNIQUE

1. What kind of introduction does Lantigua-Williams use?

2. In what point of view (first, second, or third person) does Lantigua-Williams write her essay? What tone does she use? Why do you think she chose to write her essay this way? Do you find it effective?

3. Lantigua-Williams uses several direct quotations. Locate one that you find particularly effective, and discuss why you believe she used it and why you think it is effective.

CRITICAL READING AND DISCUSSION

1. Reread paragraph 2. Describe the two arguments that are being made about incarceration.

2. Discuss the factors that lead to lower crime rates as listed in paragraph 3. Do these surprise you? Why do you think these factors have a positive impact on crime rates?

3. What does Furman mean by his statement (paragraph 4) "it cuts across party lines"?

4. What does the author mean when she says in paragraph 6, "leaving people to struggle with chronic underemployment"? Explain the term "chronic underemployment" and identify the other factors that often accompany it.

WRITING ASSIGNMENTS

Assignment 1: Writing a Paragraph

At some time in your life, you have probably had a job that didn't pay very well, or perhaps you have such a job currently. Write a paragraph about your experience, explaining to the reader why you took the job, why you still have the job or why you quit, and what you have learned from working in such a job.

Assignment 2: Writing an Essay

Many people struggle to make ends meet because of the gap between their wages and the cost of living. For this essay, you will need to research the minimum wage and the costs of living in your state. You will then need to research what the minimum wage would need to be in order for a person to be able to afford basic needs. Finally, you will write a letter to your state representative explaining why the basic minimum wage for your state should be raised. Or if, after researching wages and costs of living, you don't feel that the basic minimum wage should be raised, write a letter to your state representative explaining why the current minimum wage should be retained, even if that wage does not allow people to afford basic needs. You will want to provide solid support, including examples that you have found from your research.

In order to properly incorporate your sources, you will want to be familiar with Chapter 20, "Working with Sources" and Chapter 21, "Writing a Research Paper."

Assignment 3: Writing an Essay

Many economists don't favor a minimum wage. For this paper, research economists' arguments against a minimum wage, and then write an exemplification paper explaining their main claims against a minimum wage.

In order to properly incorporate your sources, you will want to be familiar with Chapter 20, "Working with Sources" and Chapter 21, "Writing a Research Paper."

RESPONDING TO IMAGES

Brainstorm adjectives to describe fast-food jobs. Think about these adjectives as you answer this question: Why have fast-food workers been at the forefront of demonstrating for higher wages?

©Jeff Greenberg/Getty Images

READINGS

INDEX